CHILDREN OF ALISO

CHILDREN OF ALISO

by Harriet E. Thurston Buchheim Mather, 1876-1948

Books by Harriet E. Buchheim

The Rescue (1912)

—————

The information in this book is true to the best or our knowledge, as it narrates first-hand memoirs of the author and her family members. The author specifically asserts:

"To tell this pioneer family experience in readable story form, free from fiction and full of human interest, has been the sole object and endeavor of the author. Therefore, a very great deal of matter that is most interesting in itself, has been omitted as not contributory to the main objective.

Events of an historical nature have been incorporated into the story only as they touched the lives of its characters. Yet in every such instance, painstaking care has been exercised to the end that such references be accurate, and thus truly informative.

To supplement the author's incompleteness of knowledge of memory, so far as possible, first-hand accounts have been obtained from those who participated in or had personal knowledge of the events portrayed."

Paperback ISBN: 979-8-9894715-0-8
Hardback ISBN: 979-8-9894715-1-5

Library of Congress Control Number: 2023923244

Printed in the United States of America.
First printing edition 2024.

Published by
Cheek Case Publishing
Theodore G. Cheek, Philadelphia PA
and
Scott T. Case, San Diego CA

To The

CHILDREN And The GRANDCHILDREN
Of
THE CHILDREN OF ALISO,

This Simple Narrative Is

Affectionately

Dedicated

TABLE OF CONTENTS

TABLE OF FIGURES

PREFACE

The present volume is not in any sense of the word intended as a history. Such implied comprehensiveness is entirely outside its scope. It is not offered as a history even of that local section of California's Southland comprehended in its own narrative.

Rather, it is the simple story of a single family of pioneers taken from among the many who formed an integral part of that romantic Southland in days that are forever gone—gone, not simply from the standpoint of the passing of time, but of the vanishing of an era.

To tell this pioneer family experience in readable story form, free from fiction and full of human interest, has been the sole object and endeavor of the author. Therefore, a very great deal of matter that is most interesting in itself, has been omitted as not contributory to the main objective.

Events of an historical nature have been incorporated into the story only as they touched the lives of its characters. Yet in every such instance, painstaking care has been exercised to the end that such references be accurate, and thus truly informative.

To supplement the author's incompleteness of knowledge of memory, so far as possible, first-hand accounts have been obtained from those who participated in or had personal knowledge of the events portrayed.

A few words here of sincere appreciation and acknowledgment are due and here tendered those friends and relatives and other pioneers who have contributed, little or much, toward the making of this "Saga of the Southland." Thanks also are reverently acknowledged as due those noble predecessors who have left on record the many valuable works that afford such boundless opportunities for research to those who follow after.

Harriet E. Thurston Buchheim Mather, 1948

This manuscript written from 1935-1948 took some time to appear as a published work. Harriet Thurston Buchheim Mather gave the manuscript **Children of Aliso** to her daughters Augusta and Evelyn with the hope they would publish it. Augusta had the document typed, proofread and bound in three volumes of 1322 pages. The manuscript was inherited by Harriet's grandchildren and a great grandson Ted Cheek who digitized the typewritten volumes. It remained uncirculated for many years and took on a reputation as more of a rumor than reality. Scott Case, a great grandson of Artemisia Thurston Ward, tracked down our family connection and the manuscript. Ted and Scott collaborated to format the manuscript for publication, incorporating family photographs and maps as Harriet had requested. Photographs and figures are sourced from Thurston family archives; and from the "Scott Case collection on the history of Laguna Beach, California" maintained by the University of California, Irvine within their Orange County and Regional History collections.[1] We have included End Notes to provide appropriate historical context and references, without disturbing the manuscript which is essentially unedited and faithfully represents her story in that culture's time and place.

Ted Cheek and Scott Case, 2023

PROLOGUE

Oh, the old days—the old ways are vanished in the past;
They are gone—forever they are gone.
But always, they imbue
The younger and the new
With interest, with romance and with song.

This story of the CHILDREN OF ALISO has been long in the making. First, it took twenty years to live it; then it took twice twenty years to live it down; since then, it has taken several years more to live it over. Thus, it is seen to be a story of living, which furnishes the vital element to make of it a living story.

No apology is offered for the choice of so humble a subject as an unknown, unimportant family of pioneers who transformed a little uncelebrated canyon from a barren wilderness into a little Garden of Eden; for the writer believes that no family is unimportant—that within the precincts of every home is a potential story of moving interest and that every individual born into this world is the ruler of a kingdom. The family of Aliso has been chosen, not because it is outstandingly different from other pioneer families, but because the writer happens to know more about that particular family than about any other that ever lived.

How important each individual life really is, may be emphasized by a simple direct question addressed to you who read these words: Whatever your life may be—however seemingly unimportant in the world's affairs, how unknown to the annals of achievement, how unsatisfactory it may be to yourself, would you be willing to exchange it, with all its own experiences, its own individuality, its own personality, its own thought-creations, for that of another? Would you, if you could, actually give yourself away to be somebody else—the sum total of a wholly different set of thoughts and ideas than you yourself have evolved? We venture to say that you would not: that you would rather be just you—ruler of your own individual kingdom, than to be anybody else under the sun, regardless of how wealthy, how educated, or how fortunate that somebody might be. Such a choice would simply mean that you place a true estimate upon the value of your own existence as an individual.

Only in eternity will be revealed the results of the influence for good or evil of common, everyday lives—yours, mine and those around us; though unlearned, unchronicled, unsung. And is it not these same common, everyday lives that awaken in our hearts, responsive chords of sympathy and interest? For after all, are we not, as human beings, bound together in one great family by the same eternal quest for self-expression, and the same limiting insufficiencies and mortal frailties?

This is a story of the "horse-and-buggy" days—days that will never come again, yet which had their appointed place in the scheme of things. And should this world go on, spared from its own self-destructive inventions, may not the airplane of today become the horse and buggy of tomorrow?

Times and methods may be outgrown, science and invention revolutionize the order of this world—in which "change and decay" are the ever present tragedy; but still the human heart remains unchanged. Human nature is the same today as in the horse-and-buggy days, and children will ever be children the world around.

So my simple story of the youth of yesterday, bright-eyed and hopeful, speaks to the youth of today with gentle reminder that youth itself is but the passing shadow of a dream. Roses bloom, roses fade, though some may linger on beyond their season. So the dear Children of Aliso blossomed only to fade. Yet here and there on bending stem in autumn's closing hours, one lingers still:

Not "the last rose of summer left blooming alone,"
But the rose of last summer, whose bloom long is flown;
Whose ripe seed-vessel clinging—though fruitful it grows—
Gives no sign to beholders 'twas ever a rose.

CHAPTER 1 INTRODUCED TO SAN FRANCISCO

My pioneer father and mother came to California in Eighteen Seventy-One, less than two years after the first transcontinental railroad from the Missouri river to San Francisco had been completed, connecting the East with the West. This event inadvertently celebrated the first centennial of the discovery by Portolá in Seventeen Sixty-Nine of San Francisco's inner bay, sixty-six years before the city had its first beginnings.

Great changes had taken place since William A. Richardson, the English rover, having become a citizen of the Mexican commonwealth, embraced the established religion and married in the approved manner a Spanish Señorita, had erected in Eighteen Thirty-Five his combination dwelling and trading-post of pine uprights and canvas and became the first resident of the city of San Francisco.

In the light of subsequent events, his choice of a building site at the head of a little sheltered cove on this wind-swept peninsula, had been nothing short of prophetic.

Here in this shallow cove that bluntly indented the bay shore-line at the commencement of its southward bend, Vancouver, first navigator of the inner harbor, had dropped anchor forty-three years before, setting the precedent for hide ships that, after Mexico had thrown open the ports of California to foreign trade in Twenty-One, found their way through the narrow strait into the sheltered port to trade with the Indians.

Two and a half miles to the west of this anchorage, was to be seen, flanking a small mesa, the original Spanish Presidio, a rampart built for protection against uncivilized Indians, founded in Seventeen Seventy-Six by Capitan Juan de Anza and his aide, Moraga, in the midst of a military reservation of some fifteen hundred acres. Its huge adobe walls with a height of fourteen feet and a thickness of five, enclosed an area of about twenty-six and a half acres, in which were to be found the chapel and its padres, the garrison of soldiers and officers with their living quarters, the pobladores, or colonists, with their houses, the horses and their stables, the store-buildings, workshops, wells and cisterns. Damaged and weakened by the earthquake of Eighteen Twelve, the presidio was now in a state of semi-disrepair.

On the extreme point of the higher bold rocky promontory jutting northward, the Castile de San Juan, a heavy mud-walled fort in the form of a broad horseshoe with a length of a hundred and twenty-five feet, its ten-foot-thick parapet bristling with cannon, guarded the narrow entrance to the world's most perfect natural inland harbor.

The great waterway, comprising a triad of major bays the San Francisco, San Pablo, and Suisun, linked together in an irregular fifty five mile crescent, contain both salt water and fresh. Connected on the west with the Pacific, it is fed on the extreme northeast by the Sacramento and San Joaquin rivers that drain the great Sierra basin, emptying as one into the Suisun.

The entire bay region was a vast natural resort for all the denizens of the western wilds. Bears and panthers inhabited the surrounding wooded hills. Deer, elk and antelope roamed at will through the forests, and slaked their thirst at flowing springs. Birds of every sort made vocal the wilderness, nesting undisturbed in its leafy refuge. Waterfowl moved through the reeds and rushes to their well-provisioned swimming fields. Abundant in the waters of the bays, were seal and mink and otter, sporting without fear, and sunning themselves on banks and islands; but destined for ruthless destruction in the ever-increasing fur trade.

On a small, level, brush-free area among the hills that sloped back from this little bay-shore cove, whose bordering green fields of fragrant mint had early claimed for it the name of Yerba Buena[i], was pitched the first solitary tent-house, to become the nucleus around which collected slowly a little trading community. Off from its northern shore a small island lifted its head, and bore the same name. Below its fronting banks, every ebbing of the tide frankly disclosed a considerable area of unromantic mud flats. Behind it, stretched away southward, acres and acres of rolling sand dunes, here and there interrupted by wandering lagoons.

Two miles to the southwest in a favored, well-watered arroyo selected by Anza, stood the old Mission de Dolores, established under the flag of Spain coincidental with the Presidio.

---

[i] Yerba Buena (Good Herb)

The white force of both mission and military post combined was only sixty-two souls. The entire population of the five northern missions of California with their military reservations, from Santa Cruz to San Pablo was not more than two hundred.

Who then, in the year of Eighteen Thirty-Five, could have dreamed that this infant Yerba Buena, rearing then its first tent-shanty was to develop eventually into a mighty city that should sweep all before it and fill the whole vast peninsula?

Who could have imagined that quiet little cove in the wilds, utterly obliterated by artificial infills protruding out into the bay and bristling with scores of piers and wharves that swarmed with busy life and bustling activity, or far less have visualized the mighty modern ships of steel engaged in war and commerce, that should throng its waters from every port on the globe, discharging their thousands of passengers and marines and vast cargoes of merchandise?

Who could have conceived the twentieth century engineering wonder of gigantic reinforced steel bridges spanning the many leagues of water to those far-off shores on the east and north?

And who could have envisioned the vast coastal regions of those same far-off shores divested of all their wooded wildness and welded into one great chain of interlocked cities, having not even space between for boundary lines, save where natural waterways occur?

Yerba Buena developed but slowly at first. Almost a decade of its existence saw still only about a dozen houses and fifty citizens. The secularization of the missions and the partitioning of their lands beginning coincidental with the inception of Yerba Buena gradually drew a population of traders and adventurers to settle along its sand dunes until the little pueblo straggled scatteringly southward over the hills to include the distant mission.

In Forty-Seven, its enterprising citizens discarded the name of the little cove in favor of the patron saint of the great bay, San Francisco, and the identity of Yerba Buena was swallowed up in the interests of commercial progress.

Then came the almost bloodless conquest of California, and the signing at Los Angeles of the Peace of Cahuenga in January of Forty-Seven, followed by American occupation, and the cession of California to the United States by Mexico a year later.

Scarcely was the ink of the protocol dry when into the unpretentious village so lately re-christened, strange, fantastic tales began to filter, of gold being picked up in the tail race of Sutter's new mill on the American river at Coloma, a hundred miles or so to the northeast.

The conservative San Franciscans had no notion of making fools of themselves and met the rumor at first with cautious incredulity. Then one day, trekkers, coming in from the "diggings" for supplies, let forth in the streets the infectious shout: "Gold! Gold!" with a brandishing of samples of yellow nuggets. Then pandemonium reigned supreme, and the year Forty-Eight staged its local gold-rush.

Not until Colonel Richard B. Mason had himself investigated these fabulous tales of gold nuggets rolling with the pebbles down Sutter's creek, and abundantly confirmed them in his report to Washington, was the rest of the world apprised. When given out to the public by President Polk, the news swept through the East like a prairie fire, and the great gold stampede of Forty-Nine was inaugurated.

Across the plains, over mountains and rivers, they came, by ox-team and caravan, through hardships, privation, and the grim, haunting specter of death from the rigors of winter. Tens of thousands poured into the Sacramento Valley in a mad scramble for the yellow metal.

Other thousands jammed the port of San Francisco, many of them from far distant ports and countries. They came in crafts of every description, from regular seaworthy steam-ships and sailing vessels to disreputable hulks. Everything that could float had been rigged up and pressed into service, then left anchored and empty like ghost-ships in the bay, deserted by passengers, crews and captains alike, in the mad rush for the gold-fields of El Dorado.

Excitement was everywhere at fever-heat. Thousands came to reap fortunes by their wits. Other ways, there were, to rake in the gold than by pick and shovel and pan. San Francisco, scarcely out of its swaddling clothes, became a city overnight—a city of ramshackle cabins and tents, and hybrids of the two, of abandoned boats turned into shops and living quarters, of every possible form of grotesque domicile conceivable to civilized man; a city of crooks, gamblers, riffraff, and gold-diggers by proxy.

Forty thousand came in Forty-Nine. When, a year later, California was admitted into the Union of States, its population had climbed to ninety two and a half thousand, the greater number of whom were clustered about the gold center. Twenty-five thousand of them huddled in the city of San Francisco itself.

Untold wealth flowed into the city. Crime went wild. No adequate civil government existed for the control of such a population. In Fifty-One a citizens' vigilance committee was organized to combat the lawless element—scarcely more lawless than itself—until a competent, stable government could be evolved.

Gold excitements, however well founded, do not last forever. This one, like all others, died down eventually. Hard times followed for a few years. But another rush to the West of a different character, was in the offing. When the two groups of railroad workers, building toward each other from east and west, met on the tenth of May Eighteen Sixty-Nine at Promontory, Utah, and drove the golden spike through the last tie, prepared of polished laurel, it was a triumphant challenge to adventurous home seekers the world around to turn their faces to the virgin regions of California.

Figure 1 Golden Spike Ceremony at Promontory, Utah [2]

Two years later, at the time my story opens, the population of the city on the bay had jumped to a hundred and fifty thousand, and San Francisco had become the great port of the West, the distributing center of all California, and indeed, of the whole Pacific coast, being its sole point of export and import. Steaming across the continent by rail, incoming thousands were disgorged with their goods, on the Oakland side of the bay, to be ferried across to the city. Freight and passengers, carried in the old side-wheelers, in ever increasing numbers, entered and departed through the far-famed Golden Gate, so-named in classic Greek[i] by Captain John C. Fremont in Forty-Six, from the flaming golden poppies whose springtime glory carpeted the surrounding hills and valleys.

My father and mother already were pioneers and inured to hardships. As children they had traveled in covered wagons across the plains with the Mormon emigrants in Forty-Eight, when some twelve thousand had trekked from Illinois to the far off wilderness of Utah beyond the incorporated territories of the United States. From that time

---

[i] Chrysopylae (Greek for "Golden Gate")

onward their lot had been cast, first with one pioneering adventure, then with another, in the settling up of that country.[3]

After attaining his majority, Father had been sent by the church on a self-sustaining mission—a requirement of every promising male adherent—and for four years had labored in a foreign land, experiencing great trials and hardships, having no financial support but his own hands and head.[4]

Returning from abroad, he had met for the first time the modest, sweet and popular young lady, scarcely past mid-teens, who became his bride. Eldest child of her father's household, hers was the gayest laugh, hers the slenderest waist, hers the lightest foot in the dance, and hers the hand most sought after; for aside from her charming personality, was she not a daughter of one of the "Twelve"?

Life had brought its burdens, its sorrows, and also its disillusionments, as it has a way of doing with us all. The time came when Father repudiated that system of religion with which he had been indoctrinated from childhood—the only faith either of them had ever known. With the rift had come inevitable heartache to all concerned, culminating in the severance of life-long ties, for Mother had cast in her lot with his. Now they were forsaking their homeland to start all over again in California, a country of magic lure, where land was still to be had as a gift of government, and every man was free.

It was in the bitter cold of February when the ground was covered with snow that Father and Mother, after a household sale, checked the remainder of their belongings at Morgan City, Utah, and bade goodbye to old friends and loved ones. A last lingering gaze over familiar scenes they were leaving forever, dimmed their eyes as, with their family of five young children, they boarded the emigrant train with tickets for San Francisco.

George, the eldest, was nearing twelve, Sadie, as close to nine, Artemisia[5], some months past six, Lafayette going on four, and little Joseph past two. It might be added that Baby Joan already had begun that journey of mystery on her way toward the entrance of this big world of ours. Over this lusty flock, presided our gentle, sweet-faced mother, patient, unselfish and tender.

A little less than medium height, her once slender form now broadened by much motherhood, she was still a beautiful woman, with her oval face, mild blue eyes and clear, lovely complexion; and a young woman too, just turned the corner of thirty years, being Father's junior by ten.

From a parting in the middle, her dark hair was drawn back severely, still failing to obliterate the soft natural wave over her temples, and wound in a coil at the back of her neck. From the coil, a high, ornamented backcomb rose slightly above the top of her head, adding its touch of height and dignity. Mother was never without that back-comb. It seemed as much a part of her as the heavy plain gold wedding ring that encircled her finger.

Through the lobe of each ear was a tiny hole pierced for the insertion of earrings; for in her day no girl was supposed to grow up without having her ears pierced. Though she seldom wore them, Mother had several pairs laid away in her jewel box, and in their absence kept each tiny opening in her ear-lobes from becoming closed by wearing inserted through it a short piece of white thread.

Her tight-fitting basque was closed down the front with many ornamental buttons. Below it a full-gathered skirt touched the floor, swaying gently over the hoop-skirt as she moved about, and completely concealing her high-topped shoes, the toes of which merely peeped out at intervals. The sleeves, severely plain, were finished at the wrists with white ruching to match that which rose from inside the neckband of her basque. Below the ruche was drawn around her neck a white embroidered tie that crossed in front and was fastened with a large brooch at her throat.

Hidden in the folds of her skirt was a generous pocket, the receptacle of many small articles frequently needed for use. Among them reposed when not held in her fingers, a small, heavily beaded purse of her own handiwork. Here also was tucked away her knitting, or bits of sewing during temporary interruptions of industry; for Mother's fingers were always busy with some form of needlework or knitting. Every moment must be utilized in providing wearing apparel of some kind for the family, even when journeying from place to place.

When needing a wrap, she wore a large fringed Persian shawl, whose bright oriental colors enhanced the attractiveness of her general ensemble.

From Morgan City, they traveled northwestward some twenty-seven miles to Ogden, then, turning due west, crossed the Great Salt Lake, thirty five miles wide, its eighty miles of length stretching out on either hand. A week was consumed in reaching San Francisco, a distance of seven hundred and ninety-two miles.

Mother was train-sick all the way out, and heart-sick too, yet for the sake of others, she strove to keep a cheerful countenance. Always before, she had been within visiting distance of her mother, though she had forsaken the home nest at the tender age of seventeen to venture forth upon the strange and troublous sea of matrimony. Now, fearful of the uncertain future that lay before her in a strange land and torn with the wrench of parting, her heart was struggling with a desolate homesickness and a dread lest this separation should be forever. How she should miss that precious mother and that father she had so loved and leaned upon! There was also the pain of leaving behind her the grave of little Erastus, her second son, who, had he lived, would now have been a lad of ten.

But far deeper and more inconsolable than all these immediate sorrows was the ever constant, secret grief that racked her heart over the unspeakable tragedy that had darkened their lives three winters before, when their baby of two and a half years, little brown-eyed Rosetta, had been stolen away by Indians, never again to be restored to her arms.

Initiating the Tenderfeet

At last, on the morning of Saint Valentine's Day, with shriek of whistle and clang of bell and grinding jolt of couplings, the overland came to a standstill at the terminal, whence a ferry boat was to take them across the bay into the teeming mart of San Francisco.

This trip across the bay was a restful relief from the noisy discomfort of the train. At the Oakland docks, an accommodating young man, also ferrying to the city, struck up an acquaintance with Father, to whom friendliness in a strange country was not unwelcome. This man, being familiar with the city, directed him to a "fine family hotel," and at his inquiry, named the price charged for room and board. Father, seeing that the charge was more than he could afford, mentally decided to leave his family in a waiting room somewhere while he should look around for something cheaper.

At the landing in San Francisco, waited many hotel drivers who shouted in vociferous competition, the names of their respective hostelries. Not giving Father time to choose his own hack, his new acquaintance signaled a driver, and the two immediately began to load the family luggage into the vehicle. Putting two and two together, Father began to suspect that this new friend was none other than a regular hired "hotel runner." When, instead of parting with them there, he climbed in also and took a seat beside the driver, this suspicion was confirmed beyond a doubt, and he could now see how from the first he had played right into his hand.

At the hotel, the proprietor met them smilingly. The luggage was unloaded in the lobby, and immediately the hack drove away, the new-found friend simultaneously disappearing. They were conducted up a flight of stairs to the "Ladies Waiting Room," and there Father left Mother and the children to wait while he went to look for other accommodations. This proceeding was quite disconcerting to the hotel-keeper, who had expected a fat "rake-off" from this family of "tenderfeet," and at their refusal to register there, his countenance fell unmistakably.

Not intending to be gone long, Father left without making provision for the family's noon meal and Mother had no change in her pocket. But the time lengthened, the children were getting hungry, and still he had not returned. When dinner was announced Mother did not know what to do. She could not buy even crackers to pacify the five little folks whose nostrils were assailed by appetizing aromas from the dining room. Expecting him every moment, she delayed until dinner was practically over, then finally took the hungry brood in to dinner.

They were given a family table by themselves. The meal, when it was brought in, consisted of nothing but a small dish of very poorly fried potatoes, warmed over from the day before, and a few slices of bread and butter. When this had disappeared the family were almost as hungry as ever. But Mother, knowing that finances must be conserved, and thinking that very little charge would be made for so skimpy a meal, made no complaint.

It was late in the afternoon when at last Father returned in the hack of another hotel, having found, after a long search, quarters that were much cheaper. Mother told him about their meager dinner, and Father, who had eaten nothing since landing, asked at the desk for his bill. Upon reading that document of extortion, he could hardly believe his eyes. The regular price for room and board for the whole family for a full twenty-four-hour day had been charged. Immediately he objected to so unreasonable a bill.

The clerk consulted with his superior, then coming upon the scene. He was obdurate. Father was told firmly that he would have to pay the bill.

Father said that he would not pay any such bill as that, but was willing to pay any reasonable charge, and turned to load his belongings into the hack.

The proprietor rushed up to him menacingly and forbade him to touch a thing until he had paid his bill, while the hotel assistants stood by ready to use force if necessary.

By this time, the altercation had attracted attention, and a crowd was congregating. Seeing in this publicity no benefit to his business, the irate proprietor threatened to call the police, classing Father as a "dead-beat" and disturber of the peace.

This produced an effect opposite to that desired. Father's dander was now thoroughly aroused. Raising his voice, he enumerated his reasons for objecting to the bill, and told about the "runner" who had "railroaded" him there.

Angrily interrupting, the man denied having any such runner. This brought out further details from Father that fully exposed the deception. Infuriated at having his tactics thus laid bare, the proprietor lost control of himself and fairly jumped up and down, hurling denunciations at the guest he had set out to fleece.

At this point the house officer in uniform arrived on the scene, and admonished the victim of this astuteness to speak in lower tones that others might not hear the disturbance.

"I want them to hear!" shouted Father. "I want them to know just what kind of a place this is! This bill is nothing but "highway robbery!" He finally proposed a settlement of four dollars, to be paid after he had loaded his goods, and eaten a meal himself.

This offer, the proprietor accepted "Shust to get rit of you!" and Father was allowed to proceed with the loading of his luggage, under, however, a running fire of abuse and insults. Unabashed by this fusillade, Father, when he had finished, turned to him and announced:

"Now I want my dinner."

He was seated at a table and food placed before him. Thither, the crowd collected to see the finish. Seething with suppressed fury, the proprietor taunted him during the meal with insult and ridicule:

"I vill gif you the four tollars! I vil gif it to you! I vill make you a pres-sent of it!"

For some time Father stood this in silence, eating away complacently. Finally, at the man's insistent reiteration, he thought it time to call his bluff.

"All right, I'll take it."

Stung to increased frenzy, the man kept on:

"Dondt you vant some money? Dondt you vant some money?

"No, I 'dondt vant some money'" mimicked Father, at which the bystanders laughed.

Goaded by this merriment, the outwitted man repeated his interrogation with incredulous inflection:

"Dondt you vant some money?"

Thinking it might silence him, Father again called his bluff:

"Yes, I'll take some money."

Whereupon, the generous host pulled out a quarter from his pocket and laid it on the table. Father reached out his hand and took the quarter, putting it into his own pocket, to the great amusement of the spectators, who were being highly entertained.

His meal being finished, Father arose, walked through the lobby, the kerosene lamps having meanwhile been lighted, and out onto the sidewalk where his embarrassed family had gathered. Assisting them into the hack, he climbed in after them, and in the presence of the bystanders—all witnesses to the fact that he had been given the "four tollars" as a "pressent"—he was driven off amid laughter and plaudits, richer by a quarter than when he came.

Such was their introduction to San Francisco.

CHAPTER 2 IN QUEST OF A HOME

After the wearisome journey of the past week with its long tiresome wait at the hotel and meager food rations, the family were all thankful for a good supper and welcome rest in real beds once more, and slept long hours into the following day.

At this place they stayed nearly a week. Then Father succeeded in securing cheaper quarters in a lodging house where Mother could do her own cooking for the family, with improvised furniture to help out. An old smoky wood stove in the place made everything baked taste of smoke. Their homemade flat-topped "chest" with an oilcloth for cover, served as a table, the children squatting around it as they ate. But being used to tribulations, the family made little complaint at inconveniences, the brunt of which as a matter of course, fell upon Mother, who did the work for the family.

Sadie's chief duty was the care of little Joseph. Artemisia—Mesia, for short, but by the family perverted into "Mishie"—looked after Lafie; while George—affectionately addressed as "Georgie"—did errands and accompanied Father on his expeditions here and there about the city and surrounding country.

The house was perched on a hillside in a thickly settled part of town. To reach the yard—common to all the tenants— it was necessary to descend a flight of stairs. The children of the different families, brimming with natural curiosity and social instincts, soon became acquainted with one another, and none being allowed to play in the street, they congregated in this common yard, where the newcomers were welcomed as an acquisition. There were two little girls somewhat older than Sadie, who came over dressed in the long trailing clothes of their elders, and introduced the game of "playing stage," strutting back and forth across the grassy plot, singing, in imitation of the actress, Lotta Crabtree:

> *"Shoo-fly, don't bother I;*
> *Shoo-fly, don't bother I;*
> *Shoo-fly, don't bother me,*
> *For I belong to Company 'B'".*

This ditty was long echoed thereafter in our family.

Father's reserve of capital was fast diminishing. He was anxious to get permanently located and find remunerative employment. Counting over his resources—the proceeds from his sale of household goods, team and other equipment, he found one day that he had left just five hundred dollars with which to face an unknown future with his growing family that must be clothed and fed.

It was his set purpose in coming to California, to find government land which he could preempt for a home. He had been told that there was plenty to be had, and truly there was, but most of it as yet un-surveyed, and therefore not easily located. In land offices no records of un-surveyed lands were available, which left him at a great disadvantage, and dependent upon chance discovery or the benevolence of brief acquaintances, a quality which he found to be rare in those he met. Those who knew of such land kept its location strictly secret in the hope of securing it for themselves or for their own particular friends. A stranger coming in was directed to "greener pastures" farther on. Thus Father's inquiries met with little success and much disappointment.

Finally he came in contact with a lady who owned large possessions in Lower California under the government of Mexico, and was interested in finding a man who would settle on a portion of it and care for the rest. Some agreement was entered into between her and Father to this effect—he to receive his pay mostly in land. Encouraged by this apparent good fortune, he immediately set about to make preparations for the new venture.

Knowing that San Diego was a very small place, where prices were likely to be high, and expecting from there to cross the border into a region as yet very sparsely settled where not much of anything could be bought, he budgeted his resources and with the greater portion of what remained, purchased the most important of those things he was sure to need.

These consisted of a small lumber wagon, with wooden bows and canvas cover for it, a large living tent, a single plow, a few simple farming implements, a set of carpenters tools, a four-hole wood cook stove, a small muzzle-loading thirty-two caliber rifle, and harness for a span of horses. This left him barely enough money, besides expenses for the trip, to purchase the animals after he should arrive in San Diego, for horses were cheaper there than in the north.

These articles he shipped by water to San Diego, paying the freight in advance; and with his family and their large amount of luggage, including trunks, boxes of bedding and other things, embarked on the same boat—an old side-wheeler, bound for San Diego, the only other port worthy of the name on the California coast. They took ship on Lafayette's fourth birthday, the twenty-third of March, Eighteen Seventy-One.

Figure 2 Example Side-Wheeler Steamship "Senator" in San Diego [6]

While Father was doing his business in the city before sailing. little Lafayette made the acquaintance of some boys—evidently not too honorable of principle, and afterward remembered by the family as "bad boys"—one of whom borrowed his precious jack-knife, a farewell gift from Grandfather Snow, who had given one each also to George and Father.

This designing boy dropped the knife down into a deep hole—at least it appeared impossibly deep to little Lafie, being probably a garbage pit, and told Lafie with many "ahs" and "ohs" that it was gone forever—that nobody could ever get it out of the hole again. There is little doubt that he took this method of securing the knife for himself.

Lafie's little heart was just about broken. He had been so proud of his jack knife. Now it was lost. And how he did grieve! The mother of this boy, feeling very sorry for Lafie, gave him for a birthday present, a little red tin wagon, which he proudly carried aboard the boat with him.

As he stood with Father on the deck while the boat lay at anchor, he played with this little wagon, wheeling it back and forth along the top rail of the bulwark. It was great fun. The rail was just the right width to serve as a wagon road. But alas! Little fingers lost their hold, and down went the little red tin wagon overboard.

Just at that instant, a boat loaded with sacks of grain and having two men in it, came alongside the ship exactly under the rail, and it landed "ka-plunk" in the middle of the boat. Father gave a warning shout before it struck. The men looked up. He dashed down below to try to recover the little tin wagon. But for some reason not now clear, was unsuccessful. So that was the last of Lafe's little red tin wagon—at least of his proud, but brief ownership. And birthday joy was turned into birthday weeping.

Artemisia was a very timid little girl with strangers. And when one day as she walked across the deck, a gentleman passenger caught her up in his arms and kissed her, it frightened her almost into hysteria. She fled when released, to stifle her sobs in Mother's bosom.

Four days the family lived on this freighter—if one may call seasickness living. The whole family shared in this evil disease; for this their first experience on the water, and none of them proved to be good sailors. Little Lafie was so sea-sick they almost feared he would die.

One day he was so hungry he begged for food, and as he seemed a little better, Father took him in his arms to the table. Those of the family who were able to look at food, were seated around the board with other passengers, and there, set at Lafie's place, was a real "grown-up" plate, and alongside it a big knife and fork—such things as he had never used before. But, most wonderful of all, a small plate placed close to the large plate, had on it a big, full-sized piece of pie. Never before had he been given a "grown-up" piece of pie. He smacked his lips, eager to get at it.

But as he looked, something suddenly went wrong in his insides and a queer, sick feeling came over him. Father took him quickly away. No pie for little Lafie, no big plate, no knife and fork. They went to join the little red wagon in the Land of the Unpossessed. During the whole trip he could retain no nourishment, and was sick for days afterward.

George also was insufferably sick and continued to be so for a whole week after landing. Certain articles of food served on the boat, he could never again "look in the face."

It was rather a sick looking family that disembarked at the San Diego docks. But they were greatly relieved at being once more on solid earth, even though it did seem to roll a bit as they walked.

After Father had located his family for the day, he went back to get his goods from the ship. Here, a disagreeable surprise awaited him—a circumstance that no doubt altered the whole course of life for the family. The steamship company held back his goods, refusing to release them until he had paid the second time for their transportation. They claimed that through a mistake made at the shipping point, the charges levied had been too low. And though Father held papers showing that all had been paid in full, they refused absolutely to give him possession until he had satisfied their illegal claim.

Father was helpless in their clutches. There was nothing he could do but pay the extortionate rate demanded. Far cheaper would it have been for him, had he been able to foresee such trickery, to have made all his purchases in San Diego after his arrival. But this is the way they did business in frontier California in those days.

This experience so reduced his resources that practically all of his remaining cash was consumed in the purchase of the necessary team of horses—California mustangs—the "Ted" and "Bill" of my story; which left him so stripped that he was obliged to give up his enterprise across the border in Lower California.

Had the contemplated location been made, this particular story could never have been written, for it would never have been lived.

Soon Father made the acquaintance of a man named Perrin, who had a California house and two vacant lots on the outskirts of San Diego. Mr. Perrin invited him to pitch his tent on one of these lots. And there the family lived for about two months in their new tent. Here also, he secured a little work to do which helped with dwindling finances.

Wherever he went, Father was on the look-out for some clue concerning the location of government land. He engaged men in conversation on the subject, following up every lead given him, but without success. There is no doubt that during his wanderings in search of it, he sometimes trod upon government land without being aware of it, as later he did in other places. But such knowledge came only after the opportunity had vanished beyond recall.

Their first introduction to bananas considered then a strange, foreign fruit, came from Mr. Perrin's cellar, out of which he brought one day a big bunch, giving some to each of the family.

His house was octagon in shape, which no doubt gave to Father the idea that afterward found expression in the building of his own octagon barn and cistern on the Aliso farm.

Not all of Mr. Perrin's land had been cleared of brush, there was still left growing an unsightly patch. One day he called George and said to him:

"There's that bunch of brush over there. If you'll grub that out I'll give you two pounds of walnuts."

George gladly accepted the offer. A mattock was given him and he went to work. It was heavy for a boy, but he labored away industriously, and in the course of two or three days, with a little help from Father, the job was finished, and he received his walnuts.

Soon afterward when he was dividing them for a treat among the family, Father, coming into the tent, objected to their being eaten.

"They will be good to plant when we get located," he said, and gathered them all up to save for that purpose. Father had a mental picture of a flourishing walnut orchard, which afterward materialized to fully justify his vision and foresight, if not his method of despoiling the boy.

During their sojourn here, they made the acquaintance of a man in his thirties whose hands showed that he had never done hard work. His white shirt, white collar, kid gloves and suit of immaculate appearance were supplied him by his wife from her earnings as a dressmaker.

This gentleman once brought some oranges to the tenting family. How exciting! Having heard often of oranges, still they had never seen or tasted any before. What a treat they anticipated! These oranges were no doubt seedlings, since the first Navels had just been introduced into California the year before, and not for seven or eight years in the future could fruit from them have been marketed. As all Californians know, in early spring, oranges other than the Navel are never fully ripe even though they appear of a bright color and lovely to look at. So when the family tasted these oranges their faces fell with disappointment. They were so sour that nobody could eat them with any enjoyment. They wondered how people could make the fuss they did over oranges.

Good News of Land

While still camping on Perrin's lot, Father met a man of florid complexion with auburn hair, by the name of Lovett. He had come down from his mountain home in Bear Valley to purchase supplies in town.

Bear Valley, about forty-five miles northeast of San Diego, its floor level some thirteen hundred feet above the sea, lies in an elevated plateau region of the Smith Mountains between the San Luis Rey and San Dieguito[i] rivers. Leading up to it from the north and west are other tillable valleys of lesser elevation and greater area. All through the region the encircling mountains were then heavily wooded with live oaks many of which still persist. To the east, some seven hundred feet above Bear Valley, rises a broad tableland of many thousand acres comprising the Guejito[ii] Grant that stretches southward about eight miles by airline to the upper end of San Pascual Valley.

Smith Mountain stands out westerly from the main range, its crest line six thousand feet above sea level for twenty miles. In these high mountains, the San Luis Rey has its source, fed by the drainage from many peaks and plateaus.

Mr. Lovett, in conversation with Father, mentioned that he had taken up government land in Bear Valley. Immediately Father asked him if there was any more land available there. Seeing his eager interest, Mr. Lovett questioned him cautiously to learn if possible something about his character and history. Having satisfied himself that Father and his family would make desirable neighbors, he opened up his heart in a very generous way and told him all about the place. There was a sixty acre piece of fine land still awaiting occupation, the rest of the quarter-section lying in the hills around. He himself had taken up his limit of a hundred and sixty acres in the bottom of the valley, and adjoining his with a little divide between, lay this vacant acreage. He said that he would be very glad to have good neighbors, and invited Father to accompany him up into the valley to see the land. This, Father was only too eager to do. And when Lovett was ready to go, he also was ready to follow him, light of heart and hopeful.

Father's kid-gloved friend had confided to him that he too was interested in finding government land to preempt for a farm. Inwardly, Father was greatly amused at the thought of this fine over-dressed dandy trying to farm, and the subject was a joke in the camp. Still, being inclined to offer him a chance, he gave the man an invitation to go along with him up into Bear Valley. So together they followed Lovett, seated in the covered wagon drawn by Ted and Bill.

---

[i] Dee-gee-to

[ii] Wah-hee-to

It was a long forty-five miles—for mountain roads always seem longer than they really are, and horses travel uphill slowly. To conserve their strength, they must be frequently allowed to rest and recover their "wind," and also given time for feeding. Forty-five miles on level roads would be a good two days' journey; but these roads, even where they appeared to be level, were all up-grade. After reaching the foothills, real climbing began, and now the roads became atrocious. There was just enough of the rocky earth dug out from the hillside so that the wagon wouldn't tip over sidewise, and just enough taken off from the steepness to keep it from tipping over endwise. So several nights were spent on the way up into Bear Valley, a trip which today by modern paved highway, may be covered in an hour.

The old road, meandering in a wide sweep, crawled up out of the Escondido Valley, entered another now known as Valley Center, broad and level, from which they entered a third called Wood Valley, long and narrow. This they followed for about five miles, when a fork, branching to the right, sloped up sharply to the northern pass from which they looked down upon the beautiful little valley of their destination.

Its six hundred acres of tillable land lay like a green gem in a setting of surrounding hills with sharp ridges, their sides densely wooded with live oaks that wandered with their shade and beauty down into the edges of the level valley. Lengthwise from east to west, almost in a half moon, curved a narrow, deep, willow-fringed wash, now dry from the long drowth (drought), but in the rainy season bearing a swift torrent across the valley to plunge down into a deep gorge at the western end on its journey to the sea.

The natural and unique arrangement of the walls of the valley into four canyons leading in from the four points of the compass, formed in effect a perfect cross. From this appearance the Indians had named it "Cross Valley." The length of the cross lay from east to west, its shorter arms from north to south. By the pass through the northern canyon, the road entered the valley, crossed its width, and climbed out through a corresponding pass in the southern canyon to the higher mesas of the Guejito. At tight angles to these, a long narrow canyon entered from the east bearing the stream-bed, and a fourth canyon affording a narrowing outlet to the west, drained the first three.

In the bottom of the basin thus formed, to the east and south lay Lovett's hundred and sixty acres, level and free from timber, except for the few large, beautiful oaks desired for shade. A surrounding brush fence marked the boundaries of his claim. Several springs of clear flowing water, one of which bubbled up cold and sparkling in his dooryard, gave ample assurance of a bountiful underground supply and a thriving young vineyard of three acres attested to the soil's productiveness. A short distance back from the bank of the wash stood his small adobe house, its walls a foot and a half in thickness for coolness in summer and warmth in winter. Without doubt his location was the choicest in the valley.

The western drainage canyon furnished the second-best location, a large portion of which was level farming land, the remainder on both sides of the valley running steeply up into the hills. This claim had been taken by a man named Sam Stripling who now occupied it with his family. Their adobe house stood some distance below the roadway, near which he had set out some pecan trees. Along with his farming he kept bees, and his apiary could be seen among the oaks on the hillside.

Adjoining his western boundary lay still another small acreage of unclaimed land almost entirely in the mountains. This included the deep, rocky gorge that drained the valley, and was afterward taken up for a bee ranch by another settler while our family lived in the valley.

Along the foot of the northern mountain to the left of the entering pass, and stretching eastward to include an area of low rolling hillocks, more or less covered with oaks, lay the sixty unoccupied acres of which Lovett had spoken to Father, the rest of the quarter-section lying among heavily timbered mountains. Here he decided to locate.

Mr. Lovett had lived in the valley for four years and was its first settler—in fact, its first white discoverer. Poorest of the poor, he and his family had come into the region two years after the close of the Civil War. They had passed through a period of unspeakable hardships, but at the present time were fairly comfortable, though lacking facilities for properly farming the land, most of which was still uncultivated. He possessed a few cows and yearlings and a horse or two besides his team, one of which was a stray.

In those days it was allowable that a stray animal taken up should be used by the finder until called for by the owner. In case the owner never came to claim him, the finder might sell him if desired, but only after fully explaining to the buyer his true status. The buyer then took his own chance of someday having to relinquish his purchase to the actual owner. The price of such a horse was never equal to that of one properly certified, but set with due allowance for the risk. So it happened that Lovett was working this horse he had never bought.

In the Army, Mr. Lovett had driven a Sutlers wagon and when the war was over, had come west with his family and his army savings, driving across the country from New Mexico to Yuma. There he and his wife were both laid low with Typhoid Fever, a disease then little understood, and languished for many months. When again able to travel, their money was gone.

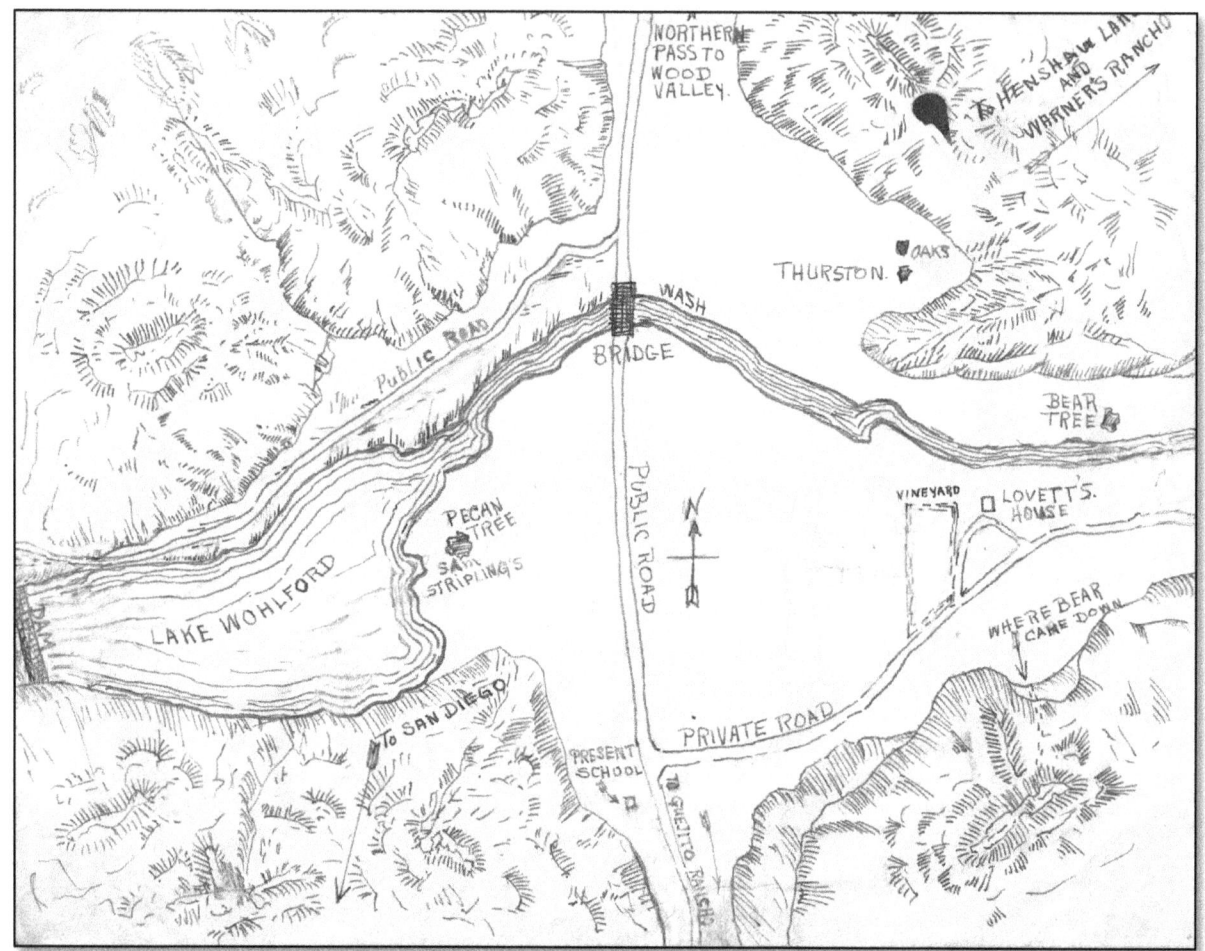

Figure 3 Map of Bear Valley Settlement

They came into the San Luis Rey Valley spent and weary, strangers in a strange land without funds, and were befriended by an Indian who took them into his own brush hut, where they remained for some time. This Indian taught Lovett how to construct a brush house like his own, and also how to manufacture adobe bricks for building.

Travelling further into the mountains from San Luis Rey, on a quest for government land, they came upon Cross Valley, where no white man's foot had yet been known to tread. There they settled, living for a time without a roof over their heads other than the canopy of an oak tree.

Soon after coming, he was apprised of the presence of bears in the valley by the discovery of their tracks. He then put up a brush house—scant protection at best—fashioned after the Indian's directions, and inside it built a high loft to be reached by a ladder, for the family sleeping quarters. He built also a brush shelter with a manger for his horses.

To earn a living for his family it was necessary that he secure work, which could be found only at a great distance from home. So for days at a time, even weeks, he was obliged to leave them alone unprotected. While thus employed in San Diego, his family passed through a harrowing experience with a huge Grizzly bear.

One day while the unsuspecting children were playing out in the manger, the mother from within the brush house, spied a big Grizzly making his way down the southern mountainside opposite. Snatching up the old "blunderbuss" her husband had left for her use and the basket in which lay her sleeping infant, she climbed up the ladder onto the loft and waited for the bear while the children at her call, snuggled down in the manger. Taking aim, as he approached, she fired, the old gun making only a great noise.

Not liking this disturbance, the bear shied around the house, and ambled off across the wash. About fifty feet up from the bank grew a leaning oak tree that stretched a long crooked arm out toward the stream. To the trunk of this tree was tied a yearling heifer, their only cow. This pioneer woman was obliged to watch helplessly while the ferocious Grizzly killed the animal and then satisfied his hunger on her warm flesh. After finishing his repast he made his way out of sight up into the eastern canyon.

When sure he was far enough away for reasonable safety, she left her children in the brush house up on the loft while she ran across the valley and up through the pass into Wood Valley where lived an old Indian, their only neighbor. He came back with her and arming himself with the old blunderbus, climbed up into the tree above the carcass of the half-eaten cow, and waited for the bear's return. Familiar with the habits of bears, he knew that this one would come again sooner or later to appease a recurring appetite.

All night he waited perched on this horizontal limb some eighteen feet above the ground. In the early dawn of the following day, sure enough the bear came back for another meal. The man in the tree, waiting till he was thus engaged, fired at him. Enraged, with his wound, the bear then endeavored to get at the man in the tree. But Grizzlys, owing to their cumbersome build and lack of coordination from the fact that their front legs are disproportionately shorter than their hind legs, are unable to climb trees. This enables the smaller tree-climbing bears to avoid their attack, as well as affording a means of escape for humans.

Wounded further by another shot, the bear desisted and left the scene, seeking refuge in the wooded canyon from which he had come. The Indian then went to secure the help of two white men who lived in another valley, and together with these men tracked the big Grizzly far up into the canyon, where they found and shot him to death. Leaving the dead bear to the buzzards, they returned in triumph with the welcome news.

When Mr. Lovett, after coming home, heard the account, he remembered that a reward of fifty dollars had been offered for the death of this big Grizzly by Colonel Maxey, who owned a ranch of five or six thousand acres over the hills beyond the Guejito.

So taking his team of horses, he started up the canyon to search for the carcass. He succeeded in finding it and dragging it down to the yard, where with some difficulty he loaded it into his wagon. He hauled it over to the headquarters of Colonel Maxey who readily paid him the promised reward. Thus Mr. Lovett was enabled to replace his lost cow.

From the death of this big Grizzly, whose depredations had been suffered far and near, Bear Valley received its present name. And gradually the old Indian name of Cross Valley was forgotten.

It was with no little enthusiasm that Father, after investigating this proposition returned to the camp on Perrin's lot, with the decision made to move his family up into Bear Valley. The whole family was happy at the prospect of at last having a place to settle permanently—a place they could call home.

The white-collared, kid-gloved friend had found the difficult experience too much for him. He said he would not live up there and travel over those roads for all the land in the country. So it was that after this trip, they parted and the family never saw him again. Doubtless, he found it much easier to go on as he was, living off his wife's labor, than to brave the hardships of a pioneer life, and roughen his pretty, soft hands.

Several days were required for preparations before starting, as necessary supplies must be secured and taken up with them. For San Diego was the nearest source of supply to Bear Valley, requiring about a week for the arduous trip there and back—a trip not to be lightly undertaken, or more frequently than absolutely necessary. When one man was making the trip, all his neighbors would send by him for whatever they needed, and thus they took turn about in supplying the community with provisions.

At length all was ready. It was early in the month of May that the family broke camp and pulled up stakes, bidding goodbye to the Perrins who had been so kind to them. George's twelfth birthday on May ninth came to him during the journey up into Bear Valley, thus furnishing another birthday landmark to fix the date of an important move.

Several nights, they camped on the way, and the journey was not completed without a slight mishap or two. Whenever they came to an especially steep grade, or dangerous place in the road, the family got out and walked to lighten the load for the straining horses. On one such occasion, Father saw that by turning out of the road a little way the grade could be made more easily. But in turning, he passed too close to a tree by the roadside whose branches were not high enough for the covered wagon to pass under, and before he realized what was happening, the stout branches had torn the canvas top and broken two of the wooden bows over which it was stretched. He stopped the team, pulled on the brake, and got out of the wagon to investigate. George, who had been walking ahead, came back down the hill and drew near just as Father was jerking out one of the broken bows somewhat viciously—for he was irritated at the accident—and the piece struck George with full force across the upper lip, cutting a nasty gash and causing severe pain and swelling. Mother was fearful that it would leave an ugly scar, but fortunately the wound healed without doing so.

They traveled for some distance up the historic San Pasqual Valley, whose Indian village of that name, twenty-five years earlier, had been the scene of the "bloodiest battle in the conquest of California," in which Colonel Stephen Kearney, with the remnant of his "Army of the West," was valiantly opposed by the Californians under Andres Pico, in the "Battle of San Pasqual." A few families, both white and Mexican, still resided in the valley.

Here the road branched, the main arm winding on to the left across the valley, and a short cut to the right leading up a long and very steep grade. Good mileage could be saved by taking this short cut, but it was impossible for a load to be pulled over it without the help of extra horses. There were men living in the vicinity who hired out their teams for this purpose.

Father, anxious to reach his destination as soon as possible, decided to take this short cut. As the hour was late he camped for the night at the foot of the grade, and the next morning hunted up a man with a team to help him over the grade. With this team in the lead, the feat was soon accomplished, and he paid the man for his services and drove on up the hill.

After a while he came to another steep pull, a short one not usually considered too much for a team. Here the family got out to walk. Just as the wagon reached the steepest part of the grade, Ted stopped and refused to go a step farther. In vain Father urged him on. Not another inch would he budge, and the wagon began slowly to slip back down the hill. It was a precarious situation. Only an experienced teamster could have handled it. He let the wagon go backward until a more level spot was reached, and there put on his brakes and let the horses rest a bit.

Then again he took the grade, using the lash to urge them onward over the sharp pitch. But again Ted balked, stopping on the exact spot as at the first. Neither persuasion nor the lash had the least effect upon him. There he stood immovable, except as the wagon, rolling back down hill, drew him with it.

Several times this attempt was repeated, with the horse balking stubbornly at the same spot, until finally Father had to give up. Somehow he must manage to turn around on that steep and narrow mountain road. Father was equal to the occasion. Letting the wagon drift down to the former resting place, he cramped the wheels and backed off the road up the hill the length of the wagon, which seemed almost to be tipping over, thereby effecting a turn, and the family climbed in. Back they came down to the foot of the grade where they had so lately camped, with half a day wasted to say nothing of the money. Then they took the long way around, spending an extra night on their journey.

In the afternoon, Father pulled out of the road where trees afforded a pleasant spot to rest for dinner, and unhitched the horses, placing nosebags of grain over their heads, and preparations for a campfire were begun. While this was going on, a flock of sheep was being driven past the place. George slipped away and went over to watch them. One of the ewes had given out on the journey and lay exhausted at the feet of the shepherd.

Usually, traveling sheep were accompanied by a wagon for the purpose of picking up any that might succumb to fatigue, but with this band, there was no wagon and no way for the shepherd to take her with him. To leave her behind meant to abandon her to the prowling coyotes, so he offered her to George.

Thrilled with delight, the boy ran back to ask Father if they might take her along. He readily assented, and came over to the place where she lay, picked her up in his arms, and carried her back to the wagon, where he made a place for her to lie among the goods, under the canvas cover.

George began immediately to pet and caress her, as she lay unafraid, while the other children perched about watching happily. He offered her water to drink and brought her bits of green stuff to eat. Dinner over, they were soon on their way again, the new pet resting comfortably in their midst, seemingly as pleased as they over the arrangement.

At evening time they camped again for the last night by the roadway, hastening to get supper over with before darkness fell. Here they lifted the sheep out to try her legs. She seemed fully recovered, and to George's delight, followed him around like Mary's little lamb of the story book. She even played hide and seek with him among the trees around the wagon. Soon all the children were playing with her unafraid, but George, she acknowledged as master and favorite. He lavished caresses upon her, and all the rest of the journey, could think and talk of nothing else. He tied her that night to the wagon-wheel for safety. After that, whenever they piled out to lighten the load, the sheep also was put out, and followed along behind as though she had always belonged to the outfit.

At last they came to the branch road that led out of Wood Valley on the last stretch of their journey. Here they passed a few primitive homes of settlers, one of whom they later came to know as Mr. Kolp. Here also, under the spreading branches of a huge old oak tree by the roadside, the public school for the whole district was conducted in the open air.

Soon they reached the pass where the canyon walls drew closer together, and looked down upon the spot in the valley below where Father had already planned to pitch his camp. Near the bottom of the descent they met one of the Stripling boys who invited them to put up at his father's place for the night. Glad to accept this hospitality, Father drove down to the Stripling house, where they received a warm welcome, and there the tired newcomers spent their first night in Bear Valley.

In this home were three almost grown young people, two sons and a daughter. So there were twelve who gathered that night around the hospitable supper table. George was the only one of the children who had ever before tasted honey. Served heavy in the comb, it was a great treat to the visitors. When Mrs. Stripling noticed what a small piece of honey Mother was serving to each of her flock, she exclaimed:

"Oh, give them a chunk!" and herself cut off a large as that Mother would have served to the whole family.

Under the Oaks

Under two huge oak trees, one of them twenty-one feet in circumference and the other fifteen feet, that grew about three rods apart, Father pitched his tent, becoming the third settler in Bear Valley. Lovett's house was something like a quarter of a mile distant around the point of the low separating hillock and on the other side of the wash.

Right away, the barefoot children found themselves tormented with intermingled sand burrs and clover burrs, cast early in the distressing drowth (drought) . In the night they would hear the fearful sound of coyotes barking, which made them huddle closer to one another and draw the covers over their heads. But soon they began to get acquainted with their new surroundings and feel more at home.

The pet sheep never strayed away from the camp, but was satisfied and happy to feed close by in the companionship of the children. But though allowed to run free in the daytime, she was tied up at night close to the tent for her protection. It was George's daily chore to feed and water her and see that she was cared for at night.

Several weeks went by, and then one evening he somehow forgot to tie up the sheep, and in the morning she was gone. For long distances on every side of the camp they searched heart-brokenly, but found no trace of her. Had she been caught by wild beasts, her carcass would have been discovered, since she was too heavy for a wildcat or coyote to have dragged away very far. So that theory was given up and it was decided that she had been stolen. Some covetous person, riding by in the night, must have lifted her up onto his horse and made away with her.

Her loss was a grievous blow to the children, especially to George, whose grief was mingled with remorse. Father and Mother, besides being fond of her, had considered her the nucleus of a whole flock of sheep in prospect. But they never saw her again.

The Lovetts had five children, corresponding in ages and sex quite remarkably to Father's own family. There was a son a few months older than George named Frank, and the two became inseparable companions. There were two girls about the ages of Sadie and Artemisia, named Kate and Ada, another little girl two years older than Lafie, called Amelia, and a boy younger than Joseph, not yet weaned. The two families soon became fast friends, the young folks being more or less together every day. Sadie and Mesia were often with these two girls, romping together in the nearby woods, exploring the mountainsides, climbing trees, hunting birds' nests and playing with their dolls. Sometimes they would dress up in the cast-off clothes of their elders and "play lady" and "keep house," with the younger ones for their "children."

Every day they had their periods of study from school books brought with them on train and boat, and would recite their lessons to Father or Mother. Artemisia possessed a remarkable aptitude for memorizing, of which Father was very proud. At the age of six he had taught her a long poem entitled "Forgive and Forget," and several songs of twelve or more stanzas, in sentiment scarcely suited to a child of her tender years.

From the Fourth Reader, she would commit to memory the definitions given at the beginning of each lesson, without even understanding their meaning. Into the low crotch of a special tree near the camp, she would climb with her book, and there study her lesson to the music of the birds, undisturbed unless perchance Frank Lovett, her hero, happened along and stopped to admire or tease her. One day he caught her sucking her thumb—a hang-over from babyhood—and made fun of her:

"For shame! For shame! A big girl seven years old sucking her thumb!"

After this she tried very hard to break herself of the unlovely habit, for she greatly admired Frank and wished to appear well in his eyes. His good-natured raillery proved to be of more benefit to her than all the cayenne pepper, asafoetida, and other ill-tasting applications that Mother had resorted to in order to make thumb-sucking disagreeable.

But though this incentive proved effective during the daytime hours when others were about, yet on the drowsy pillow at night that pale bloodless thumb, with its nail thin and brittle from overmuch use, would unconsciously find its way into her mouth again; and not until she had turned nine was the habit completely conquered.

In the adjoining valley was a young bachelor named Higgins, who claimed no land of his own, but worked around here and there for others. He affected the cowboy type of attire and manners, riding about on horseback in leather breeches and "ten-gallon" hat. Occasionally he would ride over the ridge into Bear Valley to see the Lovett family.

Sometimes Lafie would be there visiting when he came. Then he would get their little girl of six and Lafie to run races with each other. Being older, she would of course outrun Lafie. This so exasperated him that one day, in the chagrin of defeat, he bit her. This put a terminus to the racing sport.

Mr. Lovett, in the kindness of his heart, gave to Father's family all the milk obtained from a certain one of his cows. George would go over there night and morning to get the milk and carry it back to their tent under the oaks. Usually he went early in order to watch Mr. Lovett milk the cows, for George had never before had anything to do with cattle, and Mr. Lovett was giving him lessons in milking.

At these times Lafie often accompanied him that he might play with the Lovett children while the milking was going on. Mrs. Lovett was a motherly woman, kindhearted like her husband, and every time he came would seat him at the table and give him a bowl of bread and milk, for she knew that in Father's straightened circumstances, there was no sumptuous amount of food on his table at home.

The Lovett girls made much ado over Lafie. He must have been a very attractive little chap, and perhaps rather spoiled. One evening while George as usual was watching the milking, they determined to carry out a scheme to keep Lafie there with their family all night. They had an old sugar barrel in which were kept chips to burn. It was about half full. The girls put him into the chip barrel and said:

"Now you lie down and keep quiet, and when George gets ready to go home he won't know where you are, and he'll go home without you."

So Lafie squatted down in the chip barrel and waited. When George was ready to go he looked for him about the place, but not finding him, called his name loudly. This was a contingency that had not been specifically provided for. Not being able in so short a time to reason himself out of this unexpected situation, he answered the summons, and of course had to scramble out of the chip barrel and go home with George.

One day Father took Lafie with him on a trip into town. There he went into a grain and feed store which was owned and operated by a man named Mendenhall—a name that still survives in Mendenhall Canyon. There were grains and seeds of various kinds in many bags set in rows on each side of the long store, the tops rolled down exposing the contents. Father went ahead down the aisle with the storekeeper, while Lafie lagged behind. He was very fond of raw wheat, and seeing the bag so temptingly open, reached in his hand slyly and took a handful, putting it into his pocket to be eaten when alone.

Nobody had seen this act, but his conscience hurt grievously, so that for a long time afterward, even in dreams, he worried about it. The sweet relief from sin afforded by honest confession, was something in which he had never been instructed, though taught always to speak the truth; so he could only wonder what would be his punishment for stealing that wheat.

While in Bear Valley, Lafie saw his first rattlesnake—a dead one that somebody had laid out; but this was not by any means the last one he was destined to see.

He also saw for the first time, the baleful effects of liquor-drinking; for drunkenness with all its attendant laxness in moral character, was not uncommon in that section. Two men, neighbors and friends, went on a "spree" together and got into a drunken quarrel. They cut and slashed each other with knives till their faces were covered with blood. This left an impression in favor of temperance upon his young mind that a lifetime could never efface.

Here, in Bear Valley, Father saw bees for the first time, and immediately became interested in bee-culture and honey production, learning all he could about it from his neighbors. They themselves were "new at the game," having just begun to acquire a few swarms of bees from the surrounding woods, where they nested wild in rocks and hollow oak trees. Soon he began to find bees for himself in the trees about the place. He made a standing offer of two dollars and fifty cents apiece for every swarm that was shown him by others, and in this way gathered a number of swarms; Mr. Higgins himself leading him to several bee-trees.

At that time there was very little literature available on the subject of bee culture—none at all that Father could get hold of. But men in California were trying to learn by experimentation how to care for bees, and handle them and their honey. In ancient times, when a bee hive was full of honey, men knew of no other way to get the honey for their own use than to kill the bees. And this they did, sacrificing the little workers on the altar of their ignorance. Father also accidentally sacrificed a swarm through ignorant thoughtlessness.

Bees are afraid of smoke and fire. Having learned this, bee-men use smoke to control bees. In the daytime, you can drive bees where you want them to go by using the smoke on them, for they will always go away from the smoke, but when there is an artificial light, and darkness everywhere beyond its beams, bees become confused and will go toward the light—smoke or no smoke. This is one of the things Father learned about bees from his own unfortunate experience.

One afternoon, finding two bee trees not far from the camp, he proceeded to cut them down, one at a time, to get the honey and capture the bees. The first tree, he severed a few feet from the ground, the bees being in a hollow rather high up in the tree. He then cut a lengthwise slab from the face of the hollow part to get at the honey and bees, and soon had them transferred—the bees to his box-hive in the usual way by the use of smoke, and the honey in pans. But by the time he had the second tree cut down and opened up into the bee cavity, it was getting dark. Instead of waiting till the next day to secure this swarm, he continued to work by firelight, building a small bonfire nearby to afford light for the operation. This is where the "experience" came in. The bees did not act in the accepted manner, but seemed confused and agitated. Instead of going before the smoke they spread around everywhere uncontrolled, or drawn to the bonfire, many of them perishing in its flames. He could not get them to go into the box; so finally he took a sack—a closely-woven, two-bushel grain sack brought with him from Utah—and holding it closely down over the mass of bees, finally got the larger portion of them into it by scooping them up with his hands, tying its mouth to keep them from escaping. He then carried the sack down to the camp, intending, as it was very late, to put them into the hive in the morning.

But Father had overlooked the important fact that bees, like all living creatures, must have plenty of fresh air to breathe, and when he opened the sack in the morning, every bee in it was dead from suffocation.

Footprints in the Rock

Frank Lovett and George went together on various trips of exploration into the surrounding mountains and valleys, sometimes going afoot, sometimes on horseback. They rode southward into the edge of San Pasqual Valley to view the country, and northward, eastward and westward, for boys must be busy, and there was very little work to be done. Always George took with him the little thirty-two rifle, which he was learning to use and also teaching Frank to handle. Sometimes they would bring home rabbits or quail, both abundant in the region, and occasionally startled a deer, who would jump out of the brush and go bounding away, stopping at a safe distance to look back inquiringly.

One day when afoot, roaming over the hillsides, with no other object but to see what they could of their surroundings, the boys made a remarkable discovery. On the northwestern ridge between the entering pass and the Stripling place, they came across a large raised flat rock, or series of rocks, separated by fissures, concealed from view by scrub oak growing there in the rich leaf-mold soil to a height of from ten to fourteen feet. This rock sloped steeply with the mountainside and might have measured something more than twelve feet from upper to lower edges, and horizontally from eighteen to twenty feet. Its slant was so steep that it was impossible to walk across its surface except by stepping in the depressions with which it was thickly covered.

These depressions were the remarkable feature about the rock. Every one of them had been made by the bare foot of a human being—made when the rock was in a plastic state of putty consistency. They ranged in size from the track of a ten-year-old child to that of an adult, and were evidently made purposely and in play. Many of them were contorted in every conceivable manner, as though the mass had been discovered in its clay-like state by some primitive inhabitants who had stopped to have some fun in passing. In some tracks the toes were pressed down deep. In others the heels were dug in. Some were of the side of the foot, many were made by jumping, others by dragging the foot or lengthening the toes. A few were natural.

Every bit of available space was thus covered with tracks which had been left to harden and eventually had turned to stone. Naturally, the bottoms of these depressions were on a different plane than the surface of the rock, for the ancient track-makers had stood upright in the soft material and not at right angles to the steep surface. This enabled the two discoverers to walk down across its sloping face in an upright position by stepping in their predecessors, now permanently fixed in the solid rock.

This most interesting archeological formation still lies where they found it in Seventy-One. And there it may be seen. After the passing of so many years, it is spoken of as a curiosity by present-day dwellers in the community.

With the arrival of the first fall days, a delightful event took place—delightful at least to the younger members of the family. On September two, under the gigantic spreading oaks of their canvas home, Baby Joan first saw the light of day, with Father and dear kindly Mrs. Lovett as Mother's only attendants.

Mrs. Lovett told the happy inquiring children that she had found the little baby out in the ash pile under the oak tree. So the younger children supposed that it was she who had given them the baby when she might have kept it all for herself; and considered her most unusually kind. Little Joan thus had the distinction of being the first of the family to be born a "Native Daughter of the Golden West."

CHAPTER 3 SETTLED AT LAST

After Father had been in Bear Valley for a while, he discovered that his two nearest neighbors were not on the best of terms with each other. This was a peculiarly unfortunate situation since neighbors were so few. It appeared that Lovett's occupancy of the choicest quarter-section of land was the underlying cause of some jealous feeling; though being the first settler in the valley, he was naturally entitled to first choice. As he mingled with the people just over the rim in the next valley, Father could not help learning that others, though holding Lovett in high esteem, held opinions unfavorable to the other man. This condition existing among the settlers was a distinct disappointment to Father and Mother; creating within them a feeling of reserve with regard to their social contacts, and of restraint against too great intimacy with the family whose hospitality they had at first so freely accepted.

Other conditions also added to the disappointment and general discontent they began to experience. They had come to the valley in the midst of a series of several consecutive dry years; which caused everything to appear to a great disadvantage. The drowth was in evidence everywhere. Streams were dried up, grass was dead, and the prospect of making a living seemed anything but promising. In the country from which they had come there was a flowing stream in every gully. Things grew without any effort. There was green grass everywhere. One did not have to be a farmer to raise crops. And Father was really not a farmer.

He had done various things in his life, and in his own line was very proficient. He had been in the lumber and milling business and had run a saw mill at one time. He had once owned an up-to-date grist mill in his home state, and previous to that had engaged in hauling freight from Salt Lake City to the mines in Montana. He knew all about horses and how to break and train them, but actual farming was new to him—especially California farming.

The mountains of his hundred and sixty acres were covered with woods, but not such as he had been used to. There was really no milling timber. It was for the most part suitable only for fuel.

All native Californians expect the streams in summer to go dry. But to the family from verdant Utah, this was an incurable drawback. They were disgusted to find that all their water, even for stock, must be drawn up by hand out of the ground. Exasperated, George exclaimed:

"Have to haul up water out of a hole to water the horses! You couldn't even get water enough to drown yourself in!"

Yet water was close to the surface. Father dug a well eleven feet deep and found plenty of water. He had not learned that Southern California was always a dry country, that water was precious, that one must understand the methods of farming peculiar to the country, in order to produce crops here.

From the wild swarms of bees, in five months he had hived twelve or fourteen stands, which cost him nothing except for the boxes and the few dollars he had paid others for conducting him to bee-trees. He could have made a good living for his family from the bee culture alone. Honey in those days was an expensive luxury, and San Diego County produced the best honey in the world. It sold for a high price—high in those days when one dollar was like ten today—eighteen cents a pound for the choicest honey, fifteen cents for the medium good, and ten cents for the poorest.

The Lovetts were wonderful neighbors. None better could be found anywhere, and rarely are such desirable neighbors to be had.

Yet, notwithstanding these advantages—which were regarded as such only when looking backward from the viewpoint of years, then future—the whole family were homesick. This condition itself was disheartening. Poor Mother, whose heart was overburdened for many reasons besides the desolating homesickness, though by nature of a cheerful disposition, would steal out into the deep woods away from the children, and "cry her eyes out."

It was for these reasons—mostly psychological—that the decision was finally reached to abandon the claim. If only they had stayed on through that first year and had experienced the four seasons, no doubt their feelings would have undergone a change; for who can judge a place by a few dry months of summer—and that too of a dry year? Father had a "good thing" in Bear Valley had he only known it. But being so new in the country, and finding it so very different from that he had been used to, he was unable to recognize a good thing when he saw it.

Lovetts were sad at the thought of their going. A strong attachment had been formed between the two families, and they tried hard to dissuade them from their purpose. Mr. Lovett offered to give Father twenty acres adjoining his of his own good level land containing a flowing spring, so soon as he should procure a title to it, if he would only stay in the valley.

But Father had set his mind on land at lower level, and his heart was toward Los Angeles County. The advantages of his present location, even with these added inducements, he could not at that time appreciate. So he disposed of his bees, which could not be transported—the neighbors taking them off his hands—and vacated his claim five months from the time of their arrival in the valley.

The land they then abandoned became in after years very valuable. During the boom period of the eighties, when California was awakened, the active development going on in San Diego County extended up into the Escondido Valley and on up over the steeps into the valleys of Smith's Mountains. Irrigation projects were launched in various parts of the county, and water companies formed for the purpose of supplying the whole coast mesa. When the major irrigation project with its distributing system was finally completed, an abundant supply of water from the San Luis Rey River was brought down into the Escondido Valley and distributed over an area of nearly two and a half thousand acres from the mountain to the sea.

At this time the lower end of Bear Valley was selected for the site of a reservoir and dam, for which purpose the location was naturally fitted. The land formerly owned by Stripling and his western neighbor was purchased from their assigns at a great monetary advantage to them, and land values were raised throughout the whole region. Good roads were built into the valleys, little settlements sprang up here and there, and today the region is a rich farming district.

The dam, built in Ninety-two, was constructed at the top of the deep, narrow gorge and extended across the width of the canyon. Behind it is now a large lake that covers the greater portion of what was Stripling's land. A large, symmetrical Pecan tree stands alone near the margin of the water, beautiful and silent, marking the site where once stood their old adobe cabin. Both lake and dam are now known by the name of Wohlford.

When they came to break camp, it was found that their one wagon would not now hold all their belongings, so much had been accumulated during their sojourn. Mr. Kolp, of the neighboring valley, was hired to haul in his own wagon a portion of the household goods. When all was ready for departure, they bade a reluctant farewell to their neighbors and turned to leave the little valley.

But their friendship with the Lovett family did not end with this separation. For many years a correspondence was kept up between the young folks. Several years afterward, Father alone made a business trip back into the valley, and again saw their old friends. This proved to be the last time.

This Mr. Kolp was a great bee hunter. On the way down the mountain they stopped their teams below a point of hill, on which grew an old hollow tree that was seen to be inhabited by a swarm of bees. He and Father chopped down the tree, and found it stored full of honey, which they scooped out, bringing two pans full down to the wagon. It proved to be the delicious White Sage—the kind that has since made the honey of that section famous. Connoisseurs tell us that the flavor of no other flower can be compared to that of White Sage. Its delicacy is not surpassed even by the famous wild rosemary honey of sunny France, the Heather honey of the British Isles, the wild Blueberry of New England, and the wild Raspberry of northern Michigan. Nothing can be found that makes better honey than the pure White Sage of Southern California.

Though Father afterward kept bees again in our own Aliso Canyon, none of the honey produced could compare in delicacy of flavor with the honey tasted that day. Not that there was no white sage on our mountains, but it grew more sparsely and was of itself insufficient for the bees to preserve in its purity. The black sage predominated, so this and other flavors were mingled with it. From time to time also, our mountains were swept by disastrous fires that destroyed the white sage, the more hardy black sage surviving to take possession.

Often in after years the family longed for honey like that they had in Bear Valley. But not finding such flavor anywhere, they wondered if after all it could have been imagination only—just the romance of first impression that had made it so desirable. Until one day thirteen years later, when Lafe was extracting honey from some hives in San Jacinto. Taking a taste, he shouted with delight:

"It's the same honey! It's the Bear Valley honey!"

Truly it was the flavor of the pure White Sage, and only then did he learn what it was that made the difference.

After reaching the floor of the valley, they traveled northward eventually striking the old stagecoach road. This they followed for more than a hundred miles. When overtaken by darkness, they slept by the roadside, spreading their beds out on the ground under the blue sky studded with stars.

Mother had an iron "Dutch oven" in which she baked biscuit-dough bread, called by the family "fried bread." She patted it out thin and greased the bottom of the kettle heavily before putting it in. Of this they all were very fond.

On their way northward, after crossing the border into Los Angeles County, they passed through the Mexican town of San Juan Capistrano half way between San Diego and Los Angeles. That year its first schoolhouse had been dedicated. Here stood the old mission whose building was begun in Seventeen Seventy-Six, finished thirty years later, and six years after that was destroyed in the great earthquake of Eighteen Twelve. Not all of the building was shaken down in that destructive temblor. The Padre's reception room and guest hall, vestry, kitchen and chapel still remained intact, the chapel being the only remaining church of the missions of California that was dedicated by Fray Junipero Serra himself.

Late the next day, after crossing the Niguel Rancho they struck the broad acres of Rancho San Joaquin, and towards nightfall came to a large slough that straggled in from the low swamp lands on the west. Here was a sheep corral, the fold of about a thousand hungry sheep, and a tiny cabin for the herder.

Seeing the water, Father decided that the location was as good a camping place as he was likely to find. So they stopped in the vicinity, several miles southeast of the future town of Tustin. Here they pitched the tent and unloaded the wagon a short distance from this sheep corral.

The herder's cabin was hardly bigger than a piano box and could be moved in an ordinary wagon, a type of bunk-house often used by herders in early days. Mr. Kolp remained with them a few days to rest his team, then bade them goodbye and returned to his home in the Smith Mountains.

The townsite of Tustin had been laid out one year previously by Columbus Tustin, on a portion of the old Rancho Santiago de Santa Ana, purchased from the heirs. However, at this time, the town consisted of the name only, though two years later it supported a post office.

Some three miles northwest of Tustin lay the little town of Santa Ana, which had its birth a year earlier on a portion of the same rancho, about six months after the completion of the first transcontinental railroad. That year also had seen the first local railroad from Los Angeles to Wilmington, one day to become the great Los Angeles Harbor.

Santa Ana had been laid out in the midst of a field of mustard so dense and tall that its enterprising founder, W. H. Spurgeon, was obliged to climb a tree in order to look out over the new townsite. Its one business combined a general store and post office, where he waited for the expected growth of the town. Abundantly was his faith rewarded in after years. He lived to see a beautiful and thriving city with a population of many thousands and a large business section, the center of many surrounding settlements, and himself honored as "The Father of Santa Ana." A more phenomenal growth occurring since, he was not privileged to see.

Los Angeles, some thirty-three miles farther north, had a population of about five thousand when Father came into the County. Largest city of the Southland, it still had no pavements, either of walks or streets, no gas, no electric lights, since commercial lighting was still future, and not a street-car system of any kind, its first horse-drawn car appearing in Seventy-Four.

Two events made front-page news that fall. The great Chicago fire early in October, and about the time of Father's arrival at Tustin, the terrible Chinese massacre in Los Angeles. During a Tong War, an uncontrolled mob, in revenge for the Chinese shooting of an American, murdered nineteen Celestials, most of them wholly innocent, shooting them indiscriminately and hanging to the patio gates. This outrage almost created international complications, an indemnity to China being paid by the United States.

While Father was camped near this slough, he continued his search for government land. On every side of the townsite and well within the present city limits of Santa Ana, land could be bought for ten or fifteen dollars an acre. But the price might as well have been as many hundred dollars so far as Father was concerned, for he had no money at all, not even sufficient to feed his family properly. And work was well-nigh impossible to be had.

Wages were down to the vanishing point, pastures were dried up, cattle and sheep were dying everywhere from starvation. Every morning near their camp, several dead sheep would be dragged out of the corral and left there to rot. The coyotes, or Western Prairie Wolves, attracted by the odor, would come in packs and howl around the camp at night in a most dismal manner, frightening the children with their weird yappings.

Father, in his great need, seeing these dead sheep day after day, conceived a "bright idea." Why could he not save the wool from their carcasses and sell it? The thought presented possibilities. So he experimented. When the carcass had reached a certain stage of "tenderness" the wool was easily pulled out by hand. He secured the necessary wool-sacks and set George to work at this repugnant and evil-smelling task. From the decomposing carcasses, quite a number of the sacks were thus filled and before they left the place, one hundred and fifteen pounds of wool had been obtained in this manner, which, selling for fifteen cents a pound, netted Father seventeen dollars and twenty-five cents.

Meanwhile Father was hunting everywhere for work, and at last fortune favored him. A landowner nearby wanted a board fence built half a mile long through the slough. Both posts and boards for this fence had to be sawed the proper length, the post-holes dug, the posts set at correctly-measured distances apart, and every board fitted to its corresponding board to meet in the center of the post before nailing; and the fence was four boards high.

The labor on this project was easily worth a hundred dollars. But Father agreed to build it for twenty-five dollars cash, receiving as a further compensation the sawed-off ends of the boards; which ranged from eighteen inches to two and a half feet in length. These pieces afterward became of very definite use to him. When the fence was completed, Father received his twenty-five dollars, and this brought his cash capital up to forty-two dollars and twenty-five cents.

While Father and George were at work on this fence, Mother would send out their lunch to them at noontime every day, either by Mishie or by Lafie, who would carry the lunch pail in one hand and the coffeepot in the other. One day Lafie, after performing this duty, hung around while they ate their meager repast and watched them pour the coffee, the delicious aroma of which was too much for him to endure unmoved. Finally he said wistfully:

"I don't suppose there'd be enough for you, if I had a little of that."

In great extremity for food, Father shot a large, lean, white bird one day, which he afterward learned was a sandhill crane, and brought it home to be cooked for dinner. This proved to be a very unpalatable bird, and as usual, Artemisia experienced a digestive upset.

Introduced to Aliso

One day Father heard that a man batching about twelve miles south of camp in a canyon called Laguna, was desirous of renting out his place there. Mounting one of the horses, he set out to find him. After riding some miles across country, he entered the little oak-clad canyon seven or eight miles in length, following its willow-bordered creek, along a faint wagon track. After passing a crude rock wall built across the canyon, he came to the cabin, but found no one at home. Half a mile farther he stopped to inquire at another little house. But here too the occupants were gone.

As it was only about a mile and a half from there to the ocean, he rode on down to the beach to take a look at the great heaving mystery of water before returning to camp. Near the mouth of the canyon he passed a rather disreputable looking shack where lived a foreigner.

As far as the eye could see in every direction there stretched a broad and lonesome expanse of hills and sand and ocean, with no other sign of human habitation. Little did Father dream that he was standing on the site of a city of the future—a city beautiful and thriving that should extend almost as far as his vision extended up and down the coast, and from the seashore to the mountain tops behind.

As he stood fascinated by the vastness, the restlessness, the grandeur and the intonations of the mighty waters before him, his eye caught sight of an old fisherman out on the rocks to the northward patiently waiting for another "bite." Surprised and pleased at sight of a human being, and hoping it might be the man he had come to see, he started up the beach leading his horse along the sand until he came opposite. Here, in a sort of half cove, was a horse tied, and here, to some bushes, he tied his own horse, and clambered out over the rocks to the side of the fisherman.

Finding that he could tell him nothing about the man he sought, Father began, as was his wont with those he met, to sound him out on the subject of government land.

This old fellow proved to be quite interesting. He not only had knowledge, but was willing to communicate it.

"Yes, I know of a piece of government land not far from here."

"Where is it?" asked Father.

"Down in Aliso Canyon. It has been taken up and abandoned twice and is now open to the next comer."

"Where is Aliso Canyon?"

"If you'll wait till I get through fishing I'll go over and show you the place."

So, with much inward excitement, Father waited till the old man hauled in his line. They mounted their horses and rode southeastward along the coast, leaving the sandy beach with its impassable buttresses, and traveling along the gently rising mesa. Picking their way amongst brush and cactus, in and out of gulches, along the old winding and seldom-used pony trail, they came at last to the "jumping-off place," the steep high bluffs that over-looked the sandy beach lying before the mouth of Aliso Canyon.

Here they turned to their left to descend the brush-covered side of the mesa into the canyon. At the foot of the trail, separated from it by a little mustard-covered flat, lay a large pear-shaped body of water, its broadened lower end extending to the strip of white ocean beach, and its narrow upper neck merging with a little ocean-bound creek, now nearly dry, that flowed bending into it.

Crossing this flat and following up the stream, they came shortly to another bend and turned to their right. Some distance farther on appeared still another bend, where they turned northward to their left. Discerning about the same distance beyond this bend, traces of a wagon road to the right up the gently sloping bank, they followed it and entered a little clearing that nestled in an elbow-like curve of the eastern mountain on a gradual up-slope to its foot.

About midway of the clearing in the shadow of the high canyon wall, stood a small deserted cabin, manifestly the only improvement on the place. About the yard lay several dead cattle and sheep—mute evidence of the fearful drowth. The ground was treeless and rocky and pitted with squirrel holes. But to Father, it was land—government land at last! And land with a creek flowing through it.

Then he listened to the history of the place related by the old man. The cabin had been built some years previously by Mr. Rawson, the neighboring sheep rancher, for a sheepherder's cabin. A herder had squatted on the claim until dry weather burned up the feed and he had gone elsewhere.

Then a young man named Gene Salter from San Juan Capistrano, who had come to California in July of Sixty-Nine and had settled there that fall, hearing about the place and that the herder had overstayed his limit of absence, came over and jumped the claim. He made arrangements with Henry Charles, a man who had a well-stocked hog ranch in San Juan Capistrano, to raise hogs for him on shares. He was furnished with about fifty hogs and with his young brother Charlie, a lad then fourteen, drove them over to the Aliso claim, where he herded them for something like a year. These hogs were not used to the English language. When the boys would call: "Pig, Pig, Pig, Pig, Pig!" they would go on eating with supreme indifference. But when they learned to call: "Coche, Coche, Coche, Coche, Coche!" they would all come running.

But the drowth was severe and feed scarce. Hearing of what seemed to be a much better proposition some forty-five miles to the northwest near the coast, Gene had abandoned the Aliso place and gone to take up land in the Gospel Swamp. There was little likelihood that he would ever come back, and the opportunity was now Father's if he desired it.

The old fisherman was himself an employee of Mr. Rawson, and occupied a little cabin eleven miles further up the canyon. So instead of returning by the way they had come, he and Father rode on up the canyon together leaving the Aliso as it crossed the valley of the broad San Joaquin, and parting company at his cabin, Father continuing on to his camp about seven miles farther.

There was great excitement that night in the camp by the slough; with conjecture and eager anticipation. The family lost no time in beginning to pack up their effects ready for moving the next day.

While still in Bear Valley, George and Frank Lovett had made a boy's trade, in which George had received two chickens—a hen and a rooster. These, he had given to Mother, who had begun immediately to save the eggs for setting. While camped here in the slough, she had set the hen, who, that very day had hatched a brood of a dozen little chicks. For this newly-hatched brood, Mother felt great concern on account of the prowling coyotes, that she knew would scent them for many a mile. What to do with them over night was a problem.

She had an old-fashioned wooden dasher churn, and finally solved the problem by putting the hen and chicks inside it, after removing the dasher. As there was a good-sized hole in the cover, she figured there would be air enough entering to do them for the night.

In the morning she went to get them out early. Removing the lid, she lifted out the old hen in a decidedly dazed condition. But the brood, all save two, were dead in the bottom of the churn. Poor Mother! How badly she felt! To think she had killed her own little chicks of which she had been so proud! The two survivors turned out to be a pullet and a cockerel. And these with their parents making four, became the nucleus of Mother's future chicken industry.

Father could not carry all his belongings in one load down to the claim in Aliso Canyon. So he loaded up the things they would need first, taking with him Mother and the children, all except George, whom he left to guard the remaining goods until he should return for them, and set out for their future home.

They did not get a very early start, and with their heavy load, could travel but slowly. The day was cloudy, due to a sudden change in the weather, which up to that time had been very hot and dry, and a cold wind blew down the canyon. Soon it began to rain. With a roof of their own over their heads, this would have been a welcome change, but in a canvas-covered wagon with night coming on, caused no little concern. As the light of the sun failed, the horses, not being familiar with the road, lost the way, taking instead a side branch to their right. This led them out among a cluster of little hills where Father first realized that he was off the main road.

On the top of one of these low, hill-like elevations, was a large white-washed adobe house with lights streaming out of the windows. They made their way toward it. The rain increased peltingly. Then, at the foot of the hill, in a little sag filled with water, the wheels sank in a bog. Father got out of the wagon and went up to the house, greeted by the barking of dogs, to inquire the way and ask for help.

He found that the people living there were Spanish Californians by the name of Yorba. They spoke very little English, but seemed to be of a class above the ordinary Mexican, and were very hospitable and friendly. Father afterward learned more about them, that they were indeed of a fine old family at one time very wealthy, having been part owners of the broad acres over which he was now passing.

Kindly they invited Father and his family to pass the night under their roof, which he was very glad to do since he still had a long way to go and was hopelessly off his course. The men came down in the rain to help him un-hitch the horses and get the family up to the house. The covered wagon full of household goods, they left standing where it was for the night.

At first the children were afraid of these dark-complexioned people who spoke a strange language, but their genial hospitality soon established a measure of confidence. They offered to prepare supper for them all, which Father declined to allow. He accepted a bed for himself and Mother and spread out the bedding he had brought up from the wagon on the floor for the children. And before long, the house was wrapped in slumber. That day was the twenty-sixth of November, and the third birthday of little Joseph.

The following day was to be Artemisia's eighth birthday, for the birthdays of these two came only one day apart. To a child, there can be no more important occurrence than a birthday. Sometimes, when peculiarly associated with other events, birthdays may stand out clearly in memory through all the years of life; thus becoming useful in establishing dates that would otherwise be vague and misty. So it is by these remembered family birth-days that we are able to speak with assurance of definite dates in our journey through the years of long ago.

The rain was gone by morning, but the sky still was overcast, and there was a chill in the air. Artemisia had a birthday breakfast "a la Mexicana," for the big senoritas of the Yorba household made them all some tortillas which, though something new and strange, were hungrily enjoyed.

After breakfast, the men went down with the horses and helped pull the wagon out of the bog. It was about ten o'clock when they were finally ready to resume their journey. After many expressions of gratitude, com-prehended more by intuition than by clear understanding, a hearty "Adios" from their host, and promises on both sides to meet again, they took their departure. And truly, this was not the last of their acquaintance.

The long road down the canyon was scarcely more than two wagon-wheel tracks—and those seldom used—that crossed and recrossed the winding creek innumerable times. A cold wind came up again as the day wore on. It was late in the afternoon when they finally reached their destination, on that memorable twenty-seventh day of November, Eighteen Seventy-One.

Into the expectant eyes that for the first time gazed out upon their future home that day, came a look of distinct disappointment. The prospect was anything but cheering. The small battened California cabin, only about ten by eleven feet, was in a state of disrepair. The door was missing from its hinges—perhaps lying about somewhere. The one small window, opening on the south, was without glass. There were broken boards in the floor. And down under these, fallen through to the earth beneath, lay a dead sheep. Another dead sheep lay outside a little distance from the door opening, and still farther from the cabin, in an advanced state of decomposition, lay a dead cow. The only living things to greet the newcomers were the little squirrels that scampered about and chattered their protest at being thus disturbed by intruders. The ground was pitted with squirrel holes, and covered with partially embedded stones that ranged in size from pebbles to boulders, among which were sprinkled liberally, the droppings from sheep.

Upon the hard, dry surface of the sloping ground, the recent rain seemed to have left no impression. What had once been a semblance of vegetation, was now completely dead and trampled almost to invisibility—save for the stumpy parts of dried mustard stalks. Near the cabin on the downhill side, stood a scrubby elderberry tree, dwarfed to shrub-like proportions. And scattered here and there on the gray, brush-covered mountainside that half surrounded the cabin on the east and south, were a few of the same dwarf elderberries—the only things within the range of vision that might be called trees.

The sloping, treeless margins of the narrow creek that angled from northeast to southwest some fifty yards from the cabin, were carpeted with salt grass to the water's edge on either side, the grass even venturing across the stream in places where the water had dwindled to a mere trickle. No other green thing greeted the eye.

The soil was virgin. No plow had ever turned a furrow to the sun. To the lonely company that stood there, it was a scene unpromising in its barrenness and isolation. Artemisia slipped up to Mother and took her hand and looking up into her face, half whispered the doubting question:

"Ma, are we going to stay here?"

"I suppose so," Mother answered with weary resignation, "There's no other place to go."

It was impossible that they should then be able to visualize the garden of beauty it was destined to become under their persevering labors. All they could see ahead of them was hardship, loneliness and isolation; for there were no neighbors anywhere, and Father had but forty dollars to his name.

Had they sensed to the fullest extent, those future hardships, they would have remained only long enough to find another location somewhere else. But had they done so, my story would never have been written.

Father had wasted no time in these somber reflections. There was need for action, for the day was far spent. The first thing he did was to get the two sheep carcasses out of the way and repair the floor of the cabin. Then he cleaned it out and unpacked the wagon; putting inside the cabin, the beds, trunks, chairs and table. The wood stove, he set up outside near the door opening. The crowded cabin was too full to hold the stove. The open space in front was to become the kitchen, for Father had planned how he would arrange things.

They brought up water from the creek; but it was brackish and evil tasting, and so hard that the soap floated in curds instead of lathering into suds. The wood they gathered to burn was mostly old mustard stumps, damp from the recent rain, and for a time, it seemed impossible to get a fire started. The wind blew, further hindering their attempts, and the hungry children thought they would never get any supper that night.

At last, everything was unpacked, the beds made down, and the meager supper of soup eaten by the light of a candle. Mother hung up an old quilt over the door opening, and something over the window hole to help keep out the cold, and tucked the children into bed. Then Father and Mother lay down, with little Joseph under the covers across the foot of their bed, and between them, baby Joan who was nursing contentedly—the only one unaffected by their discouraging circumstances. And the tired family forgot their troubles in slumber.

When they awoke the next morning, though not early, they found it bitterly cold. The mountain, bending on two sides of their cabin held it in a cold shadow until long after the bright sunshine had warmed the atmosphere to the north and west of it.

Father fed the horses, and after a frugal breakfast scouted around to find something to burn that should serve the family until he could return with the last load of their belongings. Meanwhile the children ran about helping and getting acquainted with their surroundings. Then he hitched up the team and started on the long road back to camp and the boy who was waiting there, with intentions of being gone a day and a half, leaving his family alone in that loneliest of places.

He had proceeded but three or four miles up the canyon when he met coming down, two Mexicans in a light "rig," in the back of which could be seen a plow and a harrow. Father observed this outfit with a puzzled expression, and after they had passed, turned his head to take another look. Then he stopped his team considering for a moment what to do. The question intruded itself:

"Where can these Mexicans be going in this unfarmed country with a plow and a harrow?"

He could think of no place but his own new claim, and said to himself:

"I wonder if that is not the outfit who had the place before Salter, and knowing of his desertion, have come back to take possession. They're hurrying on account of the rain, intending to put in a crop."

Father turned his team right about face and followed the Mexicans down the canyon. In their lighter wagon they were soon lost to view, and he did not see them again until he came in sight of the cabin. Sure enough, there they were. They had stopped a little distance from it to examine the dead cow and were conversing in Spanish. Father passed them, left his team standing, and went into the cabin to the puzzled and fearful family, who had been watching the movements of the foreign strangers and were greatly relieved to see him return.

Father had never had any dealings with Mexicans and was not sure of his ground. Indians, he knew how to handle, but now was facing a new experience. He waited for them to make the first move. After a while they came toward the cabin and spoke to Father in Spanish—he greeting them in English. With gestures, they repeated their words. Father told them that he did not understand Spanish and could not talk with them unless they spoke in English. Then one of them began to speak in perfect English. He told Father that the place belonged to them, and ordered him to move out.

Father listened till he was through, then himself began to speak. He recounted to them the facts that had been told him by the old fisherman, showing that he was perfectly familiar with the history of the claim from the beginning. By the laws of California, he said, no one had a claim on the place but himself. All previous squatters had forfeited their rights by pro-longed absence.

"And now," he finished with emphasis, "You go, I stay. This place is mine. You'll never have it again as sure as your head is black"

When they saw that he was not to be intimidated and that he was well informed, they stepped back, consulted together in Spanish for a few moments, then turned and went away.

But Father was afraid of possible treachery. What if they should come back with reinforcements in his absence and make trouble? He thought best not to leave his family alone for a while, so stayed around the place for several hours, waiting and watching. But as nothing happened, he finally bade his family goodbye again and with much inward trepidation, set out once more on the road toward Tustin.

He traveled most of the night, arriving at the camp before dawn. George had been wholly unaware that rain had fallen; the area of rainfall not having extended so far north. After taking a few hours for sleep, early the next morning they loaded up the pile of lumber they had accumulated, consisting of the sawed-off fence-board ends, the trimmings from posts, and other odds and ends collected during their stay there; piling on top the remainder of their boxes and belongings, and lastly, taking down the tent. This, they rolled into a large bundle and hoisted in on top of all the other things under the canvas cover; and took their final departure from the spot where they had been camped for more than a month.

No time was lost in getting under way, for Father was anxious about his family left unprotected, and possibly at the mercy of angry Mexicans. Across the great San Joaquin rancho and down the canyon they drove, as steadily as they could with their heavy load, stopping only long enough to feed and rest the tired team. Large flocks of half-starved, bleating sheep could be seen on every hand, searching for food with noses to the ground, as they wandered over the barren pastures. It was a sight to arouse pity in the stoutest heart.

In due time they arrived at their destination, and Father was much relieved to learn that the Mexicans had not again been heard from. Nor did they ever return to the place, and nothing further came of the incident. But what if—Who on earth knows what to do with that little word "if"?—What if Father had been just one day later in getting there with his family to establish his claim? Well, this story could never have been written, that's all.

Father and George pitched the tent about eleven feet away from the cabin to the north of it, its front facing the cabin door. With the short ends of boards, he laid a much-pieced floor under the tent, extending it across the intervening space to meet the floor of the cabin itself, which it joined at the same level, but being a little wider than the cabin, passed it an equal distance on each side.

Then they took the canvas cover off from the wagon, and stretched it overhead between the tent and the cabin, for a roof to the kitchen. This gave them three rooms—if the middle one without side-walls could be called a "room." Here through winter's cold and summer's heat, they lived for several years. Not till time and weather had worn out the canvas, were walls and roof added to the floors that had been built.

CHAPTER 4 ALISO CANYON

To describe Aliso Canyon—or that part of it which might be considered our own—is our next undertaking. Not that we would describe it in its barrenness as first it came to view, but as first I knew and remember it, fruitful and beautiful under the magical hand of cultivation.

ALISO[i] is a Spanish name meaning Alder tree. Contrary to the prevailing idea, sustained by a few historical references, it does not mean Sycamore. The Spanish name for that is Sicomoro. The Alders, which originally must have given the canyon its name, in our day were to be found only in its upper end, where were plenty of rocks, more shade and a greater abundance of water. The lower portion was dotted with Sycamores.

Every foot of this part of the canyon is so fraught with interest and tender associations for one who has lived long within its sheltering walls, that in attempting its intimate description, one must be free to wander into its many bypaths, to press again the footprints of the past and linger here and there as fancy wills, breathing again the atmosphere of bygone days, sipping inspiration from its hidden springs, and touching with reverent hand its sacred shrines.

But wandering thus, would one not be likely to lose sight of the main highway, and find that after all it is not the canyon itself but the shadowy forms that live there, one has described? So then, let this first view be but a brief glimpse of its general contour that shall enable us at any future time to take our bearings from any wandering byway.

The general direction of the canyon from its source among the Santiago Hills to its outlet at the ocean, is both westward and southward. This course is accomplished by a series of nearly right-angled bends of the canyon walls, which for the sake of simplicity will be spoken of as true to the cardinal points of the compass, though actually somewhat "catawampus," for Nature has a way of disregarding man's convenient arrangements.

With the bends above our own portion of this canyon and its fascinating creek we are not concerned, though they were numerous and interesting. But the lower five of these major bends are a part of my story. Of these, we will call that the "first bend" which marks the beginning of that territory we originally claimed.

The creek, as it comes down from the north, after hugging the eastern side of the broadened canyon floor, made then at this boundary line, a right-angled turn westward directly in front of a smaller canyon from the east, opening into Aliso, thus interrupting the continuity of the Aliso canyon wall. The mouth of this branching canyon was filled with a beautiful Sycamore grove, from which it was given the name, Sycamore Canyon. Its southern wall, uniting with the Aliso wall, formed a sharp and prominent point. At the foot of this point was our "second gate," opening into Sycamore Canyon.

Though the creek here turns westward, the mountain wall continues on southward for a distance, making a curving sweep as it bends to parallel the creek, leaving between, an expansive level strip about half a mile long for our "filaree pasture." This pasture extended from the second gate to the "first gate," which opened into the upper end of our "apple orchard" where the mountain turned southward again and formed "Old Lion-Head" Point.

Now let us notice the canyon wall on the other side of the creek, beginning at the first bend. Diagonally across from the high point at the 'second gate," the canyon's opposite wall formed a corresponding point, in this case, acute, low, and almost flat on top, but rising gradually to distant high ridges, beyond which lay Laguna canyon. This region became the grazing grounds where we pastured our cattle on government land. An imaginary line crossing the creek along this diagonal slant from point to point, would indicate our supposed northern boundary, and there was built our first brush fence, met and supplemented at this low point by a rock wall with an accompanying row of pepper trees. This wall followed the foot of the receding mountain part way along the upper end of the "barley ground," the most northerly of our cultivated areas, and lying directly opposite the filaree pasture, which was never cultivated. The mountain curved westward, framing the far side of the barley ground and bringing it to an abrupt end by an impassable barrier of rock at the second bend, that turned the flow of the creek southward in a greatly widened stream as it compassed one side and end of the apple orchard. The mountain, instead of turning with the stream, first receded into a small draw or canyonette, the open face of which looked directly across stream and orchard, into the elevated features of "Old Lion Head." The indentation of this draw created an interesting half-circle nook that

---

[i] Pronounced Ah-lee-so

was known as "George's Ground." The lower side of this nook came back to meet the creek again after which the mountain receded from the foreground, leaving our somewhat triangular-shaped vineyard in the curve of its arm with a sharp inland point, which we called "Grapevine Point" or "Vineyard Point," after which the mountain receded again to encompass the main tract of orchards, in a greatly enlarged area, not meeting the creek again until the Fourth bend, beyond the walnut and almond orchards.

The end of the filaree pasture and the beginning of the fenced apple orchard cornered also on the beginning of our fenced hillside corral. The Lion's stone face from its high eminence at this turning-point commanded a magnificent view, as if set to guard the premises, looking out above a series of rocky declivities slightly resembling a stairway, that extended from the canyon floor upward for several hundred feet, and regardless of all other "points" mentioned, this one was called by the family, "The Point."

Veering away to the southward, the sloping side of the mountain soon became a series of impassable cliffs, to form, as it were, a protecting rear wall to our living quarters, and to make fencing on the upper side of the corrals unnecessary. About midway, the corral fencing was indented by our large barn and smaller cistern, which faced the public roadway as it came up from the "first gate," with the corral fence on one side and on the other the first row of apple trees. Opposite the barn, the apple orchard gave place to a general orchard, containing five or six varieties of figs, scattered apple trees, a few pears, peaches, nectarines and at the end of the plot, a group of olive trees. The barn was also the dividing line between the horse-corral and the cow-corral, and at this line the cow-corral, road, and orchard began a decided slope upward to a higher land-level that was itself also a cross-slope. The road then lay between an extensive weed patch, where were many hidden rocks, the walnut racks and sulphur house, and family dwelling on the left, or east, and the orchards, water tank, woodpiles and croquet ground on the right, or west side of the road. At the end of the large clean-swept front yard, the road, having skirted its lower edge, turned at an obtuse angle toward the creek. Where the perpendicular cliffs above the rear of the house terminated, the mountain itself continued on, assuming the form of a half-circle curve as it sent out from its shoulder a spur that gradually sloped to a low, westward-facing point about seventy yards beyond and below the house, overlooking the road and the creek, leaving our dwelling area reposing in a somewhat chilly recess, shaded by mountains. Viewed from the house, this spur presented the appearance of a sharp point; but from the creek, its face was broad and blunted; its broad and gently sloping top was threaded with many paths, from base to opposite base, worn by the treading of generations of hooves, both wild and domestic. We called this symmetrical elevation "The Little Hill." The footpaths over it led down to another cultivated plot called, "The Cart-road Garden," behind which the main mountain continued on southward. The name of this plot was taken from a short, narrow branch road that was not wide enough for a regular wagon, built from the main road across the face of the Little Hill, parallel to the stream, as an entrance to the garden plot. A large gate spanning the wagon road at this turn was distinguished as "The Cart-road Gate." In later years this Cart Road was widened to accommodate wagons and even hay racks, as the crops were changed from truck-garden vegetables and the like to alfalfa, corn, and kindred crops. This plot came to an end as the mountain turned westward at the third bend of the creek.

Almost immediately, the same mountain turned southward, away from the creek, to include in its curving sweep another and smaller plot called the "Corn Patch," the most southernly of our cultivated areas in the canyon itself.

At the fourth bend, the stream became very wide, and its two large pools very deep in winter. The base of the mountain presented a wall of solid rock to the oncoming stream, as well as to the daring foot-traveller endeavoring to negotiate the path that had been chipped out of the solid rock about a foot or two above the waters of the pool, with nothing to cling to but the slight incline itself.

The orchards ended at that bend, long rows of almonds utilizing as much as possible of the sloping hillside, and overlooking a perpendicular high muddy bank, at the base of which a narrow footpath, meeting the one across the rock, led into the walnut orchard, planted on level land, adjacent to the rows of figs and almonds. All along the southern end of this tract, between the Third and Fourth bends, extended a long dense row of beautiful and thrifty Eucalyptus trees, planted for a windbreak when the orchards were young. The outer walnut rows were protected by willows, thickly planted all along the creek as it flowed southward.

At the lower margin of the ungrubbed brush on the hillslope above the last almond row, a deep gully had formed, dry in summer, and in winter rains contributing a muddy volume to the swollen creek; as it completed its Fourth, and swept on to meet the mountain at the far corner of the "corn patch," the Fifth and last bend, veering southwestward, the creek merged with the backwaters of the pond, that stretched away seaward, narrow at first, but broadening and deepening into a large pear-shaped body that lapped the white strip of sandy beach at the lower and larger end and the curving foot of Frank Goff's Bench. The area between the foothill and the pond along its northern length, was a sort of marsh, covered with a very green soft, jointed carpet about hip-deep, a grass of unknown name, that seemed to be rooted very close to the water level; this we called "the Marsh Weed Flats." To attempt to walk across any portion of it was like trying to get through a deep mat of soft wet sponges; every step bounced one on to the next without touching bottom. We tried it as children, merely by way of experiment, and each year it grew more formidable, increasing in depth and area.

The mountain with the rock footpath across its base above the deep pool, parted immediately with the creek and turned due west, skirting the area that contained the marsh-weed flats, and the pond, above which it rose as a part of the high coastal ridge, and then suddenly swept downward in an extensive slope, becoming the broad mesa of Frank Goff's Bench, whose bluffs overlooked the western ocean and the sandy beach of Aliso.

The opposite mountain that met the creek at the Fifth bend, did not at first present to the stream a base of bare rock where it struck, but there still was enough soil left there to preserve a road to get by to the beach during my memory. Later, however, all trace of a road was swept away. Just before reaching the sand there was a small triangular shaped malvia-covered area, roughly bordering on the pond, the wagon road down onto the sand, and the other division of the road that led from it almost straight up the side of the southern mesa, of Lee Goff Bench, facing the beach and ocean on the southern side of the canyon's mouth. This road led on to Three Arches, and later, as roads were built, to San Juan Capistrano, from which roads already were travelled inland to San Diego and other points. The fork that led down past the triangle onto the beach itself, crossed the sand strip and climbed the very steep road up the face of the bluff onto Frank Goff Bench, and on past the long Cypress row and the Goff cabin, on the way to Laguna.

As may be seen from this description of Aliso Canyon, the deviations of its walls on their westerly course to the sea gave us whatever tillable land we possessed, and this, scattered in isolated patches at intervals all along both sides of the creek. This statement is subject to modifications, as afterward disclosed by a legal survey.

Figure 4 Aliso Canyon Farm, 1920

Figure 5 Aliso Canyon, 1908

CHAPTER 5 EARLY STRUGGLES

The first serious problem to be solved, if the family were to live in the canyon, was that of obtaining suitable drinking water. The water of the creek, besides being hard and brackish, was constantly defiled by stock, as it flowed through the upper pastures, and rendered utterly unfit for domestic use.

Applying himself diligently to this problem, Father spent much time exploring the country around, and more especially wherever the hillsides displayed areas of deeper green than surrounding vegetation, hoping to find a spring. One such green area, he discovered upon the mountainside above the filaree pasture. There, a seepage oozed very slowly through a rock crevice from some hidden spring, but not enough water was available from this source to answer the purpose. It offered only a possibility for future development at great outlay of labor and expense, not to be thought of in his present financial straits.

Reasoning that the sheepherders on the Rawson ranch must be getting water from some source, he sought them out. They told him of a spring three miles from where he lived, in a smaller canyon that branched off from Aliso on the north. This welcome information saved the day for the family in Aliso. Father and George located the spring, cleaned out the hole and dug it deeper, and later, as soon as the lumber could be secured, boarded up the sides, leaving an opening about three feet square and raised high enough above the earth level to prevent in-filling. From this spring, all our water for drinking and domestic use was hauled in barrels over a period of nine or ten years.

To the canyon which furnished it, we gave the name of "Spring Canyon," but later learned that its real name was "Wood Canyon," so-named either from the fact that it was well wooded, or because there lived, a mile or so above the spring, a man named Wood. But to us, it was always Spring Canyon.

Little Joan had reached the early age of speech, when, one summer day, bent upon replenishing the water supply, George hitched up the team to the wagon, loaded in the water barrels, and also the children, who all wanted to go along, and drove away up the canyon for a load of water. While filling their barrels at the spring, Mr. Wood, on his way down the canyon, stopped for a brief chat with George, then started on, as George, having finished filling the barrels, lifted Baby Joan to the high spring seat beside him and prepared to follow. When they reached the junction of Spring Canyon with Aliso, Mr. Wood, only a few paces ahead, turned to the left toward town, while George turned to the right. Baby Joan, who was so shy she had been afraid to speak to Mr. Wood or even to look at him when at the Spring he had tried to engage her in conversation, now, in great distress as she saw him leaving the only road that could be the right one—the road that led to the center of her universe, home, forgot all that painful timidity in the fear lest he should be lost, and called out to him loudly:

"Ong oad, Wood! Ong oad!"

Because Father never tired of repeating the quaint sayings and doings of his little folks, many of them escaped oblivion, becoming a family heritage. Little Joan had never seen a real well. The familiar spring was never so-called. But down in the moist creek bottom, one summer, a hole had been dug where water was dipped up in buckets. This, for lack of a better designation, the family called a well.

One day, on the site of the future almond orchard, Father and George were grubbing brush. Joan was with them. During a few moments' cessation of labor, she, with George and Father, stood by the deep, narrow, dry gulch on the upper side of the plot, looking down into it in silent meditation. Suddenly Joan broke the silence with the terse observation:

"Hi-uh well! No dink!" and this became a family byword.

To her, alfalfa was always "av-el-dy fav-el-dy." Her nickname, "Jonie", was used by all the family, her middle name being Alice. She was also called "Daughter", and Father called her "Ducky" and "Pet", or when appearances suggested it, "Dirty-Pig". So it came about that Joan claimed all these names, and whenever any stranger would inquire:

"What is your name?" she would answer by rapidly repeating the whole lingo:

"Do-nie Allie Dauty Ducky Dirty-pig Pet."

One of the first tasks set for the children was gathering up stones from the land. Beginning near the cabin, they carried them day after day toward the foot of the hill and heaped them in piles there. The task thus early begun, lasted throughout many years. There were stones everywhere, big stones and little stones, loose stones, embedded stones. Every plot of ground on which they hoped to raise their living had its share. Nor were they all on the surface. As Father and George began to cultivate, it became apparent that the land in many places was full of buried stones. Mesia, with some spasmodic help from the little boys, would follow behind the plow and pick up stones out of the furrow, carrying them either to the foot of the mountain or the bank of the creek, whichever was the nearer. Stones too heavy for her were carried by George or Father.

Of these larger stones, they built at various locations several rock walls three or four feet high and two or three feet thick, to turn water or serve as supplementary fences. Alongside of these walls, Father usually planted pepper trees in rows, which grew and flourished, beautifying the place and furnishing shade for man and beast. Some of them, grown to great size, may still be seen standing guard over stone heaps that once were walls, and dropping their red berries as of old where children play no more nor gather them up.

One day George, always on the look-out for beauty, brought home three young sucker sprouts from the base of a sycamore, with their lovely, tender, velvety leaves, and cast his eye about the yard for a suitable spot to plant them.

Two or three rods above the back door, by a little protecting pile of stones that had been gathered but not yet carried from the yard, he planted the first one, and some eighteen or twenty feet north of that, the second. There they took root and grew, little twins that became in time great, beautiful trees, a living joy to all the family. For many years the little pile of stones remained at the root of the tree.

The third sucker sprout, he set out farther away by itself, in the shelter of a long, low, curved, embedded rock that protruded like a foundation rib of the earth. This tree, well-watered by much emptying of tubs, grew to mammoth size, for in after years the family laundering operations were carried on under its friendly shelter. Never did we have any other wash house.

A Pioneer Menu

The first year on the claim was very dry like its immediate predecessors. The prophecy of the November rain that had accompanied the advent of the family into the canyon, was not fulfilled by normal rainfall. The ground remained hard and dry. Though they turned a small area of the soil and put in a few potatoes, with no means of irrigation, it was wasted effort, howbeit, when properly watered, the land proved to be very fertile. Nothing could be grown until rains came to break the succession of dry years.

No words can portray the hardship and privation of those early years. How the family managed to live through the first poverty-stricken year is indeed a mystery. Food was scarce and money scarcer. For many months they had no milk, no butter, no fruit, no vegetables. Had any member of the family been asked what he expected to have for dinner a month or two in the future, he would unhesitatingly have answered:

"Bean soup and corn bread."

"And what will you have for breakfast?"

" Bean soup and corn bread."

"And what will you have for supper?"

"We don't have any supper."

Week in, week out, month in, month out, that was their whole bill of fare, and not always all they wanted of that. Only the infant nursing at Mother's breast had milk.

When, on rare occasions, their diet was varied by a few potatoes, these were cooked only after the "eyes" had been cut out for planting.

Once in a while, Father would bring home a sack of "shorts," coarse and dark from its content of bran and germ, and cheaper than white flour. This, though commonly despised as "stock-feed," was a welcome change from so much cornmeal, and made the best of bread.

After they secured a cow, sometime later, Mother would occasionally make for a treat, delicious salt-rising bread. This is made without yeast, even the wild yeast being prevented from growth by an excess of salt in the "starter."

In the morning, she would warm some milk and water together, putting into this enough salt to properly season the whole batch. Then she would stir in some of the shorts and set it by the fire to keep warm till raised. The lightening process was accomplished by bacterial action unrelated to yeast. This batter was called the "emptings." At night she would stir in more shorts or white flour when she had it, and perhaps some cornmeal, working the dough into a smooth mass. Then she would cover the pan and wrap it warmly to rise overnight. In the morning she would make it into loaves and bake it the same as any other bread. The whole process required about twelve hours longer than for ordinary bread. The flavor and goodness of Mother's salt-rising bread has followed us all through life.

Sometimes the menu would be varied by making mush of the cornmeal instead of bread. Especially was this so after they had milk. Cornmeal in those days was ground whole and was therefore much better tasting and far more wholesome than is the bolted meal of today. Mother made this mush by sifting the dry meal through her fingers into the boiling water, a little at a time, stirring very rapidly to keep it from lumping. Though more difficult to make than by first wetting the meal, it better retained its nutty flavor.

When a young girl just learning to cook, Sadie made one morning a big pot full of this cornmeal mush, stirring it as usual with a large bread spoon. In serving it, she dipped up this spoon heaping full of boiling hot mush to carry from the stove to the table. Fearing that some of it might topple off on its precarious journey from pot to plate, she put her hand underneath as a precautionary measure to protect the floor. Sure enough, the dreaded accident happened. But the primeval instinct of self-preservation outweighed the cultivated habit of housewifely cleanliness, and automatically she jerked away her hand in time to avoid the burning mush-meteor, leaving gravity to take its natural course. So ker-splash down onto her clean, freshly-scrubbed floor, spattered the gob of mush.

In those early days, Father did not possess a shotgun. But, through practice, he learned to secure with his thirty-two rifle, a little of the wild game so plentiful everywhere. First, he tried the squirrels—very different here from the eastern varieties used for food. They proved to be sickening. Mesia again became nauseated, and the family decided to leave squirrels out of their diet. Sometimes he would succeed in bagging a few rabbits, which they ate with a relish. Quails were abundant, but with a rifle, very hard to get without mangling beyond recognition.

As yet, Father knew nothing about ocean fishing. Having no understanding of the water and its moods, he felt himself unable to cope with it. Had there been a market for fish, doubtless he would have learned the art at once as a means of livelihood, but none existed within his reach or knowledge. Fishing then, seemed to him, but a pastime for those who had leisure, and means to invest in equipment for pleasure. So, at a time when most needed, this valuable source of food supply was left untouched. Several years elapsed before fishing was discovered to be a profitable and fascinating sport.

Every member of the family went barefoot the year round, except Father and Mother, and even they were perilously near it. Mother patched and re-patched the clothes, and patched the patches. Always, she made over for the younger children things outgrown by those older. And that, by hand, for in those days Mother did not have a sewing machine.

Feeding the Wild Things

When at last the welcome rains came and softened the earth, causing vegetation to spring forth, Father and George began in earnest to cultivate the soil and plant crops. The obstacles they encountered almost beggar description.

The one-horse, single-share plow bought in San Francisco, was their only implement, besides a hoe, until supplemented by a home-made "cultivator." From beams, Father fashioned a V-shaped foundation, bracing it with cross pieces. In the point and along the sides, he bored seven two-inch augur holes on a forward slant, into which he fitted large wooden teeth, shaped with his draw-knife. With these he essayed to put in his crops.

Then commenced the battle with weeds and nettles—particularly the nettles, which came up "thick as the hair on a dog's back" and grew to a height of sixteen inches or more. So poisonous was their sting that it compared with that of bees. The home-made "harrow-cultivator" was noted for cultivating the weeds most effectively, inducing a prolific growth, but with little benefit to the crops, so utterly submerged by their more thrifty and sturdy rivals.

Unused as they were to California dry-farming, it took them several seasons to learn that weed destruction was of paramount importance in the conservation of moisture for the maturing of crops, that not one must be left growing to rob the planting. This necessitated much pulling of weeds by hand from around the growing plants.

Nettles came up in the gardens so thick that in order to find out where the hills of corn or potatoes were they had to feel about among the nettles before painfully pulling them out in a circle around the young plants so that the hoe might be used.

When Father first planted a two-acre patch of alfalfa down in the cart-road garden, it came up intermingled with a heavy crop of these nettles. There were more nettles than alfalfa, and they threatened to smother the crop. So when the nettles were about six inches tall, Father set the children to pulling them by hand. Mesia, being the "outside girl" was assigned this job, with the part-time assistance of those younger. And what a job it was! With hands and arms wrapped in old rags, she worked away at it day after day and week after week, till at last the nettles were conquered.

When the alfalfa, thus painfully and laboriously saved, had grown to a height for the first cutting, the gophers, unbelievably numerous, began to work on it from beneath, cutting off the plants just below the surface of the ground and eating the roots. Poison and traps were used day after day—a never-ending chore—but in spite of all efforts, the gophers almost took the patch. Great bare areas stood out, denuded by these sharp-toothed rodents.

Then, out of the surrounding hills, the deer began coming down in the night to feed on what was left of the alfalfa. The boys then took their two dogs down there and staked them out in the patch to frighten the deer. They would bark vociferously and run frantically about in the circle measured by the length of their chains, beating down the alfalfa and tearing it up with more damaging effect than that of the deer. As for the deer, they soon learned that the dogs were circumscribed in their activities, and grew so bold as to quietly feed on the green crop just out of reach, even within ten feet of the impotent dogs. So this ruse was soon abandoned.

As soon as young potatoes began to form on their underground stems, squirrels came out of their holes by hundreds, scattering over the fields, and dug up the young potatoes without damage to the vines themselves, carrying them away to their holes for protracted feasts, leaving the empty vines to flaunt vain promise of harvest.

For the few potatoes overlooked by the squirrels, waited innumerable voracious worms. Not a single potato escaped their visitations. From one hill alone by actual count, George dug up and destroyed seventy-five worms.

When the grass of the pastures began to dry up and the hillsides to turn a dusty gray, our plots of maturing garden stuff stood out in tempting greenness to attract the wild things whose food supply was becoming scarce. Then the rabbits ventured down from the brush and cactus of the hillsides by the dozens to comfort themselves with man's provision. What the rabbits left, the deer devoured in the night. Year after year it was the same.

The second year of his occupation, Father planted three or four acres of navy beans on the "barley ground" plot. They came up and flourished. The family all were very proud of this fine stand of beans, and hoped for a substantial harvest and income, for beans were a good price. But just when they were full of fine, promising pods, a wonderful green area among the drying hills and pastures, the deer, that came down in companies after dark to drink at the creek, began to trim the edges of the bean patch. Night after night this was repeated, the patch growing smaller and smaller, until there were scarcely any vines left. When finally the crop was harvested, there were only two rather small sacks of beans.

These experiences were most disheartening to the struggling family trying to wrest a living from the soil of their isolated farm. It seemed as though they had moved into that canyon for no other purpose than to create "happy hunting grounds" for all the wild life of the surrounding country.

But the gophers, the squirrels, the rabbits, the deer and the worms were not the only pests that preyed upon the crops. There were feathered frequenters of air-lanes and forests—thousands and thousands of them.

The "California Mockingbirds," or brown Thrashers, which we designated as "hooked-billed brown birds," were even worse in the cornfields than were the squirrels. The squirrels would dig up the kernels after planting, and carry them away to their holes, so that for several weeks the fields had to be watched to keep out these little robbers. But the brown birds would dig up and carry away both the kernels and the young plants. Someone always had to be watching these birds.

Children would be stationed at the various plots, separated one from another, to keep the birds out of fields and gardens. While Lafie would be guarding a patch at the far western side, Mesia would be watching at the cart-road garden. Taking a book with her, she would seat herself on a rock in the sunshine, and try to read while watching the birds. But it was hope-less. She would no sooner get back to her rock after driving them all out of the field, and take up her book to read, than they were all back again, to be chased away once more.

One year Father planted a field of Kaffir-corn in the cart-road garden, hoping to raise feed for the growing flock of chickens. When it came to fruitage, and the tops of the stalks were full of exposed bunches of corn, large flocks of linnets and other birds descended upon the field and devoured the ripening kernels, leaving empty hulls.

Little Joan was at this time initiated into the duties of bird-watching, and in connection with the task, received her first spanking from Father. Time and again she chased the birds away as they settled down on the corn, and time and again they came back. They were not afraid of Joan. She tried to play between times, as children will.

Even older folks find it difficult to attend to two things at once. Little Joan had only two eyes, when a whole dozen eyes would have been none too many to keep watch over all those birds. But doll houses are so interesting to build, and tassel babies so fascinating to play with, that Joan quite forgot the tiresome cornfield and the naughty birds. Her bright blue eyes were occupied with interests nearer to her heart.

Just at that inopportune time, of course, Father had to come along. It was so unfortunate, for just then the field was covered with voracious birds, and the little soldier playing contentedly, completely off guard.

Mother, who always thought tenderly of the little children at their irk-some tasks, endeavored unconsciously to make up for Father's strictness by providing little treats for them. Whenever she would bake salt-rising bread, and some of the dough from the over-light loaves would drop off onto the oven bottom, she would think of Joan and her special fondness for this crusty, crunchy "run-over," and send Hulda down to the field where she was at her task, with a big run-over of salt-rising bread. To Joan, this tasted better than any cake in the world.

Winters in Aliso Canyon were sometimes very severe. There was always a distinct draft blowing up or down the canyon. In crossing its mouth from one mesa to the other it could be distinctly felt. This draft in winter time was sharp and cold. Ice formed on the top of still water, and if shallow, it sometimes froze solid. Water left overnight in tubs or wash basins would be solid in the morning. The dew that lay heavy on grass and weeds would often be frozen, and even the ground itself. This made early morning chores particularly disagreeable for the boys; especially so since they were seldom properly clothed.

On one occasion, Lafie passed through a field of malvia, knee-high and very dense, and blanketed with frost. It was frozen so solidly that the stalks would break off as he walked through, and for a distance of about thirty feet on every side, the field would quiver and shake from communicated contact. After thawing, the bruised or broken stalks all died, but wherever it was undisturbed the malvia showed no evil effects. On the two mesas the climate was much milder. There they seldom had frost. It never snowed in the canyon, but often hailed for short periods.

No matter what the weather, little children in those early days were obliged to take their places at regular tasks along with their elders in out-side work and chores, with the added discomfort of being barefoot.

Just turned five, little Joseph began the daily task of herding ducks during the very early morning hours when coyotes were likely to be sneaking about the barnyard. Down to the icy creek he would follow them, though frost covered the ground and icicles hung from weeds and grasses. Often his little bare feet became so cold and stiff he would break the ice of the creek and wade, where the temperature was a little higher.

One frosty morning, Artemisia, leaving her own work, came down to the cornfield where he was stationed to keep out the squirrels—for after advancing day had abated the coyote menace, the squirrels were next in order and that she might have as a base of operations, standing room on a spot less cold, sat herself down on the frozen earth to thaw it out.

But when the lovely summer days came along, these outdoor tasks were good medicine and not unpleasant to take.

Joseph was a droll little fellow, with a plentiful supply of individuality. When first learning to talk, he made very hard work of some words. Members of the family would ask him to say "potato" just to hear again his amusing version of it. Puckering up his mouth for the ordeal, with great preliminary effort and expenditure of breath, he would puff out the word:

"Buh, buh, buh, buh-da-do!" finishing with an emphatic burst of triumph.

When Father and George, in preparation for building the road at the point of the little hill, were grubbing out the brush one day, Lafie and Joseph, interested in the proceedings, were standing around as boys will, when all at once the voice of Mother was heard calling in tones crescendoing to a high, sustained falsetto:

"Jo-seph! Jo-seph!" Stolidly as a stuffed toad, he stood unheeding, as though not even hearing the unwelcome summons. Lafie, always inclined to be forward, spoke up, saying:

"Joseph, Ma's calling you. You'd better go and see what she wants."

Mentally busy inventing an excuse, Joseph suddenly began to scratch his leg vigorously from hip to knee, answering with spirit:

"Well, ain't I a scratchin?"

A few days later , in the same setting, when the men were shoveling away at the new road, the two small boys again were hanging around watching—Joseph, idly, since he was really on duty with the ducks; and Lafie, a lad of seven, helping a bit and in consequence assuming a sense of importance. In the mud of the pond nearby, the ducks too were shoveling, turning up dainty morsels of food from the ooze, washing themselves, and in the manner of ducks so occupied, quacking conversationally. Hearing an old drake suddenly give a loud quack, Lafie, taking the elder-brother attitude, said:

"Joseph, you'd better go down there and look after them ducks. They gener-ly quack when they've laid an egg."

Joseph didn't move. After a moment, he said, in his slow, stolid way:

"They gin-ly quack when they haint laid no aaig."

No matter how much work children have to do, they will manage to find some time in which to play; and these were normal children.

Often, by way of diversion, Sadie and Mesia would dress up in Mother's long skirts and play "lady". The younger ones, they would have for their "children", dressing them up in their own clothes. They tried this on Lafie, dressing him up to be a "girl". Still a boy, in spite of this incumbrance, Lafie hopped about on one foot.

"You mustn't do that!" they admonished, "Girls don't hop."

"You must walk nice, like little girls do!"

This avenue of self-expression cut off, Lafie began to whistle, which brought stronger reprimands:

"Don't whistle like that! Girls don't whistle!"

"You're a girl now, you mustn't whistle."

But all their training could not make a girl out of Lafie.

Learning to read at Mother's knee, Lafie had another temperance lesson. In his First Reader, was a story with a very evident moral, about "A Little Temperance Boy" named Robert Reed. Another character in the story was a heavy liquor drinker, who because of his bad habit, fell into the ways of crime and languished in jail for two years.

"My!" said Lafie, "That's a long time—as long as we've lived here!"

At the end of the story, the moral was summed up in a poetic flourish:

"I'm going to be a 'temperance boy,"

Said little Robert Reed;

"I'll never drink the poison stuff

Nor smoke the filthy weed."

This verse with its moral made such a lasting impression upon the plastic mind of seven-year-old Lafie, that he decided to be another little "temperance boy."

Planting Trees

For three years, the family farmed in Aliso Canyon without raising enough of anything to be called a crop. There was scarcely more than enough to feed the chickens. These were years of desperate privation and hard-won experience.

Meanwhile they were busy clearing off the land, building roads, and planting orchards. In the spring of the second year, Father planted the two pounds of walnuts brought from Perrin's place. Every one of these nuts sprouted and grew into trees, with increasing promise as the years went by.

At the same time he planted a handful of hardshell almonds in a row along the margin of the cart-road garden next to the hill. When these trees, some years later, began to bear, half of them proved to be bitter. The other half were sweet and good. One tree bore especially fine nuts, and these, he replanted on the slope they had cleared of brush west of the walnut orchard. While still young, he budded the trees from these nuts with buds taken from the original good tree that bore them, thus insuring the same kind of fruit; and in time was rewarded with a most beautiful and gratifying almond orchard, earliest in the springtime to put forth a forest of snowy blossoms.

At that time, the only towns of any consequence in the county were Los Angeles, Wilmington, and Anaheim. The last named, founded in Fifty-Seven by a group of Germans from San Francisco, had become the center of an extensive district of vineyards, a place of brewers, distillers and wine-grape producers. From these vineyards, Father secured cuttings of three varieties, Malagas, Muscats, and Zinfandels, about the third year of his occupancy, and planted our vineyard across the creek from our dwelling site.

The Zinfandel, a wine grape, but excellent for table use, proved to be hardy and practical for a place so damp and cold as our little canyon. The Malagas mildewed, and a few years afterward had to be dug up; though had Father known about the use of sulphur then, he might have saved them. The Muscats also mildewed, and refused to attain normal size. These had not been planted in the vineyard proper, but stuck around in out-of-the-way places. Some of them hung from the little hill point over the bank above the road, their foliage mingling with that of the poison oak. So, even when ripe, we were afraid to gather them.

From nurseries around Anaheim, Father picked up young apple trees from time to time, and planted an orchard in installments. He wisely selected as great a variety as possible, including those that bore earliest in the summer and latest in the fall. The apple orchard that resulted became a source of continual profit and pleasure. Fruit trees of many kinds were set out in the adjoining area, to become a general family orchard.

An Irrigation Experiment

The drowth of the first year having been so profound, when the second planting season came around, Father decided to put into action a plan he had conceived for irrigating a patch of garden from the creek.

With the help of George, he built a thirty-foot rock dam four or five feet high, across the creek between the rocky base of the spur flanking George's Ground, and the lower end of the apple orchard—though neither of these parcels had yet been so-named. There was no bank at that time between the orchard areas and the creek, but only a long, gradual slant covered with grass, and hard.

Enough water collected behind the dam to supply a good-sized garden. To provide space as close as possible to the supply, Father, with his plow, broke up this smooth grassy slope almost the whole length of the three-acre plot below the house, widening the garden area almost to the stream bed.

This proved to be a costly mistake. That winter, rains came in abundance as though making up for lost time. Flood waters came down the creek in torrents, slipping over its firm, smooth, salt-grass-covered bed as in former uncounted years, without damage, until they reached this rock wall. Diverted by the obstruction, they shot around it over the plowed slope, and began to cut away the land that had been thus loosened.

Formerly, the hard, undisturbed ground of the slope had prevented erosion, the water slipping over the grass without digging in, and rising to its maximum height on either side of the stream bed and subsiding again un-eventfully. Its capacity for unobstructed widening, lessened the swiftness of the current, there being then no trees growing on either side, and the soil was firmly held in place by a matted framework of grass roots.

Now, abrupt banks were cut, progressing inland to threaten the whole cultivated areas. Alarmed by this calamity, which future winters could only intensify, Father began the planting of willows all along these newly formed banks, to stay the damaging erosion. From scattered willow trees that grew along the stream farther up the canyon, he obtained all the cutting needed, and set out a thick border of them on both sides of the creek, the whole length or our premises.

These cuttings grew luxuriantly, spreading and multiplying, becoming for the whole distance a thick, protective wall of willows, that in places along the margins, thickened into small forests. Even fence posts, cut from green willows and stuck into the ground, sent out shoots and became trees as well as posts.

Around the curve of the apple orchard area, he planted, besides willows, half a dozen or more pepper trees, all of which thrived, and in after years afforded a beautiful, shady place to play. Just inside the bank and willows that bordered the general orchard area, he planted from seeds, a row of acacia trees, which also thrived, in after years becoming an ornament of great beauty and delight to the soul.

Farther down the creek on the opposite bank, he stuck in a few poplars among the willows, which soon outstripped them in height and slender ever-green beauty.

CHAPTER 6 STOCKING THE FARM

The stocking of a farm usually begins with the humble swine. So it was with this one. Father had been in Aliso only a few months when he acquired his first pair of pigs—a beginning that multiplied into a large drove later on.

To chickens and pigs were soon added ducks, and after some years, geese, all these, for the most part, foraging for themselves.

A year and a half had gone by when he secured his first cow, which he purchased of Mr. Congdon of San Juan Capistrano, for the sum of fifty dollars. How he obtained the price is indeed a mystery. Because of her bright red color, Mother named this cow "Cherry", and a greater blessing never came onto the farm than dear old Cherry.

Cherry's first calf was a bull, whom they named Star, from the white star-shaped mark on his forehead. He became a great family pet, as well as a valuable sire. Afterward, Cherry bore twin heifers, and this gave quite a fair start with cattle.

Later on, a wild Spanish range cow, of a brindle coat and one-eyed, was brought to the farm from Mr. Congdon's herd. This cow was priced very low, for she was a dangerous and vicious fighter. To milk her required real strategy, and two men.

As yet, we had no corrals, so all the cattle had to be kept staked out, to be loosed and led to water every day and their locations changed for fresh feeding. Thus, a rope was required to be kept on the horns always. Either Father or George would approach old Brin while thus staked out, and annoy her until she stepped astraddle of the rope with her forefeet. Then, picking up the rope behind her, he would pull her head down close to the ground and hold it there while the other, with a stick, would push under her udder on the ground, a short rope having a loop in one end, deftly bringing the free end through the loop and tying her feet together, with much ineffectual struggling on the part of old Brin.

Then, while the one still held her head down, the other would extract the milk—or as much of it as she could not prevent by exerting all her powers of retention, with manifest resentment at every stroke of the hand.

The task of staking out the cows became an irksome one, and finally, a brush fence was built a good half-mile from the house at the first bend from point to point diagonally across the creek. The cows were then turned loose in the open pasture above the fence, and restrained from wandering too far away, by keeping their calves in a little pen in the near side of the fence.

There, in the shade of the beautiful grove at the mouth of Sycamore canyon, the cows often lay and chewed their cuds, and there they were milked morning and evening, and the buckets of foamy milk carried home this long distance, to be strained through a clean cheesecloth or superfine brass-mesh strainer, into broad, shallow tin pans.

Every winter, portions of this fence would be washed away by rising floodwaters, but again and again it would be rebuilt.

Mr. Lovett wrote Father from Bear Valley that he would let him have some of his cows to use and raise calves on shares. This generous offer, he was only too glad to accept, so one summer day found him setting out on horseback for Bear Valley to drive home these cows. Once again he and his former friends enjoyed a brief but pleasant visit together—which proved to be the last.

Then the two men rounded up the cows and drove them down the mountain into the Escondido valley, and there they parted, Father himself bringing them on out of San Diego County. At San Juan Capistrano, George met him, astride Ted, to lend a hand for the rest of the way.

The drove consisted of five or six head, milk cows and yearling heifers, and within a few years, Father had acquired a sizeable herd of cattle, besides those raised for Lovett.

In due time, the brush fence across the canyon was replaced by a more permanent fence. The wire used was smooth and round without barbs, and the posts were cut from willow trees. The road was spanned by a swinging gate of horizontal boards, and this was our "second gate."

When, in Seventy-Four, the newly patented Glidden barbed wire came into use, Father built a long corral for both cows and horses, extending from Lion Head point to the summit of the rise that occurred about two thirds of the way toward the house. Cornering there, the fence turned to the hill. Near this corner, Father for some time stacked his hay in one big stack, though earlier, the spot for the stack had been lower and nearer the house.

To animals unused to it, this new barbed wire proved to be a vexatious snare. Sometimes the horses would get astraddle of it and cut themselves cruelly. Poor Ted was the first victim. As fast as he was able, Father built other fences enclosing various fields to protect growing crops from invading stock. Beyond the fourth bend, for protection on the south, he strung another wire fence across the mustard flat from Frank Goff Bench to the pond, with a gate across the road. The cattle were often driven down the creek through this gate and up onto the grassy Bench to pasture, being herded there and brought back in the evening.

Brin had been separated from her calf when bought. Probably it had been sold to the butcher, which had only increased her grievance against the world. With every calf born after that, she would become almost crazy, fighting everything that came near her. Especially did she hate petticoats, and would go for a female at sight. Truly, old Brin did her best to vindicate Rudyard Kipling's "female of the species."

One day Father, Lafayette and Artemisia were driving the cattle down the creek bed toward the pond on their way to this pasture up on the mesa. Brin was in the herd, and her calf had been left at home. Mesia, her side vision obstructed by an old-fashioned blue sunbonnet, straggled along at the outer edge of the drove. As they crossed the creek, old Brin caught sight of her, and with an angry shake of the head, took after her—at first not seen by her intended victim, buried in the sunbonnet.

As soon as Mesia sensed her danger, she started for the fence ahead at top speed, with all the odds against her, for ferocious old Brin was gaining at every step. Lafe, watching the unequal race in a paralysis of fear, thought surely she was doomed. Father, who was carrying a big club, shouted at the enraged cow and leaped into a run after them, while Mesia, nearing the gate, turned her head in desperation to look at her, now bellowing and snorting with head to the ground and menacing horns almost touching her.

Just at that instant Father, in his race with death, came alongside with his club and struck the surprised animal a terrible blow on the side of her nose and jaw, which took all the fight out of her for that day. Mesia, limp and trembling, was sent home to safety and Mother, while the others drove Brin, now thoroughly subdued, with the rest of the herd up onto the mesa.

A man named Smith had come to live and farm in Tustin, whose acquaintance Father made. Because of his unusual "gift of gab" he went by the sobriquet of "Gassy" Smith, and none of us ever knew his actual name. He and Father got on very well together because both loved "politics," and neither of them could out-talk the other.

Of this man, Father, about four years after coming to Aliso bought at a very low price, a little newborn crippled mare-colt of very fine breed. She was a beautiful black from head to hoof and grew to be very large. Because of her unfortunate affliction, she was not expected to work, but as a brood mare greatly improved our stock.

One of her hind legs was stiff in both hip and knee joints. This caused her to develop a queer twisted leg and sway back. One side of her foot wore more than the other, giving a long, pointed, one-sided hoof. She would drag this foot forward in a semi-circle, leaving at every step a large half-moon track on the ground, and by this could always be traced wherever she went.

Gentle and well dispositioned, she became a family pet. We all loved dear old Nellie, and felt great compassion for her infirmity—though but for that we should never have known her. Sometimes we little folks would be placed on her back for a little ride, held there by older children while she grazed about.

Father raised some very worthwhile horses from this old favorite, among them a fine blooded stallion of great merit and local reputation, much to the improvement of our own stock.

After a few years, Father thought he would try raising goats. He reasoned that they would thrive on the rocky hillsides with very little expense for other feed. So, about the fifth or sixth year, he invested in a billy and two nannies, which soon increased to quite a flock. These goats would scamper to the sharp tip of the highest rock without seeming effort, standing poised and unafraid. All over the steep sides of Gable Rock little kids would gambol without even a slip.

But goats, though interesting and easy to raise, proved to be a great nuisance on the place, so much of our stuff being unprotected. They would go unbidden to the haystack in preference to foraging on the hillside, and not content to stand on the ground and eat around the edges, would climb all over the stack, causing large bunches of hay to slide to the ground. So another chore was born, keeping goats away from the stack. Little Joan was assigned to this task, and had her hands quite full, for goats are heady creatures and determined to do as they please.

The young apple trees were then making a good growth, the largest being about three or four years old. One day the old billy went down into the apple orchard, and with his horns began to peel the bark from the trunks of the trees. This was too much for Father. He decreed that the goats must go. Soon, he began to sell them off, and it was not long until there were no more little goats running about over the hillsides.

Father very early began to raise bees. His first hive was given him by Mr. Wood, an old bee man, who raised bees as a sideline on the small sheep ranch he and his partner Athens rented of Mr. Rawson. The second swarm, George found a mile or so ups the canyon, living wild in a rock crevice. Other wild swarms captured from their natural nests in rocks and hollow trees, were added from time to time, and Father soon had quite a stand of bees, and began to produce honey.

Bee men were then just beginning to organize for the better promotion of the industry in Southern California, the first county association having been started in the fall of Seventy-Three. Through them Father secured a copy of the book, "Langstroth On The Hive And Honey-Bee," then about seven or eight years off the press in its revised form, and from this most excellent text, studied the subject of bee raising and honey production, combining the practical with the technical, until the bee business became a major industry on the farm. It was by means thus obtained that he was enabled to put up the humble buildings that afterward adorned our premises.

Having no machinery for extracting the honey, he utilized the sunshine. A long V-shaped trough with closed ends was set up on cross-legged stilts about shoulder high, slanting to the small hole that had been bored in one V-point and finished with a tin spout. Into this would be placed the de-capped combs of honey, and the whole trough covered with glass to protect from bees and other insects. When one side of the comb became empty it would be turned over. The honey, warming in the sunshine, would run out of the tin spout into containers placed underneath. A little of the wax also would melt and run out. But this would harden into a little cake as it cooled, and could then be lifted off.

Father always attended to this part of the bee business and to the canning and marketing of the honey. But the older boys and girls grew into the work of actual bee tending, each in turn carrying the greater part of the burden. During the early period when George and Mesia had charge, the number of stands increased to a hundred and twenty. Lafe then took up the work and ten more stands were added. After him came Joseph, and the number of stands increased to a hundred and sixty, the peak of our bee industry.

The necessary equipment for handling bees is very simple. The "smoker" consists of a small bellows with a wide stocky snout, in which old rags or burlap are kept smoldering. This is used to drive the bees where you want them to go. The "bee-veil," used to protect the head and face, is made of mosquito netting, the upper edge gathered to slip over the crown of a hat and fall over the brim, the lower edge being tucked securely in at the neck. The "hive-tool" for lifting off the covers from hives, maybe a chisel or screwdriver.

The bee-tender must keep bees from overmuch swarming, by providing them with plenty of room for more comb building. This he does by adding "supers" or upper stories to their hives, for their object in swarming is to secure more room for growth. He also gives them additional comb, if needed, which may or may not be artificial. Or he may have to rob the hives of honey to give them more work to do. Sometimes when nectar is scarce, bees will rob each other, those from one hive entering other hives to carry away their stores. To prevent this demoralizing practice, when he sees it beginning, he closes the little front doors of all hives almost shut, leaving only room for about one bee at a time to pass through. Those inside the hive can then handle the intruders in their own way.

But regardless of all that is done, many swarms will be cast during the season from any apiary. The great problem is then to recapture them. This is possible due to the habit of bees to cluster in a large, hollow, cone-shaped mass on some nearby tree branch, or other convenient place, for a period of time that may vary from fifteen minutes to an hour, before taking their final flight away to the wilds of hill or canyon. If not retaken during this interval the colony will be lost to the apiary.

All through the warm summer weather we had to be constantly on the watch. Whenever would fall on our ears that peculiar, loud swarming sound of many thousands of wings buzzing in unison, we would shout:

"Bees are swarming!" and all runs to arm us with tin pans and large bread spoons with long handles to beat upon the pans, and dash out to the scene of commotion. Amidst the deafening noise made by our improvised orchestra, the whirling mass of bees would begin to concentrate into more compact formation, and finally settle on some branch in a bunch, usually high up in a tree.

Then an empty hive would be fetched and placed on its permanent base in the apiary row, with perhaps a little empty honeycomb in it to make the bees feel at home, and a broad extra board would be placed on the ground in front, slanting up to the opening. A box or pail would be brought also to receive the swarm.

One of the boys—or if no boy happened to be handy, then a girl—would climb up into the tree and shake off the bees into the receptacle, or if a small branch, it might be cut off and brought down to the hive, with its new strange fruit. The bees would be emptied out onto the platform, and begin of themselves to crawl into the hive. No special protection was needed, for bees never sting while swarming, so anybody might undertake their capture with perfect safety.

A bee's stinger should never be pulled out of the wound but scraped out, as pressure applied only presses more poison out of the poison sac attached to it into the same wound.

During the season of honey flow from April to September, the air seemed to be full of the tireless little worker bees from morning to evening, bringing in the sweet nectar, and the constant hum of busy bees accompanied the twittering of birds on every side. Bees are not able to pierce the tough skins of fruits, but after the little birds had pecked them open, there were plenty of bees to be found there busily gathering the sweetness.

Father had planted fruit trees in the apiary, but they did not do very well for lack of sufficient cultivation. When he attempted to work the ground with old Ted hitched to the cultivator, the bees objected to his presence, and Ted to theirs, so strenuously that this method had to be permanently abandoned. Yet weeds must not be allowed to grow rampant even in the apiary, and make of the place a tangled wilderness. So they had to be kept down with a hoe, a task which, for obvious reasons, nobody was anxious to tackle.

The noise and vibratory disturbance attendant upon hoeing in gravelly ground, greatly irritated the sensitive mechanism of the bees. Lafie, who had the job of watching for swarms, to which the hoeing was now added for good measure, was stung so much and so often while engaged in this occupation, that he became almost immune and a bee sting would leave only a pinpoint of red on his flesh. However, before this blissful state was acquired, he passed through many a painful experience.

George and "Old Man Meeker," a kindly-faced, full-bearded old gentleman were one day standing engaged in conversation near this bee-orchard where Lafie was hoeing, when suddenly they were interrupted by a yell of unmistakable pain. Turning quickly, they beheld Lafie whirling and swinging his arms about as if in an Indian war dance, and slapping his body with yelps of anguish. A bee, losing its way, had crawled high up inside his trouser leg and had stung him in a super-sensitive region with most agonizing results.

CHAPTER 7 BARNYARD ENEMIES

For some years after coming to Aliso there was no coop for the chickens, except a few small ones of a size for a hen with her brood. For the ducks there was a low gable-topped coop about eight feet square built of slats and just high enough for them to stand upright.

The rest of the fowls were left to roost wherever they could find a place. No trees being large enough yet to afford perches, they would seek the haystack, line up along the wagon sides, across the center ridge of the duck coop, on the woodpiles of uncut brush and fallen trees, and even in a long row on the ridge of the housetop.

In inclement weather and on hot days, they took refuge under the house, which was open at the two ends and lower side. There in the cool shade, the hens would lie and dust themselves, and there too, deposit their eggs in scratched-out depressions, far up under where the mudsill rested on the ground.

Thus it was that some small boy must be commandeered to crawl up under the house every day to gather eggs—and who so handy as Lafie? This was not quite so simple as it sounds, for chickens were not the only creatures that had their habitation under the house. Due to the abundance of wildlife such as squirrels, rabbits and gophers, together with our own domestic cats and dogs, the place was overrun with fleas that hatched there in the warm sandy soil, multiplying prolifically. Allowing fowls under the house did not help the situation any, for they kept the soil loosened and made the fleas a nice warm breeding place.

Fleas drove the family almost distracted. Restful sleeping at night was well-nigh impossible. Hunting fleas in the warm bedclothes of a morning immediately upon arising, was our first task of the day. Mother became very famous in her family as a flea-catcher, and the rest of us all aspired to the same efficiency, with plenty of material on which to practice.

So it was that before Mother would send Lafie up under the house after eggs, she first would strip him to the skin. With his bucket of eggs, he would crawl out again black with fleas—too many even to think of trying to catch, and Mother would dexterously brush them all off before putting on his clothes again.

Our domestic flocks increased in numbers in spite of coyotes, bobcats, foxes, weasels, skunks, coons and hawks that preyed upon them and their eggs.

With the first streak of daylight the fowls awakened, and since all they had to do was hop down from their various perches or walk out from under the house, they were naturally up and about at that early hour of gray dawn fraught with greatest danger.

George, who rose every morning before daylight to feed the stock, milk the cows and build a fire in the cook-stove, would frequently surprise a coyote chasing a chicken about the yard. Perhaps the coyote would have killed and made off with his prey, or even have killed several chickens before Father could be aroused and get out with his gun, and even then he might escape unharmed.

At any time of day, a frightened chorus of cackling hens might send the girls and boys running to look, and there perhaps would be seen a bobcat climbing through the brush of the hill with a chicken in his mouth. It may have been a hen caught from some stolen hillside nest, or simply picked up from among the flock without alarming the dogs, who followed too late to overtake him.

One day a great cackle and flutter on the side of the little hill brought the family running. There, sure enough, was a bobcat with a hen in his mouth making his way up the hillside. George fired, breaking the cat's back. Immediately the dogs were upon him and a terrific fight ensued that brought the struggling, snarling cat down into the apiary, still holding his own, disabled as he was.

To assist the dogs in finishing their prey, Father reached out and grabbed the cat by his stubby tail, holding him out at arm's length toward the dogs. But he had not reckoned with a cat's long legs and agility. Quicker than thought, the cat swung toward his captor, reached out and grabbed Father's trouser leg with the claws of his front foot, pulled himself over and snapped his teeth together through the flesh of Father's thigh. It was then time for all hands to help Father.

Often our hens would steal their nests among the brush and rocks of unprotected hillsides, to become, as soon as they began to sit on their eggs, a prey to wild animals. A mass of scattered feathers, discarded feet and bones, and a deserted nest of old rotten eggs found long afterward, would tell the story. If a stolen nest was suspected, there was no rest till we found it. If the "setting" process were far advanced, Mother would sometimes put a coop over hen and nest till hatching time.

Should a hen thus sitting be not discovered, and somehow escape molestation by prowlers until ready to hatch, the peculiar strong odor of hatching chicks would invariably betray her to enemies at the very last end of her long vigil, and neither hen nor chicks would survive that terrible night.

When the nest of a laying hen was found, in place of her own, a glass egg was substituted, for a hen cannot tell the difference, neither can she count, and if so much as one egg remains in the nest, she will not miss the half-dozen removed, or notice that from day to day there is no increase. If none at all were left, she would likely forsake her nest.

When all her eggs had been laid, her peculiar actions of clucking and ruffling her feathers would tell us that she was "setty." Then, after a nightfall when a fowl cannot see, we would apprehend and confine her in a coop till she had forgotten all about her desire to raise a family.

In those early days, with every available source of income so greatly needed, an egg for breakfast was an unusual treat. As an added inducement to nest-hunters, Father promised one egg out of every dozen found in new nests. So it happened sometimes that one child would enjoy an egg for his meal when no one else could have one.

Little Lafie, just big enough to hunt nests, seemed to be finding them everywhere. He had an egg for breakfast so often that George began to get suspicious, and became a self-appointed under-cover detective.

One day he watched Lafie run up onto the hill a little way, stoop down, stretch out his hand under a bush, then straighten up again, and shout:

"I've found a nest! I've found a nest!"

"Stay right there till I come!" called George, starting up the hill. There lay two eggs on the bare ground, with no evidence that a hen had ever been near the place.

"There's no nest here!" he declared sternly.

"There's the eggs," replied Lafie, pointing to the "evidence."

"Yes, and you put 'em there too! I'm going to tell Pa!"

This incident put a damper on Lafie's nest finding, and eggs for breakfast became few and far between.

As soon as Father could obtain the necessary materials, better housing was provided for the chickens, and allowing them under the house became a thing of the past.

Skunks were very numerous, and being exceedingly fond of eggs, were diligent nest-hunters, taking their own reward. But, for obvious reasons, we were very careful how we went about to effect the capture of these beautiful, innocent looking little creatures, striped with white on glossy black coats. Woe to the luckless dog that ventured to attack one of them, to receive from its hidden arsenal the noisome spray, offensive, sickening, ineffaceable. Weeks of isolation would scarcely suffice to remove the odor from his shaggy coat.

A skunk once took up temporary quarters under our dwelling, attracted, no doubt by the eggs he found there. But no effort was made to dislodge him, and the dogs were restrained on leashes till he chose to vacate.

They are very fond of watermelons. Selecting a ripe one, a skunk will gnaw a round hole through the rind, reach in and feast. One year the skunks were raising havoc with a patch of melons at Grapevine point. Someone told Father how to get them. He cut ripe melons in half, spread the cut surfaces with strychnine, covering each cut surface with paper, held on by a clod. The next morning, there lay an even dozen full-grown dead skunks.

One morning, when the boys were older, it was discovered that "setty" hens in a small coop made of slats, had been killed in the night by some unknown animal who, by reaching down from above through the slats had laid hold on them by the heads and had slit their throats wide open with sharp claws; being unable to pull them out after killing. This was a startling calamity. Traps were set the next night around the coop; but the wary animal gave these a wide berth, as though he knew all about traps and the ways of humans; but he went instead to the duck coop, and climbing up onto the low gable roof, built also of slats, reached down through the narrow openings and grabbed the heads of the ducks within, killing a number of these also in the same wholesale manner; but unable as before to secure his prey afterward. Again and again this prowler came, climbing all over the coops, which had been patched up with additional covering, and in spite of this precaution, several times succeeded in tearing loose a slat and getting hold of a fowl's head with fatal results. This went on for some time, and still the creature remained uncaptured. Every effort was made to stop this shocking destruction. The boys tried both trapping and poisoning; but without success. Neither could it be determined what kind of animal was responsible for the murderous work, since no visible tracks were left behind on the hard ground about the coops.

One day, Father butchered a calf. The boys took the offal of this calf and carried it to the point below old Lion Head, and there in the beaten path, staked it down securely to the ground, setting a cleverly concealed trap near the fresh odorous mass. Returning to the spot the next morning, they found caught by the paw, a large cat of the lynx variety, entirely at their mercy; which was scant, for he was shot without a trial. This animal was proved to have been the culprit by the fact that those particular depredations immediately ceased.

Some time later, we were again troubled by a wild prowler taking our chickens in the night; and as before, traps and poison bait near the scene of the theft proved of no avail. About that time, one of the hens was taken sick, and being about to die, Mother isolated her in a coop to protect the rest of the flock; intending, since nothing could be done for her, to have her put out of her misery.

Thinking that a live bait would be much more likely to ensnare the miscreant than a dead one, and hoping that by the sacrifice of one, many lives might be saved, the boys between themselves decided to use this sick hen to accomplish their purpose. To their way of reasoning, it seemed that since she had to die anyway, it might as well be by an animal as by an ax, since benefit might thus be derived from it. So they made a poison paste, and smearing it underneath her wings and on other parts of her body, staked her out in a path that was worn through the tall mustard growing in the corral beyond the barn. The next morning the hen was gone, and there were evidences that she had been taken by some animal who had snapped the string, and had left indistinct tracks in the path. Great hopes were indulged that this would end the thievery; but to their dismay, the depredations continued as usual. They wondered how any animal could have devoured that hen for breakfast without receiving his death potion. In the fall after the mustard was all dried up, they found the carcass of this unfortunate hen where she had been conveyed and left intact. The shrewd animal, discerning the poison, had refused to eat her. Later, however, he had been caught in a trap; which had ended his career of chicken stealing.

Coyotes were often trapped in various places about the premises or environs; the bait usually being the carcass of some fowl or beast, or the offal of some animal butchered on the farm. At one time a trap thus baited was set in the pasture up above the second gate, and in the morning it was found to be sprung and holding in its jaws two toes of a coyote. The animal had gnawed off his own toes in order to escape. A few months after this, in a trap set in another place, a coyote was caught that was found to have two toes missing from one foot; so it was thought that these two animals were one and the same.

Trapped coyotes were usually quickly dispatched with a gun, as the most humane procedure for their disposal; but it was felt by the men folks of the family that for their training, our watchdogs needed the experience of doing battle with the wild animals thus captured—at any rate, this plausible view provided the proper pretext for such mortal combats—for what male human does not enjoy watching a fight? So sometimes the dogs were turned loose on the captive animal that carried a steel trap on a broken foot at the end of a long chain. Then what a terrific battle would ensue. Many times have I seen a poor coyote foaming at the mouth and snarling with rage and pain, as he lunged at the nagging dogs and at us who were watching, to the length of his chain—from which we kept a respectful distance—the weight and strain of it all borne by the poor broken mangled foot in the trap. It seemed an uneven fight; yet even thus hampered, he was more than a match for one dog; but with two, the odds were against the frenzied coyote. After he had been worried to the point that he could no longer properly defend himself, then he was usually put out of his misery with a bullet.

All through the early years, coyotes were so numerous and destructive in California that in the early nineties the government finally put on them a bounty of five dollars a scalp, which lasted about four years. During this period, they were hunted by all the farmers in the country, and by everyone else who could use a gun and set a trap; so that they became greatly thinned out, and never afterward were such a pest.

At the same time the government placed a bounty on jackrabbits, so destructive to growing crops, and paid twenty-five cents for every pair of ears brought in; so that this pest also was greatly reduced. This, however, was about twenty years after we came into the canyon. Our men folks—especially Lafie who was then grown—secured many of these remunerative scalps.

There were also a few mountain lions in the country sometimes seen by others, though none of the family ever actually saw one. Lafie, while crossing the walnut orchard one early morning, came across huge tracks leading toward the little hill made by a cat-like animal several times larger than those of a bobcat; which could have been none other than those of a mountain lion. Also, a sheepherder once told of a mountain lion that came into the sycamore grove and killed one of the sheep in his corral up above the second gate, and having no weapon, of throwing old tin cans at him to frighten him away.

Sometimes, from far up on the Rawson pastures, the boys would bring home an inoffensive badger that had strayed away from its burrow too early in the evening, for they sleep during the daylight hours and prowl about at night. For this reason, we seldom had the privilege of seeing one of these most interesting of animals.

A relative of the skunk, weasel and martin, he yet differs distinctly from them all. When running on his short, thick legs, he is rather slow, awkward and clumsy, and if overtaken by danger away from his burrow, he will flatten to the ground, which his own color closely resembles, draw feet and nose under his body and lie motionless. He might easily be taken for a stone or clod of earth. But he is very fearless, tenacious of life, and plucky, and when cornered, will put up a fierce fight, though ordinarily a peace-loving, timid little beast.

He is beautiful too. His tawny pelt, with its broad black stripe from nose to neck on each side, and alternating with white on forehead and throat, is of some value as fur in cold, high altitudes, where he becomes of hibernating habit. But this is not the case in warm southern climates.

Badgers really are a benefit to farmers and should not be molested. They feed upon squirrels, gophers, moles, field mice, and other rodents, though if such food is scarce they will resort to vegetation. After digging out his small victim, he will enlarge the burrow thus made vacant, and himself occupy it.

The sly little weasels also fur bearing, with pelt a delicate light reddish brown, trimmed in white, was exceedingly wary and difficult to catch. Fortunately for us, weasels were not very plentiful. It was well-nigh impossible to construct a coop that would keep them out. The fine meshed wire used today was not yet invented, having made its first appearance in crude form about the year Eighteen Eighty-Three. A man named Page was the first to try it, putting up a fence of simple interlaced wires in his own yard, patenting it later.

A weasel will not eat the flesh of his prey. He lives exclusively on blood. One morning the "setty" hens—half a dozen or more in a coop built under the cider press—to our great dismay, were found dead, all of them, lying on the ground floor. Investigation revealed the tracks of a naughty little weasel who had slipped in, squeezing his slender, elongated body between the slats, and with quick, noiseless movements among the fowls, who could not see in the dark, had slit their throats one after another and sucked the blood from their veins—and this, without so much as raising a warning cackle, withdrawing from the banquet as noiselessly as he had come, without disturbing even the dozing dogs.

CHAPTER 8 BREAKING HORSES

As previously mentioned, Father understood the science of breaking wild horses. In his library was a valuable textbook on the subject entitled, "Rary's Method of Breaking and Training Colts and Horses, "from which he had learned the art. Had it not been for this accomplishment he with his family would have fared even worse than they did during those early pioneer days. Whenever the larder was low and garments would bear no more patching, out to the San Joaquin Ranch house he would go to see the manager, Mr. C. E. French, and solicit of him untamed horses to break.

For five dollars he would take a horse wild from the range and tame him to be handled and led about with a bridle. For fifteen dollars, he would further train him to the saddle, demonstrating his achievement by himself mounting and riding the animal; or if preferred, train him to be driven in harness hitched either to a wagon or plow. Two horses for one owner would be so trained at the reduced price of twenty-five dollars. There were plenty of range horses in the country to be broken and ranchmen soon came to recognize Father as an expert at this business, and his method as far superior to those of the Mexican trainers then commonly employed.

A Mexican, out in the open country, would first lasso a wild horse, and during his mad and excited efforts to escape would draw the rope around his throat tightly enough to partially cut off his breathing until faint and unable to struggle. Seated upon another horse, he would then ride up close and slip over his eyes a leather blind to cut off all vision. Then onto the back of the trembling animal now concentrating his whole effort upon obtaining enough air to sustain life, he would throw first a blanket, then a saddle, cinching it firmly in place; and over his head place a specially constructed halter of braided rawhide having two reins and falling low over the nostrils to choke off breathing when pulled tightly. To all this frightened horse gasping for breath, could make but a feeble resistance. The next indignity suffered was the mounting.

With a light step in the stirrup an expert rider booted and spurred would swing onto his back in the saddle, controlling his frantic rearing by cutting off his wind; and when fairly mounted would reach forward and raise the blind from his eyes. Immediately the animal would plunge and rear and buck in an effort to unseat his rider, who then would put spurs to his sides, at which he would leap forward and run wildly—the rider controlling his activities and speed always by the low halter. Renewed spurring kept him running until completely tired out, when the first lesson was considered finished.

This performance would be repeated from day to day until the animal learned to submit—because there was nothing else he could do. But though conquered, he had been taught no lessons of trust and confidence; neither had he been broken of kicking and biting, and his service to man was based entirely upon fear.

Father's method was very different. Its aim was to establish a mutual confidence and understanding by means that were sane, sensible and without cruelty. The first thing required was a properly built corral; the ideal being of boards about seven feet high, thirteen feet wide and thirty feet long. This corral, or some near substitute, the owner was at first expected to furnish; though later, Father built his own corral and broke the horses on his own premises; for which he raised his charges somewhat.

The next essential thing was a proper whip; which Father had made to order for himself. This whip had a hickory stock about forty inches long and a lash of well-braided buckskin that tapered down to a fine point not larger than one-fourth of an inch; to which was attached an unbraided cracker of buckskin half an inch wide—in all about eight feet of lash. The object of having this extra-unbraided cracker was that it would sting without drawing blood or injuring the animal in any way; as would a braided tip.

One more article completed his equipment; a leather strap about two and a quarter inches wide and something like a yard long, having a stout buckle and two keepers—one of which was placed on the inside a few inches from the buckle, the other being on the outside and farther distant.

The horse to be broken was usually delivered to Father after having been lassoed and tied; and would then be turned loose in this specially constructed corral. Usually the animal would immediately begin to stand on his hind legs and climb with his front feet against the fence in an effort to get out. Father would enter the corral with his whip, which he stretched out on the ground behind him, holding the whip-stock in his hand. The frightened horse would run to get away as far as he could, making frantic efforts to escape in some way. When at last he stood, shivering with excitement, his head would naturally be turned toward the fence, usually facing a corner and tail toward his trainer.

Father in clear, distinct tones would then call, "Come here!" After giving the unheeding horse time to hear this command, he would give him a slight flip with the whip cracker on his hinder parts. The horse would then change his position—perhaps run to the next corner, or to the opposite end of the corral But whatever he might do he would eventually settle down in some corner in the same position with head to the fence. Then Father would repeat distinctly this same command, "Come here!" and after a moment of waiting would again give him another light flip on the flank with the whip—afterward each time rearranging it on the ground behind himself in proper position. Whenever the horse attempted to go by him, he never interfered with him, and was particular never to strike him anywhere but on the rear. Trainer and horse repeated this procedure until finally the animal discovered the thing his trainer was endeavoring to teach him—that the safe place for his hinder parts was next to the fence; and so reversed his position. From this time on he began to comprehend a little of what was wanted. Father would then advance carefully toward the horse's nose, holding the whip-stock like a stick, its lash caught back and held with the butt in his hand. The horse, who had been seeing only obliquely while his rear was toward Father, could now watch what was going on fairly from all viewpoints. Father, talking softly and coaxingly to him, would make cautious advances to see if the horse would allow touching him anywhere with the whip-stock. Ordinarily, the animal would show nervousness and whirl about to get farther away, before he could accomplish anything definite. With arm, stock, and lash extended together, Father could reach twelve feet or more, and calculating distance, at this juncture he would step to a position from which the lash when wielded, would not strike against any part of the enclosure; arranging it as before on the ground behind him. Then, he would again issue his command: "Come here!" following it with a light, stinging cut on the flank. Before long, under these tactics, the horse would begin to comprehend that his head was not in danger, but only his heels; for Father had been exceedingly careful never to touch the animal's head with the lash. When the horse had learned this, instead of whirling about, he would begin to sidle away, keeping his head toward his trainer in an effort to protect his rear parts. The next decided advance in his submission, was when he would allow his trainer to approach near enough, while talking softly and persuasively, to touch him on the nose or head lightly with the whip-stock, and perhaps stroke his head gently with the braided lash at its end held taut. Having allowed this, he would soon permit himself to be stroked and petted more freely around the head and neck with the whip-stock held at arm's length. Should the horse become fractious and break away, and forgetting what he had learned, again turn his rear parts to Father, the same command as formerly would be given: "Come here!" followed by the inevitable sharp cut with the lash on his flank. Then, instead of allowing the horse to run past him unmolested as formerly, he would step out a little toward him and say commandingly, "Whoa!" If the horse ran past him, no attempt was made to stop or molest him or interfere in any way with his movements, until the horse of his own accord ceased running. Then the "Come here!" would be resorted to and the "Whoa!" repeated until the animal stopped at the word "Whoa!" when Father, being closer to him than formerly, might be able to touch him with his hand and pet him a little. This procedure was repeated until the horse would not only stop at the word "Whoa!" with his face toward Father, but would allow him to stroke and pet him freely about the face and head with his bare hand, while talking gently to him in a low voice. Soon the horse would be tame enough to allow himself to be rubbed and patted all over his neck and shoulders. Invariably, any turning of the heels toward his trainer would be followed by the same command: "Come here!" and the clip on his flank, till the horse had the lesson thoroughly learned that "Come here" meant at least for him to keep his head toward the trainer. All the while during this whole lesson, Father had to be on his guard against being kicked; for often a vicious horse would kick at him. But only once, is it known that Father ever was actually kicked while thus training a horse.

After caresses had been allowed as far as the shoulder, Father, using the whip-stock, would gently extend them over the sides, belly, hips, and rear as fast as permitted, and finally over both front and hind legs. The horse would now have learned that there was no danger from any quarter so long as he kept his head toward Father. Having mastered this part of his lesson, Father would next attempt to bend the horse's front knee gently so as to "break" his weight. Next, the horse would permit him to pick up his left front foot (the mounting side of the animal) stroke it and let it down to the ground; which he would repeat several times. The next thing was to strap up this leg. Holding the leg bent, he would pass the strap around the fetlock with the buckle next to himself, and slip the free end through the special keeper on the inside of the strap opposite the buckle, pulling it all the way through, and slipping the strap down close to the hoof. With the strapped foot in his hand, he then passed the strap-end around the bent leg near the shoulder joint, slipping it through the buckle and second keeper, thus rendering the leg useless and painlessly disabling the horse; while at the same time wholly eliminating the danger to himself of being kicked; for a horse unbalanced on three legs can hardly kick. The horse, thus strapped, in an effort to free his leg, would plunge and hop on three feet helplessly; but the proceeding had not increased his fear of Father.

Now, the real taming and gentling of the horse could proceed much faster than before, and without danger to himself. The trainer then might stroke the horse all over, give him little pats, gradually increasing the vigor of them till quite a slap could be given, getting rougher and rougher—yet not hurting the animal at all, until he had established a real confidence. After this, Father would jump up a little way against the side of the horse several times to get him used to the idea of a possible mount. Next, he would take hold of the horse's mane and pull himself with a jump half way up onto the horse; repeating this movement several times. Then he would jump up and lie on his stomach across the horse's back, his head beyond the other side and his feet off the ground, to let the animal feel his weight. After several repetitions of this maneuver, he would, while in this position, throw his right leg over, and lo! He was mounted, bareback and without a bridle. The horse would become disturbed, but not afraid of being hurt. Father would dismount and remount till he became used to it and suffered it without protest. Then, while mounted, he would strike him with the palm of the hand to get him to go forward; and the horse would hop around on three legs, carrying his mount without attempting to dislodge him.

The animal was now conquered; the most difficult and important part of his lesson learned. Sometimes this stage was reached within two hours of the time the horse first entered the corral. But not often so soon. Then Father would dismount and let down the foot, removing the strap; and the horse would be petted and caressed and given food and allowed to rest.

By this time, a considerable confidence between horse and trainer and knowledge of each other had been established; but still the horse did not understand fully what "Come here" meant. Another lesson would be given him that same afternoon or the next day; which often might have to overlap the first lesson considerably; but the horse in addition to the repetition of maneuvers, learned the meaning of "Come here." With whipstock in his right hand, and the lash extended in position on the ground behind him, while the horse faced him, Father again issued his command, "Come here!" By an expert movement, he then dragged the lash forward till its tip was opposite the hind feet, and flipped the horse somewhere in the rear. Four times out of five, the horse would step forward a few paces toward his trainer. Then Father would advance toward the horse and begin to pet him; after which he would step back and get his lash in position again. Before ever the command was given, the whip was invariably in position to strike him on the rear parts should he fail to obey. If the horse reared or ran around the corral, he was allowed to finish this maneuver unmolested; then the same procedure was repeated. By approaching the horse at the shoulder instead of the nose, Father taught him the valuable habit of coming to his master with shoulder next to him—the proper position for putting on or taking off a halter or bridle, and for mounting the animal. Every time the horse, at the command "Come here!" advanced toward his trainer, he received petting and commendation in approving tones till he at last learned what the command meant, and would follow his master all around the corral when thus called. When once an animal has learned this lesson, he never forgets it. So trained, he will answer to the command wherever he may be. Father once had a horse on the premises which he was training thus to make him more gentle and obedient. Somehow, this horse got loose during the night, and in the morning was missing. Father and George went far up the canyon to look for him, and found him among a herd of other horses. Their own mounts, being habitually used for heavy work, were not fast runners, and they found it difficult to get the stray separated out from the group, but finally succeeded. The horse attempted to get back again among them. Father raced ahead of him on the open range, but the renegade, being fleeter and unencumbered, got past him on his way to join his late companions. Father yelled, "Come here!" The horse stopped in his tracks as if shot, and faced him. Father then rode up a little closer to him, dismounted, went to his shoulder and put a halter on him, mounted his own horse again and led him home.

George, after watching Father train horses, himself read the book by Rary, and having seen how successfully the principles there unfolded could be put into operation on horses and colts, decided to try out the method on other animals. So he proceeded to practice on Star, the young bull born of Cherry. Here he met with admirable success and so tried it on other calves, with the same results. Then he decided to tackle vicious old Brin, an undertaking fraught with more or less danger. This wild cow had already learned that Father and George were her masters, which lessened the risk to George, and he put her through the paces with the same law of kindness practiced on other animals. The effect was wonderful. In time, she became so docile that one could sit down and milk her anywhere without binding her in any way.

CHAPTER 9 THE FIRST SCARE—BUT NOT THE LAST

The family had been in Aliso Canyon but a few weeks when they were shocked and frightened, one day, at sight of a horrible rattlesnake of unbelievable size, crawling across the yard not fifteen feet from the cabin door.

This incident was but the beginning of a long "reign of terror," and the killing of this new enemy the "opening gun" of a relentless, indefatigable war of extermination waged against the scaly foes, another of which was seen soon after, crawling out from under the house.

Unmolested by man, and left to the natural laws of growth and multiplication through uncounted years, these crawly creatures had become exceedingly numerous, and their ancient ones of enormous size. A "big rattler" then meant really a big rattler.

Father's experience with rattlesnakes up to that time had been very limited. He was unacquainted with the seasonal agility and rapidity with which they can coil and strike. One day in early spring he was mowing alfilaria for the pigs, which Lafie was carrying in armfuls to their pen. Hearing an excited call from the boy, he dropped his scythe and went to investigate. There lay a huge rattler stretched out alongside the path in a fitful patch of sunshine. Father went to the house and returned with his rifle. Seeing the snake now crawling away, he put his foot down on its tail to hold it while he took aim and fired. Fortunately for Father, the weather was cold, when snakes are sluggish. Had it been in mid-summer the story might have ended differently. Father, whose height was five feet eleven in his socks, took the dead snake over to the elderberry tree near the house, and hung it up by the tail-tip on a level with the top of his head. Its nose barely missed the ground.

Not a month of the first seven years passed by without at least one rattler being slain, and at times a rattler a fortnight, which of course did not include all that were seen.

Sometimes our poor cattle were bitten on the face as they grazed in the pastures. Though their sufferings were great and their heads enormously swollen, eventually they recovered. Our dogs also were bitten, with the same suffering, accompanied by much swelling and drooling. They too recovered, for snake venom seems to be less deadly to animals than to humans.

Many and thrilling were the hairbreadth escapes experienced by different members of this pioneer family. The constant tense anxiety and resulting nerve strain under which Mother lived, with her numerous brood scattered out over fields and hills at their various daily tasks, can hardly be imagined. Children were made "rattler-conscious" by frequent cautioning never to take a step among weeds, rocks, or dry grass without first making sure the spot held no lurking danger.

Some of these narrow escapes have become a matter of family tradition. Walking barefoot in the creek bottom along in front of his garden, one day, where the weedy growth was a foot or so high, George was just in the act of completing a step, when directly under his descending foot, he saw a coiled rattler. It was only by a superhuman effort that he managed to lengthen his step enough to miss the snake, and jump quickly aside.

At another time when there were rows of growing beets between the grapevines, George, working there in the dusk of evening, reached down and grasped by the tops a handful of young beets to pull them, when there underneath his hand lay a coiled rattler.

Wild gourds, distantly related to the pumpkin—called by some "mock orange" from the shape, size and color of its wholly inedible fruit—grew scatteringly all over the place and had to be grubbed out to bring the land under cultivation. This plant was distinguished by its very large, strong taproot, often twelve inches or more in diameter, that extended down into the ground about three feet. The roots alone would have filled a washtub. The vine itself, gray-green and hairy, with its large solitary, bell-shaped, ill-smelling yellow flowers, was sometimes sixteen feet across its circle.

George, grubbing out one of these gourds in the lower end of the barley field, one day, having cut away the vine, leaving only a tuft in the center, and dug down around the tap-root to the depth intended, struck it a severing blow and pried it loose. He then leaned forward and grasped the tuft of heavy leaves on the head of the tap-root, lifting it out of the hole, when from under his hand, a full-grown rattler fell out of the tuft back into the hole, rattling furiously. At times as he worked, its coil had been but a few inches from his head.

Mesia too had narrow escapes. Suckering corn one day in the same field, she reached down to pull out some suckers and her hand almost took hold of a young rattler coiled about the stalks. At another time, before the big flood had cut away the soil and path in front of George's Ground, she almost stepped on a large rattler lying there in the weeds. At her shrieks, George came running and killed the snake.

Father once accidentally stepped on a rattler, but near enough to the head to prevent its striking. He came home bringing the dead snake as an exhibit. I remember seeing Father at another time coming up the road past the little hill carrying an immense rattler. He held it out at arm's length by the tip of the tail higher than his shoulder to keep the head from dragging on the ground. Its body was as large around as Father's arm.

When the little walnut trees were making their first growth, corn was raised between the rows. George was hoeing weeds and thinning out and suckering the corn hills, while Lafie, then past seven, helped pile the fodder ready to be hauled to the cows. Mother cautioned him particularly about snakes, never to stop running until at least a rod away, should he see one, for rattlers could "jump a long way." Mother allowed wide margins where snakes were concerned.

The very next day Lafie had reason to remember the caution. The soil of the main orchard was soft sandy loam, but up at grapevine point where George was working at the time, it was hard and cloddy. He sent Lafie down to the far end of the orchard-field to bring up a pile of cornstalks. As the boy ran barefoot down between the cornrows, he stepped on the middle of a rattler stretched out there. Knowing by the feel of it that it must be a snake, but not seeing it, he ran on, remembering Mother's counsel. At quite a distance, he looked back. The snake was still in the same spot, but his head had been drawn back to the barefoot track directly across his back, in which position George found it upon arriving at Lafie's call. Fearful that his little brother might have been bitten, he questioned him with much concern. Together they returned to the point to collect hard clods for the battle. But still not satisfied about Lafie, he threw down his clods, lifted him on his back and ran for home. He knew that if bitten, the boy should not exercise.

Mother, seeing him brought thus, and hearing the word "rattlesnake," suffered a severe shock. Even when satisfied that he was all right, she took him up in her arms and wept over him at thought of what might have been. Father and George ran down with a gun, and trailing the snake, found and killed him.

In August snakes shed their skins. In preparation for this event, a film grows over their eyes, rendering them for a time totally blind. Then everything to them is an enemy. Constantly anticipating trouble, they strike ferociously at anything that in the least disturbs them.

One August day, Lafie was running down from the house toward the little hill point, and there across the road, and almost as long as the road was wide lay a rattler that had just come down from the hill. Lafie was running so fast he couldn't stop, so cleared the snake with a jump. When he came to a stop and looked back, the snake, who had instantly coiled, was standing up on its tail, weaving about from side to side, springing up and down, and striking this way and that in a blind effort to bury his fangs in the unseen foe.

But Lafie's most thrilling experience with a rattler was yet to come. He was guarding a field of corn, growing where the almonds were afterward planted, dressed as usual in short home-made breeches, and barelegged. The hook-billed brown thrashers were so numerous that the young crop could not be left unguarded even for an hour, so Mother would send the boy his dinner every day by one of the girls. With a boy's voracious appetite, he would watch eagerly for his sister to appear around the point, and run to meet her through the potato patch, that filled the space between them with thrifty, luxuriant foliage.

On this occasion, as he saw her coming, he started running and entered the potato patch at top speed. While running thus between two rows of potato vines, a rattlesnake sprang out from a vine on his right with rattles buzzing, and struck at his left leg as it moved forward in advance of the other. Before its fangs could reach their objective, Lafie's right leg came forward and struck the snake's body, carrying it onward with him, which caused the snake to become wrapped around both legs. In the melee, the snake, missing its mark, struck poison fangs into its own body, at which it fell away from the legs of the boy, who went on scot-free. The snake, writhing in an agony of rage and pain, and utter confusion, kept on striking its own body repeatedly. The two watching children, almost paralyzed with fear and trembling with nervous excitement, screamed for Father, who, hearing them, ran down with his gun. The snake was still fighting itself when Father shot it.

Experiencing this fright while still so young caused Lafie to be cowardly where rattlesnakes were concerned. He was so deathly afraid of them that he never even thought of trying to kill one himself. No matter where he happened to be, at sight of a rattlesnake, he would call for someone else—for Father, or George, or even for his younger brother Joseph, who, not having had such a harrowing experience, was quite adept at dispatching snakes.

CHAPTER 10 THE FIRST DEER—DISCOVERY OF THREE ARCHES

The family had been on the Aliso claim a little over a year when one morning George, having risen early as usual at the call of farm chores, while feeding the chickens, spied a deer a rifle-shot away above the yard at the foot of the cliff. Considering himself only capable of shooting small game, he ran to the house to awaken Father, who jumped out of bed, pulled on his breeches, grabbed the gun and started on a run.

The deer, meanwhile, sensing himself discovered, had sped down the hill past the house, crossed the creek and the plot where afterward the vineyard grew, and was now making his way up the hillside beyond. George, following him with his eyes, waited expectantly for Father to shoot. But somehow, Father's eye had not caught sight of the deer at all, and to the boy's great disappointment, there was no report and the game was soon gone from view.

Sometime after this, George was again out early one morning attending to the chores, when he beheld a big buck across the creek to the north, feeding in the bean patch—the plot afterward known as the barley ground. Again he raced back to the house to call Father, who, being eager to redeem his reputation, took no time to put on his shoes, but ran out barefoot in breeches only, gun in hand, to stalk the deer.

Crossing the cultivated ground—afterward to become the apple orchard—he passed into the tall, dense mustard that bordered the creek banks, emerging at the edge of the stream. There, on its farther side a few yards distant, he saw a "jackass" drinking at the creek. The animal raised his head. They looked into each other's eyes a few seconds, each wondering at the other's presence. Then suddenly the jackass whirled about and fled across the bean patch and up the mountainside. Not till then did Father's brain seem to wake up and recognize the "horns" his eyes had seen on that graceful head.

In a flash of realization, he took aim at the fleeing buck and fired. But it was too late, the prey was gone. George, completely disgusted, wished ardently that he had been in Father's place with that gun in his hands. Much chagrined, Father had to admit that he himself had been the "jackass."

When George, after finishing the chores, went into the house, he found Mother, equipped with two good eyes, patience and a pin, picking salt-grass spears out of Father's heels, a painful ordeal it took her two good hours to finish. Seeing George come in, Father, with evident irritation, said to him:

"If you see any more deer, go and hunt them yourself!"

This was all the boy needed to set him after big game, for he didn't think any too much of Father as a deer hunter. After that he felt privileged to carry the gun along wherever he went.

Not long after this, came "election day", and Father drove over to San Juan Capistrano to cast his ballot, taking with him Mother and the younger children—except Lafie, then about six, who remained with George to "keep him company."

This town could be reached by team and wagon only by driving up Aliso Canyon and connecting with the old stagecoach road that passed through San Juan Capistrano on its way from Los Angeles to San Diego, there being then no coast road, but only a horseback trail through brush and cactus. Since this increased the distance from our place by many long miles, the family was not expected home till after dark.

Seizing upon this rare opportunity to enjoy them free from parental restraint, the two boys left behind made their way to the beach—a never-failing source of pleasure. There they spent a few idle hours in complete recreation, wading in the surf, watching crabs in the holes and crevices of the wet, mossy rocks, picking up shells, dragging sea-weeds about and "popping" their bulbous fruits to see the water spurt, digging out sandfleas after receding waves left their bubbling holes behind, hunting for ripe beach-apples to consume their red pulpy contents, until growing appetites reminded them it was time to return.

On their way home, having ascended the bluff near Tunnel Rock and crossed the point of the mesa, they began the descent into Aliso Canyon by the steep, rough, narrow foot-trail, too difficult for Lafie without assistance. When about a third of the way down, they were startled by a loud crash about fifty feet below them. Three deer ran out of the brush, dashing up the hill to their left, and in less time than it takes to tell it they were fifty feet above them passing over the brow of the hill.

George, having not yet become used to carrying a gun, had not remembered to take it with him, but now his one consuming desire was to get home and back again with his gun. Hastening down the remainder of the hillside path, they ran all the way home. There, George left Lafie alone and went back after the deer, with his gun and powder horn.

Reaching the foot of the mesa, he cautiously ascended by the same trail, with gun loaded and ready. Nearing its flat top, he peered over the edge, and there, on a level with his eyes, were the three deer browsing on the dry grass. Taking aim at one of them, he fired. It reeled, evidently shot through the intestines, but did not drop. All three then fled up a trail over the ridge of mountain that formed Aliso's western wall.

George, having never before shot at a deer, was thrilled to see that his bullet had gone home. Reloading his gun, he followed them up the trail to the ridge. No deer were in sight. But as he watched, one of them suddenly jumped up out of the brush not more than forty yards away, and climbing onward a little distance up the ridge, stood for an instant looking around. George took aim at his front shoulder and fired. The deer wheeled and went crashing down the mountain with one leg broken. Immediately another deer jumped out of the brush and ran across a gully. George felt in his pouch for a bullet to reload. Not another one was there. In his eagerness and inexperience, he had overlooked the important thing, and without bullets, his powder was of no use. So, on the eve of success he was faced with defeat. As he stood helplessly watching, a third deer, evidently the one first wounded, got up more slowly and climbed the ridge. There was nothing he could do but watch them disappear from sight, and then take his disappointment and his lesson home with him. Several years afterward, being up on the same mountains one day, George came across the skeleton of a deer, no doubt the one he had shot that day through the intestines.

The proudest moment of his young life was when he brought home his first deer. One morning, going up as usual to the second gate to milk the cows, as he passed the first group of sycamores on the near side of the brush fence, out jumped three deer, a mother and two fawns, almost grown, and started toward the mountain. George dropped his milk bucket and hurried back to the house to get his gun. Two men, who had stayed all night at the farmhouse, being on their way to Santa Ana, were in conversation with Father as he rushed past, dropping scant words of explanation. When they saw his weapon, they said:

"You can't kill a deer with THAT gun!"

"Well, I'm going to try!" he called back, without slackening his pace.

The three deer, having evidently decided that their fright was uncalled for, had returned to browse around on the green grass of the pasture. But with the recurrence of danger, they lifted their graceful heads and made for the mountain again, running up the side a little way. There they stopped and looked around. George aimed at one of the fawns and fired. The shot broke its back.

In this pitiable condition, the fawn struggled to get up the hillside, which was very steep at that place, but with every effort would slide back down again, a little farther each time. The mother, in her solicitude, followed the wounded fawn down the hill while the other fawn stood above them watching the performance. It seemed quite apparent that none of these wildlings had ever before come in contact with hunters and guns. Their innocent simplicity invited compassion, while at the same time their position presented an irresistible "shot."

George, reloading with shaking fingers, knew almost as little about the nature of deer as did these trusting creatures about the nature of man, and trembled like a leaf with an attack of "buck-ague." The wounded fawn was now tumbling over and over and rolling farther down the hillside, with the mother continuing to follow, and both of them coming closer and closer. Shaking so he could hardly take aim, George finally fired at the mother doe, the shot breaking her front leg. She turned then and began to climb the hill on three legs. The fawn above her also started to climb.

The hunter took up the chase, following toilsomely after them to the mountaintop. But they, reaching it first, were then out of sight in the dense brush, and both made their escape. Giving up further chase, George returned to the foot of the hill where the young buck lay dead. Exultantly he started for home dragging the limp animal. On the way he was met by the two men who had resumed their journey, and at this, his first killing, their expressions of surprise and commendation were a triumph supreme. To this were added the delighted compliments of those at home, always more than glad when venison varied their monotonous diet.

After tanning the hide of this fawn, George sent it by Father on his next trip to San Diego to be sold. Of its two little horns, he made two corn-husking pins, which did service in the family for many years.

His second deer was secured in Sycamore Canyon on the farther side of the brush fence and second gate, and this also in the early morning at milking time. It is the habit of deer to begin feeding early with the first streak of dawn; then when the sun grows warm and men rise to stir about, they seek the protection of heavy brush and lie quietly chewing their cud, coming out again in the evening for their supper. George's custom of rising early gave him the advantage of surprising them at their breakfast.

As he came near, he discovered this deer grazing a short distance up on the hillside, and having with him his gun, shot before the animal realized his presence. The bullet took effect, and by its actions he knew the deer to be wounded. The staggering animal lay down a little distance away under a bush. George, sure of securing his prey when through, picked up his pail and began milking.

Just as he was finishing, Mesia came along the road to join him, as she sometimes did, and learned about the deer. Hanging his bucket of milk on the arm of a post out of reach of the calves, he started with Mesia in search of the wounded game. A little way up the hill they routed him out of the brush; but after running a short distance, he stopped to look back as deer do, and George shot him again, this time fatally.

Having learned that animals should be bled immediately, with his jackknife he cut a gash across the animal's throat, severing the main artery, and left him there while they went back to the barn for a horse to carry him home, for this one was no light-weight fawn, but a full-grown deer.

Mother was mixing bread at the kitchen table before the window near the back door, when George came into the backyard leading his horse with the deer lying across his back, its head hanging down exposing the slashed throat, at the same time letting out a "war-whoop" to attract attention. This, with the sudden sight of that bloody, gaping throat, so startled Mother—who was none too well, that she almost went into a nervous shock. But this part belongs to another story.[i]

Four Surprises in a Turtle

So far as is known, George was the first white man of modern times to discover the famous Three Arches, and with that discovery is linked up another thrilling deer story.

This buck also was first seen when, on an early summer morning George went up to the second gate as usual to milk the cows. He was feeding on what appeared to be the top of the mountain, and this time the boy was prepared with gun at hand. Hanging his empty bucket on a post, he started up the mountain, climbing the point where two canyon walls merged. He came upon the deer still feeding unalarmed, and taking aim under cover, fired, the bullet shattering his hind leg. Crippled as he was, the wounded animal scrambled on up the mountain, the hunter following—for his position had proved to be not the top as at first supposed.

George had with him a "deer" pup that as yet had never been trained to track. Perhaps it is due to this blundering pup that the Three Arches were discovered that day. Instead of waiting till sent by his master, he gave chase every time the fleeing buck was glimpsed through the brush. Whenever the escaping animal stopped for a moment, the pup bayed loudly, starting him on again, thus giving no opportunity for a shot. The hunter was several times all ready to fire when this occurred, obliging him to lower his gun and trudge on again. It required too much time to re-load to risk a "running shot," so on and up they climbed, and about nine-thirty reached the summit, the boy spent and weary but still determined to win.

The long hard chase, however, was but well begun. The wounded deer, slanting off toward the southeast, headed for the coast down the other side of the mountain, hunter and dog following. Now the deer had the advantage, making better time downhill, and in the widening distance soon was lost to view. Tracking was slow work, but George kept doggedly on the trail until it led him within sight of the ocean bluff between "Coffee-shell Beach" and "Three Arches"—though neither place yet bore a name in the annals of the coast.

As George gazed out over the rolling expanse of water, wondering what had become of the fugitive, he espied him far down, standing broadside knee-deep in the surf. Taking aim, he fired, but the shot went high. Just at that instant a great wave, coming in, knocked him down, rolling him over and over. Regaining his footing, the deer started northward pell-mell up the beach, bounding on his three legs along the edge of the waterline.

Following along the rim of the bluff, George came to a trail made by wild game, the only one in the vicinity that led down to the beach unaware that it was the one previously descended by the fugitive and the only one by which he might regain the mesa. Directly opposite this trail, a high prominence rose up out of the sea, shaped like the back

---

[i] Chapter 15 (Earliest Memories)

and sides of a gigantic turtle, its head and neck stretched out upon the sandy shore, its body almost surrounded by seething water that broke over piles of tumbled rocks at its base.

George descended the steep, rocky and almost impossible trail to the sand below, but could see nothing of the deer. The tide was coming in, the waves washing almost to the bluffs, and all tracks had been washed away. He looked this way and that, greatly puzzled. What could have become of the deer? In both directions he could see only impassible barriers—mighty ramparts extending out into deep waters, breasting waves that broke far up their sides. No caves or hiding places were possible unless it be on the farther side of this island-like prominence before him.

"I wonder if he could have gone around these rocks," he mused, and started picking his way over the water-sloshed, spray-showered masses at the southern side of the broad basic foundation of the promontory, its northern side presenting a sheer drop into the sea. He had gone but a short distance when, to his surprise, he came to a great "hole" piercing the turtle's shoulder from side to side, where one might walk through on a sandy floor.

As he continued to clamber further out over the rocks, another surprise confronted him—a second archway larger and higher than the first, disclosing a broadened view of scenery on the farther side, its sandy floor swept by surging waves.

"My!" he ejaculated, "Two holes! I never saw anything like that before!"

But still no sign of the missing deer rewarded his searching eyes. A few steps farther, and light shining through the huge monster revealed to his astonished gaze a third archway. Yes, there it was, now alongside, larger than either of the others and in deeper water, completing the most amazing trio of great archways through solid rock that nature could offer an astonished explorer.

But a fourth surprise immediately awaited to consummate his long effort—a surprise that thrilled him even to his toes; for there in the midst of this tunneled archway, standing belly-deep in water, was his deer, looking at him with fear-troubled eyes.

One moment for self-recovery, one shot, and the buck dropped dead in his tracks—wounded, trapped and beaten in the age-old game of huntsman and prey. Immediately he was carried by the restless waves out through the farther side of the archway whence he had entered, and drawn back into deep water. Fearful that the carcass might be swept out to sea and he be unable to land his game after all, George, for better observation, clambered still farther out around the great rock-island to its sheer side—beyond which no man has ever been able to pass.

There he could watch the floating carcass riding back and forth in the swells, and soon discerned that it was being borne slowly toward the shore. He made haste to retrace his steps around the rocks to the sand at the turtle's head, passing to the farther side. There for some time he waited and watched till the waves brought their burden near enough that he might hope to reach it.

Taking off his trousers, gun in hand—for he reasoned that the gun might be of use in prodding if necessary—he waded in, and watching his chance on an incoming swell, caught hold of one ear. The receding wave then pulled back on the heavy weight so strongly as to overbalance him, almost causing the loss of footing, gun and game. But he managed to hang on to the ear of the buck, and with the next incoming wave, succeeded in dragging him out of the water, up onto the sand, in belated triumph.

The problem now was to get that carcass up the precarious trail, very steep, crooked and dangerous in spots from sliding shale. But "where there's a will, there's a way." Having at last secured his game at so great a cost of time and strength, he had no intention of giving up now. With all his "might and main" he labored to get that dead weight up the trail and finally gave it the last pull over the rim of the bluff.

Hiding his quarry under a bush, he started for home to get a horse. Father, riding another horse, accompanied him back, and he too, for the first time, gazed on the striking phenomenon of three successive great archways piercing the body of an immense turtle, lying with head and narrower neck stretched shoreward, asleep in the sea.

The forenoon was gone, the cows not milked, George was tired, but happy, Father was pleased—they were supplied with venison for many a day.

CHAPTER 11 DEVELOPMENT OF THE DWELLING

The tent was used for a sleeping room, and George, with others, slept there until the first corncrib was built about two years after their coming. Then he changed his sleeping quarters to the corncrib, leaving more room for others in the crowded tent. This crib was a long narrow building walled up with horizontal slats having spaces between just narrow enough to prevent the passage through of ears of corn. In the south end was a door, also built of slats.

As soon as possible, this crib was duplicated by another paralleling it; and a broad gable roof built over both cribs to include also the large open space some twenty feet wide between them; which we called—rather illogically—"the shed."

Under the long ridge of this gable roof, beams extended across the open space from crib to crib, resting on the tops of their two inner walls. On the beams, lying lengthwise under the center ridge, a few long, loose boards were placed forming a sort of narrow "attic" without walls; and here Father stored various articles for which no other place could be found. There were hides, rolls of this and that, and, when not in use through the winter, receptacles used in the bee business, such as five-gallon honey cans, extra bee-frames, and large empty molasses barrels, closed at both ends, with uncorked bung-hole openings. The family designation for this crude "attic" was "up on the boards."

To this place George now transferred his bed, being able to reach it only by "shinnying" up the crib walls, clinging to the slats with fingers and toes. The vacated upper corn crib was after that devoted to the storage of farm produce, such as eggs, butter, milk and cream, salt pork, potatoes, beans, peanuts and corn.

One night soon after this change of "bedrooms," George was violently awakened from sleep with a sudden stab of pain. Not realizing where he was, he leaped out of bed, narrowly escaping a fall from his unwalled perch. Lack of artificial light precluding intelligent examination, he concluded that he had been stung by a bee, though at the point of agony, the stinger a bee always leaves was not to be found. Puzzled and suffering, but with nothing else to do, he crawled back into bed.

Daylight investigation revealed the true culprit. Yellow jackets, overtaken by darkness while feasting on molasses-barrel gleanings, had decided to pass the night with their human neighbor in a warm bed. After that the bungholes were carefully corked.

Not long after this a thunder storm came up with violent wind and pouring rain, which ripped to pieces the old canvas roof stretched between cabin and tent, and their "kitchen" was left uncovered to the elements. This catastrophe presented a problem that had to be solved immediately. Like most calamities, it proved to be a blessing in disguise, for as a result, extra housing efforts were made. A roof was built over the floor to meet that of the cabin, and walls added to enclose the kitchen, giving another warm room in place of an open shed.

Another year or so, and the tent was becoming so worn that it could no longer be used as a sleeping place through the winter. Then, over the tent, were built connecting roof and walls, to which the tent-canvas was tacked as it stood, to help keep out the cold, for the room otherwise was but a rough shell. And thus was another winter passed in Aliso.

Some years later this room was finished inside. The tent was removed, the rough walls covered, first with cheesecloth tacked on, then with wallpaper, and the ceiling was covered with a portion of the old canvas tent, tacked across the rough rafters. This canvas ceiling remained for many years.

About this time Father built an addition to the "downhill" side of the cabin for a bedroom, and a porch across the remaining part of the house, facing road, orchard and creek. In this bedroom was built the first clothes closet, standing out squarely from the corner of the room as was the architectural custom in those days—even fine houses having their symmetry spoiled by these jutting closets—and our dwelling now began to take upon it the appearance of luxury.

The original cabin had been built throughout, including even the roof, of eight-inch tongue-and-groove shipboards. In the process of remodeling, Father removed the roof and the partitioning wall between cabin and kitchen, and used the shipboards thus obtained, to help in building the new lean-to room and front porch, putting a shake roof over all the building. This threw both cabin and kitchen into one large room, divided only by the two jogs, one at each side where the kitchen widened beyond the cabin, and the straight seam across between them where the two floors met and joined together.

For years and years there were no screens on this house, either on windows or doors, and the flies swarmed. The earliest and most unique attempt at overcoming this nuisance was by the use of "clapboards." A pair of boards about three feet long and six inches wide were hinged together with leather at one end, and suspended from a rafter in the kitchen, the lower ends falling apart about five inches. The smooth inner surfaces of these boards were kept smeared with honey. When they would become black with flies, someone, coming along, would quickly clap the boards together, with great slaughter.

Next, we obtained the newly invented balloon-shaped flytraps made of closely woven wire and having removable wooden bottoms for holding the bait of sweetened water. Around this were spaces for flies to go in, but being too brainless to find the same way out again, within an amazingly short time the balloons would become buzzing hives. Then, removing the wooden bottoms, someone would hold the trapped flies over the flame of an open stove-hole and roast them, making a dainty repast for the chickens. This style of trap, made very large, for years was used as a public flycatcher. At every prominent street corner in Santa Ana stood a big balloon, which, when full, was held over a flame, probably the blacksmith's forge, to roast the victims.

After a while, black poison flypaper came into use. This, placed in saucers, moistened with water, and distributed about the rooms, was a "sure shot." Dead flies dropped around everywhere, on window ledges and shelves, and floors and tables, to be cleaned up daily.

Then someone invented sticky flypaper. The sheets were in pairs stuck face to face. These we would pull apart and spread around on tables. They filled up so fast that many sheets a day would find their way into the stove. Sometimes an unsuspecting cat, stepping onto one of these sheets, would furnish much amusement for the family.

But in spite of all our efforts, the flies made life miserable, especially for women folks. When endurance was no longer possible, a general Buhach slaughter was decreed. Just before sundown all windows and doors were left wide open, inviting those outside to the warmth within. Then closing all openings and arming themselves with towels, the women of the family would drive the flies all into one room, made attractive with light, going over the rooms again and again to get as many as possible.

The door to this buzzing hive was then closed and rags stuffed into every crack to exclude fresh air. With a small bellows full of Buhach, one of them, while holding her breath, would quickly puff the room full of the powder, step out and stuff rags around the door behind her. An hour later not a fly in the room remained alive. Then the cleaning up took place. Their carcasses, with the spent powder were swept up and burned in the kitchen stove.

Then for a few days what a blessed relief! Those that remained about the premises, as they began to increase again, would for a time be driven out of doors at mealtime, and perhaps it would be a week or so before they became obnoxiously annoying again.

There was no bathtub in this house. The family ablutions were performed in the kitchen in a large galvanized washtub set in the middle of the floor. The older members of the household made their appointments for this ceremony at night after the numerous flocks had been bathed and put to bed. There was never any undue exposure or violation of privacy upon these occasions. Far from it. Modesty in our family was considered a fundamental virtue and its preservation by all a foregone conclusion. The most profound mystery of my young life was the mystery of my mother's person.

About this time Father built our first big chicken coop. It was about twenty-five feet square and high as the roof of a house, flat on top and built entirely of laths nailed onto a stout framework spaced to retain all fowls except small chicks. It was not intended as a protection from wind and weather, but only from hawks and wild animals. Thereafter, chickens under the house became a thing of the past. Inside, along the front, nailed to the uprights, was a row of box hens' nests, lined with straw and furnished with glass nest eggs.

When this coop was in building, the piles of laths had to be soaked with water before nailing. While putting up the framework, Father set Joseph, then about seven, to carrying water from the creek in two little tin buckets to pour over the laths. All day long he worked, toting water from creek to coop and back in his endless, irksome job.

Several years later, another coop providing weather protection was constructed alongside this one.

The next building to go up was the Honey House, built to house the stores and operations of the growing honey business. Father had a hundred stands of bees before it was built. This was a substantial, one-room building, separated from the dwelling by perhaps twenty-five yards, and situated on a sudden, steeper rise of the general slope—almost a knoll.

Underneath the honey house was a large dirt-floor cellar whose rock and mortar walls served also as a foundation for the building above. This deep and roomy cellar was excavated first and while digging there, a most curious and interesting find was made.

Four or five feet down in the hard dry earth, almost to the very bottom of the excavation, Father, while digging, broke into an old closed-up cavity that had once been a hole. Within it were two or three toads, shriveled up like mummies, nothing but skin and bone, that had been sealed up in there—God only knows how long, and, "believe it or not," they were still alive.

This weird, mysterious, freakish marvel is really believable only to those who saw it. Unnumbered years, without food or water, deprived of air, they had lain there buried alive in this deep, dark grave. But when brought up to light, air and sunshine, in their frail and weakened condition, they could not long survive the shock, and soon died.

CHAPTER 12 GEORGE'S GROUND

The little draw at the second bend, abruptly recessed between the rocky, pathless point that ended the barley field and the low, jutting spur at the upper angle of the vineyard, was not without reason called "George's Ground."

From point to spur the distance might have been sixty yards by airline. A narrow, brush-bordered path led down into it from the vineyard over the top of the spur. Its floor sloped up at first rather gradually, then more steeply to the foot of low cliffs at the rear, whose upper rim was broken by a little gap where a small gully descended.

To the left of the gap, as you face it from the creek, the cliff rose precipitously, a bare, perpendicular rock surface, its upper edge, after a short distance against the blue skyline, lowering to form the roof of a long, low-ceilinged, shallow cave, its opening partly concealed by a mossy, rounded rock of some size that stood guard.

A smaller cave, in a frame of bushes, looked out invitingly from the wall in its curve toward the creek, above which the brushy rim flattened slopingly to form the jutting spur.

On the other side of the gap, against the higher mountainside, brush-covered and curving toward the point, the cliff took the form of a roomy, high-ceilinged cave having a large open front. This too was shallow except in the extreme right corner which deepened into a low dark cavity suggestive of a wild animal's den. From the walls of this cave a number of knob-like projections furnished convenient roosting places for the owls that spent their daylight hours inside, flapping out in the night on their foraging expeditions, and frightening little children with their loud:

"Too-hoo! Too-hoo! Too-hoo!"

The floors of these caves, like those of all others around the canyon walls, were covered inches deep with yellow sandstone dust, fine and powdery, and, lying about promiscuously—their beauty despoiled by ages uncounted, both within the caves and all along below the cliffs, were old seashells of different varieties that crumbled to pieces in our hands—mute evidence that these mountains were once covered by the ocean.

Opening out upon the sloping grass-covered bank of the creek, this nook in the mountain, too wide to be called a gulch, too small and steep to be classed as tillable land, filled with brush and cactus, weeds and grass and poison ivy, had long been the haunt of wild animals. Many rodents and small prey were to be hunted there, the den-like caves offered ideal shelter and concealment, and an easy climb afforded quick escape through the little gap to the ridges beyond.

About the third or fourth year after the family settled in the canyon, George, longing for a little spot of ground he could call his own where he might raise a few flowers, set his eyes on this plot, and one morning, hurrying to finish his chores before time, took his hoe over there during the short interval before breakfast, and began cutting out the weeds. Morning by morning, this activity was repeated, confined to a small central area, till he had a little clearing. Then he brought down from the hillsides and pastures around, some of the native wild flowers and transplanted them there, watering them with a bucket from the creek below.

Father, seeing the interest and diligence of the boy, with the resulting little flower garden, and willing to encourage him, told him he might have the place for his own to do with as he pleased. And thus it was that the spot came to be known as "George's Ground."

Appreciating this notice of his endeavors, George began in earnest to clear out the brush. He had no implements other than his garden hoe—which was rather dull—and an old mattock used for grubbing brush from land, and no time to devote to this new enterprise and recreation other than the short interval between milking and breakfast. This could be lengthened only by earlier rising and greater speed with the chores. Yet it was not long before he had quite a large area cleared of brush and weeds and a most interesting flower garden started.

One morning, he spied a coyote prowling about the premises, and taking his dog and gun, stole out after him. The coyote fled into this garden with the dog at his heels, and took refuge in a big patch of cactus, which cost him his life. For though the dog knew better than to follow him into the cactus, his stationary position there afforded an excellent mark for the rifle. In those days the coyotes of Aliso had not learned very much about men and their guns.

Quails by the thousands came down from the brush of the hills around to scratch and dust like chickens in the soft, newly worked earth of the garden, often digging up precious plants. Quails when resting and feeding like this, always have a sentinel stationed somewhere on guard, to give a sharp warning signal at any approach of danger.

One day a small flock of a dozen or two came into the garden to dust, and George surprised them there. They were not very much afraid, having never yet to any extent been preyed upon by man. The old male lookout gave his shrill warning call, then flew up and alighted on a cactus plant to watch while the others walked away to a distance they considered safe. Then he hopped down to follow after them. But something had happened to his foot. It had happened while he was perched on the cactus plant. Then began a comical spectacle interesting to observe. He hopped a step or two, then stopped, lifted his foot, and turning it bottom up, critically examined it; while endeavoring to keep one eye on the intruder. He pecked at it several times, then put his foot down again and took another hop or two. Again he paused, lifted his foot bottom up, squinted an eye at George, pecked at the thorn again, clumsily endeavoring to hop at the same time with the help of his wings. But his progress was slow and difficult. Thus, steadying himself with one wing, alternately hopping and pecking, with the injured foot held off the ground at an upturned angle, at the same time keeping an eye on the enemy, he made his way painfully across the clearing, while George, chuckling with amusement, quietly watched the performance till the quails all flew away into the brush of the hillside above.

At first George had not attempted to get rid of the cactus in his garden. It seemed too formidable a task to tackle with his simple implements, and there were several large patches of it. Yet, the sight of cactus in his garden was an eyesore. And as time went on, his vision of its possibilities enlarging, he began to work on the cactus, keeping at it till he had it all grubbed out, with the brush, clear to the foot of the cliffs and an equal distance up the sides of the draw all around.

In the bank of the creek near the fence across the front of the garden, he dug a little well, boarding it up and putting a crossbeam above, from which suspended a rope and bucket, to make the watering easier.

He laid out winding paths all through the garden and leading up to the caves, and bordered them with appropriate flowers. At the base of the cliffs and along in front of the caves, he set out geraniums on either side of the paths, which thrived as hardily as weeds. Even trimmings thrown up onto the bare rocks to die would keep green and go on blossoming for weeks. From the canyons around, he brought wild shrubs. There was a tobacco tree, with its bright yellow bells, a yew tree to the right of the larger cave, and not far from that, a mallow tree, or Malva Rosa, with its maple-like gray-green leaves and large, brilliant, pinkish-red, deeply-veined blossoms. From above Sycamore canyon he brought a native lilac, with its shiny ever-green leaves. In after years its fragrant blue and lavender blossoms hung in dense showy panicles over the path that led up the side of the spur on the way from garden to vineyard.

He brought from the beaches and hills around, the jeweled ice plant, and the thick-leaved, succulent plant called Stonecrop by the wise ones and also "Hunters' Rock Leek" from the fact that thirsty hunters in arid regions where it grows will extract the fluid from its leaves as a grateful temporary substitute for water. But to us ordinary folks it was "hen-and-chickens." These, with their rosettes of heavy watery leaves shooting up tall graceful spires of orange-pink blooms, bordered the paths and surrounded themselves with nesting circles of little ones. He filled the whole place with beautiful flowers, both wild and cultivated, sometimes transplanting, and sometimes sowing the seed.

From pastures and canyons came larkspurs—or wild delphinium—cream-cups, of the poppy family, buttercups—or wild ranunculas—bluebells, fiddleneck, forget-me-nots, and lupines of several varieties, scarlet bugler, daisies, and wild heliotrope. From the little hill, came monkey flowers that grew there in abundance, yellowing the whole hillside; and other flowers. Above the vineyard on the mountain, he found some California poppies—rare in the canyon, and since then adopted as the State flower—which he brought down and transplanted in his garden. Wild roses—the true "Rose of Castile"—were transplanted from the clumps found in various places on the premises; and wild sweet peas—both the small, and giant "Pride of California" varieties, were brought from the hillsides above the pasture to clamber over the fence at the border of his garden. There was also a dwarf plant of the yucca order.

Native to the garden and left growing there, were the convolvulus, yellow and red primroses, and "rattlesnake-weed," with its tiny grayish-green round leaves, which hugged the ground in a broadening circular mat, twinkling with the tiniest imaginable pink blossoms with white collars. It was believed by us all that this plant was an antidote for the rattler's venom. By the Mexicans, a poultice of the mashed leaves was bound onto the wound, while a tea made of the whole plant was drunk. Its presence here reminded us that even in this beautiful garden we must not relax our watchfulness for rattlesnakes.

The willows planted along the creek bank to which the wires of the fence were attached, grew apace, and soon concealed the garden from outside view—aided in this by a small group of tall eucalyptus in the corner of the garden by the entrance at the foot of the spur.

When campers began coming to Aliso Beach to spend their summer vacations, they would visit our place, and on such occasions, were shown this garden in the hillside nook. To them, it was a discovery. They would explore it with delight, and come back again bringing others to see it, exhibiting to their admiring friends its unique beauty. They marveled at the perseverance, industry and art that had wrought this transformation with tools so simple, and became interested in the young gardener as well. These friends began bringing and sending to George, packets of seeds, cuttings, bulbs, and plants from their own gardens at home; so that in time, the place was a mass of luxuriant bloom and greenness and mingled fragrance. Sweet geranium and honeysuckle lent their perfume, tube-roses and pinks, their rare sweet scent, Australian sweet peas climbed the fence, commingling with wild roses. One or two garden roses also grew there. Hollyhocks raised their tall stately stalks of red bloom from above beds of nasturtiums and verbenias. Marigolds and "Gilly-flowers"—our name for single stocks—and the pin-cushion Scabiosa, dark and velvety—to us, "bachelor buttons"—and "four-o'clocks" and Canterbury bells and prickly phlox all flourished in this wonderful garden.

Most of the flowers were of the single varieties, for in those days, there were but few of the glorious doubles that modern scientific methods of flower culture have developed. But there were oriental poppies of various colors, single at first, that after four years of self-seeding, became fringed, large and permanently double—a marvel to us— the delightful transfiguration giving its added beauty to the garden.

After the bloom had all fallen from the poppy stalks and their pepperbox capsules with advancing summer had become dry, and rattled with ripened seeds, we loved to gather them and shake out the little black seeds into the palms of our hands to eat—licking them up with the tongue. They were rich and oily, with a rare, subtle flavor that pleased the palate. So well did Joan and Hulda like this delicacy, that one summer they decided to gather a great quantity of the seeds to put away in receptacles for future consumption. So they brought their cans and gathered all the pepper-box shakers they could find; and were sitting there in the garden on the dry grass with their laps full, shaking out the poppy seeds into their containers; when along came George into the garden too, and seeing them engaged in this delightful occupation, asked what they were doing. When told, he looked very stern; and stooping down, to their great dismay, gathered up all they had, crushing the yet unshaken capsules, and scattered them far and wide over the ground, emptying their containers, and explaining to the girls the poisonous nature of poppy seeds.

We loved this garden—reveled in it; and long enjoyed the fruits of the labor and love of the beautiful, that dwelt in the soul of the boy who made it. Others beside the family loved it. George loved it, and cared for it faithfully as long as he remained at home. Even after more than sixty years, there are still left traces of geraniums and "gilly-flowers" growing below the caves. Always-always it will live, one of the bright spots in my memory. As I now look down through the long vista of years that are flown, I can think of nothing that more surely tells a story than does "George's Ground"—that beautiful garden in the side of the hill.

CHAPTER 13 THE FAMILY INCREASES

Meanwhile, the babies kept coming. Hulda was the first born in Aliso Canyon—born in that little one-room cabin less than twenty months after it became their home.

Little Joan, now nearing two, was delighted with the tiny new sister. Father asked her what they should name the baby. Joan, for a few moments was lost in thought. Only a short time before, she had tasted her first honey, made by the bees in their own apiary, and could think of nothing nicer and sweeter. A light shone in her blue eyes.

"Name her Honey," she said. And "Honey" it was from that day forward.

Not until their interview with the "census-taker" years afterward, did the baby have any other name than Honey. Then they called her Hulda. But long after this was recorded, the little nickname persisted. Someone was always threatening to "eat" her because honey is so eatable. This would greatly irritate her. One day when about six years old, in exasperation she exclaimed:

"I won't like any of you anymore if you don't quit calling me 'Honey!'"

A serious effort was made after this to bring her real name into common use. But Father, much to her disgust, would call her nothing but "Half-a-day."

Hulda must have been an interesting and imaginative child, as shown by amusing incidents from her baby life preserved in family tradition.

Being a bit delicate, "Honey" was given an extra cup of milk to drink night and morning, a special favor, milk being a great luxury. She was very fond of it. But one evening when George went up to the second gate to milk the cows, she accompanied him, and there for the first time saw where the milk came from. Astonished, and by her own eyes convinced that it must be something very "nasty," she refused to drink another drop of milk. Several days went by, during which coaxing and bribery had no effect. Finally, under the argument of its being "stored up food" that made little calves grow and would also make her grow up big, she succumbed to the force of reason and decided that milk was proper stuff for refreshment.

The premises were infested not only with the large ugly tarantula, but also, more numerously, with the harmless little black pinacate beetle which when disturbed would lower its head, lift up its rear on two long hind legs, and emit a fetid odor from the up-tilted tip, justly earning the common name of "stink bug."

While Father was one day at work excavating for the cellar, he heard this amusing call from little "Honey," at play nearby:

"Oh Pa! Here's a tint bud, and he keelie-up!"

Fearing tarantulas, Father ran out to see. There to his great amusement, stooped little "Honey" in the striking attitude of a "tint bud" herself, with nose to the ground and rear as high as two "hind legs" could reach, gazing intently upon the tiny creature before her in the identical position.

Around the family board, the children one day were enjoying the game of spelling out the name of each food asked for:

"I want some b-e-a-n-s," and beans would be passed.

"I want some p-o-t-a-t-o-e-s," and to potatoes they were helped.

Little Honey, gazing upon the coveted dessert while listening to this interesting game, suddenly announced:

"I want some t-e-PIE!"

She wanted to go somewhere with Father, one day, but he excused himself from taking her. Turning to her sister, she exclaimed indignantly:

"Jonie, ain't Pa SCHINGGY?"

Sixteen months to a day after Hulda's birth, little curly-headed Frank was born—their last son—on November fourteen, three years after they settled in the canyon. And six days less than sixteen months after that event, Harriet came along to grace the family register, born in that same little cabin during a terrific storm in March.

In her very nature was implanted a spirit akin to the conflicting elements that greeted her advent into the world. Mother had not wanted any more babies. She did not need any more babies. But especially did she rebel at having them come sixteen months apart. And by that mysterious alchemy beyond the pale of scientific analysis, to her latest offspring there was imparted—along with some of her sterling virtues—an unhappy admixture of all the emotions engendered by such a prenatal state of mind, modified and supplemented by paternal characteristics and other untraced ancestral legacies.

The resulting fusion was a strange composition of contradictory forces and propensities, producing a nature at contrariety with itself; a nature at once shrinking, easily repulsed, dreamy, romantic, sentimental, poetical, yet concealing all effectively behind a front of practical matter-of-fact-ness; a nature inclined to melancholy and cursed with an over-dose of "inferiority complex," yet manifesting natural leadership and dominance; a nature craving discovery and appreciation of the inner sanctuary, yet persistently guarding against its invasion from without.

With such turmoil of conflicting elements wrapped within the germinating seed of her being to follow a natural unfoldment of misinterpretations, did baby Harriet launch her little bark upon the ocean of life. And what could it mean but rough sailing?

There was nothing effeminate about Frank. As became the masculine, he struck straight from the shoulder. Hulda, one day, came weeping out of Mother's room where, at play with her younger brother, she had been sorely wounded by his pugilistic tendencies. Holding hands over abdomen, she cried bitterly between sobs:

"Ma! Ma! Frank hit me right here in my brains!"

The two were out walking one day with Father, who, between them, held a hand of each. Along the cliffs above the yard were several diminutive caves where owls roosted daytimes away from the bright light of the sun. Running over the edges of these caves were small white patches, one of which was outstanding in its resemblance to a white rag hanging down from the opening. Little Frank, looking up at this white formation, asked:

"What is that?"

Hulda, knowing the answer, did not wait for Father to reply:

"That's God's nightshirt," she said.

Our family practiced "Hooverizing" before Hoover was born, and the doctrine of the "clean plate" was rigidly observed long before the world war gave the idea to the nation.

There was one thing, however, that Hulda would not eat—the soft yolk of an egg. The very sight of it was to her, nauseating. But Father determined to teach her to eat it. At breakfast, one morning, with some of this yolk still untouched on her plate, she asked for something else. Father said:

"No. Eat what is on your plate first."

Looking at that repulsive yolk, she said disgustedly:

"Kulk ain't fit t'eat a-toll!"

After this, "yolk" was always "kulk" at our house. Starting when I was an infant, this was the only designation I knew for the yolk of an egg until told differently when quite a large girl. Thereafter, an egg yolk, to me had two names, and I much preferred the more familiar one of "kulk."

Frank and I were like twins, as indeed we were often taken to be by strangers. While very small and dressed alike, knowing nothing of sex differences, we were inseparable. Where one was, there was the other. What one did, the other did. We shared alike in everything without rivalry or jealousy.

But there came a day when they first put Frank into pants. It was the first time he had been given anything that I could not share. I cried and pleaded for pants too. In vain they explained to me that Frank was a boy and I a girl. This meant nothing to me but partiality. I wanted to be a boy too and wear pants like Frank. I couldn't see why they wouldn't let me be a boy too. Frank had been promoted. I was not. My heart was broken. I must remain only a girl, but he had been raised to the dignity of a boy, with honors I could not share—though I am sure that Frank understood the reason for it all no better than I.

The superior airs he assumed only increased my grievance. In vain did Father try to console me with flatteries:

"I don't want too many boys. Neither does Ma. We want one nice little girl."

"But the baby's a girl," I argued, "I want to be a boy! Let me be a boy like Frank and have pants too!"

Finally, Father tucked my dress into the top of my panties, fastening them on the outside, and told me that I could be his "little Bennie." But though a tiny bit mollified, I knew that this was not the same thing, but only a compromise. Frank didn't have his dress tucked into panties. They had taken it off entirely and, to complete my chagrin, had told me I could now have all Frank's dresses. But I didn't want Frank's old dresses. I wanted pants.

For some time, Father dressed me thus and called me his little Bennie. But somehow, I did not soon forgive my parents—not even after I knew that boys and girls were physically different, for I did not even then see why they had ordered a girl instead of a boy.

While a small child, Frank had the disagreeable habit, when displeased, of throwing himself to the floor on his back, kicking and "squalling." One morning while being dressed, something went wrong and he threw himself as usual onto the floor.

It so happened that someone had just taken off a hot stove lid and, because the stove hook was burning the fingers, had set it down on the floor. Onto this hot stove lid, Frank rolled. He then had something very real to cry about. His poor little back was fairly cooked, and was many a day in healing. For years he carried a great ugly scar. But never again did he throw himself onto the floor.

Perhaps his frequent spells of temper were due to his lack of ability to make himself understood. He could not pronounce words according to sound. This was a constant source of irritation. Until nearly six years of age he said "rat" for "yes" and "Doby" for "Joseph." When finally he did learn to talk, he stuttered, a habit that continued for several years.

When nearing the independent and self-conscious age of ten, he was told by some interested visitor of a sure way to break oneself of the stuttering habit. This friend told him that if he did not break himself while young it would be a lifelong handicap. Frank, who keenly felt his impediment, was interested right away.

The remedy was simple, requiring only perseverance. He was to keep two small pebbles in his mouth all the time, removing them only to eat and sleep. Frank believed this friend and put the instruction to the test, with the result that he was completely cured of the habit of stuttering.

The principle is unfailing. In an effort to keep the pebbles from falling out of the mouth it is necessary to speak very slowly and deliberately, which, when persisted in over a long period of time, will correct the nervous haste that causes stuttering.

When about nine years of age, Frank received a vicious kick from a horse on the crown of his head, which made a large half-circle gash in his scalp. With a common sewing needle and coarse white thread, Father himself sewed up this ugly wound, taking many stitches.

Frank sat in the baby's high chair like a Spartan without anesthetic of any kind, during the long and painful ordeal making never a sound above a whimper. Watching this performance, my sympathy was mingled with wonder at his "grit." Physical pain to me was a bugbear. I could not endure the thought of it and shuddered to see that needle go in and out while Frank endured it so unflinchingly. Had it been I who occupied that surgical high chair, what loud wails would have rent the air!

What Price Glory

Too late for wisdom to correct,

We analyze in retrospect.

Through early childhood, my hair was kept shingled tight to the head—not in a "girlish bob" or even a "boyish bob" such as are worn by girls today, but just an ugly short cut without bangs or other softening feature. Very often, by strangers I was taken to be a boy, for it was no uncommon thing for boys of my size to be seen dressed exactly like girls. In my presence, the question would be asked:

"Is it a girl, or a boy?"

Then, with all my heart, I would wish that the answer might be given:

"It is a boy," for never had I become reconciled to having been born a girl.

Frank and I were often mistaken for twins. Though my senior by sixteen months, he was shorter than I due to the unhappy fact that his legs were disproportionately short for the upper part of his body, which was of normal size, and but for this deficiency, though his head was a bit large, he would have grown up a well-proportioned man.

As it was, throughout life, he never could find a pair of trousers that otherwise were a good fit, but they had to be shortened. Needless to say, Frank's short legs were the bane of his existence. Though he would endeavor to conceal the fact whenever the subject came up, by passing it over with a jest, still, it rankled.

Inseparable companions from our earliest years, Frank and I doubtless would have remained so had our mutual association been left to develop naturally. But unfortunately it was not. We were still of tender age when Father began to amuse himself and chance visitors by pitting us against each other in wrestling matches. This might have been good enough sport had Frank experienced his rightful share of successes. But in these bouts, I, being heavier and taller, always won.

This seemed to "tickle" Father immensely and he would boast to others that Harriet could "lick" Frank, proving it by setting us at each other again. Poor Frank would fight desperately—even lose his temper as he felt me winning. But so far as I can remember, never once did he come off victor.

It is to be supposed that I as well as Father, enjoyed these triumphs; for what child—or grown-up either, for that matter—could fail to take pleasure in a victor's crown? But Frank did not enjoy it. And therein lay seeds of harm to both of us.

Looking back now, I see it as one of the stupidest, cruelest blunders that could have been perpetrated against child victims by parental thoughtlessness and utter ignorance of child psychology. The whole thing was entirely unfair to Frank. My being his junior and a girl besides, insulted his masculine pride. In the end, it proved unfair to me also, for it led Frank, my natural mate, to look upon me as his natural rival, undermining the early basis of comradeship and erecting between us a barrier of perpetual misunderstanding.

Thereafter, in a natural effort to regain his "face" and establish his male superiority, Frank instinctively fell into the habit of discountenancing me at every opportunity, extending this attitude beyond the physical to a general concept. While magnifying his own worth in every line, he manifested contempt for that of his supposed rival.

The reaction upon me was just as unwholesome. To be so treated hurt my personal poise, developing an attitude of self-defense that marred my character. Wholly unconscious of meriting his dislike and being utterly in the dark as to the underlying cause of it—neither of us having age or experience enough to analyze the situation—I came to consider him boastful and disagreeable, which was only one side of the picture, and that biased.

To the other girls, Frank revealed another side of his nature. He was affectionate and required affection. He liked the company of girls and showed much more appreciation of them than did the older boys, who considered him too young to be companionable to themselves. His brotherly confidences that I might have shared and returned with benefit to both of us, were bestowed upon others.

The two next older girls than we were mates together. The two next younger were natural mates. But who was there, if not Frank, to chum with me? Thus deprived, in the midst of a large family, I grew up peculiarly alone and lonely. I wanted to be his pal. I needed a brother's comradeship. I needed to give expression to that side of my nature, and Frank needed to receive it. We needed each other's sympathy and balancing attributes, and should have become mutual developers one of the other. But with this nipped in the bud by early and tragic misunderstanding, we both lost something irretrievably precious out of our lives.

CHAPTER 14 WHEN THE CLIFF FELL

Between Frank's birth and mine, a notable event took place; one not altogether unexpected, yet which came in an unprepared moment as an overwhelming surprise, and which might easily have been a tragedy.

The mountain back of our house rose up at first so gradually from the general slope that only the line of ungrubbed brush marked its beginning. But its incline soon increased to steepness and several hundred feet above the house came to an abrupt end at the foot of a perpendicular wall of overhanging cliffs. These cliffs presented a barrier precipitous and impassable, perhaps a hundred and fifty feet long and at its widest part fifty feet high, narrowing at the northern end to something like thirty feet.

Underneath them for a distance of about ten feet back, and along the greater portion of their length, the sandstone rock had disintegrated with the ravages of time, into fine yellow, powdery sand and dust, leaving, not exactly a cave below, but an overhanging ledge above.

Father did not like the look of these cliffs. Shortly after bringing his family there he had noticed and remarked about their dangerous appearance, and had warned them that someday the ledge might split away from the cliff and fall down the mountain. The house being directly below the ledge, the possibility was one to cause them uneasiness. He instructed his family, should this ever happen, to flee, everyone, toward the little hill out of the path of danger.

One day in June the man named Wood was visiting Father. They sat on the doorstep of the upper corncrib facing the young pepper row, engaged in conversation, when Wood, looking up at the cliffs, said to Father:

"Ain't you afraid of a landslide here some day?"

"No, but I'm afraid of a rock-slide," replied Father.

"Aw, them rock's'll never fall. They've been there for thousands of years," said Wood reassuringly. But Father was far from satisfied.

The next day after this confabulation, Mesia, then past eleven, noticed an old mother cat carrying her litter of newborn kittens one by one in her mouth up the hillside path to a new nest she had prepared, to escape the too frequent fondling of the children. Leaving her duties, she slipped along behind her up the trail toward the cliffs to learn the secret hiding place.

When she came down supper was in preparation. Mother and Sadie were in the house cooking, and Mesia began to set the table. Joseph, between six and seven, had gone out to the woodpile for an armful of wood. George, accompanied by Lafie, was up at the second gate half a mile or so distant milking the cows. Father was building beehives up in the shed. He had a pile of new finished hives standing outside at the north end of the shed, and Joan was playing among them.

Directly in line with these hives and lower down in the yard, stood the low gabled duck coop, six or eight feet square, in which were between sixteen and twenty ducks, just housed for the night. Little Hulda, nearing two, was sitting on the ground at the lower corner of this duck coop playing. Dusk was just beginning to fall.

Suddenly, the stillness of that quiet evening was shattered by a terrific roar so deafening it seemed fairly to split the eardrums. No one could hear his own voice. Father rushed out of the shed, grabbed Joan in his hands, and carrying her thus before him, ran toward the house yelling a frantic warning for all to run; but bringing up the rear, for Mother had already snatched up baby Frank, and screaming for the other children to follow, was on her way toward the little hill. Joseph, who had happened not to hear Father's previous instructions concerning flight, dashed toward the creek, but soon turned back and joined the others at the little hill.

A noise like prolonged and fearful thunder followed the first crash, and great mountainous rocks came rolling down the hillside above the house and outbuildings. The air was dense with suffocating dust, making both vision and breathing difficult. The family could scarcely see one another. When they had gathered together and "counted noses" it was discovered that little Hulda was missing. Joseph said he had seen her sitting down beside the duck coop just before the crash, and thither ran Mesia.

By this time the rocks had stopped rolling and were all lodged somewhere, and the noise had ceased. Running across the backyard above the house, Mesia found little Hulda there wandering blindly about in the bewildering dust, sniffling and whimpering. Snatching her up, she carried her back to the anxious, trembling family group. Sadie was hysterical, all was confusion.

Up at the second gate, when the first startling sound broke the stillness, George paused in his milking to listen. Lafie asked excitedly:

"What was that?"

"That was a big breaker! My! It must have been a whopper!" replied George. He waited to hear the inevitable second breaker follow. But none came.

"That's peculiar," he mused, in a puzzle.

He finished milking and they started home. After rounding the bend as they neared the barn, the whole atmosphere was dense with powdery dust and the ground everywhere covered with it. Crossing the yard their feet sank half buried in the dust that already had settled, leaving deep tracks. The house was full of it and everything inside covered deep with dust, the supper completely spoiled. Everybody was in commotion, some weeping with nervous excitement.

In the middle of the orchard below the woodpiles lay a great rock weighing many tons, with a deeply plowed track behind it not far from where Joseph had been standing. Another of similar size that had just missed the southern end of the house lay a little lower down in the orchard above the young olive trees.

Leaning against the upper corner of the duck coop was another large rock weighing a ton or more, which had cracked into three parts but still held its shape. This rock, on its last turn-over had shoved the duck coop full of quacking ducks about six inches, without injury to either coop or inmates, and had come to stop a few feet above the spot where Hulda had been sitting at play directly in its path. One more turn of this rock would certainly have crushed her. It had first crashed through the new-made bee hives at the spot where Joan had been playing, breaking a few of them in its mad career.

Close to the step of the corncrib where Father and Wood had held their confab the day before, another rock of about a thousand pound weight had broken through the upper front corner and now was balanced on the sill, with about two feet of it inside. A few pans of milk had been upset and several dozen eggs broken.

Father and George afterward dug a hole underneath this rock to undermine it, allowing it to fall back away from the sill into the hole.

It seemed as though some good angel had watched over that family to protect both their lives and their property from destruction. The conversation of the day previous between Father and Wood, seemed itself like a divine forewarning. Three of the children had been in special danger, yet spared unhurt, and even the ducks had cause to quack their thankfulness.

Many large rocks and innumerable smaller ones lay scattered over hillside and yards. Above the cribs a huge rock of many tons had lodged higher up the slope. Another of immense size, slender in form and pointed, extended high in the air, with a cluster of lesser rocks at its base. Northward from these nearly on a line with the cribs a rock of huge proportions had come to rest, which ever after went by the name of "Gable Rock." It was shaped like the ridge and two slants of a steep gable roof, with shorter straight sides extending to the ground, and might as appropriately have been called "Tent Rock."

Below this one a large potato-shaped rock weighing many tons was standing on one end.

The cliff now presented a smooth, perpendicular surface from base to top. The great ledge had evidently given way all at once and slid in one piece to the hard rock bed below and there had been broken up by the impact into many parts before rolling down the hill to remain where they lodged, permanent parts of the general landscape.

In their wake, the whole hillside they had passed over was beaten smooth and free from all growing vegetation and the soil ground to a fine powder. In places, the powdery yellow dust was knee-deep. A little elderberry tree that had been growing on the hillside was now planted upside-down, the top of it buried in the ground sufficiently deep to hold it in an upright position, the roots sticking straight up in the air.

The kittens were no more. A family legend of that mother cat's mournful wails for days afterward, came down to us younger children who made our advent into the world too late to have a personal part in this thrilling experience.

CHAPTER 15 EARLIEST GLIMPSES

My earliest recollection is of being rocked in a big rocking chair, held in someone's arms—either Mother's or an older sister's, and drinking in the exciting words of the lullaby crooned to me:

"Rock-a-by Baby, up in the tree top; When the wind blows, the cradle will rock.

When the bough breaks the cradle will fall, And down will come Baby, cradle and all!"

I knew then nothing of birds and nests. It did not occur to me that the "baby" could be other than myself. The meaning of "bough" and "cradle" I did not comprehend, but I knew what a tree was and what it meant to fall. I would fancy myself actually up in the top of a big tree and imagine the sensation of that terrible tumble down to the ground, shrinking with fear at the thought of it.

In my unworded ideas, I supposed it must be very wonderful to be high up in a tree, but oh, so scary, and decided that being held in safe arms in a rocking chair on the floor was much to be preferred.

Another very early memory picture comes faint and dim as to time and detail, but nevertheless standing out as a personal emotional experience of babyhood.

I was standing all by myself in the kitchen near the open door of Mother's room, looking in upon a strange process of bewildering confusion that was turning my world topsy-turvy. The meaning of it all, I could not grasp. Just what they were doing, I could not tell, but things were unfamiliar—mystifying. I did not know where to go or what to do, and so, stood all alone in the big kitchen, and seemingly alone in the world, forgotten by all who usually gave me attention—they were busy in there.

Looking back, it seems to me now that they were probably tearing off the inner tent lining that had been tacked onto the walls of the room built over it, and refinishing with cloth and paper the inside of Mother's room to make it more livable, for some such thing must have taken place about that time.

Another very early memory glimpse is of grapes hanging overhead in bunches on many wires strung back and forth across the kitchen underneath the uncovered rafters. When we would eat these grapes reached down to us by some grown-up who stood on a chair, they seemed extra sweet and rich as though half raisin. I think they represented the last picking of the crop from our young vineyard, recently come into bearing, saved, perhaps, from the many hungry robbers of the wilds.

There is the dim recollection of little goats running about the hillside and clambering over rocks back of the corncribs. One particular goat on a certain rock stands out in the picture. I remember wondering how he could skip with such ease over the big rock, onto which I could not even hope to climb.

The actual purchase of the big Charter-Oak stove in Seventy-Nine, which, after long study of catalogues, Father sent east for at great expense, freighting it to Los Angeles and hauling it down by team and wagon to Aliso, I do not remember, but I do recall distinctly, a time when the name, ''Charter-Oak'' was intensely discussed at our fireside. To me, it seemed that all the grown folks could talk about was "Charter-Oak," "Charter-Oak" "Charter-Oak," and I had not the slightest idea what they meant. What it was all about, I wished I could fathom, for the name, albeit so meaningless, sounded mysterious, fascinating, intriguing.

The burning of the haystack in Seventy-Eight, I do not recall. Yet, I know just where it stood before the burning, and the new location where they stacked the hay afterward alongside the cow corral.

Memory retains the vivid sketch of an incident when I was a year and a half, still in the majesty of babyhood, seated upon the family throne. Never yet had come into my experience cross words and scoldings, with their rude awakening. The voluntary preferment and tender solicitude of all the household and their unquestioning gratification of my every wish, accepted as a matter of course, is a part of the memory picture, epitomized in a sense of satisfied security.

I recall the appearance of chubby arms and the sound of baby words as though looking back upon a scene that pertained to someone else, yet it was I, endeavoring to comfort a sister in her grief. "Jonie" seemed like a very big girl to me. She had just celebrated her sixth birthday, the main gift of which was a little pearl-handled penknife. Sadie had borrowed this treasured penknife, and had lost it in the vineyard across the creek. All afternoon we had searched for it, turning up soft, sandy dirt along the path where Sadie had walked, but in vain.

Now, we were seated in solemn sadness around the big table, in the center of which stood the lighted lamp. Broken-hearted Joan was weeping bitterly. I stood up in my chair beside her and, with one supporting hand on the table, put the other arm around her neck, bending forward in deepest solicitude to peer up into her tear-wet face, repeating in great distress:

"Don't ky, Donie! Don't ky! Poor Donie! Don't ky!"

Another very early incident remains in memory because of being laughed at. By this time, dispossessed of my queenly throne, I was in turn, a worshipper at the shrine of the new baby. In a rapture of adoration, I watched Mother bathe and dress the tiny infant, lightly rubbing my cheek over the downy head, and touching the delicate little fingers. Then I said:

"Ma, I want a little baby too."

"You can have part of this one," she said, matter-of-factly.

"But I want one of my very own," I explained.

"You have your dollies. They're the kind of babies for little girls," said Mother.

"But I don't mean dollies," I insisted, "I want a real live meat-baby."

Then they laughed at me, which was disconcerting, for I was in dead earnest. After that, to my embarrassment, Father repeated this saying to everybody.

Still another incident made its lasting impression because of laughter evoked. The family were all at breakfast, seated around the big round-ended table. The fire glowed in the open grate where we sometimes toasted bread on the hearth before the coals. But on this occasion toast was being made on the top of the stove. All the older children were toasting bread, each for himself, but nobody made any for me. Of course I had to have some too.

So I took my slice of bread over to the stove, the top of which was about on a level with my eyes, but when I saw that stove-lid all covered with burnt crumbs and looking so black and dirty, I could not make up my mind to put that clean white bread on it. I went to the wood box and found there a small piece of paper, which I spread out cautiously on the top of the stove, then laid my bread upon the paper.

The laughter of the family group shamed me greatly. Still, I could not see what there was to laugh about. Surely, I thought, they ought to know that a dirty stove would dirty my bread.

Well do I remember the first time I ever heard thunder—a sound so terrifying that I ran for refuge into Mother's room and hid myself. But I could not hide from that awful, fearsome, pursuing, penetrating sound. I thought it must be a thousand barrels rolling down the hill, and that they would surely crush all in their path. When it ceased I ran out into the yard to see what had happened. But everything was just as usual, except that some big scattering drops of water fell on my head. I asked what that noise was, and somebody explained to me that it was thunder.

"Thunder," what was that? Nobody could tell me. It was just thunder that was all. "Thunder," a sound without cause or result, a great cracking and tearing that was meaningless. What strange things there were in the world! I was skeptical. But since nothing really happened, I supposed they must be right, and added another bit of learning to my rapidly increasing repertory.

Another incident comes to mind that transpired when I was still too young to be trusted out of sight of my elders. It was springtime. Everything was fresh and green and dewy. I wandered, unbeknown, away from the house and climbed up onto the little hill point to play a new venture for me. There, I found some beautiful glossy green and red leaves, the most beautiful I had ever seen. I thought of Mother—my world, my all. How they would please her! I would pick a bouquet for her. So I gathered my hands full of the tender red tips and carried them back down the hillside and home to Mother.

Never will I forget her reaction at sight of them, how, with horrified exclamations, she snatched them out of my hands and put them all into the stove, unmindful of my loving thought for her. And how she got the soap and wash basin of water and scrubbed my hands and face till I thought my skin would come off, all the time telling me that I must never, never touch those bushes again—that they were poison oak and would poison me all over if I touched them.

I was badly frightened, and wondered if I really were going to die. Though she watched me anxiously for several days, that immediate scrubbing saved me from any evil after-effects. But always, after that, I looked askance at the little hill whose beauties were so dangerous, and never forgot that I had been forbidden to play there.

Then there was the incident of the little green frog I swallowed—or did I swallow him? Near the open end of our long narrow front porch, stood the "water barrel" that held our drinking water from Spring Canyon. Over its top edge was hooked a dipper, the bowl hanging down inside. When a very little girl, as I once put this dipper to my lips, a little green frog perched on its brim, caught my eye just as the first mouthful went in with a gulp, too late for the frog or me either to do anything about it.

That I swallowed this frog, I firmly believed and maintained against the skepticism of those older. Exasperated by their incredulity, I declared, as last convincing evidence, probably a mixture of imagination and fabrication, that I felt him "scrape my throat as he went down." How large a place imagination had in this whole incident it is impossible to tell, but at any rate, the little green frog was real, and afterward could not be found. As a wise precautionary measure, Mother gave me a dose of physic, the family remedy for a multitude of ills, and I seemed none the worse for the experience.

Somewhere, as a tiny girl, I once visited a nest of baby owls built just inside of a cut out opening near the top of some outbuilding. A big boy helped me to climb up the ladder that leaned against the wall, to reach the square opening in front of the next. I looked in, and there squatted two of the most adorable fluffy balls of creamy down that ever came out of an eggshell.

The old mother, who must have been a Monkey-faced Barn Owl, stood a little apart from the nest, and with her keen, beady, round eyes, watched every move I made. Cautiously I reached my hand in and lifted one of the babies. It was light as a feather, though such a big ball. Its legs stretched out awkwardly, its little round eyes took on an expression of fear, as the mother owl clicked her bill with low hisses. The boy warned me not to touch them. I put it down carefully, withdrawing to a safe distance from that menacing hooked bill and those sharp claws and penetrating eyes.

I was not an enemy, but a true friend and admirer of her family. But she could not be sure of that. So I climbed down the ladder again reluctantly, loathe to leave the beautiful babies.

Where was this? I cannot tell. There was no outbuilding on our place that fulfills the mind picture I carry about with me of this scene. To me, it seems always to have been back of our own cistern, but how there could have been such an opening as this under that octagon roof, is a mystery I cannot solve. Who was the boy? I cannot say. I only know that it is not a dream—that the boy, the ladder, the attic opening, the baby owls, were real, and that the incident took place somewhere—but where, who can tell?

Roar after roar of dynamite resounding through the canyon and echoing among the mountains fixed in memory the blasting of the tunnel for the spring on the hillside above the filaree pasture. And over the horizon's rim from the indistinct to the clearer side of memory, comes the building of barn and cistern. Distinctly I recall the feeling of joyous, exhilarating excitement at the unloading in the newly built barn of the first new-mown hay, whose odorous incense haunts me still.

The same month that President Garfield was inaugurated, I became five years old—not old enough to know or care anything about the event. But four months later when the bullet of the assassin laid him low, plunging the nation into indignant sorrow, much discussion of the tragedy made its lasting impression. Perhaps the one thing more than anything else that fixed it in my young mind was the ballad that was sung all over the country, supposed to have been written in his death cell by the guilty man.

Though scarcely comprehending what it was all about, and quite hazy as to the meaning of "scaffold" and "fatal doom," with others, I sang it lustily:

"Oh my name is Charles Guiteau—

The name I'll never deny—

I leave my aged parents

In sorrow for to die.

Little did I think

When in my youthful bloom

That to the scaffold I should go

To meet my fatal doom.

"My sister came to see me
And bid me a last goodbye;
She threw her arms around my neck
And wept most bitterly,
Crying, 'Oh, my dearest brother,
This day you surely must die
For the murder of James A. Garfield
Upon the scaffold high!"

About four months after the President's death, another American of very different type and notoriety was, according to the accepted account, treacherously betrayed and shot in the back for reward, by his own cousin and pal, Bob Ford. It is to be doubted that the death of the President himself created any greater wave of national indignation than did that of the outlaw, Jesse James, so contrary was the deed to the American spirit of fair play.

Discussion of this event in our family circle, from newspaper accounts, is a matter of personal memory. Though a small child and unable to fathom the role of "Mr. Howard" in the case, I joined in singing the commemorating ballad:

"The dirty little coward that shot Mr. Howard
And laid Jesse James in his grave."

These glimpses of memory would not be complete without mention of my "beauty spot." I was born with the appearance of an ugly gash across the front and side of my throat. There could be seen the blood-red color and the grain of the flesh as it parted and rolled back from the central cut across the tissues. Father called this my "beauty spot," and I, as the family intended, taking it as a compliment, was proud as could be of possessing something that none of the others had. When requested I would, with great willingness, exhibit it to visitors, who, to keep up the kind deception, would also compliment me as having something to be pleased about.

The cause of this birthmark was well known to mother and to other grown-up members of the family. When old enough, I was told how it happened. Only a few months after the cliff fell, Mother, one morning, was mixing bread at the kitchen table directly in front of the window. Suddenly, she heard a loud whoop from George and looked up. There in the backyard, framed by the window, slung across the back of a horse, was a slain deer with head hanging down exposing a throat slashed wide open where it had been bled after the killing.

Startled "out of her wits," Mother, with a cry of horror, grasped her own throat, an instinctively nervous gesture. When I came, my throat had the same appearance as that of the deer. I am assured by those older that it could not have been a more perfect representation. The marvel of mercy is that it should have disappeared during my childhood, though I was in my teens before the last of it vanished.

George too was marked in a similar manner with a bunch of three ripe red strawberries which Mother saw pictured on a grocer's shelf and coveted, unthinkingly touching her own body where the impression was made. During his youth this also disappeared.

Modern medical science may have relegated such ideas to the discard, still, there stand the facts, supported by actual experience, and, may I add, also by Scripture (Genesis 30: 29-43).

The Song of the Fox

Inseparable from this early jumble of memories and woven into the pattern like a fadeless thread of color, is the "Song of the Fox."

Lying back contentedly in Father's arms—on those occasions of special attention vouchsafed to the very young members of the household—a sudden eager and tense interest would grip me as he began to sing in his deep voice, the Fox Song. Heard so many times before that I knew the words almost by heart, yet they thrilled me anew with a weird, inescapable fascination every time he sang the song, the last-line repetitions of each refrain rolling out in great billows of sonorous finality:

"A fox went out one moonshiny night,
And begged of the moon to afford him light

For he'd many a mile to travel that night

Before he reached the town, oh, town oh, town oh,

"For he'd many a mile to travel that night

Before he reached the town, oh."

Listening, with a brief mental struggle over the word "afford," I concluded that it must mean "spend;" then wondered why he had to "beg" that way when the night was already "moonshiny," and I wondered if the moon really knew as I did, why the fox wanted the light, but more was coming:

"At length he came to a farmer's yard

Where the geese and ducks were all at large;

Saying, 'The best of you shall grease my beard

Before I reach the town, oh, town oh, town oh, '

Saying, 'The best of you shall grease my beard

Before I reach the town, oh."

I stumbled over the expressions, "at length" and "at large," but never once did I think of asking what they meant. I wondered if all foxes had hands like Father's, and why he wanted his beard greased. A fleeting mental picture of grease dripping from long, silky whiskers, was overshadowed by the apprehension of imminent tragedy to the poor unsuspecting victim. How tense grew my muscles, and how keen my senses, as the song continued:

"He seized the old black duck by the neck

And swung her all across his back"—

A shudder of horror and an inward gasp, and a feeling of sharp teeth crunching through the flesh and bones; and a twisting pain of that long swing by her bleeding neck—"Could she breathe?" I wondered:

"Which made the old drakes go, 'Quack! quack! quack!'

And the legs came dangling down, oh, down oh, down oh,

Which made the old ducks go, 'Quack! quack! quack!'

And the legs came dangling down, oh."

And a frightened little girl huddled closer in Father's protecting arms, as he brought out in most realistic fashion, that resounding "Quack! Quack! Quack!" Imagination immediately supplied the distracted chorus from geese and ducks, that followed.

"Old Mrs. Widdle-Waddle jumped out of bed,

And out of the window, she popped her head,

Crying, 'John! John! John! the black duck's gone

And the fox is off to his den, lo!'—

The way Father shouted out that "John, John, John," scared me out of my fleeting reverie concerning old Mrs. Widdle-Waddle and her intriguing name. In that brief instant, I had seen her run to the window—strangely like our own window in the end of Mother's room—and had seen the mean old fox grab the duck out of the coop—also a facsimile of our own chicken coops—and wondered who had left the coop open so the fox could get in.

—*"den, lo! den, lo!*

Crying, 'John! John! John! The black duck's gone

And the fox is off to his den, lo!—'"

Here was another puzzle; the fox had started for town, and how he was off to his den. Perhaps it was a fox-town, or maybe he just changed his mind and didn't go where he started or his den might have been in the direction of town; but no, he must have started from his den in the first place—and so, helplessly floundering just as Father came to that last terrifying "John!" I quickly made a mental adjustment and accepted it all by faith—the unsullied faith of childhood—and went on listening:

"Old John went out upon the hill

And blew his horn both loud and shrill;

Quoth the fox, 'That's wonderful music, still
I'd rather be in my den, lo, den lo, den lo";
Quoth the fox, 'That's wonderful music, still
I'd rather be in my den, lo.'"

Here disgust and indignation rose uppermost. What a stupid old man was John to make such a noise and go up on the hill in plain sight of the old fox! He didn't know how to hunt a fox at all! Why didn't he take a gun instead of a horn, and sneak up quietly behind him and shoot the old fox dead—I guess the poor duck would have been dead though anyway, by that time.

"Quoth" was a word utterly outside my vocabulary and baffled all understanding. However, it must be connected in some way with the escape of the bad old fox. But here the next stanza, coming on, introduced the family of hungry little fox babies—and my heart softened a bit. I really was relieved that the old fox got back to his "young ones" safe. They might have starved to death.

"At length he came unto his den,
Where he had young ones, nine or ten.
They tore her up without knife or fork,
And the young ones picked the bones, oh, bones oh, bones oh,
They tore her up without knife or fork
And the young ones picked the bones."

Oh, the stark tragedy—the horror of it! I could hear the flesh tear and the bones crunch and see the scattered feathers everywhere, and old Mrs. Widdle-Waddle couldn't even save them to make a pillow of. My only consolation was that the duck must have been dead before they "tore her up" and so didn't feel the cruel teeth and sharp claws.

No matter how many times my father sang to me this song, each time I would go through the whole gamut of emotions and climaxes—of fear, wonder, indignation and pity, and at the last, would wish that I might see those cunning little fox-babies, and long, with the greed of fascination, to hear it all over again.

CHAPTER 16 IN THE VINEYARD

When our young vineyard came into bearing and its first grapes began to ripen on the vines, then the wildlings all rejoiced, communicating one to another the discovery in their midst of this strange new delicacy, seemingly imported for their especial benefit.

First to take advantage of it were the quails. Down they came in large flocks from the brush of the hills around, to settle in the vineyard and feast upon the delightsome new fruit. This invasion brought children into the vineyard to drive out the trespassers and stand their guard through daylight hours.

When darkness wrapped the world, both feathered and human, in slumber, their antlered neighbors, keen of eye, stole quietly down the mountain trails to sample the new forage, and liking it well, spent the night there banqueting.

When their tracks and their ravages came to light on the following day, George vowed vengeance, and that night, taking a cot and the dogs with him, transferred his sleeping quarters to the vineyard. At the next appearance of deer, the dogs gave chase, spoiling their anticipated feast.

The next visitors to help themselves in the gray dawn, after George had left his post for early chores, were the foxes. Then George resorted to trapping. He set a large double-spring steel trap in the vicinity of the tracks, and soon caught a grown male fox, his leg above the foot being broken by the steel jaws. Not till then was he sure of the nature of the present intruders. Mister Fox was soon dispatched with the Thirty-two.

The very next night Missis Fox stepped into that concealed trap and her leg also was broken. One snap of the trigger and a puff, and poor Missis Fox had followed her mate into oblivion.

The third night, little boy Fox came along, wondering why his father and mother had not returned with food, and he also fell a victim to that wicked trap. His poor little leg was badly mangled. The gun was brought, and soon he too was no more.

By this time George perceived that it was a family of foxes he was trapping. Desiring to secure one of them uninjured that he might tame it for a pet, he took away the big steel trap and in its place set a small one with a single spring. The very next morning he found a little girl fox in the trap. Her leg was neither broken nor seriously injured, though painfully wounded. Wild, suspicious and suffering, she put up a fight when he drew near. So George made a slip noose in the end of a rope and threw it over her head, drawing it snugly around her neck and tightening till, for lack of oxygen her strength began to fail. He then approached and tied her feet together, removing the trap. Holding her so that she could not bite him, he loosened the noose and tied a non-slip knot, then carried her up to the house, and, freeing her feet, put her into a little coop built for chickens.

His next move was to establish a basis of friendship by ministering to her physical needs, followed by a courtship to win her confidence and affection. Every day he would go out to the coop with food and water, and spend some time making cautious advances, patting her head and touching her body till she no longer feared him but allowed his caresses and seemed to like them and learned to trust him, becoming at last as tame as a dog. Then George took her out of the coop and put her on a chain, and she became the pet of the family. All the children loved the little fox playmate, and for a year or more she was one of our barnyard domestics, but always kept on a chain.

Deer would sometimes step into the traps set for other animals, but always they pulled themselves out again, leaving the trap sprung with, perhaps, a little wisp of hair from the fetlock to tell the story, and tracks, where they had jumped about to get loose.

Meanwhile, came the coons—or more properly, raccoons—making a beaten path from hillside to vineyard. These are most interesting and curious little animals. They are related to the bear, though so very much smaller, weighing from twenty to twenty-five pounds, with a length of body about a foot and a half, and an additional foot of beautiful bushy tail, ringed alternately with black and white. A coat of soft fur with longer coarse, black-tipped hairs, gives them a grizzled appearance, and very striking is the broad black stripe across both cheeks above the sharp-pointed black nose.

Like the bear, they are rather awkward and clumsy of movement, yet climb trees readily, and use their fore paws as hands, picking up food to put into their mouths. This trait and their mild innocent eyes that looked out with curious, humanly quizzical expression, their little fore paws so like a baby's small hands and the resemblance of their tracks made by rather large, flat hind feet, to those of a barefoot child, made them so human to us children that we hated to see them killed. It seemed almost like murder.

Yet they were very destructive, and being omnivorous, were fond of eggs as well as fruits. Even little chicks were not safe from them, for all kinds of small animals and birds are their prey, as well as fish from mountain streams, and shellfish along the ocean beach. Green corn and fruits were their delight, especially those wonderful new grapes in our vineyard, so we farmers could not let them go unmolested.

Lafie and Joseph, who as time went on, took over the vineyard night watch in grape season, formulated with George, a method for trapping coons that remained effective for several years. It was based on the habit of these little animals invariably to follow the same beaten path night after night.

A small steel trap attached to a chain would be staked out near the path, the stake being driven well down. After setting the trap directly in the path, it would be covered, chain, stake and all, with loose sandy soil sprinkled over it. The boys would then break up a bunch of ripe grapes into small clusters and drop them at intervals along the path, both preceding and following the trap. So the coon, coming from either direction, while picking up the grape clusters would be sure to step into the trap, and then it was just too bad for the little fellow. Many indeed were the victims thus ensnared during the years.

But in course of time, these little creatures became wise to the ways of man, and when they came to the grapes scattered along the path, would shy around them, going out of the beaten track till past the tempting bait, and coming in again on the farther side, to feast as usual among the vines. So new schemes had to be devised.

The boys then began to set unbaited traps at intervals along the path, and again they caught their game, for coons never learned not to follow the path. Poor little coons! They were after all no match for their human superiors.

As grape season came around and "coon" plottings filled the air anew, resulting in occasional victims being brought lifeless from traps to yard, we youngsters conceived in all this, the suggestion of a new "game." We too became coons.

Crawling about on hands and knees among the vines, avoiding imaginary traps and dogs, we helped ourselves to the bunches hanging down as best we could with lips and teeth, unaided by our "forepaws," for we had not yet learned that coons use theirs as hands.

But finding the grapes thus purloined too dusty to be appetizing, we carried some of the ripest bunches down the bank to the nearby creek for a cleansing souse in its pools. Then, dividing them into smaller bunches, we tied them with cord strings to the low, overhanging branches of the willows that bordered the vineyard, and there on all fours, stretched our necks as before to devour.

This gave us a real "coony" feeling, and of course, made the grapes taste ever so much better.

When grape-picking time came around, all hands went out with buckets and knives into the vineyard to gather the vintage. A horse was hitched to a sled-like affair built for the purpose, which was piled high with wooden boxes— for paper cartons had of course not yet been invented—and into these, as the horses were driven back and forth between the rows, the pickers would empty their brimming buckets.

Moon nights were coon nights. When it was very dark, coons seldom put in an appearance, but a bright moonshiny night was sure to find them abroad.

After neighbors settled on the coast, a night in the full of the moon would sometimes be set apart when, with dogs and guns, families from far and near, especially the men folks, would gather at some appointed farm where coons were known to be abundant, and engage in an old fashioned "coon hunt."

While the men were on the chase, the women would prepare supper and entertainment for all upon their return.

A coon, when started by the dogs, would run for the nearest tree and climb to the top while its maddened pursuers surrounded the base. By the marked change in the baying of the dogs from that of mere pursuit to a wild clamorous battle cry, the men with their guns at some distance behind always knew that the coon was treed. And there in the moonlight, the poor hunted, cornered creature would meet his inevitable fate.

Sometimes a weak link would develop in the chain of a trap to remain undiscovered and cause a mishap.

One night at the beginning of the grape season, a coon, caught in one of our steel traps, parted the chain and escaped with the trap on his foot.

Later on in the season, one bright moonlit night when the two boys were sleeping down at vineyard point, the dogs, dozing alongside the cot with one eye open and ears alert, suddenly scented a coon, and with loud yelps were off in hot pursuit.

The boys, thus rudely awakened, scrambled out of bed, secured their gun and followed the dogs across the plowed ground of the orchard toward the almond trees at the end of the eucalyptus row, where a "coon path" led up over the brushy point to the bench. Clambering up this trail in bare feet and shirt-tails after the dogs and fleeing coon, they heard faintly through the din, a peculiar rattling sound like the dragging of a chain over the trail ahead, and immediately thought of their lost trap. Though scratched and torn by the bushes, with quickened ardor they pressed the chase until the coon finally took refuge in a tree-size sumac shrub, where the dogs held him at bay till their arrival on the scene. And there they shot him by the light of the moon.

But there was no trap on his foot. It had been lost somewhere along the trail. Examination showed all the toes missing from one foot and the wound perfectly healed.

The following morning, anxious to recover their trap, they retraced their steps up the coon trail over the point, and sure enough found the trap. Fast in its jaws, all shriveled and dried, were the missing toes of the coon.

I am sure you are wondering what eventually became of the little fox George had caught and tamed the first season. This unfolds another coon episode.

The year following, the boys as usual slept in the vineyard on their "double" canvas cot—far from comfortable, for both sides rolled toward the middle—till the season neared its close. One night they were caught in an early rain. Though they covered up their heads, the rain, increasing to a downpour, soaked everything through and through, clothes, quilts, and even the canvas of the cot itself. The next day they took their bed home, and there had a sorry time trying to dry out their sodden quilts, while old Sol refused to show his face.

To insure crop protection for the remainder of the season, they staked out the dogs by themselves in the vineyard, hoping to frighten away the night marauders. But there were not enough dogs to guard all the main points of entry, so Father told the boys to take the tame fox down there and stake her out too along with the dogs. So they took her down on her eight-foot chain and staked her out near one of the paths. The stake when driven in, stood about four inches above the level of the ground. The next morning when they went down into the vineyard, they found the poor little pet fox dead. The chain was wound round and round the stake tight up to her neck, and the ground, for a large area all about was so padded with coon tracks as to leave not a square inch uncovered.

Upon her body they could discover no outward evidence of violence, not a bone broken, nor a joint out of place, nor an abrasion anywhere. Her death assumed the aspect of a mystery. She was so used to being on a chain it seemed hardly possible that she could have suffocated herself by winding it up so in her effort to get at the coons. Yet there she lay dead, the little fox playmate, to be mourned by all the family.

Before burying her carcass the boys took off the pelt. Had they not done so they never would have discovered the true cause of her death. They found the flesh underneath the skin black and blue all over her body and pounded to jelly. The coons had simply beaten her to death with their powerful fists.

The Catcher Caught

One morning Lafie found a young coon in his trap. Desiring to let Prinnie—a nickname for prince, our little black and tan spaniel—do battle with the coon for the experience it would give him in animal offense and defense, took him down there and set him onto the coon, who, with the encumbrance of a limiting chain and a trap dangling from one of his feet, fought at a painful disadvantage.

After a long and desperate fight, the dog finally won out. The coon, lying on the ground apparently dead, would still, once in a while open its mouth and gasp. The dog, sitting on the ground panting in front of the dying coon, was resting from the long wearisome struggle in seeming enjoyment of his victory. Every time the coon opened his mouth to gasp for breath, the watching dog grabbed him by the neck and shook him again.

Lafie pulled up the stake, and squatted down on his heels in front of dog and coon, almost ready to open the jaws of the trap and free the foot of the victim, his hands hanging idly between his knees. Some noise behind him attracting his attention, he turned his head to look. Just at that instant, the coon gave its last gasp for breath and the dog seized and shook it vigorously in front of Lafie.

When the jaws of the coon came together after that last gasp, they had between them one of Lafie's fingers in a final death grip. The boy sprang to his feet with a yell of pain, both coon and trap hanging to his finger, and swung the whole outfit around his head three or four times, whirling like a dervish in a futile effort to free himself from the death-tightened jaws.

There was no one to help him but Prinnie. After his first shock of astonishment, the dog attempted to attack the flying coon, whose strange and unaccountable behavior betokened a sudden coming to new and vicious life. A further surprise was the harsh reprimand for his willing assistance.

But those jaws were set, and not to be shaken off by dog or boy. Lafie was obliged to bear his painful burden till, with his free hand, he could pry them open sufficiently to release his lacerated forefinger, whose nail the teeth had penetrated. Thus did the coon, in death avenge his wrongs.

Uncured Walnuts

A few years after the first vintage, the walnut trees also began to bear, the first crop being very small. The peanuts Father had planted between the rows were ready to harvest at the same time and the grapes too were just beginning to ripen, guarded as usual by the boys, sleeping on their cot in the vineyard.

They had greatly enjoyed gathering and hulling this first crop of walnuts, and when finished, father spread the new nuts out on the floor of the honey house to dry and cure. Knowing something about uncured nuts that the family had not yet learned, he locked the door.

The boys, hungry for more of the delicious creamy new nut-meats tasted during harvest, stole out to the honey house to help themselves. Finding locked doors, they felt considerably "miffed" at the unfairness of being denied what they wanted to eat after themselves harvesting the crop, and decided somehow to have them anyway.

Hanging on a nail just inside the back kitchen door was a homemade wire key, fashioned as a makeshift after the disappearance of the original. Starting to bed that evening, they paused long enough to sneak this key, hoping it might unlock the door of the honey house. To their exultant satisfaction, it worked, and filling their pockets with nuts, they were soon sitting on their cot in its wide-open vineyard bedroom, enjoying the feast. They cracked and ate all the walnuts brought with them, digging holes and burying the telltale shells.

Having been harvesting peanuts that day, they had, while working, eaten their fill of these also, and now for dessert, went out by moonlight and hunted among the vines for a few bunches of half-ripe grapes to fill the remainder of their gastric cavities; after which, they lay down to enjoy a good night' s sleep.

About midnight, they were simultaneously awakened by the most terrible griping pains in their insides. Breaking out with cold sweat in their intense suffering, they writhed and groaned and rolled in agony for several hours. At last Nature, recognizing the propensity of boys to gormandize, sent nausea to their aid, and all those delicious uncured walnuts, the fresh, coarsely-masticated peanuts, the sour grapes and the regular supper besides, mercifully decided to take a trip out into the wide world—a life-saver for two sadder and wiser boys.

The First Smoke and the Last

Mr. Wood was an inveterate smoker, and used the customary pipe. He was "great on spinning yarns," having as do all, his own peculiar mannerisms. While smoking and talking, he would suddenly stop both, and taking the pipe out of his mouth, hold it caressingly while running a finger around in the bowl, then put it back, take a few puffs, and resume his yarn-spinning.

His stories, though always addressed to adult audiences, were full of appeal to boys, who would hang around on the outer edge of the circle and drink them in avidly. There were wonderful tales of gold prospecting, grizzly bears, Indians and train robbers. The Jesse James gang, then terrorizing the country, with a special penchant for robbing the rich railroads—considered by the poor a common enemy—were glorified, and their lawless raids given the semblance of daring heroism in the eyes of their youthful listeners.

In spell-bound silence, Lafie would sit listening to the thrilling entertainment, lost in admiration of the entertainer. Whenever Wood stopped to finger his pipe, Lafie fidgeted about impatient at the interruption to the fascinating story, yet admiring his deliberate composure. To him Wood was a hero.

"If only I could be a man like Mr. Wood," he thought longingly. To have a pipe dangling out of his mouth, to tell wonderful yarns with such dramatic pauses, to hold in rapt attention such admiring audiences, would, he thought, be the acme of social ambition. A close successor of admiration is imitation.

One day Lafie said to Joseph:

"Let's make us some pipes"

Joseph thought this a brilliant idea. So, suiting action to the word, they hunted up and cut down the pithy stalk of an elder tree about the diameter of a pipe bowl. From two-inch lengths of this, they dug out the pith, all but enough to form a bottom to each bowl, above which, with a penknife they cut a hole for the stem, made of hollow joint grass. And the two pipes were ready for use.

But what should they use for tobacco? Experimenting with this and that, they finally hit upon the dried leaves of the grapevine. These worked like a charm. When rolled in the palm they crumbled and stuck together like pipe tobacco, and sent up a wreath of smoke without blaze like the genuine article. So they filled their pouches with this and "drew" and "puffed" like real heroes.

But after awhile this fun grew tame. There was no real flavor to this smoke, no tang, no aroma. It was just plain smoke. Then they remembered that, growing wild about the premises, were real tobacco trees, and set out to find some. This was the Indian tobacco and very strong—really the lobelia plant. They found plenty, but the green leaves had to be dried before using, and this must be accomplished without arousing any suspicion—for tobacco was taboo.

Climbing a ladder to the loft of the honey house, they found there an old scrapbook, and between its leaves, spread out quantities of those other leaves under a weight to dry and press. This process required time but eventually their tobacco became dry and brittle.

With much anticipation of the secret delights to be enjoyed, they brought down the innocent-looking old scrapbook and removed its guilty burden, crushing their new and real tobacco between their palms till fine enough for proper smoking.

The elder tree pipes by this time were no novelty, neither were they in the best of repair. As they looked at that big pile of lovely tobacco, it occurred to them that they might make it into cigarettes, surely a fine idea. So, concealing their treasure, they went in search of "cigarette paper." The heavy, rough, dark brown wrapping paper of those days was the only kind to be had, and returning to their rendezvous, they cut it with their dull knives into proper pieces and began to roll their cigarettes. But another problem was presented. They wouldn't stay rolled. The boys had not thought of that. They must have some mucilage. Wherever borers entered the trunks of apricot trees, there would exude from the wound a soft transparent gum in globulous bunches which, when dissolved in vinegar, made excellent mucilage. Mother made all we ever had to use in this manner. So out they hied to the apricot trees in the apiary and collected as much as needed. Purloining a little vinegar from the cellar, they soon had their mucilage mixed in a small tin can and their cigarettes took on a professional appearance. There were enough of the little "coffin nails" to fill a quart cup, and carefully they laid them back between the leaves of the old scrapbook to dry.

Reserving two of those first made, now nearly dry, after depositing the bulging scrapbook up on the loft, they stole out behind the honey house for a real treat—their first genuine smoke, and lighting their cigarettes, began to puff away as do grown-up heroes.

It was great fun—for a few puffs. They sat opposite each other, one leaning against the wall of the building, the other against the crossed legs of the sun extractor, watching each the face of the other. Silence prevailed, each busy with his own thoughts. Their first impression was mutual, that tobacco was much stronger than they had supposed. There was plenty of "flavor" to this smoke, but what a flavor!

Neither of the boys being able to observe the change of expression on his own face, each observed it on the face of the other. Lafie saw Joseph turn pale around the corners of his mouth. Joseph saw Lafie do the same. Lafie saw Joseph's paleness spread to the parts around his nose. Joseph saw Lafie's do the same. Lafie saw Joseph's eyes grow dull and the parts about grow white. Joseph saw Lafie's do likewise.

Lafie began to feel queer in the pit of his stomach. Joseph felt the same way. Lafie took the cigarette out of his mouth, and Joseph did the same. Beside them was the little five-pound lard pail they had crumbled their tobacco in. Lafie picked it up and handed it to his younger brother, saying:

"Joseph, go and get a bucket of water so we can have a drink."

Joseph went. On his return, they each took a long draught, then another turn at the cigarettes. But the greatly diminished zest was growing less with every breath. Something seemed to have gone vitally wrong in their insides, and they left off smoking. But mere cessation was no cure for what ailed them.

Turning their backs on each other, the deathly-sick boys sought the gully nearby as the most convenient receptacle for their internal contents. And that was the end of their smoking career.

About six months later, Father, rummaging about up on the loft, came across the old book bulging with its forgotten contents, and took the boys to task. Somehow those beautiful cigarettes reposing between the leaves, held for them no interest. They told Father:

"We don't want them anymore."

With inward amusement, reading the old book's secret between the lines, Father gathered up the well-measured doses to use for horse medicine.

Prickly Pear Pies

On Vineyard Point were several large patches of thrifty cactus, their attractive bright red, briary fruit, challenging the passerby to brave the spiny fortifications and help themselves.

One day Sadie and Mesia took a notion to have prickly pear pies for dinner, and Lafie, then eleven or twelve, was sent over to the point to gather the fruit. It was no child's play to secure these cactus pears that bristled all over with fine needle-sharp briars, themselves attached to large fleshy leaves loaded with stout spines. But Lafie understood how to do this without getting severely pierced and carrying away briars in every finger. So, sharpening a long stick with which to pierce the fruit and hold it steady while cutting it off, he started out with this, and a knife and the little brass bucket that held four or five quarts.

One after another he lifted impaled pears on the stick and transferred them to his bucket till it was brimming over. Those older were to clean the fruit. The girls would not trust anyone but themselves with this part of the work, for it would not do for even one briar to find its way into the pie. Each pear, held at first with tongs, was rubbed in sand or grass to remove the worst of the briars, then taken with the fingers in a firmer hold and thoroughly scoured till the last briar from the fringe about the end was gone. After this they were singed over a flame to remove the least suspicion of a briar, and washed in several changes of water before peeling to take out the delicious juicy, seedy pulp for the pie filling.

Lafie brought to the house his brimming bucket of bristling fruit, and Sadie, receiving it from him, dumped it into the big dishpan and handed back the bucket empty—save for a layer of loose briars in the bottom, bidding him "clean out the bucket." Some of these were so fine as to be almost invisible, having been shaken off the fruit in transit.

He received the bucket, carrying it away some distance from the house, and thinking:

"They will be easy to blow out," lifted the bucket to his face.

Drawing in a deep breath, he blew a strong blast into it. The loose, dry, needle-fine briars came out in a jiffy. But where did they go? Where, where but into Lafie's poor eyes, as many as could stick in, filling them full.

Prickly pear pies were forgotten in the horror of the emergency. Lafie, in his agony, was taken in hand. The visible briars removed from his face then began the long, excruciatingly painful task of extracting the briars, one at a time from inside his eyes. Already they were sticking into his eyeballs, and crowded all around underneath the lids. A more painful experience it would be difficult to imagine. With tweezers and a silk handkerchief, Father, Mother, and the girls in turn worked over Lafie's eyes—not for one day, nor for two days, nor for three days, but for a whole week before the last briar was removed from those inflamed and bloodshot eyes, bringing the first relief to the suffering boy.

Experience is indeed an expensive teacher—but a thorough one.

CHAPTER 17 LAND GRABBING

Most of the land in Southern California was included in one or another of the large Spanish and Mexican grants that cursed the country in those days as a heritage from Mexico.

Since Father found himself wedged in between two of these grants, and thereby involved in controversy, a brief historical summary of their origin and the causes leading up to this experience, might be of interest.

Spain had acquired the first title to California by the threefold right of discovery, conquest and occupation. Soon after the voyage of Columbus to America in Fourteen Ninety-Two, Spanish colonists began to settle on the islands in the Gulf of Mexico, where, hearing fabulous tales of a great wealthy empire on the western mainland, they organized an expedition for its conquest in Fifteen Nineteen under Hernan Cortez.

The Aztecs, under their war-chief Montezuma, headed a confederacy of three Indian tribes, numbering twenty or thirty thousand, occupying the pueblo of Mexico among the lakes of the Valley of Mexico, with other hostile tribes in the surrounding districts. After receiving the Spanish invaders in peace, they were treacherously betrayed by their guests, who with the aid of unfriendly Indians, within two years had overpowered and destroyed them, taking possession of their city.

The conquest of Peru under Francisco Pizarro—also effected by treachery—soon followed, and by Fifteen Thirty-Six, Spanish colonization had begun along the Pacific slopes of the Andes, on up through the coasts of Central America, and on the islands of the West Indies.

Spain's first contact with the natives of California was in Fifteen Forty Two when Juan Rodriguez Cabrillo, a Portuguese under the flag of Spain, sailed from Mexico up the California coast and entered the port which he named San Diego. Here he encountered the local indigenous people living in their villages. Continuing northward along the coast, he visited other villages at places now known to us as San Juan Capistrano, San Gabriel, and Santa Catalina. Here were natives similar in appearance but speaking diverse languages.

Sixty-one years later, in Sixteen Three, Admiral Sebastián Vizcaíno, cruising up the coast of California on a voyage of exploration, discovered and named the Bay of Monterey.

After her first contact with the natives, these new-world possessions lay dormant under the hand of Spain for more than two and a quarter centuries, during which time the Atlantic states had become well colonized.

It was only six years before the war for American independence broke out at Lexington that King Carlos III of Spain, fearing encroachments upon California by England and Russia, began in Seventeen Sixty-Nine a serious effort to explore, colonize and Christianize California; sending out expeditions by land and sea.

The famous land expedition in the midsummer of that year led by Don Gaspar de Portolá who, after landing at the port of San Diego, set out to blaze a trail to Monterey where a settlement was to be established, included in the party the devout priest, Fray Junipero Serra, empowered by Spain to establish a chain of missions throughout the length and breadth of Upper California. The first of these was founded at San Diego on July sixteen, Seventeen Sixty-Nine. Not at first recognizing Monterey, Portolá passed it and pressed on northward and discovered by accident the inner bay of San Francisco, until then overlooked by maritime explorers.

With Portolá, also in the service of the Crown, was Don Jose Antonio Yorba, a young corporal not yet twenty from the Spanish province of Catalonia. This young man was destined to become an important character in the early life of the country, and owner of many broad acres over which he passed on that momentous expedition. He it was who founded the house of Yorba in Southern California.

Later, followed the expedition of Don Juan Bautista de Anza, the intrepid and successful leader of a company of colonists from Sonora, Mexico, across the desert and over the Colorado River into Southern California and Arizona. From Fort Tubac, which he founded in Arizona, his government called him in Seventeen Seventy-Six to lead another company far to the north and establish a mission and military post at San Francisco.

Accompanying Anza from Sonora and on to San Francisco, was Don Juan Pablo Grijalva, another distinguished soldier and explorer whose wife and two lovely daughters became pioneer women of California. One of these became the wife of Don Gabriel Peralta, a soldier of the same company, and the other of Don Antonio Yorba, stationed for a time at the Presidio of San Francisco. The families of these two young men with their multiplied descendants played a major part in the colorful life of Southern California in the 'days of the Dons.'

Portolá might be justly considered the first military governor of California. He was succeeded by Barri the following year, and by Felipe de Neve in Seventy-Four. As an inducement to colonists to settle up the country and bring it under cultivation, Governor Neve was ordered by the King of Spain to issue free grants of land to those who would devote themselves to agriculture and stock-raising; the beneficiaries to be Indians, worthy Spaniards, and Spaniards who had married baptized Indian girls. In Seventeen Seventy-Five Manuel Butron, a Spanish soldier who was married to an Indian convert of the San Carlos Mission, Margarita Maria, received the first and smallest grant of land, consisting of but one hundred and ten square feet.

When Pedro Fages became governor in Seventeen Eighty-Two he began to issue very large grants, ranging from fifteen thousand three hundred sixty to three hundred thousand acres. Land then, however, was not measured by miles and acres but by leagues and square leagues—a league being a fraction over two and six-tenths miles, and a square league about four thousand four hundred twenty-six and eight-tenths acres.

The measuring of these immense tracts of land was done by two men on horseback. A rope, or riata of braided rawhide fifty varas (a vara equals 33 1/3 inches and fifty varas 137 1/2 feet) in length, to each end of which was attached a sharp-pointed stake long enough to be set in the ground while held in the hand of a man on horseback, was used by two riders, each carrying one of the stakes, alternately riding in advance of the other the length of the rope and setting his stake, where he would wait for the other to ride ahead for another length of the riata and set the other stake before again carrying forward his own.

Often the rope would be trailed through wet grass, marshes or water thereby causing it to stretch and become longer than its original measurement. This difference would amount to hundreds of acres in large grants; but who was there to care about this? Land was so plentiful, there was so much more of it than was needed that a few hundred acres more or less meant nothing either to the grantee or to the government (acreages used in this chapter are only approximate, having been based on accurate leagues; figures of available authorities differ).

During the thirty-year period from the issuance of the first grant to the rebellion of Mexico in Eighteen Ten, Spain had issued thirteen of these grants in Southern California. Then followed the troublous ten-year period in which Spanish California took sides with Spain against the Mexican rebels yet lost their cause in the Mexican victory of Eighteen Twenty-One.

Mexico began immediately to follow the Spanish precedent of granting free lands, inaugurating an era of reckless land-dispensing that completely overshadowed that of Spain. Within the first ten years of Mexican independence fifty such grants had been made. A check, however, was placed upon the size of grants; eleven square leagues, or almost forty-eight thousand six hundred ninety-five acres being the maximum that could be granted to one individual.

But Mexico's territorial possession of Alta California was destined to be very brief, lasting only about twenty-five years; when she lost it to her more powerful and enterprising neighbor to the north—whose rule most of the Californians preferred, and many of them helped to gain.

When the treaty with Mexico was concluded February two, Eighteen Forty-Eight, the United States gave assurance that all land titles granted prior to the opening of hostilities on July seven, Eighteen Forty-Six would be respected. On the strength of this promise, many fictitious and antedated documents were hurriedly executed by the conniving of Mexican officials, granting immense tracts of land to their personal and political friends, in the hope that the new government would fail to discover the deception. It is said that Don Pio Pico, the last governor of California under Mexico, spent the entire night immediately preceding his flight from Los Angeles in August of Forty-Eight, in signing these illegal grants supposed, according to dates, to have been issued two years or more previously.

Thus it was that when California was admitted into the Union in Eighteen Fifty, instead of the original and genuine grants that were covered by the treaty promise, there had sprung up an innumerable crop of grants that covered practically all of the best land in California. The question of their recognition became one of the major problems of the government by which it was harassed for twenty-five years or more. Of the eight hundred and thirteen cases carried through the courts, only four hundred eighty-four were confirmed, involving nearly nine million acres of land. Three hundred and twenty-eight claims including those that had been withdrawn from the courts were rejected, so that the total number of grants finally recognized were six hundred and four.

Before American occupation, land in California had but little value. The Californians had been allowed to take possession of as much of it as they desired without being required to give strict account to the government. There were no official surveys and very little attention was given to legal descriptions. Landmarks were vague and uncertain; such objects as rocks, hills, trees, swamps, and neighboring ranchos, whose lines were equally uncertain, being used in describing boundaries. Often there were strips, spaces and corners left between adjoining grants that were actually unclaimed by anyone.

The people were simple-minded and easy-going, allowing their herds to mingle indiscriminately on the plains, to be separated and branded at their general and periodical rodeos, spending their money without reference to the future, borrowing from one another without legal formality and repaying at leisure in cattle or land, but seldom pushed for payment by their creditors, who, like themselves, adhered to a "gentleman's code."

These conditions prevailing at the time the United States took over the country, became a temptation to unprincipled Americans, with whose astuteness and subtleness the simple and trusting Californians were unable to cope; and the Americans soon began to get possession of their lands.

The American traded to his own advantage upon the fundamental difference of outlook between the two nationalities. He learned that Californians seldom paid back borrowed money in legal tender—due not to any inherent dishonesty, but because they knew not how to save and accumulate money—how to economize and budget their resources in order to cover debts. To them, money was made only to spend—never to hoard—and it was so much easier to give an insignificant piece of paper. Land was so plentiful a few acres more or less made no difference, and the reckoning day was so distant—why worry about it?

Therefore, if an American loaned money to a Californian—and some of them made a business of doing just that—he was almost sure of having eventually to take the land held as security, to settle the mortgage. When an American coveted certain lands owned by a Californian, all he had to do was place a loan upon it—always a small percent of its real value, let the interest accumulate—which was the custom in those days till the principal was due—then take over the land. Sometimes a financial lord would even offer to loan money on land—the unsuspecting and grateful Californian, always ready to borrow, eagerly seizing the bait.

When the time of payment would draw near, the owner not being prepared to meet his obligation, it sometimes occurred that a third party would step in and offer to take up the mortgage, hoping thereby eventually to secure the land for himself; or, it might be a gentleman with no desire but to help his friend. Then the mortgagee would kindly accommodate his debtor by allowing the note to run on for a longer period. He might even offer to loan him an additional sum, being the surer by this means of accomplishing his purpose.

There was then in California no fixed rate of legal interest. A lender could exact as much usury as he chose to ask, which might be from twelve to eighteen percent, and often even twenty percent. In some cases this exorbitant rate was to be compounded monthly instead of annually, which amounted to nothing less than actual robbery. Since the interest was commonly not paid till the principal became due, the whole sum would then amount to many thousands of dollars more than the original loan; making liquidation still more improbable.

Many an American in this manner acquired large holdings and became a rich cattle and sheep man. Others, even more unscrupulous, would hatch up some scheme by which an unlanded Mexican would be hired to lay claim to certain lands as a grant, and papers would be antedated and forged to show such ownership. By the help of former Mexican officials whose loss of office had engendered no particular bonds of allegiance to the new regime, and of corrupt American officials who were not above accepting bribes, such forged or deceptive papers would sometimes escape detection and become legalized, the instigator "purchasing" the land from the Mexican for a small sum, thereby securing legal title to lands taken wholly by fraud.

There were at first no United States surveys of lands in California, and many years were consumed in the process of accomplishing the survey of holdings both public and private. But until such time as a claim should be officially surveyed, no legal title could be secured from the United States; and all claimants, either by grant or purchase, were required to prove their ownership. In addition to all unclaimed lands, those reverting to the government from grants and claims proved to be fictitious, were thrown open to the public for settlement. As an inducement to the railroads to extend their lines into the frontier regions of California, they were given outright every other section to do with as they pleased—use it, hold it or sell it, and often settlers would purchase railroad land after the survey, at a low figure.

The only right to unsurveyed public lands a "squatter" could acquire was that of "possession." So long as he "stuck" no one could dispute his right of occupancy; but should he for any reason leave the premises, he must return within six months to hold his right. Abandonment of his claim for a longer period, if such could be proved at the time of settlement, or especially if someone else had meanwhile squatted upon it, forfeited all his acquired right with all permanent improvements.

The actual occupant at the time of survey was always given the first right to acquire the land on which he had settled, but the time he had lived upon it previous to the survey counted for nothing. He was obliged to fulfill the required time beginning from the date of his filing upon the land after it had been surveyed. It was therefore to the interest of possessors, whether squatters, purchasers or original grantees, to secure survey of their lands as early as possible.

A government claim could be taken up in any one of three ways: as a homestead, a simple preemption, or as a timber claim. If a homestead, the claimant must improve the land and live upon it for five consecutive years after filing before he could "prove up" and receive a title from the government. The filing fee was sixteen dollars and there was another fee of sixteen dollars at the time of proving up; making a total of thirty-two dollars; but there was no purchase price to be met, for the land was a gift from the government. All a squatter had to do was prove by two witnesses that he had fulfilled the law's requirement by improving and living upon the land continuously for the five-year period since filing, pay the required fee, and the title was issued to him. Continuous residence was interpreted to mean that the claimant had made it his only home and had been actually present on the premises— passing his nights there—for at least half of each month; some leeway being allowed him to engage in remunerative employment elsewhere.

The preemption method also required that certain specified improvements be made, but exacted only a six-months' residence on the land after filing, when it could be purchased from the government for the low price fixed; which was a dollar and a quarter to two dollars and a half an acre, depending upon its distance from a railroad. Hence, this method was most commonly used. Timber claims required that the claimant plant and raise on the land a certain number of trees to the acre, but did not require residence. Until such time as title to government land should be secured, there were no taxes to pay, and even after proving up taxes were very low.

The largest tract of land permitted to be taken up by any individual was a quarter-section consisting of one hundred and sixty acres. The object of limiting the acreage thus obtainable being to give opportunity for a greater number of home seekers to settle in the country. But dishonest and greedy men used this beneficent law to enlarge still further their immense holdings, by hiring other men to preempt for them—though this practice was specifically stated in the law to be illegal and punishable by fines and forfeitures.

Sheep-men would sometimes have their own hired herders—usually ignorant foreigners—to file on land, each putting up a cheap "dinky" cabin in which to live for six months, then proving up on the land—the employer furnishing the money and the two witnesses necessary. When the papers were all made out and signed, a farce purchase also would be shown and the title be found in the name of the grasping, scheming employer. He would then wait for a reasonable time to allay suspicion before recording the instrument. The hireling received as a bonus for such services a few dollars extra in addition to his regular wages, his job with its regular monthly income being worth more in his estimation than the land. In this way, land was misappropriated by thousands of acres from the use intended by the government.

The surveying of large holdings offered still further opportunity for fraudulent practices. An original grant would call for a certain number of square leagues, but should there be discovered adjoining it a strip or corner of government land that had somehow escaped inclusion in any grant, the covetous landholder would contrive if possible to have this included in his own possessions, and use illegal means to prove his ownership. The mere changing of a fence might offer a basis for such claim of occupancy, and, reinforced by a few dollars on the side to the surveyor, might even suffice to accomplish this end.

There was also a difference in the desirability of land. There were valley lands and mountain lands, watered lands and dry lands. But such schemers were not willing to take land as it came, good and bad alike, though legal descriptions as revised by the United States required definiteness of acreage—they wanted the best—the level watered land.

If they could get possession of all the level valley land with all the streams and springs, they knew that the mountains would be left unclaimed by anyone, and that they still could have undisputed use of them for grazing purposes without the necessity of legal ownership. So they schemed and maneuvered and bribed to get their lines so drawn as to take in as much as possible of the level watered pasturelands and leave out the mountainous portions. This made their boundary lines deviate and wind tortuously in and out between mountains to avoid including these in their holdings; which was of course all contrary to law.

By the time Father came into the country, some of the old original grants were being cut up into parcels and sold, which was the best thing that could have happened for the development of Southern California. One of these was the Rancho Santiago de Santa Ana containing eleven square leagues—almost forty-eight thousand six hundred ninety-five acres—granted in Eighteen Ten by Governor Jose Joaquin Arrillaga to Don Antonio Yorba, then a retired sergeant sixty-one years of age, as a reward for long and distinguished service to Spain. His equally honored father-in-law, Don Juan Pablo Grijalva at the time a retired ensign of the cavalry, with his large herds of cattle and horses prior to this had occupied the land jointly with Don Antonio, and himself had petitioned the governor for the grant—his death occurring before consummation of the transaction—drawing a most interesting map of the rancho which is preserved in the archives of the county to the present day.

This large tract of land was none other than our own fertile Santa Ana Valley, named by the soldiers of Portolá after the saint whose mass they had that day celebrated, in which now are located the thriving towns and cities of Santa Ana, Orange, Tustin, McPherson, El Modena, Paulerino, and perhaps others.

To the southwest of this rancho lay the broad acres of the San Joaquin, allotted in two grants of Eighteen Thirty-Seven and Forty-Two to Don Jose Andres Sepulveda, consisting originally of eleven square leagues but later added to by purchase of one thousand eight hundred acres from Jesus Dominguez, a Yorba heir, and after its transfer from Sepulveda to Flint, Bixby and Irvine, further enlarged by the acquisition in Eighteen Sixty-Eight of Rancho Lomas de Santiago to the east from assigns of other Yorba heirs; which brought the total acreage to approximately ninety-seven thousand seven hundred seventy-two acres, stretching from the mountains to the sea.

To the southeast of the San Joaquin lay Cañada de los Alisos toward the eastern mountains, and El Niguel (correctly pronounced Neg-well, the sounding of the g being almost imperceptible) west of it toward the coast and Laguna. Cañada de los Alisos, consisting of two square leagues, (about eight thousand eight hundred fifty four acres, more or less) was granted to Jose Serano in two parcels, the first by Governor Alvarado in Forty-Two and the second by Governor Pio Pico in Forty-Six. It included the upper portion of Aliso Canyon, beginning about ten miles above our own farm, with El Niguel between.

An Englishman by the name of Dwight Whiting purchased this rancho of the Serano heirs, and when the railroad went through that part of the country in Eighty-Eight, started an English settlement a mile or so above the old stage road and called the place El Toro, a name that has been associated with the location for many years.

El Niguel, consisting originally of three square leagues, (about thirteen thousand two hundred eighty-one acres) was granted in Eighteen Forty-Two by Governor Alvarado to Don Juan Ávila and his sister, Concepción Ávila Sanchéz. Of all the Ranchos now in Orange County, this is the only one that has retained its Indian name, the meaning of which is obscure.

Ávila married one of the daughters of Don Antonio Yorba, and established his rancheria, or rancho headquarters, on an elevation above the Aliso Creek where it is crossed by the old stage road southwest of El Toro. There his old adobes, opposite those of Serano, stood as landmarks for many years. There they lived with their flocks and herds and many descendants, prominent among the dons and doñas of those romantic days.

Afterward acquiring interests at San Juan Capistrano, Ávila sold this rancho to others. Domingo Yorba acquired a tenth interest and in common with other assigns, held it until they parted with it to the Americans. Members of this Yorba family were still living on a portion of the rancho when Father first came into the country. It was probably with the household of Domingo Yorba that he found shelter and hospitality for the night when driving with his family down to his own new claim at the mouth of Aliso Canyon. That very month, November of Seventy-One, Domingo Yorba and the Aguilars transferred their portion of El Niguel to the brothers Hiram A. and Cyrus B. Rawson.

The Rawson Ranch

Rawson negotiations with the various owners for the purchase of their several interests had been going on for a number of years previous to Father's appearance in the Canyon, and continued for years afterward. At that time there had been no complete United States government survey of the rancho.

Hiram Rawson, whose interests his brother eventually acquired, seems to have been a silent partner. Apparently his joint transactions were merely to furnish means for the operations of his brother, considered by everyone to be the owner.

A California ranch house had been built some distance from the old Ávila headquarters on a higher elevation north of the stream, from which could be enjoyed a beautiful view of the valley. Here lived Cyrus Rawson, an unmarried man, and the rancho, so long as he claimed an acre of it, was known far and wide as "The Rawson Ranch."

It is impossible to give an adequate description of the early hardships endured by our family without bringing into my story to some extent, the Rawson Ranch and its owner. Personal childhood memories supplement details supplied by those older, of incidents locally well-known at the time, and typical of existing rancher-settler relationships in those days of maladjustment. The accompanying pen-sketch of this rancho may serve to make more vivid and realistic the reasons for seeking boundary enlargements.

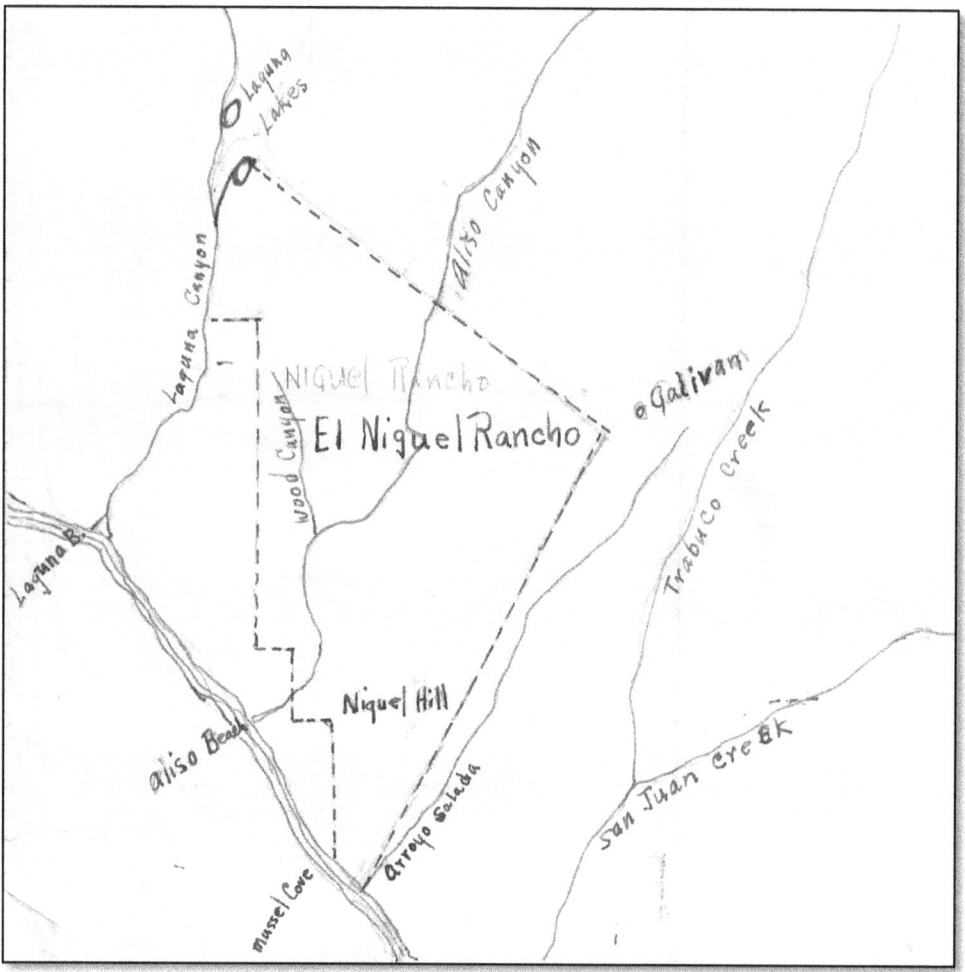

Figure 6 El Niguel Rancho

It is seen that El Niguel forms roughly the major half of a diamond which would have been a perfect half had the boundary line from north to south been cut straight instead of zigzag. Again, had the western boundary followed Laguna Canyon to its outlet at the sea and from there the coast-line to the diamond's southern point, an almost perfect whole diamond would have resulted, together with a magnificent ocean beach frontage, actually almost wholly denied the rancho which had a beach of only half a mile between Mussel Cove and Arroyo Salada (Spanish for Salt Creek).

In Laguna Canyon, about two thirds of its length up from the beach, repose, one on either side of the road, two rather large lakes from which the canyon takes its name—Laguna. Through the center of the lower lake passes the northern boundary line of El Niguel, meeting there the southeastern edge of the San Joaquin, whence the two ranchos border each other down the canyon for about two miles before diverging. The San Joaquin, continuing on down the canyon for several miles farther, then cutting across the low hills westward, meets the ocean beach at the promontory now known as Emerald Bay Point.

El Niguel, from the point of divergement, strikes off due east for about three fourths of a mile, then turning at right angles, runs due south for something like four and a half miles, then cuts east and south in a series of four short right angles till it meets the beach at Mussel Cove. The irregular boundary thus formed crosses Aliso Canyon at the upper border of our claim. Had this southward-running boundary line instead of angling progressed straight to the ocean, it would have included in El Niguel all of our Aliso farm, and have given the rancho nearly two and a half miles more of ocean beach frontage than it possessed—an advantage greatly to be desired. In this motivating situation lay the secret of the animus later disclosed.

The area left between the two ranchos not belonging to either, roughly triangular at first and extending down the coast in narrowed form like the half of an arrow head, at no point of greater width than three and a half miles and at Aliso half a mile, had doubtless been reserved by the former government for its own purposes when the original grant was made. However, from the standpoint of the grantee, for the sake of straightened lines, symmetrical proportions, and ocean frontage values, this strip of land—at least that east of Laguna Canyon—should logically have been included in the Niguel grant.

That this evident mis-apportioning was not lost upon its American purchaser is apparent from the ambition he is said to have voiced that he would eventually own every foot of the coastland from Laguna Canyon to Salt Creek. This of course included the Aliso tip on which we had settled. But the report came to Father's ears only after the truth of it had been verified by his own experience.

Though as yet the coastlands had not been settled, it was nevertheless a large boast since so many individuals held separate interests in the grant itself. In his extremity, to raise necessary funds to carry out his schemes, Rawson himself deeded and mortgaged portions of the rancho to his friends at various times, no doubt with the mutual understanding that he was to receive the land back again upon repayment of the loans. To accomplish this he would borrow from one to repay another back and forth in the risky, uncertain game of finance.

He had one friend, however, Jonathan E. Bacon, with Rawson and Eagan completing a trio of old bachelors, often seen together and wielding considerable local power in their day, who having personally purchased of Ávila assigns sixteen hundred acres islanded in the midst of the rancho, repeatedly and consistently refused to sell out to Rawson, thus becoming a thorn in the side of his friend. Tenaciously Bacon held on through the years to his possession, and only at his demise about the turn of the century was his interest in El Niguel relinquished. His heirs then parted with the land. But this was too late to benefit Cyrus Rawson.

Father's establishment in Aliso Canyon, to this ambitious ranchman must have been another annoying "fly in the ointment"—one that must somehow be dislodged. There was, however, nothing crude about his methods. He manifested toward Father a disarming neighborliness and friendly interest in his welfare from the first, generously allowing him free use of adjacent pasture lands for stock, and for family needs, of the spring on his property. Father considered himself most fortunate in having a neighbor so kind, pleasant and accommodating.

After a year or more of hard and bitter struggle for existence, he was approached one day by Mr. Rawson with an offer of a much better proposition than he had in his present location. The land he was farming, said Mr. Rawson, was so limited in extent, so stony, and in such scattered plots, and the water source so distant and inconvenient, that he was going to have an exceedingly difficult time where he was to make a living for his family.

Wouldn't he like to move farther up the canyon where there was an abundance of good level land that he himself was not utilizing? He could have the use of it as long as he wished without charge, retaining, as his own whatever improvements he should choose to make. Such a move, he believed, would be greatly to Father's advantage. He would be not only closer to the spring, but also to town and have better roads.

This offer on the face of it sounded very attractive, and had the appearance of disinterested generosity. Perhaps it sounded too generous. It may have been this interview that laid the first dim foundation in Father's breast for distrust of the man's motives. Though he could not yet perceive the "ax" to be ground, yet Father was nobody's fool. There must be something back of it.

Father had not come to California to farm another man's land, but government land that he could hope to own eventually for himself. And the kind offer was declined. If his would-be benefactor was inwardly perturbed, there was no outward evidence of it, and no change in manner or friendly attitude. And things went on as before between them.

Had Father fallen into the trap, it would have been a simple matter for Rawson to have slipped in another man, ostensibly as herder, to squat on the Aliso claim without betraying his own designs. In due time he could have had the land quietly surveyed and filed on by the squatter, from whom he could have "purchased" it as soon as he proved up. Thus for a few dollars he could have secured as he had always intended, his coveted outlet to the sea.

The land being unsurveyed, neither Father nor Rawson had any means of knowing the exact location of the boundary lines that separated between their two holdings. The brush fence Father had built diagonally across the canyon from point to point followed the supposed line according to the best information he could obtain from others. So our family had come to consider all the land in the canyon below that fence as belonging to us.

As soon as he was able to secure the necessary wire and materials for posts and gate, Father put up a more permanent fence in place of the brush fence, and built a swinging gate of horizontal boards and cross-braces to span the road. This gate at the upper end of our filaree pasture, being the second from the house, we called the "second gate"—a name which still clung to the location as a means of permanent designation long after both gate and fence had disappeared.

The only legal hold Father had on the Aliso place at that time was the right of the squatter to continue to squat until the survey of the land gave him the first right to file upon it. A survey of the claim then, would be a distinct advantage not only to the squatter, but also to anyone who might have designs upon it. If Father by any means could be induced or compelled to vacate even after filing on surveyed land the succeeding claimant could obtain legal title by preemption within the short space of six months after filing. Rawson's next move was to secure this survey.

The Survey

Sometime in Seventy-Four when the family had been there for almost three years, Mr. Rawson came down to see Father one day and asked him if he would like to have his land surveyed. There was nothing he desired more, but he told Mr. Rawson that he had no money to pay for such a survey. Mr. Rawson assured him that it would not cost him a cent. He was having his own land surveyed, he said, and since the government surveyor was already on the ground it would be but a small matter for him to set stakes on down the rest of the way to the beach. The additional expense would be but a trifle, and he was willing to stand for it.

Father assented with alacrity, and the survey was extended clear to the tide lands. Not until then was it revealed that our northernmost boundary line fell far short of the fence and its second gate. It took from us almost half of our filaree pasture and a goodly slice from the upper end of the barley ground, including both the rock wall and pepper row. The little hill also, together with a small portion of the creek bed off its point was found to be outside of our line. This took away the cart road, the only means of access to the garden patch beyond.

These losses were in a measure compensated for by changes in our favor southwesterly. It was found that our boundaries now took in a three-acre strip across the tip of the northern mesa and five acres on the tip of the southern mesa—land that we had not hitherto claimed. All told, the survey gave us something like twenty acres of level land in the canyon and eight acres on the two mesas; all separated into nine different plots entirely disconnected one from another. This included all of our available farming land. The other hundred and thirty-two acres of our quarter-section covered the surrounding mountains; most of it too steep even for grazing land.

These twenty-eight acres of tillable land improved with various fruit and nut orchards, and planted with grain and garden stuffs, together with what small hillside pastures were available for stock, our small bee business, dairy and poultry industries, cattle and hogs raised for sale, and Father's horse-training, constituted our financial resources— supplemented by occasional periods of labor for others at small wages by different members of the family, all of whom were drafted into service on the farm as soon as old enough to gather eggs or handle a hoe. With the best we could do, our large family never had more than a meager living.

While this surveying was in progress, two of the men so engaged were camped for a short time in the vicinity of our creek just below the house. One day as they were eating their lunch in the shade of the young willows, Joseph and Lafie, as is natural with small boys of six and seven, were hanging around at a distance hungrily watching them eat. Their lunch included crackers and cheese. Now crackers were something entirely new to the boys and cheese a rare treat, such luxuries being taboo on our meager table and a vast curiosity mingled with and whetted their appetites. One of the men in finishing, tossed over to them a soda cracker, which fell into the salt grass some feet away. Lafie, being the quicker of the two, dashed over and picked it up first, immediately beginning to eat it.

"Give me a taste," begged Joseph.

"No, I got it first," replied Lafie.

"Oh, just give me a nip," pleaded Joseph coaxingly.

"Well," said Lafie, relenting a little, "I'll just give you half a nip.

The men thought this quite amusing and reported the incident to Father. Thereafter "half a nip" became the family synonym for a very small portion.

After the survey, Father and George built for the cows on our own side of the new boundary line, a temporary brush corral in the midst of the filaree pasture crossing the canyon road. This necessitated two gates at entrance and exit. Each of these gates was built of three horizontal boards; and made to slide out of its socket and swing around parallel to the road when opened; having a peg to hold it there in a level position. When the corral was empty, both gates were left open. Starting up the canyon after the cows one day, George passed through these two open gates. Just then, a small flock of quails flew up and alighted on one of the gates in rows along the three boards, ten of them sitting on the upper one. George had the rifle with him as usual. He stepped to the side of the road till he was on a direct line with these rows of birds, and with his eye sighted along the topmost board. The quails on it all appeared to be just one bird on a level with his shoulder. He said within himself:

"What a pretty shot! If I hit the first one I've got them all."

Taking careful aim, he fired. Eight quails dropped off that board like a waterfall, shot through the heads and unmangled. The remaining two wounded slightly, fluttered away with the rest of the flock. Eight quails with one bullet was a shot to be remembered long after the delicious potpie they made had been forgotten.

The survey completed, Father lost no time in filing upon his land as a homestead, thus beginning in November of Seventy-Four the five-year period of occupancy that must precede the proving up. Later he learned that he could file on the lost little hill as a timber claim, by setting out timber on it. The Act of Seventy-Three had at first called for forty acres of timber to the quarter-section, but this had been reduced to ten and would amount to about two and a half acres of trees to the proposed claim, which consisted of forty acres on the hill and an eighth of an acre running down into the creek.

The Eucalyptus, a native of Australia, was a new tree in the country, having been first introduced to America some twenty years earlier. By widely advertising, the government was encouraging their use as a fast-growing tree suitable for windbreaks, fence posts, stove-wood and the like. Father sent to Washington for seeds and set out a bed to raise his own nursery stock. He filed the timber claim and set George to work grubbing off the brush to prepare the land for planting the young trees.

When large enough for transplanting, he covered the little hill with Eucalyptus trees, and having plenty left over, set out for a windbreak a dense row along the southern end of the walnut orchard. This row grew rapidly and thrived, forming in after years, a most beautiful border of luxuriant green trees visible both from the house and the ocean.

He planted a group of a dozen or so above the honey house near the rock wall and pepper row, which likewise flourished, adding to the landscape their shade and beauty. Two or three stuck in at the corner of George's Ground also thrived.

But those planted on the little hill were not a success, being too far from water, for the Eucalyptus is a tree requiring much water. Only a few stunted trees survived scattered about on the hillside where they still may be seen. The rest of them died out entirely, and Father did not succeed in holding his timber claim. So long as we lived there, however, we had undisturbed possession of the little hill, and we younger children never knew until long years afterward that it did not belong to us.

Father also planted a patch of Eucalyptus trees on the triangle between the pond and the southern mesa, where wild malvia had flourished higher than a horse's back. These trees made a fine start and grew very thriftily for a while, then slowly died out, only a scattered few persisting on for a number of years. Doubtless this was due to the periodical inundations of salty water from the mingling of pond and ocean during high winter tides. The malvia evidently liked salt, but not so the trees.

This survey revealed besides his own altered boundaries, something else of great importance that, had Father known it in time, would certainly have affected the whole course of our experience. It was then that he first learned the location of Rawson's western boundaries, and that neither that ranch nor the San Joaquin included the lower half of Laguna Canyon with its beach and the coast mesas, which were now shown to be government land and therefore open to settlement. The very land over which he had ridden horseback on that eventful morning four years before, and the very spot where he had stood when he sighted the old fisherman, he might have settled upon and had his choice of the best. There were other strips also, one between the two ranchos north of the Rawson ranch house, all level farming land, and one in the mountains above Wood Canyon.

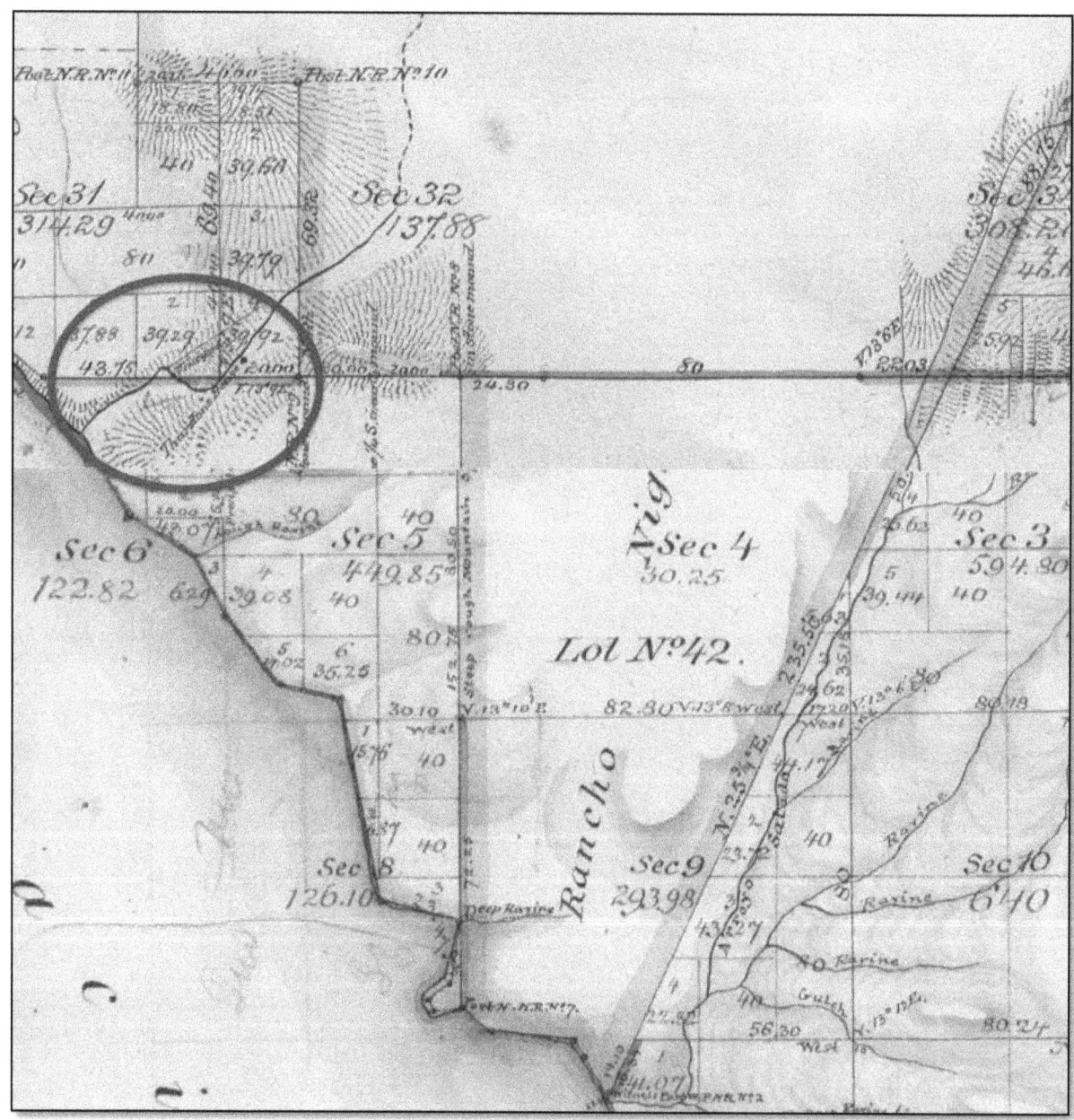

Figure 7 Extract of United States Survey Maps 1873-1875, Townships 7&8 S, Range 8 W [7]
Thurston homestead marked in the oval

Discussing these things with others, he learned from a man who had been working for the San Joaquin Rancho at the time Father had been camped near the slough a few miles out from Tustin, that the very strip on which he had been camped was at the time government land. He might have built a cabin there and secured it for a home, artesian well and all, had he but known. The man said he was witness to the illegal manipulations by which this strip of land a mile and a half wide, a short time after Father left the site, had been gobbled up and "surveyed" into the neighboring rancho. No doubt while there he had been feared as a potential settler, and swift measures taken to forestall a recurrence.

But when Father learned all this it was too late. He had used up his filing rights and invested all he had in Aliso Canyon.

A Lonesome Place

Our mother had the distinction of being the first white woman ever to live within a mile of the coast between Newport Beach and San Juan Capistrano, distant from each other about fifty-three miles by the circuitous inland roads then available.

Aliso Canyon was a lonesome place to live. There were no neighbors—unless a few men without families scattered here and there through the country, could be called neighbors. Father made contacts with the outside world on his various trading trips, often passing the night with some family by the way. But for Mother and the children, for years and years, life was almost wholly without social contacts.

At Mr. Rawson's ranch house ten miles above our place, for a few years lived his niece, Mrs. Robert Crowder, keeping house for her uncle. She was the first woman ever to visit Mother in Aliso Canyon. And no other woman came within the first six years of her life there.

Mrs. Crowder, with her husband, moved away some time in Seventy Four, taking up residence in the new town of Orange, where they opened up the first successful grocery store—a former venture by another having proved a failure. At that time the only other business in Orange was the "Hygiene Health Home," located on South Glassell. It had a solarium on the roof for the taking of sun baths.

Mrs. Crowder had conceived a great liking for Artemisia, and when they left, begged Mother and Father to let them take her to live with them for a while. So Mesia accompanied them to Orange and stayed in their home for nine months.

Orange was another town that had been located on a portion of the old Yorba estate broken up and sold in the middle Sixties. Its founders were two Los Angeles attorneys, A. B. Chapman and Andrew Glassell, whose names are perpetuated in the two principal intersecting streets.

When Mr. Crowder went there in Seventy-Four the "greenback question" was agitating the minds of voters everywhere, and culminated in the formation that year of the "Greenback Party," which loudly advocated the making of greenbacks the only form of national currency. Several years later, when this paper money of fluctuating value had risen from a par of forty cents in Civil War days, to eight-five cents on the dollar, Mr. Crowder astonished the townspeople and won their hearts by putting up a big sign on his store that read: "Greenbacks Taken At Par."

Far up in Laguna Canyon lived the Fountains, who somehow never got in touch with the family in Aliso. He it was who had put up the rock wall across the canyon, and he claimed all the land below it. Above him and within the wall, lived Mr. Simons, the bachelor, who disputed this claim, which could not be sustained.

With the Fountains, lived the fisherman, Old Joe Lucas, a native of the Azores, born in Fayal, who had been a whaler. After Mr. Fountain's death in the eighties, Old Joe moved down into the empty shack that had been occupied by the Chilian, Serray, (Pronounced Sher-ráy) near the mouth of the canyon, then belonging to Mr. Rogers, where he lived during the remainder of his life. Old Joe was a picturesque character always in evidence, greeting the stages at their arrivals and departures, known and humored by everyone, and living principally upon the bounties of others. In his later years he might be seen every day, a familiar figure going up and down the beach armed with his pail and trident—a relic of whaling days—very busy at his work, but catching little if anything.

Serray had built the old shack at the mouth of the canyon, and lived with his wife and numerous progeny for years. He was always spoken of as "the Che-la-ne-an." Being an unnaturalized foreigner, he was not legally entitled to squatter's rights. So in after years he was driven off the place, and the land taken by Mr. Sterling, who sold it to Rogers. Serray then put up another shack in the draw-back of Coward's Cove, where he lived for many years, eking out a living for his family by fishing.

Along about Seventy-Four, two stockmen came into Laguna Canyon, H. S. Pankey and his brother-in-law John Damron, neither of whom became permanent residents there. They had quite a large number of cattle and horses that were allowed to range at will through the unfenced country, often to the detriment of farmers. The family in Aliso often suffered from their depredations.

John Damron was often to be seen riding about on horseback, and sometimes would come over into our canyon to see the folks. On one of these occasions, as he rode up the creek, he discovered a deer on the plot of ground where our almonds were afterward planted. He shot the deer and hung its carcass up in a large shrub at the foot of the hill, and came on up to the house to get Father and George to help him bring it in.

While they were skinning the deer, Lafie, hanging around as small boys do, for the first time noticed the peculiar little slot-like groove that every deer carries below each eye paralleling the nose. Pointing to this slot he immediately asked young Damron:

"What made that? "

"That's where his mammy stuck a knife into him when he was a baby," replied Damron jocosely.

Lafie was silenced but not convinced. Though but a small boy he felt the rebuff.

This form of "fun" at the expense of small children was ignorantly supposed to be of value in "sharpening the wits." Too frequently they were thus humiliated and made to feel self-conscious and inferior to their "smart" elders, with consequent injury to their self-respect. In such incubation is hatched that most insidious of all vipers injurious to personal poise and happiness, the" inferiority complex."

Children are naturally questioners. That is their normal means of acquiring information. They are by natural right entitled to sensible answers and explanation. Having been thus abused when young, these same children usually grow up with similar ideas and know no better than to perpetrate the same thoughtless cruelty on the next generation, thereby keeping up the vicious cycle. In those days there was no literature available on child psychology. There were no young mother societies and parent organizations. No one had ever heard of such a thing as the "inferiority complex." But today no excuse exists—unless it be in very poor and unenlightened sections—for ignorance of proper methods of guiding and correcting children without injury to their personalities.

With Lafie again as the subject, another example of this kind of "smartness" might be recited. One day Mother sent him down to Vineyard Point to tell Father and George, who were plowing there, that dinner was ready. His message was accepted in silence. After finishing the row they began to unfasten the traces. Then still without speaking, George jumped onto one of the horses and Father prepared to mount the other. Lafie, being a very little boy and unable without assistance to properly interpret their actions, asked innocently:

"Where are you going? "

"We're going courting," replied Father with a wink at George.

Lafie appeared mystified.

"I don't suppose you know what that means, but you ask George, he knows," added Father as they both rode away without so much as offering the little messenger a ride.

Lafie was left in a mental puzzle, wondering what "courting" could mean and if they would get back in time for dinner. He watched them ride across the plowed ground through the opening between the young willows into the creek bottom. Not until he saw them turn in the direction of the house, did the truth dawn upon his consciousness that Father had been only joking and they were merely going home for dinner.

As he trudged homeward far behind them, the inevitable reaction followed of unwholesome chagrin at the unnecessary wound.

Stagecoach Days

The old stagecoach road that had been traveled from ancient times between Los Angeles and San Diego, crossed Aliso Canyon somewhere between the boundary lines of ranchos Niguel and Cañada de los Alisos, about a mile west of the location where the town of El Toro was afterward built.

For the first eight or nine years of our life in Aliso Canyon, this was the only road by which either city could be reached from our place. There were no roads following the coastline north and south between Santa Barbara and San Juan Capistrano Beach, a distance of approximately two hundred and twelve miles. The only exit from our place by team and wagon in any direction was the canyon road that crossed the old stage road ten miles up from our beach.

Los Angeles lay sixty miles away to the north and San Diego eighty miles to the south. These were the closest towns that in those early days afforded any market for produce. Whatever Father had to sell or exchange for food, clothes, and other provisions, had to be transported these great distances. A week was required for the trip to San Diego and back, and five days for the round trip to Los Angeles. No roads had yet been built over the mountains to San Bernardino, and the long and circuitous route to reach this town made it still more distant than either of these.

Often the roads were in such a state of disrepair it was with extreme difficulty that he could pass over them. With deep sand in some places and mud in others, the horses had all they could do to pull the heavily loaded lumber wagon. In winter a shovel was always taken along with which to repair washouts.

Much of Father's time was thus consumed in going and coming for although honey will keep for several months, butter and eggs must be marketed before becoming stale. Also, provisions must be replenished with comparative frequency. So far as means would permit he bought these in quantities, trading in his produce.

Along this old dirt highway, subject to the enveloping dust of summer travel and the quicksands, washouts and mud-ruts of winter, journeyed from early days the old "thoroughbrace "stagecoach drawn by four good horses. The stage was kept on the road constantly day and night, the horses being exchanged for fresh ones at the various relay stations along the route and at the terminals.

The first relay out from Los Angeles was called the Seventeen-mile House, the second, some sixteen miles farther, was at Anaheim, where the change was made in the late afternoon or evening. Here the drivers also were exchanged. A short stop usually after dark, at Santa Ana, was made to discharge and pick up mail and an occasional passenger, after that town had been put on the map. The third relay was at "Culver's Corner" three miles east of Tustin, where an ancient adobe in charge of a stock tender served as relay station. This was fifteen or sixteen miles from Anaheim. Some seventeen miles farther on was the fourth relay at San Juan Capistrano. Las Flores, the fifth, lay about twenty miles farther, and here, drivers were again exchanged at three o'clock in the morning. No station lay between this place and the terminal at San Diego some forty-six miles beyond, where drivers were again exchanged. On the return trip the hours for drivers' exchange were practically reversed, being in the evening at Las Flores and in the night at Anaheim.

Before bridges had been built crossings were hazardous, and the schedule often interrupted by swollen waters and quicksands. It was no uncommon thing to see a wagon abandoned in midstream by some traveler, where it would stand for several days until the water subsided and help could be found to extricate it.

It was during the Fifties that the first stage began to be operated, when as yet there were no towns or settlements other than San Juan Capistrano between the two terminals. No regular schedule was then possible. The driver deviated his course to stop at irregular intervals at the various rancherias located within reach along the way, where mail and passengers were picked up or left. The arrival of the stage was the big exciting event of the week. Later as towns sprang up and the route became modified in consequence, stages began to run biweekly and after some years tri-weekly.

The old thoroughbrace stagecoach used in those early days was built without springs, the body being suspended in a frame by two huge leather straps. These were formed of ten strips riveted together and measuring about five inches in width and an inch and a half in thickness. Only the very best leather was used in their manufacture, and half a dozen choice hides were required to make one set.

These thoroughbrace straps, one on each side, extended from front to back underneath the coach, so that the curved body resting on them rocked like a cradle—only from end to end instead of from side to side.

If properly loaded, riding was easy as in any carriage. But if unevenly balanced this coach would perform gymnastics all its own. If too much weight in the form of baggage were to be placed on the rear boot, the front end and the driver's seat would be hoisted into the air; and correspondingly, if too much weight were placed on the front, the rear end would fly up. So a driver's fitness for his job consisted not merely in knowing how to manage his horses.

The stage was built to carry eleven passengers, nine insides and two outside with the driver. But often it was crowded with several extra. The fare from Los Angeles to San Diego, a distance of some hundred and thirty miles, was twenty dollars.

Valuable mail and express were often carried by stage between distant points, and it sometimes happened that the monotony of these long stage drives was broken by the excitement of a daring holdup. One particular spot along the route seemed especially favored by gentlemen of this lawless profession.

A deep gulch, dry except at times of winter rains, led down from the mountains northeast of El Toro across a portion of the San Joaquin Rancho, something like a mile north of the Rawson ranch house. Where the stage road crossed it, the gulch spread out into a wide wash, lined with willow thickets, elderberry trees and patches of cactus, with a good stretch of loose sand in the bottom. Invariably, the team, after descending the slanting grade into the wash, was obliged to slow down to a walk for the pull through the sand before climbing out again up the slanting grade of the other side. This circumstance, added to the loneliness of the situation and the opportunities for concealment of any lier-in-wait, caused the spot to be dreaded by stage drivers.

One night the stage was rolling along on its way toward San Juan Capistrano, carrying three passengers and a valuable Wells Fargo express box. One of the passengers, a native of sunny France, was sharing the seat up front with the driver, Charley Smith. Of the two inside one was a Chinese. The other was Judge Eagan, the local Alcalde, or justice of the peace, known familiarly as "Dick Eagan." He had come to Capistrano to live in the days when only two others beside himself spoke the English language. Homeward bound, he was dozing comfortably as they jogged along about eleven o'clock down the easy grade into the dry wash, and slowed up for the pull across the sandy bottom.

Suddenly he jumped, startled out of his dream by a loud, harsh command uttered outside to the driver:

"Stop! And hand over that box!"

The quick crack of a whip followed, then a pistol shot, and the stage bounded forward in the darkness, as the horses, lunging and plunging in their fright, came up out of the wash and started across lots. Other shots rang out, as the Frenchman emptied his chambers in the direction of the bandit, while above the din sounded the driver's yell to the judge:

"Come up and take the reins! I'm shot!"

The stage was careening over the rough uncultivated "hog-wallow" land and tossing and pitching after the terrified horses who had left the road. The helpless Frenchman, who knew nothing about driving, was trying to keep his seat. Judge Eagan, madly endeavoring to get the door open and to hang on while he reached up and took hold of the top rail, managed to draw himself up onto the driver's seat where he got hold of the reins and brought the horses under control.

Charley had been shot in the hand and blood was spurting all over everything. Bringing the team to a stop, the Judge tied a handkerchief about the wound, and then made for the ranch house of his friend Rawson. Here, further treatment was administered before continuing on to San Juan Capistrano.

But plucky Charley Smith was crippled for life. The Express Company showed their appreciation by presenting him with an expensive engraved gold watch and chain, which he was always proud to exhibit, but which could not bring back his good right hand.

In Eighteen Seventy-Five one January day, there came steaming in from Los Angeles to Anaheim the first passenger train, shortening the stage journey by thirty-three miles and making Anaheim its terminal. Two years later the same Southern Pacific was continued on into Santa Ana, which then became the stage headquarters.

About that time the old thoroughbrace coach was supplanted by a later model built with springs. This was a "double-decker" having a cloth top and a "boat" for baggage overhead. It was intended to carry six passengers and was drawn by two horses, and was called locally a "mud-wagon." Most of the time for the next ten years, it was operated from the livery stables of Henry Neill of Santa Ana.

Even this modern stage, as it made its round trip runs three times a week to and from San Diego, was not operated without its moments of excitement. The bandit this time was the age-old lawless enemy of common sense and judgment—Alcohol.

On a certain ill-fated trip, the driver took with him besides his solitary passenger, the "cheering" bottle, from which he freely imbibed until he had attained a state of reckless irresponsibility. Seeing that his passenger was becoming nervous over his driving, he conceived the idea of giving him a "real scare" by way of a pleasant diversion. So just as they were approaching the high ocean bluff at Las Flores, he lashed his team to a foam and took at break-neck speed the precarious curve along the face of the precipice.

The jittery passenger, taking his only chance for life, jumped out of the flying vehicle, and almost immediately the horses, driver, stage and all were hurtled over the edge of the bluff before his eyes and dashed to pieces on the rocks a hundred feet below.

In Eighty-Seven and Eight, the iron horse in its march of progress, laid its track all the way into San Diego. Then the old "mud-wagon" too went into the discard, as had the picturesque old stagecoach a decade before it, passing into oblivion and decay.

In the reverent atmosphere of the museum, the place of old things made sacred by their very passing, might still be seen the old thoroughbrace stagecoach, age-worn, bedraggled, but in undisturbed composure dignified with grace, its raised dais guarded in stately honor by protecting bounds. Backward, it seems to turn the wheel of time, as if in a reverie dreaming of labors abundant, of endless roads, dangerous turns, precipitous grades, trusty and sure-footed steeds, brave and jovial drivers, tired and dusty passengers, bags of mail, boxes of bullion, the cracking of whips, the whistle of bullets—silence, freighted silence, whispering ever of a vanished past.

An Indian Outrage

Father's brother, Peter Franklin Thurston, youngest child of his parents, was twenty the year Father came to California, and just before the family left Bear Valley, was married to Miss Mary Ann Spendlove, a girl of sixteen, known to them before leaving Utah. Within eight years they had a family of five children.

In the early Eighties, Uncle Frank was freighting across the desert to the silver mines at Tombstone, the new mining town in the hills of southeastern Arizona. Six horses were required to a schooner—a large wagon built with extra wide bed and very wide iron tires, often trailing a smaller, short-tongued wagon.

The country was lonely and covered with Mesquite shrubs, the roads few and rough, sandy in some places and rocky in others, and the surrounding mountains of the San Carlos Indian Reservation were infested with Apaches, who frequently took the "war path," raiding through the country, especially during the years when the notoriously cruel Geronimo held the chieftainship.

One day as usual, Uncle Frank with his six-horse schooner, was passing through the Dragoon Mountains, when he came to a dry wash where were many clumps of shrubbery and low oak brush. Suddenly a band of yelling Apaches rushed out upon him from ambush. They caught and cruelly murdered Uncle Frank and scalped him, then cut up his body in pieces and tied the pieces to his wagon wheels, carrying off the goods and driving away the horses. They then set fire to the wagon, which was partially consumed when discovered.

The horror of that time left its impression on me, a tiny girl, when Father received the dreadful news. Another uncle, Frank Wooley, first husband of Mother's only sister, was also murdered by Indians. In those days, Indian stories took first place in current magazines.

CHAPTER 18 PERSECUTION

Southern California from earliest times had been devoted to sheep and cattle raising. Long had stock and sheep men enjoyed, irrespective of minor boundary lines, undisputed possession of the rich pasture lands that stretched away for many miles on every side from the mountains to the sea.

When farmers began to drift into the country and take up the smaller claims that lay sandwiched in between the large grants, they resented the invasion, considering them as intruders to be harassed and driven out, and endeavored to make things as difficult and unpleasant for them as possible. Never had they been obliged to keep their stock within fences, and they did not propose to do so after the farmers came. Their cattle and horses were allowed to run unrestrained over the fields of growing crops produced by the struggling farmers. This made bad blood between the two classes. Often stock would be killed by way of retaliation.

On one occasion as Father and George were driving stray cattle from our own premises far up the canyon, they saw lying dead in the ranch pasture a beautiful horse recently slain—probably by some irate farmer. Occasionally some man would lose his life over the trouble.

Father at first had no fences of his own and no means with which to procure them. As soon as his crops began to make a showing, they became a prey to all the stray stock of the country round. Some of this stock was from the Rawson ranch, and some of it from other stock raisers pasturing through the country on land they did not own.

In the evening after a day of hard work, Father and George with the help of our faithful dog Carlo, would be obliged to chase stray stock away from our premises, and like as not the same stock would return during the night following. The situation became an unbearable nuisance. And there was no redress.

When Father approached Rawson about the matter, he was apologetic and sorry, but the nuisance continued unabated, with no effort on his part to stop the devastation of crops upon which the very existence of the family in Aliso depended.

Failing by these means, apparently accidental, under a cover of friendliness, to exasperate Father into abandoning his claim, and seeing that he was at last protecting his crops with fences, this rancher set himself to devise a more effective scheme. Had the same drastic means that Rawson now employed been used a few years previously Father no doubt would have been worsted in the struggle.

He had been in the canyon more than six years, and the Aliso place, now under cultivation and covered with young orchard and vineyard, was acquiring a value aside from its peculiar location as a coast outlet. Having filed his homestead claim in Seventy-Four, the time was not far distant when actual title to the place could be secured. This would place it forever beyond the reach of the man who coveted it. Therefore, if Father's evacuation was ever to be effected no more time was to be lost.

A few families, after the survey, had drifted into Laguna Canyon and taken up claims and campers had begun coming to the beach for summer vacations, which furnished an apparently reasonable basis for Rawson's next move. One day he approached Father with a proposition. The time had come, he told him, when he found it necessary to put up a fence across the canyon in order to exclude general travel back and forth across his land, as he was afraid of possible fires that might be set out by careless campers and hunters. Father and other trusted men were to be given private keys to the gate and allowed to travel back and forth as usual, the only stipulation being that they lock the gate after them each time.

This, on the face of it, sounded very plausible and friendly, but Father did not like the idea. During the last few years of his residence in the canyon he had learned too much about the crookedness that was going on and had suffered too much from stray stock to be easily deceived by fair words. The old gentleman who had first shown him the Aliso claim, he had learned, had been summarily discharged from Rawson's employ as soon as he heard of the incident, and Father had come to regard the ranchman as two-faced. He was afraid of his principles and of his promises, though as yet little had been said about it beyond his own family circle.

The California law provided that after a road had been traveled publicly without protest or interference for five successive years, it could not again be closed to public travel. The road in question to Father's own knowledge had been traveled for nearly seven years without protest, and presumably much longer. This made it now public property and gave him a legal right to travel the canyon road unmolested at his own pleasure. Father could see in this proposal of Rawson's far more than appeared on the surface, and had no intention of surrendering this right.

There was at that time, as has been stated no other road out of the canyon in any direction, except by horseback over narrow trails up and down the coast. Should he accept a key, thereby giving consent to the placing of a gate across the wagon road, the act could be construed as conceding a right to fence it off and would be a virtual surrender of his right to travel the road at all. If his use of the road were to be by permission only, that permission might be rescinded as easily as granted, in which case he would find himself effectually "bottled up" on his own premises with no outlet except by the whim of an overlord.

Seeing through this game, Father refused his consent to the building of the fence, rejecting the offer of a key. But regardless of this unsatisfactory outcome of the interview, Rawson went ahead and built the fence across the canyon between the spring and the Aliso place about two miles up the canyon, and put a locked gate across the road.

On the near side of this fence, "Old Jake" was farming about twenty acres of land for Rawson, raising wheat, corn, potatoes and vegetables to supply the herders with garden stuff, and tobacco from which to make "sheep dip." The fence was erected alongside this garden plot, and the gate—no doubt designedly—placed conveniently near, where this farmer henchman, while innocently working in his little corn patch, could watch furtively the movements of anyone traveling the road. Besides keeping the gate locked he could keep his employer informed of any interesting occurrences, and provide as well a necessary witness at law for his master.

Rawson sent this man Jake down to the Aliso farm to bring Father a key to the lock of the new gate across the road. Father refused to accept the key, and old Jake was obliged to carry it back to his employer.

The next time Father had occasion to go up the canyon, he found this gate locked, and being prepared for the emergency, promptly smashed the lock with his hatchet. Father knew himself to be within his rights, for he had made diligent inquiries concerning the matter, but that fact did not protect him from the legal persecution, which now began openly. A few days later the sheriff came over from San Juan Capistrano and arrested him on a warrant for "malicious mischief."

This being a criminal offense, the cost of prosecution was upon the county, but Father as defendant, was left to bear his own expense of defense. When the trial came off in the San Juan Capistrano court, he was acquitted. Rawson then appealed the case. The acquittal was confirmed. But that was not the end of the matter.

While Father was away at court, Rawson took advantage of his absence to make another attempt at inducing the family to accept a key to the gate. He sent his foreman down to the Aliso place with the key. Mother and George were at home with the children and received him politely. His approach was very friendly, and after a little conversation he offered Mother a key to the gate. Having been instructed as to the principle involved, Mother told him she could not accept it. He urged her strongly as the simplest way out of the difficulty. Others had accepted keys to the lock, he told her, and were passing back and forth freely without any inconvenience. Mr. Rawson, he informed her, had no desire to cause Father any trouble. He was bringing it upon himself by his stubborn attitude.

Mother persisted in her refusal. He seemed somewhat annoyed, but still insistent. It was evident that he had come intending to accomplish his purpose. He turned to George, then a lad of about nineteen, and offered him the key, almost thrusting it into his hand. But George drew back refusing to touch it. As the man turned to go, he saw Frank, then a little fellow coming four years old, sitting on the ground at play. He tossed the key over to Frank, saying:

"Here, you can have the key," and jumping into his wagon, drove hurriedly away.

George, seeing this act, quickly snatched up the key and running with it after the fleeing foreman, threw it into the back of his wagon.

After this, in passing up the canyon road, every time Father found the gate locked he promptly smashed the lock. And every time he was caught he was again arrested for malicious mischief. It seemed he was perpetually involved with the law, either under arrest or with a case or an appeal pending in court.

Father was always acquitted. No jury could be found that would convict him. But his persecutor was cunning enough to select each time a different precinct in which to make his complaint, so there would be found no previous record of suit and acquittal on the court register.

The second time of arrest he was tried in the Santa Ana-Tustin precinct, the third time in the Anaheim precinct, and the fourth time in Los Angeles. By each time appealing the case, Rawson prolonged the expense for his victim, being at very little expense himself, thinking thus to wear him out and break him financially till he should be forced to give up the uneven fight.

The only way Father could keep out of jail was to put up bail. This he found very difficult to do in his circumstances. But through influence of lawyers, usually gained leniency enough that he was released to go and come by himself on his promise to be at court on time.

In a small mining town named Silverado situated in a canyon of that name northeast of Orange where a silver mine, "The Southern Belle" had been recently opened up, lived a lawyer known to Father, who went by the name of Judge Mecum. On the occasion of his second arrest when the time drew near to appear in court, Father drove up to Silverado to secure the services of this lawyer for his defense.

Expecting to be gone from home for several days, he took Lafie along to bring back the team which was needed daily on the farm. Lafie, not yet twelve, had never before driven a team hitched to a wagon. He went along with some trepidation at the thought of being expected to drive alone such a distance on his first try-out.

Judge Mecum accompanied them to Tustin, where Father took him into a saloon and treated him to beer. Though not a drinking man himself, Father recognized the custom of treating those who might expect it. The bartender set out three glasses, one for each of the two men and one for Lafie, the boy. Lafie took one sip of the beer and set it back on the counter. It didn't taste good to him. Mecum chaffed him a bit, and after drinking his own, picked up Lafie's glass, saying:

"I'll show you how to drink beer."

First he blew the foam off the top of the glass onto the floor—which Lafie observed with disgust, thinking him to be of very uncleanly habit—then gulped down the second glass without taking a breath. This incident left the boy still more unfavorably impressed with drinking, and might have been called "temperance lesson number three."

Lafie brought the team home alone without accident, and thereafter was considered a driver.

After Father's acquittal, Judge Mecum told the plaintiff that he was going to sue him on Father's behalf for five thousand dollars' damages. If this had any effect, it was not immediately evident, for the case was again appealed to a higher court, and again in due course of time, the defendant's acquittal was confirmed.

The last time an arrest was made for breaking the lock, George was the offender. Going up after water with Lafie, one day, he came to this gate and found it locked as usual, and as usual broke the lock, passing through without being molested—though they saw someone moving among the corn in the garden patch as they went by. On their return with the load of water, they found the gate locked again, and two men were moving about among the bare stalks pretending to husk corn—though it was fully evident that the corn had already been harvested. One of these men was old Jake, the other was Mr. Wood. This man was an habitual gambler, and as a consequence, was always either up or down financially. To settle a gambling debt, he had sold out to his partner Athens, and being then "dead broke" had hired himself out to Rawson.

George took out his tools before their faces and again smashed the lock on the gate, at the same time giving them both a "piece of his mind" for their contemptible trick. In reply to this tirade, Wood said to him:

"Well, we have to obey orders, you know."

Within a few days after this, both George and Father were arrested for "malicious mischief." Mother was at this time very sick with Erysipelas, being subject to occasional attacks of this very serious malady. She lay in bed with cow-dung poultices over eyes, side of face, and neck, and Father was waiting on her when the Sheriff came to take him away. There was never any doctor available, and it is doubtful if a doctor would have been employed had there been one nearby, for Father felt himself sufficient for the occasion, having a well-thumbed "Doctor Book" in his library, and a knowledge accumulated through the years of many medicinal herbs and natural remedies. His remedy for Erysipelas was one that today would doubtless shock the medical profession; but somehow whether by faith or accident, it seemed to do the work. Father was known to boast that he had never had a doctor in the house, and his ideas of the profession were not altogether complimentary. He seemed to overlook the fact, however, that the very books in which he placed such implicit confidence, had all been written by members of the medical profession.

This time the case was to be heard in The District Court of Los Angeles (January 1, 1880 the District Court of Los Angeles was abolished to give way to the County Court); and to this place they were taken—this sheriff not extending the same leniency that local officers had been inclined to allow—leaving the sick wife and mother to the care of inexperienced children. After putting up bail for both, Father went to see the best lawyers then in the city—

J. D. Bicknell and Stephen M. White; but when he learned what their charges would be for handling the case, he was obliged to place it in other hands less expensive, and hunted up a lawyer who took the case for forty dollars.

This lawyer happened to be a brother of the judge before whom the case was to be tried, and for that very reason, when—after several expensive trips back and forth from home on the train—it finally came to court, the judge was inclined to be strict to avoid the very suspicion of favoring his brother at the bar. During the trial, while Father was on the witness stand, he started to tell something which to him seemed important, and the judge forbade him to proceed. This was irritating to Father, and he decided to tell it anyway. Whereupon the judge, to teach him a lesson, promptly fined him ten dollars for contempt of court. At this a titter went over the courtroom. After the case had gone to the jury and the spectators had all left the room, Father's lawyer succeeded in persuading the judge to remit the fine. When the jury returned, eleven stood for acquittal and one for conviction, and the case was dismissed. So once more he was free.

Father had by this time made up his mind to go after Rawson on a charge of "malicious prosecution," and instructed his lawyer to start the suit. This sort of thing had been going on now for several years and was keeping Father financially stripped. He determined to endure it no longer. During this time, he had been busy gathering damaging evidence concerning certain crooked dealings with the government in which his tormentor was engaged. This, he could back up by substantial witnesses, and the time had come when he felt that it was his turn to strike. He wrote to Washington to the proper authorities making serious complaint against the ranchman, backing up everything he said by proof in detail. His letter revealed an intimate knowledge of names, places, and dates, incidents and descriptions that could not be ignored by those in authority. The result of this was that a secret service official from the land office at Washington was immediately sent out to California to investigate the illegal matters reported.

This man's name was D. K. Sickles. He came directly to our place and stayed in our home for some time, going out from there on his tours of investigation. Mr. Sickles had an odd way about him; no matter whether the weather was cold or hot, he always wore an overcoat. When asked why he did so he replied:

"In cold weather I wear it to keep the cold out; and in warm weather I wear it to keep the heat out."

Father took this man all over the country to interview the different parties referred to in his letter to Washington. One of these was Rawson's own cook who had been preempting land for his employer. They went to Rawson's ranch house and finding him not at home, Father took this federal officer right into his kitchen to interview the cook.

For years past, Rawson had been trying to get his Mexican title confirmed at Washington. By conniving with surveyors, he had succeeded in having the lines so drawn as to include much of the best land and the watering places, leaving out mountains that properly should have been included instead. This had made his lines so crooked that the government would not accept them. Now, under the accumulated evidence gathered by this federal secret service man, he faced the necessity of straightening out, not only his lines, but many other things beside that were much more difficult. Immediately he had something far more interesting for entertainment than the persecution of an unwanted neighbor. He removed the lock from the gate across the canyon road, and in time the fence also disappeared. And Father dropped his suit against him.

Not long after this, in the spring of Eighty-One, Mr. Rawson leased his ranch to two men by the name of Lewis F. Moulton and P. H. Look, whom he had previously known for several years. These men also leased Jonathan E. Bacon's interest in El Niguel.

Rawson left that part of the country and started again in the cattle business in Inyo County. But getting into financial difficulties, in order to raise means to clear his obligations, in January of Eighty-Four he sold El Niguel rancho—thirteen hundred and seven acres in undivided half interests to M. A. Forster and Richard Eagan, including the precious half-mile of beach frontage, and fourteen thousand acres to Lewis F. Moulton by contract, which automatically dissolved the latter's partnership with Look.

It was not until ten years later, however, that Rawson was able to give Mr. Moulton a clear deed to his land. Eventually, Mr. Rawson died a poor man in Inyo County. Mr. Look tried his fortunes in the real estate business, and investing heavily during the "boom" a few years later, went broke when the boom "busted."

Mr. Moulton prospered. He reduced the sheep raising and put more cattle on the rancho. Later, when the Santa Fe came through in Eighty Seven, he reduced the cattle and began grain farming on shares. In Ninety-Two he took a partner, a Frenchman, Jean Pierre Daguerre, who brought into the partnership money, hard work, and sound counsel. In Ninety-Six they bought out the interests of Forster and Eagan, and in Nineteen One, after Bacon's death, bought his sixteen hundred acres of his heirs, thus acquiring the whole of the original rancho. They later secured other parcels adjoining it, which brought their eastern lines to the old Stagecoach Road—in after years to become a wide concrete highway—and to the railroad south of El Toro. Land in the Laguna hills was also added on the west.

Mr. Moulton was a kindly man, a friend to everyone in need, and greatly beloved as a neighbor. He passed away in December of Nineteen Thirty-Eight in his eighty-fifth year. And California said goodbye to another of the old pioneers.

CHAPTER 19 OUR FIRST NEIGHBORS

That was a happy day in the fall of Seventy-Seven when the discovery was first made that we had neighbors. They had lived in Laguna a year and a half at least before we knew they were there.

About the time of the survey in Seventy-Four, two men, brothers-in-law, Harvey Hemenway and Henry Goff, with their families came from Kansas to Southern California and settled on the lowlands west of Santa Ana at the place called Westminster. There in partnership they began raising hogs.

After about two years of this, they heard of Laguna Canyon where government land was open for settlement, and in the spring of Seventy-Six moved over into Laguna and took up claims. Hemenway chose his quarter-section in the canyon and built his cabin about a mile from the beach, incorporating into it the little one-room shack there that formerly had been occupied by John Damron, who had left the canyon with his stock.

Goff took up land nearer the beach, and put up his cabin on the elevated spot overlooking sand and sea, where the Laguna Hotel now stands. To this first cabin, he added little by little, until within a few years when campers began coming to the beach, he had made out of it a crude hotel, the outside battened in early California style, and the inside partitions made of straight up-and-down beaded lumber.

Harvey Hemenway was a large-built angular man with a ruddy bewhiskered face and hearty manner, unaffectedly simple and honest in his dealings with others. He paid for his homesite by raising chickens, hogs and cows, selling the milk and eggs, pork, and honey from a few stands of bees, to the campers on the beach. He kept his money in a tin can hid in a geranium bush until he had accumulated enough to pay the government for his land.

His two eldest were children of a former marriage, Merittina, shortened to "Tiny," a girl of twelve, and Levy a year and a half younger, had lost their mother when the boy was an infant. Little Edna, two years old, was the child of his present wife, Mariah Betsey, and four more children were raised in Laguna, Elvin, Joe, Rubert and Lelia—three other boys having died young. Elvin Hemenway was the first child ever to be born in Laguna.

Libby, the wife of Henry Goff, was Hemenway's sister. In their family were four children, Ammon, Clinny, Addie, and Sherman, spoken of as "Big Sherm" to distinguish him from a younger cousin of the same name who was called "Little Sherm." Two girls, Cordie and Eva were later born to them in Laguna.

By Way of the Mountains

Goff and Hemenway, after living in Laguna for a year and a half, heard that just over the mountain in another canyon called Aliso, lived another family by the name of Thurston. They made up their minds to find them.

There being no wagon roads of any description south of their homes, they knew of no other way to find their neighbors than to start out blindly and drive through the brush as far southward across the rough mesa as it was possible to go and then seek for a way over the ridges of mountain that lay between. So one morning, hitching up Hemenway's span of mules to his spring wagon, these two men with their wives, all then in the prime of life, started out bravely on this most venturesome pioneer tour of exploration.

Picking their way slowly through the brush, the first real obstacle they encountered was a rather deep arroyo, dry now, but the outlet of freshets that came down in winter from the mountain to the sea. This was that gulch that in later times was spanned by a wooden bridge of crude design and in after years called "Sleepy Hollow." Scarcely can it be recognized today, built up and spanned by the grand concrete bridge of the present coast highway through the city of Laguna.

Having accomplished the feat of crossing this gulch without tipping over, they continued bumping their way across the rutty, stony, mesa, covered with brush and cactus and seamed with many more minor washes.

Two or more miles of this brought them to the verge of a deep impassable ravine, another outlet for winter freshets to the sea, its sides traced by a winding horseback trail. Here they were obliged to halt, for team and wagon could not be driven across this ravine.

There was now but one thing left for them to do if they were to proceed on their daring escapade, and that was to try driving up the side of that formidable mountain—a perilous thing to attempt. Deciding upon the spot most likely to admit of ascent, so far as they were able to ascertain from the bottom, they turned courageously to the dangerous undertaking, determined to go as far as possible. Should it prove wholly impracticable, they could at least give up the attempt and return home.

Up and up the pathless steep clambered those sure-footed mules, driven by intrepid pioneers through brush, rocks, patches of cactus and gulches. Pausing occasionally for a breathing spell, they crossed ridge after ridge, dipping down into ravine after ravine, narrowly avoiding many a disastrous tip-over, finally reaching the top at last.

Here they stopped to rest the mules and their jolted bodies, and incidentally to take in the magnificent view spread out in all directions. From their position they could gaze over into Aliso Canyon, but not knowing which way to direct their eyes, saw at first no sign of habitation. Soon, to the southeastward, they discerned in the far distance the cabin and corncribs of the family they sought, nestled up against the foot of the curving mountain on the other side of the canyon.

The little farm must have presented a rather barren aspect with its battened cabin and its two lone outbuildings, for our orchards and vineyard, planted only a few years previously, were still too young to make much of a showing at that distance. However, they could discern patches of cultivated land here and there and see signs of life.

How to get down the mountain on the other side was more of a problem than had been the ascent. It was steeper and farther. There were cliffs in places, and no mesas broke its long stretches of brush and cactus-covered declivities. They followed the ridge for some distance in its slope toward the south, and were rewarded by the discovery of a smoother decline that seemed to offer some hope of successful descent into the valley below. Near the bottom a spur jutted out toward the creek breaking the long decline and considerably lessening its steepness. At the foot of the spur towards the south could be discerned an area of land under cultivation.

Here they decided to try their "luck." Starting down hopefully but cautiously through the brush they concluded the precarious descent without mishap, easing up on the more level spur. On the north side was a cliff walled recess, in the bottom of which a little clearing showed signs of flower culture. The other side offered the shortest and most likely descent to the bottom, which they accomplished safely, and found themselves in the upper end of our young vineyard.

From there it was an easy matter to discover our private wagon road across the creek up to the house. As they drove into our yard, their unexpected arrival, especially from that impossible direction, was an overwhelming surprise to all, evoking from Father and Mother, mingled with their expressions of hearty welcome, many ejaculations of astonishment and wonder:

"How did you ever get here?"

"We just drove over the top of the mountain."

"Over that mountain?"

"How in the world did you ever get over that mountain? Where did you come down?"

Then they described the seemingly impossible feat of driving over the uncharted mountain, recounting their many narrow escapes from disaster.

"You had more courage than I would ever have had!" declared Mother with great admiration.

Indeed it had been a remarkable exhibition of courage, daring and perseverance on their part.

As the visitors passed into the house, they saw shy children everywhere; the older ones of an age to be companionable with the young people they had left behind in their homes in Laguna. The rest of the nine tapered on down to Harriet, the baby of the family then about a year and a half old, and as tall as her little brother Frank—the two being taken for twins.

These isolated families were indeed glad to become acquainted with one another. Though there were three or four mountainous miles, and no roads between their homes, yet it was a comfortable feeling to know that other people of their own race were within occasional visiting distance—and not too far to walk. As for the young people, it was to them an exciting experience, betokening future adventure.

They did not return home by the same way they had come. None of them had any appetite for reversed repetition of the adventure. Father showed them the road up Aliso Canyon that by a long circuitous route eventually connected with the road down into Laguna Canyon, and they were glad to take the long way home in assured safety.

A few weeks after this visit, Father and George took horses and set out to find the location of their new neighbors. They rode down the canyon, passing to the upper side of the pond, and on up the steep, rough, brush covered side of the mesa. Once on its almost level top, they followed a winding horse-back trail up and down gullies and through the brush, reversely over the same route that had been taken by Father in company with the old fisherman on his first trip into Aliso Canyon. They found their new neighbors, and visited with both families before again taking their departure for home. Thus interchange of communication was established between these pioneer families who were to remain neighbors and friends for many years to come.

One day Mesia, then fourteen past, recalling how their neighbors had first come down over the mountains to see them a few months before, thought to take this climb a-foot and see the tops of those towering mountains they had driven over. Starting alone up the hillside by way of George's Ground, and passing through the gap at its upper rim, she viewed from there what appeared to be the top of the mountain above her. There was no trail beyond the gap, but on and up she clambered through the brush toward the summit. When she reached the goal, she found that it was not the top at all, but only a ridge; and the summit seemed to tower high above her. Tired and panting, she renewed her climb; and at last reached this top—not the top of the mountain, but only of another ridge; and high above her, rose still another ridge that appeared to be the summit. Having gone so far, she would not turn back defeated; though fatigued beyond all her calculations and wondering if there really were any top to this mountain. Laboriously she struggled on upward toward her goal; and at last was rewarded; for this third ridge proved to be indeed the summit; and here before her lay the same immensity of view on every side that had greeted them. She stood for some time enjoying the view, gazing over her own Aliso home, now far below her, and taking in the whole canyon as far as distant mountains permitted, then the downward sweep of the western side creased with innumerable gulches, some of which crossed the mesa and continued to the sea; whose broad expanse seemed most wonderful and incomprehensible viewed from that height.

Down the slope she went to the mesa and made her way home by following the horseback trails to the farther end of it, and then the footpath down the side of it to her own familiar creek and orchards, reaching home at last very weary and lame from her mountain climb and the long walk back, but feeling well repaid for the effort.

A Malaga Stump

Some time after this our Malaga grapes, on account of mildew, with which Father then knew not how to cope, had to be dug up. Goff was desirous of trying them out on his own place so Father gave them all to him, and he divided them with Hemenway. The two men planted the vines, every one of which grew and flourished without even a taint of mildew, for in our canyon they had been hampered by extreme cold and dampness, while on the coast, the climate was milder and sunnier.

Father afterward learned more about grape culture; and no doubt could have saved them all by sulphuring, had he but known it at the time.

In digging up these grapevines, some of the stumps had been overlooked and left in the ground. Something like a year later, Lafie, then past twelve, and Joseph were cultivating the ground in the vineyard—Lafie handling the cultivator, and Joseph riding and guiding the horse between the rows. Becoming very thirsty, Lafie decided to go up to the house and get himself a drink of water. Between him and his desired object, lay the barbed wire fence, which he could pass in any one of three ways—there being no gate at that place. He could crawl under it, climb through it, or jump over it. Being athletic, full of life, daring and fond of jumping, the last-named method appealed to him. Very often had he taken a running jump and cleared a three-strand wire fence; so quickly decided that was the thing to do, and walked back to get the proper start.

Barbed wire fencing had been invented a few years before—the first patent coming out in Seventy-Four—and consisted then of two strands of wire twisted together, between the twists of which, was inserted at intervals of something more than two inches, a short, double barb cut from sheet metal, both ends of which were shaped and sharp-pointed like an arrow; the barbed ends being bent once across each other to hold them in position. The fence was built of three strands of these double twisted barbed wires strung one above another between posts set in the ground.

Lafie had on a pair of boots that were well worn, the toe of one being broken through and ragged. Having taken his position, he ran swiftly toward the fence and was about to make his leap over it, when the ragged toe of his boot caught on a Malaga stump, tripping him so that instead of making the jump, he was thrown with great force against the fence. His right leg went through the fence between the two lower strands of wire and was ripped open on a barb for three or four inches on the upper front of the thigh; at the same time this leg hooked onto the barb of the bottom wire and was also cut open under the knee. In an involuntary effort to steady himself, his right hand grasped the upper strand of wire directly over a barb, which entered his hand, one point of the double barb going in first, then, as his hand pulled back stretching the wound, the other barb entering at the same spot, thus embedding both barbs in the palm of his hand in opposite facing directions, while the wire lay straight along the surface. This painful wound was necessarily made larger by the process of removing the barbs. Poor Lafie! For many a day, he was laid up unable to work or play; and carried lifelong scars from this escapade.

Birth of Mary Tryphena

In Eighteen Seventy-Seven, not long after we made the acquaintance of Henry Goff and Hemenway, Mother and the family were presented with a very adorable Christmas present—though three days late—for on December twenty-eight of that year, little Annie was born—or rather, I should say "Pheenie." Our parents did not at first name her "Annie," but a couplet of two Bible names—"Mary Tryphena." We called her "Pheenie" for short. For two years she bore this name before it was changed to "Annie."

By that time, we had made the acquaintance of a beautiful young lady from Artesia, named Annie Vance, who had come to camp on Aliso Beach. She took quite a notion to Pheenie, but a decided dislike to her name. One day after she had walked up from the beach to our house, and was seated, as I remember it, near the front door under the high window behind the big stove, she began to coax Mother to change Pheenie's name. This was with Mother entirely a new idea. She did not refuse to consider the matter, however, though raising some objections, but listened respectfully to the young lady's proposal.

In those days, there was no compulsory registration of infants at birth; and names might be altered at will so long as the "census taker" had not been around; which might be quite a number of years after birth. For ever so often—or I might say ever so seldom—the census taker went through the country taking a record of all the children that had been born since his last trip. If a child had not been given its name before he made his appearance, it must be named before he took his departure, and after that, the name was settled and could not be changed without due process of law.

Encouraged by Mother's attitude, Annie Vance pressed her proposal, and as a special inducement, promised:

"If you will name her 'Annie' after me, I will buy her a new dress."

"Will it be a pocket dress?" asked Pheenie, at once becoming interested in this proposition.

"Yes, it will be a pocket dress. It shall have two pockets in it" said Annie.

Mother and Father and the older children took this matter under advisement; and at last all agreed to the change, and "Pheenie" became "Annie," a namesake of Annie Vance. Cloth was bought as she had promised, and the little dress made, with two little patch pockets, one on each side, which were little Annie's great delight.

But a middle name must be found that would go euphoniously with "Annie." What should it be? Father finally selected "Mariah"—much to Annie's future disgust; though at the time she was interested in nothing but the 'pocket dress.' When old enough to loathe this euphonious addition, she dropped the final "h" and wrote the name "Maria;" but that did not change the sound of it. So, years afterward, she adopted the French form of spelling and called herself: "Annie Marie;" which, though neither a family heirloom nor a biblical treasure, was nevertheless more pleasing to its possessor—and incidentally to the rest of the family.

Too often in those days helpless children were afflicted with ancestral, biblical and historical names that became the bane of their lives. Most of the children of Aliso were thus encumbered, being made perpetual reminders of parents, aunts, uncles, grandparents, and heroes and heroines of history both sacred and profane.

It was some time before the family forgot "Pheenie" and learned "Annie". But finally Pheenie faded away and vanished into the limbo of the past, and now it seems funny to recall it.

In the year that Annie was born, pennies were first introduced into California, though it was a number of years before they came into common use, the nickel being the smallest coin in circulation.

The Goffs and Other Settlers

Other families had begun to straggle in and locate up in Laguna Canyon and along the coast. The George Rogers were there, Thompsons, and several families of Brooks. There were Oliver and Will Brooks with their families, and Nate Brooks, a bachelor brother, with their mother Mrs. Draper; who also was sister to Libby Goff and Hemenway. There may have been others.

This influx to the coast very early called for a wagon road across the mesa to connect with the canyon road where it came to an end at the mouth of Aliso—the only means of access to the spring in Wood Canyon, where some of the early dwellers on the coast were obliged to go to obtain drinking water. This first road from Laguna to Aliso was built with pick and shovel by the men of the neighborhood; and at the end of the mesa was cut down the steep face of the bluff onto the sand of the ocean beach; which it crossed to the triangle to join our road up Aliso Canyon.

Nate Brooks, in partnership with his mother, had taken up a claim on a portion of the mesa adjoining the northern claim of Henry Goff and running up into the hills; but having no ocean frontage. The two towns of Laguna and Arch Beach were afterward built one on each side of it.

Figure 8 Nate Brooks

Before the year Seventy-Seven had passed, Frank Goff, brother to Henry, came from Massachusetts to the West with his family, consisting of his wife Emma, and their three children, Leon the eldest, then eleven, Nellie, not yet eight, and Mabel, not yet five; and in November settled in Compton, where then lived the two other brothers, Hubbard and Lee.

This town, first called "Comptonville," but later shortened to Compton, had been laid out in town lots in Sixty-Nine—the same year the transcontinental railroad was completed to California, when on the strength of this impetus to settlement, other Southern towns, including Santa Ana, had been started. G. D. Compton, its sole resident at that time, was the founder, having bought the tract of Temple and Gibson for five dollars an acre. Being a religious man, his intention was that it should be kept a "dry community." This town is peculiar in that its location is central to four other towns at nearly equal distances from it, in four different directions; namely, Los Angeles, ten miles to the north; Redondo Beach, ten miles to the west; Long Beach, ten miles to the south; and Norwalk, approximately the same distance to the east. From Laguna, the distance to Compton by the roads of access in those days, must have approximated fifty miles or more.

Figure 9 Frank and Emma Goff

Frank Goff was a man above average intelligence. He had been a grocery merchant and also a member of the police force in his home state. While still in Compton, in August of Seventy-Eight, another child, Lena, was added to his family; and when this babe was about six months old, probably in January of Seventy-Nine, he moved with his family from Compton to Laguna; where he went into the cattle-raising business with George Rodgers, who put up for him, a cabin on Government land on the hillside in the little canyonette now called "Bluebird Canyon." Here, with Leon's help in herding, he raised cattle on shares with Rodgers, and soon built up a sizable herd.

High up on the Laguna Mountains, pasturing them on Government land, Leon, a lad of twelve, herded these cattle. And there he and Lafie—then engaged in the same occupation with Father's smaller herd—often met and spent the day together, and the two became fast friends.

One day about this time, the Henry Goff family gave a party inviting all the young people of the community. From their big wagon they removed all seats but that of the driver, and with a layer of straw spread out over the bottom and two or three young people with him in the wagon, Ammon Goff drove down the coast to pick up those who lived at a distance and bring them to the party. Crossing the mesa, he stopped at the little cabin in the canyonette to pick up his cousin Leon; and together they came on to Aliso. There, they gathered our own young folks, George, Sadie, and Mesia into the wagon-bed with the others, and started back to Laguna; all having a merry time together, jouncing about on the straw.

On the way as they passed Leon's home his mother came out of the cabin and down the slope to meet and greet them, lifting up her dress to avoid catching it on the bushes, thus exposing her white petticoat underneath. This was embarrassing to Leon, sensitive as to his mother's appearance, and he exclaimed:

"Mother! Mother! Where is your dress?"

"Why, my dress is on me," she replied sweetly.

"Well! It doesn't look as though you had any dress!" chided her son.

This incident affords a glimpse of the extreme modesty of those times. Incidentally, it also witnesses that the idea of "bringing up Father" is not altogether a new one.

The occasion of this ride and party was the first time Artie and Leon had met each other. Many shy glances were exchanged between them and by the time the party was over and Ammon had brought them home again—Leon accompanying him once more to Aliso —they felt quite well acquainted and much interested in each other.

In the fall of Eighty-Nine, Frank Goff took up the remaining quarter-section that adjoined the two clans of his brothers Henry and Nate Brooks, and extended to the ocean bluffs at the ocean side and southern end of the long mesa. He was at first not correctly informed as to the exact location of his southern boundary line; and when he began to build his cabin, inadvertently placed it on land belonging to Father; whose claim now included a small portion of the mesa. Learning of this, Father went over to see him and showed him the surveyor's stakes. So Goff moved his cabin, this time locating it some distance back from the ocean bluff below the present coast highway on a portion of the land that afterward became known as "Goff Point."

On this point, just above the bluffs, many years before the white man came, had once been located an old Indian village. This was evidenced by the presence of wagonloads of old disintegrating seashells lying about in heaps— mostly of the shellfish varieties, the meat from which had been used for food in the long ago. There were no fresh shells or recent remains but those only of great age that crumbled at a touch. We used to gather them up by handfuls in our play and crush them to powder just for the fun of it. These old shells would fall apart in flakes, which still retained bright iridescent hues; and after the coast became more settled, art-workers would gather these bright shell-flakes to make up into shell flower bouquets and wreaths which they covered with glass in deep frames to hang on the walls for adornment as pictures are hung. This artistry required no mean skill and was very popular in those days, and very beautiful.

Many Indian relics were found along the coast regions by the early settlers, some of which are still preserved in art collections in various places. For many years we had, and used, a mortar and pestle made by the Indians, in which they ground their meal. The mortar was of gray granite about the size and shape of half a cannonball watermelon hollowed out bowl-shaped on the flat side and worn smooth with much use; the outside being rougher. The pestle was also very smooth and perhaps seven or eight inches long with both ends rounded one smaller than the other, the larger being about the size of a man's wrist. This end was worked in the bowl while the hand grasped the smaller end.

Frank Goff once found a mortar of stone that was inlaid all around the top with abalone shell, and years later Joseph came across a long pestle that had a neck and knob at one end inlaid with several rows of fine pieces of bone, and at the other end, tapered to a point. Another long round stone had the appearance of having been used as a rolling-pin, while several rocks shaped flat and smooth on top were discovered that might have served the purpose of mixing boards. Larger embedded ones suitable for games of the table sort were also to be seen.

After Frank Goff had taken up his claim, his brother Hubbard—always called "Hub"—left Compton and with his family, consisting of his wife Lottie and five children, Lula, Onnie, Effie, Sherm and Rosie came to Laguna to live near his brothers. Frank then divided his hundred and sixty acres with Hub, letting him have the northernmost thirty-five adjoining Nate's and Henry's claims and extending to the ocean opposite taking in the frontage now known as Arch Beach. Frank retained for himself the remaining hundred and twenty-five acres fronting on the ocean bluffs from Arch Beach to Aliso Beach.

Hub built his cabin toward the hills on the upper side of the roadway near his southern boundary line, and here they lived for many years, where another child, Jennie, came to join their family.

Hub Goff was a carpenter, blacksmith, and general "Jack-of-all-trades." He built houses, made wagons, sharpened plows and fashioned various farming tools. With a little scroll "jig saw," which we called a "buzz saw" that was mounted on a four-legged framework and operated by a treadle, he cut out all kinds of wooden toys, birds, animals, men and so forth, but specialized in "jumping jacks." These were little acrobatic men. He would cut out the head and trunk together, and each arm and leg separately, which he riveted in proper position loosely to the trunk—the rivets acting as pivots. He would then mount this little jointed man between two arms of a long stick shaped somewhat like a "Y" with a long stem, by running a short stiff wire through the hands from tip to tip of the prongs. This wire served as an "acting bar" from which the little man hung free suspended by his hands. Strings were attached to proper parts of his anatomy, and brought together as one at the lower end of the stick. By pulling the string this little man was made to go through all kinds of acrobatic stunts and somersaults; which varied so that one never knew what he was going to do next. Painted up appropriately in bright colors, and at times wearing a long flowing beard of hair pasted on, the jumping jack made a very interesting and amusing toy, that even the grown-ups liked to manipulate as well as the children.

Hub Goff was a personality—a genius in the community, pleasant and companionable in his family, entertaining to children, kindly as a neighbor unless others happened to cut across his own plans, and not above advantaging himself in a deal. He "played the fiddle" for all the neighborhood dances and made his own violins.

George, after watching Hub at this craft, made a violin for himself, not a mean instrument for an inexperienced boy, for upon it he played all the tunes he knew by heart.

For a year or two past, George had planned that when he became of age, he would take up the claim adjoining Father's land on the southern mesa. As the time drew near when he could qualify, he confided his intention to his new friend, Leon Goff, then past thirteen. This unwise confidence cost him a great disappointment; for just two months before his twenty-first birthday, Lee, the youngest of the four Goff brothers, with his wife Nettie and little daughter Nina, moved over from Compton to the coast and took up that identical claim. It was not until sometime afterward that George connected the two incidents together and began to suspect that he had been double-crossed.

As the northern mesa came to be called "Frank Goff Bench," so now the southern mesa became "Lee Goff Bench," and they bore these designations until long after both families had left the country—yes, as long as we lived in Aliso; and even yet, are so known by all "old-timers."

Lee Goff's family was increased while living on the coast, by two more children, a girl, Birdie, and Allie a boy. Nettie, the wife, had been the daughter of well-to-do New England parents and had no knowledge of housekeeping. Though very pleasant and sweet of manner, her woeful ignorance of domestic things made her unfitted to manage a household and bring up children. Her culinary habits were wasteful and expensive, and her little flock did about as they pleased—and they pleased to do very differently from the way we children had been brought up.

Nina was rather a good looking child with pleasing facial contour, howbeit with prominent upper front jaw and short lip that exposed the teeth. At one time, she had a birthday when her parents were to be away from home. The mother arranged for her a birthday party and invited us three to come over and spend the day with her three children during her absence, and before starting for town, prepared a very nice birthday dinner. The party was rather a boisterous affair, there being an absence of parental restraint, though it is doubtful if such a thing existed in their family anyway. Nina showed us her new toys, half of which were already broken to pieces and lying about on the floor, and after entertaining us for awhile with games and stunts about the yard, she headed the crowd as we trooped in to have dinner—the chief feature of the day.

Dinner was all cooked ready to serve and even the table set, and consisted of every inviting thing that could be thought of. The first course tasted so good and we ate so much that when dessert was mentioned we could none of us hold another bite. There stood the beautiful birthday cake uncut, candles and all, and everybody had to refuse it.

Of course we supposed it would be served us later on before going home, after a little more rough and tumble play should have jolted down our dinner a bit and made more room. But Nina was "different."

When she realized that nobody could eat any of it, she set that beautiful birthday cake down upon the floor and jumping upon it with both feet, trampled it to fine bits—her sister joining in the "fun" with high glee, while we three visitors to whom a cake was a cake—a rare, choice treat—stood looking on in horrified amazement and disappointment.

Allie, a baby of probably two and a half, while we were all out in the yard playing picked up a black pinacarta beetle—the common "stink bug" of the country—and to climax the day's enjoyment put it into his mouth and began to eat it, crunching it between his teeth. All the intervening years cannot obliterate from memory, the sound of that stink bug being crunched in Allie's mouth.

After Lee came to the coast, a road was built up the Lee Goff side—a sharp steep pull—and it was not long till it had been extended to another new claim at the Three Arches Within a few years it had lengthened clear to San Juan by the Sea, where it joined the old stagecoach road to San Diego. Although this first road across the mesa was very crooked, with many steep grades and hairpin turns, it was nevertheless a great convenience to all the coast dwellers, and especially to Father, whose frequent trips to San Diego were thus greatly shortened.

Lafe was thirteen about the time Lee Goff settled on the coast, and after the road was built Father made a proposition to him and Joseph that if they would clear the brush from his five acres on the Lee side, they might farm the land for themselves and keep what they raised on it. So the boys went to work. It was very foggy when they started though the morning was warm, and as the work was hard Lafe began to feel uncomfortably warm and rolled up his sleeves as high as they would go to help him keep cool. After a while the fog cleared away and "Old Sol" came out in all his splendor. All day they labored in the hot beach sun and at night came home tired but having made good progress with the brush-grubbing. However, that first day's work, for Lafe, was the last for many a day, for that night he began to suffer with a severe sunburn on both arms which laid him up for a whole week so that he was unable to do anything at all but to nurse his terrible burns. When at last his arms healed and the time of "peeling" began, Lafe took hold of a piece of the dead outer cuticle near his shoulder and peeled it off from shoulder to wrist in one big piece, like a snake shedding its skin.

Water was scarce on the coast; and the obtaining of it a great problem to those early settlers. The Goffs were obliged to water their stock in our Aliso creek, and to haul all their own drinking water at first, as we did from the same spring on the Rawson property in Wood Canyon, but having several miles farther to haul it. Hemenway had dug a little well near the creek in Laguna Canyon that helped out the situation for him and Henry Goff. Nate Brooks by tunneling into the mountain a little way where a seepage showed, had secured a small amount of water for his own needs; perhaps supplying a few other families. Several had cisterns to catch the rainfall for drinking purposes.

Frank and Lee found it to be an endless task for them to haul all their water for domestic use from the spring in Wood Canyon. The steep grades over which it must be brought and the gullies that made sharp dips in the wagon road caused so much sloppage from the barrels that they never reached home with more than half of their load. So they decided to dig wells on their claims, and imported into the community a red-headed Irishman named Mc Manus, a miner, to engineer the work of putting down these two wells. Frank Goff's was the first to be dug and his shaft was sunk to a depth of between eighty and ninety feet without striking so much as one sign of water. So the undertaking was given up as a failure. Then they went over to Lee Goff's claim and dug another well deeper than the first by some ten feet, with a little better success, for this well contained water, however brackish and fit only for stock.

After this they built cisterns in their yards to catch the rainfall from the roofs of their cabins during winter rains, covering over the tops with platforms of boards and installing hand pumps to raise the water.

After this unsatisfactory well-digging, Mc Manus went over beyond Lee Goff's place on the mesa above the Three Arches of old turtle-back and took up a claim for himself there. He built a little house, and shortly afterward sent away somewhere out of the country—it may have been as far as to the "ould counthry"—to fetch for himself a wife. This woman was a widow with one little girl about four years old. She was as small of build as he was large, as red-headed as himself and as Irish. She must have been very much disappointed upon discovering that he was a heavy drinker, for this habit of his caused her much grief.

In an effort to find water, Mc Manus dug a tunnel up in the hills above his house. But this too was a failure. He said that whenever he dug for gold he found water, but whenever he dug for water he could find neither water nor gold.

After this discouraging effort his wife who possibly had been observing a bit on her own account suggested to him that he go down below the house and dig in a certain gully nearer to the ocean and she thought he would find water. With all his drinking, he evidently had more wisdom than is displayed by some men, in that he was willing to listen to his wife. He took her advice and after only a few feet of digging in the gully of her choice, struck water sufficient for all their needs.

While living on this claim another child was born to them. When the time drew near, Mc Manus was in San Juan Capistrano on a protracted spree. There was no food in the house and no one in the home with his wife but her own little girl. Mable Goff was at that time herding her cattle on the hills above the southern mesa, and was in the habit of running down to the Mc Manus home while her cattle grazed, to play with this little girl. Mrs. Mc Manus sent word by her to our parents of the plight she was in and asked that Joan come down to stay awhile with her. When the word came, Joan coaxed Hulda—a girl then about twelve—to go in her stead. Hulda had never been away from home by herself, and was not yet instructed in the art of cookery, but consented to go and for two days and nights was in the Mc Manus home. She became so desperately homesick that when Joan went over to see her she refused to stay a day longer, and Joan who had come only for the afternoon, remained in her stead.

Hulda walked back home having promised Joan to send over her clothes. Joan remained with her two weeks and was the only attendant Mrs. G Mc Manus had during her trial—the drunken man being still absent—and the child was still-born.

Acquaintance had been made with another family who lived up in Trabuco Canyon, and kept stock and bees— Andrew Frame and his wife and five children—one of whom was named Idaho, who was hare-lipped, caused by his accidentally running into a clothesline when a boy which had disfigured his face for life. There were two other boys and two girls, Kittie and Ella. George and Ella took a great liking to each other, and might have made a match had Father not frowned upon it for no particularly good reason except that he needed George at home to work.

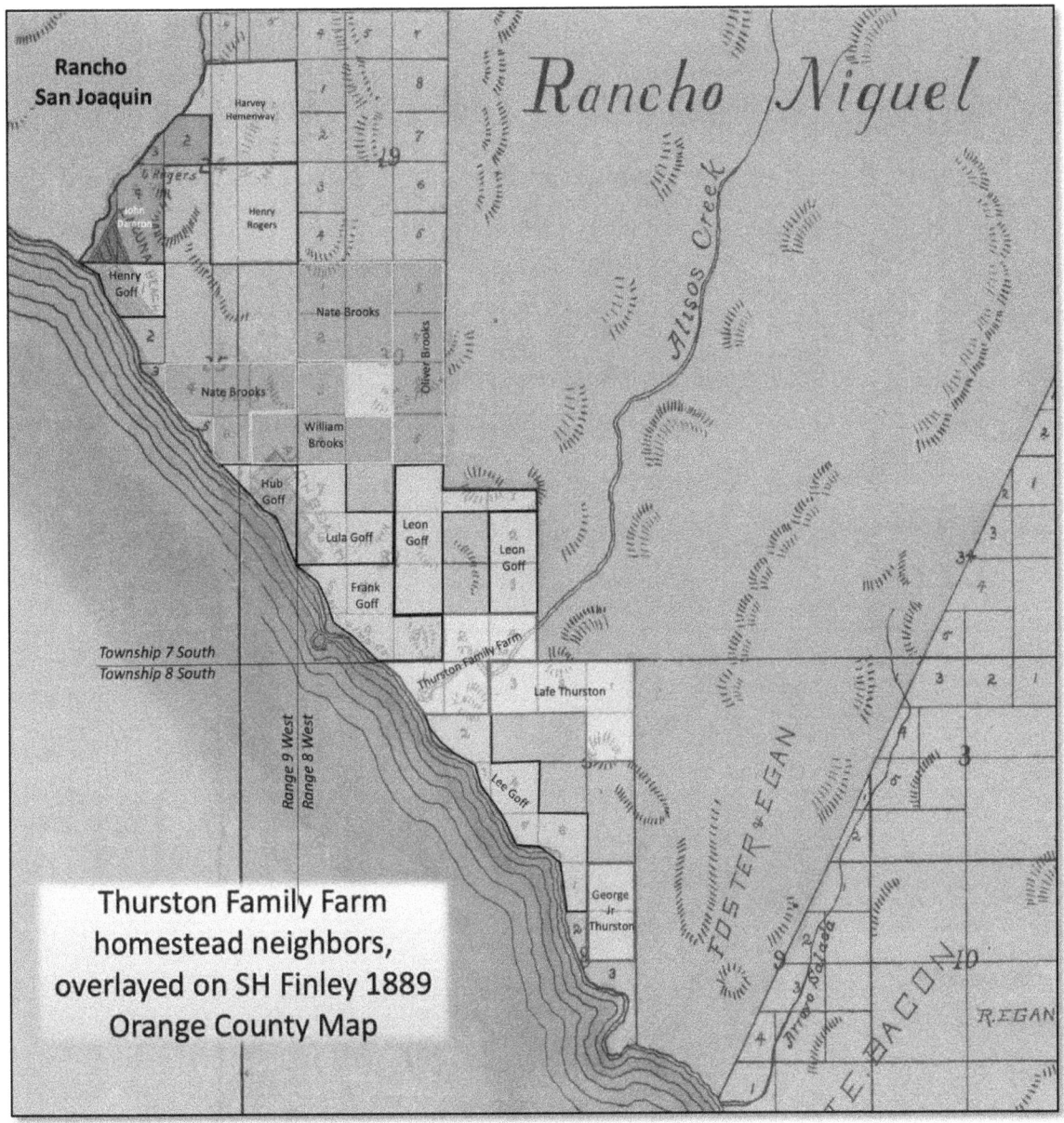

Figure 10 Homesteading Neighbors Near the Thurston Farm [8]
Brooks Families (Nate, Oliver, William), Goff Families (Lee, Frank, Henry, Hub), Rogers, Hemenway, Damron

A Calamity

About the time Frank Goff settled in Laguna, Father bought George a little saddle mare named Mollie for which he paid thirty dollars, George expecting to repay him in labor after he became of age. By trading around George secured a used saddle for her giving ten or twelve dollars in value, and was proud and happy in his new possession.

Old Man Wood used to come down occasionally to fish with George. Between them there was a good natured rivalry as to which could catch the most fish. Usually it was George who won in the contest, for he was by far the best fisherman and caught three or four times as many as Wood.

One summer day after the hay—consisting of alfalfa, alfilaree and barley—was all harvested and stacked together in one immense haystack out near the pig pen, Wood came down bringing with him another man named Hamilton, to go fishing with George. The sea was rough, the fishing rather poor, and they all got pretty wet, but caught enough so that they had plenty of fried fish for supper, which Mother cooked and served to the whole crowd. As it was late these two men crawled into the haystack and camped for the night. Hamilton was not a smoking man but Wood was an inveterate smoker. However, when he tried to light his pipe that night, the matches would not burn, for he had gotten them wet while fishing. He would scratch them and throw them down in disgust until unlighted matches were lying about everywhere. In the morning the men arose, had more fried fish for breakfast, and went home.

The next day, George, riding Mollie, went away somewhere, and on his return along about dinnertime he unsaddled his horse, put the saddle under one end of the haystack for shelter from the hot sun, and went in to dinner. Scarcely were they all seated at the table, when a loud crackling noise was heard. The family all rushed out of the house and saw to their horror that the haystack was on fire. The sun had dried out Wood's wet matches and they had ignited. It is possible that George might have stepped on one of them unknowingly causing it to smolder and burst into flame after he had gone into the house. The cause of the fire was discovered only after other unburnt matches had been found lying about. George, by quick action, succeeded in saving his saddle, but the whole stack—all their winter-feed, was a total loss.

Father fairly "tore his hair" in dismay.

"What will the poor horses do now? All their whole year's feed is burned up!" wailed Mother.

Artemisia was so tender of heart that she could not stand the sight of it, but ran crying down toward the creek. The horror of the cruel fire was too much for her. Lafe followed to offer what comfort he could; but suffering from nerve-shock she wept uncontrollably for some time. Indeed it was a harrowing experience for the whole family; and a bitter loss—one they could ill afford.

Wood offered no compensation to them for his carelessness, and after that came no more to Aliso to visit with them.

CHAPTER 20 BABY CHARLOTTE

Soon after Frank Goff settled on the mesa, before our young people and theirs had become well acquainted with one another, Baby Charlotte was born. About that time the whooping cough was going the rounds in the community and had a run in our home. Tiny Baby Charlotte took it when she was six weeks old. It was pitiful to see the little thing torn and wrenched day after day with that terrible strangling cough. Even after all the rest of us were recovered it would not leave her but lingered month after month, its dreadful paroxysms almost choking her to death. Father and Mother were fearful of losing her; but at last, after long anxiety and careful nursing, she pulled through— snatched, as it were, from the jaws of death; and the little darling became the pet of the family.

Everybody loved little Charlotte—so sweetly serious, so unselfish, so patient, and so anxious to please everyone. Nor was she ever obliged to surrender her place in our affections to the next on-coming infant; Charlotte always remained a family favorite. As for me, I fairly worshiped her.

Almost every infant sucks either a finger or a thumb; but Baby Charlotte sucked her fist. She would double it up tight and suck away at it, drawing it partially into her mouth. But one time she sucked in the whole fist and could not get it out again. In vain Father and Mother tried to draw out her hand, they could not get her to unfold the fist. She kept it doubled up tight, and was in a great predicament. Finally Father had to insert his own finger, stretching her little mouth unmercifully, to force her fingers open—with no little grief on her part, before he could draw out her hand.

Everything she got hold of went into her mouth. And everything that went into her mouth and could be swallowed disappeared down the long lane. She once put in a nail, and it went down; she put pins into her mouth as she had seen Mother do, and they went down; at least, supposedly. When she told Mother she had swallowed some pins, there was a great hubbub over it. No such thing as X-rays had ever yet been conceived in the wildest dreams of man; so there was no sure way of locating the pins. As no harm came of it, they concluded she had never swallowed them.

But the most preposterous thing that ever followed this peristaltic path did so because of the folly of someone else. Father, who suffered much from aching and decaying teeth, and was beginning to realize that he must have them out, one day went to Santa Ana to have an aching tooth pulled, taking Mother and the baby along. The dentist worked hard to get this tooth out; for all Father's teeth were difficult and painful to pull; because of great hooked prongs deeply embedded in the jaw bone.

After it was out and the bleeding stopped, and the family were preparing to return home, Father picked up this large ugly pronged tooth in his fingers and held it up before the baby's face, saying facetiously: "How would you like to have a tooth like that in your little mouth? Eh? Let me see how it fits!" He expected Charlotte to shrink away, of course; and had not the least intention of getting any nearer with it. But serious little Charlotte, not grasping the playful intent, obediently opened her mouth wide. This invited Father to carry the play a little farther than he had intended; and on the spur of the moment he put his thumb and forefinger holding the tooth into the center of the cavity, expecting to withdraw it without contacting the walls. But it is the unexpected happening that frustrates the best of intentions. Just at that instant, Father lost control of the situation and the tooth slipped out of his fingers; Baby Charlotte gave an involuntary gulp at the same time; and before he could regain it, the thing slipped down her little gullet—leaving Father distressed and foolish, and Mother disgusted and angry; "but all the king's horses and all the king's men" couldn't pull the thing out again; and for once, a scathing rebuke from Mother elicited no retort from Father.

Father must have been somewhat of a Spartan. Being so far from town and the dentist, and having so little money for extra expenses, when he learned that all his teeth had to come out, he determined to pull them himself. So he bought a pair of forceps, took them home, and began to pull his own teeth. He went out to the lone sycamore tree, and tying his head to the trunk to hold it steady, proceeded to extract those deeply embedded and hooked-pronged molars and grinders that it would have taken a strong-armed dentist to get out.

None of us ever was able to comprehend how he could have the grit to do it, and we children would stand around at a distance and watch wonderingly. Day after day he would repeat this performance pulling out a few at a time, till finally they were all extracted to the last one.

Then for a long time he was toothless before being able to have plates made. During this time he learned to eat apples of which he was very fond, by scraping them out of their halves with a table knife, after cutting them in two crosswise around the middle. When he would have finished there would be left only the peeling in a smooth half shell each with a bit of stripped core standing up in the center. In due course of time he had his plates, and then the real troubles commenced; for dentistry then and dentistry today are two very different things.

When less than two years old Baby Charlotte had another very serious illness; and again came very near the gates of death. We called it "lung fever;" but today it is spelled "pneumonia." When she was up and out of bed again, she had forgotten how to talk or how to laugh. No amount of coaxing could get her to do either. We would stand her up on the top of the little brass-bound trunk that stood about twelve or fourteen inches from the floor, and beg her to laugh for us; saying persuasively:

"Now laugh, Baby, laugh!"

She would look at us soberly with big round serious eyes and then in an effort to please, with a queer little tune-like rising and falling inflection and never the hint of a smile, would say:

"Laffy-laf, laffy-laf, laf, laf, laf."

"No, no, Baby. Laugh like this," we would coax, imitating a hearty laugh.

With that same serious wondering expression on her face, still unsmiling, but desiring greatly to please us, she would repeat in the same manner the same little sing-song lingo:

"Laffy-laf, laffy-laf, laf, laf, laf," and that was all we could get out of her for many weeks.

How relieved and happy we all were when once again our darling began to talk and laugh like her own sweet self!

As soon as we children became old enough to carry a small bucket of water, we were expected to keep the kitchen supplied from the creek for dishwashing and scrubbing. One day Mother sent Annie and me, each with a five-pound lard bucket, down to the creek for water; and Baby Charlotte, between two and three years old, accompanied us. The big cart-road gate at the little hill point which we were obliged to pass through had a disagreeable way of swinging shut when we wanted it to stay open. To avoid the labor of opening this gate twice, we left little Charlotte standing there to hold it open for us until we should dip our water and return. We went on down to the creek, and as we bent over the water intending to dip in our buckets, something interesting attracted our attention. We paused to watch it for awhile. Perhaps it was a beetle, or a water-bug—I have forgotten; there were so many interesting things to observe in that creek—in fact, so many, that we set our buckets down unfilled and began unconsciously to play—for play is second nature to children. We soon forgot all about dipping up the water—forgot Mother's need of it—forgot the open gate and little Charlotte. One thing led to another—and there was no end to the fascinating things to be seen and done in that most wonderful of all natural playgrounds; so, oblivious of all responsibilities, with no sense of the passing of time, we played on and on till the fleeting moments lengthened into an hour and longer. Then we were suddenly and rudely shocked to our senses by the shrill sound of Mother's voice hallooing for us from the front porch of the house. We jumped up quickly and guiltily; dipped up our water, and fearful of punishment, hurried back to the gate. There—remembering her only when we saw her—we found dear, patient, weary little Charlotte still standing without a protest, faithfully holding the gate open for us. How ashamed we were! The severe scolding that fell to our lot seemed to us too light a punishment for what we had done. Mother never knew about little Charlotte. We had begged her not to tell.

"You won't tell Ma, will you?" we had pleaded.

"No," she promised; and she never did.

Eagerly we would watch for the first ripe fig in summer. As the season drew near, down we would go to the orchard every day or so to hunt for ripening figs. One day Annie, Charlotte and I were playing in the sand along by the willows at the edge of the orchard under the lovely acacia trees when I thought of this quest for figs. Already earlier in the day we had searched those trees near at hand without results; and suddenly I suggested to Annie that we run down to the fig orchard to see if there were any figs getting ripe. Annie instantly agreed, but we didn't want to take Charlotte along. She was too little to run so far and we thought she would be too much bother and impede our progress. So we tried to induce her to go to the house; but she refused to budge. She wanted to go with us down to the far-away fig orchard; so finally deciding we would have to take her along, we started out.

Wading the creek, to the opposite fence, we crawled under and crossed the vineyard, followed the footpath along the base of the mountain and reaching the orchard, began our search for the first ripe fig of the season. Walking about under the trees craning our necks this way and that with upturned searching eyes ready to interpret favorably any tinge of black that might be revealed, we passed from row to row. Finally, high up overhead, I spied a fig that was turning black. At my shout: "I see one!" the others came running to look.

Sure enough, it appeared to be the first ripe fig; but how were we to get it? We had been strictly forbidden to climb the fruit trees for fear of breaking the laden branches—and I suppose, our own limbs as well. But we simply must have that fig.

Figure 11 Annie, Harriet and Charlotte, 1895

Who could resist the urge to secure the first ripe fig of the season? So up I went, shinnying the trunk to the first bough, and from there climbed up to the one that stretched out toward the coveted prize. But this, proving to be too low to reach the twig on which it grew, I sidled back, holding onto other branches, and climbed up onto a limb that was higher still, from which I hoped to reach the tempting fig that hung just out of reach.

But alas! This limb proved to be too slender to support my weight, and down I came, branch and all, tumbling ignominiously to the soft plowed ground beneath. They did not inquire: "Are you hurt?" but both exclaimed: "Oh, you broke a limb!" That was the greatest concern of us all—that broken limb. What should we do? There lay the tell-tale limb, mute evidence of deliberate disobedience; if we should hide it in the brush of the hillside, still there was the gaping, juice-dripping wound in the tree that Father would be sure to discover the first thing; then would follow the inquisition in which the truth would be ferreted out; and the threatened whipping for disobedience would follow—all the more surely for the attempted concealment; for a lie was the capital offense. There was nothing to do but tell him about it and take the punishment—and how Father did wield a whip!

While thus deliberating suddenly we heard the loud call for dinner; and reluctantly rose to go—the fig that had caused all our trouble utterly forgotten in face of this calamity. Charlotte was Father's favorite. If interceded for by this gentle little pet, the sentence might be commuted to standing on a box in a corner—a frequent penalty for minor offenses, and the greatest concession I could hope to secure. So in my distress I turned to her imploringly:

"You tell Pa about it for me, won't you, and ask him not to whip me?"

"I will," she promised, and the dread of the homeward journey was lessened by this hope of possible leniency.

When we reached the house Charlotte went in and hung around for awhile to gather the necessary courage. Father was sitting in a comfortable chair waiting for dinner to be dished up onto the table. Finally she went up to the side of his chair, and looking up into his face with her big serious eyes said persuasively:

"Pa, Harriet broke a limb; but you won't whip her, will you?"

Father was so amused at the simple eloquence of her plea that he picked her up, and only laughed about the matter; and thankful Harriet didn't get any punishment at all—not even a reprimand. Then, how glad was I that Charlotte had accompanied us to the fig orchard! It is wonderful to have a mediator—an advocate who is in high favor with the dispenser of justice.

At another time little Charlotte became responsible for my receiving an unjust punishment. While playing alone one day up at the corncrib, attempting to climb the wall by inserting fingers and toes between the slats as she had seen us older ones do, she had accidentally broken one of the slats. Father discovered it afterward, and knowing that I frequently climbed the wall, asked me if I had broken the slat. I denied knowing anything about it; which was perfectly true. He then questioned Frank and Annie, each of whom made the same denial, and furnished satisfactory alibis. Mentally limiting the possible culprits to us three, and having satisfied himself that neither of them was the guilty party he made up his mind that I was lying—the unpardonable offense. A slat might be mended; but a lie permanently marred the character—unless properly whipped out of the system. So, having not even thought of Charlotte as a possible element in the case—she being too young to climb the wall, Father sent me to the pepper tree to get a switch; for it was his custom when administering a whipping, to send the condemned to get his own instrument of chastisement.

In vain did I protest my innocence; this only made my predicament the worse. He was not punishing me, he explained, sternly, for breaking the slat, but for lying about it; and whip me he did, as only he knew how. To be punished as a liar—to be utterly unable to establish my innocence in the eyes of anyone, was more than I could bear. The whipping was a lesser calamity. But Father never did learn the truth about it, and I sobbed out my rebellious grief without redress.

Timid little Charlotte, the victim of intense and exaggerated fear of the physical punishment (from which she probably would have been exempt in any case), though conscience stricken, was utterly tongue-tied, and could not bring herself to confess her guilt. So she let the opportunity pass, only to worry over it for many months—even years. Over-severity in dealing with children is as much to be deplored for its evil effects as over-laxness in discipline. Punishments well deserved are soon forgotten; but parental injustice rankles long in the heart, and is never completely erased from memory, and "fear makes cowards of us all."

When the time came for potato planting often all hands would be called upon to cut seed potatoes. Then with our paring knives and buckets we would gather around the tub into which a sack had been emptied, ready for the cutting bee. Now as every country boy and girl knows, there is a right way and a wrong way to cut seed potatoes. Each piece must contain at least one or two good strong "eyes" from which the sprout is to start. Otherwise the plant will be weak; or else there will be no plant at all.

At one of these cutting bees, we children who were old enough to understand this principle, were squatting around the tub with our knives cutting potatoes ready for the planting, when little Charlotte came around wanting to help too. She had never cut seed potatoes before; but was sure she could do it. So Joseph showed her how it was done, and she took her paring knife and started in. At first she did it so well that Joseph praised her for her good work. Then we all began to praise her and to talk about how wonderfully she was doing—thinking that she knew why her work was good. But little Charlotte only half understood the principle; and for the most part it was only a "happen so" that her cutting was so satisfactory. She got the idea that it was because of her fast work that she was being commended, and began to increase her speed to secure more of that good-sounding commendation.

Then Nate Brooks happened along, and stopped to chat; and we began to tell him what a good potato-cutter Charlotte had become, and how apt she had been at learning. This praise went to her little head; and she began to cut so fast that even we older ones couldn't keep up with her; and her pile increased rapidly to a very big one.

Then Nate reached down and picked up a handful of her cut pieces and began to examine them. He called Joseph's attention to the manner in which they were being cut; and Joseph too examined them. Then little Charlotte was greatly humbled before our visitor and before us all; for none of the potatoes cut after the praise had grown exciting, were done right. Even the eyes were often cut across through the middle, and some chunks had no eyes at all.

116

So commendation was changed to condemnation, and poor little Charlotte was sent away from the job in disgrace; her little balloon deflated like a "flat tire"—only there were no such things as "flat tires" in those days—for nearly all that big pile she had cut was wasted, and had to be sorted carefully before any of them could be planted.

Once, when the ripe beans had all been harvested and threshed, there was left piled up in the yard, a large stack of bean straw—that is, dry, empty, crushed pods and vines—which remained there for several weeks. One evening at the supper table Frank and Charlotte were missing from their places. Anxious inquiry elicited the information that they had last been seen playing out by the bean straw stack. They were called; but no answer came. A search was begun; but they could not be found anywhere on the premises. The whole family became alarmed; for it was getting late and darkness would soon be falling. From one end to the other the farm was searched in vain. The searchers would call and listen; but no answer would come back. Darkness fell; hours went by. Mother was becoming frantic. Lights were left streaming from open doors and windows in the hope that the missing children, lost in the darkness, might see the light and by this means find their way home. It was nine o'clock at night; the distracted family was returning from every possible extreme of the farm unsuccessful. Loudly they shouted—this time nearer the house whither their fruitless search was culminating. Disturbed by the shouting at last, the two children, unconscious of the furor they had caused, awakened and came crawling out from under the bean-straw stack, where all this time they had lain sound asleep. They had been playing they were pigs, they said, and had rooted around the stack picking up stray beans; and finding a loose place, had crawled in under the pile way out of sight and had lain down. It was so much fun in there that they stayed, and fell fast asleep.

One day, not long after this, Charlotte came in to Mother boasting that she had "swallowed more beans than Frank." Upon questioning, it was discovered that the two had been "running a race" to see which could swallow the most dry beans; and both of them had disposed of as many as they could chuck down their gullets. The next interesting event in their lives was two huge doses of castor oil—not disguised with orange juice and sugar—oh, no, just plain castor oil; for then they knew of no other way to give it.

We were all shy of strangers and bashful to painfulness; blushing at the least provocation; yet even the most timid could not resist the inclination to "show off" before company. Little Charlotte was just about as shy as a child could be—absolutely tongue-tied when addressed by a stranger; yet even she was not immune to this temptation.

One day a lady camper came up from the beach to buy some eggs, bringing with her two little girls near Charlotte's age. Timid as a little deer, Charlotte would not speak a word even to the children; but still felt that somehow she must entertain them. Hospitality demanded some demonstration to show she appreciated their visit. The front door into the kitchen was closed, but the back door, exactly opposite, was open; and the company sat facing this door-to-door runway.

Charlotte went out the back door and up the sloping yard for some little distance above the house, then turning ran at top speed down the slope, through the open door, and on across the room, coming to a stop with her body against the closed front door. This performance she repeated three or four times in breathless succession; all the while soliloquizing in her little boastful heart: "My! Those girls will think I'm a fast runner!" But, as the Good Book says: "pride goeth before a fall." On the last run, just as she came pell-mell into the room through the kitchen door, she stumbled and fell ignominiously to the floor flat on her "tummy" in front of them all; with which unexpected and humiliating climax, the entertainment came to an abrupt end; and little crestfallen Charlotte slunk away and hid herself out of sight till the visitors were gone.

CHAPTER 21 MAJOR IMPROVEMENTS

During the period of litigation when strenuous efforts were being made to close the canyon road, Father, fearing that at any time he might be effectively excluded from the spring on the Rawson property, realized that the time had come when he must find some other source of water supply.

Again he went up to the spot on the hillside above the filaree pasture where water oozed slowly from a crevice between embedded rocks, to study the possibility of developing water there. He brought his neighbors over, Hub Goff, the carpenter, and Mc Manus the miner, to examine the site and counsel with him.

All agreed that sufficient water might be obtained by tunneling into the mountainside, so, engaging their help, he began preparations for the undertaking. The first thing to be done was build a wagon road from the pasture up to the location, then with plenty of dynamite, picks and shovels, he and George with these two men, began blasting out the great rock-formation that extended far back into the mountain.

The farther in they went, the more water they found, and thus encouraged, kept at the work until a tunnel thirty or more feet in length and about six or eight feet in diameter had been blasted out of the solid rock, with a basin-shaped floor to catch and hold the water that now trickled into it from all sides and dripped from the ceiling, until an abundance of pure, clear, cold water flowing into the basin proclaimed the undertaking in every way successful.

The next thing was to pipe the water thus obtained around the mountain and down to the proximity of the farmhouse, nearly half a mile distant. This done, Hub built for Father, a round wooden water storage tank sufficiently large to hold all the water he would need to store for domestic use, and set it up on a framework near the woodpiles by the roadside. It did not occur to him that he might have set the tank on a high standard at the upper side of the house and piped the water into the kitchen. Such luxuries in the country were so rare as to be outside the ordinary man's calculations. So we drew it from a spigot and carried it up the slope to the house in our buckets. And thus was completed the most important improvement on the farm.

Near this tank where it might benefit from drippings and overflow, as an experiment, Father planted a little orange tree. In spite of the canyon's frosty winters and the lack of attentions required by citrus fruits, this tree grew and thrived luxuriantly, becoming a thing of evergreen beauty.

There was one unfortunate drawback to mar the general elation over this procurement of domestic water. Though cold and sanitary, it was not pleasant to the taste, but reeked with the flavor of iron, and we could never accustom ourselves to its use for drinking purposes. So we continued to haul drinking water from the spring on the Rawson property for about a year longer till we had built a cistern.

Because of its mineral content, the water from our new spring made very poor wash water also. It first had to be "broken" with lye, which was very hard on hands. Even then soap when cooked in it formed a thick cheesy curd over the top that had to be skimmed off before using, which wasted a great deal of soap. The tin basin at the wash bench collected this curd mixed with dirt from the hands to form a hard offensive ring that had continually to be scraped off.

The Octagon Barn

The next major improvement on the farm was the building of our big octagon barn. After the burning of the haystack, it seemed more than ever imperative that we have some place for the safe storage of as finances made it possible, the project was launched.

The lumber for this building was shipped by water about four hundred miles from San Francisco to Newport, and there unloaded onto the pier, where Father and George reloaded it onto the wagon and hauled it by team to Aliso, a distance of between thirty-five and forty miles, making several trips.

The site selected for the barn lay at the bottom of the gentle down grade northward from the dwelling, and the fence, here following straight alongside the road, was taken down and reset to curve around behind the proposed buildings, leaving room also for a future cistern.

There being no level spot for the floor on the sharp slope between road and mountain, excavation became necessary, which left a high curved bank behind the barn, topped by the corral fence, and later by a flourishing row of olive trees which Father set out along the curve just outside the enclosure.

Having decided on the octagon shape as being more roomy than any other, besides lending itself admirably to the location, Father again secured the help of Hub Goff to erect this large building. I suppose there never was another barn built quite like this one. Each of the eight sides approximated fourteen feet. The roof correspondingly lay in eight triangular sections, the. long points of which met at the center peak, from which all rafters radiated to the eaves. It was supported centrally from ground to peak by a hollow pillar a foot square, on two opposing sides of which were nailed at brief intervals up its whole length, short strong cross-pieces with projecting ends, to serve as a double ladder.

One of the eight sides paralleled the road, and against this front, a lean-to stable was built, opening onto the roadway, with stalls, mangers and feed boxes to accommodate four horses. Four window openings with hinged wooden doors provided feeding convenience from barn to manger.

The two sides adjacent to the stable were each pierced by large double doors for entrance and exit of the hay racks in harvest time that were driven straight through after unloading, leaving more than half of the floor space available for storage of hay. But seldom was this ample space completely filled.

The barn was finished in time for the on-coming grain crop, and with the first harvest that ever went into it there was born an era of joy for us little folks. Playing on the haymow became our major sport. Oh, what pure delight to tumble and roll about in the deep, soft, sweet-smelling new mown hay! All other amusements were eclipsed. Sometimes the hay was piled so high that after we had climbed the pillar to the top of the mow our heads could touch the ceiling as it lowered toward the eaves. Or, by climbing the ladder a little farther we might reach the center peak itself, and from their jump down onto the soft bank of hay, that bounced us back like rubber balls. Oh, what fun was this! And how we enjoyed sliding down the steep side of the stack onto the ground floor, carrying with us a mass of hay! But this we endeavored to replace by carrying it back up the ladder, or if unable would stuff it into the mangers through the window doors. For Father did not like us to knock the hay down.

We would play we were animals and burrow into the stack, or carry old quilts up the ladder and play we were sleeping on the hay. For some time the boys had their beds there and we could play sleep on their quilts.

Sometimes, close to the eaves inside, we found clinging to the beams head downward, by the claws under their wing-joints, little furry bats that darted swiftly away at our touch, wheeling about back and forth for awhile in the semi-darkness of the big barn, then alighting again at some other spot out of our reach. Occasionally we would catch one of them, to be greeted by faint mouse-like squeaks and bitten by the tiniest of teeth, fine as those of a baby's comb. This didn't hurt much, and we thought it a small price to pay for the fun of holding them just for a few moments, stroking their soft, lustrous, mouse-colored fur and examining their queerly constructed bodies. We never hurt them, for bats were our friends, destroying many disagreeable insect pests.

Near the mangers, leaning in the corners, were pitchforks of which we must beware. Mother had so often warned us about these, exaggerating the danger, that we really thought pitchforks meant death itself.

One day we were playing in the barn, Annie and I on the hay mow, jumping from the center ladder, and Charlotte being too little for that, playing on hay that had fallen to the floor. In her play she accidentally ran against one of the terrible pitchforks, scratching her foot a little, enough to draw blood. The pain was nothing, but her fear was terrible, and expressed in blood-curdling screams. Had not Mother told us repeatedly that pitchforks would kill us if we got stuck with them? Charlotte believed herself doomed to die. Annie and I, judging by her screams that she was already half killed, were as scared as she.

Hastening to her assistance, and supposing that she must not be allowed to walk, we made a "cross-cradle" with our arms to carry her home. Mother and Joan, hearing the rumpus, thought only of rattlesnakes, and ran out of the house toward the barn, sure that someone must have been bitten.

At the first corner of the cow corral they met us carrying Charlotte, and hearing our pitchfork story, made examination. Upon discovering how slight was the wound, though relieved, they were decidedly irritated, and made Charlotte get down and walk the rest of the way home. But the real cause of her terrified outcry they never did divine.

Another example of exaggerated fear was our attitude toward spiders. We seemed to gather from Mother's repeated cautions, the idea that all spiders were deadly, and that to be bitten by one was comparable to being bitten by a rattler.

One day Charlotte and I were down in the cart-road playing at the foot of the little hill, when she began to whimper, saying something was biting her on the back of her neck. I looked, and there was a tiny spider crawling along at the spot indicated. My terror knew no bounds. To me a spider bite meant almost certain death. I began to cry and call for help, with some heroism brushing off the spider. My crying frightened Charlotte, who now joined in, due, I thought to increasing pain from the bite.

I led little Charlotte homeward by the hand as fast as she could toddle, screaming at the top of my voice:

"A spider bit her! A spider bit her!"

Our frightened elders ran out of the house to meet us scared half to death—and all over what? The innocent spider had probably merely crawled across her neck, the unpleasant sensation causing her uneasiness. Fear alone—unreasonable fear—had done the rest.

The Cistern

A few months after the building of the barn and in time for the conservation of the winter's rainfall, Father began work on the cistern, employing Lee Goff, who by this time had settled on the coast. An octagon container twelve feet deep was excavated and plastered with mortar, and an octagon room built over it, having a trap door into the cistern through the floor with a ladder leading down, and a door and window opening toward the roadway.

On the side next to the barn, was constructed a hopper-like arrangement with a spout leading into it from the trough that extended all around the eaves of the big barn, by which water from the skies was caught and conveyed to the cistern. Beside it near the window, a platform was built and a hand pump installed where buckets were to be filled from the cistern.

The pump, being second hand, developed a leaky valve that had to be coaxed by priming. Forgetting to bring with us a little water for priming, meant an extra trip back to the tank by the woodpile. Mother used to say to us:

"Make your head save your heels."

The first rains of the season were never allowed to enter the cistern. The dust and leaves that had collected on the roof and in the eaves trough must first be washed off. After this, the connecting spout was attached and the rainwater fell into the hollow emptiness of the cistern with a musical tinkle. This we were not often privileged to hear, since rainy weather usually found us under shelter of the home roof, but when occasion afforded, would listen eagerly to this enchanting sound of muffled music echoing up from the depths of the cistern.

In spite of all precautionary measures, some dirt was sure to get inside, and at long intervals the cistern had to be cleaned out and thoroughly scrubbed, a time being chosen when the water was low.

The room above became the boys' bedroom, the first Lafe and Joseph had ever known. Up to this time there had seemed to be no settled place for them to sleep except to bunk around in sheds and haystacks, and more recently, on the hay in the barn. Where they kept their private possessions is a mystery. Now at last they had a real bedroom of their own, not very large, to be sure, but at least private, where they might hang their clothes about the walls and keeps their boxes under the bed and their guns in the corner.

Whenever we spoke of "the cistern," we always meant this room, either with or without the water container underneath it. There, the boys practically lived. I used to wonder why they didn't make an effort to keep it clean. At long intervals the older girls would come down with their brooms and mops to make a general war on dirt. Perhaps they should have done this more often, but it seemed quite hopeless. Within a few days it was as bad as ever. "Boys are funny," I thought, "Disorder doesn't seem to bother them a bit."

But the boys did keep their guns clean. One day, down in this cistern room, Lafe, thinking his gun was not loaded, attempted to clean it. All of a sudden the gun went off. The bullet, passing close to his face, shot through the brim of his hat and crashed through the windowpane. This was only one of the many "thrillers" that hastened the gray in Mother's hair.

At another time Joseph was cleaning his gun in the kitchen, when the cleaning rod, tightly wedged in by the little square of cloth used on the end of it, got stuck in the barrel. Lafe was called upon to help get it out. Remembering his former experience, he asked:

"Are you sure it isn't loaded?"

Joseph assured him it was not.

So, with Lafe holding the rod and Joseph holding the stock, they pulled and jerked the gun all over the room—the little folks standing about watching. Still it wouldn't come out. Lafe had an inspiration. Taking the gun out of doors, he thrust the stock between heavy board slats that were nailed across the openings below the porch floor, and with this firm purchase, pulled and jerked on the cleaning rod in the barrel till it was dislodged. Then, upon further examination, it was discovered that all this time the gun had been loaded. Two boys, about that time, looked and felt very foolish.

From the time we began to catch rainwater in the cistern, we ceased to haul drinking water from the spring in Wood Canyon, and the water barrels disappeared from the porch at the end of Mother's room.

As Interpreted by Children

During the years that Father was having all his legal trouble with Rawson, Annie and I were too young to know what it was all about. Charlotte was born in the midst of it. Our ideas of the man himself were most hazy. It is doubtful if we had ever seen him. But our ears, like those of the proverbial "little pitchers" were wide open.

How many times had we heard that dreaded name associated with such awful and fearsome words as "land-grabber" and "prosecution," which, though unintelligible as Egyptian hieroglyphics, struck terror to our souls! No hydra-headed monster of the briny deep was ever more to be feared than Rawson, the land-grabber, and we didn't propose ever to get near enough to him to be "grabbed."

These exaggerated ideas were of course unknown to our elders, for the way of children is to take for granted as fact, the fiction created by their own feelings, and leave to chance discovery the revelation of their "inner-workings."

One day we three—the eldest probably past five—were playing behind the newly-built cistern, just inside the cow corral, when we heard on the road from the direction of the pasture, the rattle of approaching wheels. Peering out toward the roadway, of which a partial view was obtainable between barn and cistern, we beheld on its way to the house, a light spring wagon with two men in it, and gun between them leaning against the seat.

"Oh look!" I whispered, "There's a wagon with two men in it and they've got guns!"

Annie, looking too, suggested in a voice of suppressed terror:

"Oh, maybe it's Rawson!"

"Maybe it is!" I echoed, adding with sudden conviction: "I'll bet that's who it is!" Then, together:

"Let's run for our lives!"

We each gripped a hand of baby Charlotte, now thoroughly frightened, and dragging her after us, ran scrambling to the upper side of the cow pasture where the end fence was strung alongside a big gulch, and crawled through under the barbed wires, in our endeavor to keep as far as possible from the roadway and our mortal enemy.

Now, outside the corral, gathering terror with every step, we made our way, clambering through sage brush and rocks, around the hill in the general direction of the corncribs, but keeping some distance above the usual passage trails, the fence with its cactus row, and Gable Rock. Passing far above the cribs, rock wall and pepper row, across the snake infested hillside area where rocks had rolled down from the cliff some six years before—a region strictly forbidden us—we gained in time, the gully at their farther end that passed behind the honey house on its way from cliff to creek.

At this limiting gully, we began cautiously to descend the slope, headed for the safe shelter of the honey house where, from vantage ground we hoped to be able unseen to watch the enemy. As we drew near, the end door being wide open, we almost ran into the arms of the "two men with guns," who, with Father, were sitting around a little table engaged in a lively argument over "politics," wholly unaware of the furor they had caused in three little breasts.

Soon after the completion of these major enterprises, an attempt was made to irrigate the cart-road garden by water to be obtained from the neighboring creek. Hub Goff was again the chief engineer and builder. A well was dug alongside the cart road, which filled with water to the creek level, and over it a windmill was built, with an elevated tank to receive the water that should be drawn up.

Unfortunately, this venture was not a success. The height of the nearby little hill overtopped the windmill and shut off the breezes from operating the fan wheel, and it stood, a monument of money and time wasted, until, after a number of years, it was torn down.

The Winery

About this time, Father was hard put to find a suitable market for the grapes. The vineyard was now supplying far more than we could use ourselves, but there seemed no opportunity to dispose of the surplus.

Some of the brewers about Anaheim advised him to manufacture wine of the grapes. He had no experience in this line, but felt that he must do something to make his vineyard pay, so another enterprise was launched. Again Hub Goff was called into action to construct a winery with its accompanying vats and tanks.

This building was attached as a lean-to to the lower corncrib, having only a dirt floor, and was finished, furnished, and ready for the incoming vintage. Our grapes, being unirrigated, had a very rich delicious flavor, and though really a wine grape, made a fine table grape. The wine made from them brought compliments from all who used it.

We did not use the product of the winery in our own home. Every member of the family considered it simply a means of income, and not a proper beverage to use. Even Father, who in its manufacture made several different kinds of wines and brandy, and was obliged to taste in sampling the different flavors, kept himself from over-indulgence. Once or twice in his experience, he got too much, but was ashamed of the fact, laying it to unwise sampling.

He was making brandy one day when Lafe came around and acted as though he would like to have some. Father offered him a taste, and handed him a small glass. Lafe took one swallow, and almost choked. It burned his throat all the way down, and nothing could induce him to touch the stuff again. Father laughed. Perhaps that was the effect he expected and desired.

At the end of the winery, Father built also an elevated cider press for the purpose of utilizing the small and windfall apples, which augmented our income from the apple orchard. The cider, too, was not used by the family after becoming hard, but only when fresh and sweet.

CHAPTER 22 THE HOUSE OF MY MEMORY

Dear little old house of my childhood, where are you? Once, I knew you so well, so intimately. Why do you hide from me now? I cannot find you with my eyes open. Too many other things have filled my vision since you went out of my life. I close my eyelids tightly together to shut out every ray of present light, then the picture begins to form. It grows slowly and surely, details appear, and at last, there you are all complete from the knot holes in the floor to the canvas ceiling overhead with all its sooty pictures that looked at me every night from above my trundle bed in the corner of Mother' s room.

I see the swing-shelf hanging, where Mother kept choice delicacies not meant for every day, but only for special occasions, perhaps Christmas, or Thanksgiving, or it might be some family home-coming. There were raisins, coconut, home-made cookies, a small chunk of cheese, carefully wrapped, a little bag of hard striped stick candy— yes, and dried apples. Oh, those dried apples! They never make them any more like those, so tasty, so deliciously rich flavored. All the sweet things that covetous little fingers fain would purloin and that tiny ants love to swarm over, Mother kept on that high swing-shelf suspended from the rafters above the trundle bed.

Sometimes the ant marauders would find the goodies anyway, crawling in a long stream down the fly-specked wires. Then Mother would dip little rag strings in kerosene and tie them around the wires, which never failed to turn them back from their purpose.

I can see Mother climbing up and balancing herself on the edge of the bed as she reaches over her head to take from the shelf some mysterious can needed for use. Now, she is dividing a bit of cheese, giving just tiny bits to each of the teasing little folks, or it may be, she breaks a stick of candy into small pieces to distribute.

Three of us at a time always slept in that little home-made, low-built trundle bed, with its wooden slats in place of springs, its mattress stuffed with corn husks, and its long bolster pillow in calico case, that reached clear across the bed. Frank and Annie and I all in a row, lay with our heads on this long bolster, and in emergency, such as Mother being sick, or the advent of a little new baby, then Charlotte too might be tucked in crosswise at the foot, with her head toward the wall. That was before our feet grew long enough to touch the footboard.

Mother's bed was in the corner opposite ours and they stood foot to foot with a space between wide enough for a window and under it a "toilet." Oh, I don't mean what you think. Nowadays you would call it a "dresser"—only ours was a home-made one, just a big box on its side with two or three shelves in it and curtains around ends and front, and across the top a "runner" of white muslin worked in red outline stitch. There wasn't any looking glass to this toilet, and there were no drawers. Behind it, the single-sash window slid sideways in a groove, opening onto the front porch.

Mother's bed too was homemade with slats in place of springs. Her lower "tick" was stuffed with straw instead of husks. On the top of the straw tick was a feather tick, which made her bed nice and soft. We were cautioned to be careful never to climb up onto her bed or even to lean against it hard, lest it should be "all mussed up," for a featherbed musses very easily. But we could play on the trundle bed and not hurt it a bit.

Mother made her sheets of two strips of yard-wide muslin, usually unbleached, sewed together in the middle, for then there were no mills or factories that made the wide sheeting we have today. For the most part, we used thin cotton blankets for sheets. Our bed-covers being home-made quilts. Her pillows were stuffed with home-picked goose feathers, and covered daytimes with "pillow-shams."

Around the foot and front side of the bed, tacked to its wooden frame, were long pleated "valences" that almost swept the floor so that nobody might see underneath, for "under the bed" was the family storeroom. There, many an unsightly box was hidden away, and among them, our boxes of playthings. When we crawled under to get them, we would not bump our heads, for the bed was high from the floor.

There was no clothes-closet in this room, but we never missed it, for such things were luxuries. One to a house was quite sufficient, and we had one in the "Girls Room," you see, way at the farther end of the house.

On a small stand at the head of Mother's bed, stood the little brass lamp, and above it on the wall hung a comb-case for her comb and brush. There too, on a nail, hung the almanac, open at the page of the current month. In the calendar of days was a pin sticking through the page, which Mother would change the first thing every morning to the day just dawned. This was the only way we had of keeping track of time. Should Mother forget to change the pin and not discover her omission, then we would go on one day behind the rest of the world until some chance visitor or the weekly paper, by its chronicle of events, should set us straight. But Mother did not often forget. If sick and unable to reach up to the almanac, she would call for one of us children to come and change the pin. No clock could be more faithful than she. Yet even clocks get out of order occasionally, and on rare occasions—perhaps at those times when her mind was occupied with major tragedies—even memory and habit would slip a cog.

In the end of the room was the only double window in the house. It was lifted open by pulling out two spring catches that slipped into other holes higher up. Near it was the big high-backed rocking chair in which many an infant had been rocked to sleep. Perhaps close by was a large tub of freshly washed clothes ready to be sprinkled down for ironing.

Tight up in the corner was the home-made, flat-topped chest that had served as table in many a camp. The heavy lid lifted ever so hard for little hands. Our common everyday things were mostly kept in here. A little narrow "till" across one end was filled with various small articles.

On the top of this chest was the "baby box," lined with some dainty material and filled with baby things ready for use. A tiny, very fine dandruff comb, a little soft ivory-handled brush, and a big downy puff of feathers—how I loved the feel of it on my cheek!—some sweet-smelling baby powder, a piece of a bar of castile soap, a little bottle of "sweet oil," safety-pins, diapers, bands, and a folded old woolen shawl, all helped to furnish that little box. I loved to touch and fondle these things. They were so soft, so dainty, so sweetly perfumed.

The baby had no little tub for its bath. Babies then were never put into tubs, but bathed in Mothers' laps before the fire, wrapped in something woolen—for only a little of the delicate body must be exposed at a time.

After its bath, the baby was cinched up tight in a woolen belly-band, put into a flannel shirt, a long flannel pinning blanket, fastened at the back with tiny safety pins, a long flannel petticoat fastened similarly, or sometimes over the shoulders, over this the long white skirt, daintily tucked or embroidered, and then the long white dress, made usually with a yoke. Over all these was slipped a dainty woolen jacket, after which was added for good measure, a baby blanket to protect from draughts.

Poor little infants of the long ago! I wonder if half their crying was not the result of simple discomfort from overclothing and scratching of wool on the tender skin. I am glad we know better now.

After the chest was another one-sash window in the middle of the wall, sliding as did the one opposite. Through this window we could see the foliage of "Mishie's rose bush." This was a wild single rose that George had brought down from the hills when a tiny plant and presented to Mesia, planting it there under the eaves to catch the drip. It had grown into a sturdy bush, covered in the spring with deeply pink buds that opened into paler roses. I loved that rose bush, loved to gather the beautiful buds and watch them unfold in the glass of water.

Near the window stood the big cabinet Wheeler and Wilson sewing machine with its removable box head cover, its dangerous needle that sewed little meddlesome fingers, and its tall front doors that reached to the floor, concealing the treadle, wheel-band and many drawers that we never touch.

In the last corner of the room, came the little low, flat-topped brassbound leather trunk, in which were kept all the baby clothes—not only those in daily use, but also the outgrown long things that after "shortening time" were no more needed until another infant should arrive. Long flannel petticoats beautifully embroidered in silk, white ones tucked closely for a foot or more up from the lace-edged hem, dainty much-trimmed dresses of soft material, all falling nearly to the floor when Mother held the infant in her arms, were there, with dainty little lace and ribbon-trimmed hoods and a long braid-trimmed cloak for wearing out, and many other garments soft and delicate, all carefully folded and perfumed with tiny bags of sachet powder and laid away in that little brass-bound trunk. How we loved to handle ever so tenderly and sniff its sweet-smelling contents! And always, we longed for another baby to come.

Against the last wall, with only the out-going door between it and the trundle bed, stood Mother's big oval-topped metal covered chest, strapped with bands of wood, called today a trunk. In this she kept her personal belongings, treasured keepsakes, sacred mementos, and other things too of a private nature, such as the long, tube-like metal plunger-syringe the only kind she had while raising her family. This was kept carefully wrapped in flannel to protect from corrosion.

This wonderful chest was always kept locked. How eagerly we would press around her and watch, whenever Mother opened that mysterious depository of her heart-treasures that whispered of a past we had not shared! Only at such times were we privileged to gaze upon its contents, so full of fascination for us, and then with cautions not to touch. On rare occasions we might be allowed to handle some of the more sturdy keepsakes, such as the heavy glass paper-weight, whose milk-white pedestal supported a big red rose with its bright green leaf, or the large rosy apple made of china, or, it might be the small brass magnifying glass that stood on three cunning little legs.

How profoundly we admired the two beautiful black lacquered teakwood snuff boxes that had belonged to her own mother and grandmother! One of these bore on its polished cover the portrait miniature of Adelaide, Queen of Britain, Ireland and Scotland, in her consort crown and gorgeous red and gold costume with ermine cloak.

There was a jewel box about six inches long of highly polished rosewood mahogany with ornamental cover, that locked with a tiny key, a token of Father's overseas sojourn. This held Mother's earrings, brooches and rings, and Father's gold studs; a tiny gold chatelaine pencil on its silk cord, set in the end with a topaz, a little wooden hatchet which Father had cleverly carved, and a silver souvenir teaspoon of foreign design. A tablespoon of solid silver, with matching fork, bore a presentation inscription to Grandfather Snow from the "Danish Saints," with the date, Eighteen Fifty-Five.

A roundish oblong oval-topped tin box with hinged cover, about eight by three inches, brown without and blue within, contained the little brass balance scales for weighing gold dust, a relic of gold-rush days. Six or eight tiny solid brass troy weights ranging from the smallest pennyweight fraction to one ounce filled a small compartment near one end. Each of the two brass balance pans was suspended by a triad of blue silk cords from one end of an iron cross-rod, at the center of which rose under an arched indicator, a free-moving balance-pointer that deviated from side to side with the raising or lowering of the pans. In the top was strung a double loop of the blue cord for a finger-hold.

In a very tiny tin box were kept, carefully wrapped in silk for double protection, the little gold dollar, and its mate, the tiny gold half-dollar, guarded always with special care. Down in the very bottom, stood a quart-size bottle of Eau de Cologne, tightly closed with a tall ornamental stopper. How wonderful it was to be allowed the rare, infrequent treat of one deep, delirious inhalation of that marvelous perfume!

Sometimes, in the depths of that chest, Mother had things hidden which had been purchased at different times during the year, to be laid away for Christmas. Once, entering the room as she bent over the open chest, I surprised her off guard and took a peep inside. There lay a doll. By the quick manner in which she covered it up and her gentle reprimand, I was sure the doll was intended for myself. But not until Christmas Day was my joyous anticipation confirmed.

There were likenesses too in this chest. Those of her father and mother—products of the newly invented process of daguerro-typing, were faded to a dull gray, testifying to its needed improvement. Precious tintypes were framed under glass in little black embossed leather cases about three inches square, lined with red or blue embossed plush, bordered with narrow gold braid, their covers, on small brass hinges, fastening with tiny hook and knob.

One of these tintypes was of Father alone, another of Mother, sad of face, holding infant Artemisia in her arms. Still another was of little Georgie and Sadie, mere toddlers, dressed in long sacque-like garments with pantaloons hanging down below. These pictures of the children had been taken hastily in the sickening fear of losing all three in the dreadful epidemic of dysentery which had just snatched from Mother's arms their little brother Erastus, leaving not even a likeness behind for comfort.

Mother, busy with household cares and the babe at her breast, had not noticed that he was ailing. He came up to her and standing by her knee, looked up into her face with sweet wistfulness and said:

"I love you, Ma, don't I. Ma, I love you, don't I."

The next day he was seriously ill, and died before they had time to realize his danger.

Another of these little cases contained the wedding picture of Father and Mother, seated side by side in all the promise of young manhood and womanhood, her cupped right hand nested in his. From under lightly penciled brows above an oval face, her mild blue eyes look out with a peculiarly reserved expression of wistful seriousness, heightened by rather full closed lips, which awaken conjecture as to what her thoughts might be.

Her hair is parted, as always, in the middle, but otherwise varied from the style we knew, in that it is plaited and drawn down loosely on either side, partially concealing her generous ears, and caught in a spangled net. Long pendant earrings almost touch the top of her hand-embroidered collar, fastened by a large gold brooch set with a cameo encircled by twelve garnets. A long double gold chain clasped together at the throat, falls to the waist in a graceful loop.

Her dress of heavy brocaded silk taffeta, was made from material brought home by her father—a gift from converts in Denmark to his eldest daughter, but with no thought of a wedding in mind. Unending vines with leaves and small flowers spiraling gracefully over a gray-green background, alternate one with another in gold and black that show the reverse color on the opposite surface.

The tight-fitting pointed basque is elaborately trimmed across the front in graduated pattern with narrow black velvet ribbon. Its sleeve, snug at the shoulder, then double-puffed above two widely flared ribbon-bordered flounces, is lengthened at the wrist by a dainty white undersleeve. And the full-gathered skirt, ballooning out in sharp contrast to the slender waist, suggests the lavish yards of fullness at the bottom, finished with a binding of the same black velvet ribbon.

This adorable picture was the only tangible evidence we had that Mother had ever been slender—this, and the little dress itself, which, though afterward made over in a different style, still showed a waistline so small it could be spanned by Father's two hands. Joan, several times, wore this little dress, and has it in her possession, still in a good state of preservation.

Father too is handsome, seated so proudly by his bride, with one hand possessively on her shoulder and a satisfied expression on his firm lips. Keen blue eyes, heavy brows and high forehead are framed in a wealth of wavy, jet-black hair, and under the square jaw and smooth shaven chin a very short velvety beard extends upward in slight burnsides. The conventional high stiff collar meets at his throat underneath a loosely-tied black bow that tops the white gold-studded shirt front and double-breasted vest.

Figure 12 George Thurston and Sarah Snow Wedding Picture, March 28, 1858

In this chest were other garments from Mother's trousseau, and some even dating from before her marriage, long since outgrown, all neatly folded and lad away in sweet-smelling stuff mingled with the odor of camphor gum and tobacco leaves, used then to keep out moths, for this was before modern mothballs were known. A beautiful wine-colored fine wool delaine with slightly full sleeves, featured a wide border of alternating wine and black satin stripes around the skirt-bottom, and in finer, narrower duplicate, around the low pointed neckline.

A sheer dress of superfine bordercloth with tiny white dots on a pale blue background was shirred in "empire" style, called then "infantwaisted." The self-border trimming blossomed with tiny blue and pink roses.

Two long loose sacques—which might today be called smocks—were of woolen material, finest of the fine; one a magenta color trimmed in black, the other white and elaborately embroidered in silk. These were fastened with many small white embossed eye-buttons.

There were several shawls; one a large black silk-fringed alpaca, another of soft wool shallie with a fine rose-colored flower design on a lilac background. A dainty three-cornered, loose-woven "party shawl" was covered with pink and blue roses on a gray background. This was really only half of a shawl that had originally belonged to her mother but had been cut cornerwise to divide it between Mother and her sister Artemisia. Besides these, there was the large silk Persian shawl which Mother still used on occasion, bordered and fringed in black, with its oriental palm-leaf motif patterned in bright reds, clear blues, and other fadeless colors.

There were bonnets too, one a Quaker shape made of green-and-rose changeable silk; another with wide ties to form a bow under the chin, had been fashioned from a beautiful Scotch plaid scarf which Father had brought with him from the British Isles. These charming bonnets, and with them a shiny black veil, were kept in a rust-less metal bandbox of gray color, with cover edge fitted down to three inches over the box top.

There were several dainty frocks for little folks made from other outgrown dresses. Two were of very fine dimity with tiny pink rosebuds in the pattern. Little panties made of fine white material buttoned below the knee with band and narrow ruffle of embroidery.

A very long white dainty baby dress elaborately trimmed in lace had been worn by her firstborn, and there was also a precious little orchid infant sacque that had belonged to little lost Rosetta.

Mention must be made of the talisman—the tiny baby beads kept in a little Beecham's pillbox of natural thin white wood with oval bandbox cover. These were strung anew for each baby born—a semi-solemn rite that must be performed painstakingly by hand—never with the help of a needle.

The Tea Boxes

In this treasure chest were two shiny black japanned "tea boxes" in which tea had once been imported, closed with rust-less push-button latches and decorated in true Chinese fashion. The hinged lids were japanned inside as well as outside, but the interior of the boxes was rough and unfinished save for the tough tea-paper pasted in. The rectangles of sides, ends and cover-tops were outlined in gold-tinted stripes, enclosing portions of various flowering trees with foliage of soft silver-shaded browns and tans, and small or large blossoms of gorgeous red. The branches were enlivened with birds of grace and beauty or weighted down with long gourd-shaped fruit.

These tea boxes were depositories of Mother's most sacred heart mementos. Along with some of the other things described, were bundles of old and faded letters tied with bits of ancient ribbons. Two of these were from her own mother, dead long since. Several were from her father; one from her only sister, and another from her brother Frank, whose script was perfect as a copybook. But oldest of all and most full of bleeding memories, was a letter from Aunt Harriet, Father's sister, dated April twenty-two, Eighteen Sixty-Eight, penned about two weeks after the tragic disappearance of little sister Rosetta, when still they were searching for her night and day with breaking hearts.

This letter, in its yearning distress, with a hope that grasps even at a straw, makes urgent appeal to the stricken parents to get in touch with a certain occult individual who claims to be able to find the lost child if only he is given just one of her unwashed garments. What hopes and fears and grief-stricken love lie folded away with this old letter!

There were also newspaper clippings concerning the lost child written later that same year by Father himself in the hope of aiding others in their cooperative search—so earnestly prosecuted by many—so fruitless and unavailing. What anguish is written in between the lines of these old clippings! What fearful suspense and heartbreak! How vividly they bring back that tragedy of yesterday.

To us younger children, born so many years afterward, it was merely sad family history never to be mentioned before Mother, and among ourselves only in subdued tones. Annie was seven years old before she even heard the story or knew there had been a sister Rosetta. But I had heard, and one day told Annie about it.

"I don't believe it!" she exclaimed in utter incredulity.

"Well, it's true just the same," I replied.

"I don't believe it!" reiterated Annie, adding: "I'm going to ask Ma," and she did, fully expecting to have her disbelief confirmed.

"Ma, did we ever have a little sister stolen by Indians?"

Mother's lip trembled. Her eyes filled, and great tears stole down her cheeks as she quietly answered:

"Yes, it's true, Annie."

That was all she said. Never had she spoken to any of us of her own accord concerning the subject, and when pressed to do so, it was but briefly. In her later years I secured from her a dictated account of the tragedy. Even this contained but few details. It is from Father's clippings that most of those known have been obtained. Poor Mother! What must it have meant to her! No plumbline was ever deep enough to probe the depth of her incurable wound.

It was a case of Indian revenge.

Father, in the year Sixty-Six, from the proceeds of his freighting between Salt Lake City and Montana, purchased a mill site in Cache Valley, northern Utah, midway between the two settlements of Mendon and Wellsville. Mendon was but a few miles from the Idaho line and Wellsville five and a half miles farther south. The mill was located a quarter of a mile off the main road, and thus was three miles distant from each of the two towns.

Father worked hard getting started. He himself cut, snaked and hewed the timbers used in building and setting up this mill, and invested all he had in the enterprise.

No sooner were they fairly settled than he heard, one day while in Mendon on business, that an Indian had been covertly murdered by a white man in that settlement. Before leaving town he satisfied himself of the truth of these rumors and as a consequence was greatly distressed in mind. Well, he knew that the Indian code requiring vengeance on the Whites would be carried out sooner or later, and that without discrimination between the innocent and the guilty.

Filled with dread, he drove homeward deeply regretting that he had located his family in a place so isolated. But, having already invested all his means in the business, he saw no way out of the situation other than to seek by kindness and strict integrity in dealing with the Indians, to win their confidence and good will.

Others assured him that as time went on the affair would blow over. But Father was skeptical. He knew that Indians never forgive nor forget an injury.

All through those parts of the Utah territory and across the borders in southern Idaho and Wyoming, were many Indians of various tribes: Utes, Bannock, Blackfoot, Shoshone, Arapahoe, and others. Bands of Indians would come periodically to the settlements for supplies, and camp on the outskirts.

It was something over two years after the outrage, however, that the blow fell and revenge was taken on the innocent. Father and Mother at that time had a family of five living children, ranging in ages from nine to one years. Little Rosetta, next to the baby, was nearly two years and a half.

That spring, Pocatello[i], among all the Indian chiefs of the country rated the most treacherous, came, as was his wont, with his band and camped in the vicinity of Mendon. Sag-wich, another chief, was camped with his band near Wellsville. These tribes and others secured flour from Father's midway grist mill. According to his policy, followed from the beginning, in order to encourage friendly feeling and give no occasion for offense, Father made it a point to be scrupulously honest and fair in all his dealings with them, giving generous amounts of grist with their purchases.

Notwithstanding this and the lapse of time since the offense, the Indians did not depart from the community without first accomplishing their long and secretly cherished purpose of revenge on the Whites. And Father and his family were selected deliberately to be the victims. Several circumstances may have contributed to this choice. Their isolated situation presented the fewest obstacles to the carrying out of their scheme, the proximity of the mill-race and pond would serve to divert suspicion from themselves, and too, they had taken a fancy to that particular child.

---

[i] The same for whom a town in southern Idaho is named.

Different members of the tribe, as afterward recalled, from time to time had been seen to show marked admiration and preference for little Rosetta, with her happy disposition, her curly hair and brown eyes—the only brown-eyed child her parents ever had. Rosetta has been described by one outside the family who knew her at the time. He says:

> "She was a veritable rosebud, the pride and pet of the family...beautiful as a cherub, her loveliness enhanced by the care and good taste bestowed upon her attire by her idolizing mother. Her disposition was as lovable as her person. She was always as bright and sunny as a balmy day in June—full of good nature and of little sayings wise and cute."

Because of their attraction to her it is supposed that the Indians selected this child with the intention of raising her to be an honored member of their tribe, as they have been many times known to do with white children. She was still young enough to forget her past, and old enough to survive apart from maternal care.

Mother had occasionally hired certain squaws to do her washing—a circumstance that afforded them opportunity for observing the habits of the family, enabling them the more intelligently to formulate the details of their infamous plot. This familiar association also accustomed the little one to their presence and appearance, allaying any natural fears that might have existed.

Shortly before noon one cold raw morning in early April, Little Rosetta, who at the time was not well, and the day previous had been kept in bed, expressed a desire to go out of doors upon a natural errand. Mother sent her sister Sadie along to look after her. Presently Sadie came back into the house alone. It was perhaps ten minutes before Mother, busy at her work, noticed that her little charge was not among them.

"Where is Rosetta?" she asked anxiously.

"Oh, she wasn't quite ready to come in yet," replied Sadie.

"Go out at once and bring her in out of the cold," instructed Mother.

Sadie went out immediately, but she could not find her little sister anywhere. To her call there was no answer. Then Mother hurried out, calling and hunting with quickened heartbeat. But there was no little Rosetta within sight of her eyes or sound of her voice. Anxiety changed to alarm, alarm to fear, fear to distraction. Father was called from the mill. Search of the premises by all hands was begun. Then, as the day lengthened, a furious ride by Father to Mendon brought help to engage in the hunt that if possible the lost child might be found before nightfall. But she was not found. It was as though the earth had opened up and swallowed her from sight.

All night long by lantern light they searched, while the frantic mother, at home with the rest of her little flock, battled with a thousand fears. Her helpless baby lost in the darkness, ill to begin with—could she survive a night in the fearful cold? What of wild beasts, coyotes, wolves? Was she down under the water of the millpond? Dead—dead? All through the night she prayed and wept and listened with straining ears for the glad returning shout that never came.

In the gray dawn, still no nearer solution of the terrible mystery than when they began, the men returned to investigate more thoroughly the waters about the mill, that on an earlier hasty inspection had revealed no indications of drowning.

They emptied the millrace till every inch of its bottom was visible. The slough of very shallow water, into which it flowed, was several rods wide and so thickly grown up with bulrushes that nothing could float in it. Foot by foot they thoroughly searched it until no part remained unexplored. Then they turned their attention to the millpond, whose nearest margin was about six hundred feet distant.

By request, Sag-wich with some of his Indians had come over from Wellsville to join in the hunt. The first thing both Whites and Indians did was to look for tracks. But in the smooth clay soil that surrounded the banks of the pond, sloping gradually down to the water's edge, not even one baby footprint could be discerned.

Cannon were brought and fired repeatedly over its surface to aid in raising the body should it be lying beneath. This bringing no results, the pond was then thoroughly dragged until its muddy depths retained no secrets. Then a search of other distant bodies of water was undertaken, which proved equally futile.

Long days went by. Far and near the populace was stirred by the mysterious tragedy. Men from every nearby settlement joined in the search, scouring hills and canyons. This was continued until the whole country from Bear River on the west to the snow line of the Wasatch Mountains on the east and a distance from north to south of many miles had been thoroughly and systematically combed. But the fate of the missing child was still unsolved. There was, however, in the minds of many a growing conviction that the Indians had stolen her. Father was now convinced of it.

Not less than ten days had been consumed in this manner of search before it was abandoned as futile. Valuable time was thus wasted and ample opportunity afforded for the actual abductors to slip away out of the country unobserved and unhindered, leaving the tribe to follow more slowly to divert suspicion.

It has been thought, with some foundation in rumor, that one of the squaws of Pocatello's tribe who previously had made the child's acquaintance, disarming her fears, had been watching her chance that day from some hidden spot, and had snatched the little one as soon as left alone, taking her muffled in a blanket to some mounted bucks who rode swiftly away with her out of the neighborhood.

No imagination is needed to picture the anguish of that frightened babe, spirited away by red-skinned strangers of an unknown tongue, sobbing for the tender arms of a mother she was never again to see on earth. But no actual proof of guilt against any individual was ever procurable.

As was afterward ascertained, Indians had been seen loitering on the premises by several different persons on the day of her disappearance, but none of them had come to the house for bread as they customarily did when around, and no member of the family had seen them. It was also disclosed that Pocatello had that very day removed his camp from Mendon to Logan on the southeast, a good distance away and several miles beyond Wellsville, where he had camped in the Logan bottoms.

There, Father went to see him to engage him and his band to help in the search. He offered rewards for the child dead or alive. But Pocatello would not agree to come unless he was promised a sack of flour whether he found her or not. To this Father readily consented. The next day Pocatello came—but alone.

Sag-wich and his Indians were there, and the Bishop of Mendon with a large crew of his people to engage in the hunt. The Bishop and his men offered to the Indians in addition to the rewards promised by Father, ten sacks of flour and a beef to find and bring the child dead or alive, and a horse in addition to these if they brought her living. These Indians all promised to hunt, and all but Pocatello did so. He got his dinner, claimed and carried away his sack of flour, and neither he nor any of his band ever put in an appearance to join in the hunt.

At a later date, Father, in company with several others, visited his camp in Malad valley, using his best and most ingratiating diplomacy—for nothing but defeat could result from any other tactics. To take any violent measures against the tribe would have been to precipitate a general massacre of the Whites who were greatly outnumbered. Nothing in the nature of threats or force could have restored the stolen child, but might have resulted in her death as well as that of his whole family along with others.

Father called him a "good Indian," said he was sure some "bad Indians" in the west had taken the child, and asked Pocatello to hunt and find her. He offered to give him in addition to all rewards formerly promised, thirteen horses for the child's safe return.

Father adds in his pitiful account: "I sometimes think that we might have obtained her on these conditions, but for the numerous threats thrown out against the Indians by thoughtless people, by which they were intimidated."

Sag-wich afterward told others at Mendon, Paradise, and Willow Creek, that Pocatello stole the child. He told when and where they got her, where they took her, how long they kept her in Cache Valley, and the night they passed through Mendon with her when they left the valley.

A young man of Wellsville on his way to the mines, wrote to his father Mr. Kerr—who showed Father the letter— that three Indians came to his camp on Blackfoot to buy flour, and began to talk about the little girl stolen from Cache Valley. They said they knew Pocatello had her, for one of them had been at his camp and had seen her there. Young Mr. Kerr later told Father in person about the interview with these three Indians, all of whom spoke good English. The one said he had seen her in Pocatello's camp in the Logan bottoms, and that Pocatello had bribed other Indians who knew about it to keep it secret, paying them several horses to do so.

A young man named Petingall living near North Willow Creek in Salt Lake Valley, told Father that Sag-wich had been there, and that he had told him Pocatello stole the child. At another time this same man overheard two other Indians talking between themselves about the case, who said that Pocatello stole her and sent her to Salmon River.

Rumors of this character from time to time, kept the bereaved parents suspended alternately between hope and despair for years. Large rewards were offered, attractive baits held out to Indians for her recovery, clues and leads persistently followed up, repeated interviews held with the suspected chief, all to no avail. Father, in his desperate determination to leave no stone unturned, rode horseback all over the surrounding mountains and to villages and camps far and near, covering thousands of miles that summer in a vain endeavor to get some tangible evidence of the whereabouts of his child. He literally wore out a light English saddle borrowed for the purpose of Bishop Henry Hughes, who had brought it over with him from England. But at the end of every avenue came up as it were, against an impassable brick wall of baffling mystery. Not until all his resources were utterly exhausted did Father and Mother finally give up hope of ever recovering their lost darling.

Unable longer to endure life at the mill site in Cache Valley, they gave up the place and removed to Weber the year following the tragedy, continuing their efforts from there to trace the child. At this place Father took charge of a sawmill for his Father. Their next move, two years later, was to California.

Ann Hughes, the Bishop's first wife, years afterward told friends in reminiscence, that she considered our mother to be one of the noblest women she had ever known. She related that it was Mother's daily custom to conduct a little private school in her home for her own family, which some of the neighbor children also at times attended. Every day during that dreadful summer following the abduction, at a certain hour she would call the children together for school, and proceed with perfect self-control to teach them their lessons for the day. Then she would dismiss them with a smile and pleasant words. But after they were gone out of her presence, she would walk the floor in the agony of her desperate anguish.

Two years before we laid Mother away, Charlotte and her husband Howard Jennings while on a vacation tour through other states, camped for a short time in Zion National Park, located in southern Utah. There they met by accident another tourist camped in the park—a lady whose maiden name was Pratt. In the course of conversation they fell to discussing family history, in which the disclosure was made of Charlotte's relationship to our mother and the lost Rosetta. Mrs. Pratt told them that her own mother had been a bosom friend of our mother, and her special chum in early womanhood. Out of her love and sympathy for Mother in her suffering, she had come to be with her during those dark days following the tragic disappearance of the child, and was in her home for a week or two.

She said that Mother almost lost her reason, that every day for weeks after the child was gone, Mother would go out to the place where she had last been seen, and with a stick in her hand would beat about in the weeds and bushes, calling piteously:

"Rosetta! Rosetta! Rosetta! "

Figure 13 Charlotte and Howard Jennings, 1907

The Main Rooms

Memory carries me from Mother's room out through the door into the kitchen. The first thing to the right was the big Charter-Oak stove, standing out from the end wall into the room. Wedged behind it, stood the wood-box, piled up high. Underneath the stove was the chip-box, holding chips and kindling for morning fires, filled by little hands in their earliest tasks.

Never since have I seen a stove like that one. Back of the four usual top holes were two little extra holes, seldom opened, whose covers when lifted presented undersides heavily festooned with soot streamers. Back of these a raised extension held a large reservoir for heating water, whose divided cover opened on pivots from the center outward.

The large oven, having an ell-shaped door on each side, was almost always full of baking bread, for many loaves a week were required to feed so many hungry children.

In the stove front was a box hearth several inches deep whose cover also opened outward on a pivot for the removal of ashes. Above it the fire grate curved upward with two little outward-swinging doors. Before a blazing fire in this grate on cold mornings we often sat, two together in a big rocking chair and toasted our toes, stuck out straight to rest against the hearth, and while breakfast was being "taken up" for the table, "licked" the gravy skillet, dividing it through the middle, each with a spoon scraping off his half of the rich brown adhesions, while a third applicant "licked" the gravy spoon.

I see this grate glowing with red coals after smoke and blaze had subsided, and before it a row of us toasting green corn on the cob, each ear stuck on the tines of a fork gripped by eager fingers that turned and turned it till every row of kernels was a rich golden brown—a repast fit for the gods.

I see Father and the boys molding bullets out of lead which they melted in a cunning little iron dipper over coals shaken down into the open hearth, and poured into the closed molds placed on a kerosene box nearby. When the metal had "set" they opened the molds and emptied out the large shapely bullets, still very hot, that were meant for the heart of some luckless rabbit, or coyote, or maybe a deer.

I see Mother picking up piece after piece of black charcoal from the grate when the fire was out, munching it as a delicious morsel—for she craved crunchy charcoal—or laying part of it away for future medicinal use.

Once or twice a month, the big stove had to be thoroughly cleaned out, and blackened and polished all over from the tips of its toes to the top of its visible stovepipe. The soot was scraped from under the oven through a tiny, turn-button removable door, using a long-handled, double-edged stove-hoe. We carried it far away from the house, emptying it onto the plowed ground. But the clean ashes, taken from the hearth with a little iron shovel, found their way up the slope and into Mother's "lye-barrel."

Stove blacking came in a long rectangular bar. We shaved it off into a deep tin plate and moistened it with soapy water to the right consistency—the soap giving an added sheen and luster. But nobody liked this job, for though the polishing brush had a handle and a bristle dauber on its reverse tip, in spite of all precautions, our hands and fingernails suffered distressing "blackouts."

The kitchen floor also, though much pieced, rough and slivery, must be scrubbed almost daily with old brooms and hand brushes, for on none of the floors in this house was there a covering of any kind. Our mop was an old broom handle to which was nailed a cross-piece, a bunch of old rags with a hole cut through the middle, being slipped down over it. Sometimes from the rough floorboards a big sliver would be run into the hand or foot, to be remedied by tweezers and turpentine. In course of time the floor boards in places became so worn and thin as to invite sudden catastrophe, and someone would go crashing and splintering through; then, added to the turpentine would be another board, with hammer, nails and saw.

Fitted into the corner beyond the stove was the "water-bench," composed of two oilcloth-covered shelves with a pleated curtain down to the floor. Behind this curtain we kept our cooking pots, kettles and skillets that were too black from contact with open flame to be kept with cleaner utensils. On the top of the bench sat the water bucket in which reposed the dipper, immersed to the hook on its handle. The milk bucket too, inverted to protect from dust, was there ready for the night's milking.

On the side wall, opening onto the long front porch lowered a step from the kitchen floor, was another single-sash sliding window, with a chair beneath it; after which came the main front door of the house, by which guests must enter and depart, swinging toward the jog in the corner. Behind it we kept our brooms and hung our aprons, and there stood our "bread-boiler"—a covered copper boiler, demoted because leaky, in which our loaves were kept. Above it was the medicine cupboard, an open-front box nailed to the wall, with a cleat across the lower edge to keep the contents in, and a little curtain over its front. Reposing here, were many potent remedies employed in the healing art, chief of which were turpentine, castor oil, iodine, camphor, powdered borax, burnt alum, lobelia—used chiefly as an emetic—cayenne pepper, and goldenseal, so effective for "proud flesh" and canker sores.

But the most popular remedy was Mother's White Liniment. Many a time have I watched her make it. Into a long, slender "little brown jug," she would pour half a pint of home-made vinegar, the same measure of turpentine, the unbeaten whites of two eggs, and lastly, an ounce of ammonia, immediately corking the jug, and shaking vigorously till the mixture was a creamy-white emulsion. Some of this she kept handy in a small bottle. The jug was put down cellar where it was cool.

I am sure that no better liniment for stubbed toes, cut fingers, burns, skin abrasions, sprains and bruises was ever compounded by an apothecary. Before using we would shake the bottle well. It smarted a little but it cured. Mother would tie a little rag around the toe or finger to exclude the dirt, and the white liniment did the rest. Often when playing or bathing at the rocky seashore, someone would slip and scrape his shin. Sea-bathed rocks make poisonous wounds difficult to heal, but Mother's white liniment was a specific. Another poisonous wound is the scratch of a cat, but we would sop it with liniment, and forget all about it. For sprains, we sometimes used another homely but potent remedy, just as good today as ever, a saturate solution of salt and vinegar, heated before application, but not to be used on broken surfaces.

There was one remedy Mother didn't keep in this medicine cupboard—the asafoetida, that odoriferous, oriental gum, whose Latin name means fetid. She kept it in a tight tin box hidden somewhere, that its peculiar exhalations might not communicate contamination. Whenever contagious diseases were on the rampage, as a preventive measure Mother would make little "asafoetida-bags" and hang them around our necks next to the skin. She would form tiny pellets also of the evil-smelling and more evil-tasting stuff, for us to swallow whole; after which we felt securely immune from all evil.

We were cautioned never to chew it, and we never did—after the first time. Of course we had to try it just once to see how it tasted, but not the second time, oh no! That once was amply sufficient. And we didn't tell Mother, either. We knew just what she would say: "What did I tell you?" And that wasn't sympathy.

Then there was the sulfur-cream-of-tartar-honey mixture, which Mother prepared for us regularly every spring to "purify the blood," dosing us "three days on and three days off" for several weeks. This was kept in a bowl in the dish-cupboard with a tin spoon in it which we all "licked" each in turn.

The prevailing belief was that something about the returning spring put impure "humors" into the blood. When all nature was bursting with new life and pent up energy, when birds in every tree were singing wild with joy, when every young animal in the pasture frisked about with shiny coat enjoying spring to the full, when new-born calves gained so rapidly we could almost see them grow, when every barnyard fowl cackled or crowed with renewed vitality and filled their nests with eggs, we poor little human animals who had been fed all winter long as a daily diet on salt pork and the products of white flour, robbed of three fourths of its life-giving minerals—freely fed in whole grains to the horses, calves and chickens—would break out with repulsive scabby sores that spread over our faces often from ear to ear, and with painful boils on necks and arms—thought to be necessary as an outlet for said humors—and charged it all, with the hideous calumny of ignorance, to the glorious springtime! Needless to say, these "humors" all disappeared completely in after years coincidentally with our deficient diet.

Beyond the jog in the wall, interrupting a row of chairs, was the door into the girls' room, behind which hung the guns suspended horizontally in leather loops attached to the wall. Here with them, hung the leather shot flask and the powder-horn, sawed from the horn of a cow.

All along this side of the room high up under the eaves, was a concealed space, triangular and floored, which we called the "attic." Over the inside opening hung a series of short curtains. Since every house needs some kind of extra storage room, this attic was a very happy thought. Here were kept an assortment of various articles not in daily use, that had to be tucked away somewhere. Father sometimes hid here the little brass bucket containing left-over squirrel poison, considering it out of the reach of little folks. Could he have been "'a mouse in the corner" long enough to see us children—especially the obstreperous Harriet—climb on cobbled-up chairs and boxes to reach inside the attic and explore its many contents, he might not have rested so serenely sure with regard to the deadly potion. Well do I remember the day when, despondent and desperate over some "injustice" done me, I thought of taking some of that squirrel poison to end my misery and make them feel sorry for the way they had treated me. When the coast was clear, I climbed up to the attic and gazed upon the little brass kettle trying to get my courage up to the sticking point. But visions of the little squirrels I had seen writhing in agony held me back. I decided it would hurt too much, that I had better hang on a little longer before sampling the contents of that little brass bucket.

Father's private library constituted my chief interest in this dusty attic. His books were of various kinds and ancient dates. There was a family genealogy that told all about our paternal ancestors, and in it were printed the names of us all down to Charlotte, the last two names having been added in ink after publication. It was too complicated for me to enjoy.

A big calf-bound volume of Thomas Moore's complete poems and another matching volume of the poetical works of Lord Byron, I explored greedily, but a volume of Robert Burns, I considered a waste of time. Such a travesty on the English language! Such atrocious spelling! Such a twisting of plain words that are so sensible when spelled and pronounced properly! Who would waste time trying to make it out? Not I, surely.

"Heroines of History" took in all the main heroines from Queen Semiramis of old Babylonia to Victoria, Queen of Britain. There I read of Cleopatra, with the reptile in her bosom, of Zenobia, queen of Palmyra, of Mary, Elizabeth, Anne Bolleyn, laying her neck bravely on the block, of Josephine, Louise, and of Joan of Arc, perishing in the flames, and many others, invoking outbursts of wrath and pity.

Another book, and one I loved, was "Driven From Sea to Sea, Or Just A Campin'," a story of hydraulic mining in Cripple Creek. Little crippled Johnnie drew largely upon my sympathy, and his rueful question as he surveyed the mess of broken eggs: "What's 'e use o' havin' panties if'oo tan't put edds in 'e pottits?" made me love the little fellow. But the shooting of noble Erastus in the trouble about the mines, leaving poor Lucy a grieving widow, roused all my indignation and disappointment. Surely, such a man as he ought to live forever, and not die young and spoil the whole story.

There was an old English grammar, small of print and compact which fascinated me. It was too deep to understand, but I meant to study it some day when older. Another book I meant to study was an old and faded text on "The Art of Bookkeeping." This, I simply longed to master. The big geography baffled me. I longed to interpret its many queer maps, but could get neither head nor tail of it.

Father's own manuscript poems were there too, written with purple ink in a big legal sized, marbled, stiff-covered book. I feared his displeasure too much to handle these, at least to any extent.

There was a stiff-covered Danish-English New Testament, two columns to the page. The English, I might have read had not the print been so small and the words so big and the meaning so hard to understand. I had no idea that it really was the Word of God, or that it concerned me in any way. So, like many another prospector, I stumbled on over the gold mine without discovering it.

Passing by the original cabin window in the end of this room, we might come to the big unwieldy cupboard that stood in the corner, or to the organ that later displaced it; the last side-wall being occupied by chairs, or left to shove the table against on rare occasions. Though greatly needed, there was no window here. The long, extended dining table with rounded end leaves stood practically always in the center of the room, at night becoming the family study table.

In this room, Mother held her "pickings." At the season when ducks and geese are covered with thick down and past the "pin-feather" stage (when a black, moist substance in the quills shows immaturity), Mother would have a "picking day."

None of the birds would be fed or let out of the coops that morning, but we would catch and bring them one by one to her to be robbed of their feathers. This work, she never entrusted to anyone else. It had to be done just so. A novice would not know how many feathers and how much down they could spare without danger of suffering from the cold, for only in winter were these heavy enough to be plucked. Then too, the birds must not be injured in any way. If fat, their skin would easily tear, and this must under no circumstances occur.

Mother knew just how to do it, just how to handle the birds without frightening them, how many feathers to pull at once so as not to cause pain and just how much down to remove, and they seemed to recognize her skilled hands.

The picking had to be done inside away from drafts, for who does not know that a mere whiff of air will blow feathers away? So on picking day, Mother would close the window and the door of the girls' room and seat herself in a low chair, usually the small rocker, where light from the window would fall over her shoulder, then, receiving the squawking bird, she would hold it with the left hand by the legs breast up in her lap with head hanging down in front and wings held gently but firmly between her knees. With her free right hand, she would pluck two or three feathers at a time with little quick movements till a handful had been obtained, then deposit them in a large can at her side.

The bird at first would make a great fuss, but Mother would handle it so gently and talk so soothingly to it that after a while it would lie there quietly in perfect submission while she plucked away. When one bird was finished, she would call for another, and we would run and fetch it from the coop, turning the plucked one loose in the yard and giving it some food. The bird would first stretch and flap its wings as if to make sure it was really all there, and then begin to eat its breakfast.

Repeatedly, Mother would push down the feathers in the can, and when it filled up would empty it carefully into a flour sack, shake the contents down and roll the top, or if full, tie it securely ready to put away.

Although the ducks and geese did not especially enjoy this ordeal, yet it was one of the things that made them tame and unafraid of their human masters, creating a bond of friendly contact.

Half concealed by the back kitchen door as it opened across the next and last jog stood the flour barrel into which the hundred-pound sacks were emptied. In the barrel with the flour, were kept the rolling pin, its handles missing, and the sieve, shaped like a pan, with finely-woven wire bottom. A piece of oil-cloth for additional protection was spread beneath the barrel-head.

There was no back porch nor even a step, since the floor at that side was but a few inches above ground, but a heavy, short plank served as a step. After the door, another single-sash window opened above the kitchen work-table. Here, Mother kneaded her dough and here we washed dishes in a big pan, for there was no sink of any kind—nor even a water faucet in this house.

Filling the space between the next corner and the door of Mother's room, stood the large all-purpose cupboard, conveyed thither to make way for the new organ. Its upper half, shelved and curtained, held the dishes. On the highest shelf, accessible only to grown-ups, was arranged the dinner set of handsome English china, trimmed lavishly in conventional design with heavy lines of real gold. These, Father had brought across the water from abroad and afterward presented to his bride-to-be. We never used them, except on state occasions. To have broken one would have been unforgivable. On the other shelves were the common dishes, and in a corner of the lowest, the box partitioned for knives, forks, and spoons.

The lower portion of this cupboard was twice the depth from front to back of the upper, and consisted of one very large and deep bin, whose heavy, slanting lid opened like a desk-top on its stout hinges to lean against the upper. Its solitary shelf, a facsimile of those above, was used for such adjuncts of the table as the butter dish, honey pitcher, sugar bowl, five pound lard pail of grease, and bits of leftovers, all shut away from flies and dust. There too, reposed the long sharp butcher knife, with other utility knives. Within its cavernous depths lodged in an indiscriminate jumble, all the miscellany of culinary utensils—milk-pans, dish-pans, gem-pans, bread-pans, large black bake-pans, basins, colander, strainer, bread-board, chopping-bowl, cake tins, pie-plates, small tin pails, potato-masher, eggbeater, big mixing spoons and granite kettles, with whatever else might haunt a kitchen.

To obtain some needed utensil from this bin, we youngsters would drag up a small box to stand on waist-high to the top, lifting with much effort, the heavy lid. Then bending over, would reach down determinedly to fish in the far depths for the article desired, balancing mid-body across the edge of the bin and fairly standing upside down as we parted company with the box-pedestal, yet trusted it to be there when, coming up again, our descending feet should need a foothold.

The Girls' Room and Porch

The girls' room, on a level with the porch, was entered by an inside step down from the main floor, and there to the right was the closet standing out squarely from the corner, its open door just missing the end of the step. There were no clothes hangers on it, not even hooks, but nails only, driven into the walls. Every dress or skirt made had a neat little loop of the material sewn on at the shoulder seam or belt by which to hang it on the nail.

To the left, fitted into the next corner, stood a large "toilet" filled with supply linens for tables, beds and baths. The top was adorned by a long "runner," and behind it on the wall was tacked a "splasher," both done in red outline stitch, the latter with some design suggestive of water, such as frogs in a pool, ducks on a pond, or an umbrella girl in the rain. But the absence of the customary "bowl and pitcher" left the theme uncompleted.

Another sliding window in the end of the room, with a little box-stand under it, was wreathed outside with a thrifty Madeira vine that had climbed to the roof, and in season, shook out its yellowish-white tassel-like blossoms. The bed, home-made, as were the others, was shoved tightly into the next corner, and above its side another window admitted its light. In the last corner, nailed high on the wall, was the "girls' cupboard," where they had their private belongings stowed away in various boxes.

Underneath this cupboard, with sufficient operating space left between them, stood the Singer sewing machine. "What?" I hear you exclaim, "Another sewing machine?" It is peculiar, I admit, but that is what my memory picture presents to me. By this I know that the mental photograph was impressed somewhere between the years Eighty-One and Eighty-Four, for this is the time when we had two sewing machines—but that belongs to another story.

The door in the end of the room opened back against the closet, and was barely included under the narrow shed roof of the long front porch. A little unroofed ell of the porch extended out as far as the building, and across the three feet of its sunny end, stood the stationary "wash-bench," with its tin basin, where everybody washed before coming in to meals. Back in the corner, from a wooden bracket hung the long, endless roller towel that reached almost to the floor. Very convenient was this family towel, for when one place became soiled or wet, a quick pull brought a cleaner spot to view, and when all the center was in a decidedly "pulled" condition, we might still wipe around the edges. Nearby on a nail hung the comb-case with its family comb, and above it a small looking glass reflected the different physiognomies of those whom there "slicked up" before entering the house.

The porch extended a little farther than the building, ending in steps to the ground, and another and narrower unroofed ell all across the shady end of Mother's room, provided a convenient platform for reserve water barrels. Along the front were supporting posts at intervals, with open railing between. Directly in front of the kitchen door at the angle of porch and ell, another set of five or six steps led down from the little house of my childhood into the broad, hard, clean-swept front yard.

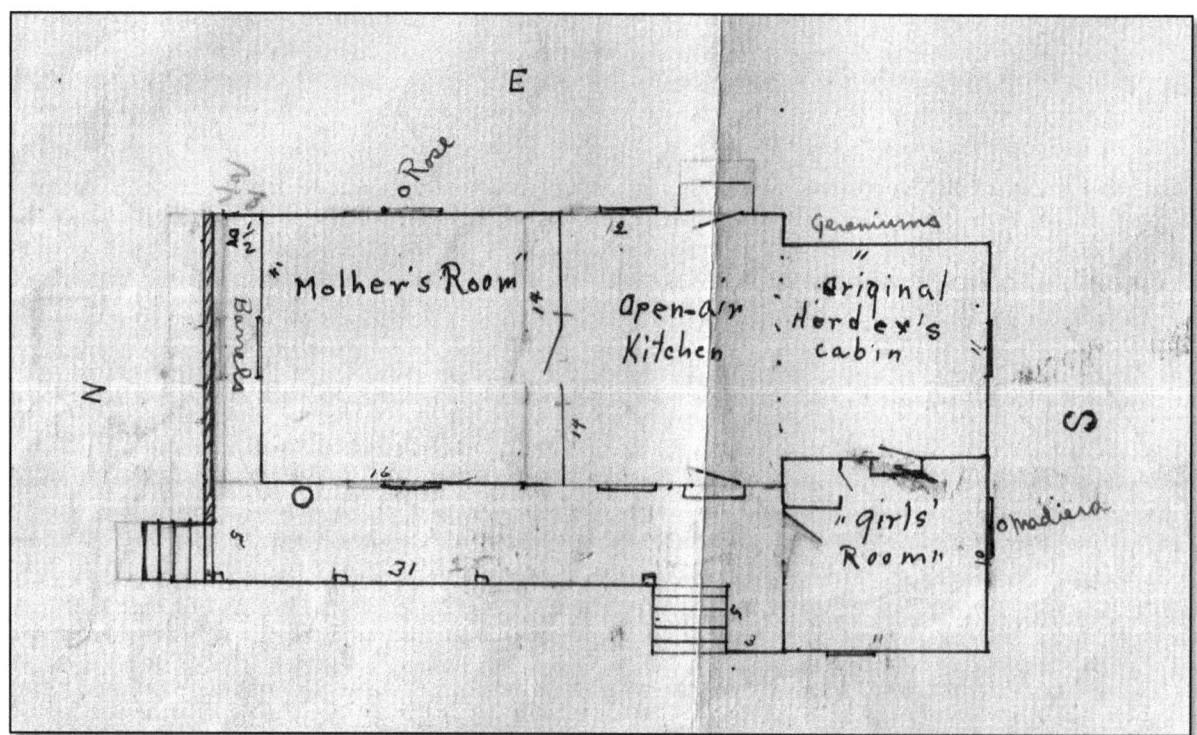

Figure 14 Old House Floor Plan

Figure 15 Old House, End View of Mother's Room & Porch, with Girl's Room at Far End

Figure 16 Old House, End View of Girl's Room & Cabin

Figure 17 Rear View of the Old House
Showing Vineyard, Walnut Orchard, Eucalyptus Row, Little Hill and Vineyard Point

CHAPTER 23 THE YARDS AND ROUNDABOUT

By the length of the front porch was measured the width of our bare, sloping front yard, ending at the road that skirted the orchard. There was no grass in this yard, and no flowers or shrubbery adorned its margins. Efforts many, had been made at such decoration. But wherever the ground was loosened and moistened for flower-raising, the chickens, in their free run of the premises, delighted to dust and scratch. And the two designs were utterly incompatible. So everybody had become discouraged with trying to raise flowers. A few scrubby geraniums and a climber of some sort had obtained a foothold at the back of the original cabin where the jog made room, but these, with Mishie's rosebush and the Madeira vine were all that survived our tussle with the chickens.

We kept this smooth front yard swept like a floor, and it was here that the outside family sports took place. When other boys came to visit our boys, here, with porch and steps as a grandstand and a bevy of children and youth as enthusiastic audience, were carried on such acrobatic contests and feats as wrestling, jumping, vaulting over bars, walking on hands with heads downward and heels in the air, and "chinning the beam." Grasping the timber under the eaves of the porch, the contestants would draw up their bodies by arm-strength until they touched with the chin the beam above.

Perched about at vantage points, we girls greatly enjoyed watching and cheering these athletic exhibitions of endurance and skill, but never dreamed of a day when girls too would go in for anything so unbecoming to them.

In this yard George once turned loose a great wounded condor whose mighty wing he had broken with a bullet from his thirty-two. Largest of the winged scavenger family, that includes the buzzard and vulture, the condor outstrips them all. This one, though not the largest, from wing tip to wingtip, measured nine feet, and weighed more than twenty pounds. I see him yet—that great sooty, brownish-black bird, sitting at bay on his reddish talons and legs, braced by the tail, his orange-red head naked all but the face, protruded with the bare neck from a thick marginal ruff of feathers, and turned as if on a pivot from side to side, as he watched with keen eyes the enemy group that surrounded him, endeavoring to keep all within his range of vision, while hissing through his open hooked beak.

Into this same front yard, a man once came bringing a tame grizzly bear who did many clever tricks at his master's command. He stood up on his hind legs and danced to the tune of a fiddle played by his master; then, putting his forelegs around his neck, hugged and kissed him. At the word, he sat down like a person, or rolled over like a dog, and walked around the circle begging and receiving bits of food from our hands. When the performance was about to close, he passed the hat to each of us.

This bear and his amusing exhibition were a great novelty to us children, but I fear the offering was lean, since we had very little to spare for entertainment.

A short distance above the back door flourished two shady old sycamores—though when or by whom they were planted we younger children knew nothing—a source of never-ending pleasure to us. Their grapevine-shaped leaves with shiny green uppers and rough undersides at maturity, when young and tender in the springtime, were things of delicate beauty. Instead of being shiny, their upper surfaces were daintily fuzzy like velvet, each a study in exquisitely blending shades of tan and henna and gold on a pale greenish background. In admiration we would gather these to play with caressingly.

In fruiting season the trees were covered with beautiful round red briar-less burs about the size of walnuts, soft-spined and harmless, strung, several together in a series, like ornaments on a Christmas tree.

Between these trees, attached to a heavy bough of each, hung a stout rope swing, with its narrow notched board seat. The hard ground underneath was grooved and pitted with many heel marks where sturdy feet had stood while strong hands pushed the swing with its delighted burden, upward, higher and higher to fly with the birds—the most enjoyable sensation aspired to by humans—only to step aside at this pinnacle of motion, and "let the old cat die."

No pen could describe and no volume contain all the unadulterated delight afforded the children of Aliso through the years by this swing under the shady sycamores. Tiny toddlers who, having no service to offer in exchange, begged: "Swing me," older ones, able to push each other to limited heights and "run under" to give the great coveted "boost," and bigger boys and girls, who, disdaining to sit, stood up on the swing-board, alone or with a partner, and worked up a self-motivated speed that carried them to the utmost limit of the rope's capacity—all alike, thrilled to the sensation of winged pleasure.

Directly above the two sycamores, the rock wall, shaded by a row of large beautiful pepper trees, formed the upper margin of our back yard, dividing its cleared slope from the brush of the foothill, ending at the verge of a small gully that provided an outlet in winter from cliff to creek for the rain-water that collected in a little draw high above on the mountain and fell in a small cataract over the face of the cliff. This gully passing behind the honey house, formed the limiting borderline of our yards in that direction, beyond which lay the apiary, embraced in the curve of mountain as it circled toward the creek.

The pepper trees waved over the wall their graceful, drooping branches of fern-like foliage the year round, and in season, flaunted their bright red berries, suspended in grape-like bunches. These, as they matured, would drop, falling apart in broken clusters to the ground. We would gather them up to crush in our small hands and see the red covering skins crumble and fall away like chaff, leaving the naked black pepper berries. Tasting these, as we did everything else that grew on the place, we found them coated with a sweetish substance, which we would suck off, without chewing the unpleasant tasting berries.

Below these, a group of tall evergreen eucalyptus trees dropped down their dead twigs and leaves and shed in long curling strips their last year's bark, leaving the new, shiny, smooth and pale green, showing beneath. These were mingled with quaint seed-vessels resembling roofs of Chinese temples, which we gathered up to play with.

At the margin of this group stood the "bone-rock" with a sledge-hammer lying conveniently near. This rock was of blue granite about a foot and a half high and roughly cubical in shape, weighing something like four hundred pounds. On its flat top, we pounded up fine with the sledge-hammer, all the bones accumulating from the carnivorous practices of the family, to be fed to the chickens. Sometimes these bones were first burned, at other times pounded up raw and juicy.

This rock was also at times the scene of real tragedy. The daily pounding of these bones was a task for which Frank cared very little. But whenever he chanced to come across any of the dismembered parts of our old china dolls, awaiting only the family surgeon for proper articular repairs, the temperature of his interest in the bone-rock rose immediately. Considering these cadaverous finds to be as legitimately his prey as rare bones, he could not resist the temptation to hammer them to bits on the bone-rock. Thus our grief was deprived even of the assuagement of a decent funeral. And what solace was there to be found in the possession of a head without arms, or arms without a head? We looked upon Frank as a doll-enemy of the first magnitude, and endeavored to keep our luckless surgical cases safely hospitalized away from his sight.

Near the bone-rock, stood Mother's lye-barrel, into which the best and cleanest of the wood ashes were deposited and left well covered with water to stand and "draw," more water being added as fast as used. The ashes would settle, the water become clear, dark of color, and strongly alkaline. This liquor was used on wash-days to "break" the hardness of the spring water, and as a water-softener could hold its own with any concoction. Frequently, the old ashes were cleaned out, the barrel rinsed, and another start made with fresh ashes.

A new and wonderful marvel, called the Bell Telephone—patented the day before my birth two years after the principle of speech transmission had been discovered—had recently been introduced into Los Angeles, whence it was beginning to spread southward—at least in fireside discussions—and hearing about this contraption you could talk into and others hear you miles away, Frank and I, near the precocious ages of eight and seven, decided we must have one.

A supplementary clothesline had been strung from one of the eucalyptus trees to the corner of the honey house, and taking two tin cans, Frank and I tied them up, one close to each end of the line, and through these primitive "mouth-pieces," he at one end, I at the other, we "telephoned" to each other, imagining our voices to be greatly amplified.

In this sloping yard were many small, sharp, embedded stones that protruded here and there just enough to catch unwary toes, and a common sight was somebody's toe done up in a rag. Though our barefoot soles grew tough as the rhino's hide, our pioneering toes, first to meet obstructions, remained tender in spite of—or perhaps because of—repeated buffetings. Sometimes, tripped and stumbling, one would go sprawling headlong by way of emphasizing the accident. But no one expected coddling. Such things were taken as a matter of course.

At the upper corncrib the rock wall was interrupted to afford a passage through from yard to mountainside, resuming again at the corner and continuing for its length along behind it. A similar wall, somewhat higher, extended from gable rock up the hillside for a short distance.

The upper corncrib was used for almost everything except corn. Behind a low curb at the far end were piled the apples after harvest, which must be sorted frequently all winter to control spoilage. Cases of eggs that in warm weather were kept in the cellar, were wintered in this crib. Here were various grains and foodstuffs for chickens and stock, in bins along the side walls. Near the door stood the pork barrel, its contents weighted down under brine by heavy stones on a large plate. Other eatables as well as non-eatables were to be found here, but never any corn.

The big wagon-shed, lying between the two cribs under their inclusive roof, was also fitted up as a workshop. Against the upper wall was built a long work-bench, at one end of which was attached a large vice reaching nearly to the ground, that tightened on its heavy screw by turning a knobbed iron rod that slipped alternately from one end to the other in its socket with every half-turn. Underneath the bench were bins containing nails of various sizes, bolts, screws, and other odds-and-ends peculiar to shops.

Here too, were kept the small farming implements, hoes, hung up by their blades between crib slats, hand rakes, one iron, the other wooden, on nails with teeth outward, the scythe, with its long curved blade and twice-curved handle, to which two pegs for hand-holds were bolted, hung high above our reach on two large spikes.

With this scythe, in the early days, all our hay was mowed, and raked with the wooden hand rake—though later, a large horse-drawn rake was purchased.

After harvest time, the large hayrack was sometimes stored in this shed, the wagons being pushed to the farther end. Then we would climb into it for an overland trip and together jounce it up and down at the fearful speed of a hundred miles an hour, thus ushering in the modern age of fast transportation.

"Up on the boards" under the long gable roof, were stored various and sundry things for which no better place could be found. Frank climbed up there one day, by holding onto the slats with fingers and toes, and was busy playing with some dried and partially tanned deer skins that retained their natural hair. Seeing the little girls come into the shed below to play, he clothed himself in one of these skins, and with a fierce growl, jumped down from above into their midst. Startled and terrified, they scattered, Frank, with horrible noises, chasing after them as they ran screaming all over the place, endeavoring to evade the clutches of this strange apparition at their heels. Even though sensing that somehow Frank was at the bottom of it, they nevertheless were filled with fright at his incomprehensible appearance and guttural noises.

The far end of the lower crib was devoted to corn, and piled high with golden ears behind a doorless slatted partition. In the front half was the heavy-lidded box of carpenter tools, and various other articles hanging upon or leaning against the walls. In one corner leaned the shovel, in another the corn-planter, whose mouth cavity when thrust into the ground and there opened, deposited the kernels a few at a time, leaving them to germinate and grow.

In the center stood the big corn-sheller, with its iron hopper. It was our daily task to shell corn for the chickens. Two persons were required to operate the sheller. While one fed the ears into the hopper the other turned the crank, and out came a golden stream of corn into the bucket on the floor underneath, the empty cobs falling into a pile at one side to be gathered up for fuel.

Mice as well as fowl liked corn, and the crib was infested with them. Charlotte was once feeding ears into the sheller when a little mouse ran out of the hopper, up her arm inside the sleeve to the shoulder. She clapped her hand over the mouse, the mouse dug his sharp teeth into her flesh, and there they held each other in this painful embrace while Charlotte ran to the house for help. Poor little mousie got the worst of it though, in the end.

A few rods below gable rock at the end of the coops, stood the large potato-shaped rock that had fallen from the cliff and lodged there years before. Now it was covered over with a sturdy old evergreen gooseberry bush that rambled in a rhapsody of beauty. Fearsome triple thorns bristled out from under the glossy, roundish, notched leaves, whose deep green set off to advantage the beautiful red branches, and glorious fuchsia-like, pendulous blossoms that fringed their spreading twigs. When blossoms had given way to fruit, almost equally beautiful were the bright red berries in briary skins, from which we pressed the delicious seedy pulp into open mouths.

From the much-pitted side of this rock, facing the mountain, the large clear-cut face of a be-whiskered old man appeared, whose rather fierce expression never relaxed through the years, and still greets the chance beholder with its age-old severity.

Beyond this rock, with a rod or so of space between, a wire fence angled down from the cliff, following the curve of mountain that here swept downward somewhat lower than the coops, then made its way to the cow corral in the distance, joining the fence there.

Along this fence in the vicinity of the rock, Father had planted a row of edible cactus, called in the catalogue, "Tunas," but by the family, "prickly pears." The fruit was large, yellow, and delicious, but, as is the nature of cactus, covered with sharp spines. Only those older could gather and prepare the fruit for eating.

Centrally located between these cacti and the house, close up against a low rambling, embedded rock, stood the grand old lone sycamore that served as our wash house, grown luxuriant and spreading from generous waterings by much emptying of tubs, its dense branches serving as roof, and as walls the atmosphere.

Strung aslant the yard from its bough to the distant crib, a long single-wire clothesline flapped its white burden to the breeze, or awaited idly the next recurring wash day. A long bench under the tree held the tubs, one of zinc, the other, half of a barrel sawed in two. Like all other wooden things, this tub could never be left without some water in it to keep it from drying out and falling to pieces. A low brick fireplace held the large square-cornered boiler full of white clothes cooking after having been washed on the board. A large kettle of solid brass with heavy bale for lifting, holding almost as much as a tub, was used as such on wash days. At other times it was put to various uses, such as the making of squirrel poison, or homemade soap.

For soap-making, a little rock fireplace to fit the kettle was built at the lower margin of the tree-shelter. Mother usually made a large batch at once, but the amount depended on the materials at hand. For twenty pounds, she used one and a half pounds of unslaked lime and three pounds of sal soda, pouring over this mixture two gallons of boiling water and letting it stand till clear. This first liquor she would drain off and discard. To the alkaline mixture left in the kettle, she would add one gallon of cold water to stand also till settled and clear. This second liquor she would drain off and reserve to be used in the process. To the mixture in the kettle, would now be added three pounds of clean fat, and these together would be boiled for about two hours. From time to time, as there was danger of its boiling over, she would add some of the liquor saved for the purpose, until it was all used up in this way.

When from past experience she decided that the batch appeared to be done, she would test it by dipping out a spoonful on a plate and letting it cool and harden. If hard enough, the soap would then be poured out into a tub—preferably one with a smooth bottom—that had first been wetted with cold water to keep it from sticking, and allowed to stand until solidified. Mother would then cut it in opposite directions across the tub into bars with a sharp knife. Of course, these bars would be of irregular shape and size and some of them oval where the tub rounded, but it was good soap, and though dark in color, was superior to the usual yellow soaps then procurable, in many of which resin was a chief ingredient.

For many years, rubbing on the board was the only method known to us of washing clothes, and this, for a family the size of ours, was a wearisome and protracted task. When I was twelve years of age, we had our first washing machine—a wooden hand-turner that made the work go a little faster, but almost broke the back to operate, as we pulled and pushed the handle back and forth across the machine, with its heavy load.

Water-carrying was a daily chore that there was no evading. On wash days it became a toilsome burden indeed, for the cistern was a long distance from the tubs, with an uphill grade between. To make it easier, the "neck yoke" was used, as long as we had it. But somewhere along the journey of years, this useful friend disappeared. By the time I had grown old enough to receive from Hulda's shoulders the mantle of official family water carrier, its services were a thing of the past, and there is no memory of what became of the good old neck yoke. Well do I remember the endless trips from cistern to wash house with two heavy buckets whose wire bales fairly cut into the flesh. How frequently they had to be let down in the road to take out the kinks from fingers and shoulders. Sometimes two of us would go together with a washtub to carry between us. It is no wonder that we fell into the habit of washing less often than once a week.

The neck yoke dated from early days when the orchard trees were first planted and had to be kept well-watered to give them a good start. There was no way to get water but carry it in buckets from the creek. It was then that Father himself fashioned the neck yoke.

Using a thick stick of timber, he hollowed it out on the under-side to fit the shoulders, indented the center to fit around the back of the neck, rounded the topside, and finished all surfaces smoothly. The ends tapered out beyond the shoulders a convenient distance, and through a hole bored in each, a stout wire was inserted and fastened, the other end of which hung down, linked to a heavy hook, which held the bucket bale at a height to be steadied by the hand. Thus balanced with a bucket on each hook, and the weight all borne by the shoulders, heavy loads could be carried with very much less effort.

On the other side of the road from this washhouse tree, stretched the long series of woodpiles. That farthest away was of trees and shrubs untrimmed in the rough, hauled from the hillsides and canyons, and perhaps cut from our own groves and orchards. Another pile was all trimmed ready to be cut, and a third, near the house was cut or in process of being cut. There stood the chopping block, a large stump sawed to shape, with the ax sticking in the top of it, and piles of cut wood lying near, and the ground covered with chips.

Near these, in olive picking time, stood the olive barrels convenient to the water tank, where we cured the olives by the water-soaking process, emptying and refilling them daily.

Between woodpile and yard the grindstone sometimes stood, so that we children might conveniently run out and turn the crank when needed. Mounted on a heavy, braced, four-legged framework, its large stone wheel passed with every revolution through a small box of water arranged underneath. Here were sharpened the farm tools and kitchen knives and shears, to be "finished" with the whetstone.

When the water tank was first placed alongside the road, Father planted a little orange tree near it where it would catch the drippings. In spite of frosts and cold weather, so contraindicated for citrus trees, this one made a rapid and luxuriant growth and in due time came into bearing.

The Honey House and Cellar

Below the group of eucalyptus trees the honey house presented its rear door, entered by one step. There, the ground was almost level, but the other door, facing the two sycamores and house, required five or six steps, so sharp was the decline on that side. The twin double windows facing creek and orchard and overlooking the slanting cellar door, disclosed a sheer drop at that end of ten or twelve feet. There were no other openings, and the room was unfinished inside. At either end overhead, were open lofts for storing miscellaneous articles. These could be reached only by employing a stepladder or by cobbling up furniture or boxes. Behind the honey house stood the two cross-legged sun extractors, separated from the apiary by the gully, from whose slanting troughs, dripped the sun-warmed honey into containers underneath.

But the delicately sweet odor of dripping honey was not more delightful than the medley of fragrant odors that greeted the nostrils as we opened the cellar door to descend the steep wooden steps into its cool, dirt-floor depths, lighted by the one small window that pierced the foundation wall above.

Here were stored all mysteries. From the long, high shelves that spanned the cellar's length, and from the floor at the side walls on every hand where leaned or stood the many jars and sacks, and from the low table of boards covered with its bottles and bags, there rose a diffusion of enticing countryside incense, that once inhaled, can never be forgotten.

There were dried apples and dried figs, raisins, cookies and mincemeat, and perhaps a fruit cake hidden away. There were crocks of spiced fruit and jars of rich preserves, cucumber pickles, cured olives, candied orange peel, pickled pigs' feet, and hop yeast. There were cans of rendered lard, onions, potatoes, beans, peanuts, walnuts, almonds, sacks of flour, and flour sacks of other things for the pharmacy: yarrow—or milfoil—for cuts and bruises, sage for washing the hair, chamomile for inducing perspiration and quieting nerves, and the exquisitely fragrant pennyroyal, for blood purifier and colic cure. There were supplies of seeds saved from ripened pods and fruiting stalks, and sometimes cases of eggs and perhaps fresh gathered fruits and vegetables.

On the long shelves extending the length of the cellar, rows and rows of pans full of creamy milk sat waiting to be skimmed, a churn half full of sour cream ready for the dasher, and pounds of butter molded for the coming trip to market, with half-pounds for our own table use shaped in a round mold that stamped each with a bunch of yellow grapes.

In this cellar also were kept the churns, two of which were dasher churns, one of them wooden, and the other crockery. The third was a barrel-shaped rotating churn built of wooden staves bound together by hoops, resting on a standard, and turned by a crank end over end. The firkins too were kept here—diminutive butter tubs, made straight-sided of wooden staves and hoops, in which Mother would pack for winter consumption the surplus butter churned when cheap and plentiful against the day when it would be scarce and high in price.

For lack of space elsewhere, many things foreign to its purpose found a place in this convenient cellar. There were little brown stone jugs long and slender as bottles with pitcher handles, stone crocks and jars, brass kettles with bales, candle moulds, wool carders—relics of former spinning days, and many other things which, had they been preserved, would not possess a decided value as antiques; beside the quilting frames and curtain dryers.

Sometimes unbeknown to our elders we would slip down into the cellar and hunt for the raisin can. Then a hand would go in and raisins come out, but we were careful not to throw any of the telltale seeds on the floor. Of the small seedless varieties so common today we knew nothing. The raisins of my memory were large and meaty with a flavor scarcely to be found now.

We loved to smother our faces in the pennyroyal bag, to sample the pickled orange peel in the stone crock that smelled so fragrant, and purloin a handful of the newly dried apples.

The Little Hill

The smooth side-slope of the little hill, rising up steeply opposite the lower end of the apiary, was covered in springtime with a carpet of velvety green grass. This tempted us one spring to seek the delightful sport of "sledding." Frank fashioned a crude sled just large enough for a single occupant, which might be described as a platform with "runners" under it, a stick across the front end to brace our feet against and a loop of rope by which to haul it up the hill. There on a level spot near the edge of the hilltop one of us would mount the sled, and the other with a push from behind would start it going downhill. Then leaping onward and downward with increasing momentum, what a wild hair-raising gravity-ride ensued, ending almost invariably in a thrilling "spill" at the bottom!

Up again we would clamber dragging the sled once more to the top, and the other would take his turn coasting down the slick beaten path of green, with exhilarating sensations no pen can describe. But Mother, attracted by our wild laughter, discovered what we were up to, and afraid of possible broken bones, in spite of vociferous protestations, put a stop to the dangerous, delightsome sport.

Upon the mountainsides about the place—its deeper green standing out against the gray background of the "rabbit-brush"—known to us familiarly as "old man brush"—that covered the mountains all about the canyon, grew the thrifty sumac shrub, or "mangla," which we called "Sour Berry Bush." Several of these grown to tree size graced the little hill. One in particular, standing on the blunt point directly above the cart road, had grown to huge proportions, the red wood of its spreading branches glimpsed through glossy green foliage, and its bitter-almond odor scenting the air. This bush we could reach by climbing for a short distance up the steep face of the hill.

From June to August its showy terminal clusters of small pink-and white sweet-smelling blossoms attracted the bees which buzzed about them continually. But when the honey-sweet blossoms fell they were replaced by fruit the antithesis of sweetness. These peculiar flat berries, each about the size of a large kernel of corn, which in shape it greatly resembled were covered with a white, sticky, frost-like substance so extremely sour that the very sight of it would cause our mouths to water. This coating was easily removed with water, to which it imparted its strong acid flavor—not unpleasant when thus diluted. So, into cups of water we would put some of these berries, stirring them about till the frost disappeared and then removing, adding to the beverage, honey or sugar if available, and drinking it as "lemonade." We called it "sour berry water" and thought it delicious.

The little hill in springtime was a riot of beautiful flowers. Its whole side slope above the apiary was covered with the sticky monkey-flower bushes—called by us "rag flowers"—which burst out in a mass of large salmon and buff-colored, ragged-edged, funnel-shaped blossoms that lasted till late in the fall. Dotting its flattened top grew the Mariposa lily which in Spanish means "Butterfly" lily, also called "Seco," or Dry lily because it thrives in arid regions, but really a wild tulip and cousin to the onion. Its three broad lavender-rose petals, each with a deep spot of brown or purple at the inside base and thickly covered with hairs, resembled butterfly wings and invited the bees to scatter their pollen and little children to gather bouquets.

The bright red Indian Paintbrush, of the figwort family, which we called "Fire on the Mountain," with its woolly stems, tiny leaves, and flowerspike that was like a brush dipped in red paint, decked the point with its rare flaming beauty, its suckered roots stealing their sustenance from other vegetation. There too was the Indian Warrior its close relative, or so thought we, who judged by the flower-spike only, which was of a rich warm claret color, and appeared to come up in the same manner. But actually this was a very different plant having fern-like leaves, crimson when young but greening with age, and not at all parasitic. Its flowerets were filled with the sweetest nectar like that of the honeysuckle, which we loved to suck out in rivalry with the bees.

White "Shooting Stars," purple-and-yellow-trimmed, their five deeply-cleft petals reflexed like the cyclamen, which we called "lampchimbley flowers," nodded in loose umbels upon stems a foot or more in height from their basal tufts of leaves, beautifying the hillside in little patches here and there. By rare accident a flaming "blood-drop" or Windpoppy—the true pepperbox kind—once sprang up on the hill-top, but prevented by our ravenous fingers from scattering its seed, never again appeared.

The Lilac-headed Brodiaea—called also by various names, "cluster lily," "grass-nut," and "onion flower"—after its basal tuft of grass-like leaves had vanished about harvest time shot up a single tall stately stalk crowned with stiffly-erect long bluish funnel-shaped flowerets in a compact head. We would pull up these stalks and often chew them for the mild mucilaginous flavor leaving perhaps stem enough to clasp in a bouquet; and sometimes would dig down deep in the soil to secure the edible bulb which was sweet and palatable. These were a favorite with the Indians who roasted them slowly in hot ashes. The flower-heads would keep fresh for a long time in water, and it was said that if packed in damp wrapping they would stand five or six days of transportation by mail and come out fresh again when placed in water at the end of their journey.

Other flowers of many hues—yellow, pink, blue and lavender—grew upon this beautiful hill in the springtime, scattered here and there among the grass and bushes and poison oak.

The Frank Goff Bench, lying half a mile distant at the mouth of the canyon, overlooking the sea, was often in springtime a solid, gorgeous field of white-flecked, magenta-colored so-called "Pink Paintbrush," named by the Mexicans, "Escobita," or "little broom"; but which we children designated as "Magenta Flowers." More appropriate, however, was its other name of "Owls' Clover." Its branching flower stalk sent up several blossom-heads, each made up of small two-lipped, clover-like blossoms, the upper lip narrow, straight and magenta-colored, the lower inflated into the form of a creamy-white sac, with bracts of magenta surrounding them and heavily topping the spike-heads. This arrangement gave to them the effect of many flower-faces, each having a queer, owlish look.

The hardy, sticky rough-leaved, bristle-stemmed sunflower grew rank and tall along the fences and borders of our cultivated fields and on sandy banks and in pastures everywhere. Its large yellow-petalled, brown-centered, composite flowers, beautiful but ill-smelling, turned on their stems to follow the sun in his circuit through the heavens—every face on the plant toward him at his rising in the morning and his sinking below the horizon in the evening.

The General Orchard

The general family orchard might be said to have begun with the apiary, where, among the beehives, were scattered fruit trees to afford them shade. Near the upper end of the bunch grass bordered gully, two seedlings bore plentifully of small but sweet apricots. There were also seedling peaches, pears and plums. At the lower end of the apiary grew a crab-apple tree loaded with diminutive fruit striped beautifully with red on an ivory background. Too sour for eating fresh, these made delicious pies and jellies. Another tree bore a hard oblong apple juicy and delicious, with red stripes on a pale-green background, whose real name was not known. This, Father had "given" to Joan, and it went by the name of "Joan's apple."

Extending from the lower corner of the dwelling straight out to the gully, was a row of the same sword-leaved bunch-grass—cause of many cut fingers—between which and the honey house, bounded by a path from cellar to kitchen door, grew a half-dozen fig trees of the brown variety, and a row of the large trees bearing small black figs bordered the little hill.

Below the bunch-grass, the orchard proper began with two luxuriant, spreading nectarine trees, budded from peach stock, that grew, one on either side of the slanting road as it angled from house to little-hill point. Below the northernmost of these stood the lone rock that so long before had come bounding down from the cliff, e're honey house, rock wall and pepper row were in existence to impede its progress. Between this rock and the fence that separated orchard from willows along the creek, flourished a group of very tall sturdy old olive trees, laden in the fall with luscious appearing fruit—but fruit that was never intended to be eaten fresh from the tree.

These enticingly deceptive drupes, clinging in cherry-like bunches to the leafy branches and showing all stages of maturity from pea-green through shades of mottled red to ripe, rich, deep black, were indeed a beautiful sight. Sometimes campers, driving up or down the road, halted with watering mouths and yielded to the temptation to help them, only to bear their punishment in silence but never to repeat the offense.

We were just naughty enough when opportunity afforded, to snare the uninitiated who, having no acquaintance with olives except as served on their tables, and supposing they would taste even better fresh from the trees, would eagerly accept the proffered beauties. For who would ever imagine that anything so charming and lovely could be so disgustingly bitter and unpleasant! Then what a spitting and choking would ensue in the midst of our laughter! The victim's only revenge was to try the same trick later on someone else.

Many of the trees in this family orchard were figs, of which there were five or six varieties. One of these, a symmetrically rounded tree of medium size, bore a small, pale-green squatty fig, whose ripe flesh was white with a flavor quite different from all the other figs. Finishing this row, were very large spreading trees that bore small black figs, delicious and rich when fully ripe. Alongside of these next the willows, the ornamental Acacia trees filled out a bulge in the outline. Scattered through the orchard at intervals, and finishing a row near barn and roadway, were large symmetrical trees of luxuriant foliage, that bore great pear-sized purple figs, less rich, perhaps, but meaty and good.

But the prize fig of the orchard for sweet, rich, concentrated goodness, grew on a tree of scanty foliage, neither large nor beautiful, as if reserving all its strength for the perfecting of the fruit, that hung in a warm brown cover, shaped like a long, blunt finger. Even the skin of this rich fig would be eaten with relish and gustatory raptures. This, however, was not our main fig orchard. That lay across the canyon adjoining the almond trees.

Various other kinds of fruit trees grew in this orchard. There were several peaches, a small black plum, a Winter Nellis pear, two large perfect Bartlets, favorites with all, another pear sweet as honey, of pygmy size that made no more than a mouthful, and a few apple trees to fill in broken rows.

Interfering with cultivation among these trees, were two other rocks. One of these, fallen long before from the cliff and lodged in the soft ground below the woodpile, the other, a deeply embedded mass that had protruded like a rocky rib of the earth for nobody knew how long, crowded the plowed furrows to either side like great knots interrupting the grain of wood.

The lower margin of this orchard at the bottom of a gentle downgrade, was indicated by a beaten footpath across the plowed ground from barn to creek, and here began the uniform rows of apple trees.

The Apple Orchard

How shall I describe that apple orchard! The wonderful apples that ripened there were famous in their day. Perhaps their unexcelled flavor was due to the coldness of the canyon and the absence of irrigation, for California is not noted as an apple country. But be that as it may, these were real apples—apples to be remembered. Not to the glamour of childhood is due this boast, for it was without exception the expressed sentiment of visitors from far and near who sampled our fruit, and came again and again for more. Easterners considered our orchard a discovery. Unbounded was their delight, unstinted their praise. How many times we heard such exclamations as the following:

"These are the first real apples I have tasted in California!"

"These are real eastern apples. Where did you get them?"

"I have been famishing for a good apple. These are like ours back home!"

There were at least a dozen different kinds, some very early, others very late, so that they strung along through fully half of the year. Near the creek fence and pepper trees, grew a row of the little delicate yellow Early June, which we children called the "White apple," appreciated because it ripened when we were apple-hungry before the main crop matured.

Of these, the first to ripen was the firm, tart, juicy Red Astrachan. Solid red they were, glossy and most beautiful. But before they began to color, we would feast upon their windfalls.

Of tempting beauty and delightsome flavor was the mellow and juicy Maiden Blush, called by us the "Flat Apple" because flattened in shape. Like the heightened flush on the cheek of a blushing maiden was the splash of bright red on one side of its polished, almost flesh-colored, pale, creamy-green surface.

There was the Roxbury Russet, so different from these that it seemed almost another kind of fruit. Its surface was rough and seamy and of a dull grayish color. Mellow and soft of texture, so tart as to set the teeth on edge, yet of a most intriguing flavor, this apple was one of which we never grew tired. And what wonderful sauce and pies it made!

Just the opposite, so mild of flavor, was the large smooth-skinned, tender Smith Cider, covered with broken pink stripes.

Near the center of the orchard grew the Rhode Island Greening, a very large apple, deep green of color, juicy, with a strong, refreshing flavor all its own. A ripe, creamy-fleshed, mellow Greening was hard to beat.

Near these were to be found two of the largest apples ever grown in the country, the true names of which we never knew? One of these, slightly oblong in shape, immense of size and of a light green color, we called the "Green Apple." It was mellow and delicious beyond description. The other, more round and fully as large, was deeply striped with red, and of a very different texture and flavor, being hard and juicy. Surrounding the core was an area of irregular, wavy lines resembling delicate, green-tinted watered ribbon. We named this the "Water Core."

There were Winesaps, perhaps the least favored, yet excellent for cooking, and the familiar Jonathans, small, red, sweet and tasty, and a larger, oblong, red-striped hard apple, which came from Oregon, and was to us otherwise nameless. We called this the "Oregon Apple."

But of all the apples that grew in the orchard, the White Winter Pearmain took the prize. This apple was a prime favorite with all the family and with neighbors far and near. Light green of color, juicy and tender-fleshed, with a flavor like ambrosia, and entrancingly fragrant, it was an apple to dream about. That marvelous flavor—that delicate, haunting perfume, like nothing else in all the world of apples, once known can never be forgotten. How many times since those far-away days have I longed for another such White Winter Pearmain! But only once has fortune so favored me. It was in a Long Beach market I saw them—the large pale beauties with their characteristic shape—I tasted, I rejoiced, and purchased all I could carry away, intending to return for more. But when I came they were all gone, and never reappeared. Nor could I find out where they were grown. There are "Pearmains" so-called, in markets everywhere so far as name and outward appearance go; but repeated disappointments with tasteless, insipid counterfeits, have taught me to shun them.

After we had gorged for many weeks on fresh apples, sold what we could, cooked the windfalls into pies and applesauce, and dried some for winter use; when campers had gone from the beaches and October had begun to sharpen the air, then all hands turned out to harvest what remained on the trees.

With buckets and boxes, we climbed and picked, and piled into the wagon-bed all the golden wealth and ruddy glory of the orchard, transporting its commingled perfumes to the upper corncrib, or in case of an overflow, to the lower—for the corn-pile was then reduced to corners.

At evening time, the day's last fragrant load would be topped by the happy face of the youngest picker—a mere baby, sitting on the bare heaped-up apples, enveloped in an aura of incense ever afterward to be remembered.

The Weed-Patch and Corrals

From the wash-house tree to the cow corral, was an area, bounded on the upper side by the angling hillside fence and on the lower by the roadway, that was uncultivated, rather rocky, and wholly given over to natural vegetation, for the most part rank malvia, which we called the "Weed Patch."

The dense malvia, rank and tall—often over our heads in the spring and summer, provided a lovely place to play. Trampling down a path from the edge to its interior, we would mat down a circular area for a "house," or it might be several adjoining areas for different "rooms" and connect them by "doors," the matted weeds forming a "carpet" of green, the high standing malvia living "walls," and the blue sky the roof. Often we made two of these "houses," one for Annie and her "family" and the other for me and my "family." Many happy hours, spring after spring, we spent in this weed patch, our houses fresh made each season, yet with never varying style of architecture.

We endeavored to build our houses away from the windward side of the pig pen, just inside the weedy margin from the skirting road, for this picketed enclosure gave forth an odor all its own. One corner partitioned off afforded a little pen for the calves while being weaned from their bovine mothers, who stood often with their heads over the cow-corral fence gazing toward their offspring, and "mooed" plaintively.

On the upper slope of the weed patch lay a large rock—or pile of rocks—of huge proportion, that once had been a part of the cliff, and climbing over it were most beautiful wild roses, mingled as usual, with poison oak as a protection from our covetous fingers. We were afraid of snakes also in the many crevices and dense undergrowth about this splintered rock so gave the place a rather wide berth.

One of its parts had rolled farther down to lodge nearer the roadway. In this rock were many little cup-like depressions, which caught and held the water that fell as dew or rain. We played these were "tubs" and in them gave our weed dolls many a bath. We loved to climb up onto the top of this rock, which was many times higher than our heads.

Little Charlotte, the youngest, was one day entrusted to Annie and me to look after. Playing in the weed patch till tired of such fare, we essayed to clamber up onto this rock for dessert. We instructed Charlotte to stay down on the ground, telling her she was too little to keep her hold and would fall off. She, however, thought otherwise, and was determined to follow us to our high perch. In vain we remonstrated. Up she clambered till half way to the top, then, losing her hold, promptly fell off, waking the echoes with her loud screams.

Mother, always on a tension for fear of snakes, hearing the uproar, rushed out of the house and came on a run. Upon learning the cause of the disturbance, she unbuttoned our panties and gave Annie and me each a spanking. Charlotte went to the house with a guilty conscience—Annie and I to sulk till our smarting bottoms recovered, sputtering over the injustice of this cruel world.

The cow corral sloped two ways, down from the weed-patch barn-ward, and down from the hills behind it, to a more level spot near the cistern. There was no dividing fence between this and the horse corral on the other side of the barn, all was one long enclosure, indented by the buildings, yet the animals seemed to recognize their own side. The cows collected at evening time to be milked, chewed their cuds, lying on the sloping ground at night, and waited again in the morning to be fed and milked, before filing out along the many little trails, beaten hard by frequent hoofs, that focused at the far corral gate through its descending end fence. From the gate a little path led around Lion Head Point into the filaree pasture beyond.

We liked to watch the boys milk the cows. The sound of streaming milk beating against the bottom of the tin bucket, changing to softer music as the foam rose higher and higher, was both soothing and alluring. It was interesting too, the way the milker balanced himself on the one-legged stool, holding the bucket between his knees while relieving "bossy" of her stored-up goodness, as she chewed her cud contentedly. Whenever she switched her tail, the white foam was dotted with little specks of dust, that Mother must carefully strain out through a fine cheesecloth or superfine wire strainer.

But often when we came out to enjoy this evening treat, Joseph used the occasion to enjoy himself, at our expense. In a manner quite disconcerting to our female dignity, he practiced straight-shooting by turning full upon our faces the white stream that never missed its mark, filling eyes, ears, and noses; then laughed hugely at our discomfiture, as indignantly, we started for the house to wash up.

In those days, quite a stir was created by some would-be scientist who claimed that milk while warm from the cow, contained a "vital element," which he called "glame," not to be found in the same milk when cold. So he was urging people to drink their milk warm from the cow.

We always hastened past the disagreeable stable that faced the road nearby, with its inevitable manure piles, from whose odorous topography rose up swarms of flies, to settle back again after each temporary disturbance.

On the horses' side, piercing the fence where it came back from behind the barn to the roadway, was a gate through which they might be led when wanted for service. Here, under the dripping faucet of a branch pipeline from the hillside spring, stood the large horse trough, built half inside and half outside, that the horses might drink either from corral or roadway.

The Point and Beyond

The lower portion of Lion Head Point was one great embedded mass of rock that rose step-like upward in a series of rock terraces to a high eminence, above which the mountain brush commenced. Here trails began, leading up to the first two caves of a series that continued around the bend at intervals, helping to form the cliff above the filaree pasture.

Lion Head itself, a huge rock topping the bluff of the receding ridge, viewed from nearby positions, bore no resemblance to the head of a lion. But distantly, from a southwesterly direction the likeness was striking.

This rock terrace, which we called simply "the point," teems with memories of early childhood. Here we played day after day, venturing sometimes as far up as the caves, though fearfully, for we had been told that coyotes and wildcats lived there. But for the most part we found the lower point more fascinating. Annie and I would "divide" it along its natural seams and ridges, each claiming a specified portion for her "house," and "visit" back and forth.

Our only knowledge of two-story dwellings was derived from Frank Goff's story and a half cabin home, the stairway of which we had on occasion ascended to their attic bedrooms. Afterward we never ceased to long for an "upstairs house," and wished Father had thought of building ours that way. Going up and down these terraces over the slippery moss and lichen to "play like" we were "going up stairs" was delightfully near the genuine experience.

The rock moss was thin and barely noticeable on sunny prominences, but in crevices and shady places where soil had collected, grew rank and beautiful like a deep-piled carpet. Mingled with it were polypody ferns standing up out of the moss like miniature trees from a soft green lawn. To me this was most beautiful. I wanted Mother to enjoy it. Nothing was too good for Mother, and every beautiful thing reminded me of her. I peeled off a slab of the velvety stuff with its little fern trees and carried it home to her. But how should it be preserved? Mother suggested the big platter, a happy thought. So there I arranged it with its adherent soil, a deep velvety green carpet with trees of fern— a thing of beauty indeed. Mother was appreciative of my efforts, which made me very happy. She set the platter in her own room where it retained its lovely freshness for a long time, even until the platter was needed for use.

It was on the rocky base of this point that I first learned how baby kittens came into the world. One day, coming suddenly upon our old housecat squatting upon the rock, I found her in great pain and making her sufferings vocal. I stood, wondering what could be the matter, yet afraid to touch her for fear of being scratched, when to my amazement, a little transparent sac slipped out onto the rock, enclosing a tiny, mummy-like baby. My eyes grew big with astonishment, as she turned and snipped with her teeth the thin covering, and began to dress the little thing in cat-mother fashion with her tongue. It was not long before another followed, and still another, with pauses between accompanied by dismal yeaouls, until four or five babies lay on the rock like little "drowned rats," which she continued to lick till clean and dry, pausing at intervals to purr contentedly.

Those few minutes had taught me more about baby things than all my previous years. My first desire was to tell Mother about it. But what if she should think me immodest for watching, and say, "For shame!" But who could help watching a thing so interesting. It seemed evident that I had stumbled on to something that was better kept to myself. But I did whisper the secret to Annie, who wished, oh so much, that she might have seen it too. Afterward, in a similar accidental manner, I beheld a baby calf make its entrance into the world, and thus, my knowledge grew.

Always, we were entranced with babies of every kind. How we loved the new-born colts and calves, the little pigs, the puppies and kittens, the little downy chicks and ducklings! And the little wild birdies too! But we loved the kittens best of all, for we could play with these, and caress them to our heart's content. Every baby animal born on the farm was "given" to one or the other of us, and so long as it remained a baby, we would call it our very own and glory in the possession.

Some distance around the point at the base of the hillside grew a very large circular clump of wild roses, generously mingled with the glossy foliage of poison oak in a tangled riot of dangerous beauty. Its base fortified by many broken, tumbled rocks, this clump was an ideal harbor for snakes. Thus doubly forbidden, we often stood gazing on the glorious beauty beyond possession, venturing perhaps to reach up for one delicate pink bud that leaned out farther than the others—a temptation too hard to resist.

On the grassy slope above grew many springtime flowers, creamcups, buttercups, fiddleneck, forget-me-nots, and the exquisitely dainty azure baby-blue-eyes. Wild lettuce, or purselain, too grew on this hillside, which we ate, and often brought home for greens.

Above the filaree pasture rose the cliffs, a broad yellow stripe across the face of the mountain, which receded to unseen heights beyond. At the immediate foot of the cliffs, mingled gourd vines and poison oak ran riot, forming with the brush, tangled mats of vegetation that required no little hardihood to penetrate. Below these, the slopes were grassy with a sprinkling of brush and an occasional elderberry or sumac or patch of cactus all interspersed with rocks of every size and shape from small stones to great rocks the size of a house. In and around these sandstone caves and along the base of the cliffs, lay the characteristic deep yellow, powdery dust, and the age-old seashells in advanced stages of decomposition.

These cliffs and caves were yearly scenes of busy activity. Returning every spring to their deserted cities, the swallows built their habitations of mud obtained from the creek-bottom nearby, repairing as well, their homes of former seasons. All day long through the nesting season, the atmosphere in the vicinity of the caves was darkened by many thousands skimming and wheeling about and uttering their peculiar purring notes, as they passed to and fro fetching materials for their masonry. Hundreds of them might be seen at the same spot in the creek-bottom, standing on their bills, a forest of tails in the air, and wings whirling.

The Spring

Midway of the "Filaree" pasture, the mountain that formed the canyon's south wall, was curiously divided by a distinct ridge from top to bottom, resembling a corner. Here the sandstone cliffs that had begun around the Point, came to an end with their caves, changing the entire aspect of the mountain. From this apparent corner, it seemed to be receded, or set back, leaving the pasture wider at its foot than elsewhere.

Some distance up this hillside, an area of deeper green and more luxuriant foliage marked the location of the cold mountain spring from which our domestic water was now obtained. The naked embankment of slate-gray clay and rock that had been dumped at the time of excavation, stood out as a further betrayal.

A narrow road, built for temporary use, being scarcely more than two wagon-wheel tracks through brush and poison oak, wound up the hillside from pasture to spring, quickly overspreading the road again after its abandonment. Especially in the spring, when the sap was flowing freely, and the Poison Ivy festooned the bushes all along these trails, we had only to pass on the windward side without visible contact to receive the windborne pollen and suffer its baneful effects. But "go," we would. The attractions of that interesting place were so overpowering as to shrink the risk into insignificance. Even poor Mother's warnings and pleadings were but lightly regarded. It was fascinating to stand within the entry way of that cold dripping tunnel, with its ceiling high overhead, and its length lost in far dark regions beyond our exploration, and almost concealed by luxuriant climbers, to shout aloud into its hollow depths and hear the deafening echoes answer. Excavated from solid rock, its long basin-like floor, a foot or more in depth, gently overflowed with icy cold water, that trickled away down the hillside to disappear somewhere on its unfinished journey. The place teemed with animal and bird life, since the smaller creatures from far and near, came to the spring to drink. Always there were quail about and these, though so tame and trusting, we considered our legitimate prey. Following the pattern of those older, Frank built a coop-like trap of laths with a little door in the top. It was "set" by raising up one side from the ground to be held by a trigger contraption with a small wooden "pan" on which the bait was placed. One or two pecks of an inquisitive bill on this pan were sufficient to "spring" the trap, and the coop would fall, imprisoning all within it.

We would scatter bits of grain along the path leading up to the trap and place a little on the ground inside as an inducement, and leave it overnight. In the morning we might find half a dozen or more birds inside. Then, what a moment of exultation for us! Through the little door in the top, we would chase them around with reaching arms, till the last one had found its place in our "gunny-sack," and then, proud as any hunter in the land, hie us homeward, with game enough for a potpie or a dumpling stew.

The Filaree Pasture

The area of several acres that formed our filaree pasture was carpeted like turf with mingled alfilaria and clover, growing deep and rank in the springtime.

When the tiny yellow clover blossoms, shaped like the pea flower—to which family they belong—would drop in summer, behind them would be left curious little green pods, twice coiled and covered with soft hooked prickles. Hardening and browning as the plant matured and withered, these burs would lie on the ground to torment our bare feet, as we walked through the pasture.

The ripening alfilaria left no such briary burs behind, but its seed vessel was to us a fascinating mystery. The plant is often miscalled "pingrass," though not a grass at all, but its name, "alfilaria" translated from the Spanish, means "little pin," and quite an appropriate name it is. Actually, it belongs to the geranium family.

The tiny magenta blossoms that compose its loose umbels are of themselves insignificant, but when they fall there is left a cluster of sheath-points which grow into long, round, slender tapering pins disposed in circular group arrangement, each with its diminutive calyx at the base. When these points ripen and burst open, every one of them proves to be a separate quiver containing five thread-like arrows, which spring apart from a supporting stalk of minute proportions, each dragging its pointed, arrow-shaped seed-tip from its snug bed in the calyx, and immediately beginning to wriggle and twist about like a live thing, and to coil itself up into a corkscrew-like spiral.

By this means it buries itself in the earth, thus insuring another crop. We would pluck off these interesting pins when ready to burst open, and giving the point of one a little twist to start the process by cracking the sheath, would hold them in our hands to watch the fascinating procedure.

At the upper end of the filaree pasture in the curve of the mountain, flourished a group of sycamores, oaks, and box-elders, where the birds held high carnival. We would gather the strong-smelling, whitish-yellow elder blossoms flowering in flat, compact umbels, whose succeeding bluish ripe berries we sometimes plucked to eat, and of which Mother at times made pies. The Indians of former days not only ate the fruit, but used the dried blossoms for medicine. Among these trees lay rocks scattered about, half concealed by rank, waist-high grass, an ideal haunt for snakes. So we seldom played here, even though the blackbirds might build nests in every tree, and music fill the glen; and though, a small apiary of unknown ownership, far up the ravine behind in the mountain's bent elbow, might tempt us to try the steep trail through the brush.

Close by the skirting road of the filaree pasture, midway between the first and second gates, stood a large rock of many tons that in times remote had broken from the cliffs above, with others that now lay scattered over the hillside, and rolling farther than they all, had found its present lodgment not far from the bank of the creek.

Here at this lone rock, we frequently played. Like the one in the weed patch it was much pitted and full of basin-like depressions. In the summer time these became filled with dust mingled with many wind-borne seeds of weeds and grasses, and in the rainy season they collected water. Thus it was that in the springtime this "barren rock" became the fertile nursery of many little miniature gardens, to flourish for a brief while, then perish in the summer sun.

Under our resourceful genius, these "gardens" became transformed into cattle ranches and prosperous farms, the homes of many a weed-doll family with their busy activities, occupations and conversations, guided by "remote control," as day after day we sought again this fascinating diversion.

The Dirt Fight

It was near this "historic" rock, one Midsummer Day, that the "famous" dirt fight took place, in which four of us had a hand, Frank and I, Annie and Charlotte, ranging in ages from nine to four.

The immediate scene of this engagement was the road itself, at this season inches deep with soft, powdery, gray dust of flour-like fineness, superimposed upon the underlying hard-beaten roadbed. We were scuffing our bare feet through it to get the soothing reaction of soft, delicious dirt "squashing" up between our toes with all its delightful sensations, and enjoying also the clouds of dust that rose responsively upward.

Just what started the bombardment is not now recalled, nor is it of importance, but somebody—most likely Frank—cast the first handful. Then the battle was on. Soon we were all at it full swing in a "free-for-all, hit-or-miss," indiscriminate combat, vying each with the others as to which could throw the most handfuls of this soft, powdery dirt at the other contestants.

How the dirt flew! How it filled four pairs of ears to the brim—eyes not escaping, though, except at intervals of scooping up more dirt, blindly closed for their preservation! How the hairs of four heads were loaded to the depths of their follicles! How our clothes dripped with it!

It was great fun while it lasted. With the consequences, we were not at that time concerned. Interrupted by the ringing call: "Din-ner-r-r-r!" that woke the echoes of cliff and cave, what a sight we must have been from the crowns of our heads to the soles of our feet, as, with the appetites of young wolves, increased by this strenuous exertion, we presented ourselves at dinner time in the presence of our elders!

Did we partake of that delicious repast whose savory odors regaled our nostrils and bathed our taste buds with salivary unction? Not we four. Our older sisters, who had the care of us and of our clothes were now our judges, and their untempered wrath fell heavy upon us.

Did they strip us! Did they jerk us about and spill their wordy ire! Did they soap us and scrub us from heads to heels, unmindful even of suds dripping, in spite of tightly squinted lids, into smarting eyes—borne stoically by culprits convinced of the futility of protest! Let imagination do its worst; for once it cannot outstrip reality.

At last they put us, clean but sorrowful, into separate beds under the awful sentence that there we must stay dinnerless, supperless, companionless, with not a sound out of us, till morning. Then they left us, "unwept, unhonored and unsung," to our doleful doom—themselves returning to their belated meal and, with the righteous members of the clan, eating up everything.

If—as I have since suspected—a certain grim humor lurked underneath their harshness, it was assiduously hidden from the wrongdoers, whose lesson must not be weakened by sentiment. By not so much as a softened tone would they condone the offense or encourage its repetition. And so the lesson went home. Somehow, soft, powdery road-dirt, as a means of offense and defense, lost suddenly its charm and potency for four sadder and wiser little mortals, as they writhed in bed through the longest day ever calendared in the world's history, and thereafter, temptation was obliged to look for other ports of entry.

CHAPTER 24 ON THE OUTSIDE

There were places outside our own special dominions, around which the heart's memories cluster with equal possessiveness. Among these was the spring in Wood Canyon.

One of our earliest sources of pleasure was accompanying older brothers on journeys after water, sitting in the high spring seat, or squatting on the straw in the back of the wagon among the barrels.

The round trip, though only six miles, consumed the better part of half a day, for we seldom traveled faster than a walk, since Ted and Bill, taken perhaps from the plow, must not be abused by overwork.

Near the "first gate," at the end of the bordering row of apple trees, grew clumps of "sweet anise," or fennel, often as high as our heads—their long green, thread-like leaves and bright yellow flowerets enticing us to snatch a handful to chew, as we opened the gate.

Driving through, we rounded the bend into the filaree pasture and followed the bank of the willow-bordered creek to the "second gate," which somebody would again jump out to open, while we passed through, now outside of our own boundaries. Before crossing the creek, that here made a sharp bend to the left, the road descended along the face of a high bank in front of Sycamore Canyon. Just as we started down this grade, a gnarled old willow tree leaned over invitingly, and passing under, we would reach up above our heads to catch hold of overhanging leafy tips, retaining in our grasp some of the broken green leaves, as the moving team bore us away. It seemed ever so delightful to be able to reach from the height of the wagon, branches that were from the ground so high and unattainable.

The road continued to hug the bank for some distance before angling across the creek into the midst of the mustard patch, from which it emerged on the other side of the canyon. Soon, we passed an old abandoned chimney of stone standing all-alone like a specter of the past, where a cabin once had been. This old landmark was used for years as a milepost, and whenever we came to the "old stone chimney," we knew we were just a mile from home.

In measuring distance from one place to another, a white rag was tied around the rim of one of the wagon wheels, whose circumference was known. Someone then, watching closely, would count the revolutions made, which were then reduced to miles. Of course this measurement would not be accurate, but qualified by all the deviations of the wheel in its progress. And since the roads were often very crooked, a later straightening of these would greatly modify our calculations.

What a wonderfully interesting trip that was, winding up through pastures, first on one side of the creek, then on the other, as we crossed it time after time. Occasionally, stretches of willows marked the course of the stream, and patches of tules grew in its sandy bed. Waving green fields of wild oats, that knew no sickle but the teeth of living herds, stretched away on every hand.

Bands of bleating sheep compelled us to wait while their thousands, led by an old bellwether, filed across the roadway. Hundreds of little mottled gray-and-buff ground squirrels, their bushy tails arched and streaming out behind, scuttled away to their holes at our approach.

Often we passed a little speckled, brownish-white and tail-barred "Johnnie Owl" (burrowing owl) no bigger than a squirrel, sitting solemnly like an elfin sentinel, by one of these holes near the roadside. His habit was to catch and eat the squirrel, then occupy the hole himself. Though wary, he would never raise a wing, for he knew we were his friends, but without moving his body, would turn his head, to follow us with his keen little eyes, so far around it seemed surely he would twist it off.

Then we would hear, thrice repeated, the sharp warning call: "Take care sir! Take care sir! Take care sir!" and a flock of quail would rise with a whirr, to settle down farther away near the foothill.

We were almost sure, either going or coming, to start a roadrunner, that most interesting and friendly of birds, who loved nothing more than to run lightly and swiftly along the road in front of us, his long pointed tail erect, his crested, blackish-blue head stretched forward, and his long, stout legs moving easily and smoothly over the ground as if without effort, stopping every now and then for a moment, then starting on again, keeping just out of reach in a roguish dare: "Catch me if you can!" but never allowing himself to be overtaken.

Often, near the foothills, we would start a rabbit from some bush or clump of cactus, who would go bounding on ahead in the roadway, or strike off across the pasture, his little cottony tail bobbing up and down as he leaped over the ground. Or it might be, a large jackrabbit leaped forward, fleeing in long jumps across the countryside, the tips of his long, pointed ears rising with every bound above the wild-oat heads, followed by the dog in hot pursuit.

Sometimes this trip to the spring would be turned into a rabbit hunt. Then we little folks would be left sitting in the wagon while the boys explored their haunts. They were sure to find some around cactus patches, where rabbits love to hide, coming out early, mornings and evenings to nibble on green grass shoots—and meeting a doleful fate when confronted with guns.

It was not uncommon, on such occasions, to reach home late in the afternoon with a whole "gunnysack" full of game—all we could hope to use before it should spoil. Then followed the evening task of cleaning the game—a task much greater than that of securing it, and far less thrilling, but compensated for by later feasts of delicious fried rabbit and quail pot-pie.

In due time, we reached the mouth of Spring Canyon where the road branched, crossing its small tributary creek and entering a region forested with beautiful oak and elder trees. Soon we came to the cool refreshing spring bubbling up between low embankments in the bed of a little wash that furrowed the canyon floor. Short pieces of plank, lying prone, afforded a slightly elevated approach from the muddy margin to the overflowing spring, with its low, square curb. On every side of it, water oozed from the saturated ground, and flecked with dancing patches of sunlight that filtered through dense overhanging branches, trickled away in miniature streamlets to the little meadows below, which in turn responded with a wealth of green and purple beauty.

Every springtime, in these meadows and all around would spring up lovely lavender and bluish-purple fields of rank and aromatic pennyroyal, or mustang mint, perfuming the air with its entrancing fragrance. It was our joyous duty to gather this for Mother, who would dry and store it away in clean flour sacks for future medicinal use. How we delighted in the task, and sniffed the blossoms as we plucked! And in the fall how we loved to hug the bags of dried sweetness to our noses, for time did not destroy its royal incense. So, while the boys were dipping up their buckets of clear, cold water from the spring, and carrying it up the muddy bank in many trips back and forth, to fill the waiting barrels, we younger helpers were gathering the lovely pennyroyal in fragrant armfuls to carry home to Mother.

All too soon, before we had half-finished our happy task, the barrels were brimming full and covered tightly with gunnysacks, over which hoops were placed and driven part way down, and the boys were ready to return home. But in spite of precaution, the water was bound to slop more or less as we jolted along over the rough roads with the precious liquid that must last us for all household purposes until our next trip should be made.

Sycamore Grove

Another lovely spot that belonged to us by right of use and appreciation, was the beautiful grove of sycamore trees, then in their prime that filled the mouth of Sycamore Canyon just beyond the second gate.

This small forest of broad spreading sycamores shaded a grassy flat, unbroken save for a solitary gully that carried mountain freshets in wintertime to the creek flowing along its front. Their clustering leafy garments, rich in subdued tones of tan and gray-green, parted coyly like those of enticing maidens, leaving open spaces for the exposure of graceful bare limbs, mottled in varying shades of gray. Here and there, enhancing by contrast the general beauty of the grove, the brilliant deep green foliage of an oak tree came shining through. Always and ever, we delighted to explore this place. It was a paradise for birds of every description, and no less so for children.

My earliest memory of it—somewhat hazy, yet definite enough to be more than imagination—was of family picnics, supplemented on occasion by others, perhaps neighbors from the coast, or it might be campers from the beach newly acquired as friends. Memories of long tables improvised of boards set up across "saw-horses" and loaded with good things, of a small rock fireplace that smelled of potatoes roasting in the ashes, and of coffee boiling over, vie for recognition with those of stout rope swings suspended from overhanging boughs, where we swung far out into the open spaces to greet the birds and the sunshine, and to gaze down upon the creek and pastures beyond.

There are dim mental visions of older young folks standing up on the swing-board, two together, facing each other, alternately bending and pushing, till the swing rose so high they would be stretched out for a frightening moment at each alternating extreme, on a horizontal level high overhead. We would hold our breath in suspense till the wild flight was allowed to slacken to saner paces.

In clearer memories of this delightful place, I am wading through tall grass or climbing trees with Frank and Annie after birds' nests, or, as often happened, wandering about alone, listening to all the mingled sounds of the woods; to bird-calls, to the mysterious rustle of dead leaves, stirred perhaps, by small life, or by vagrant winds, or it may be a gliding snake to be avoided. It always meant peering cautiously about to discover, without startling, some nesting bird, and searching every hollow tree-trunk for signs of a wren's nest, and dreaming—always day-dreaming, and "making up poetry" in a vain effort to express all the strange feelings and longings that well up within the inner consciousness. I loved that sycamore grove. It influenced my life.

One spring, a lovely group of royal Matilija poppies burst into bloom to the north of the grove, their white blossoms four or five inches across, with crepe-like petals and golden centers, that, so far as I know, appeared neither before nor afterward. At another time, straying far up into the canyon, I came across a gorgeous mahogany-red peony— the "Christmas Rose," several inches across its blossom and featuring a center of heavy yellow stamens. I had never seen the like of this before, and gathered the lovely thing to carry home to Mother.

The Mustard Patch

One of our most interesting playgrounds was the Mustard patch, a broad level area on the southern tip of the Rawson pastures north of the creek. Here, in season, grew a dense forest of tall mustard, often high enough to conceal a man on horseback. This field in blossom time was a most magnificent sight, acres and acres of waving yellow bloom so thick and even it appeared to have been sown and cultivated by the hand of man.

Here was the haunt of the red-winged blackbirds that would settle like a cloud upon the swaying tips that bent to their weight, and warble in a rippling chorus of joy. Birds of many kinds fluttered and hopped about among the branches, larks and linnets built their nests in its dense seclusion. Butterflies and bees helped themselves to the sweetness it afforded, as they flitted and buzzed over the Yellow Sea. Little wild rodents scuttled about on the ground within its concealment. Snakes also found rich provision there, and swarms of insect life hovered over its golden surface.

There was plenty to be discovered here in this mustard patch, and bird nests we might easily reach. And in its depths we loved to play, showered with its golden snow, and after the four-petaled blossoms all had fallen, to pluck the long, slender, thread-like pods and sample their peppery contents.

When the advent of autumn dried up the mustard, we would have more fun than ever "playing horses." It would then be a field of barren stalks, but every stalk was a potential steed. At the point where the young mustard plant first breaks through the earth just above the root attachment, it forms a double bend that in the mature stalk greatly resembles the ankle joint and upper part of a horse's hoof. The stalk when dry can be easily pulled out of the ground and above this bend is very straight and tough. Selecting a "good one," we would trim off all the short, dry branches and the slender top, break off the root mass below the bend, and then on a sandstone rock by brisk rubbing, grind the lower surface smooth for the sole of the foot, and we had our horse's hoof; the peculiar bend making the resemblance very realistic.

Each of us must needs have two of these modified stalks, one in each hand—by which means they were very dexterously operated—to form our front feet and legs. Our "hind feet"—well, they may have borne a closer resemblance to the feet of a bear than of a horse, since they really were "bare" feet, but we didn't mind that, we couldn't see our own hind feet, we were too much occupied with the novelty of our front ones; besides, who cares about a little matter like that?

We champed, we ran, we trotted, we loped; we kicked with our hoofs and pawed the ground; we ate imaginary green grass, and drank imaginary water from the very real creek—for of course, our necks were not quite long enough to reach the real water. We whinnied, we bucked, we carried imaginary riders; we rested one foot at a time as horses do; we had our feet shod, we talked to each other about our masters and other subjects supposed to be of interest to horses.

Day after day, for hours at a stretch, we would give ourselves up in abandonment to this game. If we had herding duties to perform, all the better, this play relieved the irksomeness of our task. Could we not as gallant steeds chase the cattle and hogs with greater speed and effectiveness than as humans unaided? We felt that our fleetness was increased fourfold. Thus invested with all the equine attributes, these "horses," assistants in labor, companions in play, grew into our affections, and when the day was over we would bed them down for the night in some secret place where no stupid elder, who wouldn't know a horse when he saw it, would accidentally use them for kindling wood.

Of all the famed "make-believes," this one I think would have taken the prize for furnishing pure delight. Perhaps to Frank belongs the chief credit for this "invention"—or discovery—or was it both? though each developed it along individual lines. At any rate, Frank led out in the "horsey" imitations.

Never did we tire of this captivating game. Each recurring season found us with a brand new set of prancing steeds. It seemed to fill us with a rare, exhilarating sense of freedom—the freedom of the open spaces, and even yet thrills me with the memory of outgrown joys.

The Playground Eternal

Of all our wonderful playgrounds, the most fraught with memories, the most invigorating, the most broadening in influence, was the long series of white sandy beaches framed in a background of mountains and mesas, jutting bluffs and overhanging cliffs, and fronting the grand, the beautiful, the loved old ocean.

Here, we played, we bathed, we hunted the sea's treasures, we picnicked, we explored, we fished, we reveled in freedom, we lived.

Aliso Beach, possessively and intimately our own, lay short and wide before the mouth of the canyon. Narrowing to the north, its strip of sand terminates with "Tunnel Rock"—really, a rock of three tunnels, two being minor—that steps out into the sea to bar the way. On the south of Aliso Beach, two points, closely connected, each with its overhanging face, permitted us to pass, by clambering over tumbled masses of rocks piled indiscriminately below, and jumping from boulder to boulder with foaming waters sloshing between, to reach our bathing place around the bend.

Here, another face of the same bluff looked southward, and leaning out with high overhanging wall, formed almost a cave that with its white sandy floor, afforded us a fairly well sheltered "dressing room."

From the solid rock base of this bluff, extending out into the sea, and accessible only at lowered tides, lie the broad, flat-topped, wave-washed "mussel rocks," crowded with upward pointed, tightly clinging mussels, each of which, during the year, might reproduce a hundred thousand others. These, in proper season, we gathered for food.

Between mussel rocks and a higher ridge to the south, stretches the "channel," a narrow, dangerous gorge where surging seas come swiftly in, and go out with a great suction, its wide mouth perilously close to our dressing room. In passing this death trap, we guarded well our steps and closely watched the little ones.

From the channel, the ridge of rock half-circles away to form a sort of protected basin, lined with sand, whose rocky rim shatters the force of incoming breakers. Within this rough enclosure the water was more or less shallow, but deepened to a long, roomy pool, sheltered and quiet, at the side of a protecting ridge, which we called our "bathing pool." Except at high tide when nobody bathed, this was considered a safe place for women and children.

But for swimming room, the men would go farther south around the next point, to reach which, they must clamber over a long rough stretch of rock-ridges and channels bare of sand, and low, narrow caves running far up under the bluff, where waters rushed with cavernous roar. Beyond this low, sharp point, huge breakers, challenging the prowess of swimmers, rolled in upon another long white beach that stretched away to "Flat Rock."

Swimming was a man's sport. No one thought seriously of teaching girls to swim. Indeed, it is a question how they could have managed it anyway with their hampering skirts. Women dressed in those days to go into the water. A girl past the age of childhood would have thought it shamelessly immodest to appear on the beach, even before men of her own family, without stockings. To have donned a man's abbreviated, tight-fitted suit would have been unthinkable. Women made their own modest dresses, knee-length and belted, with full bloomers meeting stockings at the knee in a fitted band. They had never heard of rubber bathing caps, so usually had to wash their long hair free of the salt, after returning home.

For chewing gum, we used black brea gathered from ocean rocks, whenever we could find it free of sand. It had a wholesome tarry flavor. We seldom returned from bathing without some of this brea-gum.

Opposite our bathing pool was a long, narrow fissure in the slanting face of the cliff. In passing, one day, I discerned faint squeaky sounds issuing from its depths. Thinking of a possible nest of beach mice, I began to prod in the crevice with my stick. All of a sudden, zip, zip, zip, out shot a multitude of bats in an ever lengthening stream that almost bowled me over. In haste and wonderment, I sought a safer position from which to view the astonishing spectacle. Hundreds and increasing hundreds of bats in startled confusion darkened the air like a cloud. How so many could find lodgement in a place so small, and why they should, was a double mystery.

After bathing and swimming were over, and the last garment donned safe from intrusion where no intruders existed, we would be joined by the men folks and all troop back around the point and along the sand to the triangle, where waited the team and wagon. Perhaps we stooped to pick up a few shells or pebbles on our way, or to snip the lilac bloom of the Sand-Verbena, or the golden flowers and silvery leaves of the Beach Primrose, or the bright yellow daisy-like bloom of the Sea-Coreopsis. Or we paused at the foot of the hill to look for ripe Beach-Apples (Sea Fig), squeezing into our mouths the ripe seedy pulp with its sweetish-salty taste.

Then, that we might be home in time for evening chores, again hitching up the horses, who had munched their hay over the end-gate of the old lumber wagon while tied to its wheels, we all climbed in to sit on the hay in its jolting bed. Perhaps Father was in a jovial mood. Then, driving homeward, how lustily, in his stentorian tones, would ring out—and still are ringing down the long corridor of years—the words of "The Boatman's Song":

"Oh, the boatman's song

Is pouring along

All over the beautiful blue;

And loud and clear

Are the notes we hear

From the boatman so honest and true.

He's rowing, rowing, rowing along,

He's rowing, rowing, rowing along,

He's rowing, rowing, rowing along,

He's rowing and singing his song."

Flat Rock, standing out in the sea, was the first of two impassable barriers that locked between them a short stretch of coves and caves, all but inaccessible. Trails led up in a steep panting climb to the mesa, to go down again onto the farther beach. Viewed from the other side, Flat Rock presented a perfect resemblance to the head of an alligator, its long nose lying out in deep water, and has since been named "Alligator Point." Swells, forming at its nose, would divide, passing shoreward on either side before breaking into foam, and this made the spot ideal for fishing.

Tied down with a man's work, George at seventeen, was seldom permitted to indulge in such pastime. But when possible so to plan his work, he would slip away in secret, and for such occasions, kept a pole and tackle hidden in the brush. One late afternoon, finishing his chores earlier than usual, he hastened down to Flat Rock to indulge his favorite sport.

Scarcely had his line touched the water when he had a "bite," and to his great satisfaction, drew out a large fish, with much thrashing and floundering. Casting again, his bait was snapped up immediately, and he landed another as large as the first, with increasing jubilation. Once more he cast his line, and a third great fish was hauled out onto the rock. He had not lost even a nibble. Thrilled with exultation, he strung them on his hunting hook, and as the hour was getting late, and these three were all he thought he could carry, he quit and started for home. When he weighed them, they tipped the scales at almost thirty pounds. Father was so pleased with the catch and the supper of fried fish, that he asked no awkward questions of the boy.

Below the nose-tip of the alligator, across the waters of a cove stood "Eagle Rock," so named from its long occupancy by a pair of fish eagles, or sea ospreys, the surest fishermen of any land or clime. Year by year, they built their nest on its top-most tip above the reach of human-kind and reared their young without molestation.

Black of wing and white of breast, save for one dark stripe, this great bird might be seen soaring above the heaving water, watching, keen of eye, alert, for a finny shadow near the surface. Suddenly, folding those outspread wings tight to his body, swift as a bullet downward he plunged beneath the waves, to rise with a luckless fish in his talons. Never did he miss his prey.

Inaccessible to all but the most recklessly daring, Eagle Rock stood, a lone peak rising from a base of indiscriminate, tumbled rocks, guarded on either side by impassable buttresses and often surrounded by surging waters, whose pounding roar disturbed not its serene dignity. Today, it may be seen only in rare pictures. The topmost peak long ago fell from this towering haunt of eagles, changing its general appearance to resemble the "ship of the desert." For years it was known by the less romantic name of "Camel Rock," the eagles having long before disappeared from the coast. Further disintegrating with the ravages of time, the head and neck of the camel have also disappeared. Now it is "just another rock."

Figure 18 Camel / Eagle Rock

As restless tides and pounding waves wash in or out the shifting sands many and frequent changes occur along the coastline. Old familiar rocks and landmarks may one day be buried out of sight and long banks of sand raise the beaches to a higher level. Then again, all these rocks and many others unseen before will be exposed in all their skeleton nakedness.

An instance unique in the history of the coast took place in Seventy Five, about four years after Father's advent to Aliso, when the incoming tide piled sand so high all along the beaches that even flat rock was left high and dry, and George walked on dry sand around this point and through the coves below. Then Eagle Rock stood on a white sandy beach.

That winter, the pond, being prevented by much sand from breaking through to the ocean in flood time according to its customary manner, became a mighty lake, backing up to the third bend at the cart-road garden and walnut orchard.

A year or so later, the very opposite extreme occurred, an instance also unique. Father and George, one winter day, went down to the beach, and to their tremendous surprise, there was no beach. Not an ounce of sand could be seen anywhere, nothing but bare, jagged masses of rock as far as they explored in either direction, or could see beyond.

As they clambered over these naked rocks, they perceived down in the cracks and crevices, shining particles like gold. Thinking they might have stumbled onto a rich discovery, they scraped off some of it and had it assayed. But it proved to be only "fools' gold" after all, just pyrites of iron.

Walking one day along the beach past the lower end of the pond, George, then a boy of fourteen, found lying at his feet in the sand—of all places the most unlikely for recovery of lost articles—a razor in its case. Undoubtedly, it had slipped out of the pocket or saddle-pack of some unlucky horseman recently passed that way.

It was an English razor, fashioned by hand and made of the best of steel, its handle inlaid with tortoise shell. On its rather thick blade appeared in beautiful hand scroll, the inscription: "I stand A No. 1." When of age to need a razor, George thinned its blade on the grindstone, regretfully removing also the beautiful script, and sent it away to be hollow-ground.

From that time on, this razor served George constantly until he became an old man. Then, when thin and fragile from sixty-three years' service, and no longer able to stand hard knocks, it was accidentally dropped and broken. Still, he proudly exhibited the pieces as a souvenir of that long-ago day when he picked it up as a boy on the sands of Aliso Beach.

"Dragon's Cave," half a mile or so below Eagle Rock, is really not a true cave, but a long, wide open tunnel having at its farther end a smaller exit, and at low tide may be clambered through. Fearsome echoes answer to the shouting voice and to the breaker's roar.

Figure 19 Dragon's Cave

"Ladder Rock" was somewhere near, so-called from a crude ladder attached to its face by some intrepid fisherman of an older day. Below these and other barriers, came "Three Arches," the far-famed, thrice pierced, turtleback promontory, where George had claimed his deer. Then followed "Autograph Cave," reached only from the mesa, its sides and ceilings carved with countless names, among them, those of the children of Aliso.

Mussel Cove, or "Coffee-Shell Beach" lay next, always thickly strewn with pebbles of various colors and sizes, among which might be found the rare and much-sought coffee-bean shell, of a pale chocolate color and corrugated surface. Its cousin also the unribbed sea-button of similar size and shape, with its larger relative, the chestnut cowrie, were found, and many other shells.

Heaped about the point here, were large masses of sea-bathed rocks, bare at low tide, where we gathered the living abalones, famed for their beautiful and useful shells, exquisitely iridescent with predominant shades of green and rose. Only the unlovely exterior, however, would be visible, the occupant clinging so tenaciously to the rocks that only strong, thin, instruments thrust under the shell without warning could dislodge him. We gathered them by the sackful at low tide, but now those days are no more. Abalones are scarce and protected by law.

Figure 20 Three Arches

Salt Creek was close by, and after that came Dana Point, its rugged profile ever gazing out to sea. This point was named in honor of Richard Henry Dana, who in Eighteen Thirty-Five, as sailor on a hide ship, there risked his life by swinging on a rope out over the bluff to kick off hides that had lodged on a ledge part way down. Hides were thrown from the top of the bluff to the sand below to be picked up by boatmen who rowed them out to ship. After this point, came Capistrano Beach, since known by other names. We never visited these farther beaches except by team and wagon.

Driving homeward along the mesa, we skirted a series of large, seaward-facing amphitheater-like chasms devoid of all vegetation, washed out of the red earth and battered to stony hardness by the oft-repeated action of water that for untold winters past had drained down from the hills behind. Their floors and sides, fluted in natural artistry with innumerable strange and fantastic carvings, sent up red steeples, spires and castles chiseled as with a graver's tool, their minutia arresting and tempting the lingering eye in passing, to ferret out the intricacy of some never-ending individual tracery.

Tunnel Rock, north of Aliso, once had a path over its roof. But the top has long since fallen in, and now it may no longer be called a tunnel. Beyond it lies one of the most interesting of landmarks—"Goff Island," a mountainous rock standing alone in the edge of the surf directly opposite "Goff Point." Back on the mesa above near the old road is the site where Frank Goff built his cabin in the long ago. Only a few scattered trees are left, reminders of a long cypress row that once bordered that old road, now disinherited in favor of a broad, concrete highway.

Goff Island is an island only at high tide, being at other times easily accessible from the dry sandy beach. Upon its broad shelving base, extensive and much fissured, we often played, sometimes in company with the Goff children, among its numerous periwinkle-bordered rock-pools, some shallow, others very deep and narrow. In their still depths, far below our reach, living starfish moved, slowly flexing their prickled rays. Sea urchins too, with their small forests of purple spines, and great golden brown turbines housing their tiny gastropods, crept about among delicate lacy seaweeds and mosses.

Figure 21 Goff Island, Looking South

In the sun-warmed water of the shallow pools often floated the smooth, oval or oblong sea cucumbers, resembling greenish-brown rocks. We would give them a shove to watch the water darken with their purple dye; and ram our ruthless fingers down the throats of the fringed, flower-like sea-anemones that rimmed the basins, to see them instantly close with an upward squirt of water and shrink back tightly to the rocks.

This beach, abounding in mosses and other sea treasures, was flanked by several narrow rock-ridges extending rib-like from the bluffs out into the surf, buried often almost to the tip-tops by the shifting sands. These lessened the force of incoming breakers, transmuting them into gentle swells, delightful for surf bathing.

Close up against the other side of Goff Point, a major mountain gulch broadened into a sandy recess filled with great sand dunes like giant anthills, and down their sides we would slide with great glee. Here, we must again revert to the mesa to reach unconquered worlds beyond. There were "Old Sea-Lion," "Rainbow Cave," and the great lone arch that pierced the partitioning ridge and afterward gave its name to "Arch Beach." There was the broad Laguna Beach, whose gradual slope far out into the surf made bathing both safe and pleasant, followed by numerous coves abounding in shells, the ferociously spouting "Devil's Hole," "Boat Canyon" where fishermen beached their boats, and beautiful curving "Emerald Bay," with its point beyond, named in much later times.

This long coastline with its many rock-ribbed beaches, belonged to us by the natural right of discovery and possession. There was none to dispute our ownership except sea birds of many kinds that shared it with us. Great solitary pelicans, with their enormous bills, long necks and pouches for prey, perched solemnly on inaccessible rock turrets, or flapped their great strong wings low over billows in search of marine provision. Scavenger seagulls flocked in companies to the sands, crying incessantly to one another, rising to swoop down upon some object beneath the waves, or settling to fight noisily over some carcass on the beach. Stately blue herons stood in quiet dignity, then rose to flap away as if on important business. Curlews, in compact flocks, would wheel and circle in unison before alighting to parade up and down the beach, on the watch for crustaceans to pull with their long curved bills, out of their hiding places. Little gray streaked snipes, or knots, would patter about at low tide on the sands, running swiftly down after each receding wave to snatch up in the act of self-burial, the quickly disappearing sandfleas, and hurrying back again up the slope before the incoming wave. Little gray plovers ran ahead of us on the sand, picking food morsels from the kelp, scattered along the wave—scallop margins.

At almost any time during the season of migration, high overhead in the blue might be seen thousands upon thousands of honking geese and quacking ducks, traveling northward with military precision in orderly formation, to settle down in the ponds, lakes and swamps of the southern coastal regions, where they were hunted without mercy, for "open season" was every season in those days. Wild ducks sailed about unconcernedly on the ocean's bosom, and filled the Laguna lakes and our own Aliso pond. There, floated the royal Mallard in all his green, blue and violet glory, the big drab Canvasback, the small, but strikingly beautiful Teal, with his iridescent colorings of wine-purple, blue, chestnut and bronzy-green, and the fat round butterball with his crest of blue, green and purple.

There also, in her mud-colored dress, paddled the inedible mudhen, or coot, her red eye and white bill in vivid contrast with the velvet black of her head as it jerked forward with every stroke, distinguishing her from the smooth-swimming duck.

Truly, this natural theater of knowledge and entertainment, once free to all, was a most wonderful ocean playground, contributing its subtle, character-building influence all through the formative days of childhood and youth. Its appropriation today by private interests kindles in my breast a fire of emotion akin to that of the dispossessed Red Man.

We grew up in the atmosphere of the ocean with all its varied moods; the playfulness of wavelets petting the pebbly beach, the hopefulness of the oncoming swell, the power and action of the mighty breaker, the ambition of rising waters climbing higher and higher for the great leap against the resisting cliffs, the accomplishment of the final crash with volumes of white spray flung high in the air, only to be perseveringly repeated, the discontent of choppy seas, the sadness of outgoing tides, the restful peace and gently waving seaweeds of quiet inlets, the constancy of its unchangeableness, the variations of its constant changing, the calmness of its quiet depths, the soothing of its lullabies, the eternities of its broad expansiveness—and the cliffs themselves—the impregnable rocks—the jutting points, that dared step out into those swirling waters and keep their foothold day and night with faces to the sea.

OLD COMPANION

Welcome me back to thy presence once more,
Dear old Companion;
Back where the sands of thy white, pebbly shore
Front my home in the Canyon;

Where the high mesas that smile on your moods—
Frightening and fleeting—
Push out their feet where your surging intrudes
And heed not your beating;

Where the encircling, re-echoing hills,
Always and after,
Lift up their cliffs where your foaming cup spills
And throw back your laughter;

While o'er their gullies and steep, rugged trails,
Winding all seaward,
Wheels the great bird of the mountain, or wails
The white, flapping sea bird.

Cradled in rock-ribbed and sand-cushioned deeps,
Creation's sigel,
Over thee arched, the blue canopy keeps
Starry-eyed vigil.

Here at my feet among eddies and rocks,
Lie children crustacean,
Heedless of whirlpool, upheaval and shocks,
Gleaning their ration.

Stealthily stealing between, and submerging
Jagged rock-masses,
Tumbling pebbles and shells, swishing and urging
Green, clinging sea-grasses,

On, come thy swells, in their shoreward succession,
Thrilled with all blisses,
Lapping, caressing the beach in possession,
With white, scalloped kisses.

So, hast thou wooed since thy waters first gathered
Into their border;
So, shalt thou woo till the cosmos there fathered
Changes its order.

Oh, woo me also, caress me with spray,
In blest reunion,
Croon to me, lave me, restore me today
The old, sweet communion.

Prone, let me lie on thy sands in the sun,
Dreaming, inhaling;
Down wave-wet stretches, again let me run,
Long seaweeds trailing.

Thou art the echo of all that is gone—
Vanished forever
Out in the distant and endless beyond,
Returning, never;

Childhood and youth, with their shadowed delights,
Now scarce remembered;
Life's stern bereavements that followed their flight,
Time-mellowed, tendered;

Strivings, ambitions that beckoned and called,
Emotions pleading,
Yearnings, submissions, and moments that galled,
And the heart's bleeding.

Scattered and changed, are the landmarks of old,
Gone, are the faces,
All, all but thou, with thy billows that roll
Still in their places.

Thou are the symbol of all that endures,
Changeless, eternal;
Thou are the essence of memory's lure,
Constantly vernal.

Thou bringest back to me, held in thine arms,
All the dear dreamings,
Unfinished still, with their pathos and charm
And tender sweet meanings.

Care free, in fancy, troop playmates I knew,
Eager feet crushing
Deep carpets where salty-sweet beach-apples grew,
Temptingly blushing;

Down the long stretches of sand-banked seashore,
Skipping and sliding,
Over rocks clambering to seek and explore
Treasure in hiding.

And out from the rock-crevice, mystery-stored,
(And probed for so seeming)
Still is envisioned the frightening horde
Of startled bats, streaming;

And the spray-showered flats where the rock-mussels grew
In colonies crowded,
And the deep-sounding caverns where seas gurgled through;
And islands, mist-shrouded,

Where fronded anemones, sensitive, shrink
Fast closing their swallows,
And sea-cucumbers offer their violet ink,
Disturbed in their shallows;

And the deep, limpid pool, in whose green, mossy depths
Of water-spread tracery,
Shiny starfish and purple-spined sea-urchins crept
In gardens of lacery;

And fast to the rocks, in the rush and the swirl,
Rough-shelled abalones
Clung with their houses, whose mother-of-pearl
Waits the polisher only;

Like the wilderness temple, whose drab covers hung,
Inward splendors, concealing,
Of the pure heart a type, glories hidden, unsung,
To its Maker, revealing.

And when, at low tide with beach widened, were brought
The sea's richer dowries,
In the ripples among the wet pebbles, we sought
Coffees and cowries.

Open thy treasures again to my soul,
Long-loved Companion,
Welcome me back to thy heart as of old—
To my home in the Canyon.

IN A SEASHELL
From the far coast line is borne to my ear,
Music, unresting;
Who can describe or explain its allure,
Ceaselessly questing?

Undulant, rhythmical, breathing in speech
Unresignation;
No other voice like the surf on the beach
In all creation.

Now, a vast concourse of world-mother hearts,
Lullabies, crooning ;
Then, sounds the siege of some far-away fort's
Dull, distant booming.

Who can fathom the spell of their variant moods,
Moon-made in mystery,
Soothing or saddening or vengefully rude,
Baffling all history?

All down the shore is a sob and a moan—
A nameless sighing
Like a slow requiem's low monotone,
Tides ebbing, dying.

Flood tides return, and grim furies in leash,
Fume at retarding
Until their wrath's intermittent increase
Swells to bombarding.
Fearsome, the oncoming breakers uproar,

Crashing in thunder,
Drenching the headlands, and high in the air,
Flinging white wonder.

Swift, in the breach, fresh artilleries pour,
Deafening, resounding;
Spent, they still mutter a-down the long shore,
Sullenly pounding.

Hark! In this seashell I press to my ear,
Rising and falling—
Mingling in one, all thy voices,
I hear Evermore calling.

CHAPTER 25 HERMIT'S CAVE

Wood Canyon, branching off from Aliso almost due north, is broad and open at its mouth, but narrows gradually as the receding walls draw closer together.

Somewhat less than half a mile up this canyon, the course of the western wall is interrupted and the floor suddenly widened by what might be called a "canyonette"—a large amphitheater-like recession in the mountainside that rather resembles the major portion of a broken bowl, its northern broken edge, slanting down to an acute point that shuts off a view of a little valley where once bubbled up the cool flowing spring that furnished us our drinking water in the long ago, and gave it the name of Spring Canyon.

High up on the mountainside a little to the right of its center, the bowl is decorated by a large rock of peculiar shape that closely resembles the elongated skull of some animal, greatly magnified, its two eye-sockets standing out boldly.

To the right of this skull, the rim of the ridge lowers to form a dip, from which a small gully zigzags to the bottom, finding its way among cattle trails to the main watercourse.

Just over the other side of this separating ridge, and out of sight from the canyon, lies an elevated area of grazing land, more or less level, skirted by a large ravine that leads down into Laguna Canyon past the old Hemenway homestead, a mile or so from the ocean beach.

Slightly to the left of the skull is a steep, narrow, rocky ravine, which holds the center of interest in the picture. Approaching this ravine from any direction, one would never suspect the existence of the long, narrow, sloping cave that parallels it, completely hidden in its southern side. To this spot attaches an unknown history that has resolved itself into a legend.

When the Salter family came into the southland in Sixty-Nine, this cave was inhabited by a man from Mexico, who lived there alone and was known as "the hermit." He possessed a set of assayers' implements, kept a few hogs, and had a little gray mule on which he rode about the country. How long he had been there was not known, but it was no secret that he was a political refugee.

An elderly man, he was, tall, slim, fine-looking, intelligent, with keen eyes, gray hair, and a pointed gray beard. In his book, "California Coast Trails, A Horseback Ride From Mexico to Oregon," J. Smeaton Chase mentions having visited this hermit's cave. The Salter boys, Gene and Charlie, met and conversed with him. But shortly after they left Aliso in Seventy-One to take up land in the Gospel Swamp, this unobtrusive hermit died, and the cave was left silent and deserted.

Soon after his arrival at Aliso, Father discovered and explored this cave. The ceiling was blackened with the smoke of many fires, and in the walls were holes drilled, into which had been driven wooden pegs, where doubtless had been hung saddles and other equipment. He brought back with him to the farm a number of articles left there by its recent tenant, among which were an old blacksmith's bellows and the large heavy head of an iron anvil, both of which served us on the farm for many years afterward.

Through many decades following, this place was known as "Hermit's Cave." But more recently it has been associated with the legend of a "Robbers' Cave" that is supposed to have been the rendezvous of bandits in the early days of California, and located somewhere in Laguna Canyon—but nobody knew where. No cave that could answer such a purpose has ever been discovered in Laguna Canyon, and the legendary cave was incredulously considered a mystery or a myth.

Its location in Laguna is now believed to be a misconception. The reason for it can be understood quite readily when the proximity and accessibility of Hermit's Cave is considered. Over the low dividing wall with its gap, bandits might easily have ridden, thus identifying themselves with Laguna Canyon while actually having their habitation in Wood Canyon—a deception greatly to their advantage.

In itself, this cave could not be considered extraordinary, though affording fair housing. But a cave more valuable for strategic position and purposes of concealment could hardly be desired or imagined. With its opening buttressed by masses of rock jutting out from the opposite wall of the ravine, and its outer end-fronting wall presenting the appearance of an ordinary mountainside, the location furnishes unique features that render the cave completely invisible until the ravine itself is entered.

A large group of oak, elder and willow trees in front of the ravine further aided in its concealment long ago, while at the same time enabling those within its recesses to watch unseen any approach from without. Behind this little forest of trees at its mouth, there was room for a number of horses to be kept out of sight ready for mounting at a moment's notice. Any luckless intruder entering the ravine or climbing the bulwark of ledges opposite the opening to look into the cave would be directly exposed to the fire of its defenders. On the other hand, a lookout stationed there and hidden by the trees would be able to watch unseen anyone approaching from any direction, and have the drop on him. On this lookout ledge in a convenient spot to furnish a handhold for the one stationed there, was another wooden peg that had been firmly driven into the hole drilled for it.

Thus entrenched in this small natural fortress, a posse of at least five times their number would have been required to dislodge a bandit gang—and that too fraught with grave danger to the officers of the law. And if so dislodged, or warned of an attack, escape over the low divide nearby into Laguna Canyon would have been a simple matter; whence, a short, furious ride either to the north or south could have afforded a puzzling vanishment to those following more cautiously.

Some distance from the foot of this ravine and within easy rifle-shot of the cave lookout, once stood a solitary old adobe house, the crumbling walls of which were some still upright when Father first came into the canyon. Standing wholly detached out in the open, offering no suggestion of secrecy and unassociated with any evidence of guilt, this building might have been used for the regular living quarters and have passed for a perfectly respectable dwelling, its outlaw connection unsuspected; while in the background, the little cave in the ravine, used as an emergency retreat, kept well its own secret of the mysteries of crime.

Only the semblance of an insignificant mound under the grass now marks the site of this old adobe house. The trees, ruthlessly cut for wood in the days of sheep herding on the rancho, are no more. The whole canyon is denuded of all save a few trees now bent and decrepit with age and pitiably futile, still left as guardians of this secluded retreat. One other, far up on the southern side of the bowl, solitary, superbly beautiful, has sprung up since those far days, and stands, a lone sentinel, its perfect spreading symmetry silhouetted against the green of hill and blue of sky, a living witness to the glories of the past.

The little spring-valley around the bend, also denuded of its beautiful forest, still bears in its floor the old muddy wash, now somewhat deepened. But no trace remains of the board wall-walk and little bubbling spring that once dispensed so freely to all. A lone and aged willow still marks the spot where it was. Gone is the shady meadow with its rank and purple fields of fragrant pennyroyal that our childish hands delighted to gather. Naught remains but a barren treeless pastureland.

When recently I visited these scenes of other days, spring clothed the canyon with greenness and streamlets followed many small waterways. In front of the sloping cave with its long opening, a clear mountain rivulet, bordered with ferns, coming down from above, tumbled musically from one mossy pool to another on its way down the rocky ravine. But at its foot now are tethered no steeds, saddled and bridled, to be refreshed by its coolness. And the hidden cave, deserted and silent, but for the scurrying squirrels, regardless of all conjecture, still holds fast its secret.

CHAPTER 26 MY FIRST TRIP—CHRISTMAS JOYS

An early waymark in my experience was my first trip to town with father, shortly after turning six; the first time I had ever spent a night away from home and Mother.

We did not get an early start, owing to the long-drawn-out discussion—a never-failing prelude to such trips—between my parents over the "bill," as they called the list of prospective purchases. This list, Mother had made by jotting down items as they occurred to her during the interval of months since the last trip to town, endeavoring to keep it within the limits of actual needs. Besides the groceries to be replenished, there might be some calico needed to make into dresses for us children, or perhaps shoes and stockings for those whose duties exposed them to inclement weather or who were now too old to go barefoot. There might, perchance, be some little gift for the approaching holidays.

The problem now was to cut this list down to absolute indispensables to make it fit the pocketbook. Poor Mother would be obliged to yield to the elimination, one after another, of things she greatly desired and sorely needed, knowing there was no hope of obtaining them until the next trip, months in the future, and in all likelihood, not even then.

Many a time on these occasions, as some cherished desire was relinquished, have I seen a tear glisten on her cheek, of which at the time, I comprehended not the meaning. It was never for herself that Mother wanted things. Always, it was for others.

She wore the same hat—old but carefully preserved for untold years, and I never knew her to ask for another. Never shall I forget that old brown straw hat, shaped like a limpet seashell, with a plain band of brown ribbon around the crown, ending in a bow at the back. It seemed a part of herself. Whenever I think of Mother in a hat, it is always this hat that comes first into mind.

I had been ready to go for hours; it seemed to me, before we at last got started. Mother and I exchanged a final goodbye kiss, and Father lifted me up onto the high spring seat and climbed in beside me, and together we jogged and jolted along over the rough canyon road. We passed the old stone chimney on our right, and the entrance to Spring Canyon on our left, and somewhere along that side of the canyon, standing out in relief against the mountain, the two little mound-like, grass-covered twin hills with a mere passageway between, to which—much to our embarrassment—Father never failed to call attention as being the perfect representation of a woman's breasts. We would listen to this in silence with shamed and downcast eyes, thinking it very immodest of him to speak so openly of things so sacredly intimate.

Through acres and acres of mustard, and other acres of wild oats, we drove, coming out at last into the broad Santa Ana Valley and long stretches of pasture lands with their occasional tiny one-room sheepherder cabins, each with its stovepipe sticking up through the roof.

Here on all sides were large bands of sheep, each attended by its lone herder afoot, with his indispensable dogs. Often our progress was interrupted by the sheep crossing the road in front of us. If even one should start across, the whole flock was bound to follow, in great rising clouds of dust, with many a "Ba-a-a-a!" mingled with calls of the shepherd, while the dogs rounded up the stragglers.

Once on the San Joaquin, we hugged the low westerly hills and the creek that flowed from their watersheds to join the Santa Ana River. Not until many years later when sheep pastures had given place to farming lands, thriving orchards and villages, was this old road changed to the center of the valley, approximately where it is today.

Dusk overtook us long before we reached our destination. But Father knew a family living not far ahead, whose hospitality he had often enjoyed on similar occasions, and there we stopped to pass the night. They were as glad to see us as were we to see them, for neighbors in those days were few and far between, and nothing was surer than a hospitable welcome.

Their house and out-buildings were close to the banks of the creek, the yards sloping down to its bordering willows and the crossing nearby. Here were cattle and horses, barnyard fowls, cats, and welcoming dogs, with evening chores in progress. Father joined his host outside at milking, while I timidly allowed the rest of the family to make my acquaintance.

Being in a strange house at night without Mother was a brand new experience to me, and one not the most happy. But, full of solicitous interest, they did their best to fill the lonesome gap, bestowing upon me so much more attention than I was used to that I quite forgot to be homesick. All this kindness and hospitality seemed so wonderful to me that for years it was a bright, unforgettable spot in my experience.

In this family, there were three, father, mother and daughter—possibly others who have faded from memory. But, to the exclusion of all beside, one stands out preeminently, the little girl, several years my senior, with whom I slept that night. This girl was a cripple—something absolutely new in my range of ideas. I do not remember seeing any crutches. Possibly they were too poor to afford them. The way she got around the house was to sit down on the floor and slide forward, using hands and the one good leg, the other being helpless from some incurable bone disease. That night after we had gone to bed, she removed the bandage to show me the deep ulcer at the knee.

Though her face and name are gone from me, there is one thing I shall never forget—the sweet, cheerful, happy disposition of this little girl. Though suffering and handicapped, with no hope of ever being able like other children, to hop, skip and run about, she was still a most uncomplaining, good-natured, unselfish little mortal. This was a marvel to me. Filled with pity, I somehow sensed that she felt no need of pity. Her time, during my visit, was wholly given over to making me happy, with apparently no thought for herself at all. Though thankful for my two sturdy legs, I coveted the secret of her happiness.

In the morning, leaving these kind friends, whom I probably never saw again, we started on our last lap for town. Santa Ana, so big to me, was in reality a very small village. Father got his mail at the general store where they carried groceries, dry goods, shoes and notions. Sometimes between trips, mail was brought to us by friends traveling our way. In this store were no fresh fruits and vegetables, for every farmer raised his own. You couldn't have bought a cake, a pie, or a loaf of bread, for every housewife made these for her family. At the drugstore, Father bought his castor oil in bulk. The proprietor siphoned it out of a tank by putting his mouth over the end of a tube inserted in the oil, and sucking on it to get the oil started running into the vessel Father had brought with him.

There were a livery stable, a blacksmith shop, and a jewelry store run by Mr. Hollingsworth, to whose house we went for dinner. A number of dwellings—the kind frontiersmen build—separated by areas of weed covered land with footpaths running between houses, completed the town, with hitching posts and drinking troughs for the farmers' horses, and a few blocks of wooden sidewalks in front of the stores.

The Hollingsworths had a green grass lawn in their front yard, which was quite a novelty to me. I greatly admired the pretty flowers that bordered the lawn just inside the surrounding field of mustard and pigweed. This couple had one child, a little boy several years younger than I did, dressed in kilts. We played together for some time. Though I thought him a little spoiled, he took quite a notion to me, being lonesome for other children.

His parents then put a request to Father, that he leave me there with them for a while as companion to this little boy. They reasoned that from so many children at our house, one would hardly be missed, and promised Father they would take good care of me. I listened to this conversation with growing alarm that deepened to consternation when Father approached me with the proposal. Seeing that he really and seriously entertained the idea, I burst into a storm of tears, which settled that matter then and there.

In those days when newspapers paid only occasional visits, about the only subject of general interest men found to talk about was "politics." Father simply loved it. Everywhere he went, he seemed to fall in with other men who had just as much time as he to spend in such discussions. Whenever he got started on his favorite theme, he never knew when to stop. He would lose all track of time. Hours would pass by unnoticed. Errands would be forgotten, places and people cease to exist. And so it happened on this memorable day on the board sidewalk in Santa Ana.

I stood around, first on one foot and then on the other to ease the foot-ache, while Father talked and talked and talked. We had been taught never to interrupt him when in conversation with others, and for fear of a reprimand, I dared not open my mouth. But I fidgeted about trying in vain to attract his attention. At last, the situation becoming unendurable, I reached up and took hold of his hand, saying timidly:

"Pa, let's go now."

He seemed not even to hear me. Soon, I repeated the suggestion a little louder.

"Pa, let's go now. Let's go, Pa."

Still no response. He was so absorbed I might have been an ant crawling in the dust for all the attention he gave me. Finally, I pulled on his hand—even dared to jerk it. He paused long enough to say:

"Pretty soon; pretty soon," and went on talking.

I waited, and waited, and waited. He seemed to have forgotten my existence. At last, the limit of endurance reached, I burst out sobbing. This brought him down to solid earth. He picked me up in his arms, comforted me a little, continued talking till he had finished his argument—for Father was never known to yield a point—and finally said goodbye and started for the wagon.

There is no memory of that homeward trip. I must have slept most of the way, for I was a very, very tired little girl. For many days after returning home, as the center of attraction, I recounted my interesting experiences—meeting the lame girl, the little Hollingsworth boy, my narrow escape from exile, the green lawn and flowers, the stores, the wonderful toys of all descriptions on display, and of one in particular, a large, gorgeous wax doll with wax head, hands and feet, painted face, yellow hair, and blue eyes, and a lovely lace-trimmed gauzy dress and petticoats that covered her sawdust body—the most "be-eu-te-ful" doll that ever was made. This doll, I coveted above everything I had ever seen in my life. But nothing seemed farther beyond my reach or expectations.

At the time, I little suspected the influence my glowing account was having on Father and Mother as silent listeners. But unbounded was my joy on Christmas morning to find this doll of my dreams hanging up beside my own stocking—because too big to go inside. A more delighted little girl it would have been impossible to find in the whole world. My big wax doll, I considered the most wonderful gift ever found on a Christmas morning.

This doll, however, was more showy than expensive—a fact I did not discern. A few weeks later, when spanking my baby for being "a naughty girl," to my great grief, her head fell off. A little glue applied by skillful family surgeons remedied the disaster and I was soon happy again. But always I spanked more gently after that. No calamity is without its moral.

Christmas Joys

Oh, those Christmases! Will memory of their joys ever fail me! For many weeks—even months beforehand, how we counted the days! Oh, how hard we tried to be "good!" With what stoicism we refrained from being "saucy" to our elder sisters, in whose hands lay much of our Christmas fate! For our joys were mostly home-made.

During those weeks, behind locked doors, much mysterious preparation was going on. There were surreptitious conclaves of our elders, and quick hidings away of things not to be seen, with unconcerned pretense on both sides that nothing unusual was taking place.

Old dilapidated, dismembered dolls would mysteriously disappear from their usual haunts, which we would wisely content ourselves without mentioning, after looking for them in vain, going doll-less till the dawn of Christmas morning. When, behold, a marvelous transformation! The old was new. Breaks and tears had been mended, arms and legs reunited to their bodies, worn and dirty clothes superseded by brand-new ones, and our old darlings were re-presented to us fresh as new beginnings.

Old toys of other kinds had been mended with glue or nails. Doll beds and cradles, with their covers, pillows and ticks had been renovated or replaced with new-made. At least one gift for each had been bought new from the store. Inexpensive to be sure, but thoughtfully selected to give the most pleasure by those whose ears had been open to our chance expressions of desires. For Frank, there might be a ball, a top, a whistle, a slingshot or a new knife. But most of these, he later learned to fashion for himself.

First of all, our actual needs were considered. New home-made underwear, dresses, or shoes and stockings were as gladly appreciated as anything else was.

In the days just preceding Christmas, there was much sweet smelling cookery going on. Peanuts were roasted in the shell, cookies baked and heaped up in a stone crock and hidden away, a big batch of twisted "fried cakes" cooked in hot fat, fruit-cake, made first of all and likewise hidden, and "boiled pudding." Corn was popped, and the biggest, reddest apples selected and added to the other delectables to perfume the cellar atmosphere, and on Christmas morning to bulge out the stocking just above the foot.

The toe of the stocking always contained the roasted peanuts, with maybe a few almonds and walnuts. A bunch of big raisins dried on the stems, followed, and always some rock candy, pink or white, either in large chunks, or formed in small jagged pieces on a long cord string like irregular beads. There were gumdrops too, and mixed candies, hard and highly colored, and stick candy in three-inch lengths, flavored with wintergreen, sassafras, cinnamon, or peppermint. Of more fancy confections we knew nothing, and therefore never missed them. Cookies followed these, and then came the big red apple, fried cakes, and popcorn shoveled in loose.

On top of all these goodies, were the real gifts, well-wrapped in parcels to whet the curiosity and lengthen the joy of discovery? If the gifts were few, the goodies were increased, so the stocking was always full and overflowing to give the impression of ample abundance. Not infrequently, that over-the-top gift was the welcome and welcoming face of a brand new doll, which never was wrapped. China heads, hands, and feet to the knees, with features, hair and shoes all painted on, and sawdust bodies, composed these beloved dolls, and they gave us as much pleasure as any more elaborate doll gives her little mistress today.

At our house, anything false, however pleasing, was treated with scorn, and nobody pretended to believe in the Santa Claus myth. The deception having once been discovered by older children, was promptly unmasked to those younger as fast as they came along.

Christmas trees, we never missed. They were outside of our experience. In later years when we heard others talk about their trees, we felt sorry for them. How could it seem like Christmas, getting your presents the night before, with no time left in which to play with them before that tiresome bedtime? And how disappointing it must be to see the most attractive gift on the tree handed to someone else? How could sitting around waiting your turn while the presents were handed out one at a time, be compared with the joy of pulling things out of a bulging stocking all by yourself as fast or as slow as you pleased, knowing that every blessed thing in it was all your own, and with a full day ahead of you in which to enjoy them?

But though there was no tree, there was always decoration. The wild Hawthorne, or California Holly, with its glossy evergreen leaves and bright red berries, in full glory at that season, was brought down from the mountains around, in lavish armfuls, to hang over doors, windows and picture frames and fill into jugs of water.

Or these might be supplemented by graceful, fern-leaved pepper branches from our own yard, heavy with bunches of rose-red berries. Always a little mistletoe, parasitic on the oak trees of groves and canyons, was hung inconspicuously over doors; and whosoever was caught passing under became subject to the delightful penalty of a kiss.

Our own stockings being too small, we always borrowed those of the grown-ups that better corresponded with our expectations, and with much ado, each selected the particular spot where his was to be hung and carefully informed the seniors of its exact location.

On Christmas Eve we went to bed early, a family rule not to be broken. For how otherwise could they fill our stockings? But bedtime for the "big folks" was some late hour in the night. It required a great deal of time to stuff those many stockings. Perhaps there remained some "last minute" gift yet to be finished, and the soft purr of the sewing machine caused us to wonder what they were making and who it was for, as we listened with intense curiosity, talking in animated whispers lest they discover our wakefulness. For "early to bed" did not mean "early to sleep," oh no! For an hour or more, the Sandman would not take even a peep at us in our joyous excitement.

The "Santa Clause" folks hung up their own stockings too, and after even they had all gone to bed, would slip out one by one to put their reserved gifts into one another's stockings—the toes having already been stuffed with the regulation goodies.

At last eyelids would close and slumber conquer, to hold sway till the dawn of that most glorious day of all the year—Christmas. According to rule, we must remain in bed till someone older had lighted the fire in the stove, for December mornings were usually icy cold. But rule or no rule, the one first awakening, would creep softly out of bed in bare feet and nighty, to steal out into the cold, enchanted kitchen and for one blissful moment feast enraptured eyes upon those rows of full-stuffed and overflowing stockings.

Some delighted exclamation would rouse the grown-ups, one of whom would come out, as we scampered away, light the fire and then go back to bed, leaving us with our joy. We lost no time in securing our stockings, together with such overflow as might be heaped up below them, and trooped back to bed, covering up our freezing toes and exploring our treasures while the room warmed a bit.

Beforehand, we had been told not to expect much for Christmas because there was no money to buy presents with—which was all too true—but ingenuity, deft fingers, and loving hearts supplied what the purse could not, and always we were surprised at the number of our gifts. The secrets of Mother's locked trunk had been revealed to help swell the bulging stockings, and seldom was our happiness marred.

Though we always knew what would be found in the foot, we enjoyed the goodies as a complete surprise, beginning to sample them whether hungry or not. But no one would eat all he had while others held reserves; they lasted throughout the day—a day of unbridled between-meal gorging. The regular heavy Christmas dinner was a meal of innumerable delights, most of which were produced on the farm. Fowl, roasted with rich dressing, rich gravy, mashed potatoes, peas or other vegetable, mince pies, fruitcake and plum pudding, were added to our candy, cookies, fried-cakes, raisins, nuts, apples and popcorn.

Since it could not be that any of these yearly treats should be slighted, it is little wonder that after the holidays, someone was sure to be ailing. And who could be blamed for a gastric strike?

The first to greet another on Christmas morning with the shout:

"Christmas gift!" earned from him some gift out of his own stocking.

The "gift" usually turned out to be a peanut or a walnut from the toe. This first shout was immediately followed by such a chorus shouting:

"Christmas gift" that it was not possible to tell which addressed the other first. Then followed the inevitable altercation:

"I said it first!"

"No you didn't, I did!"

"Yes I did too; I said it first. You've got to give me a gift!"

"All right then. I'll give you one peanut," and that settled the scores. But Christmas wasn't Christmas without this.

To the older folks, coming on the scene, we shouted: "Merry Christmas!" Everyone tried to say it first.

Should some visitor chance to come onto the premises that day, he was greeted in chorus with a hearty:

"Merry Christmas!" to which he replied in kind.

It was considered quite inglorious not to have said it first.

Homesickness

Sometime after my first visit to Santa Ana, I made a second and longer one. The Hollingsworths, with whom we had taken dinner that day, had not given up the idea of my serving as companion to their young son. Sometime before, they had lost an infant daughter by death, and the little boy was lonely for some child to play with. Sadie, who about two years previously had gone out into the world to shift for herself, was now staying with Mrs. Hollingsworth. While on a brief visit home, as their ambassador, she invited me to return with her and stay for awhile.

This proposition was quite different from that other which had involved my being left there without any of the home folks. I thought it would be great fun to go away with my big sister Sadie, who had always made a pet of me. So, Mother being willing, Sadie took me back with her.

I had a perfectly wonderful time playing with the little boy—then began to grow desperately homesick. Sadie had hardly counted on that. Neither had I. Oh, how I wanted my mother, my sisters, my brothers, my kittens, my dolls, my playthings! I began to beg to go home. But how was I to get home? There were no trains to Aliso, no streetcars, no busses, no automobiles, no airplanes, I was twenty-five miles from home. That would be more than five hundred miles today.

Sadie promised that if I would be a "good girl" and not beg to go home, she would send me home by the Goffs the very first time any of them came to town. How I watched and waited for some of the Goffs to come! For two long lonesome weeks I tried my best to be happy, but in vain. A dozen times a day I questioned:

"Do you think they will come today, Sadie?"

"I don't know; we'll watch and see. Now you be a good girl and run out and play."

But homesickness was an incurable disease and time dragged by on "ball and chain."

At last, the joyful day arrived. Hubbard Goff had come to town in his spring wagon, and as a good neighbor should, had dropped around to see how Sadie was getting along. With him was his little daughter Rosie, somewhat older than I, and Sadie made arrangements for me to go home with them. I was so happy I could scarcely wait for them to get ready to leave. Long before the time came to say goodbye I had my little bundle of clothes tied up with a string.

It was afternoon when at last we got started, and what a long journey it was! That was the first time I had ever seen Laguna Canyon, and everything was unfamiliar and strange in the gathering darkness. I was not used to being with these neighbors. Though known to me, yet the friendship was not intimate. I felt weirdly strange and lonely, even with Rosie. Night came on and the air grew chilly. We both became sleepy too. Hubbard Goff had brought with him an old quilt, and now he wrapped us in it and bade us lie down in the wagon bed behind the seat. He drove faster than Father, and the jouncing and jolting along over the rough road made sleep difficult.

Away off in the dark distance somewhere, a coyote began to yap. I was afraid and almost held my breath at the penetrating sound. I wondered if by any chance he could get into the wagon should he catch up with us. Then I was glad to be traveling so fast.

At last, in spite of the jolting, we fell asleep and knew nothing more until awakened at their door to get out and finish our sleep in a warm quiet bed.

In the morning our eyes opened upon a dense fog that wrapped the world in a blanket of white. I was all turned around. The ocean was on the wrong side of the world. Had I then started for home alone, I should have headed directly back again toward Santa Ana. They pointed out to me the true direction of my home, nearly two miles farther on, but in bewilderment, I thought they surely must be mistaken. I had never been at their house before, and felt lost and woebegone.

They were getting breakfast. But I wasn't hungry. All I wanted was to get home. Hardly could I wait till the meal was ended. I supposed that Hubbard Goff would get right up from the table and take me home. But apparently he had no such idea. He was taking his time. Didn't he know how important it was for me to get home? I began to beg him to take me home, and finally he did—that is, he took me part way.

To me, in my mental confusion, we started out in the wrong direction. Not one single thing on the way appeared familiar. I was timid and said nothing of all this to Mr. Goff. At last we reached the end of Frank Goff Bench, where the road went steeply down the bluff onto the white sand below. Here, he drew rein. A path branched off from the road to the left, which he told me led down into Aliso Canyon. He said, to my dismay, that he would leave me there, and I could walk home alone the rest of the way.

Perhaps he did not realize what a very small girl I was and how little I had been away from home. He knew nothing of my bewilderment—how that everything was wrong-side-to, the ocean where the mountains ought to be, and vice versa, that the road down onto the sand faced opposite from the way it used to, and that the path he pointed out to me was as strange and new as though I had never seen it before. He was so self-assured, so perfectly confident that I understood just where we were and how to get home that I was ashamed to tell him I was utterly lost.

He lifted me out of the wagon, waved a cheery goodbye, turned his team around and started back, leaving me there, half a mile from home, a lonely, bewildered, forlorn little waif, standing alone on the top of a world draped in white. Fog outside is bad enough, but fog inside is worse. If my lips quivered and tears fell, who was the wiser?

I took that path blindly because it was the only path there was to take. Reason told me also that the path had to be in a direction away from the sea, and this one was. It had to be down a mountainside as was this one, but what mountain, I could not make out.

Not until I had descended to the very bottom and there through the fog saw the old familiar row of Eucalyptus trees, did the world suddenly turn a somersault and right itself. The rest of the way I fairly flew. How beautiful were the old familiar things. How astonished was everyone to see me so early in the morning, arriving alone unescorted and unexpected, like dropping down from the skies! How marvelous was the welcome accorded me! It is great to be a heroine.

Having dwelt in town this time sufficiently long to take concrete observations, I showed Annie and Charlotte how to make whole villages along the sandy creek banks; how to lay out streets, plant trees to outline them, pat down hard walks, build stores, houses, and all the other things that go to make up a town. And soon we became expert city builders.

CHAPTER 27

Harriet skips Chapter 27 but no text is lost (manuscript pages are consecutive)

CHAPTER 28 PLAYTHINGS AND PASTIMES

The ingenuity of children is amazing. Especially is this true in the country, where there are so many avenues for inventive expression and so many simple materials at hand. Although we scarcely ever saw a store-bought toy, still we were never without plenty of things to play with; and I think appreciated the toys we made ourselves much more than do children nowadays the fine expensive toys made for them in factories.

There is a peculiar joy, as well as training, in making things from unworked materials that boys and girls who have everything ready-made and placed in their hands to play with, miss, to their great loss. To be the proud possessor of something that has taxed your own skill and patience to produce—something that bears the stamp of your own individuality, and to have your workmanship praised by your elders and envied by your youngers, is almost the pinnacle of gratification.

From the time we were old enough to make corn-tassel babies and malvia-leaf dolls, our creative imagination never lacked an outlet. It took so little then to make us happy. The tiny, misplaced, abnormal ears that sometimes appeared, growing inside the husks of large ears, when discovered by our elders in preparing these for the dinner-pot, were never thrown away, but given to us little folks, always eagerly watching for such treasures. From these, we would make the most adorable babies. Carefully removing one by one, all the delicate wrappings but the last, we would retain that one for the cape, the long tassel of corn-silk hanging down below it being the dress, and the protruding stem above it, the head. There we had our tender, delicate darling little cob-baby to mother and caress, in a long cream-silk dress and lovely pale-green wrap that supposedly concealed the arms from view.

A malvia-leaf doll too is easily made if you understand how. For a foundation, we would pick one large leaf, leaving attached enough stem to give the desired body height, and upon this build other leaves, each creeping up on the stem a little above its predecessors till just enough for the head remained exposed. A malvia leaf, if you pinch off its stem close up, is shaped like a little hoodless cape finely scalloped all around the edges—only it naturally hangs wrong-side out. After preparing many leaves in this way, we would wrap them one at a time around the foundation, alternately facing first the front of the doll then the back. It mattered not if these many petticoats were wrong-side out, for they would not show much anyway; but the last one to go on, being the dress, must have the shiny side turned outward. At the neck, a small leaf was usually added for a cape. The resulting effect was a little lady with many ruffled flounces. True, the head was hardly large enough for the body, but such a minor matter could easily be disregarded. She had no arms, but these were supposed to be hidden underneath the cape she wore. Altogether you would go far to find a more beautiful weed doll.

Sometimes we would play "cattle" and make great numbers of domestic animals, and well-fenced corrals in which to keep them. For these, our materials were unripe figs, burnt matches, small chicken feathers, sticks and cord strings. The figs must be picked when barely beginning to ripen that they might be sufficiently soft for the insertion of matches and feathers, yet firm enough to retain these in place.

The neck of a ripening fig, with its small attached stem, is seldom straight, but just crooked enough to represent either the downward stretch of an animal's head and neck as he feeds on the vegetation, or by turning the fig over, the erect posture with head held up above the body. While holding the fig in either position desired, we would insert for legs, four match-pieces, slanted sufficiently to balance the creature in standing alone, and just above the blossom-end, for a tail would insert the quill-end of a feather. In making these for cattle, the feather would first be stripped all but a tuft at the tip. For horses, more slender figs would be selected, longer legs added and the tail left unstripped. Small figs would be made into calves; or by shortening the legs, into pigs; and for these latter, tails must be found that would curl. Little filaree seed-spirals, when available, made excellent tails.

Corral posts were made of many sticks broken the proper length, the fence-wires being several strands of cord string tied one below another, around the sticks, whose lower ends were left longer than the upper, to allow for planting in the ground, and the posts would be placed several inches apart. These fences could be planted in any size and shape we desired our corral to be, and could be pulled up and laid away for future playtimes, to be reset in any location desired. The animals also were good for a number of weeks, till they should begin to shrivel.

This play was worlds of fun. We would herd our cattle and hogs in pastures of green during play-daytime, and confine them in corrals at play-nighttime. Our horses we would "ride" around over the ranges limited by pasture fences they could not pass, all through the fig season, till autumn frosts and fogs cut off our source of supply.

We would manufacture doll baskets out of the curious prickly burrs of the Chilicothe—called also Wild Cucumber from its similar leaves—that grew afresh each spring out of its immense undying root, clambering over bushes and sage brush, to which it clung by many strong, curling tendrils. Its racemes of small yellowish-white flowers developed into large pendant burrs covered with prickles, at first soft and harmless, but ripening into hard sharp spines, changing from deep green to straw color.

Late in the season, these burrs would crack open at the point of attachment and the outer spiny layer peel back a little way to let the seeds escape. Then we would pull them off the vines and finish the peeling process cautiously. With the spines all removed, there would be left an oblong cage of beautifully meshed lacy openwork that was partitioned off lengthwise into four equal divisions, in each of which lay several hard, oblong, and slightly flattened seeds about the size of marbles, and of a rich, glossy, brownish-red color, most attractive and ornamental. Of these, the Spanish Californians used to make bead necklaces for their lovely ladies to wear; and we also, captivated by their beauty, would shake them out of their cases to play with.

By exercising care, the partitions too could be lifted out; leaving a deep receptacle that needed only a little trimming off of its ragged open top to make of it a lovely basket that would endure as long as we cared to play with it, both baskets and seeds becoming permanent parts of our doll-house equipment.

We also played with the "Mock Orange" gourd, whose small hard seeds when dry would rattle inside their hard shells. These were also used by Mother and the girls for stocking darners.

Sister Hulda, who was always doing something nice for us youngsters, made Annie and me each a big rag doll the size of a real baby, first cutting them out of unbleached muslin after a pattern of her own manufacture, sewing up the seams by machine, and after stuffing with cotton, finishing and sewing the parts by hand. On their heads, she painted facial features and plenty of black hair, and on hands and feet, painted fingers and toes. She dressed them completely, not omitting full sets of underclothes, shoes and stockings, hoods and jackets, and how we loved them! They lasted for years the old darlings, sometimes appearing in short dresses, sometimes in long, but never growing up.

But though a most ardent and devoted lover of doll babies, to my mind there was nothing so fascinatingly interesting to play with as a real live toad baby. Toads made such adorable infants, with their bright popping blinking eyes and wide mouths, their little five-fingered hands and five-toed feet—even though the middle toe was disproportionately long—and their spankable bottoms that one could put didies[i] on and be sure they would get wet and have to be changed.

This baby, while I was endeavoring to dress it up properly in my doll clothes, would "fuss about" trying to flop over, and move its little hands and feet, wriggling and squirming like a really truly baby. It wouldn't lie still at all when told as dolls do, and so just naturally had to be spanked to make it behave—not just pretend—when naughty. And oh, it was just like having a real baby thrilling, entertaining, fascinating! From the toad's standpoint I cannot speak.

The only disadvantage about a toad-baby was that you couldn't lay it away when through playing as you would a doll to be found again where you put it when wanted; but you had to turn it loose and never could be sure that you would ever find it again.

When not in the mood for playing baby, for diversion I would sometimes tie a string about the toad's front foot and attempt to lead him about as one would a pet poodle.

None of the others would play with toads, and for the most part were afraid to touch them, looking askance at me when picking up these little warty playfellows. Everybody knew that they would make warts on the hands, and nobody wanted warts. I didn't want any more either for I had plenty already; but I never allowed the thought of warts to interfere with my toad play. In fact, nobody ever quite convinced me that toads were the cause of warts. Hadn't I had warts before ever playing with toads? And didn't others of the family have warts who never handled toads? These facts were to me quite conclusive arguments.

Yes, most of us had warts, big warts and little warts that persisted in coming back even after being treated with muriatic acid or burned out with a needle. Did you ever try to burn out a wart with a needle? When a little older I

---

[i] Informal expression for diapers

became so desperate about a big seed wart in the joint of my forefinger that I resorted to this expedient to get rid of it. Inserting the point of a needle down into the wart as deeply as I could stand it, I held the other end of it in the flame of a candle. But I didn't hold it there long—oh no! I jerked my hand away and danced a double jig howling like a whirling dervish. But I didn't give up and remove the needle from my wart. Determinedly, I put it back into the flame, and again danced a wild whirling jig. But my mind was made up to kill that wart, pain or no pain. So as soon as the worst subsided and my courage revived sufficiently, I tried it again and still again, repeating the performance till pretty sure that the wart was cooked. Though it wasn't any fun, and produced a very sore finger, yet this severe treatment accomplished the expected result. Within a few days, the wart had loosened till I could pull it out by the roots. But not quite all the roots; for that pesky wart, after a number of months, grew back again and I had it all to do over. One more persevering repetition of the process however, proved to be sufficient, and that big seed wart was effectually destroyed never to return.

Father allowed the use of certain of his carpenter tools to those of us who were able to manipulate them without too much abuse, consisting of hammer, plane, wood-file, compass, brace and bit, and a little key-hole saw. By means of these, with materials obtained from old boxes and scraps from his shop in the shed, we would fashion the most wonderful doll-beds, cradles and wagons—these last being our specialty. When boxes of suitable sizes could be found ready-made for wagon beds, but little work was required to convert them into wagons. A cigar box left by some camper or visitor—for no one at our house used the "filthy weed"—provided a most excellent one.

The lid being discarded, two sticks for the hubs were secured and whittled down at the ends smooth and round of a size to turn loosely in the hole of a spool, and nailed across under the bottom of the box ends the round portions extending out a little beyond the box. Two spools were then sawed through the middle crosswise for the four wheels, and slipped cutsides inward over the hub-ends, through each of which a small slender nail was then driven to hold them on. A string tied through a hole in the top center of the front end by which to draw the wagon completed the ensemble.

But let no one imagine that it is a simple and easy matter to saw a spool in two. In the first place, a spool is too small to handle well; in the second place, it is built to roll and is certain to roll out of position "eleventy-leven" times without fail; in the third place, it is easily broken when just about finished and then you must begin all over again with a new spool. So if one can master a spool he can saw almost anything.

When the box was too large for spool wheels, we would be obliged to make our own wheels. Drawing a circle with the compass on a rather thick board, the size desired for the wheel, and with bit and brace boring a hole in the exact center the size of the hub for free turning, we would cut out the circle with the little key-hole saw as neatly as we could, finishing with a wood-file to make smooth from any jagged ridges, and the wheel was ready. The hub was more simple. Two sticks trimmed the right size to nail across under the bottom of the wagon, one at each end, with a projecting portion filed round for the wheel to turn on, finished with a small nail to hold the wheel on. Then, while standing on its four wheels, a small hole was drilled near the center top in front for the insertion of a suitable string by which to draw the wagon.

Store dolls, presented to us on special occasions such as Christmases and birthdays, we always treasured. Such dolls would seem funny to the modern little mistress, with bodies stuffed with sawdust and only head, hands, and feet of china. The face, and the hair, which might be either light or dark, had always been painted on before glazing. Those features were attractive and smiling, were naturally considered to be girlchildren; but when less pleasing to the eye were chosen to be boy-children, as lesser contestants in the field of beauty. The stiff, all-over china dolls from one to several inches in height, were always made the baby members of our doll families; for we believed in family life, the larger dolls being parents, and the smaller dolls their children.

But if short on store dolls we were by no means straightened. It was easy as anything to make dolls. Just roll up a piece of rag, tie a little square of white cloth over the even end for a head, make two small rolls and sew them up tight for the arms, attaching them to the neck (never mind about legs, clothes cover them anyway), imagine face and hair, and presto! you have a doll any size you wish to make it.

If we wanted a man-doll, then we had to make legs of course, and manufacture pants and coat. That was much more difficult. But I once accomplished this feat, and my noble "Rufus," standing eight inches in his footless socks, was the envy of all the other families around. For years he remained the "head" of my doll house, and the father of a numerous and rapidly increasing progeny.

It was such fun to have families that you could add to, and to pick out names for the diminutive "newborn," and to build for them wonderful houses—roofless of course—in choice locations along the roadside up in the filaree pasture or down in the sandy creek. We would build our low walls just high enough to serve as enclosures, and partition them off into numerous rooms with doors between, and place within them such immovable furniture as could be molded out of damp sand—stoves, tables, chairs and beds. We would plant trees all about the front and back yards, and have sometimes a tree-bordered lane leading from door to roadway, adding such individual features as occurred to us.

Within these farm houses family life was made to carry on much as did our own—the same words and actions, duties and pleasures, and routines and activities of daily occurrence, being vividly reproduced and interpreted by our own "master minds" and voices.

The grave difficulty with these farms and houses obviously was that they had to be so frequently replaced. There was no permanency, the trees would wither and had often to be replanted and the houses rebuilt. In an effort to overcome this difficulty of frequent rebuilding I once set my fertile brain to work to fashion a permanent house.

Having had some past experience in the use of tools, I set to work in earnest with saw, hammer and nails, and in due time the house was finished even to gable roof, with a partition in which a door opening was left, and an outside door hinged with leather straps, and two windowless windows—a house to make an architect swell with pride (if he were not too particular). But it had one irremediable fault. It was all enclosed and I couldn't get inside of it to manipulate my dolls. All that could be done was to put them in there and let them sit like mummies and that wasn't any fun. So I decided that after all roofless houses were the nicest to play with, and we went back to our sand-farms. Really, you know, when you are playing "keep house" and making doll families live and carry on, you just have to imagine some things, like roofs and windows.

Frank, besides helping with wagons and girls' toys, made other things too as the older boys did. Whistles that would play a clear sweet note, or warble, if you put just a little water inside; wonderful bows and arrows, the points of those for boys finished with sharpened nails, but those for girls left blunt; slingshots, made with plain, stout, elastic bands attached to the two prongs of a Y-shaped stick, and joined in the middle with a diamond-shaped piece of leather to hold the stone that went whizzing through the crotch of the Y; tops out of spools whittled to shape, the holes filled with pointed pegs, which would spin merrily with a smooth, even hum like any factory-made top of that day. Frank would produce other things too that boys know how to make, that we girls got as much fun out of as he. There were the high stilts, on which we tried our skill, ambling awkwardly around the yards. It gave us quite a feeling of elation to be elevated to a height that equaled, or surpassed that of the grown-ups.

Then there was the game of merchandising. With Father's pair of big tin-shears, we cut out little circles from the lids of tin cans, or other sources, for money; buying and selling our wares as did our elder merchants. We sold our toys back and forth, and these were sold for "keeps" unless and until we bought them back. This was a game of dignity. It made us feel that we were men and women of affairs.

One of our most delightsome pastimes was blowing soap-bubbles. At first our blowpipes were home-made, the bowls from cane, using a solid joint for the base, and the stems from the smaller joint-grass. But later on, clay pipes were bought for us from the general store. If we succeeded in getting the suds just the right strength, oh! What gorgeous bubbles would balloon out from those filmy soap-dips into globes of delicate beauty! All the colors of their surroundings were reflected, and the commonest things glorified. We would climb up onto the work-bench or other elevation, and blow them as big as we dared to without breaking, then flip them off gently, high overhead, to sail away through space, until they would touch something more solid than air—then Piff! There was nothing.

Father had bought for our enjoyment a handsome double croquet set. Instead of four, there were eight long-handled, gaily-striped wooden mallets, each two of a different color arrangement, and eight large wooden balls to match. The same colors were enameled on the two end posts. In the set were also ten stout wire wickets and an instruction book. The boys had leveled off an area below the first woodpile in the edge of the orchard, and in close proximity to the big front yard, tamping it down hard and setting the wickets in proper order, with two crossed in the center for a "basket. This game when mastered, became a never-ending source of pleasure to us all. We thought ourselves quite proficient when we were able to become "rovers" and assist our partners. There was, however, one drawback; the spot selected was partially shaded by a large thrifty fig tree, which kept the ground rather mussy. In summer season, the ripe figs would fall onto the croquet ground and in the autumn the dying leaves, so that each time it must be tidied up in preparation for a game.

As eldest of the last group of five, all girls, I fell naturally (and that includes dispositionally), into the position of group-leader. I was always thinking up some "wonderful" invention, or scheme for entertainment, to the admiration and delight of my younger playfellows. Though inwardly resenting my autocratic leadership, still they acknowledged with awe and respect, the originality, fertility of imagination, and inventive ability thus displayed. Knowing that if Harriet should refuse to play with them their good times were bound to be decidedly limited, they refrained from incurring her displeasure. This unwilling dependence grew at times impossibly irksome, and brought various reactions. Whenever Annie would get enough of my lordly rule, she would grow sullen and sulk; though still "hanging around" unwilling to miss anything that might make life interesting. Little Charlotte, usually meek and submissive, once reached a stage of resentment herself that bordered on rebellion. By way of revenge, she sneaked up behind me stealthily and grabbing my pigtail, gave it a big jerk, then ran away satisfied with her even score. But not knowing why she did this little stunt, it is to be feared the rebuke was lost on me and so failed to effect the intended reform.

One of the most primitive of these original games was the game of "King"—a good and powerful word, but one whose real meaning was decidedly hazy in the minds of democratic American children, who wondered only why some people had kings, and some didn't. Due to the peculiar nature of the game, it was never suggested except when accompanied by the qualification: "I'll be the king!" "Oh, let's play 'King.' I'll be the King." If it be true (as say some evil-minded critics), that the inventor of the game was the most frequent applicant for that royal office, is that to be wondered at? Who wouldn't want to be a king when the slightest command of that august personage elicited from his subject's instant and servile obedience?

Mounted upon an elevated throne, this monarch issued his commands, however trivial and devoid of rhyme or reason, in imperial authority, voluminous voice, and spirit of intolerance: "Come all before the King!" All obeyed; "Bow before the King!" All bowed; "Pass in order and kiss the King's toe!" None refused. "All kneel before the King!" To an individual he might say, "Fetch a drink of water for the King!" "Pick up the King's handkerchief!" Hang it on the doorknob!" Or, "Run around the room!" "Stand in a corner!" And so on ad infinitum.

The Game Par Excellence

Did you ever play "Flooper Birds"? What! Never even heard of them! Why, how much you've missed! Oh, I was forgetting; of course you never did, because it too was an original invention, and nobody ever heard of it except just us Children of Aliso. But oh, it was such fun! Just a game for girls, for no boy would play any game that called for the wearing of capes. Every Flooper bird, little or big, had to wear a cape. We couldn't play without them at all, for they were our wings; and oh, such wonderful wings they made! There were plenty of capes to be had, for all the womenfolk wore them, and whenever they made new ones they would let us play with the old ones. When they had hoods, these were our topknots. But if not, we would play our hair was feathers, you know.

Our arms were just our wing-bones, of course. All we needed them for—after we had buttoned the cape at the neck—was to operate our wings. We would stretch them down straight, take hold of the two front edges of the cape, and hold on tight. Then we would raise our wings high and "floop" them down again; up and down, up and down, as we ran—for then we were flying—and all the time we were repeating the only word we knew how to say—for birds can't talk, of course—"Floop-er, floop-er, floop-er, floop-er!" With the first and accented syllable uttered on a lower note, we brought our wings down, and with the last syllable on a higher note, we raised them up. It sounded just like a bird language—sort of mournful like, with a falling and rising inflection as we flapped our wings.

We would go up the slope to the pepper trees or the bone rock and come sailing down as fast as we could fly "floopering" all the way—the capes rising and falling and ballooning out behind in undulant waves. Never, except in rare dreams, have I so nearly realized the supreme sensation of flight through the air, as when I stretched out my wings—my ''flooper wings—my super-wings—and "cape-ered" down the hill. Perhaps it was this exhilarating sensation that made the game such a favorite with us.

When we hovered our little ones we would say "Flooper" very softly, over and over in a crooning way, to put them to sleep. I was always the mother Flooper, partly because my cape was the largest and would hover the most, and partly—perhaps mostly—because that was the star position, and being the inventor of the whole ensemble I claimed the right of first choice as a sort of "royalty" due to genius.

Charlotte, Luella and Clara were the little Flooper birds and Annie was the father Flooper. He would climb the tree and pick the figs and bring them to the mother Flooper for her to feed to their young, who would all open their mouths wide as little Flooper birds should, and wait for her to drop pieces of fig into them in turn. Sometimes, forgetting their limited vehicle of expression, they would chirp quite humanly: "me-some, me-some, me-some."

Sometimes Annie would beg me to let her be the mother bird for a while, and occasionally I would graciously consent. Then I would show her by example just what a father Flooper should be like. I would make the office of father Flooper so attractive that she would be perfectly willing to take it back again. Then I could be happy once more.

But I am sure you are wondering by this time where these little birds were hovered and if we had a nest of any kind. Of course we did. Flooper birds must have nests the same as other birds, and they must be built up in a tree, too. Near the end of the croquet ground was a large fig tree with crotches low enough for the Mother and Father birds to climb, and the baby birds with some boosting. But they didn't go up till we had the nest built, and what a nest it was!

Though Frank stooped not to join in such a girls' game, he often watched at a distance with envious eye and when it came to building the nest took right hold and helped us. Of course we Floopers all said "King's Ex" while we built the nest, for little birds are supposed to be in the shell while such things are going on. But these little King's exed Floopers helped all they could to build the nest. They packed straw and other things needful and ran errands galore, for this was a nest of some proportions and sturdily built to stand many a season of wear and tear, and all hands were brought into service.

The first step was to hunt boards, and the next to lay them across the branches and fasten them securely with pieces of rope so they would not fall off, for it must not be that little Flooper birds should have any unfortunate tumbles. After that, gunnysacks were laid on the boards and then straw from the manger where the horses had eaten off the heads of grain. This was brought in armfuls and piled high on the boards and a depression was made in the center, leaving a circle of sidewall around a well-lined nest.

When all was complete the parent birds—like the evolutionist generously dispensing with the "missing link," in this case useless intermediary eggs—the baby Floopers were boosted up the tree and of themselves cuddled down in the nest most happily, and the hovering began in the most wonderful nest a Flooper bird ever had.

The voluminous cape wings of the mother bird were ample to cover all three of the little ones huddled in the nest, in which she squatted uncomfortably while the father bird sat on a limb nearby and preened his feathers or hopped about hunting rare morsels of food for the fledglings.

When the mother bird would tire of her squatting position and the prickles were beginning to run up her legs, she would decide that the time had come to teach the little Floopers to fly. So, with a great ballooning, billowy bound, she would leave the nest alighting on the soft plowed ground beneath, afterward assisting with her featherless wing-ribs the little ones to do likewise. The father joining them, the whole family would then go "floopering" all over the place from peppers to willows and from bone-rock to barn, seeking the nest again at nightfall in their imaginary cycle of time.

For many seasons that nest foundation remained in the tree, each spring needing only to be repaired for another round of "flooper" joys. This game we never outgrew till we outgrew capes and the last rag of the last cape had gone over the mop-handle.

Another yard game we played was "Blindfolding." One of us would submit to being blinded and led about by the others from place to place over the premises, at intervals making guesses as to where we were, guided by the senses of smell, hearing and touch.

"Where are we now?" would be asked.

"We're by the pig-pen," might be the answer, based on the "piggy" odor or a casual grunt or the soft sound of munching.

"Where are we now?"

"We're by the chicken coop," guided by another distinctive odor, a rustle of feathers, or a low clucky sound.

"We're in the orchard," might be the venture, the location betrayed by soft plowed ground or perhaps the bare foot pressing down on an overripe fallen fig.

"We're in the road," would be guessed if the ground was hard and beaten, with superimposed soft dirt, or marked with ruts.

"We're under the Eucalyptus trees," if pieces of bark and dead leaves were underfoot. Or if a rattle of dishes was heard, or the smell of food became evident, the answer might be:

"We're near the kitchen."

But far more often our guesses were wrong, and very amusing, a false and ridiculous guess bringing gales of laughter. At such times the blindfold might be lifted enough to let one see how outlandish her guess had been. When we guessed aright, the blindfold would be removed and placed on another, and the fun continued.

Sometimes we marked off "bases" in the yard and played "Pomp, pomp pull-a-way"; in which Frank and perhaps Hulda would join heartily, or we played 'Throw the Ball," usually a triangle game, the littlest running to fetch stray balls.

We would play "Hide and Seek" and hie us away to a neighborhood of good hiding places.

One day we were playing this game down in the walnut orchard along by the creek fence and bank, heavy with undergrowth and willow trees. Our "goal" was a walnut tree nearby, which we would strike three times while shouting triumphantly: "One, two, three for ME!"

I had squatted down on a small bare spot of sand among the willows and weeds, awaiting my opportunity to run to the goal. The "seeker" had just finished his warning call:

"A bushel of wheat, a bushel of rye; who ain't hid must holler 'I'"—a brief pause, then, "All eyes open!"

At this psychological instant, a peculiar movement underneath me brought my glance downward, and behold a hideous snake was crawling out from underneath my clothes, who sensing discovery immediately set up a terrifying "kettledrum" that made my hair stand on end and curdled the blood in my veins—but not in my feet. With a shriek: "Rattlesnake! Rattlesnake!" and a coordinated bound such as no deliberate effort could ever have accomplished, I landed far from the source of danger in the soft plowed ground of the orchard shocked and screaming, which broke up the game in a hurry and brought the others running.

"I sat right down on him! He was right under me!"

"Where did he go?"

"He crawled into the bushes right there!"

Then bidding them guard the spot at a safe distance to be sure he didn't get away out of reach unbeknown, I ran as fast as two legs could carry me up to the house to find Joseph.

When found, he was sardonically skeptical and very reluctant about taking the time to investigate. "It was probably only a gopher snake," he said, unimpressed. "If you had sat down on a rattler, he would have bit you."

"It was too, a rattler!" I protested indignantly, in feverish excitement; "I heard him rattle right under my dress! Come quick before he gets away!"

The tale sounded fantastic to Joseph and childishly imaginative. I was almost in tears before he reluctantly got his hoe and started back with me.

When we reached the spot there were the others watching around but not a sound had they heard nor a glimpse had of the crawly beast. I showed Joseph the exact spot where I had been sitting, and there sure enough was a faint snake trail passing into the thicket. Joseph, with his hoe prodded about among the tangled undergrowth for some time, and finally to my great joy and triumph, found the rattlesnake coiled up in the weeds. It didn't take him long to dispatch the enemy and I claimed the rattles.

The Masterpiece

Under the Eucalyptus trees above the bone-rock, some of our most interesting playtimes were spent, and here was made and put into operation my most famous invention. As leader of the younger group and the most dependable, I was allowed by Mother the use of some things ordinarily forbidden, such as matches, hatchet, tin-shears, can-opener and so forth, being held strictly accountable for their proper use and safe return.

From a five-gallon kerosene can, with tin shears and can-opener, I fashion a most wonderful cook stove. The side of the can was to be the top of the stove and the top of the can the front end, and in the corner where was the small spout and shut-off, which I intended for a convenient door handle, I cut the end door all but one side leaving that for the hinge.

On the top of the stove I marked out and cut four round holes properly spaced for small sized cooking pots and frying pans, which were to expose their unprotected bottoms to the smoke and soot.

The stove-pipe was next to be considered. A space was left for an oblong hole to the rear of the cooking holes, but I thought wisely that the size of the stove-pipe should first be determined before cutting a hole for it so cast about for proper material. We searched the premises over for tin cans, far less plentiful then than now, collecting those of similar diameter until we had enough to total a stovepipe's proper height; after which I laboriously cut off both ends of each can below the rims. Being of the same size, one would not fit down over the other, so a short slash cut in the upper edge of each enabled it to be lapped sufficiently to allow the next joint to fit over it. The free end of the lower can was then pressed into an oblong shape and held resting upon the top of the stove while marking around it with a nail point. And on this line the hole was cut for the stove-pipe. When set up, it wabbled ingloriously, which showed me that I should not have cut the hole out, but should have slashed it from the center outward in pie-shaped wedges and bent these downward to hold the stove-pipe steady. It was too late to remedy this defect, but I mentally decided that if ever-another stove was made, this idea should be followed without fail. As it was, the weight of so many joints with no steadying brace made the stovepipe somewhat top-heavy. So some of the carefully made joints had to be discarded and the stove-pipe shortened. A place was now leveled for the new stove to rest upon, and we were all set ready to go.

There were plenty of dead branches and strips of bark lying on the ground under the trees for our first fuel, and with this we filled the stove and then applied the match. It was a triumphant moment when the first smoke began to rise up out of that beautiful chimney, and real fire to glow inside the stove! This increased with a fearsome roar, even sweeping up the whole length of the stovepipe replacing the smoke, and shooting out its tongue at us over the topmost joint.

But close on the heels of this glorious success followed disaster—as it has an unpleasant way of doing. The proud inventor had not reckoned on the liquid nature of solder when mixed with fire. First, the little doorknob tumbled off leaving instead of a handle a round hole, which after all might be just as serviceable as a handle in opening the door. This afterward proved to afford sufficient draft so that no door was really needed—except when some stick too large for the top hole was to be inserted. Next, the noble stovepipe began to part at every soldered seam, and toppled over with a disconcerting clatter—the cause revealed only by after-investigation.

But some of the cans had remained intact, and these, we discovered by close inspection had seams pressed instead of soldered. So, undaunted by this setback, we began a thorough search for cans with pressed seams. These were very scarce, but we found a few more, though not all we needed. So a substitute was improvised by wiring the parted seam of some cans together through nail holes made near the edges. Thus, the stove-pipe difficulty was overcome.

The oily Eucalyptus twigs made the fire so fierce, that it was necessary to cover the top of the stove; so rounds were cut from other pieces of tin, larger than the holes and laid thereon, and we were ready to cook our first meal.

Mother loaned us a small frying pan, and with cans for kettles and teakettle, we began our first culinary enterprise, that never ceased so long as that stove held together. One never-to-be-forgotten delectable dish was fried potatoes a-la half-raw; and was they good! Yum! Yum! We had fried apples and fried salt pork, and made coffee out of wild triangular brown buckwheat seed. Never was banquet served in palace on finest china to be compared with that delicious repast served out under the Eucalyptus trees, with a box for a table, a dish towel for linen, and odds and ends of kitchen ware, broken dishes, old spoons, and what-not for our table service. Satisfaction was complete. Nothing lacked to mar the perfection of that magnificent repast.

Thus began a wonderful period of culinary pleasures that lasted through the years. For a while till the "bran new" wore off, we cooked and ate out under the trees every day and after that with varying frequency. Hulda, ever mindful of us, would send up delectable things from the kitchen to be cooked or warmed over. Should there happen to be some tasty dessert for dinner, she would see to it that some of this found its way up to the picnickers under the trees.

Never did we tire of this fascinating game. We pitied the poor grownups who were obliged to eat in the stuffy house. Our own cooking we enjoyed far more than theirs. There was a zest and a tang and a taint of smoke that could be had only in the great out-of-doors; and every meal was a fresh delight.

When our stove grew old and began to wear out, we made another one even better, improving upon our former patent as a good inventor should. And in time, we made still another; for we had at least three of these stoves before outgrowing our zeal for this delightsome game.

CHAPTER 29 HERDING CATTLE AND HOGS

As the herd of cattle which Father was raising on shares with Lovett increased, it became necessary during the spring and summer months while crops were being raised and harvested, to make use of the free government pasture lands on the tops of the hills around. This called for the supervision of a herder. George being engaged in the heavy work of the farm, as soon as Lafe was old enough to drive a cow, he was set to herding cattle, first on the coast mesa, and after that on the Laguna Hills and ranges west of Aliso Canyon.

During the long and lonesome hours he would think up things to do by way of diversion. While the cattle grazed on the flattened top of the Bench, he spent as much time as he dared leave them unwatched, down on the beach where the breakers pounded along the rocky surf and so many things invited investigation. At "Tunnel Rock," the northern boundary of Aliso Beach, was a large pool which he called a "bathing hole" about eight or ten feet across and six feet deep, in which were to be seen many small fish and minnows swimming about. These he longed to catch, and so one day, decided to manufacture some fishing tackle and try his luck at fishing.

He collected equipment, consisting of sack twine, pins and pieces of lead, and on his way down to the grazing fields as he passed through the creek, cut down a willow sapling and trimmed it for a pole, fastening to it, the sack twine. He bent the pins for hooks and fastened one near the end of the line, tying below it an oblong piece of lead for a sinker. Down among the rocks, he hunted about for bait; and discovering mussels, pulled some off prying open their shells with his pocketknife, and baited his pinhook with the meat. Then, with eager anticipation, he took his position and dropped the hook into the pool.

It was not long before he had a "bite," then another. He gave his line a jerk and there was a little fish on the pin-hook bending and flopping about on the end of the line as it came up out of the pool. Lafe was thrilled at catching his first fish, and overjoyed with such grand success. He kept on fishing as long as he dared absent himself from his charges, and that evening carried home with him quite a little bunch of small fish for supper. Needless to say this fun was after that often repeated.

While herding up on the mountains above Laguna, he made a bow and arrows with which to amuse himself and while away the hours. Selecting a good thrifty Holly shoot without knots and three or four feet in length, he cut it for a bow and leaving in the center of it a space the width of his hand to serve as a hand-hold, whittled from that point toward the ends each way until both were even in size, flattened, and of the proper thinness to make it limber as a bow should be. Then, after notching around each end, he stretched a stout twine tightly from tip to tip, so that it held the bow bent in a slightly crescent shape.

For arrows he had carried with him material from our "bunch grass" row. The stems of this grass were hollow and segmented with partitions from four to six inches apart. The blunt end of his arrow that should rest on the bow-string, he cut close to a joint to give it a solid end, notching it to fit over the taut string. The other end, he cut an inch or so past its last joint and into this inserted a nail—one of the old-fashioned square iron nails then in use—of proper size to fit into the tube snugly. This he had first prepared at home by hammering the head flat and then grinding it on the grindstone to a diamond point. The other end was pressed tightly against the joint in the tube and the pointed head left extended for deadly effect. Half a dozen or so of these arrows furnished his ammunition, and with them the long pliable bow constituted a most formidable weapon.

Armed with these munitions of war, Lafe would hunt rats which infested the mountain top having their coarse nests built of many sticks in the thick bushes. Many a luckless rat fell a victim to his practiced aim. Now all will agree that rats are a natural enemy of man and exist to be destroyed if possible. But Lafe did not stop with rats. With the lust for conquest that dwells in the heart of a boy, he sometimes aimed his barbed arrows at less legitimate objects. Occasionally, an inoffensive roadrunner, though decidedly the friend of man from his propensity to destroy rattlesnakes would receive the more deadly arrow in his trusting breast.

Sometimes Lafe would try his aim on smaller game. When crickets chirped merrily from their hiding places in the cracks of the dry adobe soil, he would search them out and with careful aim and a "twang" of the bow-string, put an end to their cheerful songs.

After the Goffs moved to the coast and Leon was tending cattle for his father upon these same hills, the two boys, being almost of an age—Leon Lafe's senior by six months—would drive their respective herds onto neighboring feeding grounds in order to visit and play together as boys will, which took out of the herding task its irksomeness.

In Lafe's herd was the pet bull Star, raised from old Cherry our first cow, and he would insist on visiting with Leon's herd, so that it would be very difficult to separate him from them when the time came to return home.

The hill at this particular place was a smooth slope almost without brush and covered with wild oats and other grass. In places, it was rough, rocky, very gravelly, and plentifully perforated with badger holes about ten inches across the opening, and the smaller gopher holes, the presence of which was often concealed by the grass.

One evening Lafe was trying to get this young bull away from Leon's herd to bring him home with the rest of the cattle. But the bull had other ideas, and persisted in breaking away and returning to the herd each time he was driven out. Lafe was chasing him at top speed down the hill, when he accidentally stepped into one of these hidden badger holes and went sprawling headlong down the hill. He struck with full force on his chest, knocking the wind out of him and seriously injuring himself. No longer able to contend with the bull, he left him behind and slowly and painfully followed the rest of his herd homeward, suffering intensely with every step.

When nearing the outskirts of the premises, he was met by Father in company with a butcher who had come out from Santa Ana to purchase of him some beef cattle. He was bringing him out to meet the herd. Lafe's face was so pale and drawn that immediately Father asked him:

"What is the matter?"

"I stepped in a hole and fell down and couldn't get the bull to come home!" explained Lafe.

Being preoccupied and slightly irritated at this failure, Father failed to give due importance to Lafe's condition, dismissing from his mind the fall as a trifling accident from which he would of course soon recover. The other man could see by Lafe's appearance that it was more serious than Father thought and he was very solicitous of the boy, favoring him by himself helping to get the cattle in. Lafe did not soon recover. For many years he could neither run nor ride a trotting horse without pain in his chest, and it was still longer before he fully outgrew the effects of this accident.

Ever since his narrow escapes from rattlers when very young, Lafe had been afflicted with an abnormal fear and horror of them. When about the age of ten, he was once herding cattle a mile above the upper limit of our place on the Rawson pastures in a dense thicket of tall mustard much higher than his head. The cattle ranged out in the mustard, but Lafe kept to the road for fear of getting lost. The road was just two wheel tracks through the mustard that had been trampled and beaten down by wheels and horses in traveling, and was no wider than a wagon, the mustard forming a high wall on each side of the road. As he walked along this wagon trail at noon eating his lunch, he came across a rattlesnake stretched out across the road in a patch of sunshine that filtered through the mustard at a spot less dense.

Lafe began to shout as loudly as he could:

"Here's a big rattlesnake! Here's a big rattlesnake!"

There was no one about to hear him, but for nearly an hour he shouted at random with one yell after another, the snake still lying unperturbed in the sun. Never once did it occur to him that he might kill the snake himself; nor did he consider such a thing as allowing the snake to get away without exhausting every possible means of obtaining help to kill it. Doubtless, he would have stayed as long as the snake did even had it been all day and into the night, shouting for someone to come and kill it. Old Jake, the farmer of the Rawson Ranch who raised garden stuff for the sheepherders half a mile away, finally heard him calling, and leaving his own affairs, came to see what was the matter and killed the snake for him.

At another time as Lafe was driving his cattle up the mountainside to the elevated pastures, coming to a boulder in a patch of wild oats, he clambered up onto the top of it. In this boulder was a wide fissure; and as he stood there looking down into it he saw within a small black rattler. Immediately he began to call for help to kill it. Joseph, not yet nine, who was working down in the field below, heard him calling and came to his rescue carrying a hard wood stick in his hand. He said to Lafe rather disgustedly:

"Why don't you kill it?"

That was a new thought to Lafe but the idea took root in his mind. Together, they killed the snake, and Joseph went back down the mountain to his work.

Farther up on the mountain the cattle had worn a series of trails through the brush and between boulders, covering a width of about seventy five feet, which was flanked on either side with heavy brush. About a week later, as the cattle he was driving, thirty or more in number, passed again up these trails, Lafe saw a large rattler attempting to cross this open area, dodging between the cattle with tail-tip in the air rattling loudly. Fearful that some of the cattle would be bitten, he picked up stones and went after the rattler. The cattle passed on safely and the snake got out into the brush taking refuge in a large black-sage bush.

Lafe from a safe distance heaved rocks at the snake in the bush, but the denseness of the low branches prevented any of the rocks from touching him. He kept up this bombardment, the snake rattling intermittently, until the rocks thrown had formed a perfect fortress for the snake by weighting the brush over him in a protecting mass, when the snake, realizing his security, finally ceased rattling altogether.

But Lafe had started out to kill. With Joseph's disgusted sneer ringing in his ears, he determined not to give up. As he stood trying to figure out some way of getting at the snake without danger to himself, an idea struck him.

Down the hillside about two hundred yards, grew a California Holly shrub. He hastened down to it and selecting a long unbranching stalk out of the clump cut it off at the base with his old jackknife, as dull as well could be and cut at all, and trimmed it up free of foliage, cutting off and sharpening the top end with much labor.

Armed with this sharp-pointed stick about four feet long and an inch and a half thick at the end he grasped, Lafe made his way back to the snake entrenched in its stronghold, on the way picking up a smooth rock to use as a hammer. With the point of the stick he prodded about among the rocks until he could see a portion of the snake's coiled body. Then with careful aim and a powerful thrust, he pierced the snake through with the sharp stick, hammering it nervously well down into the ground and securely pinning him there. After this impalement he left the snake to its agony and went to look for his cattle.

For two miles, he followed before catching up with them and found them over in the Laguna Hills with Leon's herd. He told Leon about the rattler, and the two boys left their cattle there and together went back to kill the snake. They found him already dead and dug him out. Leon holding him up by the tail, found him to be two inches longer than Lafe was tall. His fourteen rattles Lafe kept as a trophy of the first rattlesnake he had ever killed. By this accomplishment, he gained the victory over his fear and dependence upon others, and never again asked for help to kill a rattlesnake.

Dear Experience

One year, the barley was planted early and came up in a very fine stand. There was plenty of rain, and everything grew beautifully; the alfalfa as well as the barley being rank and tall. After the rains we had some warm, pleasant weather, and the grain grew so fast that Father was afraid it would lodge with the next rainfall, so it could not be cut, and we would lose our hay.

He worried considerably about this, hardly knowing what to do to save the crop from lodgement[i]. Finally, he decided to turn the cattle into the fields and let them eat off the grain; which had not yet begun to put out heads, and thus give it a setback in its growth. George suggested to him that so much green feed might not be good for the cattle; but Father was not much impressed with this thought; he had the welfare of the grain in mind, and the other side of the matter did not sink very deeply into his consciousness. A very cold spell came along; everything was white with frost, and the grain was bending with the weight in perilous nearness to a lodgement. A rain following the frost, Father thought, would finish it and lay it like a mat on the ground. So Father told the boys to leave the gates to the barley and alfalfa fields open, and let the cattle go in on it. This was done; and they went in and ate their fill. By noon, when the menfolk went out to see how things were going, they found dead and dying cattle all over the field. Poor old Brin and one of her half-grown heifer calves lay all bloated up to twice their normal size, dead in the barley field; and another with them. Others were bloated and suffering the most intense pain.

This was a shocking calamity. Father and George worked over these cattle to save them—Father performing a surgical operation upon each; cutting in to let out the gas that was ballooning up their insides. But in spite of all that they could do, two or three more of the cattle died—died in horrible agony; cattle that we needed so much and would miss so terribly. It was thus, at such a cost, that Father saved the barley stand. Experience is sometimes a very dear teacher.

---

[i] Lodgement refers to the bending over of grain crop stems near the ground level, which makes them very difficult to harvest and can reduce yield.

Joseph Falls Heir

Lafe was the regular cattle herder until past ten years of age. Then, Joseph's eighth birthday having come and gone, he was considered old enough to assist with the job, while Lafe in turn shouldered some of the heavier farm work (though still retaining much responsibility for the cattle). There was a season in the fall and winter when it was not necessary to herd the cattle; but in the times of growing crops and harvest, when they had to be looked after closely, and driven far up on the hills to find pasture, this was a real responsibility for a boy so young as Joseph, and in some ways a strenuous experience.

Joseph would take his lunch with him, which consisted of bread and honey, or bread and butter, whichever he preferred. No one was allowed both butter and honey on the same bread—not until more prosperous days came along. He carried it wrapped in a piece of brown paper and tied with a string, for paper bags were very rare indeed and there were seldom any to be had at our house. Many such convenient articles considered now so indispensable and common were in those days scarce and hardly ever seen.

In the region where he usually herded his cattle this first year, not far from the roadway was a heap of old lumber where an abandoned sheepherder's cabin had tumbled down. And their Joseph would sit and eat his lunch in the afternoon. He would leave there the little bundle of lunch while busy with the cattle, and when he became hungry would come back for it.

One day when he came for his lunch, it was missing. A little squirrel had carried it away to his hole. That day he had no dinner. He was almost ready to cry, for he was only a little boy and ravenously hungry as boys always are, and he didn't like that little squirrel one bit.

A few days after this, when he came to the pile of lumber a squirrel ran out, and Joseph took after him with his stick. He gave such a close chase that the squirrel ran down into the first hole he came to. Joseph rammed his stick down into the hole and prodded about. It proved to be a very shallow hole, and the squirrel ran out. Quick as a wink Joseph grabbed and caught him by the nape of the neck. He struggled to get away, scratching, kicking, and trying to bite him with his sharp teeth. But Joseph cut off his wind and soon had him limp and lifeless, and that little squirrel never ate his lunch again. There were others though, and more than once he lost his lunch.

The first year Joseph kept a stick and cut a notch in it for every day he herded the cattle. At the end of the year he had seventy-two notches in his stick. The herd at that time numbered ten or more. Some had been sold to the butcher, some returned to Mr. Lovett, and some had died of bloat, so that for a time the herd was greatly reduced. Joseph herded cattle off and on till he was about fifteen years old.

Much of the time he went barefoot, but sometimes he had shoes. These shoes were not like the shoes of today. They were not factory-made but made by hand in cobbler shops, for in those days cobblers made, as well as mended the shoes. The heels of these were not shaped to the foot as shoes are today, but were straighter and would slip up and down on the foot as one walked. So Joseph's shoes wore blisters on his heels and he was obliged to keep them off while the blisters were healing. Work shoes and children's shoes in those days, had each a strip of brass about half an inch wide across the toe to make them wear longer. We would think them very clumsy nowadays.

Sometimes a little squirrel was caught alive and brought home to be tamed for a pet. Squirrels make interesting pets and are very easily tamed. We once had a little pet squirrel that was given the run of the house. We never allowed cats indoors so he was comparatively safe. He would run up onto anyone's shoulder and sit there with his bushy tail curved up over his back and cock his little head in a most knowing way. He would run along the window grooves, sit on the tops of the chair backs, and climb up onto the tables. He liked nuts, and when given peanuts or walnuts, would crack them and always put the shells behind Mother's trunk. After a while Father bought a little cage for him with a tread wheel in it, and he would spin that wheel so fast that both squirrel and wheel would look like one big blur. Sometimes this cage was hung outside the house on a limb of one of the Sycamores in the back yard. I remember once—being then a very little girl—standing and watching him spin the wheel under the tree.

Ground squirrels were naughty little pests. All through the years, the depredation of squirrels which bred in countless thousands on the neighboring cattle and sheep ranches, had to be systematically fought by poison raids. So numerous were they in the pastures that the ground was perforated with their holes till it was dangerous to ride a horse outside of the beaten track for fear of his stepping into a hole and spraining his ankle or breaking his leg.

Several times a year at breeding seasons, Father would repeat his campaign of war by poisoning, against these destructive rodents. He would mix up a large batch of poison wheat in our big brass kettle, warming it on the Little

Rock fireplace where Mother made her soap out under the lone Sycamore tree. He always used honey to add to the attraction of taste and smell and to make it stick together, and would stir the poison wheat and honey mass together as it warmed. At first he used phosphorus which came in sticks like candy, and being very dangerous and inflammable was kept buried under the ground until needed, when he would dig it up to make his deadly potion. Later on he came to use strychnine in the place of phosphorus. Sometimes instead of wheat he used windfall apples for bait, treating them the same way, for he had discovered that squirrels like apples too.

Then the little brass bucket, a small duplicate of the big one, would be filled up with this poison bait, and Father, with sometimes the boys, would tramp over the whole territory of our farm and adjacent pastures, hunting for squirrel holes to be sure not to miss one. And into every hole would drop a bit of the bait. Whatever might be left over, would be scraped into the little brass bucket and set away high up in the "attic" out of reach of babies, and everything washed up clean. We children were cautioned at such times never to pick up any pieces of apple we might chance to find lying about, for it might be that a squirrel would have brought it up out of his hole.

Always it would make me sad to think of the terrible suffering of the little squirrels that innocently partook of the deadly stuff. Usually they would die inside their holes, but occasionally we would find dead squirrels lying about outside.

Carlo and Prinnie

Whenever stock died on the range, the cattlemen's herders would put poison into the carcass in order to destroy the marauding coyotes, whose keen scent could detect the odor of decomposing flesh for many miles around. Many of them would gather in the night to the fatal feast thus provided. Dogs also have this keen scent and enjoy a putrefactive feast. So this practice of poisoning the flesh of dead animals often acted as a two-edged sword, bringing disaster upon valuable dogs far and near.

The poison-mongers would of course tie up their own sheep-dogs at such times but unwarned neighbors would suffer the consequences without redress, their unprotected dogs dying in agony with no evidence available as to where the poison was obtained. Such was the fate of dear old Carlo, our white and yellow Shepherd-Collie, whom we loved almost as one of the family, and who was more than worthy of this affectionate regard.

Gentle and protective with the little children, whom he loved as they loved him, Carlo played or worked with equal faithfulness, and with more real sense than is manifested by many humans. He always seemed to understand just what was wanted of him and to be even more eager to do it than his master was to have it done, rendering the highest possible quality of willing, faithful service—the service of love.

The boys never thought of rounding up the cattle without his help. He knew just how to handle them. Never would he go to their heads, jumping and barking as do some foolish dogs, but always, he went behind them. He had trained them to know that he meant business, by just nipping their heels enough to suggest what might happen should they become belligerent. In this way, without injuring one of them, he never failed to bring every one of the cattle into the corral at night.

One evening when Lafe was ready to round up the cattle, he missed Carlo, and called him lustily. When the dog returned there was plenty of odorous evidence that he had been visiting some carcass. As they neared the second gate, Carlo plunged into a deep pool of water, lapped up a drink, and swam for a few moments, as though feverishly thirsty and uncomfortable. He helped corral the cattle, and the two went on to the house. Hardly had they reached it when he fell to the ground in convulsions. Soon the spell passed, and he rose, whining piteously. Straight to his young master, he went, as if pleading, for help. He raised up on his hind feet, put his forepaws on Lafe's shoulders, and for a moment gazed in dumb agony into his face. Then, without further warning, dropped to the ground, limp and dead.

That was a sad and bitter day on the farm. Lafe's grief was almost as though he had lost a brother. How we children wept for our dear old Carlo! How we hated the unknown enemy who had put out the poison without warning us to tie up our dogs. How we missed him! So often, we had played with him under the beautiful acacia trees, and there, in the soft earth of the orchard, they buried him. For years, the spot had a special sacredness for us. We felt that somewhere near, just out of sight, lay Carlo, the loved playmate we should never see again.

Our other dog, contemporaneous with Carlo, was little black-and-tan Prinnie, whom we also loved dearly, and even more so after Carlo was gone. Jealously we guarded him as well as we could from meeting the same fate.

Carlo had been a farm ranger with definite work to do, but Prinnie was more of a yard dog and pet, having no regular duties, but still useful in many ways. Though small he was very fearless, and as a watch-dog was quick to sense danger and scent wild intruders giving chase regardless of size or ferocity in defense of his master's premises and property.

Once little Prinnie was bitten by a rattlesnake on his nose. We thought surely he would die. His face swelled up to twice its usual size, and he lay around slobbering with tongue lolling, and eyes speaking misery for a week or more. During this time we doped him with what remedies we knew, and tried to make him as comfortable as we could. To our great joy, he recovered, and lived for some time after that experience.

However, Prinnie too eventually succumbed to the drug Strychnine—more deadly than the venom of rattlesnakes, and once more we wept for a lost pet and hated the poisoner of dogs. Such were some of our early tragedies. Other dogs we had through the years, but Carlo and Prinnie were dogs to be remembered—dogs that fastened themselves in our early affections, and still hold a sacred place in our memories after other dogs have been forgotten.

Frank Becomes Herder

When Frank was nine years old, the mantle of cattle-herder fell upon him from the shoulders of Joseph, upon whom now rested the extra burden of Lafe's work, he having gone from home.

One day Frank, with the help of his shepherd dog, was herding cattle in the Laguna hills. While they grazed, he lay down on a grassy slope and fell asleep. The dog too settled down close by his side, dozing, with head on paws. Awakening at some slight sound, Frank raised up head and shoulders, thus arousing the dog, who also sat up. This movement disturbed a third creature, who, unseen and unsuspected, lay coiled and ready. In a flash, the rattler struck, burying his poison fangs in the lolling tongue of the dog.

Frank hurried home with him, where the poor suffering dog made for the first water he saw. There in a mud-hole of the shallow creek, his face held against the bank and open mouth half filled with mud, he lay hour after hour in his misery; the boys watching helplessly while the day wore away.

Recovery came at last, but the area of the tongue where the poison fangs entered, in time rotted away, leaving a life-long deformity. Also the dog was left with a permanent deafness.

A young bull once broke the fence escaping from the corral, and took after Frank, who ran into the apple orchard nearby putting a tree between himself and the bull. Around this tree he dodged from side to side keeping the bull at bay, the bull also changing his course whenever Frank did his in an endeavor to meet him face to face that he might gore him with his half-grown horns. At last Father saw them from the barn and came running with a pitchfork in his hand, and soon had the bull back again inside the corral.

Mr. Moulton used to let his beef stock run loose all over the hills to multiply naturally as they would, and among them were several dangerous bulls. Frank was herding one day on the top of the Laguna mountains, having his cattle on a small flat up there. Other cattle also were roaming the hilltops, without herders. Suddenly one of these vicious bulls sighted Frank and came after him with head down and bellowing. There were no fences or trees up there or anything else to offer refuge—nothing but scrubby bushes on every side.

Frank knew that unaided he could not cope with that bull. He could not depend on his speed and agility to save him, for though he ran, the bull was gaining on him with every step. He must use his wits. One thing he must contrive to do—frighten the bull. But how? There was nothing in sight but the bushes. So, with his eyes ahead, selecting one of these shrubs while running, he stopped upon reaching it, and pulled it up by the roots, tugging frantically, for he had no time to lose. It was of the biggest and bushiest growing there and came up with a jerk that almost overbalanced him. Quickly he jammed this bush down over his own head, and crouching to simulate an animal. ran toward the bull, yelling at the top of his voice. The bull stopped and snorted. This was something he did not understand. As the strange apparition kept coming toward him unafraid, looking so fierce and making such terrifying noises, he became suddenly frightened, and turning, fled precipitately in the opposite direction. So Frank was saved by his own ingenuity, alertness, and courage.

Herding Hogs

We were never without hogs on our farm; and, increasing year by year, they grew into a large herd of fifty or more. Our barbed wire fences, built of three strands, were of no use in keeping hogs out of fields and gardens; therefore it became necessary that they be watched and herded at all times when outside of their own pens, except at those seasons when there were no crops they could damage.

Whatever profit lay in hog-raising, was largely due to their ability to find their own food. So they must be out foraging around over the premises the greater part of every day. At night they were fed the contents of the "swill-barrel," and perhaps given some corn, matured on the cob, if thought necessary. But other than that, their nutriment was for the most part picked as they roamed and rooted about over the premises and pastures. They usually found plenty, for there is nothing a hog will not eat.

Thus it was that I too, at an early age, became a herder—not successor to Frank, but contemporary with him; since it was not cattle, but hogs that fell to my lot. So I became the official family hog-herder. Annie, as she grew old enough, was assigned to be my assistant, but in matters of responsibility, the job was mine, and I was held to give strict account of my charges.

Let none suppose that herding hogs is an easy task; though that might be said of a few months of the year; for of all "ornery critters," the hog takes the prize. Drive him out of a grain-field, and before you can turn your back he is in again. Multiply such a case by fifty, and you have your hands full. During the season of growing crops, we had all we both could do to keep them under control; for no substitute could be devised to take the place of constant supervision. One moment of relaxed vigilance, and there were the hogs, all over the fields munching the grain or the vegetables. When utterly weary of this one-sided game, we would sometimes drive them up Aliso canyon far beyond our own borders, where there were no cultivated lands to be guarded. Here we could play around on the creek bottom between high banks, which served as effective barriers to such as had a yen for wandering, especially since there were no richer feeding grounds outside to offer temptations. There we could play with weed dolls, boats, and whatever could be devised, while the hogs were busily occupied along the streams of shallow sluggish moving water turning up with their snouts all kinds of roots and grasses, and other eatables dead or alive, buried in the mud. Carcasses, snails, snakes, and lizards were greedily devoured when discovered, for a hog revels in such provender and refuses nothing.

On these occasions, we really enjoyed our task, having plenty of time to play, and but little trouble in keeping our charges within bounds. We would build houses in the damp sand and fill them with little people made of weeds, which carried on at our bidding all the activities of life in a much varied and interesting kaleidoscope.

When we herded them nearer the coveted grain fields and gardens, it was a different story. There was then little time to play. After the grain was harvested, we must herd them in the stubble fields to fatten upon the rich barley gleanings, at the same time keeping them out of other garden plots nearby still producing crops. When the fallen overripe figs lay upon the ground under the trees in all stages of decomposition, we would drive the hogs into the orchard to feed upon this delicacy. Likewise when the apple trees dropped their wormy fruit and windfalls, we would allow them to help themselves to these, but always under close surveillance. Sometimes we herded them around in the filaree pasture, where they found much forage.

The Little Lamb

One day while driving his cattle home from the hilltop feeding grounds, Frank found a little lone lamb abandoned by the sheep men on the Rawson pastures, and joyfully brought it home intending to raise it as a pet. Immediately we loved this little lamb as we did all the baby things, and especially did little Charlotte love it and carry it about in her arms most tenderly.

One day soon after this find, Annie and I were herding our pack of fifty hogs in the filaree pasture, when little Charlotte came down from the house to be with us. We saw her walking toward us from the apple orchard around the bend, carrying this little lamb lovingly in her arms. Around its neck was a short piece of rope with which it had been tied, that dangled down dragging a little on the ground.

She had scarcely reached us when the little lamb caught sight of the hogs and became frightened. Struggling out of her arms, it leaped to the ground and ran a little way up the hillside dragging the rope. The instant those hogs spied the lamb, they all rushed in a body, led by the biggest old boar, and closing in around it like maddened devils, devoured it before we had time even to see what was happening.

Fleeing in fright from the ferocious pack we children climbed up onto a large rock where we stood trembling and shouting in impotent rage at the savage hogs that had so ruthlessly and suddenly robbed us of our pet. After the pack had scattered, we came down from off the rock and hunted about the place, but could find not so much as a bone or a wisp of wool. Even the rope around its neck had been devoured, and the hogs were champing for more, with their snouts to the ground.

Enraged and heartbroken, we took up our big sticks and whacked those hogs about right and left in vengeance dire. But not a sign could we find that there ever had been a little lamb in the world. So quickly had he perished that his sufferings must have been over in an instant, but not so with our own. How we mourned the untimely and horrible death that had robbed us of our little innocent pet! And how we hated those greedy beasts for their wicked deed! Sometimes I wonder with a shudder what might have happened had they spied the lamb while still in little Charlotte's arms. Would they have devoured our little sister too with him?

In this herd were two big old boars, the largest and leader of the pack, weighing about four hundred and fifty pounds more or less, the other somewhat smaller. They were fierce old fellows; but they recognized Annie and me as their masters and with us were usually docile. They would scamper ahead of our threatening sticks, seeming utterly unconscious of their own ability to "turn again and rend" us with their cruel tusks. But let any other member of the family try to manage them or force them against their wills to do anything, and they would immediately bristle up and show fight.

Hulda, though nearly three years my senior, was desperately afraid of them. Knowing this only too well, they gave her every reason to be afraid. Especially did this biggest old boar have a "pick" on her. He never would let go by an opportunity to chase her. Always, she would run for the nearest tree, screaming loudly for "Harriet!" to come to her rescue. This fear she communicated in large measure to Charlotte, who being in her care was often with her.

I still carry a mental picture of Hulda up in a certain fig tree just above the reach of her tormenter, trembling with terror and yelling at the top of her voice for help. The old boar, with all the bristles along his spine standing up straight and foaming at the mouth, would rise up on his hind feet in an effort to get at her. When I came running with my inevitable stick, his fight vanished and he suffered himself to be driven away as though it were all a part of the game. But it was no "game" to Hulda. She verily believed that he would have torn her limb from limb had he been able to reach her. After that experience with the little lamb, I could hardly doubt it. Even Annie and I, ordinarily not in the least afraid of him, were frightened then.

On another similar occasion, Hulda and Charlotte were down in the cart-road garden playing, while the hogs, under the usual supervision, were feeding in the creek opposite the gate among the tules and thick young willows. The biggest old boar, whose name was "Buck," hearing them down there slipped away from the herd among the willows quietly without my noticing his absence, and ran along the cart road to find them and have another "good time" with Hulda. The next thing that happened was a series of piercing and terrified screams coming from the cart-road garden.

Hulda had seen him coming, and dragging little Charlotte to one of the nearby almond trees, had "shinnied" it with her precious charge just in time to escape his ugly bared tusks. And there I found them, the boar all bristled up and standing on his hind feet with his snout up almost to where their bare feet clung to the limb of the tree. His "fun" was all over when I got there with my stick.

Two Doughty Steeds

If hog herding was not without its diversions, neither was it without its compensations. Some of the best times Annie and I ever had were furnished us by these two big boars. Old Buck, the larger and fiercer, "belonged" to me, I being correspondingly larger than Annie, while the smaller one, called Tim, "belonged" to her. These two boars, perseveringly "broken," were our respective "mounts."

Seated astride the backs of these doughty "stallions," we would ride them bridle-less all over the stubble field, while they munched along with their snouts to the ground. We guided them with sticks. A smack with the stick on the left jowl, accompanied by a loud "Gee" would turn the steed to the right, while a smack on the right jowl and a "Haw" would turn him to the left. A sharp clip on the "curl" in the rear would send him forward at a quickened pace. And thus would we "gee-haw" them about among the hard clods of the stubble field, here and there, according to our own sweet wills in truly imperialistic fashion.

It was great fun for us, relieving our daily task of its irksomeness. As for the hogs, they did not seem to mind it in the least—within certain limits. Those "limits" were of two kinds, equally effective. Taken singly, they might have been overcome, but together, were invincible. The first, was the degree of exasperation at which even a hog's docility finally succumbs. The second was the enclosing barbed wire fence.

When these animals would decide that they had been "gee-hawed" about quite enough for one day, they would simultaneously lift up their stubborn snouts, give a preliminary snort, kick up their heels, and make a "bee-line" for the fence. Just before reaching it, their imperious riders, having suddenly lost all their powers of persuasion, would precipitate ignominious backward somersaults, allowing the runaways to pass on through unhampered by human encumbrances; thus tendering a complete, if undignified, acknowledgment of the potency of barbed wires and pigs' wills.

The road that led across the creek to this stubble field, otherwise known as the "barley ground," led down the bank from the "filaree pasture" opposite, where the gradual slope was terraced by a stretch of white sand from the "big flood," nearly level and dry in summer. At this place grew an isolated clump of shady green willow trees some distance from the flowing water below.

A family of Southerners once camped for a few days on the sand under these willows, and all unbeknown to the chief performers, watched this hogback-riding stunt. The next day, as we were passing by their encampment, they stopped us and coaxed and begged us to repeat the exhibition for their especial benefit. But, seeing nothing ourselves of an unusual or "show" nature in the performance, and being very shy and diffident country children, we utterly refused to accommodate them.

Meanwhile, standing at a respectful distance from the camp, we stared in amazed disgust at the spectacle of a dirty pipe dangling filthily out of the old lady's mouth—a sight, the like of which had never before met our eyes. So it happened that the "free-for-all" show was in reality two-sided, had they but known it.

CHAPTER 30 EVENING GAMES AND PARTIES

On long winter evenings when early darkness shut us in, when the chores were all done and supper things out of the way, and perhaps the rain was coming down softly, then someone would suggest "games."

"Oh, let's play 'Hunt the Thimble!'"

"Oh yes, let's do!" and forthwith the drawers of the sewing machine would be invaded in search of Mother's thimble.

"I thought of it first. Let me be 'it!'" one would say.

"All right, you're 'it,'" and the others all would troop into the girls' room and shut the door.

The thimble must never be hidden completely out of sight, but placed where some lamplight would fall upon it so that it might be found with eyes alone.

When the hiding was finally accomplished—often with some suggestions from a non-interested grown-up who might be trying to read with one eye on his book while watching the game with the other—the signal would be given, the hunters all rush out from banishment, and the hunt begin.

"Am I warm?" someone would ask. And every such question called for a truthful answer.

"No, you're cold—freezing cold!" And the seeker would forsake that spot.

"Am I warm now?"

"Cold as ice and getting colder."

"Now what am I?"

"You're getting warm." At this everybody would rush over to the "warm" region.

"Am I warm now?"

"Yes, you're getting hot!" How tense all would become!

"You're hot! You're almost burning up!"

Now how concentrated grows the search! How excited the group, each eager to be the first to catch a glimpse of the shining thimble! Soon someone shouts:

"I see it! I see it! I see it!" and the finder climbs up to recover it from clock-shelf or niche or nail where it had been reposing in plain sight all the time. Then the lucky finder becomes the hider in the next round. In this game the very littlest could join.

Perhaps the game selected would be, "Button, button, button." Then Mother's button bag would be invaded. Sometimes bigger folks would take a hand in this game.

The players, all but two, leader and guesser, seated themselves in a circle around the room, their hands placed palms together fingers matched, in the lap or between the knees. The leader, holding his hands together in the same manner but having between them the button, passing from one to another around the circle, inserted his own hands between the palms of the others each in turn, while repeating the instruction:

"Hold fast all I give you."

At some point in this procedure, he left the button secretly between the hands of someone without changing his motions to indicate it—though to confuse the guesser often pretending to leave it where he had not. All this time the guesser had been silently following him around closely observant in an effort to obtain some clue as to who might have received the button. The leader after finishing the round, stepped back with the announcing question:

"Button, button, button! Who's got the button?"

Then guessing was in order. Any one asked had to open his hands, and when the guesser found the button he became the leader in the next round.

"Pussy Wants a Corner" was another familiar game we played; in which the players arranged themselves around the room in stated positions in corners or against the walls—there being one less such position than players. The one left out of a place was "poor Pussy," and must go to each in turn with the plea:

"Pussy wants a corner."

"Go to the next door neighbor," was answered.

But while he was going, someone behind his back might beckon to another to exchange places. Pussy, on the watch for such opportunities, if he saw the attempted exchange, would endeavor to secure one of the two corners for himself. If he succeeded the one left out became "pussy."

If he failed and had gone the round without getting a "corner," he might shout: "Everybody wants a corner!" the signal for a general exchange of places, and everybody was obliged to vacate his corner. In the general scramble Pussy was almost sure to secure one, and somebody else would be left out to become "Poor Pussy." This was a lively game that afforded much exercise and laughter.

Often, after the smaller ones had been put to bed, we would gather around the table and play Dominoes; for in order to have a part in this game one had to be old enough to count and add numbers quickly. Or it might be, the card game of "Musical Authors" was selected for the evening's entertainment, in which we formed "books" of four cards, each set bearing titles of different compositions by the same author. Unwilling opponents would be obliged to yield up incomplete "Books," card by card to those who called them in turn. Such authors as Handel, Bach, Wagner, Beethoven, and a host of lesser lights, were inscribed on those ancient cards, together with the title of many a notable composition. Among these stand out in memory with persistent prominence the "Air from Lucia Di Lammermoor" and "Lucretia Borgia."

Then there were the "string games": "Twirl the Button"—which even the small children could play, and "Cat's Cradle, Quilt, Rack and Corncrib," played for their amusement by those older.

For the first, a very large two-hole button would be selected, or a larger round piece of tin cut having two nail-driven holes through the center. A long cord string would then be threaded through the two holes and the ends tied together. The button or tin being shoved to the center of the double string, with a thumb through each end loop, while holding the left hand stationary the right would be swung round and round describing a circle till the string was well wound up. Gentle alternate pulling and relaxing of the string with both thumbs in unison allowing no slack, would start the centrally-located button or tin to twirling, swiftly unwinding and rewinding itself alternately and endlessly so long as the proper tension was maintained, giving forth its busy, musical hum. This was quite fascinating to operate.

For the "Cat's Cradle," a longer string was required—about six and a half feet. The two ends were tied together and the hands, inserted in the loop, fingers up and palms facing each other, with the string stretched out taut resting in the crotch of each thumb. The fingertips of both hands, one at a time, would then be dipped toward the body over the string, underneath it, and up again through the center to the same position; so that now the string lay twice across the back of each hand and once across the palm. Each middle finger in turn was then inserted from below under the string that lay across the palm of the other hand, and drawn back with it to position. The hands were then inverted with fingers pointing downward, and the result was the outline of a little cradle, having on each side a straight top string, and below this two diagonally crossed, leaving on each side of the cradle two half-diamond spaces with points meeting at the center.

This might then be transformed into a quilt for the cradle by a second party's transferring it onto his own hands. Using only thumbs and forefingers, he reaches down into the cradle and firmly grasps the two opposite string-crossings, or points of diamonds, through the half-diamond spaces. Then lifting these crossed strings, both sides at once, straight up over the top strings, then down on the outside, under them, and up through the center space together, without letting any part slip, he lifts the whole off the hands of the other person. Parting thumbs and fingers, and stretching out the slack upon them, there is formed the pattern of a pretty little quilt having one complete diamond in the center.

This quilt may now be turned into a long flat rack, with pattern running in straight lines lengthwise, by the first player's lifting it from the hands of the second player. With thumbs and forefingers, he grasps the two sides of the center diamond at the two points of crossing, lifting them simultaneously up over the outside strings, under and up again through the center, straightening the rack out on his own fingers.

This flat rack may then be changed into a corncrib. The free player first crosses his hands. Then with the right hand he lifts in the crook of his little finger the left outside double string drawing it over to the other side. With the left hand he does the same with the right double string, drawing that over oppositely to the left, so that the hands are no longer crossed. Then drawing these strings wider apart, on the little fingers, with thumb and forefinger of each hand pressed tightly together he dips them both at once from the outside, down under the two remaining strings of the rack and up through the center space, holding them thus loosely without slipping while the other player disengages his own hands. Without tangling or releasing the string in any way, he then straightens it out gently on his own fingers into a long corncrib with narrow bottom and depressed sides from which the horses are supposed to eat.

This whole process might then be reversed. To turn the corncrib into a flat rack, the two string-crossings on the sides are grasped, one by each hand, using thumb and forefinger, from the inside and pressed straight down outside, around and under the two bottom strings and up through the center space, and the rack straightened out on the fingers and thumbs. Or if a quilt be preferred (and this must always come second if all of the four are to be reversed) the two crosses are grasped from the outside—not lifted, but drawn down under the string and up through the center. We have already told how the quilt is converted into a rack, in the first process.

To convert the flat rack into the original cradle, the hands are crossed as before but instead of lifting the outside double strings with the little fingers, the inside single strings are lifted, and pulled back out over the outside strings, while thumbs and forefingers pressed together, are dipped down on the outside, under and up through the center as usual. Now we are back where we started, with a cat's cradle. The cycle may be repeated indefinitely. We never tired of this fascinating game.

Then there was the sleight-of-hand string performance, which, to baffle the audience, had to be done deftly and quickly and required previous practice. In this, a long endless string was slipped by the performer over the upturned finger of another person, and the announcement made that he would proceed to take it off without untying the string or slipping it over the end—a thing that appeared impossible (and indeed, was).

This, by sleight-of-hand manipulations he would quickly accomplish, to the amazement of his audience.

On pleasant evenings we might occasionally have company, when the young people—and older ones as well—of Laguna and vicinity would drop in to enjoy an impromptu party. At such times invariably we played games. Sometimes it would be "Blind Man Buff." One person was blindfolded and given a whirl to confuse him. The rest all formed a ring around him holding hands and moving silently to right or left, taking care not to betray to him their identity.

From inside the ring, Blind Man Buff feeling about and grasping someone, the circle would stop moving until he had made a guess at the captive's identity. He might examine the person's clothing, hair, or features, or ask questions to hear his voice. An answer must be given even if only in a disguised squeak. When the guess was finally made, if it proved to be wrong, the circle moved on, and the poor blind man had to try again. But if correct, the captive exchanged places with him, receiving the transferred blindfold.

There were two games we played with music—often from the harmonica, which we called a "mouth organ." One of these was "Musical Chairs" a noisy game in which all but one was given a seat. The music would start, and from the center of the circle this one would await his chance. So long as the music continued there was nothing he could do to get a chair. But at the caprice of the music-maker, the music would suddenly stop when all were obliged to exchange seats. Then was his opportunity. In the scramble he would have as good a chance as anyone else. There was always much laughter and excitement, and often ludicrous situations would result; such as two persons attempting to fill the same chair and finding themselves for a brief instant one in the other's lap—it might be a blushing young lady in the lap of an embarrassed young man or vice versa. Whoever failed to get a seat became the "seeker."

The other musical game, "Magic Music," was the direct opposite of this in that it was the most quiet and decorous game we knew. No one was to speak a word during the game. Its interest consisted in the musician's versatility of performance and the seeker's being able properly to interpret the music which was to guide his movements. Someone, chosen to be seeker, would be sent out of the room, while those remaining, in consultation would decide upon some certain object that was to be sought.

The seeker was recalled from banishment by the sound of loud music, which became soft as he entered the room. Immediately he would begin to touch different objects about him, listening to the music for its reaction to his touch. The farther he retreated from the chosen object, the softer and fainter became the music, and the closer he approached, the louder it grew.

Thus, guided by music alone, he would try touching this and that until the general location of the object was perceived. Then he would concentrate his attention on that locality, discovering at last that he had touched the right thing, by a final loud burst of music and its cessation.

We played also, several "joker" games; whenever there were present some ignorant of the joke. One of these was called "Introductions." Those to be introduced were excluded from the room during preparations, and recalled one at a time. The first "stranger" upon entering beheld three very demure maidens with downcast eyes, seated in three chairs in a row in the center of the room, hands folded in laps. The leader stepped forward to greet him with extended hand, and words something like this:

"Good evening, Mr. So-and-so, I would like you to meet my friends the Misses Fly."

Then leading him to the first of these young ladies, he proceeded to introduce him in the most approved manner:

"Miss Butter Fly, allow me to present to you my friend, Mr. So-and so. Mr. So-and-so, Miss Butter Fly."

This introduction was acknowledged by the young lady who extended her hand to be shaken, with a bow of the head. Proceeding to the next young lady, whose name was Miss Shoo Fly, introductions were made in the same manner, with more or less amusement on all sides. The third young lady was Miss Let Fly. He would repeat:

"Miss Let Fly, allow me to introduce to you my friend Mr. So-and-so. Mr. So-and-so, Miss Let Fly."

Miss Let Fly would now extend her hand as if to meet his in a handshake, but instead would let fly a thimbleful of water in the face of the gentleman, to his discomfiture, amid loud laughter from the audience. Whereupon, after he had wiped his face, the next victim would be called in, and the game repeated until all had been "introduced."

"Brother, I'm struck," was another joker. Gentlemen unacquainted with the game were banished from the room, to be called in singly in turn. Upon entering, the victim beheld two chairs placed back to back in the center, and learned that he and some other man were to occupy them, both blindfolded. Someone in the room was then to strike one of the two upon the head, who was to announce: "Brother, I'm struck." His companion was to ask: "Who struck you?" then he was to guess which one of the audience, who, having joined hands were slowly circling around the two, had done so. The guess was always incorrect; and after a number of strikes and failures, the two were unblinded, and another victim was called in. The former one watching the proceedings, learned by observation how he himself had been tricked. After the new victim had been blinded and seated, the same "partner" was again seated in the other chair, and a blind tied around his head, but high enough to expose his eyes, and a tightly-folded newspaper handed him to strike with. While the company circled, he struck himself on the head, saying "Brother, I'm struck." The other innocently asked: "Who struck you?" then followed a guess, and the next strike was on the head of the man behind him, to aim which, he partially turned in his chair. By this time the first victim was sheepishly comprehending, and all were chuckling, supposedly at the failure of either one to guess correctly, but actually at the amusing pantomime, and the look on the face of the last victim, whose guesses, of course, could never have been right since he did not suspect the deception. The joker usually managed to give the other fellow the hardest whacks, with understanding winks and grimaces to the on-lookers the while, in a monkey-like manner. But he himself never laughed outright for fear of betraying his duplicity to the victim. It was all very amusing to the crowd in the room, who could hardly keep within bounds for laughter.

This would be kept up for some time, nobody guessing correctly till finally they would decide to let the unfortunate guessers have a rest, and call in another. Whereupon, the paper cudgel would be first recovered, then the blindfolds removed, and the victim would not suspect that he had been made the fool till he beheld as a bystander the scene reenacted.

Though himself highly amused, and feeling utterly foolish, he could say nothing till the game was over. Then invariably would "vow vengeance" for the whacks he had been given.

Some games we played as "puzzlers." These would be carried on by a leader and his secret accomplice in the audience. Should there be present anyone else who understood the game, he was by "unwritten law," as in the joker games, bound in honor to keep his knowledge to himself. Of such were the two games, "Spirit Rappings" and "Colors."

The first was represented as being done by the aid of "spooks." Lights were turned low, and an air of mystery and subdued quietness prevailed. The leader, walking about on tip-toe announced in sepulchral tones that after he should retire from the room, a certain designated person in the audience, (naming his secret accomplice) would shake the hand of someone in the audience, and that upon his return, he himself would proceed to shake hands with the same person. Opening the door, perhaps lingering a moment to hear whatever remarks were being made, he would then suddenly turn and go out, closing the door gently after him.

His accomplice, rising and walking about the room for a bit as if deciding in his mind with whom to shake hands, would then extend his hand to some individual, after which he would go softly to the door and rap.

Answering raps would come from outside, and immediately be returned. Back and forth with suggestive pauses, they rapped as though conveying some hidden meaning, the object being to mystify and mislead the audience into supposing the secret to lie in the raps.

The door being opened, the leader would come spookily in, look about for a moment, then tip-toe over and shake hands with the same individual.

"They had it all fixed up beforehand," someone would likely declare.

"Well, if that's what you think, we will do it all over, and he can shake hands with someone else—anyone he pleases." Saying which the leader would again leave the room and the performance is repeated, some other person being selected for the handshake.

The same accurate results would again mystify the audience, the conspirators insisting that the "spooks" were responsible for it all. Then many wild guesses would be hazarded as to the secret.

But in their efforts to discover the "key," the focus of all guessing was likely to be the secret code of the raps.

Between you and me, however, the trick is very simple. The last person to speak a word in the presence of both accomplices before the leader turned his back to go out the door, automatically became the one selected to receive the handshake.

The game of "Colors" had a similar trick. The guesser having left the room, those remaining would decide upon some particular object to be guessed. Whereupon the banished, being recalled, would come in and seat himself. The accomplice, then rising, would walk about the room, touching objects one after another, with the inquiry:

"Is this it?"

"No."

"Is it this?"

"No."

Passing around the room, he would continue to touch this and that with the same inquiry. Finally, he would touch the right object, repeating:

"Is this it?"

"Yes, that's it," would be the reply, utterly mystifying those present.

Some would insist that it was all in the way the question was asked. So the two accomplices obligingly would play it all over again, and the mystery would deepen.

But no one noticed that always immediately before touching the right object, the accomplice for the first time had touched something black.

No party was every quite complete unless we played "Spin the Platter." A tin pie-plate would be brought in, and while all the company sat around in a semi-circle, the leader seated opposite would spin the plate on the floor some distance from them, calling at the same time the name of some member of the group. The person called must catch it before it fell over, or pay a forfeit. If successful, he took his turn at spinning the plate, but if not, the leader would go on with the spinning until someone did catch it.

Many would be the forfeits paid. They might consist of any small thing personally owned, such as a handkerchief, a watch, a ring, a brooch, a stick-pin, a pencil, a pocketknife, a back-comb, a ribbon, or just anything that the player could temporarily dispense with. When a sufficient number had been collected, the order of the game would be changed, and the forfeits "redeemed."

All the forfeits would be placed in a receptacle by the leader, who stood behind a chair placed in the center of the room. In this chair was seated the "Judge," selected for his cleverness and originality. He must now know whose forfeit was put up for redemption.

The leader would hold one of these articles above the head of the judge, with the announcement:

"Heavy, heavy hangs over your head."

"Fine, or super-fine?" the judge would ask (fine indicating a gentleman as owner of the forfeit and super-fine a lady).

"Fine," (or super-fine). What shall the owner do to redeem it?"

The sentence would then be pronounced by the judge. He might order the owner to sing a song, speak a piece, dance a jig, even propose to a certain person of the opposite sex, ask for a kiss, say a certain rigmarole a definite number of times, or to perform any silly or crazy stunt that might be supposed to furnish amusement for the company. He might be asked to pat his head while rubbing his stomach, or rub his head while patting his stomach; and any person who thinks this is easy, should try it. This latter part of the game produced much amusement.

Perhaps instead of the usual evening of games, we would have a "candy pull." The candy was always made of honey and cooked in a large iron skillet; a little cream of tartar being added to keep it from graining. After being boiled until it tested the right consistency, it was poured out into large well-buttered platters and set in a cool place to stiffen. While waiting, games would be played, the candy being examined at frequent intervals.

When cool and thick enough to handle, everybody would wash their hands and afterward butter them thoroughly to keep the candy from sticking. A large portion was then given to each, and all would begin to pull, double, and pull till the mass, at first very dark, became a beautiful cream color. To get it started, we would work fast, but after that it was easy, and plenty of fun. Anyone who liked would put a lump of it into his mouth and chew as he pulled.

During the pulling, someone invariably would start a game of "grab." This was a "free-for-all" in which everybody would try to snatch some from his neighbor, thus adding to his own store; and anyone so robbed would replenish his own by the same method. As the candy would be pulled out in a long string, it was easy to snatch a bit of the string, and sometimes in so doing, fine threads would be spun that would float away out of control, and mayhap stick to a lady's dress or hair. This was not so delightful for her, though furnishing entertainment for the one responsible. But it was all "in the game" and taken good-naturedly. Nobody even once thought of such things as "germs," called in that day's "microbes," the very existence of which was sometimes scoffed at.

When the game came to a close, some would be found having much candy and others very little. But all would have had "bushels of fun," and be abundantly gorged with sweet. The guests if they chose, might take home with them what they had. We little folks would lay ours away on a big platter side by side, marking it as to ownership; and next day would feast on the leftovers. Of course it would not pull any more after becoming thoroughly cold and "set."

Sometimes, instead of making "pully candy," we would make nut candy. This was cooked exactly the same except that just before removing from the stove, a quantity of chopped nutmeats—walnuts, almonds or peanuts—would be stirred in. Then the candy would be poured into platters as before, and when cool enough cut into squares. This was very delicious. We hardly knew what it was to make candy of sugar. It was too expensive—not being a home-product as was honey and nuts; which was most likely better for us than we knew.

Saint Valentine Parties

Every year, on February fourteen, somebody in the neighborhood would give a Valentine party; a custom that began, in our vicinity, with the coming of the Goffs to the coast—for of course there were no young folks before then to give a party of any kind. In later times, young people from San Juan Capistrano were included. One of these very early parties was held at our house when Mesia was a little past sixteen, and Sadie was soon to be "of age" (eighteen) and leave home.

The older young folks of the coast then included, besides our own three or four, Clinny, Addie and Ammon Goff from Henry's home; Tiny and Levi Hemenway; Lulu from Hub's family; and Nellie and Leon from Frank's family; besides these, there might have been one or two others; and a few of the married couples were still young enough to enjoy a party. Hub was always there if dancing was thought of; for he was the community "fiddler."

Of all these guests, Leon was the youngest, though no stranger would have suspected it. Large for his age, well built, of fine appearance, strong pleasant features, and grown-up ways, Leon would have been taken to be several years older than his birth record indicated—which placed him at almost thirteen and a half. Being an only son, he could hardly have escaped being spoilt by his adoring parents and one older and two younger sisters, who fairly worshiped him.

Mesia was a slim, graceful girl, very retiring, with refined, winsome features, straightforward, unassuming manner, and maturity beyond her years—the result of carrying responsibilities in the home; yet withal, peculiarly immature as to experience outside the home, and even childlike in innocence. She and Leon from the first of their acquaintance had been attracted to each other; which gave to the neighborhood parties, for them at least, an added zest. From time to time they had visited back and forth, spending an evening at playing Dominoes, or Authors; and if at his house, then he would see her home afterward.

Once, wishing to make for Leon a little remembrance of her own handiwork for his birthday, and having no means of obtaining colored embroidery thread, Mesia made some dye from the juice of the prickly pear and dyed her white thread a bright rose-red color; with which she then worked his initials in the corner of the white muslin handkerchief she had made for him.

Valentine parties were silly things; though furnishing much fun. Such an occasion was a time of mock and pseudo-lovemaking. The valentines written at home and brought to the party were always unsigned, and usually were intended to mislead the recipients into supposing themselves to be addressed by someone "dead in love" with them; when as a matter of fact, the writers more often were mere acquaintances. But this was all a "part of the game" and taken as intended. However, it was a time also when genuine admiration might be expressed in an anonymous missive without compromising the writer. The public reading of these valentines—always of a sentimental order—invariably would cause embarrassment and blushes to the recipient, and much laughter on the part of others.

These homemade valentines were usually self-composed and written in the author's script on tiny sheets of notepaper, folded small and placed in home-made envelopes for delivery. Often they were decorated with tiny colored pictures of flowers, birds, clasped hands, overlapping hearts, or boy-and-girl lovers—sheets of such pictures being factory-produced for the purpose.

One of the valentines from this very party now reposes in my box of mementos, fifty-nine years old. It is a curious little relic of the past, its mushy sweetness still breathing of bygone romance and a measure of poetic skill.

The tiny envelope made of thin wrapping paper, in which this much folded little sheet of pinkish notepaper is inserted, measures about one and a quarter by two and a half inches. Its flap is cut in three deep scallops, each of which is itself very finely scalloped, and has been sealed with red sealing wax. This particular valentine is unadorned with pictures. Perhaps they had not come into use quite so early in history, or at least not so far from the larger social centers; or it may have been simply lack of means or of opportunity to obtain them so far from town. The verses are in the form of an acrostic on the name of the recipient—the initial letter of the added line revealing a clue to its authorship.

"An Acrostic Valentine
To
Leon Arthur Goff Feb. 14th, 1880

"Lovely charmer that thou art,

Ever joyful, light of heart,

Oh, may sorrow never cloud—

Never wrap Thee in its shroud;

Ah, it could not cloud Thee long.

Gay and witty, brave and strong,

Oft, I've seen Thine eyes so bright

Filled with sweet love's tender light—

Felt the heart that through them shines.

Might become thy Valentine."

All valentines brought to the party were dropped unopened into a box. When the time came for the public reading of these missives, they would be stirred, shaken up, and drawn out one at a time by a selected person, who customarily would open and read them personally before passing on to the recipients.

The fair writer of this most complimentary valentine had expected the usual custom to be followed. But to her utter confusion, the routine was in this instance unexpectedly varied, and the valentines passed unopened to those addressed to be read aloud by them to the audience. Leon read his with a very flushed face, and several glances cast in the writer's direction, at which the telltale blushes covered her own face and drew to her the unwelcome attention of other listeners, so that she wished herself many miles away and the valentine in limbo. But Leon, though embarrassed, treasured it.

After this feature of the party was over, there would be a general attempt carried on by individuals to discover the authorship of the valentines received. Sometimes this was easy, but not always; for authorship would nearly always be denied even if correctly guessed—the object being to mystify and tantalize the one so complimented. Questions would be asked on every hand, such as:

"Did you write this?"

"Do you know anything about this valentine?" or

"I'll bet I know who wrote this one!"

The author might want him or her to guess aright, but never to know for sure; so evasive and misleading answers would be given and expected.

Another valentine of later origin, relic of a valentine party held in San Juan Capistrano, was written by a young lady in early teens, placed in its home-made envelope and dropped in the box, addressed to an acquaintance of a short time, who had another girl. He therefore was puzzled somewhat as to its authorship at the time, but later assured. This one read thus:

> *"Forgotten am I, Dear One, say—*
> *Hast thought of me when far away?*
> *I've dreamed and dreamed, and thought that thou*
> *With welcome sweet would greet me now."*

This one brought, sometime later, through the mail, a gaily-decorated missive to the greatly embarrassed girl, who had hoped not to be found out:

> *"Nay, not forgotten, Precious One,*
> *Methinks I see your sweet face now;*
> *And with welcome sweet as in your dreams,*
> *I plant my greeting kiss upon your brow."*

Sometimes "comic" valentines were given. These were always bought at the stores, and might refer to some past amusing experience of the recipient, or some joke. More often they were presented to express dislike, or by way of revenge for some fancied slight.

One of these, cartooned in loud colors, representing a wrinkled Old Maid before the mirror attempting to resuscitate some of her lost attractions by means of cosmetics, was sent for the purpose of insulting a young and very sweet girl; who reacted to it with wholesome mirth:

> *"You wily, foolish creature;*
> *You' re eaten up with pride.*
> *You think of hats and dresses*
> *And little else beside.*
>
> *Your friends are always laughing*
> *At your imitation sacque;*
> *They know you starve your appetite*
> *To clothe your worthless back."*

An invariable feature at such parties was conversations carried on by means of candies. Flat sugar candies, either heart-shaped or diamond, flavored with peppermint, musk, or some other favorite flavor, and printed in red letters with brief, and often silly mottoes, or with questions or answers to supposed questions, were freely passed around, and used to carry on these secret and silent communications. Search among the candies would be made by recipients to find appropriate answers to candy questions received, even exchanges with others to find appropriate replies.

Hard mixed candies also, flavored with peppermint, sassafras, or wintergreen, came wrapped in narrow strips of paper containing longer messages. These would be used for the same purpose and passed back and forth between the young people.

Partners would be chosen for supper, and two eat from the same big plate together. There would be several kinds of cake, maybe two kinds of pie, candy and sandwiches; with lemonade, tea or coffee.

The usual games would be played. Or if the evening were moonlit, the young folks might go out of doors and carry on such rollicking games as "Drop the Handkerchief," "Ruth and Jacob," and other similar games.

Sometimes when something was going on in which we little folks could not very well join, Hub Goff would slip away with us into the girls' room for a while and entertain us with amusing silhouettes or shadow-pictures on the wall, made in the lamplight with his hands. He would produce the most lifelike donkeys with long ears, that munched hay, and brayed; ducks with long bills, rabbits, horses, dogs, cats, monkeys, and birds—all different, moving in lifelike manner, and vocalizing, with his help, in a most realistic fashion. This was to us a pure delight; and we would wish we might have him with us always.

Country Dances

Perhaps the floor might be cleared for dancing—all chairs shoved back against the walls tables folded up and placed in corners, and a little bees-wax shaved over the floor. Then the good old square dances, quadrilles, hornpipes, and reels were entered into with hearty enjoyment; while Hub would play the fiddle, tapping his foot the while rhythmically on the floor. Often, if the dance was impromptu and the company small, Hub was also the caller. But as the community increased in numbers, and the gatherings became more formal—especially if invited for dancing only—then a separate caller was engaged for the occasion and made master of ceremonies.

The caller, always a genius in his line, often would dance right along with the others in the set while calling to the rhythm of the music, stamping his foot hard on the emphasized notes that betokened change of figure. I hear him yet singing out the various calls of those old-time quadrilles, snatches of which come surging back into memory, as I see the couples moving through the measures of the various dances:

"Swing that girl, that pretty little girl, the girl you left behind you!"

"Then Pass right through and Balance Too, and Swing That Girl Behind You!"

"First Gent Out to the Couple on the Right, Swing or Cheat. Do as You Like!"

"First Couple Out to the Couple on the Right; Swing When You Meet and Meet when You Swing."

"Swing Your Honey and She'll Swing You!"

"Swing Your Honey With a Pretty Little Whirl, and Then Run Away With the Corner Girl!"

"Ladies Go Gee and Gents Go Haw!"

"Swing Your Paw and Swing Your Maw!"

"Birdie in the Cage and Three Hands Round, Birdie Hops Out and the Crow Hops In!" the crow meaning the gentleman and the birdie a lady.

"I'll Swing Your Girl and You Swing Mine! You Swing Your Girl and I'll Swing Mine!"

"Swing When You Meet, Both Head and Feet!"

"Single File Indian Style, Stop and Swing Her Once in a While!"

"Down the Center and Then Chasse!" The caller always pronounced "chasse" "sashay." And when the time of the music permitted, he would sing a bar of the words, or throw in a rhyme, nonsensical or humorous, of his own clever improvising, besides the customary jingles.

Quadrilles proper were always danced with four couples, being as the name indicated, a drill of four. They stood in square formation, constituting a "set." The head couple, always nearest the music, led out in every figure to form different patterns, guided by the "caller" whose calls acquainted them with the figures to be formed. Though the patterns and tunes varied, they were all fashioned after the same general principle.

The Contra Dance required six couples, and the formation was different. They would line up in two rows—ladies in one row and gentlemen in the other, with partners opposite.

The Lancers, requiring eight couples, was stately and dignified and a more complicated dance.

The round dances—those for one couple only—were then not much engaged in. Occasionally a waltz, or schottische, or polka would be indulged, but this was the exception. These dances were considered selfish and not entertaining to anyone but the dancers. Also they encouraged too much intimacy between partners. That this objection was well founded has been demonstrated amply by the sensual degeneration expressed in many so-called modern round dances. In reality many of these are importations of ancient heathen dances practiced among primitive peoples in connection with heathenish and degrading rites. In the days of the old square dances, there were no "Bunny Hugs" and "Turkey Trots," but sane and modest figures that required real skill and grace and were carried out in beautiful patterns of drills and marches to the swing of the music, in which all, young and old, might engage.

Sometimes when gatherings were solely for the purpose of dancing, confetti would be thrown—handfuls of tiny bits of bright and varicolored paper, manufactured for the purpose and showered over those it was desired to compliment. Or the old Spanish "cascarones"—empty eggshells filled with confetti and sealed—would be broken over the head of a lady or a gentleman; and the bright bits of silver, gilt and vermilion would lodge in hair and on clothes that retained some of the sparkling particles for the rest of the evening.

In dancing Old Dan Tucker any number of couples, not less than four, could join. But there must be one extra man without a partner who would be "Old Dan Tucker." With couples arranged in a circle about him, the music and calling would start:

"Balance all to Old Dan Tucker!"

All would balance forward on the right foot and backward on the left.

"Allemande left!" Each man would join right hands with the lady on his left and turn her once around, then with his left hand take his own partner and turn her once around.

"Grand Right and Left!"

All partners would face each other and start around the circle by clasping right hands, giving their left hands to the next in line then the right to the next as they progressed around the circle, which always brought those of the opposite sex together, the gentlemen all going in the same direction and the ladies in the other. It was then that Old Dan Tucker would get his chance to "horn in" and secure a partner by hanging to the last lady he had when the call changed to "All Promenade," leaving someone else to be forced into the role of Dan Tucker.

Then the caller might sing out: "Clear the way for Old Dan Tucker! He's too late to get his supper!" in which others sometimes joined, and the dance would proceed with a new "Dan Tucker" in the center.

"Forward and Back!"

"All Hands Around!"

"Balance All and Swing Your Partners!"

"Promenade Around the Room to Your Seats!" This ended the dance; as the gentlemen took their ladies with a galloping or marching step, first around the set, then to their seats against the walls.

In promenading, couples had three choices as to style. They might gallop, march, or glide. When going to seats, they usually started out in one of these steps, and finished by walking.

The Money Musk was a contra dance with either six or nine couples. In the first figure the head couple and simultaneously, the fourth and seventh, were going through the same figure of the dance in succeeding formations that ended with each couple taking positions one step lower in line.

"Swing Once and a Half Around!"

"Forward and Back Six!" brought to formation two groups of three each, facing the sides.

"Swing Three Quarters Round!" and "Forward and Back Six!" brought the same formation of dancers looking up and down the set instead of toward its sides.

"Swing Three Quarters Round to Place!" and each leading couple came to rest one position still lower in line.

"Right and Left!" finished the figure for the first dancing groups the whole dance being repeated till all had their turn, and

"Forward and Swing Partners" "All Promenade!" brought the dance to a close.

For the Arkansas Traveler the measures were different. Separate units of three ladies and three gentlemen were formed, dancing all down the line to the same calls.

"Balance Six!"

"Six Hands Half Around!" left them in opposite lines.

"Balance Six!"

"Six Hands Half Around!" brought them back to original positions.

"Right Hand Mill!"

The first and second couples would cross right hands, each joined with the other's partner, forming a "mill," and swing half around finishing on opposite sides.

"Swing Your Partners!" called them to break the mill.

"Left Hand Mill!" repeated the figure, joining left hands instead of right.

"Swing Half Round" to original positions.

"First Couple Swing!"

"Down the Center and Back!"

"Cast Off!" and they would separate passing behind the next in line to take new places below them in the set.

"Right and Left!" and "Forward and Swing Partners!" and "All Promenade!"

Chase the Squirrel was another of those beautiful and interesting old contra dances for six couples.

"Down the Outside and Up the Center!" was executed first with the head lady followed by her partner dancing down the outside of her line of women to the foot of the set and up the center again to the head; then the same figure repeated by the gentleman dancing down his line of men and she following. The third and fifth couples, waiting till passed by the previous ones, would then follow, executing the same figure.

"Down the Center and Back!" The first couple joining crossed hands would execute this measure then "Cast Off!" and take the place next lower in the set, finishing with a "Right and Left," "Forward and Swing Partners" and "All Promenade" to seats as usual.

Once in a while in the more complicated movements of a dance a tangle would occur which would require a bit of explanation and straightening out by the "Caller."

The Virginia Reel, another contra dance, was a favorite with all. There were three general divisions. The first, preliminary and executed entirely by the head and foot couples alternately, dancing cater-cornered to the set in a light and springy step, in response to each call advancing to meet in the center and backing to their places.

"Forward and Back and Honor Each Other!" (with a bow).

"Swing with Right Hands!"

"Swing with Left Hands!"

"Dos a Dos!"—meaning back to back—the couple passing around each other, danced backward to their places.

The next division began with the call:

"Head Couple Down the Center!" Joining hands they would chasse (move with a light gliding step sidewise) down to the foot and back again without turning.

"Right Hand to Partner and Reel!"

Clasping hands or linking right arms, the first couple would turn once and a half around. Then releasing each other link up and turn in the same way with the second couple, then releasing turn partners again, repeating this movement on down to the foot of the line till every couple had been reeled and left in their original places. Then the reeling couple would join both hands at the foot and chasse up the center to their own first positions.

The third division of the dance began with: "March!"

Every couple then faced toward the head of the line. The leaders turned outward away from each other and passed down the outside of their respective lines followed by all in the set, and took their position at the foot, every follower taking a position below the last preceding, which left them still at the head of the lines.

They then formed an arch with clasped hands raised high, and under this arch all couples passed, beginning with the lowest. These took their original positions just above the arch, the next lowest taking the next place, and so on till the last couple had passed through, and stood at the head of the lines. This left the former head couple down at the foot again as their permanent position and the original second couple at the head, who were now to lead out in the next round.

The whole dance would repeat till each couple having gone through all the figures held the head position.

"Forward and Swing Partners," and "All Promenade to You Know Where!" ended the dance.

No dance evening would be complete without "Pop Goes the Weasel!" After formation in lines the call:

"Down the Outside and Back!" would be followed by:

"Down the Center and Back!" and the head couple after passing separately down the outside of their respective lines and back would join hands and promenade down between the lines to the foot, turn, join their other hands and promenade back.

"Three Hands Round With Lady!" A "threesome" was formed by joining hands with the second lady in line, all swinging once and a half times around, bringing the odd lady to the opposite side, facing her original position. Meanwhile, somebody on the floor might be singing:

"Every time that I come home, the monkey's on the table. Take a stick and knock him off—Pop, goes the weasel!"

At the word "Pop" with the proper note of music, the couple would drop her hands, lift their own high joined together in an arch, and she would pop under gaining her former position and moving up one place in line.

"Three Hands Round With Gent!" and the same figure would be executed with the lady's partner. All other odd-numbered couples had followed and been leading out in the same figure and dancing to the same calls as they progressed down the line so that several were popping through at the same time making a very interesting pattern.

How They Dressed

In those early days, the women wore hoops and bustles with either tight-fitting basques, or polonaise, draped and looped up in graceful folds over their bustles and often ruffle-trimmed. Their heavy, full-gathered skirts with several petticoats underneath, swept the floor in a most unsanitary manner, completely concealing the cotton or lisle stockings, always either black or white—for no such innovation as silk stockings and varieties of colors had yet been manufactured.

Hidden in the folds of these skirts were generous pockets, without which no dress was complete. Ladies in those days did not carry handbags as they do today but only small coin purses, often beaded or otherwise ornamented, that could be kept in the pocket. Their hands were thus left free for carrying fan or umbrella—a distinct advantage over our modern custom. Purses then were seldom lost.

Women and young ladies were cinched up tight in corsets that gave them wasp-waists and womb-trouble, considered then in their ignorance of its causes, to be women's natural heritage. Their long tight-fitting sleeves were edged at the wrists with white rushing, sometimes gold or silver bordered, which also stood up around the neck from inside the high choke collars. A long white tie or scarf of lace-trimmed net was often passed around the neck below the collar and tied at the throat in a large bow, fastened usually with a brooch.

Half-gloves were worn, called "mitts" that allowed the fingers and thumbs beyond the second joint to protrude. These too were made only in black and white.

Many ladies wore their hair down on their shoulders in either half-braids or ringlets. Especially was naturally curly hair so worn. Emma Goff in those early days always wore her long natural curls so. Others combed the hair back into a snug "pug" at the nape of the neck, covering it—the pug only—with a net made of woven cotton thread; no attempt at invisibility being made. Later they began doing it up very high on the top of the head, with hidden "rats" made of "combings" to hold it in place and give the appearance of generous amounts; ornamenting it with ribbon bows, fancy combs, or flowers. Practically all little girls wore circular combs that went half around the head, pushing them in straight from the front toward the back; where the hair would bulge out around the comb.

Ladies' hats in winter time, were richly trimmed with bird-wings, aigrettes, and feathers, or even whole birds; and in summer were veritable "flower gardens." Always they were worn straight on the head, with none of our modern jaunty tilt, and fastened with the inevitable hat-pin—considered as well a woman's weapon of defense in case of molestation. For every-day wear around home, and at the beach and on other outings, the universal sunbonnet was worn; made with deep front to shade the eyes and protect the complexion and with short cape to cover the neck from the sun. At the throat there were strings of self-material to tie.

In those days, a great stir was being made about women's wearing birds on their headgear. A man by the name of Audubon had started the ball rolling almost half a century before, by making a study of bird life, and sketching our feathered friends of America. He had pleaded for the preservation of our beautiful birds. Others had taken up the idea, and societies were being formed in different cities bearing the name of the great bird lover of the century. All fine winter hats for the ladies at that time were decorated with real birds—or wings and aigrettes that involved the death of the bird—the most beautiful being in greatest demand.

Women at first resented this invasion of their "rights"; but soon the movement gained such momentum that the subject was agitated everywhere, and women began to get ashamed to appear in public with birds on their hats, and afraid of becoming unpopular, or considered indifferently cruel. Many there were whose hearts were touched when the subject was brought to their attention, and willingly lent their support to the humane movement.

So the styles switched from birds to ostrich feathers; which could be removed without involving pain or injury to the bird; and our magnificent hummingbirds, orioles, scarlet tanagers, bluebirds and woodpeckers were allowed to live.

The ladies wraps of those days were for the most part, shawls, capes, and perhaps long, loose wrap-around cloaks with places for the arms to protrude, but without sleeves. On their heads for evening, they wore "fascinators," or three-cornered crocheted head-wraps that crossed in front at the neck and fastened at the back; and the "kiss-me-quick," a sort of crocheted and beaded hood, having a rosette of beaded crochet-work over the forehead—usually homemade.

The gentlemen wore long fringed neck-scarfs, crocheted by the women, and "wristlets," also crocheted, to slip over the hand and fill up the space below the cuff or sleeve, for protection from the cold when exposed to inclement weather. These too were made by wives, sisters or sweethearts; and upon occasion, women also wore them.

As I grew up styles changed materially from what they were in my childhood days. Long, heavily-lined and gored skirts and shirtwaists came into style. The dances also underwent a change. Round dances came into popularity, and the old-fashioned square dances gradually went out; and these evening entertainments lost much of their former charm and friendliness.

The "Basket Social" then came into vogue—usually a "benefit" of some kind for a community purpose—in which dancing was always a main feature. Every lady would make a lunch basket and put up a lunch for two. These baskets varied greatly according to individual taste, style and skill and sometimes were real works of art. Each basket was auctioned off to the highest bidder and the prettier the basket, the higher the price it was likely to bring. The lunch was shared by the purchaser as a supper partner with the lady who had prepared it, whose name was concealed in the basket.

No one but herself was supposed to know whose the basket was until after the sale, when the purchaser should discover the name. But any young lady who had a sweetheart, would likely find a way to let him know which was hers so they might eat together. However, for this favor, he often paid dearly, for as soon as he would begin to bid on a basket, other men would bid against him to force him to pay a high price, and unless he was very clever in "fooling" them by adroitly bidding on several, he would have a very expensive supper and tete-a-tete.

People of all ages from far and near came to these basket socials, and as well as affording pleasure and entertainment they were a source of revenue for any worthy community purpose that came along. There were however many disappointments, as names in attractive baskets often were found to belong to old ladies, or very young misses— partners not likely to be entertaining—while the preferred one might be observed across the hall eating supper with some other gallant. The young lady's basket might be purchased by some old or uninteresting man, and her preferred be seen eating supper with some beautiful rival.

On the whole, men preferred to choose their own supper partners and treat them to what they wanted rather than buy baskets, and girls who were popular much preferred this order. However, those not so popular stood a better chance of getting an interesting partner than otherwise.

Perhaps it was for such reasons as these that the basket social passed away within a few years of its rise.

CHAPTER 31 LEAVING HOME

When Father returned from one of his market trips to San Diego, he brought back the sad news that Mr. Lovett, their old-time friend of Bear Valley days, was dead. Mr. Lovett had become sick at his home in the Smith Mountains, and had been taken down to a hospital in San Diego for care. His ailment was not such as should have caused death, nor was such a termination expected either by the family or by the hospital, but came as a sudden shock to all concerned.

To make it all the more heartrending his death, it seemed, was entirely unnecessary and preventable. From diligent inquiries as to the nature of the ailment and the suddenly changing symptoms, Father was sure that the patient had been accidentally poisoned, and had died from an over-dose of strychnine (used all too commonly in those days) though of course, the thing was hushed up. Following his death the heartbroken family sold out their mountain home and went back to Texas, their native state. After this move, Kate Lovett wrote to Sadie, telling her all about their sorrow and trouble but the family saw them no more.

In May of Eighteen Eighty, the same month that George attained his majority, Sadie also became of legal age, and at eighteen was the first one of the family to leave home to shift for herself. She went to Laguna to help out our neighbors Will and Annie Brooks at the birth of one of their children. Supposedly, she was to be gone from home only temporarily, but actually, her intention was to make her own way in the world from that time forward. She hoped by keeping this purpose to herself to ease the wrench for Mother, but never was she at home after that except on brief visits.

The winter of Eighty-One and Eighty-Two found her at Hollingsworth's in Santa Ana, after having worked at various places in the interim; after which she went to be with the family of "Gassy Smith" in Tustin for a short time; whose daughter Minnie she accompanied to Arizona the following June. Minnie died within the year; and Sadie remained in Phoenix, where she attended school for a term or two; working her way at the same time.

Figure 22 Sadie Thurston Byers, ~1885

It was during this period that she met and loved Arthur Byers, to whom she was married two years after leaving California. Before me lies a faded girlish letter written to Artemisia, then working in Los Angeles and dated about four months previous to that happy event. From this letter the following extracts are taken, dripping with the sweetness of that old love story:

"My Darling little sweet Sister:

Your second charming letter is at hand. How good and loving they both are and how happy they make me!

You have asked so many questions I scarcely know where to begin to answer. In reference to how I am progressing with my studies, I enclose two slips clipped from the Phoenix paper…When I leave school, I have not decided what I shall do, as the day for my wedding is not so much as set…Arthur was down New Year's afternoon to hope me a happy New Year, and had a good laugh because he was a few hours ahead of me, for we were engaged near Christmas, but never mind, I am pleased. I send you one of his photographs which will speak for him. He begs me to tell you that the artist was a poor one, and the picture is not nearly so good looking as he is.

I made a mistake in my description of him. He has brown eyes instead of blue, but really, they were so bright and his tones so charming, that I failed to notice their shade, so doubtless you will excuse the mistake. 'Has he got any bad habits?' What a question! Now what answer did you expect? Well, I will tell you what he says; that I will find plenty after I get better acquainted; so I will wait till then to tell you.

Yes, I expect to make my home in Arizona—to live and die here, for aught I know. When we consent to unite our life with that of another, we must make up our minds to give former pleasures and ties up, and follow them through good and ill; to follow them not for a month, or a year, but a lifetime. They must come first; all others second in our mind and heart.

Mesia, do you think I will make a wilful, stubborn, selfish companion? I am so afraid I shall. He is just about a head taller than I am, and often quotes: 'Katy Lee and Willie Gray,' our old favorite and his too. Can you be my bridesmaid? A thousand times yes—one and all of them! I only wish you might. And as for what I am going to wear, I have not decided—perhaps calico. Yes, I remember how we used to plan that you would get married first—and perhaps you will yet for aught I know. I can not find out anything by you."

The two newspaper clippings are as follows:

(Number One): "PHOENIX PUBLIC SCHOOL REPORT FOR JANUARY

"Number of pupils enrolled	179
Average daily attendance	164

Names of pupils averaging in studies ninety or over, who have been neither tardy nor absent:

Oliver Bewley,	91
Robert Linville,	90
George Linville,	92
Eddie Rodgers,	91
Freddie Ingalls,	90
Sarah Thurston,	92
Ada Kelly,	92
Addie Kelly,	90

Mrs. F. Stanton, Teacher."

(Number two): "A school paper is now one of the features of the Phoenix public schools. It is read once a month, and contains all the compositions of the several classes. Sarah Thurston and Brookie Gregory are the editors." On the back of this one, Sadie has scribbled: "And you bet we have lots of work to do. Want a sample copy?"

Figure 23 Sadie and Arthur Byers

At the time Sadie left home, George felt that he had the same right and privilege to go out and make his own way in the world, however, he chose to stay on at the farm long enough to help Father harvest the summer's crops. The following August, gathering together his few personal belongings into a saddle pack, he set out early one morning with his little mare Mollie, to hunt for himself a job. His saddle he left behind for the use of those upon whose shoulders his work should fall—Lafe, aged thirteen past and Joseph, nearing twelve; and bareback, with nothing but the saddle blankets under him, headed for Norwalk. Father had given him ten silver dollars when he left, and with this capital he intended to buy himself a used saddle somewhere on his journey. Up Aliso Canyon he rode, crossed the San Joaquin Rancho, passed the site near the slough where the family had camped in Seventy-One, and on to Tustin, now a village having its own post office. Here he spent a night with the family friend Gassy Smith, resuming his journey the next day through Santa Ana now beginning really to look like a village. On he went through the old town of Anaheim, whose reputation was then that of breweries and distilleries, where he turned westward toward Artesia—more a small settlement than a town—and here took the road northward for Norwalk.

Arriving at Norwalk, he had no difficulty in obtaining work on the thresher, and went to work with a will. He was no shirker, and with the other seasoned men held up his end of the job all day in the hot sun. The water, of which he drank freely, was different from that he was used to, and somehow the combination of heat, over-work and strange water, was against him. That night he crawled all perspiring into a stack of straw to sleep, and took cold. The next day he was sick and unable to go to work with the others. For half a day he lay around endeavoring to overcome the disability, and then went out to the machine to try it again. But he found that his job had been taken by another man—for such large outfits cannot be bothered or inconvenienced by trifles like sick men—especially new hands; so once more he was jobless.

Again he set out, this time headed for Los Angeles, arriving in due time at the city. Here he looked about for a saddle, but decided that the wiser thing was to wait until he should secure work; for even the cheapest saddle he could find was more than he could afford in his present situation.

Hearing while in Los Angeles that there was plenty of work to be had in the San Fernando Valley, he continued on northward in the stifling heat to San Fernando. Sure enough, work was plentiful; and here he secured a job on a ranch at a dollar and fifty cents a day with board. Placing what was left of his precious ten dollars in the possession of his new employer for safekeeping, he went to work.

Within a few weeks, some of the Goffs came up to see him, and by them he sent Mollie back to the farm in Aliso; for there was no pasture for her where he was and nothing she could do to earn her keep.

In three months George had earned a hundred and thirty-eight dollars—more than he had ever before in his life possessed. One hundred of this he immediately sent to Father to help pay his lawyers' bills and other expenses from the suits with Rawson, up to this time not finally settled.

Father was still having to sacrifice time and money over this unjust law business, and the farm work was piling up again. For these reasons George quit his job after holding it for four months, and returned home to help on the farm. Having bought another little mare to team with Mollie, which he named "Kittie," he rode her to Aliso.

George then worked on the farm off and on as he was needed, and in between times, at other places for short periods. A Deputy Sheriff of Los Angeles, named Dunlap was at that time opening up the old abandoned gold mine in Silverado Canyon; and George, in company with Mr. Mc Manus, went up to work in this mine. Mr. Mc Manus, being unable to irrigate his land at Three Arches, was not trying to raise anything on it, but merely staying there the time required to hold the claim, and between times made prospecting trips and worked in mines.

George took Mollie with him up to this mine in Silverado, and for a month or six weeks packed timbers strapped to her back up a hillside to the mine which was being timbered. During this time he spent his evenings whittling, having nothing else with which to occupy himself; and with no tool but a one-bladed pocketknife, from an old piece of hard wood, carved out a beautiful fiddle neck—keys and all—a work of art, which is still in existence.

This job at the mine proved to be nothing but a "sell." The mine did not "pan out" and none of the men received a cent for their arduous labors. So George with Mollie returned home feeling somewhat disgruntled and cheated, but there was nothing that could be done about it since Dunlap had no money.

A Tale of Sewing Machines

About this time we had our first contact with a sewing machine agent. This was about four years after the first appearance of sewing machines with treadles. Machines for sewing seem to have first originated in France. They were invented in Eighteen Thirty by a Parisian named Barthélemy Thimonnier, and a few of them distributed about Paris. When Charles the Tenth lost his throne in the revolution about July of that year, the tailors and seamstresses of the city, fearing unemployment, searched out and smashed up all the sewing machines they could find. The unfortunate inventor left for England with his one and only original model, and died insolvent of a broken heart in Fifty-Seven. His death brought newspaper publicity concerning his invention, and three years later, in Sixty, someone took up the manufacture of sewing machines. In ten more years, they were in common use throughout the English world. Not, however, till Eighteen Seventy-Seven did the machine appear with treadles.

One day a sewing machine agent, whom we will call Mr. Brown (which might be correct) found his way down Aliso Canyon and stayed all night at our place. In the back of his wagon securely tied in place, was a large lovely Wheeler and Wilson Cabinet Sewing Machine, which he lifted out and brought into the house to demonstrate to the family. The large full-length doors, closed when not in use, when open, displayed six or eight drawers divided equally on the two sides. A leaf dropped down on the left end to be raised when desired, and the head was covered with a removable box—for this was before the days of drop-heads—and it was operated by the new foot treadle, with a long endless belt connecting the upper and lower wheels.

Mother had great need of a sewing machine. Up to this time she had done every stitch of her sewing by hand with thread and needle, often sitting up half the night and sewing by the light of a Kerosene lamp; to the great detriment of her eyes. But there was no money for such a luxury as a sewing machine. Everybody wanted her to have it, and no one more than she herself, for no one else so realized the need, or so keenly visualized the help it would be in expediting the vast amount of sewing necessary to keep the large family in clothes. All the mens' shirts and boys' trousers and coats had to be made by hand, as well as underwear, bed and table linens, towels and so forth; besides the clothes for the female side of the family and the infants. All this, with the vast amount of other work, left little time for sleep. So it is no wonder that our mother became a "night owl."

The agent offered to make a trade for stock, but there was none that could be spared. George greatly admired the well-matched span of horses driven by Mr. Brown, for his own little team of mares were not so well mated. Noticing this admiration, Mr. Brown asked George if he had anything he could trade for his team and the sewing machine. George had a little money left from his work in the San Fernando Valley, and he greatly desired that Mother should have the machine, so showed the man his own team of mares, Mollie and Kittie. Mr. Brown offered to trade, with a certain cash difference from George—Father agreeing to put in a little cash also; and the deal was made, George paying a sum equal to the difference in value of the two teams as he saw it. He considered the deal a good bargain at that, and Father signed for the machine.

But as this was the only machine Mr. Brown had with him, and as there were a few more families he wished to contact while on the coast, he made arrangement with Father to retain and exhibit the machine until the following day, when he was to return and make the delivery.

Before leaving, he warned Father that there was another Machine agent in the country who was making it his business to follow him up and try to break up his sales. He told Father that he might expect a call from him also, but to remember that the deal was made. Mr. Brown then took his departure, promising to return the next day.

Sure enough, the other agent came in the meantime bringing a Singer. This man limped in his walk and his name was Gage—the slickest salesman that had ever visited Aliso. After some friendly preliminaries in which he completely won Father's confidence, he proceeded to convince him that the Singer was the only machine on the market worth buying. Then he began to ridicule the "cumbersome old-fashioned Cabinet" and the man who would spend his time trying to sell it. He chuckled as he recalled the times that Brown's commodity had been turned down in favor of his own, and his so-called "sales" repudiated when once his own superior product had been exhibited. He indulged in a little friendly ridicule of Father for being so gullible as to swallow the bait, and advised him to do as so many of the others had done—give Brown the "go-by." Father, feeling decidedly foolish, reminded him that he had already bought it, and it was now too late to make the change. But this Mr. Gage "poo pooed" with a smile, and assured Father that Brown could do nothing at all about it, that since he had not delivered the machine, and no money had changed hands, Father was in nowise bound to take it. With good natured freedom, he boldly put the Singer into the house "just to try it, no obligations," brushing aside all objections as though doing the family a great favor.

But somehow, before he left, he had by some hypnotic spell, induced Father to sign on the dotted line. Then Brown came back with the Cabinet. He had it off the wagon and into the house before anybody could explain a thing to him. It was too late for argument. Brown reminded Father of the warning that he had given him, and with a few well-chosen words, restored to the Cabinet all its previous virtues. This, with the hypnotizing Gage out of the way, was not hard to do. He convinced Father of the absolute legality of the first transaction and the uselessness of attempting an evasion of it, then took his departure with the cash and team of mares, leaving George his own span and Father in a decided "pickle."

Thus it was that we became the possessors of two sewing machines. We greatly needed one sewing machine; but we needed two about as much as a donkey needs two tails. Father felt exceedingly foolish, and to cover up this chagrin in a "manly" way, as is natural to many members of the masculine sex when it becomes too humiliating for them to bear their own infirmities, tried to "lay it onto" Mother. But that didn't pay the bill; neither did it convince anybody that a donkey ought to have two caudal appendages. It was many a day before the nagging monthly installment payments ceased to remind him of his folly.

By that time Artemisia too was gone from the home nest and was out in the world making her own way. After the Singer had been in the house, a needless piece of furniture, for about three years, Father took it up to Los Angeles, one day in Eighty-Four where Mesia was at that time working on Ninth Street, and made her a present of it.

Now Mesia was the one girl in the family who never did take to sewing. She did not like it, could not do it well, and had no desire to learn. Therefore, she had no more need for that sewing machine than a Guinea-Pig has for a tail. Add to this the fact that she was not settled in any one location, but working about from place to place, and moving her belongings with every new job, and it is evident that she could not be bothered with "carting around" that lovely sewing machine. So the first opportunity that presented itself she sold it, receiving the sum of twenty-five dollars—only a fraction of what it had cost. So this is the end of that story.

Likenesses

About this time, the Zahn brothers, Otto and Oswald operated a carrier pigeon service between Santa Catalina Island and the mainland. Messages were fastened to the legs of the birds, and it took them about an hour to cross the intervening water and reach their cotes on the other side, one of the men receiving them at each end. A service of this kind had been carried on intermittently since Eighteen Seventy-One.

Eighteen Eighty-One, the year that the cabinet sewing machine came into our house to stay, Los Angeles was celebrating as the first centennial of its existence, and boasting a population of twelve thousand. Photography was then in its infancy; and the great and much coveted event was to have one's "likeness taken." A photographer would come into a town, pitch a canvas tent, and advertise that he took "likenesses." Then everybody would flock to the tent. When he had "done" the town, he would move on to the next. On the back of some of these pictures is printed pretentiously: "San Francisco Gallery, Santa Ana, Cal." The photograph of oneself to a loved one was the gift "par excellence"; and an album in which to keep such gifts was only second to it. That Christmas Sadie presented George with a beautiful photograph album, which bears the date on its flyleaf; being still in a good state of preservation.

To have the likeness taken, then became an outstanding ambition of every member of the family who was old enough to care about such things; and they and the children were one by one taken to town as money could be spared for the purpose, to pose for their likenesses in a setting of "rustic art." Only the older ones were allowed to smile; the children were told not to do so as it would "spoil the picture"; for that was the idea held by the artists of those days concerning the picture-taking of little folks. The results were as might be expected—sour faces all around.

Baby Charlotte, about two, shows in her sober little face and big round eyes the great timidity she was experiencing, while Annie, a year and ten months her senior, was turned into a sour little pickle when the man tossed up a gaudy toy bird and tried to interest her in it. She had seen better birds than that thing, and they didn't "whistle" like that one either. The brass pieces across the toes of her little shoes, the way they made shoes "durable" for children in those days may be plainly seen. Well do I remember the little pink calico dresses ruffled and piped in white, which they have on. How they must have resented the "straight jacket" effect of the stiff iron post behind them supposed to be needed to keep them in position!

Hulda, at eight, is dressed after the same pattern and has on her face the same worried expression. George went with her to town and also sat for his own picture at the "San Francisco Gallery." Somehow, Frank and I were missed entirely in this picture-taking; for neither of us appears in any childhood picture. Perhaps the money gave out, and the expected "better time" for taking us was overlooked. It was about a year later that I made my first trip to town; but then there was no picture-taking.

Joseph, then a little past twelve, was taken to town by Father for the first time in his life in order to sit for his likeness in that canvas tent. It took them about eight hours driving Ted and Bill in the lumber wagon, to make the journey of twenty-five miles—time enough for an airplane of today to travel two thousand miles or more. To the lad, it was a very tedious trip, and Father's thoughtless failure to "show him around" after their arrival, made it doubly so. When finished with his own business, Father took him to the tent to sit for his picture, but by that time the boy was so worn out from sitting around and waiting with nothing to do, that picture-taking to him was just another bore. So his expression of discontent was registered for all time on the little tintype that resulted.

Lafe was also taken to this place for his tintype, and Father sat for his—a very good likeness of him. Sadie and Artemisia, then about eighteen and sixteen, had theirs taken at a different studio conducted by "C. A. B. Hall."

Figure 24 Joseph and Lafe Thurston, 1880

Figure 25 Sadie and Artemisia Thurston, 1881

Figure 26 George Sr (Father) and George Jr Thurston, 1880

A Snake Twice Killed

George now had a beautifully-matched span of horses; and as Ted and Bill were getting old, these younger horses were used that spring for practically all the team work of the farm; as well as for driving.

One August day while Father was away from home, George took the rest of the family down to the ocean to bathe and gather mussels. When the afternoon began to wane, Lafe and Joseph started home afoot ahead of the others in order to begin the evening's chores at the usual hour. At the third bend of the creek, between the corn patch and the cart-road garden, where the southern mountain now rises a bare wall of rock, there was at that time, a stretch of sandy soil on a wide, sloping grassy bank, with a footpath leading along the base of the mountain. On the upper side of the path, grew a large clump of vegetation composed of wild roses, bull nettles, and poison oak, all mingled together in rank profusion.

Lafe, who was some distance in the lead, had passed this clump and had entered the cart-road garden by crawling through the fence, when Joseph came walking barefoot along the path beside the clump. There in front of him, lay a rattlesnake coiled as if to strike. So large was this snake that the coil was about ten inches across. Joseph's foot was already lifted for the next step to be planted exactly where the snake lay, when he saw it. Greatly startled, but too late to retreat, with a desperate effort, he made a quick half-jump and lengthened his step, setting his foot down beyond the coil of the snake; and then began to call loudly for Lafe. At the sound of his voice, the ugly creature began to move away; for it was in August, the season when all snakes are blind, and govern their actions by sound instead of sight. No doubt, he had heard Lafe pass, and had immediately coiled in an attitude of defense. By the time Lafe, retracing his steps, had reached the spot, the crawling snake was almost out of sight in the thicket. Arming themselves with sticks and stones, the boys followed him into the dense tangle, and regardless of nettles, thorns or poison oak, drove him clear through the thicket out on the other side; and there beat him to death.

Knowing that the wagon load of bathers would in a little while be coming along the road up the creek bottom, one of them suggested: "Let's fool the folks!" So they took the dead snake and stretched him out across the roadway in a very life-like manner; and leaving him there, went on up to the house to begin their chores.

In due time the family arrived; and George proudly exhibited the rattles and a long reed with which he had measured the "big rattler" that had been "killed by the wagon wheel rolling right over his head" as he lay stretched across the road. Joseph then "took all the wind out of his sails" with his sardonic:

"Yes? But we killed him first."

After the season's heavy work was done, George engaged in fishing for the market with Hub and Frank Goff. The fishing was done, not with hook and line, but with dynamite and dip net—a practice long since outlawed. From a row boat, a school of fish would be located; then a charge of dynamite set off among them, killing the fish wholesale. As they floated to the surface, they were easily gathered up with the dip net.

George was never a seaman; he would become sick every time he got into a boat; so the others did the fishing and he managed the selling end of the game; using his own team and wagon. He would load up in the middle of the night, and travel till morning getting into Santa Ana just as the people were beginning to stir about. Then, after eating his meager breakfast of crackers and cheese, which he had brought with him, he would curl up in his blanket and sleep till the town had finished its breakfast.

Beginning then, he would peddle his fish from house to house; keeping at it as long as he had a fish left to sell—often till late in the evening.

Then he would drive back the twenty-five miles to the Aliso farm, and there, snatch a few more hours of sleep, rising in the night again to go down to the beach and load up.

But George proved to be a poor financier. Instead of requiring that his partners share with him the expense of horse feed, he divided up with them the proceeds of each day's sales equally, and fed his own horses out of his third of the profits; with the result that for him there were no profits. Fish were cheap in those days; but horse feed was not. So at the end of the summer, he had just about broken even, and there was nothing left with which to buy horse feed through the winter.

Horses Play a Cold Joke

The creek bottom was rich in delicious vegetation, and by way of supplementary feeding George would turn these two young horses loose at night to forage for themselves up and down the creek—it being flimsily fenced away from orchards and fields.

Early one crisp, cold morning, Mable Goff, having as usual, driven her cattle afoot by way of our creek bottom, up onto the mountain pastures above our place and left them there to graze, was returning home, and, as on other occasions, stopped at our house to rest and chat with the young folks for a few moments before continuing on her way. We youngsters thought it would be fun to go with her part way home; so when she started on, we trooped along with her—Hulda, then nearing nine, and only a little her junior; Harriet, not yet six; Annie, past four, and Charlotte, past two, the baby of the family and Hulda's special charge.

The creek had receded from a recent high-water mark; and was then a broadened area of small streamlets separated by island spaces, partly covered with the inevitable salt-grass and whatever of the other well-rooted weeds and grasses had been able to hold their footing during the freshet. These, and everything else were covered with a white frost; for it was bitter cold, and the sun not yet risen in our shaded nook of the canyon, though shining brightly on the surrounding hilltops.

The creek, aside from its freezing temperature, offered no obstacle to the progress of this barefoot brigade; and we started across in high spirits, stepping lively to keep warm. But when about half way across, something happened. The two young horses, new and strange to us all, which George was pasturing in the creek that winter, seeing us invading their territory, left their occupation of feeding on the succulent herbage farther up the creek, and came running at top speed directly to the spot where we then were in the middle of the creek.

We scattered in a hurry, some this way and some that, to get out of their path, our purpose to go farther with Mable forgotten in our fright. Annie and I crawled under the fence on the home side, and went on up to the house; but Hulda, pulling little Charlotte after her, ran for refuge to the opposite side of the creek with Mabel, and crawled under the fence into the vineyard; the horses following them as far as the fence. Afraid that the two strands of wire would be insufficient to check the horses the children ran clear to the hill at vineyard point before stopping to catch their breath.

Mabel, being older, and well used to animals, thought nothing of the matter and went on home alone; leaving Hulda and Charlotte behind in an unsuspected state of terror. The horses stood with their heads hanging over the fence watching the children; evidently waiting for them to return their way. But the frightened children were watching the horses; and not until they saw them leave the fence and meander off again for a distance, munching the luscious vegetation, did they venture to start back again toward the fence, which they must pass through in order to get home.

As soon as the two horses spied them coming toward the fence, they cantered back again and hung their heads over as before; the children retreating in fear. Again, they waited, growing colder every moment in the icy air, for the horses to retreat and give them another chance to escape; and again the opportunity seemed to be theirs. The two horses wandered off up the creek, and the girls cautiously made their way toward the fence, intending to crawl under and run across the intervening creek for the opposite side. But the horses were not to be taken off guard; they seemed to sense this intention as soon as the girls made a move, and reached the fence before them; intruding their heads again over the top wire of their prison enclosure.

Again and again this performance was repeated; the horses returning, the children retreating, and growing colder and colder every moment in the frosty morning air; tearful prisoners of fear, vainly trying to make their voices heard at the farmhouse.

Annie and I not having taken the incident so seriously, and utterly ignorant of their plight, had not even mentioned the circumstance to the rest of the family. Busy with our play, we had forgotten all about the episode and the two participants, who had been with Mabel the last we knew of them; until all of a sudden, Mother asked:

"Where is Charlotte?"

"Oh, she's with Hulda"; we answered.

"Well, where is Hulda?" Mother persisted.

"I don't know"; was the answer.

"Weren't you playing together?" Mother asked probingly.

"Yes, but some horses scared us and we all ran away"; I told her.

"Well, you go back there Harriet, and see if you can find them, and tell them to come home"; commanded Mother. This was an hour or more after the scattering.

When I reached the creek, there stood the two horses with their heads hanging over the fence; and in response to my calling, the two girls appeared on the other side and explained their plight in voices so hoarse with weeping and shouting they could scarcely make a sound. They were stiff with the bitter cold—chilled fairly to the bone, and afraid of freezing to death. I broke off a willow branch, and with it drove the two horses away, far up the creek, while the girls made their escape.

Once more in the safety and warmth of the home shelter, they sobbed out their story hoarsely in Mother's arms; who fixed them up an internal heating potion of Jamaica ginger, and tucked them up in a blanket by the fire to secure them against catching cold.

That the horses would have injured the children, is very doubtful; but be that as it may, their absolute fear made them nevertheless prisoners under circumstances that might easily have been fraught with serious consequences. No doubt it was this fear which the animals sensed, that put into them the mischievous spirit that delighted to torment the children. With me, they showed no such disposition; but accepted my mastery of the situation, and suffered themselves to be driven away from the scene without protest; because they saw that I was not afraid of them.

From early childhood, it seemed instinctive with me, if ever I were afraid of an animal, never to let him suspect it. But poor Hulda, though admiring my "bravery," could not hide her fear; and suffered much in consequence, during her whole period of farm life.

A Delightful Visit and a Harrowing Experience

George kept his beautiful span of horses for a year or so, then after Mesia went away from home, sold them to Mr. Sheets of Tustin for a good price. About this time, he met the inventor of a patented singletree, who wanted him to take the agency for it. This singletree was so constructed that the iron couplings at the ends were turned away from the usual position in which they were always "barking" the trees when cultivating, and the ends cushioned with rawhide which protected the trees from this nuisance. This appeared to be something that would fill a long felt want among the farmers of the country; and George allowed himself to be persuaded to take it up.

But one thing called for another. Having sold his team, he had now no means of conveyance by which to get around among the possible purchasers, scattered widely over the country. The inventor had an outfit consisting of a buckboard, horse and harness, which he offered George for seventy-five dollars; and the young would-be agent took it. After this, he drove down to the factory in San Diego—the round trip amounting to about a hundred and sixty miles—to secure a supply of singletrees, and incidentally to assure himself that everything was as represented concerning the factory and its output. Finding these as represented, he returned with his singletrees sometime in October, intending to begin at once to devote himself to their distribution.

But something grand had happened at our house during his absence. Dear Grandpa Snow, Mother's own father, had come to see us from his home hundreds and hundreds of miles away in another state. None of us who were younger than Joseph had ever met him before—and Joseph having been then a baby, did not remember him. This was a rare treat for Mother, who had not seen either of her parents for eleven years. Grandpa's son-in-law, Mr. Thatcher, was with him, and also a stranger whom he had hired to drive him down from the railroad terminal in Santa Ana.

So, finding Grandpa there, George delayed his business operations to enjoy this visit with the rest of the family—since it was an extraordinary occasion for all of us. Grandpa was a dear, kindly, quiet-voiced old gentleman, whom we loved at sight. With ordinary strangers, we were shy as wild deer; but not so with him. He showed that he loved us, was interested in all our affairs; and won our hearts and confidence completely.

One incident connected with his visit, will stay with me, I suppose, as long as intelligence remains. We came out of the back kitchen door and up the slope of the yard a little way; Grandpa in the middle, Frank on his right and I on his left, each clinging to one of his hands as we walked; and both jabbering in a race to see which one of us could tell him the same thing first. I was winning out as usual, for Frank stuttered, and it took him forever to tell anything.

Grandpa listened quietly for awhile, at the unintelligible jumble; then he suddenly stopped in his walk, and turned, disengaging his hands—thereby gaining our attention. Quietly he spoke:

"Now, which of you is the older?"

Quickly, I replied: "I'm six and Frank's seven."

"Alright then, Harriet"; said Grandpa gently, "Since Frank is the older, you let him tell it"; and I did.

During this visit of Grandfather's, George had a very harrowing experience; one that left its lifelong effects upon him. One day in company with Joseph, then nearing fourteen, Uncle Thatcher, and the driver who had brought the visitors to Aliso, went down to the ocean for a swim. Reaching the water front, they found the waves so rough that the two visitors declined to go in. However, they all went "around the rocks" to the men's usual swimming place, and George and Joseph disrobed and went into the water; both of them being swimmers, but neither as yet expert.

Joseph stayed pretty close to shore; but George went farther out, and for awhile enjoyed the sport of diving through the tips of the breakers and being swept in on their crests toward the shore. But after some time at this, he made a miscalculation, and dived through a big comber too far out beyond its swell; and instead of being carried shoreward, he was left in its trough behind, and the receding water swept him farther out to sea with a strong undertow.

George now began to get frightened, and to swim with all his might toward shore; but without making any real progress. Soon he became very tired; then, to rest himself, paddled dog-fashion for awhile. He had never learned to float, because he would strangle every time he tried it; so could not now avail himself of that means of respite.

The two men had gone up a little way onto the side of the bluff, and were sitting there idly watching him, but utterly unconscious of his distress. George called out to them; but they, hearing, thought he was hallooing in fun, and took it as an evidence that he was enjoying his swim. They could see nothing wrong. But Joseph, in the water near the shore, noticed that he was not getting in as he should.

For awhile alternately stroking and paddling, George kept working to get in to shore; but finally grew so desperately tired that he could no longer change his stroke to a paddle; and at last was so utterly without strength that he could not take another stroke. Then summoning all his remaining energy he concentrated it in one last call for help which reached the men on shore. They took the alarm, instantly jumped up and ran down the hill toward the water. George, taking courage from this, was inspired to make one more feeble effort to keep from sinking.

Just at that instant, a huge breaker came combing in. It lifted him up in his utter exhaustion, and bore him on its crest for a little distance shoreward. George knew that these huge waves always come in groups of three, alternated by a number of lesser breakers between the groups, as is the habit of the sea, and that now was the opportune time to get in to shore if ever he was to do so; for after the third one should be spent, if not then safe, his plight would be beyond remedy; for he would be again returned to the merciless sea.

Before Thatcher reached the water, the second big breaker came along and brought him a little nearer to the shore. Then he saw Thatcher begin to roll up his breeches; and his heart sunk to zero. He knew that no help was to be expected from that source. The third big comber, and last of the series, was drawing near; and George considered it absolutely his last chance for life. From this high peak the following waves would dwindle and again carry him out to sea unless this one brought him in safely; then he was lost.

But the breaker brought him in, rolling him over and over in the churning sand and water of the surf. Thatcher, his precious pants rolled up high and dry, waded in and caught hold of George's arm; dragging him out above waterline, too exhausted to help himself in any way. As the water receded, his feet dragged toes down, bottoms up, as though broken. When helped to his feet, supported between two, he essayed to walk; but was so utterly without strength that he could not lift his foot from the sand, but would drag it forward toes down and bottom up and with a great effort plant it in front of him while the other foot was being brought in the same manner to a position for a step. When dry sand was reached in this way, he slumped in complete exhaustion; and lay there unable to move or speak for nearly half an hour. His eyes were flashing fire as though being struck with heavy blows of the fist.

After his strength came back, George arose, dressed, and went fishing out on the rocks; but his attitude toward ocean swimming had undergone a complete change. Never again was he known to go in swimming. After this experience, whenever he bathed in the ocean, it was with the women and children in the surf. And this is by far the wisest course for one who has lost his confidence so completely.

Father and Grandfather came down to the beach after a while; and the occurrence was related to them. Thatcher, in reciting his part in it, said that he had "prayed that God would give George strength to get in." This relation of friendly importuning, however, had the opposite effect than that desired, upon George; who could see nothing else but Thatcher rolling up his breeches. He felt like asking him if he had prayed that God would give him courage to go in after a drowning man even at the risk of wetting his best pants. "Oh Consistency, thou art a jewel!"

Artemisia was working at Mrs. Rice's in Tustin when Grandfather came that October and there he went to see her on his way out of the canyon, regretful to have missed Sadie, who had gone to Phoenix in the spring.

Before he left Aliso, Grandfather invited George to go back with him and take a business course in school. George would greatly have liked to do this, and might have done so had he not already spent his money in equipment for the singletree agency. It did not occur to him to accept charity at the hands of relatives who were interested in his welfare; nor did he think how entirely possible it would be to obtain work in another state among friends; and that singletrees were needed there as well as in California. As it was, he worked at the agency only for the period of about a month; which was long enough to convince him that there was no money in it. His expenses and horse feed took all he could make; so he became discouraged with salesmanship and gave it up, as many another has done before and after him. He then hunted a job at ranch work; leaving his buckboard outfit with Gassy Smith to use in return for feeding the horse.

Mother said goodbye to her dear father that fall with forebodings that she might never see him again. From him, she had learned that her mother was ailing, and about two months after his return home, the sad news came to her that her dear mother, on the twenty-first of December had passed away, thus leaving them both to mourn.

Some Early Beginnings

When Father first came to Southern California, there was no town of San Pedro. But that very year, Seventy-One, the government started a man-made harbor, building a low rock jetty between Terminal Island (formerly called Rattlesnake Island) and Dead Man's Island—so named in Eighteen Forty-Six by United States Captain Mervine, because after Mervine's retreat from the fire of Flores the Mexican captain, six American soldiers killed in the Battle of Dominguez Ranch were buried there. From this time, a town began slowly to build up, partly on the bluff, and partly down on the low land bordering the bay. Some activity, however, had been there before this. As early as Eighteen Ten the mission fathers of San Gabriel had built a small warehouse on the bluff half way between Timm's Point and Point Firmin (not Fort McDowell), for the storage of hides to be shipped out and mission supplies that were brought in. This is described by Richard Henry Dana about Eighteen Thirty-Five in his book "Two Years Before the Mast," as:

"A small low building with one room containing a fireplace, cooking apparatus, etc., and the rest of it unfinished, and used as a place to store hides and goods."

This was the only building in San Pedro at the time of the American conquest. After this, a few buildings were erected on the bluff and at Timm's Landing, where a rude wharf had been built. Goods and passengers were conveyed to and from the Pueblo de Los Angeles and the old original building on the bluff, in the old Mexican ox-drawn Carretas.

In Fifty-One, D. W. Alexander and Phineas Banning formed a business firm as Commission and Forwarding merchants, and in Fifty-Two, started a stage line between Timm's Landing and the Pueblo Los Angeles. J. J. Tomlinson then bought out the original stage line to Sepulveda's Landing, becoming their rival in business, and in Fifty-Three, the old building was used for passengers instead of goods, and a small storehouse was built below it.

In Fifty-Eight, the old wharf was badly damaged in a storm, and Banning and Alexander abandoned Timm's Landing and built a wharf and warehouse at the head of the slough six miles north of the old shipping point and that much nearer to Los Angeles, and named the place New San Pedro, or San Pedro New Town; and from then on, this place became the center of activities and the port for Los Angeles commerce. A village sprung up there. Banning, who came from Wilmington, Delaware, in its honor later changed the name of the place to Wilmington, and his choice was afterward confirmed by the government (in Seventy-Three).

In Sixty-Nine, the Los Angeles San Pedro Railroad was completed to Wilmington, due largely to the perseverance of Banning. This public-spirited man also kept agitating the need of improving the harbor until the government took the matter up and in Seventy-One built a breakwater between Rattlesnake Island and Dead Man's Island which deepened the water in the channel from eighteen inches to eighteen feet. Up to this time, passengers had been rowed out to their vessels over the sandbars, only eighteen inches at low tide flowing over the bars.

In Eighteen Eighty, the railroad was extended from Wilmington to Sepulveda's Landing; and two years later, the town of San Pedro was laid out and mapped on the Rancho Los Palos Verdes; which was then divided up into individual plots. This place has grown up into the San Pedro of today, and the little harbor to another great port of the West.

The business section of Santa Ana in Eighteen Eighty-Two stood in the form of a cross three blocks long on Fourth Street by two wide on Main Street, set in a frame of mustard and weeds, interspersed by scattered residences. The town had grown eastward from the first general store built by its founder, W. H. Spurgeon, on the Southwest corner of Fourth and Sycamore. The old original frame structure, in which were both store and post office, had been torn down in Seventy-Five, and a two-story, also of frame construction, erected in its place, with a hall upstairs for lodge meetings and community gatherings, and a board sidewalk laid in front of it.

The length of the cross, embracing West—afterward renamed Broadway—Sycamore, Main and Bush Streets, was slightly extended into the next block by the livery stable of Henry Neill, who operated the stages to and from San Diego—his being the last place of business eastward in the town, with Spurgeon Street beyond him. In the center of this business section, on the southwest corner of Fourth and Main, Mr. Tichenal, the constable had his private residence; from which heart it is to be inferred that a stream of law and order pulsated through the arteries of the town. The prominent business men of town then were Spurgeon, and his brother-partner Granville, John McFadden, Henry Neill, Hollingsworth, Horace Dibble, Jeff T. Harlan, Jim Hickey, Jim Layman, Lake, Bob Cummings, and Ira Chandler, who had come later to town and opened up a grocery store. There were also the saloon keepers Tucker and Bassonett.

Chandler also owned a twenty-acre ranch toward Tustin; fifteen acres of which were in oranges and five in grapes—all bought for the sum of sixteen hundred dollars. At the present time this property is all within the incorporated city limits of Santa Ana and almost beyond price.

George Makes a Purchase

On this ranch of Chandler's George went to work. He took his meals at the residence, three quarters of a mile distant, and at night, slept in the barn with the horses. In the evenings after work for the day was done, he "bummed" around the store in town; wishing that he too might learn the grocery business, and work in the store; which secret desire grew from day to day. W. H. Marquis, who had come to town in the fall of Seventy-Nine was also working for Chandler at that time inside the store.

Occasionally, he would be commissioned to haul merchandise from Newport pier to Chandler's store to restock his shelves. In those days, a ship called The Newport, owned by John McFadden and his brother, plied between the southern coast and San Francisco, and would drop anchor off Newport where they had maintained a landing as early as Seventy-Three, bought of D. M. Dorman and Captain Daniel, and a small steamboat from Newport would go out to meet it and bring back to the pier whatever merchandise was intended for the merchants of Santa Ana. These goods would be unloaded onto the pier in the open; for there was no warehouse in the place, and teamsters would come down from Santa Ana when the boat was expected, and haul away the goods to their respective purchasers in town.

Occasionally, a ship would drop anchor off Balboa Island, then uninhabited. Balboa Island was a part of a hundred and sixty acre claim, on which the owner had recently proved up—having purchased it from the government for a dollar and a quarter an acre. Soon after proving up on it, he sold the island for five hundred dollars; which was three hundred more than he had paid for the whole quarter-section. He was elated over his bargain; little dreaming that a little while in the future it would be worth as many millions.

The job on Chandler's ranch proved to be not a full-time job. After the season's work was done up, Chandler would lay George off, and wait till again overwhelmed with work before sending for him. Then George would have to work "like a house afire" in order to "catch up"; when he would again be laid off till work accumulated. During these "off times," George would have to shift for a job wherever he could find one, and he did not like the arrangement. He thought that Chandler might have provided him some work in the store to fill in the slack times, but instead of doing this he hired another boy to work in the store, leaving George to fill in his "lean times" with short jobs here and there as he could. This became an irritation to him.

During his second season at Chandler's, Hub and Frank Goff came one day to see him. While hunting for stock pasture in the San Jacinto country, they had made the discovery of some government land and also of some railroad land; and told him that if he was interested, they would go back up there with him and show him the location.

So George took a week's vacation from Chandler's, went over to Smith of Tustin and "borrowed" his own horse and buckboard, and drove with the Goffs up to the San Jacinto Valley. The land lay some four miles west of the town of San Jacinto—then unincorporated. The old town had been started in Seventy-Two, by H. T. Hewett and J. C. Jordan; but in the early Eighties, the railroad coming into the valley, stopped two miles west of the town; which put a period to its growth in that location. A new town then began to form about the railroad two miles to the west, and grew into the present town of San Jacinto, which was incorporated in Eighty-Eight. Hemet also, a few miles distant, began with the coming of the railroad.

The upshot of the visit was that they all bought land. George loaned Hub money for a down payment on eighty acres; giving the two their choice of the land, and himself bought two hundred acres of railroad land, that was offered at from two fifty to four dollars an acre.

About two years later, George sold Hub's land for him to young Sprowle of Norwalk, at a profit to Hub of five hundred dollars. Two years after that sale, in Eighty-Seven, he sold the same piece of land again for Sprowle, at a profit to him also of five hundred dollars; so greatly had values increased.

The Sprowle family had been brought in touch with us by our mutual friends, the Thompsons. Besides Willie, there were three sisters, Marcia, Susie and Nellie, and two younger brothers. Marcia became a close friend of Artemisia.

George was back at his job on Chandler's ranch again within the week. He had worked hard that season, as was his wont, and when the work was almost done—all but trimming the hedges about the house—the hired boy from the store came out where he was working and on the side informed him that he was to be "let out" that Saturday night. This news coming from the source it did showing the boy to be so evidently in his employer's confidence with regard to George's affairs, nettled him greatly; and instead of waiting to be discharged he quit work Saturday morning, leaving his employer to get the hedge done as best he could. George never went back. At the beginning of the third season, in the early spring of Eighty-Four, Chandler sent for him to come and begin work again; but George informed him that he had other plans, and went to San Jacinto to farm his own land. Breaking a drowth, rains had begun with every indication that the year would be one of bountiful crops everywhere.

Mesia Follows: A First Romance

In November of Eighteen Eighty-One, Mesia celebrated her eighteenth birthday an event to which she had long looked forward; for she intended then to go out and make her own way in the world. But Joan was very young to assume the responsibility she was laying down, and she lingered on at home for several months. George, who was then fishing with the Goffs and marketing his fish in town, heard of a place out on a ranch five miles from town toward El Modena, where a family by the name of Fletcher wanted a girl. So he secured the position for Mesia, and made arrangements for her to ride out to town with Hub Goff, since his own trips were made in the night, and there at Santa Ana the Fletchers were to meet her and take her out to their ranch. George himself took her baggage over to Goff's place ahead of her, arranging for her to stay all night there in order to be ready for the early start to town the following morning.

So, on the afternoon of the first of February, Mesia said a quiet goodbye to the folks, and started out to walk over to Hub's place. On the way, she stopped at Frank Goff's where she spent the evening, Leon proposing to accompany her from there to his uncle's. After his evening chores were done, they played table games till it was getting late then together started out. But this walk was different from any that she and Leon had ever taken together before.

About half way between the two places, was a deep gulch where the road leading down to the bottom, made a "hairpin" turn before coming out on the other side. Just as they reached this turn after the descent, Leon, who had been unusually tender in his manner toward her since leaving the house, suddenly stopped, facing her. Pinioning her arms to her side in a vice-like grip with his own strong hands and transfixing her to the spot, he told her with the eloquence of ardent emotion of his great love and asked her to become his wife. Mesia was utterly speechless and embarrassed, and began to tremble with nervous excitement at the unexpected situation, for she had never before experienced anything like this. Leon was very dear to her, she had loved him for years; but marriage was something far from her thoughts and intentions. She wanted to see something of the world, before thinking of such a thing and felt that they both were far too young and inexperienced to talk of matrimony. But nothing of all this could she tell the ardent young lover so eagerly encouraging her to give him an answer. Something seemed to have stolen away her power of speech. Leon, though only fifteen, was in appearance and manner a grown man, seeming much older than his fair companion with her three years' seniority. He was tall and masterful, fine looking and magnetic, and very much in love. Mesia, so retiring and timid and with it all so extremely "proper," and having never really "made love" in earnest in her life, was utterly at a loss to know what to do or say. So she stood tongue tied and dumb while he poured out his hopeful pleading and hurried on to tell her that he would not ask her to marry until after he had made a start financially and was able to support her properly. He did not kiss her. For in those days a gentleman did not kiss a lady without her permission having first been obtained and a kiss was almost equal to a betrothal. But for some time, speech would not come. Mesia could not think clearly. All she knew was that he expected an answer and it did not seem right or possible to utterly disappoint one so in earnest, so purposeful, and withal so dear.

He relaxed his hold, and they began to walk on together up the grade. Finally after they had reached the top and were going on, Mesia found her voice. He was talking to her still and pressing his suit and when her answer came it was a timidly whispered "Yes." The boy felt that he had won his sweetheart. But even then he did not offer to kiss her since her manner did not invite it. Not until they reached the door of his Uncle's home where the lamps were now out and the family retired for the night did Leon claim his privilege. Then he took her in his arms and made her kiss him. So when they parted that night they were betrothed. As Leon turned to leave her, Mesia went into the house quietly and with as little disturbance as possible to bed, but not to sleep. Shaking with nervousness, she lay awake pondering over what had taken place, and condemning herself for not talking to him sensibly of all the thoughts that had sought expression and ought to have been said to him while she stood absolutely dumb. But she had not been able to help it.

The next day she was taken out to her first position to work for her living. The position had been represented to George as a "very easy" one; but it was not long before Mesia discovered that it was everything else but an "easy place." She, as the hired girl was given all the work of the house to do—all the washing and ironing, skimming milk and churning, baking of bread—and two kinds of bread at that; for some liked white and some graham—all the sweeping, scrubbing and dusting, besides the cooking and dishwashing for the family of five and three hired men—and all for sixteen dollars a month! The work was far too hard and strenuous for any other woman however experienced, for that matter. There was work enough to keep two strong women busy, and the hours were from daylight till late at night when all the supper work was done up. There were no days off.

Leon, enthusiastic and eager to get out into the world and make a start towards securing a home for his future wife, had gone to work in the mines with Mr. Mc Manus, and from there he wrote his sweetheart. Mesia was too burdened with the ceaseless work to answer his letters. There was absolutely no time. At night she was so "dead tired" that all she could do was to tumble into bed and get what sleep she could before the early rising hour should roll around. But Leon did not understand this. She kept intending to write him if ever she should find the time. But it did not occur to her that half a dozen words would be better than nothing. She felt that he would expect a real letter, and that, she could not find time to write. So immediately, a misunderstanding arose between them. He thought she was mean not to answer his letters, and that she was trying to jilt him. So he wrote her a hurt and angry letter which made her also angry, for she felt it was unjust. Yet he was not to blame. Neither was she. It was just "one of those things" that are unfortunate and distressing and hard to adjust. Both of them were very unhappy and Leon felt downright injured. To him her silence was inexcusable and could only be due to a betrayal of their troth or a change of mind toward him. He thought that if she really cared for him, she could write at least once in a while.

It is always easy when too late, to see where we made our mistake. Life would be different for us all could we see our mistakes before making them. The position being so hard and thankless, and so far beyond her strength, was not worth keeping anyway, especially at the price of friendship. She should have risked letting some of the work go, or have demanded some time to herself, and written to her lover. She owed him that. Though it was true that she did not wish to marry him for years to come, yet neither did she wish to forfeit his regard. But Mesia's mistake was one of inexperience –both in working out for her living, and in conducting a love affair. And who of us has not made mistakes as foolish?

Mesia could not long stand the hard work at Fletchers, and long before her first month was up was tired out. So after her first payday, within a very short time, she left the place, seeking refuge for a few days with her friends the Gassy Smiths in Tustin. Sadie was at work in Santa Ana, and contemplating leaving California soon. Through her help, within two days of leaving Fletchers Mesia had secured another situation this time with a family named Cohn in Santa Ana. As she took up her work, Sadie, knowing the Cohn reputation for close dealing, gave her a bit of sisterly advice:

> "Be sure that you collect your pay at the end of every week, (for their custom was to pay weekly) or you might not get it at all."

Mesia, being so inexperienced, took this sisterly counsel too literally without the proper admixture of common sense. At the end of the first week, since they did not pay her promptly, she went to Mr. Cohn and asked for her money. He paid her without hesitancy. The second week it was the same. He did not come to her with the money, so she went to him again and asked for it. He was surprised and undoubtedly displeased, though he paid her without a word. But when she came to him the third week, he lost his temper completely, "blew up" and fired her on the spot. So again, after twenty-two days at the Cohns, she was out of a job.

Sadie, on March twenty-six, two or three days before this, had bidden her goodbye, and in company with Minnie, daughter of Gassy Smith, had taken her departure for Phoenix, Arizona, wholly unaware of the effect of her well-meaning counsel.

A few days spent with friends in town, finished the month, and on the last day of March Mesia secured another position at two dollars a week with Mrs. Minter, a worker in the young town library she was helping to foster. After several months her salary was doubled, and Mesia remained with Mrs. Minter for six and a half months.

All this time, the relationship between her and Leon had remained the same—a state of misunderstanding and estrangement. When at long last they met and she in her diffident way tried to explain, to him in his bitter mood, it was only an excuse. Mesia was not gifted with fluency of speech as was the boy, and neither was she in the habit of equivocating, but a girl of peculiar candor. She felt that he should have taken her word without question. So, failing to make him understand, she had let the matter drop, leaving him to smart under the lash of wounded pride and fancied insult to his love. Just children? Yes. But aren't we all, even as they? So the misunderstanding grew, Mesia being under his blame for her neglect of him, and Leon under hers for not accepting her statement of the situation, and both of them being miserable over the whole affair.

Mrs. Minter had a sick child which had been the reason for Mesia's employment and as the case was not improving properly, she went to Los Angeles taking Mesia with her to consult a specialist. But the child did not recover; and when it was finally laid away, Mesia's help was no longer required so again she was out of work.

Her next position taken October fourteen, was with Mrs. James Rice, the sweet singer of Tustin, at sixteen dollars a month; where she was working when Grandpa Snow visited us in Aliso and called on her in departing.

About a month before Mesia left Mrs. Rice's, the whole country was horrified by the news of a terrible train wreck in which more than a score of people, many of whom belonged in the Southland, lost their lives, including Mrs. Downey, the very popular wife of our former state Governor—all through a little thoughtlessness of a train brakeman. The southward-bound Express pulled into the station near the summit at Tehachapi Pass one bitter cold night in January several hours before dawn. Here the locomotive and tender were uncoupled from the rest of the train to take on water and fuel; which service engaged the engineer and fireman. The conductor had gone into the office to make his report. The brakeman was the only one in charge of the passenger cars standing on the track. The wind was blowing a furious gale and he stepped off the train to escort a young lady across the yard into the station. But he had neglected to take the precaution to put on the brakes and the fierce wind began to move the cars along the track toward the steep grade. Before anyone realized what was happening, the unmanned train was plunging headlong down the incline gaining momentum with every second. Near the bottom, it jumped the tracks and was hurtled into a deep ravine below, all in a splintered heap. From the old-fashioned kerosene lamps and coal stoves, immediately the wreck was set on fire and soon became a raging inferno. Many were burned to death, and some beyond identification. Ex-Governor Downey escaped, but was so overcome by shock and grief that for years he was not himself.

A short time before Saint Valentine's day, Mr. Rice came into the house with a message for Mesia, telling her there was a young man outside inquiring of him if a girl by her name was working there, and being told that she was, wished to speak to her. Wondering who it could be, she went out; and there stood Leon. He was engaged in selling fish, and having heard she was employed there had driven around to look her up. After conversing for a little while, he asked her to accompany him to a Saint Valentine's party that was soon to be held in Laguna. Mesia hesitated. She would have liked to go. But something restrained her. She was afraid of Leon—afraid that when he should have her all alone to himself, he would again make love to her—that he would kiss her again as he had that other time— the very memory of which made her afraid. But she felt that it would not stop there—that by the power of his personality and magnetic persuasion, he would break down her resolve not to marry—a thing she was determined not to do for years yet—that she would yield to the fascination of his ardent lovemaking, and be swept into matrimony in spite of herself; so Mesia said she could not go; giving for a reason what he could see was only an excuse. So Leon, hurt worse than ever, again turned away for the last time, not knowing how much she really did think of him. It was hard for her to do that; but Mesia was meticulously honest, and felt that since she had no intention of marrying for a long time yet, she should not be making love with him; for he was not the type of lad to wait for years for his bride. He would have pressed his suit so ardently as to shatter all her resolves; and this she knew; so she did the hard thing; for she really did care for him very much. If Leon had not made his declaration so early—if he could have schooled himself to be just friends for a few more years until both should be of proper age and experience, they might have continued to enjoy a very sweet and worthwhile friendship, and perhaps have married in the end when conditions were right. But being of the demonstrative type, and used to having what he very much wanted—for the womenfolk of his own family denied him nothing, he being the pride of their home— his chances were lost by his own precipitate wooing. From this turning point, they drifted apart; and their young romance came to an untimely end. Leon never married. Whether this experience had anything to do with that, can be only a matter of conjecture. Had Mesia been of the same mind as he regarding matrimony, they might have been very happy together; for they were young enough to have adjusted themselves to each other's ways with less friction than is usual in later life.

Mesia stayed at Mrs. Rice's four months, until Father came out from home to bring her the news of the birth on February ninth, of another little sister, who was then about nine days old, and to take her back with him to help Mother for a few weeks. So Mesia gave up her position, and went home with him to Mother, who was just beginning to be up and dressed.

"Mishie Changed to "Artie"

When Mesia came home this time to stay with us for awhile, after being gone from home for more than a year, she made announcement to the family that she had changed her nickname from "Mishie" to "Artie"; and that thenceforth we must all call her "Artie." This seemed very strange and awkward to, us who had never called her anything but "Mishie." Perhaps if we had always given her name the proper pronunciation, she would never have found it irksome, for "Artemisia" is not a mean-sounding name, but musical and pleasing to the ear. Even Mesia for short, when pronounced as it should be, is not too bad; but "Mishie"! –who could endure that forever? None of us really blamed her for discarding it; and we tried hard to effect the requested change. It was years, however, before our lesson was thoroughly learned and we could say "Artie" without first thinking "Mishie." But in time, it grew to be natural; just as "Annie" had superseded "Pheenie"; and everybody almost forgot that her name had ever been anything but "Artie."

CHAPTER 32 LUELLA JOINS THE FAMILY

Charlotte during her reign as baby of the family, always slept in the middle of the bed between Pa and Ma and. But one mysterious night at the termination of this regency, they tucked her up crosswise in the foot of the bed, where she soon fell sound asleep. When she awoke it was morning, and she found herself no longer at the foot nor yet in her own place in the middle, but over against the wall in Father's vacated place. So she clambered over Mother to get back into her own place in the middle again. But there wrapped in a soft woolen shawl she found a little bundle and immediately interested to learn what it might be, started to investigate. Mother watched to see what she would do.

Unwrapping the folds of the shawl, she soon uncovered the sleeping infant's face, and shrieked with delight:

"It's a baby! I've found a little baby!"

After showing her "find" to Mother, who simulated surprise, she climbed out of bed and ran to find Father, exclaiming excitedly:

"Oh Pa! I found a little bump in the bed; and I opened it, and I found it was a baby!"

In the most natural manner imaginable, she claimed it as her own find, and therefore her personal property. So from that time on this baby was her very own.

Father made a proposition to her. He said that since he would have to buy clothes for it and food when it grew old enough to eat, and since Mother would have to take care of it and nurse it, that they would like to have half of the baby, but that she could have the other half. To which Charlotte agreed, and the bargain was made. The baby was half hers always and forever.

Whenever a new baby came to our house, we children were all happy. We loved to watch Mother give the infant its morning bath as it lay on a soft piece of blanket across her knees, its cunning little hands and feet hardly larger than a doll's inviting caresses and rapturous adoration. We would hang around Mother's chair, eager to wait on her and hand her anything she needed. I loved to hold my nose close to the infant's downy head and rub it gently back and forth, inhaling the delicate sweetness of its little body. I had begun this with Annie, and continued it with Charlotte, and now another little treasure, coming just a month before my seventh birthday, invited the same mute worship.

This was the first family baby, little Charlotte had ever seen in her three years and four months of life—the longest interval in which any one of us had enjoyed the distinction of being the baby of the family. But this usurpation did not awaken the least spark of jealousy in her little breast. She considered this infant to be her very own baby, and promptly adopted the little trick of rubbing her nose over the infant's head, adding to it features of her own. As Mother washed and dressed the infant she would hover over it in rapturous adoration, and with lips closed and making a queer little sucking sound with her tongue, would rub her nose and mouth back and forth gently over the little one's soft, downy, perfumed head like a little purring kitten in the most happy manner, enjoying to the full her partial possession of the tiny newborn baby. We thought her most adorable in the performance of this invariable act of worship during the infant's daily ablutions, and all the family humored her by recognizing her proprietorship.

In a special sense the child "belonged" to her until she was old enough to understand the "why" and "how" of babies. And even to this day there is a peculiar tie between the two.

This little one went by the exclusive name of "Charlotte's Baby" until it was time to wean her. Then Hulda, nearing eleven, took her from Mother's bed to her own at night, cuddling her up in the middle to sleep between herself and Joan and from that time on Hulda assumed the special care of the baby. It then fell to my lot to look after Charlotte and become accountable for her welfare—a task I was most happy to assume for Charlotte was my special favorite and I loved her very dearly.

"Charlotte's Baby" soon acquired the additional name of "Hulda's Baby." When her first birthday came Mother and Father thought it time to give her a name indeed, and by mutual consent chose "Luella." But Father wanted a "Belle" on the end of it. He had once had a sweetheart named "Belle," and was partial to the name. So he insisted on calling her "Luella Belle." Mother, however, very naturally was opposed to this; for what woman wants to call a child of hers by the name of an old rival? Mother stood for "Luella May." Then Father wanted to compromise by having it "Luella May Belle." But Mother would not tolerate even this, and for once stood her ground. Not being able to come to an agreement between themselves, they both decided to leave the matter up to Hulda as to whether the name should be "Luella Belle" or "Luella May." Hulda pondered the two names for awhile and then announced that she thought the names "Luella May" sounded the best together, and that settled it. "Luella May" it was. But Father always called her "Welly."

Luella was a beautiful child, with dark, curly hair that hung in ringlets down on her shoulders. From the very first, she revealed great personality. When beginning to try to talk, she made up a language all her own, that doubtless, no infant has ever duplicated before or since. For "water," her word was "dugan"; if she had to wait for it, her desire was emphasized by repetition with addition: "Dugan! Dugany!" meaning hurry up with it. Food in general was "Nap." When she became very hungry, "nap-pum" indicated the fact. If delay aroused her impatience, she would repeat this word, with additional suffixes and increasing emphasis: "Nap! Nappum! Nappenny!!" "Ee" and "ee-up" were used to attract attention to some particular thing; "ee" meaning "that," and "ee-up" "pay attention; that's what I want." If in a great hurry, it took the form of an emphatic: "Ee-up-an!" When in a desperate hurry and very impatient it became "Ee-up-an-y!" as for instance, if there was a failure to understand what she meant, this was supposed to fully convey her idea; even though the powers of interpretation were stretched to the utmost.

When Luella was a tiny girl, she put on her little sunbonnet one day and went out of doors by herself, wandering down below the bunch-grass row where a few beehives were standing at that time—the overflow from a full apiary—and being too young to know anything about bees, sat down in front of a hive to play. It was not long until we heard terrible screams, and ran out to find her. There she was, literally covered with bees, her face and neck black with them where they had settled in her little sunbonnet like a cloud.

Snatched from her perilous position, the sunbonnet torn from her head, and the bees slapped from her face and head right and left, she was borne screaming with pain and terror, into the house, where safe in Mother's arms, the cruel stingers were removed one by one until a total of thirteen had been extracted—all about the face and neck. Left a little longer to their mercy, they would doubtless have stung the little darling to death.

In Luella's day, all the cows in our herd were gentle and used to children. They might enter the corral in perfect safety at any time; and as the cows lay at rest chewing their cud, would often climb up onto their backs unresisted and unmolested to pet and play with them to their heart's content, the cows seemingly enjoying it as much as the children. To them the cow was a playfellow.

One evening at milking time, Joseph, the usual milker, being absent, Father, with George, then visiting at the farm, were occupying the milking stools. Charlotte and Luella left the supper table, carrying with them their unfinished ears of green corn, and followed them out to the corral to watch the milking—always an interesting procedure. Entering the corral in perfect confidence as usual, still eating away at that good corn on the cob, they noticed that a stranger cow was among the herd waiting to be milked. Such visitors were not uncommon, but children were forbidden in the corral during their presence. However, the entrance of the two children on this occasion had not yet been noticed. Luella, seeing this visiting cow, saved a little of the delicious corn on her cob, and approaching in the spirit of friendly welcome, and genuine hospitality, trustfully held out to her the cob of corn.

The vicious animal lowered her head, and before the astonished child could utter a cry, or the men could realize what was going on, rushed the child and tossed her high in the air. Down she came with a thud on the hard ground. Instantly the cow tossed her again on those cruel horns, and still a third time in rapid succession, before the men could make a move to the rescue. As she struck the ground the third time, Luella lost consciousness. George picked her up and carried her home to Mother; while Father beat the cow unmercifully. It was some time before the precious child came to her senses.

Fortunately, Luella's physical injuries were limited to nervous shock; but this, however severe, was not to be compared with the anguished shock to her sensibilities. The grief-stricken child could not understand why her kind and loving gesture had been so cruelly rewarded.

Whatever hurt Luella, hurt Charlotte, for she worshipped her. She dearly loved to tease her, however, in a harmless way. She would go out to the weed patch with her to play, and running a little way ahead would enter the tall malvia that rose much above their heads, and drop down into it out of sight so that her little sister would not know where she was. Luella would call and call, but Charlotte would lie still and not answer; then suddenly would jump up and surprise her.

When a little older and they were sleeping together out in the honey house along with the rest of us, Charlotte would waken very early and slip out of bed without disturbing her companion, dress quietly, and run down to the apple orchard to pick up the first red apples off the ground that had fallen during the night, before Luella had the chance.

This always teased Luella, who dearly loved to do the same thing; but she was not such an early riser and so missed the fun. She loved to sleep in the morning, while Charlotte loved to get out in the crisp cold air and run about before anybody else was up.

Luella furnished another example of the spirit of entertainment when too shy to be conversational. Again a company of campers had come up from the beach to purchase supplies. They were in the kitchen in conversation with Mother; but Luella felt that she must acknowledge their visit by some sort of celebration; so she went out of the house, found herself a formidable stick, and began to drive the flock of squawking geese—loudly protesting in true goose fashion—around and round the house outside. Since at least one member of the family was desperately afraid of geese, this performance in her estimation, meant a good-sized "feather in her cap"—and not a "white feather" either. So round and round and round they went, time after time, urged on by Luella with the big bold stick—all for the entertainment of the unsuspecting guests. But upon said guests, their eardrums fairly cracking with the deafening hubbub, in which no one could even hear himself think, let alone carry on a conversation, the magnanimous intention was wholly lost.

From earliest childhood, Luella manifested remarkable judgment, having a head on her little shoulders worthy of a much older person. Her sense of right and wrong, of fair play and justice, was very decided. Since it was her habitual intention to do right as she saw it, she deeply resented anything that cast aspersion on her motives or savored of unfairness. Any corporal punishment wounded her pride—of which there was a large "bump," and roused in her a spirit of stubborn rebellion that was difficult to handle. Compulsion, she could not brook; but possessed an indomitable spirit that was not to be broken or coerced into good behavior.

Mother, whose hands and heart were full of many and diversified problems, did not always choose the most happy method of dealing with this imperious little individual who had come to be a member of our family circle; for with Luella, stereotyped and customary methods often would not work. Instead of quietly reasoning things out with her and giving her time to subdue her own rebellious propensities and to exercise her own power of choice, Mother according to the usual accepted standards in dealing with children would administer some punishment. This was always disastrous.

I remember once seeing Luella tied by a stout cord to a doorknob; which indignity had stirred up an internal fury of resentment that was being vented by vicious jerking of the offending cord and violent kicking of the door, alternated with pounding of her fists; her long dark curls bobbing wildly about a very flushed face set in angry lines. Would she admit that she was "sorry" in order to obtain release from the hated captivity? Not she! Nor was she in the least "sorry," only stormily rebellious, for in her own estimation she was being "abused."

At another time Mother shut her in the upper corncrib. The occasion for this punishment was a disagreement with Charlotte over the question of "precedence." We had visitors. Sadie and her little first-born son were out from Phoenix and as usual when extra plates were set, there were not enough chairs to go round. Someone had to sit on an up-ended kerosene box. Thus far it had been Luella who had occupied this uncomfortable seat. So when Mother asked her and Charlotte to "set the table," she, having decided in her own mind that it was Charlotte's turn to sit on the box, took advantage of the occasion to set a chair at her own place and the box before Charlotte's plate.

Luella being only four and Charlotte eight, this was a breach of etiquette, and Charlotte promptly remedied it by exchanging seats. Luella, being more concerned with "justice" than with "etiquette," held the fort determinedly changing the seats back again as fast as Charlotte fixed them "according to Hoyle." After box and chair had exchanged places a number of times, Mother, annoyed by the contention, and being somewhat heated from cooking over the hot wood stove, interfered in the interests of peace. Utterly ignoring Luella's side of the question, and failing to secure her submission by milder means, she took down her little switch—kept handy for such emergencies—to use it on the recalcitrant. This being a thing seldom resorted to where Luella was concerned, her proud spirit rose in resentment and she rushed out of doors, followed unwisely by Mother, now fully determined to bring the rebellious child to order.

The two played "tag" around the house outside, Luella winning in the game, while Father, much amused, looked on. At last he said:

"Come, Welly, come, and I'll give you a piece of candy."

For a moment she wavered, undecided whether or not to yield to his tempting offer. But deciding that it was not quite "sporting" in him to interfere in Mother's affair of discipline, she gave up the game of "dodge," and disdaining the candy, surrendered to Mother. It was then that Mother took her up to the corncrib and shut her in, securing the door with a shoestring passed through the slats and tied in a series of knots on the outside.

Mother then went back to the house to resume her cooking, intending to free Luella in time for the repast. But to Luella, being tied in instead of being trusted to stay there of her own accord, after having surrendered voluntarily, was an insult to her integrity. So she began to scheme a way to escape from her prison. There was no possible way but by the door, so that string must be undone some way. Thrusting her arm into a crack between the slats, which was so narrow she could barely force her elbow through, she got hold of the string, and patiently grappling with the knots one after another, finally succeeded in undoing them to the last one, and jubilant, attempted to withdraw her arm. But alas! The elbow stuck. It would never do for Mother to come up and find her in that embarrassing situation, so she worked perseveringly to get her arm out of the crack, reasoning that since it had gone out, it would certainly come back in again. And at last it did.

It was a thrilling moment when, opening the door, she walked out free—free, but with no place to go. Her eye cast about for some means of concealment. The pepper row was just before her—their thick drooping branches offering a friendly retreat. So selecting one with limbs low enough for her to reach, she climbed up into the tree with her little bare feet, and perched on a big high bough awaited developments.

It was not long until Mother came up. Finding "the bird flown," she instituted a search, resolving upon further discipline for this flouting of her authority. Out under the pepper trees she went, turning over upside down every one of a pile of boxes that were there to look inside for the fugitive. Straightening up, she called for Frank to come and bring a little piece of rope, intending to secure that door the next time so well that no such impudent little rascal could ever unfasten it.

Luella, watching unseen from her perch directly overhead, realized that she had freed herself from one prison only to become her own jailor in another, and though still glorying in her pride, wished she didn't have quite so much of it.

When Mother and Frank, after a fruitless search, were gone back into the house, she saw Father come out and go to the nectarine tree. Shaking it till the ripe fruit came rattling down onto the ground, he called loudly for all the children to come and help themselves. This unusual treat was tempting indeed. But the fugitive, rightly interpreting it as a bait for her small self, dared not "come," though from her high perch, she could see the others running. She had become a voluntary "tree-sitter," antedating by many decades the modern marathons. Not till all was over, the last ripe nectarine gathered and the crowd dispersed did she clamber down from her perch and sneak over to the gully at the end of the pepper row. Following it down behind the honey house to the lower corner, she there sought the shadow behind the open cellar door. At this point she came unexpectedly upon Frank, who would not betray her but gave her a nectarine and the bit of good advice to give herself up and tell Mother she was sorry.

This advice, Luella took, being tired of the game that eventually she must lose any way. And Mother then sent her back up to the corncrib by herself to go inside and wait till she should come up and release her. Charlotte, who had watched her more closely than anyone else and with a greater pull on her heart strings, and feeling herself to be somewhat to blame in the matter, knew all the time where she was hidden in the tree, but would not tell anyone.

Luella waited in the corncrib obediently until the belated dinner was on the table. Then Mother came up and set her at liberty. This time she went out free indeed. Thereafter she sat on the kerosene box unprotestingly as a younger sister should, thankful that there was a box to sit on. For sometimes she had stood at the table as others before her had stood when company overflowed. Yes, and even worse than that, she with others had waited around in that limbo of a back yard through the long meal, wondering hungrily if there would be anything left after the big folks and company had finished. How older folks could eat at all with hungry children unfed, is a mystery I leave for the reader to solve. But that was the "custom" then. Children were not only "made to be seen not heard," but to "wait not eat" till their elders were satisfied. How well do I recall similar occasions on my own account! How hungrily I waited around till the company had finished, or if allowed at the table, sat on a box or even stood to eat when all the boxes too were in use, or there was not room enough to put one in place!

One such occasion I shall never forget because it led to the tragedy of an unjust punishment—and that by Mother herself. We had company. The big extension table was let out to its fullest capacity. There were places enough to go round and plates enough, but seats were lacking. Even the boxes were all appropriated so my place was left without any. I had searched everywhere and could find nothing to sit on. The dinner was just about to be put on the table, after which all present would take their places. It was no fun to stand while eating dinner, but I was not complaining, since it evidently could not be helped.

At the last moment, in passing the front door leading onto the porch that opened against the jog, I partially closed it and there to my delight stood behind it a perfectly good chair that it seemed had been overlooked. Quickly I appropriated it and well pleased with my find, set it at my place. But my joy was short-lived. Hulda soon came and accused me of stealing her chair for myself. Indignantly I denied it.

"You did too!" she said.

"I didn't!" I retorted.

"You did!"

"I didn't!"

"You did!"

"I didn't!"

Then she went to Mother and firmly accused me, pointing out her chair-less place and my sudden find to fill my own.

"I found this chair behind the door," I told Mother. But knowing that I had not been given one and that Hulda had, Mother did not believe me. Again I was the victim of circumstantial evidence. Promptly she unbuttoned my panties and gave me a sound spanking. My rebellion knew no bounds. The injustice of it was like "gall and wormwood." For some time I sobbed in angry insubordination; not even coming to the table where the rest were all sitting to partake of the savory dinner. Finally Mother threatened to make me go without entirely if I didn't "stop crying" and "sober up and come to the table." Being ravenously hungry, I could not let the last chance go by of something to eat, so came to my place and choked down the food while standing on my two feet, still unsubdued and thirsting for justice.

After the dinner was over, the company gone before whom I had been disgraced, Hulda slipped quietly up to Mother and confessed to her that while we were eating she remembered that she had drawn her chair over to the wall to hang up her apron and had forgotten to put it back and didn't remember the incident until all of a sudden it came to her at the table. Mother then came to me humbly and exonerated me from blame. She said that Hulda didn't mean to—that she was very sorry; which was all true. But somehow that did not reverse the shame I had endured and still must suffer in the minds of others who understood not the truth. I held it against Hulda for a long time unforgivingly, and against Mother too, not only for arbitrary belief and acceptance of her word against mine, but for acceptance as sufficient of a whispered apology to herself, which should have rather been made directly and openly to the injured party who had suffered the indignity of unjust punishment, publicly.

CHAPTER 33 CATS AND GOPHERS

Gophers were among our most aggravating pests. We were always after them with traps and cats and poison. On account of the gophers and mice, we always kept large numbers of cats on the farm; and much to our joy, we children were allowed to keep the kittens that came—at least some of them; the surplus being dispatched secretly to spare our feelings.

To us, kittens were made to play with, the gopher question being entirely secondary. And how we loved them! The advent of a new litter of kittens was a most delightful event surpassed only by the arrival of a new baby. Some of our cats grew to be remarkable hunters, the squirrels and gophers suffering much in consequence. Even rabbits were sometimes brought in, and as for mice, one dared scarcely to show his head.

At one time gophers were so numerous and destructive that Father offered to give us children five cents apiece for every gopher scalp we brought in to him. There were not enough traps to go round, so the older ones had the traps and caught most of the gophers. For a time when money was very scarce, the bounty was cut to three cents a scalp and the boys had to catch thirty-five gophers to earn a dollar and five cents.

Whenever a gopher was caught, the first thing was to bring him up to the yard and scalp him. The boys' pocketknives being too dull for this work, table knives were used. These were not silver knives, but black steel; for only rich folks could have silver knives in those days. But scalping a gopher was not so easy even if the knife was sharp. There were so many cats around during the operation, it was "nip and tuck" as to which would get the scalp. If the cats should succeed in seizing the gopher before he was scalped, it would be goodbye to that scalp, and the promised reward.

Joseph once brought into the back yard a defunct gopher to be scalped. Several of us youngsters were standing around in a huddle helping to keep the cats away, and watching the operation, when Frank, not knowing what was going on but supposing it to be a treat of some kind to attract so many of us like flies around a honey-pot, came running to get his share of whatever it might be, calling as he ran:

"Can I have some too? Give me some too!"

By the time he got there, Joseph had finished scalping the gopher, and answered:

"Yes, you can have some," and handed the scalped gopher to Frank, who turned away chagrined and crestfallen.

Joseph, when a small boy, was once on his way down to the cart-road garden where he was to watch the corn to keep the squirrels and birds out of it, when a gopher popped his head up out of his hole and retreated again. Joseph had his bow and arrows with him, and stood very still poised with arrow across bow ready for a shot. In a few moments the gopher again showed his head. "Twang!" went the arrow, and the little rodent stiffened in death. Father had not liked for Joseph to play with his bow and arrows for fear he would neglect his work; but when he saw the gopher he changed his mind.

I once spied a gopher that had wandered a little too far from his hole in quest of food, and pouncing upon him with bare hands before he could get away, soon had him in my clutches. But just about as soon, he had me in his clutches—his four long sharp front teeth that clamped together on my thumb like a vice. There was but one thing to do—choke him. That I did releasing him not till he let go and lay limp and dead; after which there was plenty of time to nurse my wounded thumb.

Long after the bounty was removed from gopher scalps, we still were encouraged to catch as many of them as we could; and whenever we would find a gopher-hole, would run for a trap. In setting a gopher trap, the main hole must first be opened by digging, and its mouth enlarged to enable the trap to fit over it properly. The box-shaped trap is fitted with a heavy wire loop that lets down over the entrance and is held there by a trigger. When sprung it flies up through a slot in the top, drawing the victim tight against the top of the box and cutting off his breath. So that is the end of Mr. Gopher. Before this kind of trap was invented, a small steel flat trap was used, which is not such a "sure catch." Of course still better traps are used nowadays.

Little Charlotte, being the youngest trapper, pleased Father so much by her efforts that he bought her a jumping-jack and a whirling monkey in a little red jacket—toys that were enjoyed by the entire family for a long, long time—even grown-ups amusing themselves with their acrobatic stunts.

Gopher skins were so soft and furry that we often thought what delicate, dainty rugs for dolls they would make. It remained for Luella, however, to try the experiment of curing some of them. They did indeed make beautiful rugs, but the moths seemed to suppose that all this work had been done for no other purpose than to provide them with a nice warm place to live and feed their capacious maws. So the rugs didn't last long.

Charlotte when a tiny girl once had a little gray kitten only a week or two old, which she dearly loved. Often she would go out to its nest in the box and fondle its tender little coat, longing for the day when it should run about and play with her. One day she essayed to lift it out of the box, and by some awkward movement, dropped it and stepped on it, crushing out its little life. Filled with horror and grief at the "crime" she had committed, her imagination inventing fearful punishments to befall her should it become known, yet faced with the necessity of giving some account of the kitten's death, she took the only way out that her little terrified mind could invent as feasible to account for it without disclosure of the real cause.

Snatching up the kitten, she ran weeping with it to the house, crying out in heartbroken excitement:

"Look what I found! Look what I found!"

Nobody suspected for a moment any deception. Her grief and horror were too evident and genuine to be questioned. Everyone was sympathetic over her loss and greatly puzzled as to the cause of the tragedy. We children held a "funeral" for the deceased, burying it in a little box, with greenery placed above its grave. But little Charlotte had no peace. For years, she suffered under the burden of her guilty secret, before finally unburdening her breast for relief.

Another incident of exaggerated seriousness and immature judgement, occurred later with Annie as a co-partner in the "crime," and a toad for the victim. One day, the two of them emboldened by Harriet's example-yet not openly for they were unconvinced as to the propriety of it—caught a toad and were playing with it, when they accidentally hurt it so that it began to bleed. Having done this, they thought it was of course doomed to die; and for some unaccountable reason, felt that they should dispose of it. But toads, according to all family tradition, were among the animals that were never under any circumstances to be injured, being justly considered the farmers' friends. So, in taking the life of this toad, they felt guilty of "murder," even granting it to be a necessary act.

Who can fathom the mental processes of a child? Quickly digging a little hole, they buried the dead toad, covering the place with malvia leaves. Not a soul did they tell about it until many years later. But ever afterward that spot to them was haunted. The shame and remorse of a dreadful deed hung over them. Never after, would they go near that spot to play or even look at it if avoidable, but would pass by with averted eyes as far as possible from the secret grave of their innocent victim. A murderer indeed could scarcely have suffered more remorse at taking human life.

Mother, who for some unaccountable reason, seemed to trust me with tasks beyond my years, one day sent me to the chopping block with a sick and dying hen, to end her misery by cutting off her head, thus preventing contagion among the flock. I laid her head upon the block—she being too nearly dead to offer resistance—and holding her in position by the feet with my left hand, endeavored, as I had seen the men folks do, to raise the heavy ax with the other hand, aiming the downward stroke at her stretched out neck. But alas! Both of my hands would have been no more than sufficient to guide that unwieldy ax, and one of them was occupied in holding her legs; so down came the ax—not on her neck, but across her poor bill, chopping it off close to the head.

Though I live to be a hundred, I can never forget that one agonized, bill-less squawk that followed the blow. Horrified, I hastened to finish the sickening job. But now nervousness added to awkwardness, still further muddled the coordination of hand and head, and two more whacks were needed to end her misery. Did I tell my Mother? Oh, no! Never! Not even Annie, the recipient of my deepest secrets.

Once, discovering among the brood a very sick chick that could not be expected to live, Mother sentenced that too to the chopping block for the same reasons, and being very busy herself, committed to me the merciful execution. I was young to be entrusted with an errand of this kind; but Mother seemed to think more highly of my dependability than was warranted.

Now, if there was ever one thing more than another that I loved and vainly wished to play with, it was a little yellow downy baby chick, strictly forbidden, of course, as inimical to the chick's well-being. So this definite temptation was presented to me accompanied by the coveted opportunity to indulge the desire. I reasoned that since the chick had to die anyway, I might as well have a little fun playing with it first—if that could be done without Mother's finding it out. The suffering that would thus be imposed I could not visualize because it was mute. So, starting obediently toward the chopping block, but when out of sight changing my course, I sneaked away with the chick to have my forbidden play.

For half an hour or so, I carried it about, putting it through one playful torture after another, wrapping it up, putting it to bed, patting it, stroking its downy body, and crowning the series by "swimming" it around as a little duckling in a pan of water, before giving it the ax. Quite ignorant of this cruel and shameful conduct, Mother kept on trusting me with tasks beyond my years.

A Boy's Sorrowful Blunder

Once we had an immense gray tomcat, in appearance and size closely resembling the wild variety, but a beloved family pet, tame and gentle as a kitten. He was a wonderful hunter, who roamed all over the mountains and pasture lands, daily bringing in his prey, consisting of snakes, squirrels, rabbits, gophers, rats, birds, and what not. He was considered a valuable asset to the farm, and was called "Frank's cat."

One day Frank came running into the house after the gun in great excitement, shouting in a suppressed voice: "There's a wildcat up on the hill!" Out again he rushed with the shotgun, and immediately taking aim, fired. The cat gave one bound and fell to the ground dead. Frank dashed up on the hill to secure his prey. To his horror, dismay, chagrin, and sorrow, he found it to be our dear old tomcat he had killed—his own cat, and one of his best friends! Oh how every member of the family deplored that stupid accident! We were all sick over it; but poor Frank was sickest of all. It seemed as though he could never get over it.

Another large old cat I remember because of her mottled appearance, yellow, brown, white and black all mingled in scattered patches over her body. She was indeed a beautiful cat; and each succeeding generation of kittens always had at least one like her, a great mouser and mother of mousers, and named "Smokey" after the family tradition.

But my old cream-and-yellow cat, who could forget her? She was the most beautiful cat we ever had on the place, and none surpassed her in size but old gray Tom. Pure dark yellow on back and head, shading to tan on lower sides, with creamy white belly and feet. She was my pride and joy, and she belonged to me. She would rub her face against my shin, trotting along like a dog at my side wherever I went. I longed for the time when she should have baby kittens, and was sure they would be beautiful like their mother. At last, the long-awaited event took place, and I began to hunt for her kittens. It was a happy moment when at last I found her next under a sheltering rock up on the hillside, with two beautiful yellow kittens in it just recently born.

I went next day up to the nest, but they were not there. "Why, she has moved them to another place," I thought, viewing with disappointment the empty nest. After that I watched her closely to see where she would go. But she stayed about the yard all day, and apparently all night too, like a cat who had no kittens at all. In vain I hunted for them far and near, all over the hill slopes and in the barn and shed and every place I could think of. But no kittens could be found. I waited for her to bring them half-grown into the yard. But they never came. And these two beautiful yellow kittens were never seen again. It was evident to us that some wild animal had made away with them. So, all I could do by way of self-consolation, was to wait patiently till she should have some more babies.

Quite a number of months later Mother said to me:

"She's going to get some more kittens someday soon."

How Mother knew this, was more than I could make out; but every day after that I watched her movements.

One day I saw her coming down the hillside, and waited for her. She rubbed her head affectionately against my shins. Picking her up in my arms, I felt something damp and investigated. There were her little breasts all suckled and damp from baby mouths, and I knew the kittens had come. Over-joyed, I began immediately to search for her babies, climbing up the hill in the direction from which she had come. She followed by my side for a while, then going ahead led me straight to the same nest formerly occupied. There, to my grief, lay two little yellow kittens, one dead and half eaten, the other cold from neglect and almost dead—too far gone for recovery by any possible means.

"Some wild animal has attacked them!" was my first anguished thought, as I looked with grief and disappointment upon the violated nest.

But before I had time to recover from this shock, another and worse one followed. That unnatural cat fell upon her own half-eaten baby, and resumed her meal. She was eating them up. And thus I learned what had become of her former kittens which had so mysteriously disappeared.

With a revulsion of feeling from sympathy to horror and indignation too terrible to describe, I fell upon her with blows and kicks and curses, driving her far from me; nevermore to feel for her anything but hatred. Whenever she would come near me, I would drive her away, resenting her overtures of affection and henceforth regarding her as "a monster of so frightful mien as to be hated needs but to be seen."

Charming Snakes? Or Cats?

It was commonly believed that snakes charmed cats, who becoming helpless in their power, were finally devoured by the charmers. So far as we were concerned, this belief was greatly strengthened by an incident that took place when I was a little girl.

Directly in front of our house below the road that skirted the front yard, in the edge of the orchard, one warm summer afternoon, we discovered one of our cats walking 'round and 'round in an ever-narrowing circle, uttering a monotonous wail, low-toned and weird, and seemingly of helpless distress. His eyes were fixed unwaveringly in evident fascination upon the eyes that never left his own, of a gopher snake coiled with head up, in the center of the ring. Squatting around the circle on our heels at a respectful distance, we watched this performance until the circle became so narrow that we feared for the outcome to the cat. At this juncture we threw stones and broke up the charm.

Many years after this, I learned from the lips of one who seemed to know what he was talking about, that the reverse of what we supposed, was true. The cat was charming the snake. To substantiate his statement, this man told of a case that had come under his personal observation, almost an exact duplicate to this one except that the onlookers watched the chief actors through to its ultimate conclusion.

The big cat weirdly moaning drew closer and closer to the snake, that seemed transfixed in the center of the circle as if unable to move. At last when the two were in close proximity to each other, the cat suddenly lifted his paw with bared claws, and gave a vicious strike at the head of the snake instantly breaking its neck, which sent it writhing and senseless to the earth; and shortly thereafter dispatched it with his sharp strong teeth.

Well do I remember two coal-black toms—brothers—which we raised from kittens; one belonging to Charlotte which we named "Rodger" in an attempt to find a name worthy of so distinguished a cat, and the other, "Bleeker," conjured up in my search for a name out of the ordinary that would go euphoniously with "Rodger." Large and beautiful cats they grew to be, and mates through all the years. They were unsurpassed as mousers and hunters, and would follow us about like dogs.

These two felines were not ignorant concerning the advantages of fruits and vegetables in the diet. They would go down to the cart-road garden and help themselves to onion tops, tomatoes, and muskmelons, biting into these and eating half a melon at a time.

We had for some time known that a rattler lived in the woodpile. But so far had not been able to catch him outside and kill him. One day as Charlotte went out to the wash house under the lone Sycamore, the dismal yowling of a cat arrested her attention. Listening, she discerned mingled with it the unmistakable buzzing of a rattlesnake—all in the direction of the woodpile.

She flew to the rescue. There on a stump with his back to her, sat her own beloved Rodger emitting that dreadful wail, poised stiff and ridged on his forepaws and haunches, his long tail moving silently and rhythmically from side to side, and his eyes riveted upon the beady eyes only a few inches from his own, of a rattler, his head alone visible, peering intently into the eyes of the cat from under the covering brush, as he shook his terrifying rattles.

With never a thought of her own danger, but fearful only for the safety of her pet which she supposed was being "charmed" by the rattler, she drew close and snatched her cat away, carrying him into the house with much solicitude.

But somehow, that ungrateful cat seemed to be utterly disgusted. Putting his ears back he frowned disappointedly, as he blinked his eyes and licked his chops, thinking perhaps of what he had lost by way of a good fat snake-dinner.

CHAPTER 34 CRAWFISHING AND THE SANDMAN: GUN REVENGE

Joseph, when a boy, seemed never able to get enough sleep. Always it was difficult to awaken him of a morning, especially after any unusual loss of sleep. His risings depended more or less upon Lafe, who, being opposite in makeup, was an early and regular riser. Arousing the boy from slumber ofttimes produced somnambulant effects that were very amusing. He would hear what was said, reply to questions, walk about, talk, and perform all manner of ludicrous acts while still sound asleep and utterly unconscious of his surroundings and of his own actions.

The boys and girls of study age, after their hard day's work, used to gather around the table of an evening to get their lessons by lamp-light. Joseph invariably fell asleep. It would then be almost impossible to awaken him and get him off to bed.

Once, when he was sent to bed after falling asleep at the table, he imagined he had dropped a string out of the window at the south end of the house, and insisted on getting it before going to bed. Not until after Father had picked him up and held him by the heels head-downward out of the window to recover his imaginary string, did he finally awaken and come to himself.

One evening at their books, both boys became very sleepy and began to nod. Father, seeing that for them, study was out of the question, sent them off to bed. Joseph was seated on a low three-legged stool. As he rose to obey, he reached down, picked up this stool, and, imagining it to be his hat, placed it upside down on the top of his head. While steadying it with one hand, he started out the door. But as the legs of the stool sticking up in the air, struck the door-frame above, he failed to get through with it. Again and again he made the attempt, unsuccessfully, readjusting his queer hat as it wobbled. Yet even this did not awaken him, nor yet the loud laughter of the family, who fairly shrieked with amusement at the comical sight. Seemingly, all this had no effect; and not until he had been engaged in argument and roughly handled, did he come to his senses and go sheepishly off to bed.

Although it was a common thing for Joseph to talk in his sleep, with Lafe, it was very uncommon and rare; but occasionally the dream-wizard slipped up on him also. Shortly after the barn was built, and the boys had their beds on the sweet-smelling new-mown hay, Father, for the enjoyment and novelty of it, joined them for a few nights. On one of these occasions, Lafe suddenly called out in the darkness:

"Oh Pa! "

"What?" asked Father.

"Here's the old cat! And she's got nine kittens!"

With this announcement Lafe awoke, feeling so foolish that he shut his mouth like a trap, pretending to be still asleep. Father, amused, tried to lead him on to say more. But not another word did he get out of Lafe. Simulating slumber, he kept on breathing with rhythmical regularity, lying still as a mouse till the others had fallen asleep again, only too glad to be thought immune to their chaffing. In the morning he listened to the recital of the incident with pretended surprise.

Crawfishing was a sport the boys greatly enjoyed. Since these creatures would never bite in the daylight, it was always carried on at night. Moonlight was very much to be desired, and a lantern was always part of the equipment. Crawfish were caught in shallow water, in crevices and pockets among the submerged rocks and seaweeds. It was essential that the weather be fair and the sea smooth; otherwise, fishing on the ocean rocks at night would be dangerous.

A line and bait were used, but no hook; and usually no sinker other than the bait. If this proved not heavy enough, a small sinker was added. Very frequently, abalone was used for bait, being first allowed to become stale. Crawfish, being scavengers, live on dead things and offal. A tough piece of rind from bacon or side pork, or even a bone made a good bait. If it had begun to spoil, so much the better; for the more smelly it was, the more effectively it would draw the crawfish.

Each fisherman must have two poles with lines and carry extra line for emergency. The poles must be short and rather stiff. After dropping the first line into a pool, the fisherman would lay the pole down on the rocks, and if thought necessary, place his foot upon it to keep the waves from washing it away, and to enable him the more quickly to sense a nibble. Then he would drop the line of the second pole into the water, holding that one in his hand. Should the one on the rock show signs of a nibble, it would be taken up and the other laid down; the two being alternated as indicated by the nibbling.

A crawfish will nibble and pull intermittently at a bait, and must be given time to take it in with teeth and claws. Then he must be drawn up very gradually and gently so as not to startle him into a realization that he is being moved. When near the surface, he must be landed with a sudden quick jerk out onto the rock, after which he may be put into the sack alive. Unless this procedure is managed just right, he will let go his hold and be lost.

With crawfish were always associated eels or lampreys. These were caught with the same equipment, but the eel must be handled differently. He will grab the bait and swallow it quickly, and unless drawn out immediately with a strong quick jerk, will swish away to a rock or a piece of kelp rooted in a rock and wrapping his long snaky body around it, hold on tightly. He will never let go the bait, for once a thing is taken in between his two even rows of sharp fine hooked teeth it is there to stay and there is no danger of his letting go his hold and dropping back into the water. This propensity enabled the fisherman to land him the more certainly if alert enough to sense the bite instantly and quick enough to pull him out with no loss of time before he could reach a rock. However, if once he succeeds in fastening himself to a rock, he cannot be dislodged by any means, and so cannot be drawn out of the water. The only way in such case that a fisherman could save his line was to cut it as low as possible and let him have the end of it with the bait. Sometimes the line might be sawed in two on a sharp rock lower down in the water than could be reached with a knife. An eel must be killed as soon as landed or he will get away, so he was put into the sack lifeless along with the living crawfish.

If, in the location first chosen the crawfish would not bite, it was abandoned and another spot selected, the fishermen moving repeatedly if necessary until success rewarded their efforts. This was the simple method of those days; but now the sport is carried on differently, with traps previously set.

One bright moonlit night, Lafe and Joseph decided to go crawfishing; which meant that they would lose a night's sleep. Taking with them the usual equipment of poles, lines, lantern, gunnysack, plenty of bait and extra fishline, the boys trudged down the canyon and up the side of the mesa, crossing it to Goff Point. Here, descending the bluffs by a trail to the sandy beach, they clambered over the rocks at Goff Island to the well-known feeding places of the crawfish, and took their stand in the best location they could find.

On this occasion they fished all night with wonderful success, and when ready to start for home near daybreak, had a gunnysack almost full of crawfish and eels. It was a heavy load to pack up the steep embankment and over the mesa, and they struggled with it together carrying the sack between them to the other side overlooking Aliso Canyon. This accomplished, they let it down too tired to bear it a step farther. Leaving the sack under a bush at the top of the hill, they then decided to go home and get a horse to pack it the rest of the way.

Day was just breaking and the birds beginning their early matins as the two weary but satisfied fisher boys dragged their feet across the plowed ground of the walnut orchard, waded the creek and met the greeting dogs with familiar pats of approval to insure silence.

Reaching at last their room in the cistern house, they decided to snatch first a little sleep at this opportune hour of gray dawn while everything was still quiet and the family wrapped in slumber. Well did they know that this was to be their only chance, for farm work cannot stop on account of all-night sport. The crawfish, they reasoned, could be brought home after the cows were milked. So undressing, they went to bed and were asleep as soon as their heads touched the pillows.

Just at sunrise, the usual getting-up time, Lafe awoke, and after arousing Joseph, began to dress himself. When finished, he turned to Joseph, but saw that he, at the beginning of his dressing operations, had been overcome with sleep again. He was lying doubled up on top of the bed, forehead on hands, face on pillow, knees drawn up under him, and with only his shirt on. Giving him a resounding slap on the spanking-place, Lafe commanded him to dress and went out.

It was his custom of a morning to go first up to the house after the milk bucket and awaken the girls. Having done this, he came back down to the cow corral to start the milking. Taking a look first into the cistern room, he found that Joseph was still asleep, and again awoke him roughly with a slap and proceeded to the milking.

Presently he heard a sound, and looking up, saw Joseph walking toward the road that led up to the house, with nothing on but his shirt.

"Where are you going?" he asked.

"Up to the house," replied Joseph.

"What for?" asked Lafe.

"To get the milk bucket," answered Joseph.

"I've been up to the house and got the milk bucket," said Lafe, adding: "Where are your clothes?"

"I don't know," said Joseph, stopping to look at himself.

"You ain't dressed," insisted Lafe.

Not till then did the boy awaken and realize his condition. Then he went into the room and dressed himself. Lafe finished the milking while Joseph fed the stock. Then taking one of the horses, Lafe went down to the mesa and brought home the sack of crawfish.

After a breakfast of fried eel, they both repaired to the corn patch beyond the third bend—the corn being about waist high—to hoe weeds which were scattered somewhat sparingly over the patch. Each took a row beginning at the hill and worked toward the creek, then back again on another row. Upon reaching the hill again, Lafe was beginning to feel his lack of sleep and rest, and overcome with weariness, suggested:

"Let's sit down and rest awhile."

"All right," agreed Joseph, and they seated themselves.

Presently Lafe felt himself dropping off to sleep, and jumped up, saying "This will never do! Let's get to work again" and suited the action to the word. Lafe worked away getting ahead of Joseph, but conscious without looking back that he was following. About midway down the row, he turned about to see why it was that Joseph was getting so far behind, and observed him in the act of trying to kick up a weed with his heel.

"What are you trying to do?" he asked.

"Trying to get this weed up" answered Joseph.

"Where's your hoe?"

"I don't know. Ain't you got it?"

"No I ain't got it. I've got my own hoe. Yours must be back at the hill."

Then Joseph awoke from sleep and went back to the hill and got his hoe.

Bonfires

After the cornstalks had grown to full height and the ears, having set and ripened, had been husked and hauled to the crib, when the old denuded stalks had withered and dried in the field, here in this corn patch we used to have wonderful times watching bonfires after nightfall.

No one then ever thought of using cornstalks for fodder. They were but refuse fit only to be burned. So when the time had come to clear off the ground in readiness for the next year's crop, we would pull up the old stalks by the roots and stack them high in four or five huge cones at intervals over the field in anticipation of a "bonfire night."

After these stacks had been allowed to stand till thoroughly crisp and dry clear through to the center and were sure to make good fuel, while still the sun shone hot before the first rains carne, and the nights were dark, Joseph would make the thrilling announcement:

"This'll be a good night to burn the cornstalks."

"Oh, goodie, goodie! A bonfire!" would be shouted in gleeful chorus.

After supper down to the corn patch we would troop, and ignite one at a time these huge piles to watch them burn with a great crackling noise and clouds of sparks sailing high up into the air against the blue sky, the glare and glow of shooting flames turning night into day. In this firelight we romped and sported, yelled and laughed to our heart's content. Oh what fun it was! How we looked forward to these bonfire nights!

As soon as one pile would burn down to a smoldering heap of stumps and cinders, fire would be carried on a burning stalk to the next pile for another bonfire. Then another and another would be ignited till all were gone and the last one had become a smoldering heap. Then when all was over, the last spark extinguished from the heaps of ashes to prevent fires that might be started by the breeze and escape to the surrounding hills, we would all troop home at bedtime through the darkness led by Joseph with the lantern.

A Prank, Odorous and Odious

One evening a little after sundown, Lafe and Joseph when rounding up the milk cows feeding in the filaree pasture, came across a skunk, who fled from their presence to hide in the formidable fortress of a large patch of cactus near the foot of the hill.

He was a big fellow having a beautiful striped black-and-white coat and a bushy tail with white rings which he held up high and waved like a pampas plume as he ran. But beauty to be appreciated must be inside as well as outside, and a skunk bears such an unenviable reputation for his egg-sucking and other forbidden acts, to say nothing of the odors he dispenses, that his carcass is more to be desired than his living presence.

The boys, having no gun at hand, were still determined to get him somehow. Gathering up a supply of loose stones lying about, they began to heave them at the fugitive entrenched in his spiny refuge. In retaliation he filled the air with his peculiar brand of perfume, as is the way with his kind. But his attackers knew better than to get close enough to receive on their persons any of the fine, obnoxious spray he was showering around with such lavish prodigality.

Even a cactus patch will succumb in time to a persistent bombardment of stones fired in rapid succession by two energetic boys, and soon not only was his protection weakened, but his own body itself mangled and bleeding. His odorous mode of defense had proved all too inadequate.

Darkness had fallen by the time the last projectile fired was deemed sufficient and the job finished. Then the natural desire of boys to exhibit their trophy asserted itself, and they began to scheme a way to get him out of his death-trap bristling with formidable spines and reeking with devastating odors. It was evident that a long stick would be the only thing advisable to use in reaching the untouchable. So, hunting up an elder tree having shoots growing up from its base, they cut one that was long and slender, trimming it free of branches and sharpening the small end to a point. With this they began to prod the lifeless victim, and finally succeeded in twisting it firmly into the long hair of his bushy tail, and thus drew him out of the bed of cactus.

Hoisting this stick with its odorous and odious burden over one of their shoulders they started for the house; the cows by themselves having long since gone into the corral. On the way the mischievous desire came into their hearts to play a joke on the unsuspecting family, the details of the plot being hatched up as they walked along.

Light was streaming from the windows of the house and all outside was quiet as the two conspirators slipped around to the end window of the living room that slid open sidewise in its groove four feet or so up from the ground. Fortunately for the success of their prank, the sliding window was wide open. There were no screens. They looked in cautiously. The kerosene lamp was standing in the center of the long table, and all the other members of the family were seated around it with their books absorbed in study or reading, with the smaller ones looking at pictures.

Without making a sound, Lafe and Joseph together lifted the stick, from the end of which dangled the skunk, and cautiously thrust it inside the room a little way letting it rest on the sill. Holding the other end firmly, they crouched below the range of vision of those inside and awaited developments.

It was not long before the olfactory nerves of the unsuspecting family began to be bombarded by an odoriferous diffusion; and the culprits under the window outside heard someone say:

"I smell a skunk!" and another concur:

"So do I!" and a third:

"It must be somewhere near; I'll bet it's under the house!" and then a chorus:

"My! This is awful!"

It was with difficulty that the two accomplices outside could suppress their chuckles. The family began to get up from the table and hold their noses to exclude the fetid odor—then someone spied the odious creature suspended in mid-air between them and the window.

Backing away from it, they began to hurl epithets at the hidden perpetrators who then could no longer contain themselves, and with loud laughter withdrew the stick with its offensive burden and ran hilariously away, chased half way to the barn by some of the girls.

Milking that night was not a task but a communion of kindred spirits in which were mingled jubilant chuckles and snickers that rose above the tattoo of streaming milk into the tin buckets till the last bossy had yielded up her contribution; after which the offending skunk, with its bushy tail and beautiful black-and-white fur was buried out of sight and smell.

Blue Falcon Hawks

Among the most troublesome of the creatures that preyed upon our flocks of chickens were the Blue Falcon Hawks, or Peregrine Falcons, also known as the Great-Footed Falcon, and because of their swift pursuit and capture of wild ducks on the wing, called by others, the Duck Hawk. For years, a pair of these birds lived up in the bluff above the house, seeming to have for their domicile a very small cave that indented the sheer face of the cliff at its widest part some distance down from the upper edge.

These shrewd, fearless, magnificent birds of prey, swift and easy of flight, with their large strong talons, heavy hooked beaks, and keen brown eyes, were the pest of the whole countryside, preying not only upon our own chickens, but upon those of every family that had come to the coast. Especially were they destructive to the little chicks, destroying hundreds of those in our own flocks in a season. From their position high in the air espying a young brood, they would fold their wings and drop like bullets catching the chicks in their cruel talons, killing and mutilating, but very often failing to secure a firm hold and throwing the chicks by the impact twenty-five or thirty feet, thus destroying and losing several for every one they retained.

They were very noisy birds, by their unearthly screeching and their fierce front, keeping every other hawk away from their feeding grounds. It seemed impossible to get them with a gun. They were too quick and too constantly on the move for a rifle shot, and no one could get near enough for the short range of a shotgun.

Mr. Frank Goff and Father were walking together, one day through our walnut orchard, engaged in conversation, when these hawks set up a discordant screeching overhead; until Mr. Goff, exasperated, and speaking to no one in particular, uttered this open challenge:

> "I would be willing to pay five dollars apiece for those two hawks to anybody who could rid the country of them."

Lafe, quietly following the two men and overhearing the remark, in secret accepted the challenge. He determined to find a way to get those hawks and earn that money. The next day, keeping his own counsel, he went up above the back yard and stood studying the face of the cliff, until he had definitely fixed in his mind the location of the little cave with reference to its surroundings, so that he could make his way by landmarks, to their habitat, without becoming confused by his roundabout approach. In his mind he was formulating a scheme for trapping the birds.

Without taking anyone but Joseph into his confidence, he started out to climb the mountainside, armed with a small steel trap having a three-foot chain attached, and a piece of wire in his pocket. Where the cliff narrowed at its northern end he began the ascent, climbing around and above the cliff. Then following a line he had previously marked out with his eye, he made for the spot directly over this little cave. Having reached it, his next problem was to get down to the cave.

A very narrow and precarious ledge extended horizontally to the cave from the southern and wider end of the cliff not far distant where winter cataracts had worn a gully. Going over to this end, Lafe clambered down onto the ledge along which he carefully worked his way to the cave keeping his foothold by clinging with his hands to small projections on the surface. One careless slip from this ledge would have precipitated him to the bottom of the precipice more than fifty feet below.

The floor of this little cave he found covered with the usual pulverized yellow sandstone dust, with which he covered the trap after setting it inside near the edge. A small projection outside nearby furnished a convenient knob to which he fastened the chain of the trap by means of the wire he had brought, winding it around the knob securely. He then sidled back along the perilous ledge to the gully and clambered up to the top. Then by the way he had gone up, he returned to the house to await developments.

Not long after there was heard a terrible screeching up at the cliff, loud and distracting. One of the hawks was repeatedly diving down to the cave and rising again, while the other fluttered at the edge of its opening, and the noise was more deafening than ever it had been before. Father, who at the disturbance had gone out of the house, exclaimed:

> "What's the matter with those hawks up there?"

> "I'll tell you what's the matter," said Lafe bursting with excitement.

"One of 'em's in my trap!" and running for the shotgun he started with it up the mountainside.

After a good stiff climb he approached the scene of disturbance where the distracted bird still executed his diving performance. Without difficulty advancing near enough to take an effective shot, he pulled the trigger and down fell the blue hawk to the base of the cliff, dead at last, nevermore to harass the farmers and terrorize the domestic flocks of the coast. By taking a position at the end of the ledge, it was an easy matter to dispatch the captive mate with another shot. Then after edging his way out to the cave, he released the dead bird to join her lifeless consort with a thud at the base of the cliff, after which he secured his trap and retraced his steps along the ledge and back to the farmhouse.

Joseph, losing no time in getting up to the spot where the dead birds lay, had brought them down to the yard for exhibition. And there the family gathered around in jubilant triumph, showering upon Lafe justly-earned approbation. They were beautiful birds with their backs and wings dark bluish ash, their heads slaty-black, with sooty marked faces, white throats and black concentric bars across their breasts. But now their reign of terror was ended, and all the family rested in the thought that their trouble with hawks was over. But they did not know all there was to know about Blue Falcon Hawks.

Within twenty-four hours another pair of the same hawks had taken up their abode on the premises thus vacated. Having been kept out by the first pair, they now had everything their own way, and in their turn kept every other hawk from intruding upon their territory. And the nagging depredations continued without even an interruption.

But Lafe's dander was up. Spurred by the disappointment of the family, his appetite for Blue Falcon Hawks was only whetted by the appearance of these successors in this dynasty. He determined to accomplish their destruction also. Relentlessly he pursued his purpose, and it was not long until by means of patient maneuvers, one of these hawks fell before his gun. Within a day or two the survivor had secured a new mate, and things went on as usual.

Down at the farther end of the cart-road garden plot, the high mountain rose up having in its rim a distinct dip which we called "the gap." Below this gap were steep craggy cliffs, in an aperture of which was another roosting place for these hawks. In his eagerness to get them, Lafe in the attempt, even risked his life.

Taking with him besides his shotgun, a long rope, he climbed this mountain to the gap, and there finding a well-rooted mahogany shrub, fastened one end of it, tying it firmly around the trunk. The other end of the rope he tied about his own body to insure him against being dashed to the bottom of the precipitous bluff in case he should slip and fall. Then he began to creep along the face of the cliff clinging to a narrow horizontal crevice across its surface till he reached this roosting place of the hawks. But after reaching the spot he could accomplish nothing, and this hazardous and foolhardy undertaking proved to be such a harrowing and nerve-racking experience for him that he was only too glad to get back alive without any prey.

Still he kept after the hawks, till finally he shot one of these also. No sooner was this done till another mate came to take the place of the fallen one, and these two continued as formerly to prevent any invasion of their territory by other hawks while feasting as usual upon our flocks of chickens.

After a time, Lafe succeeded in killing one of these two, and immediately another mate was brought to fill the vacated place on the kingly throne of hawkdom. So the game continued over a long period of time until Lafe and Joseph had killed thirteen of these Blue Falcon Hawks. As soon as one was gone the survivor would bring another mate and together they would maintain their right to the same territory.

But after a while they became so "skittish" that a pair of them would be seen around for days before they dared make a noise, which must have been a character test for such loud noise-making birds. Toward the last it became so difficult for the one bereaved to find another mate that quite a time would elapse before two of them would be seen in the sky. The time spent in silence afterward before making their presence known by screeching, lengthened accordingly. Finally the last one, unable to find a mate at all, vacated that part of the country. Thus, after an incessant fight of two years or more, the coast country was absolutely ridded of Blue Falcon Hawks.

The suggested reward, however, which had given Lafe his first incentive to make war on the hawks, and which had been earned by the boys many times over, was never paid; for though Lafe felt it was well due him, he never did openly present his claim to Mr. Goff.

But still there remained other hawks in the country. A smaller one, yellow with black and white stripes across its tail, we called the "Chicken Hawk." He also caught chickens, but in depredations was not to be compared with those that had been eliminated. There were also hawks that preyed upon rodents and let chickens alone. These "Big Yellow-tail Hawks" we never thought of killing but considered them very beneficial friends.

Two of these birds maintained a nest in a diminutive cave set in the face of the high precipice topped by old "Lion Head," which was much higher up the mountain than the several caves we children were wont to visit. Below this nest was a sheer drop of three hundred feet to a large irregular mass of boulders below.

Lafe greatly desired some hawk eggs for his collection. But as hawks always nested in inaccessible places these were very hard to get. Seeing that this cave was very evidently the location of a nest, Lafe eyed it longingly. Looking up from the point at the corral gate far below with an examining eye, the nest in the little cave appeared—by the enchantment of distance—to be very accessible from the mountain above it; and Lafe decided that he would perform the glorious achievement of climbing up to this nest in the cave, and securing the coveted hawk eggs.

His plan was to climb the mountain around and above the bluffs till directly on a line with the little cave, and then descend to reach it. This appeared entirely feasible, and the ascent was begun. He reached this objective point after a long hard climb and not without some difficulty, and from there began the descent which he had thought would be so easy. But it proved to be very hazardous indeed. That which from below had appeared to be mountain soil, he found to be a rock surface covered over with patches of moss that would loosen under pressure and slip downward as he stepped upon it. To depend upon its holding weight was entirely out of the question, and one incautious step might precipitate a plunge of three hundred feet to the boulders below. The farther down he went, the more hazardous it became. He debated whether or not to go on. But it was not like Lafe to turn back and give up in defeat when so near the goal. He wanted triumph and glory and he wanted the eggs, so kept on slowly and perseveringly. Finally he reached the cave and a foothold of reasonable safety.

But here he was awaited by an overwhelming disappointment. It had not occurred to him that there could be anything but eggs in the nest. But as he neared it, his ear was greeted by a chorus of "cheeps," and several wide-open mouths of young fledglings recently out of the shell rose upward on stretched out necks for expected food.

Overcome by a sudden realization of the futility and foolhardiness of his daring and arduous escapade, whose peril was by no means yet ended, the consciousness of which intensified his inward wrath at the disappointing climax, a great revulsion of feeling against the whole business and against all such risky undertakings in general welled up in his bosom and thirsted for revenge against his own folly and everything connected with it. To vent this impulse he seized the nest of fledglings and pitched them all out of the cave down onto the rocks far below, and then wondered how he was to get out of this scrape without following them in their fatal plunge.

He dreaded even to begin the ascent. Surely it was bound to be more perilous and difficult than had been the dangerous descent. But it had not only to be attempted but also accomplished if he were to go on living. So he started up, inching his way across the face of the bluff clinging to this and that and testing every foothold well before trusting it. At last without mishap he reached a place of safety where he could breathe freely once more. Never before had life seemed so precious to him. There and then he registered a vow that never again would he be so foolhardy as to risk life in such a manner. And that was the end of his bluff-climbing.

The Scrawny Fawn

The next spring Father put to the boys the proposition that if they would grub off the brush from a piece of raw foothill land that lay beyond the almond orchard, extending to the dry gulch, he would give them the use of it to farm for themselves. So they worked away industriously around the edges and during spare moments from regular farm work and chores, and finally at the end of the summer had the ground all cleared and ready for cultivation. It was too late to plant anything that season; but after winter rains came they plowed and prepared it for spring crops.

Father made an advance offer to pay them a cent a pound for all the corn they could raise on the piece. So they planted corn and tended it faithfully till the crop matured raising five hundred pounds of shelled corn. At the price paid, this netted them two dollars and fifty cents apiece—quite a sum for a half year's work.

The next spring they planted potatoes, which were harvested about May; and after digging these they decided to experiment with watermelons as a second crop—though it was very late to plant melons. Father bought their potatoes from them, and with part of the proceeds they put in a melon crop, which came up and made a fine stand— the vines blossoming well and filling out. But being a month later than they should have been, the melons, which should have matured in July were just beginning to ripen when August rolled around.

The boys watched these melons with pride, every day examining the curl and curl-leaf and tapping the melons, listening to hear whether the sound would be a "pank" indicating "green," or a "punk" for ripeness, and counting the days when they should be ready for picking. There were two large beauties ahead of all the rest that were ripening fast. These were almost ready to pick, and only waiting a few days longer for the sun to add a little more rich red color to the meat. Then something happened.

One morning as usual Lafe went down to look at the melons, taking along the little thirty-two as they frequently did—for no one knew when he might run onto some game. He went first to these two ripening melons. What was his wrath and disappointment at discovering that both of them had been selected by a discriminating deer for a delicious feast in the night! There they lay half-eaten, their red meat open to the sun. Lafe made a vow that he would get that deer before night.

Now Lafe had never yet shot a deer, and that gun, though George had accomplished the unusual with it, was considered much too small for such big game. Lafe had been trying for weeks to secure a deer without getting even a shot at one. The very day before, Mother had taken him to task for wasting his time and energy. He had reminded Mother of George's success with the gun. Why couldn't he do the same? Mother in turn had reminded him that George was a good hunter and though a good shot, even he could hardly ever hit a deer with it. Besides, the gun was old now and wearing out, and he might as well quit and do something more profitable.

So when Lafe made up his mind to get this deer, he said nothing at all to Mother about it, but started at once on the chase. The tracks led him first across the creek then along by the corn patch and up the eastern mountain. When about half way up he began to reason that the charge in the gun was not heavy enough for such big game. There should be a double charge of powder back of the bullet to send it with extra force. So he fired the gun to empty it and reloaded to his satisfaction before proceeding up the mountain.

He had climbed over the top of ridge after ridge without sighting any deer, when suddenly, there he was—a great buck with branching horns, his beautiful head poised, as he stood looking back at the pursuer from another ridge farther on, too far away to risk a shot. Lafe carefully worked his way around behind a bush out of sight of the animal, and then began to sneak up closer, keeping the bushes between them.

Suddenly, two does jumped up out of a gulch and ran along down the ridge; the buck following them down a canyon where they were soon out of sight. Taking the track, Lafe hurried after. Before long they were started again, being routed out of a patch of denser tree-size shrubbery. He raised his gun to position, and waited for them to stop and look back as fleeing deer always do, covering the big buck. At the precise moment that he stopped at a distance of about two hundred yards and looked back, Lafe fired. The buck dropped in his tracks.

With a yell like that of a Paiute Indian, Lafe threw his hat into the air. He had shot his first deer. Hastening over to the fallen buck, he discovered that the animal was not dead at all—scarcely injured in fact—for the bullet had been so spent before striking that it had only slightly dented the surface of the skull and could be picked out with the fingers. The buck was only stunned and if left alone would in a short time undoubtedly recover consciousness and regain his former powers. Had Lafe not reloaded his gun with a heavier charge the shot would have fallen short of its mark and the prey been lost. It was left for the young hunter then to cut the jugular vein—a customary act in any event to let out the blood. Then, thrilled beyond words, he made his way across the mountains for home to secure help to bring him in.

The deer had led him many a mile from his starting place at the melon patch, and now Lafe headed for the top of the bluff that overlooked the dwelling house from the rear where he had trapped his first hawk. Cupping his hands to his mouth, he gave a loud "Halloo!" which brought Father out of the house to see what it was all about. Then Lafe shouted:

"Saddle up old Ted and come up here! I've killed a deer!!!"

When Mother heard this, she said with good-natured incredulity:

"It's probably some scrawny little fawn that couldn't get out of the way!"

Father went up the mountain with Ted to meet Lafe, and together they made their way across the ridges to the slain buck, who was so large and heavy that they could scarcely get him onto the horse's back. Then, highly pleased over Lafe's achievement Father led Ted back down the mountains to the yard and deposited his burden at the end of the shed. No one could be more surprised than was Mother when she saw that big buck. Her face fairly glowed with pride. In her estimation, Lafe, as a deer-hunter rose to the top notch.

At the end of the shed they hung up the deer by the heels on a pulley and proceeded to skin him. When this part of the job was finished; their next move was to cut open the carcass down the front with the sharp butcher knife. As they were doing this, out from the cud-stomach of the deer fell the ripe watermelon eaten that morning in the boys' melon patch. Thus the culprit was identified and Lafe felt amply avenged for their loss. His vow had been fulfilled.

Father remarked to Lafe that now he was a real hunter he would have to get him a real rifle. This he did almost immediately, trading in his old revolver with some cash contributed by the boys, for a second-hand Smith and Wesson Winchester Repeater. And the days of muzzle-loading guns were at an end.

Two weeks after acquiring possession of this breech-loading rifle, Lafe killed his second deer, another buck, smaller than the first, and one that had been wounded at some time in the past, for he carried an old scar. Then we had so much venison on our hands, the two having been slain so close together, that the folks decided to "jerk" it—another term for drying.

We cut it up in small strips and strung it all along the clothesline from one end of the yard to the other, hanging each piece folded over the wire. When in a few days it had finished drying, we had almost a full flour sack of jerked venison. And was it good? Yes indeed! For many months we enjoyed that jerked venison. No meat ever tasted better. It made wonderful gravy, the rich sweet flavor remaining uninjured to the last; though it became so hard that it had to be well soaked before cooking.

But it didn't have to be cooked to taste good. The sun had both cooked and sweetened it. We children ate it ravenously just out of the sack. No matter how hard it was we would chew away at it enjoying every morsel. In walnut-gathering time before going down to the orchard to work, we would fill our pockets with it and munch as we picked up our nuts. When our own pocket was empty we would wheedle a bit more from someone else. Yes, it was delicious. Half a century has not effaced the memory of the wonder-fully intriguing flavor of that jerked venison.

CHAPTER 35 THE RUNAWAY

Shortly after Lafe secured his second deer, he and Father had a disagreement that led to serious consequences. Starting from a very trivial matter, as most such things do, it had grown to unnecessary proportions. During the altercation that ensued, Father lost his temper, and forgetting that the boy was now sixteen and a half and almost a man, administered to him a humiliating whipping.

For three days and nights the thing rankled in Lafe's bosom so that he could not sleep. He would get up during the night and wander about over the farm battling with a great resentment. Finally he came to the decision to run away and sever forever his allegiance to parental authority.

Lafe owned a little mare which had been given him when a newborn colt by Frank Goff who at the time was working the mother and did not want to be bothered by raising a colt. With Father's permission Lafe had taken this baby colt to raise, feeding her while very young on cows' milk with great solicitude, and when grown had broken her to the saddle. Now she was to carry him away into the unknown future.

In a little cabin up in Spring Canyon at this time, lived Bill Cousins, an American citizen of light complexion, who herded sheep on the Rawson Ranch, at that time rented to Look and Moulton. This man was well educated and friendly being one of the very few herders who was considered by the family in the light of an associate and friend. Often he visited us in Aliso, the boys and Father returning his visits.

Lafe, in order to accomplish his design of leaving home without betraying his purpose, asked permission to pass the night with Bill Cousins. This request being granted, he secretly collected together his few necessary belongings into a bundle, and keeping his intentions secret from all but Joseph, rode this little mare up the canyon to the cabin of Bill Cousins.

This friend, to whom he unfolded his grievance, endeavored to dissuade him from his purpose. For a time Lafe wavered, but finally came to the settled conclusion that he should carry out his original intention, and rode away from the cabin headed toward town. That day was the nineteenth of September Eighteen Eighty-Three.

Father afterward mistakenly blamed Bill Cousins for aiding and abetting Lafe in his getaway, and likewise Joseph for not informing him of Lafe's intention. This involved an undeserved chastisement for Joseph, whose young shoulders with his brother gone, were now to be weighted with an extra heavy burden of farm work.

We all felt grieved and lonesome over Lafe's departure, especially poor Mother who shed many secret tears over the whole affair. But none of us aside from Father, really blamed him for going. We little folks missed Lafe in more ways than one, for not only was he lively about the place, whistling and cutting up capers, but was also an inveterate tease.

One of his disconcerting tricks was to come up to one of us very small fry, the oldest not more than seven, and playfully but painfully tweak an ear, asking as he did so:

"Do you want that?"

"Of course I do!" was always the rather indignant answer with a move to protect the offended organ.

"All right then, I'll pull it off and give it to you," he would reply, proceeding forthwith to do so. This time it would be more than a tweak and just painful enough to extract from the victim a protesting:

"Ouch! "

Sometimes he would grab hold of a nose, scraping it none too gently, and immediately exhibiting before our eyes the protruding end of his thumb between two fingers of his fist, would announce:

"Now I've got your nose. See?" Highly amused to see us feel of our noses to make sure they were all there, he would finish by saying:

"Here it is, and your face is all bleeding." But it was not so much fun for his little victims. However, we liked him anyway, and it was rather dull around the place after he was gone.

Lafe set out for Tustin, where George was working temporarily for Gassy Smith at threshing beans, during an off-season from Chandler's ranch, where he had then been employed off and on for a year or so. The method then used for bean-threshing, was rather crude. A spot in the corral had been selected and swept clean of all loose earth down to the hard ground. The vines full of dry beans were then spread out on this clean hard area, and the men drove their teams over them back and forth, round and round to thresh out the beans. Smith drove one of his own teams and George drove his own horse hitched to the buckboard. After the beans were thus trampled out of their pods the crushed empty vines were gathered up into piles to be burned; and the loose beans collected, winnowed and sacked.

It was two o'clock in the night when Lafe arrived at Smith's place, so tying his horse to a hayrack, he crawled into the haystack for the rest of the night. There George found him when he arose in the morning to do the chores, and listened sympathetically to his story. Expecting that Father might look for him at Smith's, Lafe was anxious to get on as far as possible from home that day. Smith had a son-in-law in Los Angeles who, he said, was looking for a boy to work for him, and on the strength of this Lafe set out for Los Angeles.

He got only as far as Norwalk. That second night he stayed with a family friend who advised him against going to the city. Lafe then changed his mind and decided to look for a job in Norwalk. In order to raise money to live on meanwhile, he sold his horse and saddle to this man, who gave him twenty-five dollars cash for them. Soon he began work for a resident there by the name of Tabor at fifteen dollars a month and board. This man was a carpenter, and here Lafe had his first introduction to carpentry.

Artemisia, after staying with Mother about two months following the advent of baby Luella, had gone again in April to the home of Mrs. Chilton in Santa Ana, but was now in Norwalk, having recently taken a position at the home of Dr. Clark. Here Lafe looked her up in September and the two enjoyed a good visit, glad for the opportunity to be again together; for they had much to talk about.

Father, having discovered Lafe's whereabouts, came to see him at Norwalk and endeavored to persuade him to return home. Failing in this, he stated that he would bind him out as an apprentice to learn a trade. This pronouncement, however, he did not carry out, and within a month Lafe left Tabor's and went to Artesia, a small settlement about three miles to the south, which had been started some eight years previously. Here he made arrangements to attend school the remainder of the term, living with John Branch and his son Frank, old family friends, and working mornings, evenings, Saturdays and Sundays for his board and room.

At this time Artemisia was receiving attentions from a young man in Norwalk who had been introduced to her at the home of her friend Marcia Sprowle. He was very much in earnest but Mesia as usual was not deeply affected and did not at all realize how much he actually thought of her. Early in December she left her position there and went to San Pedro with a Mrs. Burkel, who was to give her music lessons, always an attractive bait for her, to supplement the eleven dollars offered as wages. To San Pedro the young man followed her, continuing to pay court.

Just before Christmas he came down to the waterfront to see her, and that evening as they stood on the porch of Mrs. Burkel's in the half-light, he produced from his vest pocket, a beautiful engagement ring which he essayed to place upon her finger, pouring out in burning words the love he had for her. Mesia was taken utterly by surprise. She had not expected this. There was nothing she could do but refuse his offer of marriage, for she did not care for him in the same way he cared for her. It was friendship merely. To give him pain was a grief to her, and when he went away deeply hurt, she knew that the pleasant friendship was ended. He came to see her no more.

With the forty dollars Lafe had received as the price of horse and saddle and a month's labor in Norwalk, he had bought for himself bedding, clothes and shoes, and when school was out the following spring, had still enough left to buy himself an ax, and went to cutting wood in the neighborhood.

Artesia at that time was little else than a name. There was a store and a schoolhouse, and a number of scattered residences, that was all. It was here that Annie Vance had lived at the time Sister Annie was named for her. Now she was married to Dick Thompson, and they had a little son Johnnie, the idol of his mother's heart.

Young Burden-Bearers

Joseph, not yet fifteen, had been left to bear the brunt of the heavy farm work; for Frank was six years younger than he and still a child. So upon his young shoulders rested a great burden of responsibility from which there was to be no release through the years to follow.

As the crop of late melons—the first two of which the buck had sampled—matured, Joseph would take them over to Laguna in the spring wagon, and sell them from house to house; continuing till the melons were all ripened and sold. From this persevering effort, he realized the sum of forty dollars—more money than he had ever before possessed. This signal success became an incentive for future adventures along the same line. He continued to raise melons and sell them during the summer, to dwellers in Laguna and to campers on the beach; and thus began what proved to be a long career of summer peddling of produce raised on the farm. Little by little, other farm produce besides watermelons was added to his load, until he was handling not only a variety of these, but also musk-melons and casabas, apples, grapes, figs, honey, corn, beans, cucumbers, tomatoes, potatoes, olives, nuts, eggs and poultry; with other things added occasionally.

Figure 27 Campers at Aliso Beach, 1915 [9]

Figure 28 Joseph and a Melon Crop, 1900

Figure 29 Joseph Thurston, 1883

This peddling added much extra work to the regular farm routine, and required that he toil very hard indeed early and late, with such help as the growing children could render. At an early age, I began to pick up potatoes, hoe weeds, sucker corn, ride the horse to cultivate, rake hay after the shocks were loaded onto the rack, help in harvesting apples, figs and nuts; besides my regular job of herding hogs, and my share of the lighter household tasks such as washing dishes and carrying water. We all worked. It never once occurred to us that working was anything else but a normal life. I am sure it was good for us and went far toward keeping us clean and moral; for idle hands and mischief are, and have always been boon companions. Still, there is such a thing as overwork. At least three of the children of Aliso, George, Joseph and Joan, were compelled in their turn to bear more responsibility and hard work than they should have.

Joan was only ten years old when Mesia, the next older sister left home; and upon her young shoulders descended a great burden of household duties far too arduous for a child so young. At an early age, she began to sew for the large family of children and more and more the burden of all the sewing of the family fell upon her; and as the years went by, the responsibility of the cooking, washing and ironing. At twelve, she was a woman doing a woman's work; and much more work than most American women do today. Undoubtedly, this hard work in her early youth laid the foundation of the ill health that hampered her during all her after life.

Hulda, of course, assisted with the housework, and always with the washings. But the burden of the managing and accomplishing was left to rest upon Joan's shoulders. Though well intentioned, Hulda was inclined to be a dreamer and irresponsible. For years her regular task was to look after the little folks of the household. Often she would take long pleasant walks with the babies in her charge, a diversion denied to Joan because of weightier tasks, but nevertheless longed for most ardently.

When the morning's early work was done, often Hulda, taking a basket of socks and stockings to darn or other mending, perhaps buttonholes to be worked, would go far away from the household's confusion and responsibilities, and finding a shady seat on some creek-side bank, would sit and darn and dream where the wild birds were singing, the stream murmuring, the trees whispering and the blue skies smiling. Because so employed there was no thought in her mind but that she was fulfilling her share of the home duties, the more arduous of which must therefore devolve upon Joan, for whom there were no such pleasures.

Upon her return, perhaps at sundown, or when the call of appetite drew her to the supper table and evening dishes, invariably Mother would compliment her upon her neatness and dexterity with the needle, never seeming to realize that a compliment might be due to Joan who meanwhile had been occupied incessantly with heavier and far less romantic tasks amid the heat and confusion of the steamy kitchen, or perhaps treading the sewing machine with bent back, or cutting out and planning new garments, laying out work that would take her far into the night to finish. No singing birds, murmuring streams, blue skies and whispering winds for her, but a treadmill of drudgery hour after hour and day after day; while her own young heart longed too for the out-of-doors and relief from responsibilities. Only the memory was hers now past of happier and more care-free days when she had been assigned the joyful duty of hunting hens' nests among the brush of the hillsides around and was free to roam at will unfettered in pursuance of this pleasant task.

So much of Mother's time was occupied with raising chickens, making butter, and other such tasks, along with child-bearing, nursing and tending infants, that as she grew older and less inclined to hard work, gradually more and more, she slipped out from under the burden of housework and let it fall upon younger shoulders. This was as it should be had Joan been older, but the child was too young to have borne so much as came to devolve upon her while immature.

Father, years before had slackened up his pace, allowing the heavy burdens of farm work to be carried by those younger. He attended to honey extracting, wine-making, general errands into town, and the discussion of politics while others worked the farm under his supervision.

In the very nature of the case, George, being the oldest child, had been early overloaded with farm work, having scarcely any time for recreations; and so it came about that these three, George, Joseph and Joan, stood as keystones in the arch, each in turn holding upon shoulders too young, the weight of the structure.

CHAPTER 36 THE LOST CREEK OF MY CHILDHOOD

The creek of my earliest childhood memory was broken at intervals throughout its whole length by little waterfalls, varying in height from one to three feet; which added charm and interest to its general beauty. There were no less than a dozen of these within a mile and a half of the pond, but the series extended clear to the source of the stream, and a goodly number were in our own creek-bottom, near at hand.

All these waterfalls had their origin at the spot where the creek emptied into the upper end of the pond and were started at the time of winter floods. Some of the salt-grass at this junction would be cut away by the swift current, and the stream, as it became normal again, flowing from the firmer salt-grassed portion of the bed onto the softer un-grassed portion, would wash some of its earth away; and there would begin the process of receding erosion by which the tiny waterfall thus formed would travel backward gradually up the creek, gaining in height perhaps, in its progress, but never catching up with those that had preceded it; and always new ones were forming below to follow in their turn. During the winter season they would cut back rapidly, but in summer barely perceptibly.

The pond was prevented from filling up with sediment by the thorough scouring out it received frequently when a flood, sweeping down its whole length would break through its lower end, cutting a channel across the stretch of sandy beach to the ocean itself; which later would retaliate by again filling up the channel with sand. Thus salt water was more or less mingled with the fresh water of the pond, favoring the growth of salt-loving vegetation.

When the family first came to the canyon, the pond was somewhat smaller and narrower than it afterward became, and more distinctly pear-shaped, and the marsh weeds were confined to the banks alone. Its banks were not then abrupt and steep as in later times, but sloped gradually to the water's edge. And on either side of the pond was good rich soil—howbeit somewhat affected by the salty nature of the water that lapped its borders and occasionally overflowed.

The triangle was at first covered with rank malvia, and the flats on the opposite side of the pond with tall mustard. For a time Father raised corn and potatoes on this land, and also found it useful as pasture. But repeated inundations and resulting erosions extended the permanent area of the pond, leaving precipitous banks and paving the way for the overspreading of the marsh weeds, which eventually took almost the whole flat. In my childhood it was covered several feet deep with a solid, thick, spongy mat in which anyone attempting to cross would flounder helplessly and be obliged to retreat.

There were years when drowth lessened the season's rainfall so much that the creek would almost dry up in summer, leaving only puddles with here and there a mere trickle of moving water. At such times the salt-grass thrived, forming an unbroken carpet throughout much of its length and breadth. Not that it was soft and velvety like a carpet; salt-grass is not of that nature. It forms hard sharp-pointed sheaths in maturing, that spear even the tough soles of bare feet. To avoid this, we would scuff through it, striking the points sidewise. But if speared, as often occurred, we would hop or limp to a seat on the bank, and turning up the sole, search for the small offending spear-point sticking there; meanwhile calling: "Wait for me!" to the others forging on ahead. After extracting it we would limp philosophically after them, soon forgetting the wound—for who could be bothered by little things like salt-grass spears?

All along the banks of the creek scattered here and there in moist sheltered places, grew wild celery, often tough, strong and smarting to the tongue, but when young and tender, quite palatable. And we snapped off its stalks to munch as we walked along.

Wild Indian Rhubarb, which we children called "soury dock," sending up in the springtime its tall, leafless flowerscapes panicled with white or rose-colored bloom, was another edible plant that flourished along the creek. Of this, we ate sparingly, for it was so sour our mouths watered even to look at it. Still, it must be that we sample it in passing.

Among other plants in the wet, sandy creek-bottom, grew the wild yerba manza in rank luxuriance, its broad green leaves spreading out from a center stalk like those of the sour dock. Its semi-pyramidal center of closely-packed insignificant flowerets surrounded by showy white bracts sat jauntily on the top of the stem like a Mexican sombrero. This plant was considered to be of value medicinally, and found its place in Mother's cellar.

When the willow buds first came out in the spring and every bough flaunted its burden of challenging fingers, before they burst into white cotton we gathered the long tender green tassels, covered like berries with tiny protuberances, and nibbled them off to the midrib to chew for awhile and then swallow. But if the cottony process were too far advanced we found our mouths filling with cotton, only to be quickly emptied again with some effort.

Directly below the house grew the largest and rankest patch of tules. Through these, narrow beaten footpaths crossed the creek to the fence where we entered the vineyard by crawling under the wires. On that side, just below this tule patch, was a series of pools in the creek—or more properly puddles—that had been cut into the creek-bed by swirling waters in flood time and never after completely refilled. These pools had become lined with salt-grass and were usually full of water. Some of the neighbor children had told us that horse hairs when pulled unbroken from horses' tails with a tiny raw fleshy speck adhering, if left undisturbed in water for several weeks would turn into snakes. So, forsooth, we must put this to the test.

Securing some of these hairs, we put them into one of the little puddles where we thought they would not be disturbed and left them there. Scarcely a day passed but we went down to see if there had yet been any change in the hairs. After a while, as we watched, they began to swell up and grow a little bit thicker, and in several weeks' time began to wiggle a little snake-like in the water. We looked in vain for heads to appear and complete the transmutation. But greatly encouraged by the snake-like indications, we concluded that perhaps everything had not been conducted just right, and that if we only persisted in our experiment the promised snakes would eventually be forthcoming. So all summer long we were putting new hairs into puddles, hoping for snakes indeed. But never were we able to make conditions exactly right for the production of snakes with heads, and finally concluded they must have meant headless snakes.

Sometimes in the many little pools of the creek were real snakes-water snakes, darting about under the surface. Often I tried to catch them. But they were very swift little fellows and had no notion of allowing themselves to be apprehended. Every time I made a dive with my hand to catch one of them, lo, he had slipped through my fingers and was gone.

But sometimes when the weather was very warm, the water would lower so much in these little pools that the snakes would find themselves imprisoned in a very small amount of water with a very narrow basin in which to swim about. Then was my chance to make a capture. So rapidly did they dart hither and yon across the pool that even then it was far from an easy matter to lay hold of one. However, I would not give up, and at last, my efforts rewarded with success, I held a wriggling snake in my hand.

Lifting him by the tail before an admiring audience of younger sisters, I swung him in triumphant glee several times about my head before tossing him out into the weeds, where he wriggled away as swiftly as he had moved in the water. I-laving once succeeded, my appetite for snake-fishing grew, and the performance was often repeated, even broadening out into land-snakes.

We made watermelon boats for the navigation of these and other pools, the melon being cut in halves lengthwise instead of the usual slices.

"Oh, save that one for a boat!" we would plead concerning one of a specially suitable shape. Then our elders would cut it in halves, dig out the center for eating, and give us the rind; which we would scrape very smooth, making a hole in the stem end for a steering string, and carry it down to the creek to sail about on all the "seven seas" giving many a weed doll a joyous voyage and carrying many a cargo from port to port.

That part of the creek that lay within our limits—barring a lesser portion at either end—was lined along both its banks with willows; which in places from fence to water-mark had become dense hedges. In one stretch extending the length of the general orchard, the hedge by voluntary multiplication, had widened into a thicket, dense with undergrowth and swampy.

In the shadowed coolness of this thicket, near its terminus where the interrupting road coming down from the house passed through the cart-road gate and crossed the sandy strip to the creek, reposed the duck-pond-a shallow oblong muddy pool, deepening to the center from sloping sides, its surface splotched with patches of sunshine that filtered through the dense overhanging branches.

Here, the ducks held forth, swimming about and digging their bills down under the water into the mud of the bottom to obtain various delicacies, and at evening time came contentedly quacking home in a long string.

I once stood watching the ducks swimming about in this little pond, when an old mother hen that had been set on duck eggs brought her newly hatched brood down to the creek to scratch in the moist earth of the banks for worms and bugs. To her intense alarm the babies all left her and went boldly into the water to swim, paying no attention whatever to her excited cluckings and frantic efforts to induce them to come out again. With mingled pity for the poor mother hen and envy of the disobedient but more highly accomplished ducklings, I watched this episode marveling that the little ducklings just out of their shells should swim quite as well as their elders and dive about in the same fashion without the trouble of learning, while I, though quite a big girl, could not swim even one stroke. I envied them and almost wished that I too, were a little yellow duckling.

At the northern end of this thicket, where was a treeless "gap," a footpath went from the creek up the bank under the gateless wire fence and crossed the plowed ground to the barn; thus becoming a dividing line between the apple trees and the general orchard. Here, where the thicket narrowed back from the creek toward the fence, partly in the shade and partly in the sun, was a bed of black genuine clay—though we called it "mud"—which Mother Nature seemed to have deposited there for our especial benefit; for there was not another bed of it anywhere so far as we knew. This was one of our most interesting and delightful possessions. Hour after hour we played here—or worked—in this natural factory, busily turning out our wares; which varied all the way from pies and cakes, to the pans in which they were to be baked and the dishes in which they were to be served-yes, even to the little black people that were supposed to eat them.

These last were our chief product—dolls; dolls of all sizes, from tiny infants of an inch or two in height to great mother-dolls and father-dolls eighteen and twenty inches tall. These were none of your modern movable jointed beauties, to be sure; but of such we knew nothing, and that which is not known is not missed. Besides, no child has ever had the privilege of manufacturing such dolls as these moderns; and since the joy of creation is infinitely greater than the joy of possession, were not we the more richly blest?

The larger dolls, we reinforced with willow bones at the joining places, sticking them one half into the trunk and the other half into head, or arm or leg; and though these articulations were thus rendered somewhat ankylosed, still, we had for our pattern the china store-dolls made by our betters of those days, and stiff as any mummy.

The heads we fashioned either round—rolling them like a ball in our palms—or oblong by flattening the ball, according to fancy, sometimes attempting features. We bent the ends of arms for hands and legs for feet not bothering with little things like fingers and toes, and when finished laid them out prone in the hot sun to dry for several days; after which they were hard enough to stand any ordinary usage without breaking. Though crude, they served their day and generation admirably. However, it must be confessed that their color was against them. It was much more fun to make them than to play with them afterward. What mattered it if our own bare arms and legs became splotched with mud? Was mud not easily washed off? And our dresses—were not dresses made to play in? The washing of them was no affair of ours. So the doll-and-pottery factory flourished.

Just up the bank opposite the location of our factory, inside and along the fence, was a short row of most beautiful acacia trees; their lacey, fernlike foliage lending grace and charm to the practical orchards. In blooming time these were covered with gorgeous yellow, furry tassels of exquisite beauty. Every spring we watched with eager delight this developing glory from the first unfolding bud, drawn by their magic attraction to play underneath these trees in the sandy ground. We loved these tassels and gathered them to play with, drawing them caressingly across our faces, inhaling their subtle and delicate fragrance. They reminded us of nothing so much as little newly-hatched downy yellow chicks.

On the other side of the creek just opposite the clay factory was "George's Ground" in its hillside nook, beckoning us to play over there in the flower garden whenever we should tire of the clay beds. We liked to pull on the rope and bucket that hung in the little well on its sloping bank, and try to lift water for the flowers.

But more often we stayed on the near side, and sought the sandy strip under the curving row of huge old willows that hugged the northern end of the apple orchard just outside the fence; supplemented around the bend by a number of shady old pepper trees that straggled as far south as the treeless gap and dividing path.

From underneath this crescent of willows and peppers a wide strip of clean curving sand sloped gently downward, becoming grassy as it neared the low bank of the stream with its little singing waterfalls; making a most wonderful playground. Here we spent long summer hours in sun or shade as fancy willed, in the pure enjoyment of carefree early childhood. We built doll houses with extensive farms in the moist sand, or whole cities with tree-bordered streets, transplanting as we built from the supply always near at hand of wild nursery stock.

There was a low, spreading, bunchy grass that grew all along the creek bottom in the damp sand, whose soft, furry tassels very much resembled miniature Pampas Grass plumes. These, for lack of a better name, we called "pussy-tails." Sometimes we planted their velvet-tipped center stalks in our streets and yards for ornamental trees, and sometimes, shortening the stems, we used them for people.

We climbed the old spreading low-crotched willow trees hunting for birds' nests, munched the celery found hidden in the weeds at their feet, sucked the sweet from the pepper berries after rubbing off their skins, and sometimes, when Autumn's mellowing days drew on, we slipped up the bank and under the fence into the apple orchard and helped ourselves to the half-ripe fallen apples.

On the northern side of the creek bend, directly across from this curving sandy playground, was a picturesque old-fashioned gate that opened into the lower end of the barley ground. Its horizontal poles and crossbeams were built of young slender Eucalyptus trees, cut whole and roughly trimmed, and hung to upright posts of the same.

The narrow wagon-road entered the creek-bottom from its southern side farther up the creek. Descending the gradual slope of the saltgrass covered bank to the edge of the narrow stream, it followed alongside for some distance, passing little waterfalls, and finally, crossing the creek, windingly in and out among the dense young willows in the bottoms, then up the easy slope to the bare trampled earth at the gate. After passing through the gate, the road turned abruptly to the right, and now inside followed the fence for some distance under the shade of bordering old willows.

Farther up the creek was the old "swimming hole," a large oblong indentation of twenty-five or thirty feet in length, in the middle of the creek bed, rimmed with weedy vegetation and margins of salt-grass, and nearly always full of clear water from the little falls above it. The sides of it sloped rather steeply and muddily down to the center, where its depth was far over the heads of us very young bathers, who played and dabbled around in its edges not venturing far down the slippery sides. Only the older children dared go in so far, the boys swimming like ducks across its length.

Sometimes the flock of ducks would leave their own special feeding grounds and the pool in the thicket, and come waddling in a long file up the creek-bottom to our swimming hole. And here they would sail about in grand style at times when their use of it was undisputed. But if found there when we came to bathe, we would unceremoniously drive them out and take possession.

There were other pools farther on in this wonderful creek. Memory recalls one that was quite deep but not very broad, and bordered all around with clumps of vegetation higher than my head; where I stood and watched the "darning needles" dart swiftly back and forth above its surface, poising for an instant after every swift movement, each with his double pair of long silver gauzy wings extended straight out from his slender black body like the wings of an airplane—only such a word had never yet been coined. For a long time I tried to catch one, but in vain. No clumsy human movements could match such easy speed and grace. We had not yet learned that these beautiful creatures should be called "Dragon-flies."

There were "skaters" on this pool too, that with one deft kick skated more than a foot at a time—though scarcely as large as mosquitoes—leaving the tiniest of riffles in their wake.

Then there were the more clumsy "water bugs" that dived beneath the water and the gnats that swarmed above it. I did not like the gnats; but most likely it was their presence there that drew the darning needles-for whom a few good fat gnats would make a most delectable dinner.

Still farther up the creek, almost as far as the "second gate" on the southern side, just opposite the "mustard patch," lay a series of narrow deep muddy pools, tucked closely together up against and under the foot of a shelving bank that was hard and weedy above, but muddy near and under the water; and here lived the "mud turtles." At any time of day we might surprise half a dozen or so sunning themselves on this shelving bank; but at the first sound of our approach down they would slide as quick as a wink with little "splash-splashes" into the water, leaving no more than a ripple to show that such a creature as a mud turtle existed. In vain would we wait around hoping to catch another glimpse of them. All was still and quiet in "mud-turtle heaven."

A short distance farther on, were pools shallower and more stagnant where the "pollywogs" lived. Sometimes we found in these pools, long loops of countless little black frog-eggs, each in a separate globule of transparent jelly and all strung together like beads, floating in the sun-warmed water. Little pollywogs in all stages of development were there, from tiny ones just hatched to great puffy ones with transparent hindquarters, revealing distinct outlines of a pair of legs just waiting to break through. Or it might be that they were already through, emerging with increasing size from under a diminishing tail. We scooped up cans full of this water containing as many as we could catch of the larger pollywogs, and carried them home to watch the completion of the metamorphosis; and within a week or so little green frogs were hopping about among our cans and everywhere, but the pollywogs were all gone.

After that, when there were no more pollywogs anywhere, oh, what choruses of frog-songs we would hear every evening down in the creek!

CHAPTER 37 THE FLOOD

The winter of Eighteen Eighty-Four is said to have been the wettest this country of the Southland has ever seen. The year also is unique in that at least some rain came down from the skies during every month of the entire twelve. Breaking the protracted drowth of a "dry year," rain began to fall on the twentieth day of January and continued incessantly and at broken intervals for weeks at a time all through the remainder of the winter and spring. The total rainfall for the year, most of which fell before the end of May, is recorded as forty-eight inches.

The whole country was soaked so full of water that it bogged everywhere. Large areas of lower lands became vast lakes. One could take a row boat at Yorba and row over submerged farming lands westward clear to Wilmington, a distance of something like forty-five miles. Roads were impassable. Floods raged and rampaged. Bridges were washed out. Trains were held up. And grocery prices soared. For some time, flour purchases were limited to one sack for a family, and other articles accordingly.

Supplies of dry goods and groceries for the merchants of Santa Ana and other towns of that area were brought in from San Francisco to Newport by boat, then the only means of transportation, where they were unloaded onto the pier. To get the goods up from Newport to Santa Ana was a muddy, boggy job, and much of the time impossible.

There were only two wagon bridges in the southern part of the country that escaped being washed out, one over the Santa Ana River and the other over the San Gabriel. Between these lay the town of Anaheim. To obtain the United States mail, the four-horse stage floundered through the mud from Santa Ana to Los Angeles making a great detour to cross these bridges.

Into the Santa Ana River flows its tributary, the Santiago Creek, at their junction west of town. Beginning at a point below this junction, the river that winter cut an entirely new channel to the sea, so that it emptied as it still does about three miles below its old outlet, leaving a territory between the old and new channels that varied in width from one to three miles.

During this time torrents of rain fell in the Los Angeles area and floods followed in that region with great damage. Upwards of fifty houses were washed away with vineyards and orchards in the low-lying sections of the city, and several lives were lost, a state that existed generally throughout the country.

The whole Artesia district where Lafe was then attending school, was a boggy mess of water and slush. For long stretches roads were unfit for travel. For a distance of several hundred yards through the center of the community, men of the place, joined by Lafe, built up the road by cutting branches from cypress hedges and strewing them thickly along its surface to enable the teams to pass through. Roads then being very narrow, two teams happening to meet, could not pass each other without bogging to the hubs.

Aliso Canyon is the natural watershed of the coast ranges for a distance of about twenty miles north and south. Laguna Canyon immediately to the north of it drains only a small area of adjacent territory, its two lakes catching and holding the water and distributing it gradually, and so mitigating the danger of floods in that region. North of that, the Santa Ana River, cutting through Bedrock Canyon between the Santa Ana Mountains and the Chino Hills, drains these and the San Bernardino ranges as well as portions of the nearer Santiago Mountains including the beautiful Orange County Park.

To the south of Aliso, the nearest outlet of any consequence is San Juan Creek, reinforced by the Trabuco, that drains the mountain ranges in that territory and empties into the ocean at the Capistrano beach.

Aliso Creek then, is the only outlet for all the waters collected from the mountains intervening between these two sets of ranges. This is why we were subject to so many floods that roared down the creek past our dwelling in winter, swelling the otherwise modest stream into a raging torrent, whose murky waters when lowered left their "flood-stuffs" clinging to trees, fence posts and ledges along its course.

Most of these floods made changes of a more or less minor nature along the course of the stream-bed. But the great flood of Eighteen Eighty-Four, beginning February fourteen, so far exceeded all its predecessors in changes wrought and damage done that it has ever since by common consent been designated as "the flood." Great trees were uprooted, fences torn out, sloping banks cut away, and with them valuable land, leaving instead perpendicular declivities along unprotected orchards. And old roads were destroyed.

Rains in the latter part of January had been heavy, and the ground was saturated with water. February opened with intermittent showers and sunny days smiling between. On the evening of that eventful Saint Valentine's Day, a party in its celebration was to be given at the home of Hubbard Goff, and our three young folks had been invited: Joseph, aged fifteen, Joan about twelve and a half, and Hulda not yet eleven.

The girls decided to walk over early, a distance of nearly two mountainous miles, and spend the afternoon preceding the party; while Joseph, who had the usual farm chores to do in the evening, planned to drive over afterward with the spring wagon to join them at the party and bring them home afterward.

It was a long walk over the hilly road from Aliso to Hub Goff's Hubbard place. After climbing the narrow trail through the brush up the side of Frank Goff Bench and crossing the first part of the mesa, there was a deep ravine to descend and ascend again, followed by several smaller gullies, and the road was rough and gravelly. They would endeavor to keep in one or the other of the wheel-ruts to keep from scuffing their party shoes and staining them from the weeds that occupied the center of the road between, and to protect their party dresses from catching on the bushes growing close alongside or leaning over banks above the grades.

By the time they reached their destination, the sky had become overcast, and dark clouds gathering over the ocean foreboded rain. But everyone was so glad to see them, and they were soon having such a good time that not much attention was given to the weather until about dusk when it began to rain. Then was felt concern for the success of the party.

In spite of the rain most of the guests arrived, and they went ahead with the festivities, having a merry time with indoor games and refreshments. But Joseph did not appear. Discerning the ominous portents of a storm, he had wisely given up the party.

The rain kept falling steadily, increasing till it became a torrential downpour; which continued without abatement all night long. It was late the next day before the weather cleared sufficiently to allow the girls to start for home. Their friends urged them to stay on until Joseph should come for them after the storm was over. But they were determined to go. There was work to be done. They were needed at home. Permission to stay so long had not been granted, and besides Mother would be worried. They knew too that the creek was likely to rise so high they could not get across it, and the longer it should rain the more difficult would it be. Had they not persisted in this determination it would have been about two weeks before they could have returned home or anyone from Aliso could have reached them.

The Goff boys, Onnie and Sherman, about their own ages, hitched up their team to the wagon to take the girls home. Over the slippery muddy road, they made their way until they reached the high bluffs overlooking the sandy beach road that rounded the pond and the triangle. Here, to their dismay, they saw that the pond had broken through the strip of beach to the ocean and a great impassable channel was cut across the road filled with surging water. Having gone as far as was possible with the team, there was then only one way for the girls to proceed. That was to descend afoot the steep and muddy trail among the wet overhanging bushes down the side of the bench into Aliso Canyon. The creek being very evidently high, it was with many misgivings that they climbed out of the wagon and after bidding goodbye to their escorts, started down the slippery trail.

They had not reached the bottom before perceiving that a really great flood was before them, and the usual footpath around the point at the fourth bend above the stream, was now buried under many feet of rolling, turbid waters. There was no other path around this bend. The high, brush covered point jutting out from the bench, at the foot of which was the submerged path, they had never before assayed to climb, and no trails had been beaten up its side. But now this seemed the only way out of their dilemma, for only by scaling this point and again descending its other side opposite the almond orchard, could they hope to get around the raging waters into the orchards and vineyard beyond.

So up they started, clinging to the wet bushes to keep from slipping back down its steep incline, their party shoes seeking foothold in the muddy soil and gravel and their party dresses drenched and soiled by contact with the dripping vegetation. Finally they reached the top and went down on the other side. Between them and the almond orchard lay the deep gully, where recently a roaring freshet had contributed its quota to the swollen waters of the creek, and in the depths of which a muddy trickle still flowed. This gully could be crossed only at a higher and narrower spot. So following the mountain's foot for a distance, they at length crossed the gully and entered the orchard, intending to take the diagonal path that led through it to the crossing below the house; for the flood still lay between them and home.

But the cultivated ground proved to be so soaked and miry that walking upon it even in the path meant sinking almost to the knees. So it was necessary to detour, skirting the orchards and keeping close to the foot of the curving mountain where the ground was firm, till they came to Vineyard Point. From there, they could look across the muddy expanse of orchard and vineyard to the Little Hill on the farther side of the creek almost opposite; and through the willows discern the dwelling house, nestled against the farther hillside, separated from them by the roaring waters.

It happened that Joseph had come down from the house to watch the rolling flood, and was standing directly opposite on the further bank. He saw the girls and shouted to them—his welcome voice carrying to their ears above the deafening roar. So, with vineyard and flood between them, they shouted back and forth to each other till the girls understood Joseph's directions as to how they might be helped across to the home side of the home side of the torrent. He told them to go up two points farther to the north, where the bed of the stream was wider and the water shallower and less swift; and that he would go to the barn and get a horse to bring them across the flood there. No horse could make it in the swift deep current where he then was at the roadway. So Joseph departed on his errand and the girls went on, following the hill at the rear of the vineyard as it curved to the low, flat-topped spur that jutted out from the hill almost into the creek, whose swollen waters now lapped its front.

Here, they followed the well-worn path up over the top of the spur, and down on the other side into George's Ground. Crossing the garden, which along its lower edge was flooded, they climbed for the first time in their lives up over the next rocky pathless point that separated the garden from the "barley ground" at the second bend, and descended into the open field below. Here was the broader stretch of rolling yellow water spread out before them, sweeping past the fence and rustic gate near at hand, and the apple orchard on the farther shore. Though lowered from the highwater mark of the night before, it still presented a formidable obstacle and they wondered fearfully how it was to be overcome.

But when they saw Joseph on the opposite shore leading faithful old Ted to the edge of the river, their fears all vanished for to them a boy and a horse made everything all right. Into the surging waters went this boy and horse, carefully feeling their way, knee-deep, belly-deep, up on the sides with nose raised high, safely fording the turbid stream and clambering up the muddy bank where waited the marooned sisters. Then with Hulda astride the horse behind him, Joseph guided him back again to the home-side, leaving her there while he returned to fetch Joan.

Dusk was falling when they stood at last together on the safe side of the flood—two of the happiest girls imaginable, in spite of the poor bedraggled party dresses and ruined shoes that never again could grace the festive scenes of a Valentine party.

But with the first feelings of relief were soon mingled emotions of deep concern for the havoc beheld on every side. The great flood had risen higher than any that had preceded it since the family had settled in the canyon. The whole of the apple orchard had been submerged; the water sweeping even to the stable and barn. All the lower land from there to the little hill, most of the vineyard and walnut orchard and the cart-road garden had been under water when the flood was at its height. Some of the orchard trees were leaning, their foothold weakened in the mucky soil. And wrapped around them, piled to a height of several feet, was a tangle of flood refuse lodged against practically every tree and grapevine in the path of the over-flow. Fence posts were washed out and lay wherever they had lodged partly buried in a tangle of barbed wire and flood refuse. Great trees that had stood along the creek banks were missing. The sturdy old willows and pepper trees at the end of the apple orchard were being torn out one by one, and land now unprotected was caving and falling into the racing waters—and the end was not yet.

I remember standing—a child of eight—with others after the rain had ceased and the overflow subsided, near the end of the apple orchard, now stripped and denuded, and watching the swirling current continue to undermine the banks. Slab after slab would slip off with hardly a splash into the swift depths below—for here it was very deep and moving rapidly. We wondered where it would end. What a forlorn and bewildered feeling came over me at sight of all this heart-sickening devastation! It seemed to me as though the whole world was changing.

That week Father and Joseph worked hard in the mud and rain in an effort to protect the land from further erosion. They set green willow posts deep in the ground along the banks and strung them with several strands of barbed wire, piling brush and flood refuse tightly against them. But the elements of destruction were not yet through with their baleful work.

The rains, resuming, continued to pour out their vials upon a saturated earth, preventing the creek from returning to its normal waterline. And just one week from the first flood another of almost equal severity swept down in its wake and completed the devastation, washing away all their work of the past week, with many more trees, some of them apple trees, whose root-holds had been weakened, and adding greatly to the general erosion.

After this second overflow had subsided, while still the flood was raging, Joseph, Joan and Hulda, putting on old shoes for the muddy tramp, started out afoot to see how far they could go toward the beach on the home side of the unfordable flood. Their purpose was to ascertain what was taking place by way of damage along its course below. Avoiding the muddy wagon-road, they entered the cart-road garden by way of the path over the little hill, and at its southern tip came up against the towering canyon wall at the third bend. Here the flood was pounding against the bare rock of the hill, piling up high in its forced turn, and submerging all the path below, together with the clump of mingled wild roses, nettles, and poison oak where the boys had slain their rattler.

They could go no further without scaling the mountain. Not to be baffled, they started up its steep, pathless, brush-covered side toward the "gap" that dipped into the high rocky bluff at its rim. It was a toilsome climb, but finally reaching the summit, they were rewarded with a grand view of the whole scene. Looking down toward the "corn patch" and the fifth bend, they saw that there also the water was piling up against the wall of the canyon as it turned toward the pond.

Descending the other side of the mountain and Lee Goff Bench, they came to the beach and the triangle, where they stood and watched the process of erosion taking place along both banks of the pond. Occasionally large slabs would break off and sink down into the roily waters below.

The flood was pouring through the temporary channel out across the beach into the ocean and mingling there with the tossing waves, which in return pounded their way through the channel into the pond, as they sped far up the beach to the foot of the triangle and the bluff on the farther side. The area of the pond had widened clear to the foot-line of Frank Goff Bench.

There, facing the pond, a series of broad steps had been cut out of the hill, reaching up to the foot-trail that meandered above them to the top of the bench. The erosion was progressing toward these steps.

Returning homeward by the way they had come, they once again paused on the summit to enjoy the view afforded on every side—range after range of mountains in the distance, the white beaches, and the broad expanse of ocean stretching away to the far horizon. Reaching home, their report of conditions below included the expressed fear that the steps up the bench would also be taken away before long.

A few days later when the flood had subsided to a depth that could be waded, Hulda, then the official baby-tender of the family, took the three youngest, Annie, Charlotte, and Baby Luella, a tiny tot of one year whom she carried on her back, and with them started out to visit the pond again. They waded the creek below the house, traversed the diagonal path across the walnut orchard that led to the far end of the Eucalyptus row, and there forded the stream again where it broadened at the fourth bend, climbed the bank beyond, and made for these steps. She found that several of the lower steps had been cut away entirely, the upper ones only remaining with some appearance of solidarity. She seated herself with her precious charges upon the topmost of these, and gave herself up to dreamy meditation, as she watched the wide pond below and the distant play of restless waves along the beach. The children too were quiet.

The channel from pond to sea had been again filled in with sand, and the pond, having now no outlet to the sea, and still fed by the steadily flowing creek, was backing up again to the high-water mark and lapping gently the lower steps of their perch.

For some time they sat there, then when it was time to return home, left the steps and climbed down the bank, recrossing the creek and orchards as they had come.

The next day Joseph returning from a trip to the pond, reported that all the steps had now disappeared, having collapsed and fallen into the water below. Hulda shuddered. What if the climax had come while she sat with her precious little charges on that dangerous perch only the day before? How foolhardy she had been! Surely the old saying must be true that "A special Providence watches over fools and little children."

Gone With The Flood

After the flood was over, it was a strange and unfamiliar scene that greeted us for the whole length of the waterway. The channel of the creek had been widened and deepened and its appearance changed completely. At every bend of the creek the earth was cut away to the bare rocks of the canyon walls. Familiar paths over which we had trodden for years were now no more. Wagon roads that had been travelled around these points ever since we children could remember were gone forever. There could be no repairing of the old. New roads must be built in new places.

At the first bend where had stood the old leaning willow, the second gate, and downward-turning road before Sycamore Canyon, the land was cut away to the foot of the mountain, leaving barely room enough for a footpath around the point. Gate, fence, gnarled old willow tree, slanting road and sloping bank, all were gone, giving place to a perpendicular wall of naked earth twenty feet high, and changing the right-angled bend to a deep curve.

Near the second bend, nothing was left of the entrance to the barley ground save a tangle of broken wire fencing. The picturesque old gate of poles, the forest of young willows, the winding road among them up the sloping bank, could never more be anything but a memory.

The curving row of shady old willows opposite that had joined the pepper trees in a crescent around the upper end of the apple orchard, had all been ruthlessly torn up by the roots and carried away in the cruel flood. Of that loved sandy playground beneath them not a vestige was left, only high precipitous banks, naked and unfamiliar, that had been cut back into the orchard almost to the apple trees themselves.

In front of George's Ground, the little well with its cross-beam and bucket, was no more, and the sloping grass-covered bank of earth with its footpath into the barley ground was all cut away and great bare rocks left exposed. The largest of these was shaped like one half of a gable roof, and so steep that no path could be built across its face. At the base of this roof-like rock and all along the front of the garden, lay now a long narrow deep pool, dug there by the churning waters, and soon found to be bordered with dangerous quicksand.

To enter the flower garden we now must clamber across a large embedded rock that formed the lower limit of the pool, jutting out from the base of the boundary spur. Over this rock, its higher edge covered with earth, a path was gradually worn, passable, but always difficult for little feet.

The quicksand of the pool against this rock constantly dared us to seek the thrilling sensation of a sudden drop into their depths. Though frightening, this experience possessed a peculiar fascination—especially since forbidden—the others, with warnings flouted, pulling us out with threats to "tell" on us.

This long deep pool, from its proximity to the garden, was ever afterward called "George's Pond." More fittingly might it have been named "Mud-turtle Paradise," for soon after the flood, the mud-turtles, their former abiding places completely swept away, got another start here lower down in a much more favorable environment where they multiplied in great numbers. They would come up out of the water—dozens at a time—to sun themselves on the broad sloping surface of the roof-shaped rock at the upper end of the pool. At the least sound of any approach, they would slip off simultaneously into the water below, leaving not one in sight, yet scarcely disturbing its surface with a ripple.

The clay beds of our doll factory at the upper end of the wide willow thicket, which no former floods had ever seemed to disturb, were now completely taken away, or buried, leaving in childish hearts a lonesome void.

The thicket itself, extending south from the clay beds, to the cart-road gate was not destroyed. The willows had bent to the waters that swept over them, and were left only leaning dejectedly. But the low bank behind them, topped by the fence along which grew the row of beautiful acacias, was cut ruthlessly away, exposing the bare roots of these beloved lacey tree-friends so that soon they began to die and had all to be dug up. Nevermore would they shake their yellow blossoms in the springtime. Never again could we play in their fern-flecked shade and pluck the furry tassels we so loved to fondle.

All our loved, familiar playgrounds up and down the creek from one end of it to the other, were completely devastated. The happy little singing waterfalls all were gone, the pools bordered with vegetation where the darning needles had darted in the sun and the water bugs had dived and the skaters had skimmed across, the clumps of nettles and weeds where the larks had built, the old swimming hole, the turtle-banks and mud-holes beneath, the duck pond, the celery along the shady banks, and the forests of tules—all were gone forever and the creek swept clean of their beauty.

At the third bend where Lafe and Joseph had killed their snake when returning home from the beach, there was left not a trace of the large clump of mingled wild roses, nettles and poison oak with its skirting footpath, but instead was a deep pool with a sheer cliff of rock above it and quicksand before it.

At the fourth bend the path around the point that the girls had found submerged by flood waters, was all cut away so that after this we were obliged to clamber around on a narrow ledge of rock hardly wide enough to be called a path. Above it the huge wall of rock, somewhat concave, afforded a place where we might lean the hands for support to keep our balance above the deep water waiting to swallow us up should a slip be made.

At the fifth bend the havoc was still more lamentable. There, the road on its way to the triangle had formerly rounded the curve on a gradually rising slope, gaining the Lee Goff side of the stream and pond without crossing the creek at all, but merely turning with it. Now all this earth with the road was completely gone leaving not even a bank, but a bare wall of rock under which was a cave full of deep water. This necessitated changing the road to cross the creek at the headwaters of the pond, where now a perpendicular bank had been left ten or more feet in height.

Through this bank, a narrow steep road was afterward cut leading up out of the pond. Often in winter time the water was so deep at this crossing as to be unfordable. But there being then no other road, we frequently were obliged to risk a crossing before it was safe to do so. The old spring wagon would nearly float—the water flowing into the bed of it, and the horses would be almost forced to swim. To this day I retain a mental picture of such a scene—the horses lunging and plunging through the water, then struggling for a foothold as they scrambled dripping up the slippery bank. And distinctly do I remember the feeling of intense relief and of breathing freely again at being safely across, while at the same time dreading the necessary return.

Compensations

With our playground thus swept away, the world to us seemed a strange and dreary place for some time after the flood. Yet we were not left wholly without compensations, for nature has a wonderful way of balancing the scores. All along underneath the wide stretch of willows below the house that had been a swampy, mosquito-infested thicket, the unsightly undergrowth had been cleaned out or deeply buried and in its place white sand deposited, carpeting the place like a fairyland and shaded still by the beautiful old willows that remained. It was like being on the beach, only with trees overhead instead of blistering sun. The swamp was gone. The old duck pond at its lower end was no more. The place where it had been, together with all the other marshy depressions and recesses were filled in level with this lovely, clean, white sand for us to play in. And how we reveled in it! Though greatly missing the duck pond, the paths and trails of former days, the clay beds, the swimming hole, the little tule-bordered pools, the beautiful murmuring waterfalls, and the shady playground at the end of the apple orchard, we soon learned to love this new playground quite as well—though long mourning the destruction of the beloved acacia trees and the clay beds—and new forms of enjoyment were invented.

Resourceful as ever, I soon decided that we must have tents and play "camping out"; for what more appropriate use could be found for a beach like this? So we besieged Mother with requests for old quilts and blankets out of which to make our tents. And these were somehow forthcoming, for dear Mother liked to do what she could to help us have good times. Next, we must have ropes and safety pins—big ones—to help hold our tents in position. Ropes strung from tree to tree formed our ridge poles, over which the quilts and blankets were hung by their centers. Then other ropes attached by safety pins to the sides and ends, drew them apart from each other tent-shaped, and were tied to other trees lower down to hold them in position. And presto! We had our tents, one for Annie and her family, and one for me and my family. Some of the quilts, we folded and laid down on the sand inside for our beds, other furnishings of a primitive nature being added from time to time.

All summer long until winter's necessary intervention, these tents remained on the sand under the willows needing only occasional straightening and tightening of the ridge-poles and side ropes, and the replacing of safety pins, as the strain becoming too great would cause them to "lose their grip." And what wonderful times we had there! No tongue can ever tell the story.

The usual activities of home life were carried on with what limited facilities we possessed, while our "children"— consisting of Charlotte, Luella, and our two big rag dolls—were alternately spanked and loved, dressed and undressed, put to bed and awakened from sleep, sent to play, or set at tasks, or—"tell it not in Gath"—nursed.

Too young to support even the faintest outward semblance of mammary glands, we substituted cloth-made pads— another invention of mine—their centers lifted and tied with strings in nipple-like bunches, from which our doll-offspring drew their lacteal nourishment. Had my old-fashioned, super-modest mother known of this last brilliant idea and its practical application, she would probably have "shamed" me to a sickly green. But needless to say, it was not intended that she should know, though any sense of guilt was wholly artificial. I had in the past done some things of the same nature that had called forth her withering rebuke: "For shame! For shame!" and never did I let her catch me pinning diapers on this same rag doll for fear of hearing it repeated. Child minds cannot differentiate between the fine shades of meaning that are by their elders attached to certain natural acts. Poor Mother! She never knew what outlandish thing Harriet would be doing next.

As the days of October drew to a close and autumn winds warned us that tenting days were limited, we were treated to a delightful surprise. Little sister Clarabel was born, immediately superseding in interest and regard, the old rag doll. For nothing was ever quite so wonderful to me, as a "real live meat-baby." This proved to be the last of all those happy events, for Clara remained for all time the "baby of the family."

The sour dock survived the flood, getting a fresh start afterward in the creek bottom, but the celery after that was very scarce. The yerba manza and the "pussy tails" came back, and of course the nettles returned. But the tules were gone to stay. After awhile we became accustomed to the changes that we had not been able to prevent, and became acquainted with the new creek-bed that had superseded the old. It too was interesting.

One happy day, while playing barefoot along the banks of the stream below the walnut orchard between the third and fourth bends, we stepped into some mud that seemed unusually sticky, and began to investigate. To our joy, we found that it was real clay—perhaps our old clay beds washed down from above and deposited here, for there had never been clay in that neighborhood before the flood. It seemed too good to be true. We were overjoyed. No time was lost in getting to work again, and it was not long before our new factory was running full force and overtime. Though much farther away from home than the old, it was still not too far for frequent visiting. Besides we were older now since another winter had passed over our heads, and many were the good times we spent at our old occupation. We now had banks of salt grass on which to spread out our products to dry in the sun, and not far away were willows out of which we made reinforcing bones, though too far for shade. Things were different, still it was clay, and that was the main thing. I think we appreciated it all the more for having lost it for awhile. This time Charlotte too, being older, was trying her hand at the business and doing her best to imitate the "perfect beauties" turned out by our more experienced hands.

With our "swimming hole" in the creek destroyed, ingenuity soon provided another. Garbed—Frank in an old pair of short pants and waist, and we girls in old panties and dresses—we would go "swimming" in the shallow upper end of the pond where the water was just deep enough for us to crawl on our hands and float the rest of our bodies out behind. With every disturbance of the slippery bottom, there would rise up a muddy cloud to darken the clear water—and incidentally the clear skin of the mudcrawler. But this, though disconcerting, did not by any means destroy our appetite for "swimming" like the grown-ups. Mud to us was a very small matter. Though not particularly enjoyed on our bodies and from that standpoint considered a drawback, yet the "feel" of it as we waded in was rather pleasing to our feet, and we liked the soothing sensation of mud "squishing" up between our toes.

In this portion of the pond there were water snakes as there had been in the pools of the creek; the muddy bottom furnishing a wonderful growth medium for the reedy grasses that had a foothold there, among which the snakes loved to sport. So we bathed along with the snakes, neither interfering with the other.

This closer familiarity with the pond put ideas into our heads not before conceived. We longed to sail over its smooth surface in a boat. With the pond thus tempting him to marine experiments, Frank's aspirations toward pleasure craft took definite shape. Out of an old dry goods box, he fashioned a boat, and launched it on the pond, paddling it about with a piece of board.

This first trial, however, proved not wholly successful—as is usually the case with first inventions—for the boat leaked and the girls refused to get into it. So, not to be daunted, Frank tried again with a bigger and better dry goods box. This water craft he improved by first stuffing all the cracks with rag strings and then daubing them over with the sticky black "brea" that was plentiful on the ocean rocks. This same brea had also furnished us our chewing-gum, unsweetened of course, but possessing a peculiarly attractive tarry flavor.

This second boat was a tremendous success. It did not leak a bit. Being larger too, it would carry two passengers at once beside the boatman—that is, by squeezing, and if they were small and would sit very still so as not to overbalance the boat; for it was rudderless.

All over the pond he paddled this boat with its precious cargo. The water at the lower end was deep enough to have drowned the whole boat-load ten times over, had the craft capsized. If our busy mother, half a mile away at the house, had been aware of what was going on, doubtless this new game would have been squelched before the fun began. But Mother didn't know. That sixth sense possessed by children, sometimes called "intuition," usually warns them what to tell the "powers that be" of their escapades, and what not to tell.

<u>A Flood Letter</u>

Artie, who had gone to San Pedro in December of Eighty-Three, was at the time of the flood in Los Angeles. Finding the promised music lessons not amounting to much and being dissatisfied with wages so low, she left Mrs. Burkel's and went to the city to look for work. She rented a little attic room at Mrs. Hughes' rooming house on the corner of Ninth and Hill. Here she did her own cooking on a one-burner coal-oil stove, which also furnished the meager heat for warming her room, paying for the accommodations, eight dollars a month. Two blocks away, was the horse-car line that then came as far south as Ninth on Spring Street.

Soon, she secured work in a store and factory run by Mr. Zech, and after a month or so, she and another girl went in together and took a better room downstairs, for which they each paid eight dollars. It was here that Artie was living when Father brought her the Singer sewing machine.

While Artie was at this place, Joan, a twelve-year-old, very soon after the flood, wrote her a letter; which was begun on the ninth of March, finished on the twenty-sixth, and posted on April the seventh—an eloquent commentary on postal conditions that spring. This childish letter, preserved from the long ago, might be of interest here.

"March 9, 1884
Aliso Canyon, Santa Ana.

Miss Artemisia Thurston

My Dear Sweet Loving Sister Mishey

Your letter was received the day before yesterday and I guess I shal procede to answer it as it is the first chance I have had cince.

It has been raining off and on for a week—not raining hard enough to make any very large flood but just enough to make it dismal and gloomy. Oh I do hate such weather so damp dark and cold.

Yes, we did have a big flood during the hard rains. It came up to the barn and all over the vineyard swift enough and deep enough to wash away a plow that was in them at the time. It rains quite hard now and quite a large flood has come cince I began righting.

The 8 of this month is Harriet's birthday, and Lafayette's is coming, and Dear Sweet little Luella May's has passed. We named her on her birthday and we call her Luella. Her hair is quite curly and she can walk 8 or 9 steps at a time. She is just as sweet and good as can be all the time. She is a little beauty. I do wish we could have her likeness taken while she is small.

Oh she thought the world of your picture. She wanted it as soon as she seen it. I think the one in black is the best. I do not think the other hardly looks like you. I think the first one you ever had taken—the one taken at home is the best and most natural. If I were to have only one I would take that. But you know it is nice to have one of all so a person can see how you change. I wish I could have mine taken so I could send you all one. But I do not know when that will be. The other night I dreamed of you and I dremp you come home. I often dream of you but I never did dream of your being dead. I dream something more pleasant than that, and when I wake up instead of being glad it is only a dream, I am quite disappointed, but I do not think there is much in a dream.

All the apples are gone and the trees are in blossom and there are wild flowers on the hills. The flower garden gets but little care. We still call it George's Ground, so we have that much left to keep his name in exercise.

We had a little party on Valentines day at Lottie Goffs. Hulda and I went down before dark. It rained so Joseph did not come so we stayed all night. It rained all night. It was then the big flood come. We stayed all day and the water lowered and we came home beyond the vineyard and came acrost there on horse. You would be surprised to see the valley as it stands now the floods has changed it so. We had two floods as big as that one.

We have not heard from Sadie cince new years she has 2 letters not answered. We got a letter from Lafay he is well.

March 26 1884

As no male has been able to pass ever cince the big flood on account of the bridges being distroyed so the cars could not run, I knew it was of no use to finish my letter until I saw some signs of disposing of it, and then I could not tell when any boddy was going to town so it is all luck and chance. I do not see how it is that I have not received any answer to my letter yet. I rote to Lafay before I began this letter and I have not received one from him or Sadie yet...I must close now with ever so many good wishes and lots of kisses and love from all,

I remain your loveing sister

Joan."

In Anaheim lived a lady by the name of Parker who was about Father's age and of the same political opinions, a rank "woman suffragist" and "Freethinker." In her home she was the one who "wore the pants" and could discuss "politics" with any man alive. Father and she were great political friends. This woman wanted a young girl to live with her and work for her board and asked Father to let her have Joan. Many promises were made as to the advantages it would be for the girl, and Father was persuaded to let Joan go for awhile. On the way to Anaheim they stopped in Santa Ana and Joan sat for her picture, so it turned out that she had her wish granted for pictures to give around. Howbeit they were of the same sober cast of countenance and the same scraggly style of hair dressing as other children of the period.

Artie, after quitting the factory which she found was not to her liking because she could not approve of the business conducted by her employer, apprenticed herself to a milliner by the name of Mrs. Hammond to learn the trade, at which she worked for two weeks. But not being handy with the needle, she soon found that this was not an occupation to which she was adapted, and the apprenticeship was dissolved by mutual consent. Mrs. Hammond gave her a beautiful hat in payment for her two weeks' work and Artie decided to make a visit home before seeking other work; so she gave up her room at Mrs. Hughes, and after writing Joseph to meet her, took the train for El Toro. She put the box containing her new hat high up on the rack in the train and being tired dozed for a time. When her station was reached she got off the train without remembering the box, and that was the last she ever saw of that beautiful hat.

Joan's experience at Mrs. Parker's proved to be a bitter one. She almost worked her to death, and was very unkind to her. All Joan's letters home were censored, and only those that voiced no complaint were allowed to go into the mail, all others being destroyed. So poor Joan had no means of letting the folks know what was going on. While there, she had her thirteenth birthday on September two. Not long after that, Father, having occasion to go to Anaheim, went to see her. It was then that Joan had her opportunity to acquaint him with the way she was being treated, and Father had her pack up her box of things, and without any ceremony took her home. Mother needed her help anyway; for this was only a few weeks before Baby Clarabel was born on October twenty-four; so Father had a very good reason to offer for his action. But never after that was the friendship between them quite so strong.

Driftwood

The big flood left our farm scattered over with driftwood, some of which had come sailing and rolling down from the canyons above us, and some from our own fences and trees along the channel. Much of it was uprooted trees, but there were many fence posts, mostly trimmed saplings, but a few of timber, and occasionally boards from sheepherders' cabins, gates, and other sources. Much of our lower land had been under the flood water, and none of this escaped the aftermath of driftwood. Tangled up with long matted grass, mustard, weeds and brush washed down from the pastures and hillsides north of us, and with the barbed wire of the fences that clung to the uprooted and half-buried posts scattered about, the driftwood had to be dug out and cut out and pulled out from its matted tangle in order to extricate the fence posts and wires and the good pieces of lumber that might be of use, and to sort out that which was fit only for fuel in the kitchen. All this was to be hauled up to the yards. The refuse and flood-stuff pulled away from the trees and vines could then be piled up and burned. In this work all hands were commandeered to assist.

One day during that summer just following the flood, Joseph, taking the lumber wagon with Ted and Bill, was sent down to the lower parts of the farm to gather driftwood. Frank and four of us girls—Hulda, Harriet, Annie and Charlotte—went along to help. As we climbed into the back of the wagon behind Joseph preparatory to leaving the yard, Father cautioned us to be sure and walk home and not burden the team with our extra weight to haul across the sandy creek bottom, as the load would be heavy enough without us. And away we drove with this warning in our ears.

After we had worked for a number of hours gathering and loading the driftwood we were very tired—all of us. And when the time came to return home none of us felt like walking. We were rather rebellious at the instruction that had been given. So before starting back a council was held concerning the matter and we all together decided that it wouldn't hurt the horses to carry us too on top of the load.

To keep Father from discovering our disobedience, it was agreed that just before coming within sight of the house around the little hill point, we would, all but Joseph, jump off and loiter around in the creek while he drove the load on home, to give the appearance of having walked in dutiful obedience to Father's command.

So when we came to the elevated strip of sand that preceded the cart-road gate at the little hill point, and had climbed the bank and gone half way across its white length, Joseph stopped the team and the five of us all scrambled off the load of wood and jumped over the side of the wagon to the sandy roadside as planned—all except Hulda. She too jumped, but hardly as planned. Just as she made the leap, her rather narrow skirt caught on one of the projecting stumps of the load, which threw her, and she fell down in the road on her stomach and face, half under the wagon and half out, exactly between the two front and back wheels on the left side of the wagon.

Joseph, being wholly unaware of what had happened, started up the team to go on. Hulda, with no loss of time, flopped over on her back, and realizing that the rear wheel was about to go over her body with all that heavy load on top, drew up her knees to her chin and wrapped her arms around them to shield her vital organs as much as possible from the brunt of the weight.

By the time the rear wheel had climbed up onto her right arm and knee, we who were in a position to see the performance, were yelling wildly to Joseph:

"Hulda's under the wheels! Stop! Hulda's under the wheels! You're going over her! You're going over her!"

Joseph then reversed the outfit and began to go backward. But not knowing her exact location and being wholly unable to see her, he backed a little too far, and the front wheel rolled up onto her left arm and shank. Again we yelled:

"You're rolling over her the other way! You're rolling over her the other way!"

Just as the front wheel eased up in response to our yells, Hulda made a desperate lunge and threw herself under the wagon free from the wheels, and came crawling out from under its rear end.

Father, hearing our wild commotion, came running down to the gate to find out what was the matter, arriving just as Hulda was shaking herself clear of the sand. Of course we were all loath to explain to him exactly how it had happened and thus expose our disobedient act. But when he understood what had been Hulda's perilous position, he inquired if she were hurt. Though trembling like a leaf from the nervous shock, she told him no she wasn't hurt at all. Being much relieved to hear it, he forgot all about the discipline due us, for which we were profoundly thankful. He seemed not even to remember having forbidden us to ride.

But Hulda was hurt. Nothing was said about the matter when we reached the house, for all were content to let well enough alone and not reopen a subject so ticklish that might possibly raise the question of punishment as well as sympathy, and so considered the whole thing a closed incident.

Mother knew nothing about the accident until that night when Hulda undressed for bed. On the outer surface of each arm and thigh, there was an area about the size of her palm where the outer layer of skin was all ground off and the flesh badly bruised. The symmetrical occurrence of these four branding marks astonished Mother beyond measure, until Hulda told her the whole story. Then in great perturbation she called Father asking:

"Did you know that Hulda was under the wagon wheels today and nearly got run over?"

"Yes," answered Father, "I knew it but she said she wasn't hurt any."

"Well she was hurt!" said Mother with a touch of severity in her tone;

"Come here and look at these arms and legs!"

Tears fell from her eyes at the thought of what might have happened, and that she had not known all day long how badly the child needed attention.

"Cuckle-Burrs"

Another aftermath of the flood was the deluge of "cuckle-burrs" left in its wake. Up to this time we had scarcely known what a "cuckle-burr" was—whose other names are Cockle Button and Burdock. This great weed attaining a height of from three to five feet with its broad, oval, rough-lined, heart-shaped leaves and rough hairy stems and its enormous roots that grew straight down for about a foot then branched off in all directions to give a very firm hold in the soil as well as a large area from which to steal the nourishment that rightly belonged to domestic crops, proved to be a greater curse to the farm than all the other damages added together.

They sprang up everywhere thick as the hair on a dog's back, and had gained a firm foothold all up and down the creek and areas that had been overflowed by the flood before Father really recognized the nature of the plant. Since it does not come into fruitage until the second year of its growth, it was at first considered to be just another weed to be hoed up from the cultivated plots without serious attempt at complete eradication, but left undisturbed along the fences and margins and up and down the creek bed, even as other less harmful weeds were left to propagate themselves. But when the ugly, prickly burrs began to show their unwelcome heads, Father took the alarm, and another irksome and endless task was added to the burden of the farm work in making war on this extremely obnoxious and pernicious pest.

The whole channel of the creek was lined with them along its wide margins, so mingled with other growth and so hidden from sight in nooks and corners and among willows and fences, that it was impossible to find them all, and those overlooked would thrive and come to maturity to cast their baneful hooked-spined burrs on every side, resowing again and again the territory already gone over, and becoming so stout and big, that when discovered it was almost impossible to dislodge them from their hold in the soil.

We younger children that could best be spared for the task, were set to work systematically to rid the premises of them. But the whole family at all times were made to feel a personal responsibility for every such plant they came across in their work or play, and see to it that they were destroyed. Hour after hour, day after day, we would tramp along the creek banks up and down the whole length of our premises and pull these noxious "cockle burrs." But for every one we pulled, a hundred more would seem to come to its funeral. They seemed to know no season—all the time was the season for "cuckle-burrs." As fast as we thinned them out, another crop would spring up.

Not only our own premises were affected but in all the length of the creek above us the same thing had taken place— only there was no one up there to pull them. So they would yearly go to seed undisturbed, and at every time of high water countless numbers of the seeds would wash down to re-sow the areas we had worked so hard to clean out. And we would have the same thing to do over again.

When our young horses would come home from the canyon pastures above, their tails and manes would be nothing but thick tangled mats of burrs that could not be extracted, and the only relief from these that could be given was to cut off the hair and the burrs with it. The long hair, their only means of protection from the nagging horse-flies— was now useless as such, for these unsightly wads of burrs were no more switches but clubs.

All through the years, constantly fighting these noxious plants, we still could never get rid of them. How we hated the sight of a cuckle-burr! It was necessary that they be pulled up root and all for if merely cut off at ground level they would send up shoots and nothing had been accomplished. Often they would grow up among the clumps of "bull nettles," where getting at them meant to be badly stung. Yet so desperate and determined was our warfare that we never knowingly skipped one even in the nettle clumps; reaching with a hoe those we could not get at with our hands. These nettles often grew high as a horse's back and their sting was almost like that of a bumble bee, so, ordinarily, we gave them a wide berth.

Little Clara was pulling burrs with us one day on a bank that sloped rather sharply and had tackled a big old burr whose roots didn't want to loosen their hold. She was straining with all her might to dislodge it when suddenly it let go and Clara went tumbling heels over head down the bank and landed in a large clump of these bull nettles. By the time we got her out, both she and her rescuers were badly stung.

Whenever the cows would eat of these burrs in the spring, their milk would be made bitter. We thought them utterly good for nothing, but had we then known that the burdock has medicinal properties and therefore a market value, we might at least have made enough out of them to pay for our labor. The roots of the young plants, when sliced lengthwise and carefully dried, brought on the market at the close of the century from three to eight cents a pound, and the seeds when ripe, from five to ten cents a pound. But of all this we were wholly ignorant, so reaped no benefit from them.

So tiresome became our daily task that anything that came along for a diversion was welcomed, and we played more or less as we worked. One day while pulling burrs below the house, seeing a big gopher snake slithering along through the grass and weeds, I seized him by the tail and held him out at arm's length just to show the others what I was not afraid to do.

CHAPTER 38 THE LAST OF THE DYNASTY

When the last baby came into our house, came also with her the old controversy concerning a name. "Clara," a name in use on Father's side of the house, was acceptable to Mother. But when he insisted on "Belle" for the middle name, Mother again objected. However, he had his way, for it would not do that a man should yield the same point twice, and "Clara Belle" it was until the census-taker came around. Father was not present at the time, and Mother turned the name in as Clarabel. So again the woman in the case had the last word and scored one for woman-suffrage.

From the day of her birth, Clarabel—or Clara, as we called her-was very delicate. She seemed to "take" every sickness that came along. Often it was feared by the family that she would never live to grow up. Her constant demands upon Mother's time and attention and her shrill voice when she cried, penetrating every nerve, made the care of her very wearing. But, as was natural, these frailties only endeared her the more to the household.

A wee mite of a thing, she grew very slowly, weighing at the age of five years only thirty pounds. When Artie, being at home on a visit, would work around the kitchen, Clara would beg for a "ride" on her bustle. Seated astride of it and holding on by reaching her arms as far as possible around Artie's body, she would ride all about the house with the greatest enjoyment. Such a sight would today seem very funny indeed, and even then was not without its humor.

At the age of six she was still too small to see the top of the table while standing on the floor, but without stooping in the least, could walk about underneath it. She still used her little high chair at eight and was taken by strangers to be but a baby.

Our geese, always running loose about the yard, delighted to pick on defenseless little children, who would flee at the sound of their terrifying squawks. Clara, hardly taller than the old gander himself, could not be allowed out of doors when they were around. One day when just a baby, she put on her little sunbonnet and went out into the back yard to play. Immediately an old gander, leader of the flock, came hissing after her with "blood in his eye," the whole flock of a dozen or more following. Had rescue not been at hand, undoubtedly they would have killed her. But in response to her screams someone ran out and snatched her from them just as the birds had gotten her down, and saved her from their cruel mauling.

But in the flock there was one member of whom she had never any need to be afraid. This was "Runty," a little pet gander that Mother had given her when a gosling. He was "cross-billed"—that is, his bill, through malformation did not fit together properly. The upper half, being out of line, closed down upon the lower midway, making it very difficult for the little thing to get enough to eat. So he never grew very big. From early goslinghood, Clara carried him about and gave him bits of food, so he became a great pet and was very fond of his little mistress.

Clara was always getting hurt in one way or another, which kept the family in a state of constant concern for her. One day when running away from Mother and a threatened punishment for some misdemeanor, she came violently in contact with another that was worse. A board with an ugly nail sticking out of its side lay in her path. Against this she struck her foot, cutting across its top a deep and dangerous gash. Six stitches were necessary to draw the edges of this wound together so it could heal properly. With Father then gone and no surgeon to be had, Lafe himself performed this operation.

One day after cooking a good dinner, Joan and Hulda were getting it onto the table preparatory to calling the waiting family to dinner. The little folks were chasing each other around the room in play, and laughing in breathless excitement. Hulda had just dished up a bowl of boiling hot gravy and was carrying it from the stove to the table when Clara quick as a flash, darted against her unexpectedly and knocked the bowl of gravy out of her hand. It turned upside down on the top of Clara's head, dowsing her with its scalding contents before smashing to bits on the floor. They grabbed the screaming child and ran to the water bucket, with dippers of cold water washing off the worst of the gravy. Mother came running to the scene. Emptying the contents of the soda box into a dish, she made a paste of it with water, spreading it—while others held the frantic child—over her head and face. And there they kept it all the rest of the day, wetting it at intervals. Holding the child in their arms they rocked her till, exhausted with the pain and nerve-shock, she had sobbed herself to sleep. Clara carried a white patch on her head and a white streak across her forehead—the marks of this burn—for many a year, even far into her teens.

When Luella and Clara were both very small, one day Clara came in to Mother complaining that she had a "bean" up her nose, and couldn't "get it out." Sure enough, there it was well lodged high up in the nostril. When asked anxiously how it came to be in there, she explained that she and Luella were "running a race" to see which could stuff the most beans up their noses. Mother in great anxiety, held her up by the heels head downward and "whacked" her soundly on the back to dislodge the offending bean, which finally fell out of her nostril.

Clara was very fond of the odor of pickled orange-peel, and whenever she saw Mother going down cellar, would follow her and beg for a smell. Mother would remove the cork of the wide-mouthed bottle and hold it near her nose to gratify her craving for the sweet fragrance. Thus her experience with bottles—at least cellar bottles—was very limited and associated with pleasant sensations. One day the little mischief went down by herself into the cellar, for the purpose of smelling the pickled orange-peel. She was a very little girl, and could not remember where to look for the bottle or just what was its appearance. All bottles looked alike to her. So seeing a bottle sitting on the lower shelf she reached up and lifted it down. She tugged at the cork till it came out and took a deep inhalation of its contents—strong ammonia. It was almost a "knock-down." How she managed to keep the bottle from following the flying cork, to smash on the cellar floor and envelop her in its suffocating fumes, is indeed a mystery. Only that strong sense of guilty secrecy which accompanies forbidden acts, enabled her to set the bottle back upon the shelf without mishap, and when she found the overwhelming stuff had not killed her, to retrieve and replace the recalcitrant cork—a sadder and wiser little maiden. Again was proved the truth of Mother's old proverb: "A special Providence watches over fools and little children."

While still too young herself to read, Clara, after listening to us who were older, would imitate our efforts in her own way. One day after a session with "Tom Sawyer" and "Huckleberry Finn", she was observed going over it again with the book upside down, muttering into its pages:

"Huck said Pap warn't feelin' very brash and Tom wasn't feelin' very flabbergash, either."

She was intrigued with the old negro spiritual: "Ain't I glad I got out o' de wildeness, got out o' de wildeness, got out o' de wildeness," which we sometimes sang. Then would follow her own version in her high-keyed falsetto: "Ain't I glad I got out o' de wilderson, got out o' de wilderson, got out o' de wilderson."

Always a nervous little thing, while learning to talk, she had developed the habit of stuttering when excited, and this grew upon her as the years went by. Finally Mother determined if possible to break her of the habit. By this time she was getting acquainted with books. While reciting her lesson to Mother one day, she began to talk so fast that her words ran together in a stuttering jumble.

"Clara! Stop right where you are! Don't say another word!" commanded Mother.

She stopped. And after a time of wordless waiting, having again grown calm, was allowed to proceed with her lesson, which she then recited in a normal manner. By this method, persevered in over a long period of time, Mother broke her completely of the stuttering habit.

Clara and her sister Luella were some time getting acquainted with their big brothers and sisters, having been born after they left home. George, being always very fond of little folks, whenever he would come home on a visit would bring them a small bag of hard candy. But there came a time when he was out of work while holding down his claim, and finances being at a very low ebb, was obliged to omit the customary treat. As he drove up into the front yard one day, Clara ran out to meet him and be the first to receive the gift of sweets. Greeting him expectantly, she stood about waiting while he tied up his horses and did something to the wagon. But as he came into the house and still no candy was forthcoming, she assayed to assist his delinquent memory.

"Georgie! "

"What? "

"You know when you uste to come home other times to visit us, you uste to bring us a whole sack of candy. You uste to just stuff us. But—now—you don't do it—anymore." Deep and disconsolate was that finishing sigh, whose amusing pathos George never forgot.

Clara was a natural-born imitator and mimic. Whatever she saw or heard that seemed to her interesting or funny, she would straightway proceed to reproduce in a life-like manner. Sometimes the family were entertained by seeing her get down on her hands and knees before a saucer of milk which she had previously set on the floor, and lap it up in imitation of the cat. To escape the family's laughter, which to her seemed ridicule, she carried a dish of sliced figs and cream outside and away from the house, placing it upon the top of a flat coop to avoid close contact with loose dirt, and mounting the coop, ate it with her mouth in the dish in imitation of the dog. She would crow, cackle, grunt, moo and whinny in simulation of the various barnyard creatures about the farm.

Peculiar brogues, modes of speech, mannerisms, tones and gestures noticed in others would be reproduced for the mere sport of it. Whether her audience consisted of one, none, or a dozen, the performance came forth spontaneously just the same, seemingly from sheer love of mimicry. Those older often said that if they wanted to see a minstrel show, they would just as soon send Clara to see the show and afterward listen to her reproduction of it, as to go themselves.

Clara was unmistakably spoiled. This is not to be wondered at. Nor is it strange that selfish traits were often manifested; since everybody yielded habitually to her. Children, though having decided individualities of their own, are as to outward behavior at least, largely what their elders make them.

Sweet as pie when everything went off to please her but violently tempestuous whenever crossed in her desires, she was wont to designate anyone who opposed her will as "Mean possel can be!" Nobody wanted to rouse unnecessarily her swift tempers and cutting tongue—a tongue that spared no one and never dissembled—so she was indulged and spoiled and given her own way by everybody. A tempest of storm, a burst of sunshine, a jolly, rollicking, mimicking, hoydenish spitfire, was little Clarabel, whom everybody loved and petted; knowing there would never be another baby in the family.

But though Clara was a spitfire she never nursed a grudge, but recovered quickly from her "mad spells" and expected everybody else to do the same. Always, she had her own version—or perversion—of the Golden Rule. Paraphrased and abbreviated it might have read something like this: "Whatsoever ye would do to others, that do." Her idea of "fun" often involved the feelings of others adversely. But to annoy or tease was her delight regardless of the discomfort or discomfiture of others.

One of her pet annoyances, when still too young to understand the game herself, was to climb up into the big fig tree that overshadowed the croquet ground, and pelt the players with ripe figs, to smash over heads, hats or clothes. There were threats. But nobody ever really made her behave.

Unlike the rest of us, she was not taught to work and carry her share of life's burdens in a regular manner, but whatever she did in that line was of her own choosing. When she wanted to work, she worked, and was as good a worker as anybody could ask, until the novelty wore off. But when she wanted to play, she likewise played, and nobody said her nay. An incident will suffice to illustrate the disposition of this little scamp.

Whoever has lived on a farm knows how well a hog lives to have his back scratched with a hoe, and how he will settle down with a contented grunt under this soothing ministration. Well, Father was like this about having his hair combed. His fondness for this diversion amounted to a passion. Seated in a large rocker with something to read and one of us youngsters standing on a box behind his chair drawing the small fine-toothed comb through his hair endlessly, he was the very picture of contentment. Because this was pleasant to him he had allowed it to become a regular evening routine. So, when Father would come in of an evening, pick up his "Weekly," draw up his rocking chair and sit down, we all knew what was coming and wondered with an inward groan which one of us would be selected for the onerous task.

Sometimes, under the soothing influence of comb or brush, he would begin to doze. Then we would stealthily lay aside the instrument to steal away. But the moment the combing motion ceased he would waken, and the ruse was never a success. We wouldn't have minded it so much if Father had been reasonable about it—if he had understood just how much he had a right to expect of a child. But Father seemed not to realize that little feet grew weary standing still on a box, that little hands rebelled at performing the same motions over and over again, and little minds grew uneasy to be at their own interesting occupations. So he was never known to say:

"That will do Dear, for this time, thank you."

No. He would wait till the little sufferer begged timidly:

"Pa, is that enough? Pa, can I stop now?" and maybe this supplication would be repeated a number of times before he even seemed to hear, so reluctant was he to forego the pleasure.

Therefore the task which, with the right psychology, might have been made a mutual pleasure—for I think normal children like just a little of that sort of thing—became instead a disagreeable bugbear.

Father had recently purchased a wire hairbrush—then a new invention—and liked it so well that it had superseded the fine comb in the nightly hair-combing. One evening after seating himself in the rocker with his paper, Father looked around as usual. But all of us youngsters had become suddenly very busy with our books—except Clara, a mere baby, who had no use for books as books, and who had never yet been commandeered to this task. Perhaps he sensed the unwillingness in the atmosphere. But be that as it may, for the first time he asked Clara if she would like to brush his hair.

Clara assented eagerly thinking it would be a wonderful diversion as well as an honor to be doing what the bigger girls did. So she hastened to get the little box we always stood on, and with this wire brush in hand climbed upon it behind Father's high-backed rocking chair. There she began to draw the brush through his hair as she had watched us do so many times, while we inwardly rejoiced at the new deliverance.

It was great fun—for awhile. But all too soon Clara's relish for hair-brushing began to wane. She was used to following her own sweet fancy like the little flitting butterfly that skips from one flower to another, resting barely an instant on each bending tip. Soon deciding to cease operations, she climbed down from the box. But Father's enjoyment had only just begun and he had no notion of condoning such fickleness, so instructed her to keep on with the brushing. Sulkily she mounted the box again and resumed the now disagreeable task. But after a few strokes began to wriggle about uncomfortably and heave great sighs, which eloquent pleas for release seemed blissfully ignored.

All of a sudden, she lifted that wire hairbrush and brought it down with a terrific whack on the top of his head, which brought Father out of that chair in a hurry. None of us dared to laugh, for just then he was in a mood to "spank" the first one of us that should give him the ghost of a provocation—Clara being too little for such violent punishment. Mother hurriedly brought the liniment bottle, to soothe the rising welt—and incidentally the irritated temper—while the rest of us dug noses into our books with sudden interest until we could get perfect control of twitching facial muscles. But never again did Father invite Clara to brush his hair. She had won for herself permanent immunity.

This method of handling a disturbing situation, was characteristic of Clara all through her growing period. Whenever things didn't go to suit her, she would "fly off the handle" and throw the first thing that came to hand. Years afterward, when the family having left the farm were living in Santa Ana, she was one day blackening her shoes with the blacking brush in her hand, when Luella did or said something that roused her trigger-like temper. Quick as a flash she hurled at her the heavy brush, which narrowly missing Luella, almost struck Charlotte in the head and went crashing through the glass door beyond. This incident seems to have broken her of such manifestations.

That she and Luella—only seventeen and a half months apart—did not get on well together, is not to be wondered at, for Luella was the essence of all that is opposite in disposition, and Clara disturbed her equanimity. Her peculiar interpretation of enjoyment did not appeal to Luella. Being herself too young and too near Clara's own age to share the indulgent attitude manifested by those older, instead of charity, it was defensive scorn and sarcasm that marked her attitude toward this baby sister, whose constant pranks and irritating ridicule invited nothing else. So it was that Luella's "sarcasm" become proverbial in the family. Frank, who was eight years her senior—the two being very fond of each other—once gave her a brotherly rebuke which set Luella to the task of trying very determinedly to overcome this propensity. She had not before realized how obnoxious are scorn and sarcasm in the character. "Luella," he said to her kindly one day, "It isn't smart or cute to be sarcastic;" and this, she never forgot.

Luella once contracted a cold which settled on her lungs. Mother, in much concern told her to melt some lard in a tablespoon, mix with it some turpentine, and rub this on her chest before going to bed that night. Endeavoring to follow instructions implicitly, Luella melted the lard, mixed in the turpentine, and carried it out to the honey house where we were then sleeping—she and Clara together. After undressing, she began to rub this mixture carefully over her abdomen. Clara, who happened to know that the abdominal part of her anatomy was not the chest—though the word was a new one in their vocabulary, burst into a guffaw and jeered her unmercifully, afterward telling everybody else about it who likewise laughed, thus humiliating Luella beyond endurance.

To get the best of Luella, was "meat and drink" to this remorseless little tease. When the two had grown older and were going to school in Santa Ana, Clara paid as much attention to the games and funny things that went on as to her lessons. Luella, on the other hand was serious and studious, being especially good in arithmetic. One day when Luella was sitting at the table "doing sums" for the next day's recitation, Clara coming in said to her:

"You are a good mathematician. See if you can do this one: There were twelve men and each man had twelve pigs, each pig had twelve little pigs. Each man had also twelve buckets of slop—have you got all that down?"

"Yes, I've got that down"; replied Luella.

"Well!" ejaculated her tormentor. "You must be pretty full with a hundred and forty-four buckets of slop down you! Ha! Ha! Ha!"

Luella, crimson and furious, retorted: "I never said I had it down me; you never got me at all, Smarty!"

But Clara danced around in high glee, repeating, while pointing the finger:

"Luella's got one hundred and forty-four buckets of slop down her! Ha! Ha! Ha!"

With such a brand of one-sided fun between them, it is no wonder that the two had frequent disagreements, and that Luella's scorn and sarcasm developed as a buffer.

In all fairness to Clara, it must here be said that in spite of these early characteristics, Clara grew up and developed into as wholesome a woman as any of the daughters of Aliso; but always possessed the ability to see the funny side of life.

CHAPTER 39 NUT GATHERING

Our almond crop ripened before the walnuts, and their harvest was over before that of the walnuts was begun. We children always rejoiced when the time came to gather the almonds. There was something fascinating about a cone-shaped heap of almonds on the ground in their popped-open hulls, around which we knelt in a circle for the first shucking of the year. There was something fascinating too about the taste of those uncured nuts that haunts the memory even to this day.

Nothing more delicious can be imagined than the fresh creamy almond eaten before the thin, tough reddish skin adheres to the nut. After taking off the outer hull and cracking open the hard shell we would peel off this thin skin that held the two white halves together, and chew them to a creamy consistency, enjoying to the full the rich flavor and goodness.

But our parents did not like to have us eat the new almonds, partly because they were a good price on the market, and partly because of the fear that we would overeat of the uncured nuts and become ill, which was by no means improbable. But what can stop the urge of a child's appetite for such forbidden treats? Parental authority? Yes, if under its direct supervision. But in most cases this is its limitation. About most such prohibitions, there was the more or less salutary fear of discovery through some less guilty accomplice turning "state's evidence." Nothing was more to be dreaded than the threat: "I'll tell Pa on you!" But when it came to almonds, such a unanimity of guilty partnership existed that we felt quite secure so long as none of the actual Royalty was about.

Anticipating the harvest, we kept a close watch on the ripening nuts and would slip off down to the orchard unbeknown and feast on the half-ripe nuts to our heart's content, digging little graves for the tell-tale shells. So nobody was the wiser. However, when working we were usually under supervision, and at such times paid strict attention to duty and orders. But only we ourselves knew the secret of little piles of buried shells left behind at times of unguarded feasting.

That we were never physically inconvenienced by this gorging, is due no doubt to the fact not then so well known, that almonds contain within them in well-balanced proportion, the three essential minerals, calcium, phosphorus, and iron, in addition to the perfect protein that is akin to that of milk; and that these furnish not only excellent body-building materials, but a ration easy of digestion and assimilation. Walnuts, though valuable in the diet, are less so than almonds, and far less digestible.

Though eating almonds while shucking was discouraged, it was not altogether forbidden, neither were the shuckers always under surveillance. And whenever we would come across an extra-large almond, we would shake it to see if it rattled in the shell and if not, then volunteer: "I'll bet that's a double!" and proceed to crack it open—often with the teeth—to investigate. A "double" was two complete almonds like twins in the same shell, their adjacent sides flattened and curved to fit each other. If it proved to be not a double after all, the cracker promptly ate it himself. But if it proved to be indeed a double, he immediately suggested to one of the others:

"Let's play Philipino!"

This is a game for two players only, and a double almond is required to play it. A word is chosen—usually "yes" or "no" and agreed upon between the two. This word is to be avoided in conversation with each other. Then each player eats one almond of the double and the game is begun. After eating, neither one may use the forbidden word in addressing the other, though either may use it in conversing with anyone else. By adroit, but seemingly unconcerned questioning, each player seeks to entrap the other into using the prohibited word. Then when it slips unconsciously from the tongue, he shouts: "Philipino!" and the other is "caught." But if the one who utters the word tabooed, remembers in time his error, and says: "Philippino" first, he has redeemed himself from being caught, and the game goes on.

The penalty for the vanquished is that he must pay to the victor some kind of gift, anything he may himself choose to give from his own possessions—a rule rigidly adhered to among us. If both players were equally alert, the game might run on for a whole day or more, even for several days without either one being caught. But eventually one or the other would forget and be taken off guard, when the disconcerting and triumphant shout of "Philippino!" would win the game for his opponent. Then the humiliated loser would have to give thought as to which of his possessions he could afford to part with in paying the required forfeit.

When the time would draw near for the walnuts to begin to ripen, Joseph would cultivate the orchard, harrowing the furrows down evenly or "smooching" them smooth with a "smoocher" made of heavy planks, in order to eliminate hollows and hiding places for fallen nuts, so that we might gather them the more easily and thoroughly. Unlike the coarse, gravelly soil of the almond orchard, that of the walnut orchard was soft sandy loam with sand predominating, and could be made almost as level as a floor.

Walnuts in those days had not reached the point of cultivation that we find in later times. Hard shells were then the only walnuts found in the markets of California. The commercial culture of walnuts had but barely begun about four years before Father came into Aliso, and grafting had not yet begun to be practiced. Seedlings were used almost exclusively until the middle nineties, when soft shells began to be raised on a scale to market. It was another decade before hard shells disappeared in favor of soft shells.

When the leaves began to fall in the autumn—usually sometime in September—the thick outer hulls of the walnuts would begin to pop open and let the clean new nuts fall to the ground. Then Joseph, armed with a short thick club heavily padded to insure against bruising the trees, would precede us to the orchard, and climbing up into the trees, would strike each of the large limbs a heavy blow or two with the club to jar loose the nuts from their opening hulls. Then they would come rattling down onto the ground under the trees. Since many of the nuts would not yet be ripe enough, he was careful not to strike too hard, for green nuts must not be disturbed. As it was, a few of these would fall along with the rest. Many leaves also would be jarred loose; so that the fallen nuts would be often covered with leaves, which we would later scratch away with sticks or hands to disclose hidden nuts beneath.

After doing a few rows thus to get a head-start, Joseph, when he came home to dinner, would announce to us that the time had come for work to begin in earnest. Then down to the orchard, would troop the "bucket brigade" to begin the season's harvest. This was always prolonged over a period of six weeks or so, as not all the nuts ripened at the same time. So the orchard had to be gone over again and again to get them all.

Some of the trees were very large and bore prolifically. These we would take one at a time as a group, arranging ourselves in a row from the trunk to the outer edge of the nut-circle, each taking a strip graduated in width from very wide at the tree-trunk to very narrow at the outer edge; and kneeling down in the soft sandy earth would pick up and hull the nuts, as we progressed around the tree till the entire circle was completed, emptying our buckets as they were filled, into sacks placed between the rows.

Often we would "run a race" to see who would fill his bucket first, or if we were using separate sacks, to see whose sack would first be filled. The smaller trees and those that bore meagerly, we did not bother to do this way but took them alone or by twos. Many of the nuts needed no hulling but dropped free of hulls.

Not always were the nuts easily freed from the outer hull. Occasionally one would be found soft and "squishy" and very messy to handle. Other nuts might have hulls tightly adherent to the shells and very difficult to remove. Sometimes a big solid green immature one would be found that was not ready to open at all, which had been knocked off too soon. These we would have to cut open on the edge of the bucket, and we disliked to handle them for our hands received dark stains from the green juice. Always at the end of the season, our hands would be so stained that many weeks would be required for the stain to disappear.

Having freed the green nut from its hull, we would often pocket it to be eaten later, for these unripe nuts with the thin inner skin peeled off were as delicious as almonds treated the same way. Those who have never been privileged to taste a nut in this immature stage, can hardly imagine the rich goodness they have missed.

Some seasons through unfavorable weather conditions or the attack of some disease, the hulls instead of splitting open in a normal way, would for the greater portion of the crop, be closely adherent to the shells and dried on so that we could hardly get them off, sometimes not at all. Then the nuts inside would almost certainly be blighted and unsaleable. This would betoken a "poor crop." We would not attempt to shuck these nuts while gathering but would pour them out of our buckets in a cone-shaped heap on the ground in the shade. When our tree or row was finished, we would all gather round the heap sitting on our heels, with individual buckets beside us and hold a "shucking bee." Joseph, though doing very little if any of the picking-up, would frequently join in the shucking.

Often, to pass the time away we would start some game to be played while we worked. An interesting and endless favorite was "Boat's Afloat," which could be carried all down through the alphabet if desired, beginning with the letter "A."

The one to introduce the game, would first determine in his own mind what was to be his "cargo"—usually something beginning with "A" to start with, which the others were to guess in turn. Then he would announce:

"Boat's afloat. What's it loaded with? It isn't Apples" (or anything he might choose to name thus giving the clue that the cargo was an article beginning with "A") and the others would begin to guess:

"Apes?"

"No."

"Apricots?"

"No."

"Africans?" and so on till someone guessed correctly. Perhaps it might be "Asafoetida," or "Aphids" or "Arnica," or something equally hard to guess.

The one who was successful could then take his turn with a cargo beginning with "B." Thus, many otherwise tedious hours would be pleasantly passed; and before we knew it, the big pile of hard nuts was finished, and perhaps the welcome sound in Mother's ringing voice halloed from the front porch, "Din-ner-r-r!" would summon us to the delicious hot meal of boiled potatoes and gravy and fresh vegetables—and the inevitable salt pork. Then we would spring up and race for home with appetites like those of winter wolves.

Often our tasks were enlivened by conversation being carried on in a foreign tongue, namely "Hog-latin." Not that it was the language spoken by hogs, nor that we took our instructions from hogs. Not that it even sounded hoggy, though it must be noted that the main character used in it was hard "g" sounded as in "hog." But certainly it was—and is of latin derivation. We say "is" advisedly; for it must by no means considered a "dead language" so long as children live.

Hog-latin is not difficult to learn. Very little education is required to master it. Once the foundation principle is understood, it can be spoken fluently by anyone, even the tongue-tied and those with poor linguistic talents. In fact, it is much more easily spoken than interpreted by the hearers; though with a little meditation and ingenuity on the part of the listener, its meaning grows upon the consciousness. The main thing to remember by both speaker and interpreter is that the endings are all alike; and the key to each word lies in the vowel sound of the first syllable. Thus:

"I-ger-ry wig-ger-ry nog-ger-ry do-ger-ry ig-ger-ry," deciphers into: "I will not do it."

"See-ger-ry thig-ger-ry prig-ger-ry flow-ger-ry!" resolves itself into: "See this pretty flower!"

"Why-ger-ry dig-ger-ry you-ger-ry do-ger-ry thag-ger-ry?" obviously asks: "Why did you do that?" and so on ad-infinitum. To this brief explanation, add a little originality, and presto! The language is yours.

After we had gone over the whole orchard in this way, the first trees done would be ready for another shaking, more nuts having ripened in the meantime. Then the whole process would be repeated, but still without getting all of the nuts. The last—and usually the third time over the orchard, we took long bamboo fishing poles with us and knocked off the belated nuts in the tops of the trees that had persisted in clinging to "the old forsaken bough" after all their fellows were gone.

It was a day of rejoicing when the walnut-picking was at last finished. Many weeks had been spent out-of-doors in our oldest clothes. We were sun tanned and dirty, our hands hopelessly stained, but no doubt healthier and happier for the experience. At first we had greatly enjoyed working under the shady trees, crawling in the soft sandy earth, and inhaling the sweet subtle perfume of the walnut leaves. But by the time the job was finished, we were all tired and glad to be able to put on clean clothes once more, and do some other kind of work.

But though our part of the harvest was over, the work was not yet finished for our elders. Every evening we had brought home the nuts gathered that day, and emptied them out onto the long racks that paralleled the woodpiles on the opposite side of the road, to dry and cure. They had been stirred every day to give the sun a chance at them all, and when the first were ready, the sorting and sacking had begun. With a large flat, square-cornered shovel having built-up sides graduating higher from front to back, the nuts were scooped up from the drying racks into large walnut sacks, and these when filled to the brim were "sewn up" ready for the market.

One black-walnut tree grew at the far end of the vineyard. This tree we never harvested in the regular manner. Its nuts were not saleable. We gathered them when and how we pleased and did as we would with them. Frank and I would take some of them up to the bone rock and crack them open with the sledge hammer, filching from their hard crannies little bits of goodness.

Then would come the fun of gleaning. All the gleanings we children could have for our very own. This is what made it so interesting. The knowledge that each could keep what he found made gleaning happiness unalloyed. This was our wages for the long weeks of labor in the harvest. To have something saleable of our own—to be able to increase our finances by ever so little, was worth many weeks of additional effort.

Though having done our best to get all the nuts while gathering the crop, it was truly surprising how many we had missed that came to light when autumn winds had blown away the covering leaves. After other duties were done, every day would find us roaming about over the orchard from one end of it to the other, wherever our fancies willed, singly, or in groups, scratching away leaves with forked sticks secured and kept for the purpose from day to day, gleaning, gleaning, gleaning; while the mourning doves called their pensive: "Oo-Coo-oo-o, oo-oo-o, oo-oo-o, oo-oo-o," fading to a distant echo. Little Luella, often all alone by herself gleaning to the tune of these soft mournful notes, felt so lonesome and far away from home—miles and miles away, though not at any time more than a quarter of a mile—so plaintive was the call of the doves.

Our gleaned nuts were never sulphured. They were brought in a few at a time, over a period of many weeks, for we kept at it till the first rains of winter put a final stop to the remunerative occupation. After the rains came, the nuts left on the ground would begin to swell up and pop open at the seam. And some day early in the year shooting up here and there over the orchard we would find little walnut trees that had come out at the gaping point of the nut and sent down a bunch of little rootlets into the soil.

Joseph would take our nuts over to Laguna with him on his peddling trips and sell them to his customers, and he never charged us any commission, so whatever they brought in nickels and dimes, we could claim as our own. Nothing was ever said by anybody as to what we should do with our money. Often these gleaned nuts sold for a higher price per pound than the main crop, and we felt quite rich.

Olive picking would usually begin in October and last a number of weeks; being sandwiched in between other duties; for olives, unlike other fruit, can hang a long while on the tree after they are ready to gather, without material damage. Instead of going over the trees again and again to get only ripe fruit, we would wait till most of them were ripe and then gather them all; for green ones, though somewhat inferior to ripe, could be pickled just the same, and it did not pay us to be too particular.

The smaller children could not help much with olive picking, because for the most part it was done from stepladders; the picker often standing perilously near the top rung, and reaching high overhead. Even then it was impossible to reach them all, and the boys had to use other very long ladders, and afterward climb the trees to get the last ones high in the tops—or failing, were obliged to leave the topmost hanging ungathered to wither on the trees; for even the birds would let them alone.

Being evergreen, the trees remained beautiful all through the winter time; their stiff, pointed, gray-green leaves shedding a few at a time, dropping in little brown curls to the ground. The leaves of the olive tree are peculiarly resistant to the action of water, and if soaked over a long period of time will not soften or spoil. Though their color might fade a trifle, yet their texture remains the same. Leaves would get into the barrels sometimes and remain under water for six weeks or two months without being affected. This quality is perhaps significant with reference to the Bible story of the great flood in Noah's time, which the leaves of the olive tree must have survived; for it was "an olive leaf plucked off" that the dove brought back in her bill to the ark on Ararat.

Demons of the Dust

Sometimes when crossing the sandy orchard, we would come across a mysterious little pit several inches deep, having perfectly smooth sides, and shaped like an open top inverted cone, with point at the bottom.

"Oh, here's an ant-lion's den!" we would exclaim; and drop down onto the ground to examine the fascinating pitfall and watch the little creature that had made it. But no ant-lion would be in sight. We knew he could be found concealed in the very bottom just under the surface, and could almost tell which way he would be facing. For if there happened to be a little patch of sunlight on one side of the pit, he would very likely be found with his head toward it, waiting for some hapless little bug or ant to straggle along that way, get too near the edge, and go sliding down the smooth steep slope literally into the jaws of death.

If we could find an ant or other small insect, we sometimes would push him over the edge to watch the performance. Mr. Ant-lion was ready for him with his strong jaws that could open very wide and his sharp eyes that could see even through the sand that covered his body. As soon as the tiny victim struck bottom, he had him in his jaws and would drag him struggling under the sand and hold him there till he was dead or paralyzed by some secretion injected. Then he would feast on his internal juices till the body was just a hull, which he would discard as rubbish.

Sometimes not getting a good hold on him at the first grab, he would toss him up and let him fall again in the right position for a proper hold before dragging him under. If he thought the victim was going to escape, he would shower him with sand till he came land-sliding down again into the pit. These cunning vicious little beasts of prey have been justly called "Demons of the Dust."

Hardly ever can you find one actually making his pitfall. They begin after dusk has fallen and their enemies have all gone to bed, when they can work in safety. Working their hind legs and bodies into the ground and tossing out the dirt with their heads, they dig always backward around and around with perfect geometrical precision in an ever narrowing and deepening circle, their first round always outlining the size of the top of the finished pit.

When we could find no little victim for his rapacity, we would capture the lion in his den by dipping a hand into the pit with fingers pressed together and lifting out a small amount of the bottom sand. There would be Mr. Ant-lion himself, backing around in the palm of the hand, trying in vain to bury himself again, and tossing the dirt around with his head.

So long as we would hold him thus in the palm, he would seem not to realize what had happened to him, and that he was in the hand of an enemy. But if we just touched him he would stop moving and lie as if dead. After awhile we would let him go to live his life in his own way, and proceed to our own duties.

Riddles

Down in the orchard one day, Joseph told me that he knew of a wonderful way to get rich quick—so quick that one's wealth would amount to over five million dollars in thirty days. And more wonderful still, all the capital you had to have to start with was one penny. I was incredulous. Joseph was surely springing another joke. But he seemed so sober and earnest, and assured me so confidently that he could prove it by figures, that my attentive interest was secured.

And this is the method he set before me: Just begin with one cent on the first day, double it the second day, double what you have the third day, double that the fourth day, and keep on doubling all you have every day for thirty days; at the end of which time you will assuredly have over five and a third million dollars.

I secured pencil and paper and began to figure it out. It required very little to finance the proposition for the first week—only sixty-four cents. I had that much myself—even a little more. I kept on figuring, and sure enough, to my amazement at the end of thirty days the total was actually the astounding sum of five million, three hundred and sixty-eight thousand, seven hundred nine dollars and twelve cents.

How wonderful! Yet how simple! What an easy way to amass a fortune! Why, I might try that myself. I could carry it on alone for maybe ten days if careful and saving and if I gleaned a little harder, for that would amount to only five dollars and twelve cents. And ten days was actually one third of the whole period. But—there is always a "but" to everything nice—when my own resources should give out what was I to do then? Borrow a little, I suppose. But if the lender should find out what I wanted the money for, he wouldn't loan it to me and let a fortune slip through his own fingers that easy. So I would have to keep my purpose to myself.

But—there's that "but" again—from whom should I borrow? Just then I could think of no one. So I decided to wait until a little older and then think up some scheme for financing the project.

I am still waiting. Figures do indeed prove it to be a quick way to get rich, but hardly a way to get rich quick.

Joseph always had another one "up his sleeve" for me. One day it was "Saint Ives," the age-old favorite—but new as fresh milk to me.

"As I was going to St. Ives," began Joseph, and my thoughts said;

("I never heard of that place before. Wonder where it is.")

"I met a man with seven wives."

("My! He must have been a Mormon. Oh, now I know! 'Ives' isn't a place at all. He just had to have something to rhyme with 'wives.') I could sympathize with that. "Each wife had seven sacks";

("I wonder what for!")

"Each sack had seven cats";

("My! I'd hate to carry seven cats in a sack. How they would yeoul!") "Each cat had seven kits";

("I wish our old cat would have that many.")

"Kits, cats, sacks and wives, how many were going to St. Ives?"

Here I needed a pencil. I had one, and paper too. Always I carried such scraps about with me in my pocket for poetic emergencies.

("Let's see. We must begin with the wives. Multiply them by the sacks—oh no! The 'rithmetic book says never to multiply different objects together. So we'll have to call it just seven times seven wives. That makes forty-nine. Then the cats make seven times forty-nine. That's three hundred forty-three. Now for the kittens. Seven times three hundred forty-three makes two thousand, four hundred and one.")

This answer I announced.

"Nope," said Joseph.

Then I figured it all over again and it came out just the same.

"That must be right—oh, I forgot to count the husband. He would make two thousand four hundred and two."

"Nope," said Joseph again.

"Well, why ain't it right? How many were there then?"

"Just one," said Joseph. "Those I met were none of them going to Saint Ives."

"Oh-o-o-o!"

Joseph grinned at me. But I knew he had been fooled first by somebody. After that I could try it on Annie, and do the grinning myself.

Then there was the man who had a fox and a goose and a bucket of corn which he had to get across the river in his little boat that was so small it would carry only one of them at a time. How should he manage to get them across? He couldn't let the goose and the fox stay together alone while he carried the corn across, or the old fox would eat up the goose. He couldn't leave the goose and the corn together while he carried the fox across, because the goose would eat up the corn. So what was he to do? How could he get them all safely across the river?

I worked on this one several days without success, the pond serving in my mental world for a river, since I had never seen one. Then, discovering that Frank knew the answer, I persuaded him to tell me, and the mystery was solved. He just took the old goose across, left her there till he went back and got the corn. Then he left the corn there and took the goose back with him and left her on shore alone while he took the fox across; he then went back the fourth time and got the goose who thus had three boat rides; and there they all were safe across the river.

Then there was the man who with his goose was up in a high prison. The question was, how can the man get down without descending? We would pucker our brows over this one, and then give up, to be told: "Why, he just picks it off the goose's breast."

Then there was the man in prison who was visited by another man in company with a friend. After the two had returned home, the friend asked: "Who was that man we visited in prison?" The other replied: "Brothers and sisters have I none. Yet that man's father was my father's son." What was their relationship?

Another riddle was put to us in which the answer must be visualized. "A flock of ducks was going by, one duck between two ducks, one duck behind two ducks, one duck ahead of two ducks, and one duck on each side of two ducks. How many ducks were in the flock?" The answer is three ducks. But the propounder always had to draw a diagram to convince his audience.

But the best one to test the gray matter put to me one day by Joseph during apple-gathering season is a legitimate mathematical problem. "A man had a hundred dollars, with which he purchased a hundred head of stock, paying ten dollars apiece for cows, three dollars apiece for sheep, and fifty cents apiece for hogs. How many of each did he buy?" Perhaps you can do this one.

CHAPTER 40 FOODS AND FOIBLES

Mother was the most unselfish of women. Always, she felt she must share with others whatever was pleasant or delectable. If presented with something out of the ordinary, such as a big extra-fine apple or a luscious sweet orange—a rare treat in those days—she would divide it to the last section with all the others, even against their united protest—for we all wanted Mother to eat it herself—or else she would lay it away in contemplation of such division in the future. Occasionally, having laid something of that kind away in anticipation of a pleasant little surprise for the children, in the constant press of work she would forget about it entirely and later come across it accidentally, only to find that it was spoiled so that nobody could eat it.

Rigid economy—absolutely necessary in the very early days—became such a habit with Mother that she never really outgrew it even when times became somewhat easier; although it cannot be said that times ever became easy enough to dispense with economy or even to relegate it to the background. In her later days, when she would consider long and carefully before making a needed purchase, or drive a close bargain for the lowest price, others unacquainted with her history might possibly have mistaken her attitude to be stinginess. But this was not stinginess at all but merely habitual economy over-stressed, a trait born in adversity and practiced from necessity, for which she could not be justly censured. Even in this, the thought was always for others. A penny saved, was saved that she might have more to impart to her loved ones or to protect them from want.

According to the standards of those days, Mother was considered a good cook. She understood the art of seasoning, always made things taste good, and could make the most out of the materials on hand. The word, "dietetics," if indeed it had yet been coined, was entirely outside of the general vocabulary. And had it been a familiar word would have meant practically nothing, for the subject of foods was shrouded in the densest ignorance. Our present knowledge gained from modern biological experimentation was as yet a dark secret. Many things that little school children of today discuss with intelligence were then unknown to the wisest scientific mind, and the scattered few who departed from the established order in the matter of foods, were regarded as "cranks."

Of such, were the "graham-bread" advocates, originating before the fifties through the teachings of Sylvester Graham, who endeavored to educate the people to go back to the old-fashioned whole-grain breads; insisting that white flour was robbed of its life and health-giving qualities. Bread made of the whole grains including outer coatings and germ, was called after him "Graham Bread"—a term today abused. A small amount of bran added to a large amount of white flour with none of the germ is today sufficient for so-called "graham bread."! The one hundred per cent bread is more nearly like that he used. However, to be sure of getting the same, requires that the whole kernels be ground together with nothing added and nothing taken away. This man who might be called, "The Morning-Star of Dietetics," as Wycliffe was of the Reformation, also left off flesh-foods and adopted a vegetable diet. But few in our day had ever heard of him or his teachings, and white flour was regarded as superior in every way to the dark flours such as "middlings," "shorts," or "Graham."

Of the mysteries of food and the body's requirements, we knew neither more nor less than other ordinary folk around us. And popular misconceptions were regarded with respect. Cabbage was supposed to be indigestible and even poisonous unless cooked about two hours. When it came out of the pot, it was very brown and very strong, and we ate it always with vinegar.

As for cucumbers, they were considered particularly indigestible, and to contain a poisonous substance that must be thoroughly soaked out in salt water before they were fir to eat at all. So they were sliced thin and soaked in salt solution until wilted, tough and leathery, then seasoned with pepper, salt and vinegar and slightly sweetened. The water in which they had been soaked, which now contained practically all the precious food-minerals and no doubt the vitamins, was of course thrown away.

In one of our old readers there was a poem that reflected this popular idea. It consisted of a description of a nightmarish, sleepless night, the cause of which was vainly sought till revealed in the last line: "'Tis that confounded cucumber I've eat and can't digest." The "confounded" soaking, pepper and vinegar had never once been thought of as a factor in the trouble. And so another wholesome food was maligned.

Tomatoes too were connected by a superstition with rheumatism and other ailments laid at their door. Today they are used to cure the very ailments they were supposed to induce. Even oranges were supposed to be bad for rheumatism.

The usual way of serving lettuce was to "wilt" it. Instead of putting it on the table crisp and raw, it was heaped into a skillet in which was smoking-hot grease, salted, covered and cooked till wilted, then eaten with vinegar. For "greens,"! we used beet-tops and turnip-tops from the garden, tender wild mustard and wild lettuce. All wholesome and good had we but omitted the inevitable pork.

White navy beans were our standby. No other bean was considered fit to bake, and but few fit to eat. No one thought of putting colored beans on the table; they were only for the stock. So we needlessly deprived ourselves of a delicious dish—a dish that many still have not discovered. There was a large white bean—not the Lima Bean—shaped like the navy, but as large as a kidney bean, which we used, and called the "butter-bean." It was good, with a flavor different from the navy. This bean is never seen anymore in western markets—for what reason, I do not know.

For dessert, Mother sometimes made "Minute Pudding." Into a pot of boiling water slightly salted and slightly sweetened, she would sift through her fingers while stirring vigorously, dry white flour, which of course would lump immediately as was intended, adding a cup or two of washed raisins unseeded; and with a few minutes of cooking the pudding was ready to serve. We ate it with a "sweet gravy" made of water, vinegar, sugar and a lump of butter, boiled and thickened slightly to a thin gravy consistency. This pudding tasted good, the important criterion of cookery then, and the raisins at least were wholesome. But from the half-raw starch and the vinegar may have come some of those "belly-aches" we sometimes complained of.

Cornmeal mush was a family standby. Often, when there were leftovers, we had fried mush, always enjoyed. But sometimes—especially if anybody was ailing—Mother would serve us with a delicious "gruel" made of half water and half milk salted and slightly thickened with a mixture of cornmeal and flour. Though so simple this was considered a treat.

Bread and milk we often had, the milk being poured over crumbled bread in the bowl. When in season, grapes pulled from the stem would be added, making a delightful variation. This with all was a favorite dish.

Another dish enjoyed was "sop"; which we usually made each one for himself.

"Oh, let's have some sop!" someone would say as supper time arrived.

"Let's do!" we would chorus, and forthwith proceed to make it. Into each of our tin cups we would put crumbled bread, salt, pepper and a lump of butter, and over this pour boiling water carefully, till we had just enough to soften the bread; when it was ready to be eaten—each one cooling his spoonful by blowing.

Sometimes we had popcorn for supper. Mother or the girls would pop an immense pan of corn and set it in the middle of the table. All would gather around to enjoy the feast, we children always making a "game" of it. First we would build a "corral" of popcorn on the oilcloth-covered table, placing at one side those kernels that were especially big and fluffy to be the "sheep." An immense one was selected to be the "dog," and a burnt or ugly-looking one for the "wolf." Then we would put the sheep inside the corral and set the dog to guard them. The wolf, we made to prowl about and break through the fence killing the sheep in spite of the dog. All these unfortunate sheep we ate with gusto, becoming the "big bad wolf" in person. All the hard unpopped kernels we saved and later ground in the coffee mill to be eaten with milk as a cereal. This meal was rich, nutty and delicious.

In winter time, when the hail came popping down thick and fast with a loud rattle on the roof, we would rush outside with dishpans and milkpans to catch all the hail we could, bringing it in for an "ice cream" feast. Dishing it out into bowls, and covering it with sugar and cream, we would eat it immediately with aching teeth and freezing buccal cavities. The only trouble with this ice cream was that we could have it only when we were cold enough already both inside and out and needed nothing to increase our shivering, while the hot summer days were doomed to pass ice-creamless.

We all were fond of watermelons, and raised the best; slicing them lengthwise and eating them out-of-doors a la natural and from ear to ear.

Quantities of sour milk would accumulate which Mother let clabber and made into cottage cheese, filling the big iron pot and setting on the back of the wood stove to heat gently. This too was a favorite dish and one very wholesome and valuable in the diet.

One of our main standbys was applesauce. This, we had almost daily as long as the fresh apples lasted. And it was delicious; we never could get enough of it. Somebody was always peeling apples for sauce. The endless apple and potato peeling kept the fingers discolored, for paring knives were not then made of stainless steel.

When the fresh apples were all gone, we would begin on the dried apples. The sauce of these was if possible even better. Oh, how good and rich and tasty was that dried applesauce! Nearly always it had plenty of raisins in it; but either way was unsurpassed in flavor and goodness. It was cooked in a great kettle-full quantities at a time so that the whole family could have all they wanted, and a pot full lasted no time at all. What wouldn't I give for a big dish of it now! Buy it? I would if I could. But the dried apples they sell today bear very little resemblance to those. They seem so flat and tasteless by comparison.

Sometimes we had "fried apples"; and if you have never tried this dish, you are missing something good. For frying, we sliced the apples without paring to keep them from "mushing," merely digging out the cores and cutting them in rings crosswise skins and all. With a spoonful of sizzling hot fat in the bottom of a big iron skillet, we would heap in the sliced apples till it would hold no more, sprinkling over them a small amount of sugar and a shake or two of salt, and covering the skillet till the apples sank down a bit, well penetrated by the heat. Then removing the cover we would cook them over the flame, turning frequently with a lifter—but not stirring—till most of them were a rich brown. Eaten hot with bread and butter they were delicious, and cold leftovers were still good.

In the fall, we always dried apples enough to last us till the next crop would begin to ripen. This meant a great deal of work; for every apple had to be not only peeled, quartered and cored but each quarter cut smaller the same as for apple sauce before spreading on the racks in the sun. At first, all this apple paring had to be done with only paring knives. But later on Father bought a little apple parer that fastened onto the table by a turnscrew much as does the food chopper of today. An apple could be slipped onto the round fork composed of three strong sharp tines, the knife with its spring hinge adjusted, the crank turned, and presto, the apple would come off not only peeled, but also cored and sliced in one continuous cork-screw coil, ready to spread apart on the drying racks, or cook in the kettle. This little wonder device greatly facilitated the work of utilizing our apples.

Fruit that was drying, had either to be covered at night, or brought in under shelter from the fog and dampness and the racks put out again at sun-up. Later on, Father invented a fruit dryer, which would dry apples, figs, or any other fruit independently of the sun. It was built in sections and consisted of a basal stove, lined with fire-brick, on which rested a low boiler from which steam confined in pipes was carried all around the removable drying racks in the high oven above, two and a half foot square of galvanized iron. This arrangement would keep the oven at a constant, even temperature of warmth in any kind of weather. In this oven wide doors provided for admitting and removing the racks.

This dryer was really an excellent invention, adaptable either to families or factories, and one that was needed much at that time. It was Father's dream to patent and promote it, but lack of means was an insurmountable obstacle. So our own family industry became the limit of its usefulness; and like many another useful invention, it died with its inventor.[10]

Mother and the girls always canned fruit for winter use. There was then no such thing as class containers. We used tin cans altogether—plain tin without lacquer or other inside finish. These were made each with a shoulder on the open end, finished with a small sunken groove having a sharp upturned edge over which the lid fitted. No one as yet had introduced the cold-pack method of home canning, and fruits of every kind were cooked in the open kettle over the flame. After the can had been filled with the hot fruit and the lid fitted on, into the groove around it was poured the hot melted red sealing-wax, which then cooled to a hard resinous brittle substance that had to be chipped out of the groove with a heavy knife-point when the contents were needed later. In thus opening, fine chips and dust of the bitter stuff would often get into the fruit, and had to be carefully removed before serving.

A great improvement over this method of sealing was the "wax-string" invented when I was quite a young girl. These consisted of strings that had been cut just the proper length to fit around the lid in the groove and then heavily dipped in melted beeswax, cooled, and packed by dozens in long narrow pasteboard boxes. After closing the hot can of fruit, one of these wax strings would be laid in the groove, its coat of wax melting immediately and filling the groove, thus effectually excluding the air. A can thus sealed was very easily opened. With a knife, one end of the string was lifted and by this the whole string wax and all could be pulled out clean. The lid was then very easily pried off. Mother used to put up the most wonderful fig preserves one ever tasted in these tin cans that filled our cellar shelves.

There was then no such thing as seeded raisins on the market. They had to be painstakingly seeded at home by hand or used seeds and all. To prepare raisins and nuts for a cake or pudding was a real task and such pains were not taken for ordinary dishes such as applesauce and minute pudding. But we did not mind the seeds then so much as we would now. We took them as a matter of course just as we take fresh grape seeds for granted, discarding them as we ate.

For a pacifier, Baby was given a large raisin tied up in a little square of cheesecloth, to which was left attached a length of string by which to rescue it—or rescue the baby—in case it should be sucked down too far. Sometimes we who were still but babies would fix up these "sugarteats" for ourselves, getting an older sister to tie the strings.

There were then no bakeries in small towns and bread was never sold in grocery stores. Even if it had been one could not go twenty-five miles to town to buy a loaf of bread. So all the cakes, pies, and other sweet pastries, and all bread must be baked at home. It was a part of every girl's education to learn how to make good bread. Housekeeping then was a real job—a job that would frighten a young housewife of today. Even the yeast had to be made at home. No such thing as fresh compressed yeast-cakes were then known. Hops for yeast were sold pressed in large bricks, and one of these lasted Mother a long time. She would break off a little piece of the brick and steep it in a large amount of water, making a hop tea for a foundation of her batch of yeast. A grated raw potato scalded with some of the hot hop-tea was added to it with a little honey or sugar and a small amount of flour stirred in, or perhaps part cornmeal, to which was added enough warm water to make the amount desired. While the mixture was lukewarm, a cupful of yeast from the old batch was stirred in to start the "working" process, and the whole poured into the stone crock used for that purpose and set away in a warm place to rise. When light, it would be covered tightly and taken down into the cellar where the fermentation process would be arrested by the cold. A cupful or two of this yeast would be used to a batch of bread. Always the last cupful was reserved for the next batch to be made. Should it happen that no "starter" was available, the yeast could be made just the same only it took much longer for it to "work"—the process depending upon the wild yeast always in the air.

No such thing as ready roasted and ground coffee could be bought then. Coffee was sold green as imported fresh from the tree. We roasted it ourselves at home and ground it in our little hand mill. Later, when ready-roasted coffee came into use, it was more expensive than the green and only those well-to-do could afford it.

Our little coffee mill was a cubical shaped wooden affair, eight or nine inches to a side. In the top of it was a little iron hopper below which revolved the crushing and grinding plates operated by a small crank at one side. The coffee put in whole at the top, was received ground in a little drawer at the bottom. While grinding, we held the mill in our laps between the knees or set it on the table holding it firm with one hand and our weight, while turning the crank with the other. Usually we prepared only one brewing at a time. Some families had little iron mills that were screwed onto the corner of a wall.

In those days we knew nothing at all about curing olives with lye, and to extract the bitter required much time and daily attention, though the process itself was very simple. We would soak them for six weeks or two months in barrels of fresh water, changing it regularly every day, and after the bitter was all soaked out would preserve them in strong brine. When so prepared they were much superior to olives cured by the modern lye process, being richer and more valuable in the diet. Though we knew nothing then of "vitamins" still they were there just the same, and it is now well known that alkalies destroy the vitamins of foods.

Olives however, have other important properties besides vitamins, and even those properly cured with lye—especially when fresh and uncanned, are very excellent food, delicious and wholesome. Those bought in the markets have been heated to preserve them and cannot be compared in flavor with those fresh cured that have never been subject to heat. Olive lovers will be well repaid for their trouble if they will find a place in the country where olives may be picked fresh from the trees—always cheap by comparison with the cured—and cure them at home.

Containers must be such as lye will not affect—stone, glass, pottery, unchipped porcelain, or good hard wood. Here is an old and valuable recipe for lye-curing that will not disappoint you: Measure enough cold water to cover the olives well. To each gallon of water add one tablespoonful of concentrated lye and dissolve well. Let olives stand in this solution exactly twenty-four hours, then drain and discard the water. Make a second solution twice as strong, using two tablespoonfuls of lye to each gallon of water, and let olives stand in this solution exactly forty-eight hours, then drain and discard. Now rinse the olives well in fresh water.

Make a solution of brine, using one teaspoon of salt to each gallon of water, and let olives stand in this solution for twenty-four hours. Drain and discard the brine. Repeat this process each day for five successive days, except that the strength of the brine is increased by one additional teaspoonful of salt to the gallon every day—the last day having five teaspoonfuls to the gallon, and this last time letting the olives stand in the brine for forty-eight hours. Then for the last time drain and discard the brine. Now make a permanent brine using five teaspoonfuls of salt to each gallon of water, and in this leave the olives while using. Should they be too salty, soak each serving for a time in fresh water before putting on the table.

Olives thus cured will keep for a long time without softening. But should softening begin before all are used, heat and can them in the usual way, cooking only enough to heat thoroughly through.

As children, we were not taught much about the evils of eating between meals. The stomach was supposed to have no rights of its own and its protests were usually misinterpreted or disregarded. We were constantly nibbling at this and that—whatever came our way, whether ripe or half ripe; apples, figs, nuts, raw turnips from the garden, or edible wild plants, regardless of meals, or appetites—though these seemed never to be satisfied.

We were careful, however, to avoid those things that had been pointed out to us as "poison"; such as the castor bean, tobacco plant, black nightshade—called by the Indians, "Toluache"—the black berries of which were thought to be poison. Actually they were not so when ripe, and were used for food by the Indians in former times.

Then there was the Jimson Weed or "Deadly Nightshade," which grew in the pastures, and was indeed a virulent poison, containing narcotic properties that produce hallucinations, stupefaction, or frenzy; and which were employed by ancient "medicine men" in their ceremonial rites.

There was also the "Loco Weed," or "Rattleweed," a plant having leaves similar to those of the pepper tree, from the leafy axils of which arise spikes, or racemes of small flowers that turn into dry seed pods like bladders, inside of which the seeds rattle. This plant varies in poison content it is said, according to the soil in which it grows, whether it contains much or little barium and may produce insanity. Often we would come across this plant in wandering over the premises, and were taught to destroy it to protect the cattle, who might partake of it and go "crazy."

Mushrooms and toadstools were plentiful, but as we knew not how to distinguish one from the other, we wisely left alone all such confusing fungi.

Nuts, such as walnuts, almonds, and others imported into California and sold around the holidays, together with peanuts—really not a true nut but a legume—were then considered to be, not a staple article of diet to be put on the table as a regular part of the meal, but just as extra nicknacks to be eaten as candy is usually eaten, between meals and whenever desired to "piece on," and to be used occasionally for cakes and candies. Therefore the demand for nuts on the market was very limited, and the price low. Such a thing as ready-shelled nuts being sold on the markets had never yet been heard of but all kinds of nuts, including peanuts, were to be had in the shell only, and must be cracked by the consumer at home. A hammer was usually used for this purpose, the soft-shelled varieties of nuts found on the markets today being then unknown.

Of fish we caught many kinds. There were bass, rock-cod, smelts, surf-fish, gold-fish, perch, halibut, barracuda—a common favorite—and other kinds. Other seafoods included eels, fat and tender, having their own distinct flavor. These we sliced round-wise and fried.

Crawfish, whose red shell yielded snow-white meat, different in flavor from anything else in the sea—unless it be crab meat—which we never ate. We prepared them by dropping alive into kettles of boiling water, afterward removing the flesh from tail and legs. Always the backs of the shells with their two protruding eyes were saved for children to play with.

Abalones, taken out of the shell alive we sliced and, because "tough as whitleather," pounded to a pulp before frying, the grayish-colored meat having a distinctly different flavor all its own. The ornamental shells we always saved, cleaning and sometimes polishing them by grinding off the outer rough layer on the grindstone; then they were very beautiful.

Mussels, we pulled off from the rocks in large quantities when the season was right, dropping them into boiling water to open—the red meat, fringed with black as it lay in the open shell, resembling nothing so much as a duck sitting on its nest. This meat we chopped and made into soups with milk as oyster-soup is made. It had a very different flavor of which we were very fond. Or we dredged the mussels whole in flour, cornmeal or crumbs, after salting, and fried as oysters are fried—a tasty dish indeed. Thus, we ate all manner of seafoods, clean and unclean alike without regard to or knowledge of Scripture rule, as do many thousands still.

Father slaughtered his own hogs for family consumption, and pickled the pork in strong brine; from which it would be taken out and sliced as needed to fry or stew for the table.

Hog-killing time was not pleasant. My soul shrank from the sound of that peculiar shrill squeal that betokened the death stroke. The tanks of boiling water having been prepared for pouring over it to loosen the bristles, and the platform upon which the carcass was to rest, placed upon the two wooden sawhorses in readiness for the scraping, the slaughter then took place. The animal still warm was brought in the wheelbarrow, dragged from it and raised onto the platform. Then the pouring and scraping was begun. Soon, there were black bristles lying all about, and the carcass began to take upon it a decidedly naked appearance.

Sometimes I too would take a scraper and help while someone else poured the boiling water over the area to be worked on. When all this was finished, Father would remove the animal to the shed and draw it up by the hind feet with a windlass and pulley and proceed to open up the abdominal and thoracic cavities to draw out the contents.

After this, the work of the womenfolk would begin. The fat from all the internal organs must be removed—a delicate operation requiring skillful manipulation of the knives that had been always previously sharpened and were dangerous to handle. Artemisia when a child of nine, in performing this task cut her hand so terribly on the sharp butcher-knife that Father had to sew up her hand with four or five stitches.

The first day, after stripping the fat off we cut it up into small pieces on a cutting board ready to "render, "filling all the pots we possessed and setting them to cook over a slow fire. That night we had fried liver for supper. The second day Mother finished rendering the lard, cooking it slowly in large iron kettles till no tissues were left but a few crisp, brown "cracklings" which she strained out, setting away the many small buckets, jars and cans of hot lard to cool and solidify into white cooking fat.

Meanwhile, there was "head-cheese" to be made and packed away in stone jars, sausage meat also to be chopped in the large wooden bowl by hand—for there were then no meat-grinders for family use. The sausage meat full of savory seasoning was then packed away in crocks and carried to the cellar. Mincemeat also was to be prepared for the coming holidays, tasty and fragrant with apples, raisins, pickled orange peel and vinegar, and likewise packed away. Sometimes the pig's feet were cleaned, boiled, and pickled. With all this necessary chopping we little folks could help. So all hands were kept busy till the smelly, greasy tasks were finished.

Then, nearly always Mother would make a big batch of "fried cakes." We knew nothing at all about doughnuts with holes through the center, but fried cakes were made from the same kind of dough rolled out thick, cut into strips, and twisted together before frying in the deep fat. For many days after this we had "spare ribs," or sausage, or head-cheese—all rich and greasy and difficult of digestion—for almost every meal, with rich fried cakes to cap the climax.

After all the fresh meat was gone, and we had reveled in the sausage and headcheese till we were filled to satiety, then we would begin on the salt pork which Father had cut up into convenient pieces and pickled in strong brine.

Well do I remember one unsavory experience when a whole barrelful of salt pork that was supposed to last us through the winter, started to spoil—the result either of poor salt, or failure to reheat the brine soon enough. For always the brine had to be poured off, re-heated and skimmed and more salt added, several times during the curing process.

As soon as this unfortunate condition was discovered, prompt measures were taken to counteract it and the process was checked; but not before the flavor of all the meat in the barrel had been impaired—tainted just enough to make it unappetizing. This was indeed a calamity. Our parents could not afford to throw it all away. Times were too hard and food too scarce. We had no other meat, and so were obliged to eat it. For many months it lasted. They tried in various ways to prepare it so as to cover up the flavor, but all in vain. Oh, how glad we all were when at long last it was gone!

Jimcracks

In those days, people believed in "jim-crack" decorations—that is, in decorating the rooms with small articles of all sorts and kinds that had no other use than to be looked at, and simply cluttered up shelves and walls and added needlessly to the burden of keeping the house clean. Wainscoting all around rooms would be built wide enough to serve as narrow shelves for the display of china and bric-a-brac, becoming catchalls for almost everything for which there was no other place.

In one corner of almost every house would be a "what-not"—a tall, three-cornered, open case containing a series of ornamental shelves, crowded with exhibits of every imaginable sort; among which would be seen, foreign seashells, glass-blown scenes enclosed in bottles, bits of bright ore-bearing rock, odd-shaped containers made of china, brass or silver, collections of abalone shells, large "turbines" (shells), vases, china animals, small savings banks sometimes covered with seashells, and numerous other dirt-catching odds and ends of every sort, accumulated through the years, to be kept dusted and cleaned.

A house seemed bare unless every available foot of wall space was dressed up in some manner. Everything that could be hung, went onto the walls. Always there were enlarged family portraits in heavy, deep-set frames, besides other pictures such as still are seen. Other deep frames contained hair-work under glass—hair, skillfully woven into flowers and wreaths. There were other frames of moss-work—flowers and wreaths of moss, and still others of shell-work—flowers, wreaths and baskets made of seashells and pebbles—all very beautiful indeed and exhibitions of great skill and patience, and of course all done by hand.

Then there were plaques of this and that—ornaments shaped like some style of plate, which might be made of wood, clay, paper-mache, or china, with flowers or other representations painted or modeled in colors inside them.

There were banners of Kensington painting—that is, oil-painting on velvet, and "crazy-patch-work"—irregular-shaped pieces of silk sewn together and outlined with various ornamental stitches, all lined and furnished with brass rods and chains for hanging over nails driven into walls.

There were deer-antlers for cloak and hat racks, and various receptacles for this and that—combs, handkerchiefs, whisk-brooms, and such things. Our own family whisk broom was very choice and kept in Mother's trunk. It must not be used for anything that would soil it or damage the straws.

In place of brushes that might be needed to brush off chairs, crumb the table, or sweep the hearth, we used the wings of large birds, such as ducks, geese, and hawks, severing them at the first joint and searing the raw surfaces over the coals to preserve them. These brushes did their work admirably, being put to innumerable uses, and had the advantage of being easily obtained without cost, and could be discarded for fresher ones at any time.

Our pillows were hidden behind "pillow shams," made of large squares of bleached muslin, widely hemmed all around, with borders and central designs worked in outline stitch with red cotton thread. On one might be worked the motto: "Sweet Dreams" or "Goodnight," and on the other, "Good Morning," with perhaps a sleepy touseled head on a pillow, or a little bird singing.

On the wall behind bowl and pitcher 'Lavatories, would be tacked protecting "splashers," made in a similar manner, or fringed at the ends, with some scene suggesting water, such as umbrella girls in the rain or frogs near a pool, worked in the same red outline stitch. Runners of similar make for "toilets" (dressers) and stands would be worked in many and varied designs, of flowers, birds on their nests, ducks, rabbits, bees, butterflies, kittens, puppies, little chicks, sunbonnet babies, and Dutch boys and girls.

Forerunners of the Picture Show

Colored picture cards in those early days were a rare treat. One would rather receive a bright picture card for a gift than almost anything else. Merchants would bait their customers with colored picture cards for prizes. At some stores every twenty-five cent purchase would entitle the buyer to a small card, and a fifty-cent purchase to a larger card. These cards, though very beautiful, always bore advertising matter on the back and the merchant's name on the front; yet were eagerly collected by the grown-ups and saved as photographs are saved to be taken out upon occasion and exhibited.

Double-faced cards, consisting of two picture cards pasted back to back, with a silk fringe protruding from between all around, were manufactured for Christmas cards, and these contained no advertising matter, but beautiful winter scenes of white snow glistening with powdered mica as snow sparkles in the sun. These were always sold in protecting folders to preserve the fringe and the snow. The prices ranged all the way from twenty-five cents to a dollar and a half according to the size and elaborateness of the card. Happy the recipient of such a Christmas gift, whether child or adult! They were preserved immaculate as treasured keepsakes throughout long years.

"Visiting cards," or "name cards" were also made either with highly embossed colored pictures and the name in print or script on one side, or with a separate cut-out picture fastened at one end to the card, the other end to be lifted disclosing the name underneath the concealing beauty of bright flowers, cooing doves, clasped hands, birds with nests, seashells and other designs. These were moderately priced, at about fifteen cents or a quarter a dozen, and were in use not so much as calling cards, but more as favors to be presented to friends much as snapshots are given today.

Father once took an agency for colored picture cards of all descriptions, and went about the country taking orders for them. He had a very large square, folding, sample sheet of several feet in dimensions to which were attached picture cards of every size and description, from an inch or two to six or eight in length, each with its price indicated below. With what eager delight we children used to "hang around" whenever he would take out this big unwieldy sample sheet and unfold it before our admiring eyes, and how we would gaze with reverent joy at the beautiful display! It was hard to "mind" when he would tell us not to touch. People bought these cards for the pleasure of looking at them, an homage paid to the love of the beautiful, an esthetic luxury that ministered to the finer part of their natures, just as do beautiful paintings today.

The magazines of that time, rarely if ever, contained a colored picture. Their illustrations were done in black and white. Colored postcards also were many years in the future. And there were no bright colored calendars distributed by banks and merchants as we have them today. The inevitable somber black-and-white almanac, put out by advertisers of patent medicines, hung upon its nail in every home.

Children's picture books were beginning to have colored covers and a few bright colored pictures inside among the black-and-white ones; but these were quite expensive and poor families often had to go without.

Never shall I forget the bitter disappointment one Christmas brought to me when a small child. Two Mother-Goose rhyme books with colored pictures were presented, one to Annie and the other to Charlotte; while to me, who was supposed to be past the "mother-goose" stage, was given a board-covered book which I found upon opening to be illustrated with utterly black silhouettes. My heart was broken. I cried bitterly protesting: "I don't want them old pictures." They seemed an insult to my beauty-loving soul. In vain Mother tried to change my viewpoint, telling me the stories were lovely; I could not be comforted. The sight of those ugly black pictures spoiled every story for me. A fatal mistake had been made and my Christmas spoiled. As long as that book lasted I never liked it. I loved a book more than anything else in the world—unless it be a doll-and to be given one that was so utterly unlovely to look at when I so craved beauty was—well, I could hardly bear it. I thought the man that made that book must have been a fool. And I'm not sure but that opinion still holds.

Father's agency included, along with his picture cards, a most wonderful book of penmanship. One would never dream that designs and lettering so beautiful and perfect in symmetry could be produced by any human being in free-hand drawing with pen and ink. Birds life-sized hovered over nests of eggs built in shrubbery, all done in scroll work for the most part with circular motions of the pen. And the book proposed to teach the art. To pore over that book was an inspiration and never-failing pleasure that half a century cannot obliterate from memory. Somewhere, one at least of those penmanship books is still preserved in the family.

One happy day, Father brought home for us a marvelous "Magic Lantern" for winter evenings' entertainment. The "big folks" would tack up a white sheet on the wall in Mother's bedroom and out in the middle of the floor set up the "lantern" at the right height, distance and angle to focus on the sheet, and light the small kerosene lamp within the machine behind the slide slot. Then they would run the long, narrow colored slides slowly through the slot between lamp and lens one at a time, by hand.

There, greatly magnified on the screen would pass before us an array of beautiful colored pictures twenty or thirty times as large as the tiny ones on the slide that had to be held up to the window light before we could tell what they were. There were revealed beautifully colored boys and girls at play, cunning babies with golden locks, kittens, birds, flowers, trees and houses, all standing out on the wall in almost half life size. Old and young would gather around to enjoy the marvelous sight. It was our first "picture show," and the only kind then available. For an evening's entertainment, the "Magic Lantern" surely took the prize.

CHAPTER 41 HUNTING BIRDS' NESTS

Aliso Canyon with its environs was a delightsome haunt for birds every description, not only those that lived at our expense, but those it befriended us by destroying insect pests, and regaled us with their sweet and tuneful melodies.

A source of never-ending springtime joy was hunting birds' nests, each one intent on building up an individual bird-egg collection. Perhaps this quest had its earliest inception in those trusting and credulous days when, pursuing the ambition latent in every child's heart actually to capture a wildling, we wandered about with handfuls of salt watching covertly some little bird as he flitted from twig to twig, or hopped down onto the ground after a tasty morsel or straw to weave, and seizing the opportunity as directed by the wise ones, threw it eagerly, hopefully, only to find where that little tail had been, nothing but the salty seeds of a painful doubt.

But bird-nest hunting had its sure rewards, though some, there were those eggs we could never hope to acquire. Of these, were the hawks, owls, and vultures, nesting high on the crags above the canyon walls, the sea-birds, who favored home-sites far away from our coasts and the scavenger of the air, the Turkey Buzzard, with naked red pate, who sailed high overhead with never a flap of his tip-frayed wing, and nested we knew not where. Even the nest of the familiar hammering woodpecker was inaccessible to us younger collectors.

But delightful possibilities for other treasures lay all about us everywhere. Up and down the willow-lined banks of the creek, and along its weed-grown fences, through vineyard and orchards, among the vines and brush and rocks of the hillsides, the caves of the cliffs, and all through the oak and sycamore groves with their rank, weedy undergrowths, we would wander with prying eyes and sly footsteps, examining the many hiding-places and peering into decaying tree-trunks, while closely observing the actions of the birds and following every clue unwittingly given of the whereabouts of their hidden nests.

What thrills of delight would accompany each discovery—that is, if the nest were accessible! But how often did I wish I might have been provided with a long, long arm—one that would stretch to unimagined lengths at the desire or need of its possessor, contracting again to normal, at will! How marvelously thrilling and convenient it would have been just to reach my arm out and up and up without effort, to explore that little nest in the high tree-top!

Though ardently loving the birds, there was one thing about them I could never understand—their choice of viands. Watching the mama and papa birds dropping into the gaping mouths of their naked, cheeping nestful of birdlings, the bugs, flies and worms, that went down at a gulp with cries for "more, more, more," a sickening disgust always possessed my soul, at their strange bill of fare. I could understand their liking for seeds of all kinds, but bugs, flies, worms! Ugh! After all, birds were funny creatures to eat such things as those. I had sampled practically everything in the vegetable kingdom that grew in our domain, but never, never, could a bug or a beetle or a fly or a worm excite my curiosity to the point of sampling its delectability.

To preserve the eggshells for our collections, we would empty them by puncturing both ends with a sharp pin and blowing out the contents. Sometimes in the process the shells would break, for many were very delicate indeed. So we would handle them with the greatest caution—especially the more rare and valuable, laying them in our boxes on beds of cotton. We could not be satisfied until samples of eggs had been secured from every bird we knew—except the impossibles.

Certain of the birds, we were strongly cautioned against injuring in any way, or completely robbing of eggs, on account of their habits of feeding on injurious insect life. These endeared themselves to us by constantly filling their crops with our small enemies, delighting our eyes with their beauty, and regaling our ears with their sweet songs.

Others of the birds, we had been taught to consider as natural enemies because of their destructive natures and prolific numbers, and were encouraged to rob and tear down their nests and even to destroy their young. But this last, we were reluctant to do, for young things of every kind possessed a tender appeal for us children. As to robbing their nests, however, we had not the same compunction, and performed many a ruthless deed in the woodland as a consequence of these instructions. Such birds were wont to destroy our fruits in great quantities, despoiling much more than they ever ate and leaving the pecked ones to sour and waste. In summer the fig trees would be festooned overhead with dangling, gaping, half eaten fruit, filled with foraging bees, who were always on the watch for such opportunities to gather sweets. Often too, could be seen the large wasp-like black-bodied, red-winged tarantula hawk, feasting among them on the same sweet juices.

Among the most destructive was the Linnet, or common House Finch, always a prolific breeder and in evidence everywhere. Though actually beautiful little birds—the male with red feathers on his forehead, throat and rump, that set off the rest of his gray-brown plumage to advantage, outshining his somber, mottled-gray little mate; and interesting too with their cheerful chatter and friendly natures, nesting in the trees around the house, in the willows along the creek, in hedges and vines along the fences, under the eaves of the barn, cistern and sheds—even bold enough at times to build under the eaves of the porch; yet, constantly presented as we were with mangled reminders of their depredations, it was hardly possible for us to appreciate their good qualities.

But no matter how frequently their nests were robbed or torn down, they never seemed to learn that we had anything against them and would build again and again in the same places, in locations more open and accessible and closer to the house than any other bird. Their nests, constructed coarsely of dried grasses, were well-lined with delicate fibers, bits of string or bright calico, wisps of cotton, chicken feathers, and anything else they could collect about the yards and pastures, and held always four, and more often five thin-shelled bluish-white eggs, the larger end speckled with black. In these our egg-collections always abounded.

Another bird that we not only considered an enemy, but actually hated, was the Butcher Bird, or Shrike. He was about the size and slate-gray color of the mocker—only less slender—showing the same white feathers in flight, but flying lower and more swiftly and having a distinctive heavy black mask across face and eyes. Our enmity was not due to any personal damage suffered as to crops, for his diet was preponderantly carnivorous-and that was the trouble. Not only did he destroy insects that we were glad to part company with—such as beetles and grasshoppers, which his keen eye could detect even at fifty yards—which trait alone might have endeared him to us, even though he did include the innocent lizard at times, and occasionally a harmless snake—but he waged a cruel and relentless war upon the young fledglings of other birds; and it was this that roused our ire. A butcher he was—and still is, for such as he are bound to persist though innocent victims may decrease—a real bird-murderer, terrorizing all the other feathered inhabitants of the neighborhood, robbing their nests of both eggs and young—of which he killed many more than he could eat, impaling them gruesomely head-downward on thorns of bushes or barbs of wire fences to feast upon at his leisure, beginning at the dangling head. To come upon such a mangled victim suspended from the barbed wire fence would fill our sympathetic hearts with futile wrath. Not only was he a murderer, but a bird of deceitful strategy who would play an unfair game. Hiding himself in a dense clump, he would imitate the calls of other innocent and unsuspecting birds, who thus enticed would come trustingly in response, only to fall victims to his rapacity.

Mrs. Shrike liked to line her nest with cotton from the willow buds, or bits found about the yards, and inside it deposited five large bluish-white eggs thickly spotted with brown, which we gobbled up revengefully for our collections.

After the summer was gone the male, as he prepared to take his flight to unknown regions, though he had not before so favored us, would burst out into the sweetest of songs, as if to redeem himself from ill-favor.

There were two kinds of Blue Jays that visited our canyon, though less common residents, and these also, besides being destructive to fruits of various kinds, were a terror to other small birds, destroying the young and eggs in every nest they found, and sometimes even eating hens' eggs and killing little chicks to feast upon their brains. In spring and summer they would select a regular territory in which to work, with impudent boldness taking possession and suffering no other bird to thrive within its range. Woe to the luckless bird who would attempt such a thing. Not until eggs appeared would their nests be bothered, then the finished laying of eggs would be devoured, or if by chance any should escape notice till hatched, the young fledglings would fall a prey to the systematic cruelty and rapacity of these jays. Their voices were harsh and raucous—betraying their relationship to the crow family—frightening the more timid birds with their noisy: "Cheach! Cheach! Cheach!"

But in spite of these unlovely traits, the jays were so entrancingly beautiful that we could almost forgive them, for the pleasure it afforded us to catch a glimpse of their bright blue plumage among the trees. One of these jays was a much larger bird than the other, with a high pointed crest of sooty brownish-black, the same color extending to throat, upper back and wing portions. But the rest of the bird was a bright blue all over, with a dab of blue on the crest-front. He loved to climb up the trees spirally near the trunk from limb to limb, with jerky restless movements, always keeping an eye upon us as we would watch him. His more somber wife laid in a coarse nest four or five eggs covered with brown speckles and splotches.

The other jay was smaller and sported no crest, but a long, dark-blue tail, which he flicked downward at a saucy angle. His head and wings also were dark blue, in contrast with a coat of dull brown and a white-bibbed shirt front of pale blue, with a white tie at his throat, and over his impudent eye a saucy white streak.

Of him, we saw more than of the other jay. He loved the willow bottoms and the oak and sycamore groves, and was fond of acorns from the live-oak, which he would bury for future consumption. And should he forget to return and dig them out, little oak trees would soon spring up to reforest the groves, so it must be that he had some good use besides his beauty.

His nest was a very rough affair outside built of twigs and other coarse materials; but inside was lined with soft root fibers. Sometimes he plastered his materials together with mud in a manner invisible to the casual observer. In this nest, would be found four or five pale bluish-green eggs spotted sparingly with olive-brown.

The Mocker was another bold and aggressive bird, with a dress of soft gray, darker tail, and wings that showed white markings in flight. He would perch on the highest eminence he could find, usually the topmost twig of some tall tree, and run the gamut of all his notes and imitations, without revealing his whereabouts, as though certain ventriloquistic qualities in his song drew us to look for him where he was not. Yet he seemed not purposely to hide himself. On the contrary, his boldness was conspicuous. As he sang, he would lift himself from his perch afoot or two and drop back again, or change his location frequently, finally flitting away without a break in his song—a song that had in it the notes of every other bird in the country, and of chickens and cats thrown in. Often he would start his vesper at ten or twelve o'clock at night and keep it up unceasingly for hours, driving sleep from weary eyes. With the first gray dawn of morning light, he would arouse them again from slumber with his sudden loud matin, and continue to hold the sandman at bay for hours with his interesting and changeful variations.

Mrs. Mocker knew well how to take care of herself and protect her nest from invasion; and seemed not to be afraid of anything. It was a foolish snake that would venture to put his head into a mocker's nest of eggs or young. For such a mistake he would pay dearly. Like a bolt from the blue she would fall swiftly upon him, with her strong, sharp beak piercing his snaky head. Even dogs and cats made themselves scarce when she took after them. And it might be added, little children also. Once a mocker, mistaking me for an enemy, when I came near her nesting tree, flew at me menacingly with loud threatening screeches, and I lost no time in scudding away.

Coarse twigs formed the foundation of her nest, and upon this, a variety of trashy materials were woven in with weeds and grass stems; the whole being lined with fine rootlets, dainty grasses, and horsehair. Up in the canyons, they were found in thickets of vines and bushes, but near the farmhouse, always in tall trees on account of our many cats. Her eggs were very pretty, of a pale-green color clouded and spotted with russet brown. After raising one brood, she would nest again the same season.

Summer and winter, the mocker stayed by, and could be heard far and near, flinging out the greatest variety of notes and calls that ever came out of a bird's little throat and that never seemed twice alike, till one would get lost in a maze in trying to follow or imitate.

Another naughty bird was the California brown Thrasher, also known as the California Mockingbird, because his song, though far less resourceful; resembles that of the Mocker. But we, not then knowing his name, spoke of him as the "Hooked-Billed Brown Bird'!—the same that has been mentioned elsewhere in connection with his depredations in our newly-planted cornfields of the early days.

He was all-over brown of varying shades, a dress that was not only becoming, but most convenient for concealment among the brown bushes in which he rustled around, turning over the fallen leaves for seeds, beetles, ants and other dainties. He loved the ground, and when startled, instead of flying he would run into the shrubbery of the foothills and scoot along under it with now and then a hop or two, till well out of harm's way, always thrashing his long tail about jerkily like the wren to whom—though so much larger—he is related. And how he loved to dig after a rain in the freshly moistened earth for worms, grubs, bugs, and planted seeds; his long curved bill making an excellent shovel for unearthing buried treasures.

But he was very shy of mankind. He built in the thickest and thorniest bushes he could find for protection; his nest being a rough, coarse bowl of interlaced sticks, roots and twigs, lined nicely with brown grasses and rootlets. Three, or possibly four beautiful eggs of a light-green ground-color, mottled sparingly with reddish-brown, were deposited in this nest; which we did not often find because it was so difficult to get through the thick brush.

He was somewhat of a mimic of other birds, deceiving us often; and when we would hear aloud "Kly-ack kee-yer!" of the woodpecker, or a jay's noisy "Cheach! Cheach! ", it would sometimes turn out to be only a brown-bird in a bush. But he would never sing in nesting time for fear of betraying his family secrets.

The variety of woodpecker that most frequented our woods was the Red-Shafted Flicker, upon whose bright plumage we delighted to feast our eyes. So whenever we would hear the resonant "tat, tat, tattoo" on a lofty tree-trunk—often a dead one—we would slip quietly through the grove to catch a gorgeous glimpse before he should flit away. Then when, becoming suspicious, he would leave his location, all the glory of the flaming orange linings of wings and three-pointed tail under upper feathers of jet, would be spread out before us in one fleeting view, with the red dash on the side of his head and bib of jet setting off the spotted gray and tan under feathers, as he dashed rapidly through the trees. Sometimes his presence would be betrayed by a piercing call from very high up overhead: "Kly-ak kee-yer!"; or we would hear him cattering to himself as he perched for a restless moment before flight; "Flee-ko, flee-ko, wee-ko, wa-ko, wa-ko, wa-kup, wa-kup!" Though so noisy, he was a gentle bird, and his only depredation was the holes he drilled in the trees.

The Flicker is very fond of ants. Finding a nest of them or a long line moving on tree-trunk or ground, he will run out his tongue, longer than his bill itself, and let it lie in their path till covered with ants caught and held in its sticky secretion, then draw it in which its delicious load that tastes so "moorish" where thousands more are to be had. Another delicacy is the acorn which he will bury to the cap by hundreds in holes he has drilled in the dead wood of trees.

Mrs. Flicker's nest is excavated far down inside a hollow tree-trunk, and lined with flakes of rotten wood, and entered from above through an aperture shaped roughly like a great keyhole. There she hovers from seven to nine snow-white eggs; and when they hatch, is kept unusually busy feeding so many mouths. As she draws near with a bill full of food, oh what a babble of hissing noises issues from the aperture! One would imagine there were a thousand young snakes or bats in there.

Sometimes a bunch of orange-lined tail and wing feathers found lying among the fallen leaves in the grove, would speak mutely of a tragedy in which the prowling horned owl probably had a part.

There were also beautiful, harmless and gentle birds in our woods, the largest of which, and among the most appealing, was the Mourning Dove, or Turtle Dove. Both names were appropriate. The love-note of the male, soft and penetrating and full of alluring tenderness: "Oo-coo-oo-o, oo-oo-o, oo-oo-o, oo-oo-o!" could be heard at great distances sounding through the orchards and groves in plaintive, mournful tones, to which we never failed to listen, charmed with its melody, sadness, persuasion. The other sound, "Turtle, turtle, turtle" was made when taking to the wing, especially by the female surprised on her nest, as she dropped flutteringly off to the ground as if wounded, grovelling along, simulating inability to fly, keeping just out of reach with wing apparently broken, and offering every inducement to believe she could be caught. Knowing her to be the greatest of the forest humbugs, we still liked to follow her as she expected, for it seemed a shame to disappoint her.

The sweet dove was one of the birds that we children loved; so innocent, so harmless, so entertaining in the great outdoors, such an example of fidelity; and it would hurt us immeasurably to see the hunter make them a prey.

Doves mate not for a season only, but for life, and cleave to each other with the greatest devotion. They are always found in pairs even as are eggs and young. The father dove is a wonderful example to husbands everywhere, if only they would heed the lesson. Though mated for life, he never ceases to woo and show her his love, thoughtful and tender to the last, seeing no other charmer, uttering no harsh note to mar their unity. Though spring is the special nesting season for doves, yet for more than half the year through they continue to raise more young. When the babies are old enough to leave the nest, the father bird takes care of them, while the mother begins to sit on another laying of eggs.

Her nest is a very crude affair; just a few coarse twigs and grasses laid loosely on the upper surface of a large bough without any attempt at fastening it there. Yet it never seems to fall or become unbalanced or cause the young any trouble about keeping inside. So it must be amply sufficient for their needs. The two beautiful milk-white eggs even at both ends and of rather large size are hovered there for weeks without danger, and the nest if undisturbed, is repaired and used again.

Though the dove's dress is not brilliant, it is beautiful with blending harmonies of varying shades of olive-brown and blue-gray, trimmed sparingly and most becomingly with white and black on tail and wings, and above two red legs, a breast of light buff. On the sides of the neck are faint iridescent colors, changing and mingling in the sunlight in which may be discerned red, green and purple tints.

The doves would never drink at the creek where the water was befouled by cattle, but would fly away in the evening to the clear fresh spring on the mountainside to slake their thirst.

Another bird, smaller of size, that had an air about him and a note of mournful melancholy, was the Western Wood Pewee. He was a drab little bird of grayish-brown, shading to whitish underneath with a pale greenish yellow tint; and a light gray bar slanted across his wings. In the daytime he would sit on a branch or on the fence under the trees, and repeat at intervals, the plaintive: "Pee-a-wee!" making an occasional sally forth after some insect he had caught a glimpse of in the sun, returning always to his perch, and uttering his single note: "Pee-a-wee!" in an apologetic tone, as if from some urge to give a reason for his action. Occasionally, for long stretches at a time, he would call: "Pee-a-wee" slowly and mournfully till it almost made one sad to listen, while carrying his tail at a drooping angle as if lamenting someone loved and lost. So far as one could discern, he was always alone. But of course he knew where his little mate was keeping herself. At dusk when there were many flies and other insects around, he would be kept busy filling his little crop and calling, "Pee-a-wee." But no other note did we ever hear him utter.

Mrs. Pewee built a beautiful compact, cup-shaped little nest of grass and plant fibers, finishing it in subdued gray with cobwebs outside, and lining it inside with very fine grasses and feathers. She fastened it securely to a small branch by means of cobwebs and other such material. Being an unsuspicious trusting little bird, she seemed not to care about concealing her nest from view to any great extent, depending no doubt on it's color-likeness to the surroundings for protection. But with all her apparent confidence, she was a very watchful little mother-bird, pouncing quickly upon any small enemy that would disturb her young. Her eggs were a beautiful pure creamy white, or ivory, with a finely-spotted chocolate wreath about the larger end or occasional blotches, or they might be finely spotted on the sides.

Another Flycatcher we had was the Black Phoebe, himself sometimes called a Pewee. But we knew him only as the "'Dobe Bird," because he built his house of adobe, or mud. On the sheltered side of some large rock that graced the hillside above our house, was where we most often found his nest, plastered there in the form of an open cup that had one side sacrificed to meet the rock's flat surface, and coming to a thick point below as a brace. Often the nest was low enough for us to reach it with the hand, or even to look inside it, where three or four milk-white eggs would meet our admiring gaze, one or two of which might be spotted with a few scattering reddish dots.

Like the doves, he and his modest little wife were mated for life, and were never seen in flocks or groups, and they spent their winters with us. He liked to be around water, and would hang about the horse trough, or over stagnant pools in the creek, where insects were more numerous or he frequented the breeding places of flies, of which he was very fond. In the daytime he might be seen sitting quietly on the edge of the eaves trough of the barn, or on the wire fence, or on the low branch of a tree, ever and anon making short sallies after insects on the wing, always returning to his perch again.

He was dull black all over except underneath, and there was pure white—the white coming to an upward point in front on his breast. On his head was a slight crest, or ruffing up of the feathers, giving his head a bushy appearance. While perching, he was always seen to move his tail in jerks, while giving his brief but rather sweet call: "Phe-be, phe-be, che-du?" or perhaps a shorter: "Tsip, tsip."

Another and similar bird, probably Traill's Flycatcher, frequented our farmyard; and against him we had a grudge. We called him the "Bee Bird," for, not content with such insects as satisfied the others of his kindred, he feasted upon the busy little workers of our apiary who visited the fields and gardens for honey nectar. Hidden in the thick foliage of nearby trees or bushes, or in a dense willow thicket, he would watch them at their labors, and as they winged their way homeward laden with sweetness, would dart out after them with sure and fatal aim. Sometimes he would sit in the near vicinity of the apiary for his delectable feast. But there, was almost sure to be found by a strange, belching shotgun.

His back was olive-gray, his underparts tinged with yellow, with a gray breast-band below a whitish throat. Around his eye was a whitish ring, and his wings were barred with grayish-white. "Prit! Whit! Pe-deea! E-eeps-i-pe-deea! Pe-deer!" he might utter disjointedly and with abstraction, as he sat near the water in the shade.

Low in the crotch of a bush or small tree near the water, his little mate set her nest, where she soon deposited three or four creamy-white or buff eggs, marked with brown about the larger end, or even scattered further to the point.

The most thrillingly beautiful of our birds was the Bullock Oriole, dashing like a flash of flame through the air, with his bright orange plumage, trimmed in white and glossy black—a glorious bird, somewhat boisterous with his noisy music, but industrious and rather trustful like the blackbird, to which he is related. He came near our domicile to establish his own. His nest was a pouch seven or eight inches long built of loosely-woven yellowish grasses perhaps the long narrow leaves stripped from the ever-present foxtail plant, and the wild oats in the pasture—softly lined inside with feathers and plant-fibers. It hung high overhead securely anchored at the top by stout, well-dried grasses in the uppermost branches of a poplar, or willow, or sycamore tree, where it was almost impossible for anyone to reach it.

Within its cozy depths snuggled five of the most exquisitely beautiful eggs that ever were found in the nest of a bird. On a grayish white, or bluish tinted background, each eggshell was decorated with the most wonderful artistry imaginable, as if a pen in the hand of a master, dipped in purplish-black ink, had drawn all at random, most intricately delicate scrolls and scrawls with here and there a tiny drop, forming a zigzag crown about the larger end, daringly approaching the slender end in places, yet always veering away from it as from a forbidden area; and no two of them ever done alike. No bird-egg collection was worthy of the name that did not contain one or more of these rare creations.

Mr. Oriole was very useful to us as farmers, for he gorged on grubs, worms and caterpillars, even consuming their cocoons; besides catching innumerable flies.

Another extremely beautiful bird visited us occasionally, who was not native to Aliso Canyon, but who was sometimes mistaken for the oriole. Yet he was different, with his bright orange-red head and throat, black wings, and tail and trimmings of bright lemon-yellow. This glorious winged creature, the Western Tanager, whenever he appeared among the willows or the orchard trees, we would watch in an ecstasy of delight; but soon he would fly away, and it might be weeks, even months before he would ever be seen again—perhaps never, and his nests we never found, for they were built far from our canyon, among pines and fir trees which he loved.

But the little bird that built the most marvelous nest was the soberest, most inconspicuous bird of all. For protection and compactness of structure, it could not be surpassed. As a pensile nest, it far outstripped the oriole's. Shaped somewhat like an elongated pear, or a longer-necked gourd, it was completely closed overhead, with just a tiny hole left in the side of the neck near the top for entrance and exit. Softly and heavily was it lined with felted plant-down, fur and feathers to hold tenderly its seven diminutive pearl-white eggs, suspended from seven to nine inches downward from the entrance, fastened with stoutly woven cobwebs from the topmost twigs of one of our tall old olive trees.

Tirelessly the tiny drab, grayish architects toiled to decorate the exterior of this wonderful nest for their family. It never seemed to be finished to their entire satisfaction, but must needs be added to long after nesting began. They covered it with lichens bound together with cobwebs, and festooned it with mossy drapes of gray and drab shades, to blend in with the gray-green of surrounding foliage.

At first we did not know the name of this little bird. Later we learned that the builder was none other than the dainty and wise little Bush-tit, who was supposed to favor a site nearer the ground in some shrub or bush. But then there were the terrible roving and climbing cats, as well as numerous snakes, and what spot could offer greater immunity than the topmost branch of the great gray olive tree? Even the cruel jays might overlook it there, and take it to be just a huddle of gray-green leaves.

After nesting season was over, not connecting them with the hanging nests, we would see these little Bush-tits in small flocks of a dozen or two as they foraged about, hopping and dodging here and there in search of infinitesimals overlooked by larger birds. For they loved such tidbits as black scale, which they stripped in abundance from our olive trees, plant lice and their eggs, and the eggs of insects. Their sharp little eyes missed nothing at all. "Kree-e. Kree-e," they called incessantly to each other, as much as to say: "Here I am, don't leave me behind." And when I would stealthily follow, they would rise stragglingly to move farther on, so that I never could quite catch up with them. But they seemed not much afraid, only wisely cautious. But oh what a hubbub they were capable of making when any real danger threatened!

There was the dear little "Good-Bird," which when older, we learned was the Wild Canary—not the Goldfinch, but a genuine canary, with all the canary's tones and movements, closely resembling the tame songsters. They were smaller, with brownish-drab back and wings and pale yellow underparts. A tender, plaintively sweet, mellow note uttered while on the wing in a pianissimo—for the voice as well as the bird was small-floated back to us as the "Good-bird" moved in wavy undulations through the air, sinking as into the trough with wings folded to the body, rising again with spread of wing to the crest of the billow, asking and answering the while its own question: "Twee-eet, twee-eet? Twee-eerr, twee-eerr." The very sweetness of its minor tones entering at the ear, would ooze out at the eye, as to watch its passing we rose from our play exclaiming:

"Oh, there's a little Good-Bird!"

Father had early told us never to harm these little birds or injure their nests or young, because they were good birds and helped the farmer. So ever after we knew them as "Good-Birds," and by no other name.

Such a beautiful, neat, tiny, cup-like nest they built! Compact, delicately woven, and lined within to velvety softness, a wonderful work of art it was, and saddled upon some slender horizontal branch among thick foliage—to hold their four tiny, milk-white eggs of exquisite daintiness.

Another bird, quaint and friendly, was the Western Lark Sparrow, by us simply denominated the "Lark." Slightly longer than the linnet, though sometimes called the "Lark-Finch," he was distinguished by his striped, quail-like head done in black and white, and a rounded tail with a broad white tip that plainly showed in flight. His white shirt front was decorated with one small black button in attractive contrast to the sandy-brown underparts and coat rather brownish with faint blackish streaks. He loved the sage brush, and the edges of the streams, and would perch upon the fences with others of his kind or hop along in front of travellers in the road till forced to flit away. His sweet gay song, melodious as gushing waterfall, rose in tender trills and lowered in chanting strains, tremulous with sweet and tender appeal.

Low down in clumps of weeds or bull-nettles, in sheltered spots among bushes, and usually close to the creek, we would find the lark's nest, built sturdily of twigs, stout grasses, strings and stems, securely swung from upright stalks, and lined with horsehair and fine rootlets. There were four or five white, or faintly tinted eggs, quite roundish in shape, and beautifully marked in spots and zigzag scrawls in purplish tinted brown, resembling often the scroll work of the oriole's eggs. Always, it was a special joy to come upon a lark's nest, for we could look within without disturbing it and without the effort of climbing a tree.

There was another lark, of larger size, who had a tuft of tiny black curled feathers over each eye, which gave him the name of "Horned Lark." This bird was almost the color of the ground and upon this he depended as a means of concealment. You would not notice him till he rose to fly after waiting till the last minute before being trampled. He too was similarly marked, and sang a sweet song.

Another little bird which I loved was the tiny wren. Though denominated the "Western House Wren," he would never come near our house. Perhaps this also was due to our many cats. But be that as it may, the place to look for these saucy little bits of individuality was up in the old Sycamore Grove beyond the Second Gate.

Across his cinnamon-brown back stretched fine dusky bars that became more distinct and plainly visible on wings and tail, while underneath was spread a lighter color approaching white but falling short of it. The wren was scarcely larger than the Bush-tit but plumper in form, and had a longer and more versatile tail, which he constantly used to express his emotions, cocking it at a saucy angle, or switching it about—holding it straight up at times, as he jumped from rock to stump with quick jerky movements, trying to frighten us away by his menacing: "Cheet! Cheet! Cheet!"

But from this bold front, we inferred that not far away, down in a hollow stump where he himself had packed through a small opening innumerable sticks and twigs as a foundation, Mrs. Wren was sitting on seven tiny eggs, flesh-colored and thickly covered with pin-points of rose-brown, in a soft fur or feather-lined nest that perhaps the two had occupied every summer for years past.

So, by all this fuss we were only encouraged to hunt the more determinedly for that hidden nest in every likely-looking old tree stump. This would fairly drive him into a frenzy of anxiety. Not that we had any intention of destroying his nest, or of completely robbing it, but we wanted just a few of those rare little eggs for our collections. At such times of danger, he would have boldly attacked any other intruder near his own size, but what could he do about such giant monsters as we?

How thrilling would be the moment when that well-protected nest would be discovered and our eager hands possessed those diminutive eggs! But more often our quest was unsuccessful, and little Mrs. Wren was left undisturbed to hatch and rear her babies.

Mr. Wren was the most cheerful and enthusiastic of singers, putting all his might into the ecstasy of it till it would seem as though his little throat would split open with the melodies, themes and flutings that issued forth from it.

But this time of love-song came before the eggs were laid, when he was busily packing his materials and courting his tiny bride. Now his attitude was wholly protective.

When he was building, he might choose a site that some other bird had already pre-empted; but that made no difference to him, he went ahead and covered up the other bird's eggs and nest with his heavy twigs, thus forcing the first tenant to depart.

A SNUG LITTLE HOME

I know a snug little home,
Just the queerest and dearest you ever did see,
Lined with the softest down
And built in the trunk of an old hollow tree.
'Tis so cleverly made
Where a branch has decayed
Not very high up from the ground,
And the door is so small,
'Tis the hardest of all
For this quaint little nest to be found.
Close by it, I'm sure you would pass,
So wisely and well is it hidden away,
Were it not for a blade of dry grass
That slyly protruding, its presence betrays.
'Tis so shadowed and deep,
If you took but a peep
You scarcely would spy, far down,
The seven wee eggs
All peppered with red
That is blended rose and brown.

Oh, a dear little bird lives here,
Just the fluffiest, daintiest, brown little thing;
You surely would see her near
Should you grow very bold in your trespassing.
With fear and surprise
In her wise little eyes
That you should discover her nest,
She would flutter and "Cheet!"
So alarmed and discreet,
Imploring you not to molest.
How often, in days gone by,
Amongst the old sycamores down by the gate,
Where the grass of the pasture was high
And the air seemed a-twitter from early till late,
Have I wandered at will
Through the carpeted trails
In Birdland's beautiful glen,
And my heart, it would bound

Whenever I found
The home of a dear little wren.

There were three different birds of black plumage in our region, all of which we called "Blackbirds," who companied indiscriminately together. The most beautiful of these and the sweetest singers, were the Bi-Colored Redwings, distinguished as to the males, by the pure bright red of their shoulder-caps, unedged by yellow or white. How beautiful they were, in their sleek glossy, jet-black coats whose sheen, fairly glistening in the sun, was thus moderately and tastefully trimmed in gorgeous crimson! The ladies of the tribe were of a dull brownish black, who with their cheerful mates when foraging for seeds, walked sedately over the ground with never a hop or flutter of wing. They would hold their places till we came dangerously near. Then, one would say "Dink!" and join others "Dink!" "Dink!" Then all rising at once together, they would sweep like a red tinted cloud to the waving treetops, or across the creek to the mustard patch, to sway on the tips of its slender stalks, or in the season of growing grain, to the barley patch, whichever way fancy dictated, alighting on bending heads of grain and talking together in a babbling chorus. Then when the danger was past they returned again to resume their interrupted occupation.

Insects and seeds and grains were their food. Crops suffered, yes, but the good they did outweighed the damage by wide margins, I am sure, especially where grain was a minor crop.

Always mingled with these birds, except when paired off and nesting, were the all-over black, Brewer's Blackbird. The glossy-black coats of their males with metallic sheen of steel-blue and violet on their heads and bronzy-steel-blue elsewhere, with the faintest tinge of green, gave them a handsome appearance, as they strutted with their plainer wives that resembled those of the Bi-color; with whom they foraged about for seeds and grubs. They loved to follow behind the plow to pick up cutworms and angleworms from the new-made furrow; and would frequent the corrals and pastures where the cattle and horses fed, and followed them about to a great extent, sometimes alighting upon their backs—perhaps in search of parasites.

In building their nests, they used the manure as a foundation layer to bind the coarse grass together, lining them with the hair from manes and tails. Their nests were sturdy affairs, and placed a distance apart, not in close colonies as some Redwings build, but individually, yet several might be found in the same general neighborhood. They might be high, or low, in stalks or trees, anywhere a good site was available. Their eggs were not all alike, though having the same general appearance. Some might be greenish, some grayish, with spots and blotches of brown that allowed the ground color to show through. But by far the greater number of the eggs we found were so blotched with confluence of sepia that the ground color could scarce be discerned if at all. The habits of both these species were very much alike, and we made no distinction between them.

The third black bird was a bit smaller than either of the others, but very similar in appearance, howbeit, his head was not jet black, but more of a brown, and his coat was without the sheen. These birds were always with the cattle, following them about continually, and for this they long ago earned the name of "Cowbird."

But the strange thing about them was that they never built nests of their own at all, but deposited their eggs one or two to a host in the nests of other smaller birds, shirking entirely the responsibility of parenthood. Their growing offspring consumed the major portion of the time and food provided by the foster mother to the detriment of the rightful fledglings-often crowding them out of the nest entirely to starve and die in the cold. Thus it was that sometimes, we would find a strange egg unlike others in the nest of a bird. Truly a shiftless, unnatural bird was this, whose only good point was his fondness for bugs, slugs, worms and insects detrimental to the farmer.

How interesting and melodious was a flock of all these blackbirds together! Especially after a rain, when the sun was bright and the air cold; how they sang then! Nothing else in all birddom could equal it. The individual notes of "Kink, kink, dink, dink, chup, ke-ring, koo-ree, kong-kee-ree! are soon lost in the chorusing medley of a thousand or two warbling at the same time in the most perfectly blended harmony. Cooperation, inspiration, harmony, melody, music, thrillingly exuberant, wild in its abandon, a veritable "shower of blessing," every individual doing his best in this mammoth choir, determined to fill the whole world with song. Trees black with them—or it may be the great mustard patch—blackbirds as far as the eye could reach across it, swaying and singing. It has begun suddenly, and as suddenly it stops, for no visible reason. A last "kink!" or two, and then a black cloud rises, and all together they make away without collision or accident to some more distant point.

Watching such a performance one day long ago in my early twenties, and listening with soul uplifted, this poem was born:

THE BLACKBIRDS
On a bright and glorious morning,
When the earth is drenched with rain,
And through clouds and dripping branches,
Bursts the blazing sun again,

How the blackbirds flock and gather
In a joyous company,
And with one accord together
Pour a stream of melody

Like a liquid, leaping river,
Out upon the freshened air,
Till the valley's overflowing
And there's music everywhere!

Wild, spontaneous joy outpouring,
All their power of song, they bring.
How ecstatic their abandon!
How delirious—ravishing!

How my soul is thrilled with listening!
How the sluggish pulses start,
As beneath its mask of culture,
Throbs again the primal heart!

Oh, the blackbirds! Oh, the blackbirds!
How they warble! How they sing!
How they flaunt their rich cadences
Till the air with music rings!

In a trilling, rippling chorus,
How they carol loud and long
Till the very hills are echoing
With the gladness of their song!

As from one wide-throated warbler,
All this sound melodious, floats
Without break, or jar, or jangle,
From a thousand happy throats.

Then, by some mysterious signal,
All at once the song will cease;
And a dark, red-tinted shadow
Rises upward from the trees,

And away they go, together,
Like a billow's rise and fall,

Wafting back the broken snatches
Of their final chirp and call.

Oh, the blackbirds, Oh, the blackbirds,
How they love the morning rain;
And for very joy of living,
Put their human friends to shame!

A plain little bird, all-over brown, shading to reddish-brown under tail and belly, and about the size of a blackbird, but entirely unlike him in character, would be seen hopping and rustling about among the fallen leaves of autumn and winter. Under the trees and shrubbery near the yards, searching for the tiny creatures that live in moist places, he would come as near as he dared to the house and chicken runs to pick up left-overs, and such dainties as might have been thrown out from the kitchen. Tame as the linnet, without fear of our presence, he was seen always by himself in solitary trustfulness, unobtrusive, taken for granted, hardly noticed, called simply a "brownbird," this little Towhee, who is related to the sparrow, lived with us summer and winter. In the spring two would be seen together, but they never came in flocks. Just over our heads out of reach in dense clumps of the larger shrubs or bushy trees, they would build their nests of small twigs, stems and grasses, lining them with horsehair. We would find them sometimes, with three or four pale blue eggs covered sparingly with inky-black spots and lines. One of these little towhees once flew up to the window ledge and pecked at the window pane, as much as to say: "Let me in"; but perhaps he saw another little towhee like himself in the glass and was pecking at him; who knows?

Another bird, which we sometimes called a "nighthawk" but mistakenly, was the interesting little Dusky Poorwill. He was beautifully mottled all over from head to tail in the lighter shades of tan and brown intermingled with white, with a white half-collar across the throat. His underparts were somewhat lighter and barred. He would fly about in the dusk of evening after large winged insects, crying in plaintive tremulous tones: "Poorwill, poorwill, poorwill." In the daytime he slept, squatting on his short delicate legs, under a sage bush or rock on the ground, whose color he so much resembled that we could almost step on him without seeing him at all. But he would always fly up before that happened, with a "quirp! quirp!" to flit away for a short distance and settle down again.

The Poorwill lady got along very nicely without a nest, and laid her two white eggs under a bush or sheltering rock on the ground. The little birdies when hatched were soon able to take care of themselves, with a little help at first from Mother and Daddy. They looked like little motionless clods of dirt under the bush, to one who was not aware of their presence.

The friendly Meadowlark was not often found in our immediate vicinity, but always on the way to town we would be sure to see plenty of them-always singly—perched on a fence post or low shrub, and never failing to greet and refresh us with their brief, rippling song, sweet, loud, clear, melodious, and repeated at frequent intervals. Chunky of body, with square, short tail edged broadly at the sides with white, and a prominent black bib worn on his chest, he was otherwise all clear yellow as to underparts, and above on wings and back, streaked with a mixture of brown, black and white, giving a mottled appearance. From his short sharp bill backward over his center crown and two eyes, were three streaks of white that gave him a distinguished appearance.

On the wide stretches of the San Joaquin Rancho, he made his home. He was not a bird of orchards and groves, but loved the open spaces, the cultivated fields, and pasture lands.

Mrs. Meadowlark nested on the ground, lining a slight hollow with grass and weed stems, and would pull the tall surrounding grasses down over her nest for concealment and shelter. Her eggs, we did not often find because the bird's haunts were far from our home, but in passing, if we could mark the spot from which we had seen her fly up, we might find the nest, with its five or six eggs, rather large, and white with dark red and purple dots circling about the larger end.

The Roadrunner too, kept himself farther up the canyon than our own premises, but was frequently to be seen as we travelled back and forth or herded our cattle and hogs in the pastures. One of his other names is "Ground Cuckoo," for he is related to the cuckoos and magpies. He is called also "Chaparral Cock," and "Prairie Cock," and by Mexicans, "Corre Camino," which is Spanish for "Roadrunner."

He is a peculiar bird, who, though able to fly with perfect ease, and to perch like others of his feathered kind, yet disdains to live in the air but prefers the ground; running along the roads for the sheer love of it. His feet are built with this propensity in view, for the outer toe is so jointed that it may be switched forward for climbing or perching; though usually, two of his toes point forward and two backward, the position for running.

His tail is easily a foot long, and very expressive; as he moves it freely up and down and rakishly from side to side, enabling him to assume the most grotesque positions. His dark, blackish-blue crown is topped with a crest, which he raises and lowers at will and around his keen eyes are naked areas. Above dull-white underparts, his dark, olive-green coat is scantily trimmed with black, white and brown, giving him a streaked and somewhat roughened appearance. We could not call him a sleek dandy such as Mr. Redwing, but certainly a bird of individuality, original ideas, and initiative.

Cautious, vigilant and wary, he is expert at catching his prey, which consists of about all the small creatures—insects, snails, beetles, grasshoppers, lizards, ticks, mice, small birds and snakes. If necessary he will jump by the help of wings and tail, to a height of eight or ten feet to secure it. Being exceedingly clean and orderly, he will take his food always to the same spot to eat it, and there leave in a pile all the refuse he has rejected.

The thing that most endeared him to us was his penchant for killing the hated rattler. Cornering one of these deadly enemies, he would deftly pick out his eyes and peck him to pieces without injury to himself. The Mexicans tell a tale, which they verily believe, declaring that they have seen it enacted, in which the bird is made the hero of a unique contest. He finds a rattler coiled asleep. Silently, without awakening him, he picks up, or cuts off, and brings to the spot, one after another, the large, spined cactus balls, placing them in a circle entirely surrounding the sleeper. He then flies at him with a swift peck, awakening and enraging the snake, who starts to go but striking the spines, recoils and tries in another direction with the same result. All the while the bird is dabbing at him with his sharp strong bill till the snake is in a perfect frenzy, striking this way and that at his vanishing enemy, always missing, and soon losing his own eyes, for which the bird has been aiming. It is then but a small matter to dispatch him, and drag his carcass to the dining-table, so handy to the garbage pile.

Though this shy, quiet and harmless bird seldom uttered a sound, yet he had his vocalizations nevertheless. When excited, it was a harsh chatter, delivered while jerking his tail and working his crest up and down. At other times, he might utter a sort of small scream repeated with increasing volume, then diminishing; while in mating season his evening song was the sweetest and tenderest note, resembling the soft "coo" of a dove, sounding through the chaparral and pastures: "Ookh-oo, ookh-oo, ookh-oo-OO-oo-o, trailing away in soft musical echoes, and so ventriloquistic in quality that to locate its source was next to impossible. It was seldom attributed to the bird that produced it.

What this friendly bird thinks of the swift automobile now roaring along the country highways at the margins of his chaparral, can only be imagined; but in the olden days of team and wagon, or saddlehorse, he took a very definite delight in accompanying travelers, running along a little ahead down the roadway, pausing to look back as if to say: "Come on, I'm here!" then speeding on again, always ahead and challenging to a race. Sometimes this dare would be taken up by a horseman; then the bird would run a bit faster, and as the pursuer began to gain, would slightly expand his wing, increase his speed, and finally, rising six or eight feet from the ground would sail on ahead down the road for a few hundred yards, then drop to the ground again, resuming his footmanship without a break, and go speeding along as before, again pausing to lure his pursuer on in tireless fun.

Mrs. Roadrunner built a clumsy nest of rough sticks heaped crisscross in angles made by cactus leaves, growing in dense patches, or on the low horizontal bough of a bent trunk, in a tangled mesquite tree, or hollow stump, or even a cranny of the cliff. But of all locations, she favored the cactus patch. Her laying was very irregular at varying intervals apart, and the number of eggs might be anywhere from two to nine, but usually three or four. They were about the size of a bantam hen's, yellowish-white with a somewhat roughened surface. Her habit was to begin sitting on her eggs as soon as the first one was deposited, which caused them to hatch out one at a time with long intervals between; so that in the same nest might be found eggs, newly-hatched fledglings, and half-grown birds. This seemed rather queer, but not such a bad idea at that, for it saved much strenuous work. She had only one or two at a time to feed, and by the time the younger ones came along, those older were able to forage for themselves.

Young roadrunners have at times been caught and domesticated and have made home-loving pets, as mischievous as any magpie and getting into more deviltry than "Peck's Bad Boy"; stealing and hiding everything that could be carried off, overturning things, and tearing up papers. During the daytime they would wander far afield, but at night would return without fail to the premises, which they kept as free from mice as would any Tabby cat.

There was but one kind of swallow that frequented our canyon, and that was the Cliff—today sometimes spoken of as the Eaves Swallow. These are not to be confused with the Barn Swallow, whose physical appearance, habits and nests are very different. This swallow was distinguished by a square tail, which, with back and head were dusky, except for a white forehead, with a steel-blue sheen on the back and a cinnamon patch on the rump. A steel-blue spot marked the center of the brownish-gray throat, that shaded to dull-whitish underparts.

These birds wintered far south in the tropics, but with the advent of spring, flocked in great colonies to Southern California, to nest, and leave again at the first hint of cold weather in the fall.

At the old San Juan Capistrano mission, observations made by the mission priests over a period of seventy years, record the strange, unvarying phenomenon of swallows arriving at the mission and departing at exactly the same day of the same month every year. From a local newspaper clipping of a few years ago, the following is taken:

> *"SAN JUAN CAPISTRANO, March 18.—With the arrival of about fifty scout swallows early this morning, the stage is all set at the old mission here for the spectacular return of its renowned flock which is scheduled tomorrow to re-enact one of the strangest dramas ever witnessed. No group of human players ever attracted so much countrywide attention as these feathered performers whose fame is attributed to the fact that their curtain has never failed to rise on time...For seventy years, a flock of swallows has descended on the mission each March 19...The only variableness in their punctuality is the hour of arrival, which in the past has seemed to depend on the weather. Old residents have noticed that on sunny days the birds often have appeared at dawn, while in stormy or cloudy weather their arrival may not take place until afternoon, but the day itself never changes..."*

This account is resumed the following day:

> *"SAN JUAN CAPISTRANO, March 19 (Exclusive)—An old hawk with frayed wings and graying breast, sheared the sky above this city today...Right on schedule, the swallows came back to the mission here to make their nests and rear their young as they have done for seventy years, and the old hawk knew...High, high up, he waited and only those who watched closely saw him close his wings and drop until he fell on a swallow. And then there was only a flutter in the flock while the old hawk rose with something in his talons. This is an annual event...a part of the migration...When the swallows come in, they find their little mud nests occupied by the swifts and sparrows, who wait out the winter in Southern California...The swallows dive into the nests. There is a great chattering, and the swifts and sparrows come out...Not long after, there are flights of swifts and sparrows seen departing northward. The swallows have won the battle..."*

At their usual time, the swallows came also into our own Aliso Canyon year after year, and swarmed about the face of the cliffs, where the same dispossessions took place and the same tragedies were enacted, as the annual work of repair and building was recommenced. Then in the whole vicinity of cliffs and creek, the air was made vocal with the busy unceasing soft purring notes of thousands of swallows; punctuated by frequent, less musical squeaks in a rising key, with relapses again to the even, busy purring note, that, once familiar, can never be forgotten.

And what wonderful houses they built with the pellets of mud brought from the bed of the creek! The individual nests of this inaccessible city lay, each shaped like the lengthwise half of a great pear, its cut side plastered against the sheer face of a cliff or ceiling of a cave, and was entered through a small aperture at the tip of a short neck that pointed down ward. These openings lay all in the same direction so far as possible. They were very cozy inside, lined with fine grasses and leaves, and finished with a bed of feathers. Sometimes a group of birds could be seen working (in neighborly fashion) on the same nest. Laying would begin often before the outside was completed; and while others went on with the work, the little mother-bird would attend to her domestic duties. Then as she would sit on her eggs, either her tail or bill might be seen protruding through the little entryway.

Located high above our reach on surfaces that could not be scaled by clumsy beings such as we, nor yet by snakes and other such enemies, these abodes of masonry afforded unusual security from molestation.

Still, it must needs be that we find a way to obtain some of these coveted eggs for our collections. So, braving the tangle of twisted vines and poison oak that trailed over bushes and rocks at the base of the cliffs, and heedless of the gathering cloud of excited feathered defenders that wheeled and circled closely over our heads, their erstwhile genial notes changed to loud cries of alarm with sound of snapping bills, we would gather up stones and clods, and selecting some certain nest high overhead, cast our missiles again and again, often missing, sometimes striking, until the house of clay was demolished and came tumbling down in pieces, together with the frail eggs we coveted. The deep, powdery dust below usually received them without much breakage; but should all be ruined, we would try again, repeating the ruthless method of attack until rewarded with success—success that would be sad indeed should the nest happen to contain young birds instead of eggs. Regrets could not remedy such a calamity, since nothing could then be done to save them. This tragedy, however, seldom took place; for by close scrutiny of the actions of parent swallows, we could usually discern between eggs and fledglings hidden within; and we never desired to harm the young.

We were proud of our swallows' eggs secured at such hazard, and carried them home carefully, to place in our cotton-padded boxes. Their blotches and dots of reddish brown over milky whiteness were collected chiefly about the larger end, but varied in density and distribution.

As we wandered about over the farm and pasturelands, whenever we would hear at a distance the shrill clear call: "Take care sir! Take care sir! Take care sir!" followed by a pause, then repeated: "Take care sir! Take care sir! Take care sir!" we knew that a flock of quails were likely to be started before long, to rise with a great whirring of wings and settle down again farther away.

Quails, now so scarce, were then most plentiful in our canyon. The stately-stepping males were decorated in knightly style, each with his tall, slender crest composed of about half a dozen glossy, jet-black, plume-like feathers, broadened at the tips and so closely packed together as to appear like one feather. These, he held normally erect, but might incline them forward coaxingly over his short bill as he fed and talked to his flock, or fluff them apart at will when excited.

He wore a glossy black bib under his chin, bordered, in sharp contrast, with a broad line of white; and an oblong trim of white almost encircled his jetty crown that shaded to olive-brown at the nape. The sides of his neck were slaty-gray finely penciled with black and delicately dotted with white, resembling fine needlework.

With a glossy coat of the same gray over back, wings and tail that glinted in the sun, with a white-bordered breast, shell-marked like fish scales with black and white, and underneath from breast to tail a bright chestnut, he was a personage of proud beauty as he strutted about followed by his similarly—but less conspicuously—garbed consort and their family.

From the last month of spring to the first of fall, we would search for quail nests under the bushes of the dry hillsides and in the tall grass about large rocks, but very cautiously, for we knew that our finding a nest would be the only signal needed for Mrs. Quail to forsake it. She would never by any sign betray the whereabouts of her nest, but always knew when it had been discovered and would have nothing to do with it afterward—not even if the eggs were dark with young, but would begin all over again somewhere else.

So far as the nest itself was concerned, it was easy enough to make another, for it consisted of nothing but a slight scratched-out hollow in the ground sparingly lined with dead leaves and grasses and perhaps a few feathers, which might have been plucked from her own breast. But her normal number of eggs might be cut down anywhere from twenty to ten for the next laying, accordingly as few or many had been abandoned.

Her sharply-pointed eggs were large, almost approaching the size of a Bantam hen's, of a deep cream or yellowish white background, and varied much as to markings. Some would be very finely and evenly dotted all over; others daubed with confluent blotches of pale golden-brown, while still others would be splotched and streaked with deeper brown.

Her brood when hatched were lively little things, able within an hour or so to run about everywhere. It was a most delightful experience for us to come upon a newly-hatched brood of baby quails following the mother about. But how they would scatter at sight of us human monsters, instantly disappearing as if by magic! So wonderfully were they marked that against their natural setting of grass and weeds they were almost completely invisible, as they squatted perfectly still waiting for us to give up the hunt. But we were likely to be exceedingly persistent, always persevering until we had discovered at least one or two. Even then it was well-nigh impossible to catch them. Seeming to sense that discerning instant when our eyes rested upon them, they would dash away with amazing swiftness and soon were hidden again from our view by the same instinctive camouflage. We never harmed the little things when caught, but after taking a good long look at them and stroking the soft downy backs, turned them loose again to live their little lives in their own free way.

In the creek-bed just above the bend near the second gate, the flood left a broad stretch of level sand thickly covered with pebbles, lying above the stream, yet below the main bank that bordered the mustard patch. And here, among the pebbles, the Killdeers loved to nest. Whenever, as we drew near, we would hear them begin to make a great fuss, screaming out their high-keyed: "Killdeer! Killdeer! Killdeer!" we could be almost sure that a nest was located somewhere on this flat. The old mother-bird would roll and tumble and flounder along over the ground ahead of us as if wounded and in mortal agony, shrieking at the top of her voice, while the male would fly in wide low circles about us taking in an acre or two, and adding to the din by his loud cries of "Dear! Dear! Dear! Killdeer!" in order to draw us away from the spot. Whenever we followed the floundering bird, as we often did just to see what she would do, it would not be long before she recovered from her disability and pattered along quite easily on her long slender legs ahead of us, till we would give up the chase and turn back again toward the pebbly flats. Then the whole noisy performance of hysterical convulsions would be re-enacted.

Even though this pebbly area was not large, that we would find the nest was very doubtful. For one might step directly over a nest full of eggs and not see it, so much did both resemble the surrounding pebbles. But if lucky in our search, we would shout gleefully over the discovery in a little depression smoothly lined with small even sized pebbles of four beautiful eggs, the color of the pebbles, about the size of a quail's and like them pointedly shaped at one end and bulb-like at the other, placed symmetrically with points all slightly downward and all toward the center. For us, that would be a moment of utmost triumph, but for the poor birds a tragedy. For they nested only once during a season, and losing those four eggs was losing a year out of their lives. However, we didn't know that then or we might have been more considerate and left them at least one or two eggs. We would take them all for our collections, supposing that they could get plenty more, and turn deaf ears to their frantic protests. The eggs were beautiful, being of a yellowish-white covered with brownish-black splotches, speckles and dots, that rendered them invisible among the pebbles.

How beautiful also were the birds themselves; brownish-black with white-trimmed wings, two black bands across the breast, another across the tail—white-tipped except for the center—and another still above the white of the forehead! Sometimes they would wade in the water to snatch insects that hovered over its surface, or patter about on mud flats and along the edges of pools where many insects were to be found. And always, might be heard their vociferous, penetrating scream at sight of a human being. Hunters, for this reason, would shoot them because they would alarm all the other creatures within hearing and spoil their prospects for game.

But we children loved these little plovers, that seemed to manifest so much individuality. And oh what a treat it was to find their little newly hatched babies! Like the little quail, they would run as soon as hatched, and at the first signal of danger, would scatter and hide by snuggling down and lying perfectly still among the grasses along the bank, while the old birds would nearly scream their heads off and go through all the humbuggery they knew, to lead us away from their jewels. What a joy to catch one and hold it for just a moment in spite of all the fuss, then turn it loose again to disappear as before by natural magic!

But of all our feathered friends of Aliso, none could surpass the gorgeous little hummingbirds with their glorious plumage and their incomprehensibly-swift-beating wings; by which they are enabled to move in any direction upward or downward, forward or backward, and from side to side; darting with the swiftness of an arrow through the air, or poising at a standstill treading the air before a flower—their wings one indistinct blur. Who can describe the iridescently-swift-changing colors—the flaming rose of head and throat turning to purplish tints; the indescribable green of back and wings to copper and gold and bronze and greenish-blue; the velvet of shining black to rich violet?

One swift dive from a tree, accompanied by that loud humming sound, and we knew as we glimpsed the little lady that a nest must be somewhere near—but where? So sudden had been the move—so startling the surprise-that it was impossible to be sure even of which tree. But it would set us to hunting.

Perhaps by close searching, we would find the nest at last, saddled upon the terminal twig of a sweet-smelling walnut branch, or a willow along the creek, or an apple tree, or a sycamore up in the grove, or it might be an olive or even a grapevine. So delicate, so marvelous in its finely-woven construction, was the tiny nest that it must have been made of little else than cobwebs gathered from the weavings of spiders. Even the littlest of the children would want to be lifted up high enough to see it with its dainty contents. We would not molest them as a rule; not unless someone greatly needed an egg to fill out his collection. And only after the hatching would we sometimes cut down the tiny nest, twig and all to put on special exhibition.

We would guard jealously the little treasure with its two jewels of milk-whiteness—always only two—and so small and delicate that we scarcely dared touch them for fear our clumsy fingers would break the shells. Daily they would darken under the hovering breast of the little mother, until at the end of about two weeks the little pearls were no more, but in their place lay two sprawling black bugs that seemed to be all mouth. So utterly tiny were they that for the first few days we would not dare even to touch them but how amazingly fast they grew!

The little mother-bird had become so tame while sitting and so used to our daily visits that she would hardly ever fly off the nest when we drew near to stand at a respectful distance and watch for awhile, then slip away without disturbing her. But often we would find the nest open and the birdlings asleep, while she was away on a foraging expedition after honey or insects to feed them. The papa bird seemed never to be around, either to feed his family or to sing to them; so the little ones were left all alone for a great deal of the time. And how they did grow!

By and by the day would come when the two little black bugs would begin to feather out, and would soon take on the proper appearance of little hummingbirds. We would handle them then a little for we just couldn't help it they were so cunning. And then one day they would begin to take short flights away from the nest, humming just as mama did, and soon we would see them no more in the nest. For awhile they would linger in the vicinity, but before long were as large as any other hummer, and we could no longer recognize them.

They tell us that there are six hundred different species of hummingbirds in the whole wide world, and at least seven species in Southern California. I am sure we must have had several species in our canyon, for some of them were different in their colorings than others; but all indescribably beautiful and interesting. They have a great deal of character, and as for fear, they know not the meaning of the word. Though of such pygmy size, they are well able to take care of themselves, and are not afraid to attack any other bird in the woodland who might show a disposition to do them harm. Their long sharp bills, their bullet-like flight are attributes to be respected in birddom. It is said that even an eagle is afraid of the hummingbird.

COLOR FLASH
Bird of the honeysuckle,
Infinitesimal thing
Of bronzy velvet and violet-blue
Changing your hue with every view;
Whence came you, elfin King,
In gorget and cap of radiant sheen,
Rose and purple, copper and green,
With your whirring, shimmering wing?
An instant only, you cling,
Neither hop nor fly, but shoot through the skies
Like an arrow painted with sunset dyes,
For a gorgeous, glorious fling
On whirling, hummering wing?

Bird with the flair for sweetness,
Who taught you that source of power-
Sent you afield to the cups that yield
Your marvelous energy dower,
In tireless quest at a silent hest,
Meadow and hill to scour;
Muzzing and buzzing from bush to bower,
Dipping and sipping from flower to flower
Through every springtime hour?
Who shaped your bill for the nectar?
Gave fire to your tiny form?
Or taught you that gossamer cobwebs
For building were snug and warm?
Not all the craft of the woodland,
Nor weavers of all the world

Could rival that dainty and exquisite nest
Tied fast to a burl, or a twig up-curled,
That a single leaf, from its bud unfurled,
Hides from view, with its two white pearls
Under their brooding breast.

CHAPTER 42 FARMING IN THE SAN JACINTO VALLEY

The summer after the flood while Lafe was cutting wood in Artesia, he received a letter from George then on his land in the San Jacinto Valley—at that time a part of San Diego County, but five years later incorporated into the new county of Riverside—inviting him to come and help him harvest his crops. For this assistance he offered to give him a share. The prospects for an abundant crop of beans were excellent. As for the wheat, as a stand it was unsurpassed, he told him, but had been injured by a stretch of foggy weather that had come just at the wrong time, and he would have to cut it for hay instead of grain.

Figure 30 Lafe Thurston, 1883

He also informed Lafe that he had filed on a quarter-section of "school land" adjoining his own and hoped to pay for it out of the year's harvest. Out of every township, consisting of six square miles, or thirty-six sections, the government had set aside every sixteenth section for educational purposes, dedicating it to the establishment and support of public schools. One could file on a quarter-section of this land, make a payment, build a cabin on it, and prove up all within one year's time, at a cost of one dollar and twenty-five cents an acre.

In response to this invitation, On July five of Eighty-Four, Lafe left Artesia to join his brother in San Jacinto. Securing a ride with friends as far as Riverside, he set out on foot from there and walked the whole remaining distance of some thirty-five or forty miles, reaching his destination within a few days. He found that George had located about four miles west of town, having built himself a ten by ten cabin out of rough boards he had purchased from a Spanish sheep-man by the name of Artego, and in this cabin he was living.

But since it now became necessary for him to live on the new land he had purchased of the government, another cabin must be put up, and this was the first task to be accomplished after Lafe's arrival. When completed it was a tiny shed-roofed affair; and after they had packed in their stuff, consisting of stove, table, dishes, cupboard, wood box, trunk, valise, water-bucket, stool-seats, clothes, small tools, Lafe's box of belongings, the horse's harness—all they had except the bed, one could stand in the middle of the floor and reach everything in the cabin almost without moving from his tracks. There was no room at all inside for the bed. So they left it at the other cabin and built for themselves a bunkbed out of sycamore boughs, against the side of the cabin, packed with straw in lieu of a mattress;

and to shelter it, put up a lean-to of sycamore boughs, roofing it over flimsily and walling it in with gunny-sacking stretched over sticks, in which a flap was left for a door. In this cabin they lived while cultivating the growing crops.

The whole country was full of most beautiful wheat fields, the finest stand ever seen in the country—luxuriant, level as a floor, with heads four and five inches long, but every acre of it rusty and blighted. Just as the heads had begun to set, the weather had turned densely foggy, remaining so long enough to ruin the wheat. There was not enough grain in all those beautiful waving wheat-fields to pay for their threshing. Even had the heads been properly filled out, the rust would have made threshing unpractical for thrashing outfits do not like to handle rusty grain, as it is poisonous to the workmen.

So George, in common with all the other valley farmers, was obliged to cut his whole twenty acres for—what? not hay, for rusty hay gives horses the "heaves," and of course nobody would buy it for horse-feed; neither could he give it to his own horse. Not a dollar's worth was saleable. All it could be used for was stock-bedding; and every farmer had plenty of the same stuff for his own bedding. So it was that on the wettest and most favorable year for wheat known, the total crop of the valley was a complete failure.

The beans, however, appeared thrifty and beautiful, giving promise of a wonderful crop, which George was planning to haul when ripe to the mines in Arizona where beans commanded a good price and ought to bring him in a small fortune. There were sixteen acres of Pink and Lima beans and fourteen of Byo-beans; all of which were just beginning to blossom when Lafe arrived. And upon this thirty acres their hopes were set. He had also several acres of peanuts that promised a good harvest, several acres of Egyptian corn, and three rows half a mile long of table beets.

The San Jacinto farming country was infested with a variety of large black ant. All through the bean fields where Lafe was cultivating, at frequent intervals appeared "ant beds" where these ants had piled up dirt in digging holes for their underground nests, and had cut down all the green vegetation in a circular area of about ten feet across. Lafe, who was wearing neither socks nor underwear, was often attacked by these ants who would get into his shoes and sometimes crawl up his legs.

One day after having been stung several times in other locations, an ant got pinched in the top of his shoe and stung him on a tendon just below the shin. Within a few minutes the cords under his knee were all knotted up and he was in terrible pain, being scarcely able to walk. Leaving the horse and cultivator in the bean patch, he made his way painfully to the cabin and fell upon the bed in an agony. Other knots formed in the groin and armpit where are located more of the buffer lymphatic glands that guard the general circulation from infection. For more than half an hour he rolled and groaned in terrible pain before being able to get up on his feet again. Never before had he been so affected by the poison of ants. This sting was far worse than that of any bee, bumble bee or hornet he had ever experienced.

The beans continued to blossom and set. But just at this inopportune time the weather turned intensely hot and the little sets began to fall off the vines onto the ground. The pods would attain a length of something over an inch, and then off they would fall, and there wasn't a thing that could be done about it. Day after day this kept up all through the blossoming season. It was sickening. The whole of that promising bean crop, tended with such tireless care, on which such hopes had been built, fell to the earth in its infancy. At the end of the season, exactly three pods of beans had come to maturity.

The same thing happened to the peanuts. Though the vines were luxurious there was no crop at all to harvest. And—strange as the coincident may seem—they found also just three peanuts. Three lima beans and three peanuts were the only souvenirs of their lost crops to arrive at maturity.

When the Egyptian, or Kaffir corn began to ripen, whose kernels are not on ears enclosed in husks as is other corn, but in open bunches, countless thousands of blackbirds came into the field and settling down like a cloud devoured the whole of the corn crop. Not even one kernel was left as a souvenir.

As for the three long half-mile rows of beets that stretched out the length of the field, all the benefit derived from them was what the boys had eaten in opposition to the rabbits while they were growing. For the rabbits, coming down from the hills by scores to a nightly feast, literally devoured them all, till at the end of the season there was not even one beet left.

Thus were the hopes of these young farmers dashed to the ground and their year of labor wasted. Not only had they made no money, but had nothing to live on through the year to follow and no capital with which to put in another crop in the fall. Disappointed and gloomy, they were obliged to hunt jobs for themselves at whatever wages they might be able to get. The crop failure being general, there was left in the country almost no money and little demand for labor, with consequent low wages.

The Blue Flannel Shirt

That fall Lafe was fortunate enough to secure a little work. His employer was Frank Clapp, who was farming two miles to the south. Soon after taking this job, he and Clapp went together to San Bernardino hauling a load of grain. While in that city, this farmer picked up a Mexican for an additional farm hand, who rode back to San Jacinto with them, the three sitting on the high front spring seat of the wagon, with Lafe in the middle. While driving along homeward, they overtook the brother of Mr. Clapp in his wagon, also returning to San Jacinto. Turning the reins over to Lafe, Frank got out of his own and climbed into his brother's wagon to finish the journey in his company, leaving Lafe and the Mexican to themselves on the seat.

Upon reaching their destination, the stranger was given a canvas shelter at one end of the haystack, where he was to live, sleep, and eat during his stay on the farm. The rest of the men slept in the house with Lafe with a Mr. Billie Jones as bed-fellow, and a Mr. McClain with the "boss."

Lafe was wearing at the time, a blue flannel shirt, in which he also slept—the usual custom of farm hands being to sleep in shirts worn during the day. But that night something seemed to be wrong with his shirt. The others, immediately upon retiring, all fell into sound sleep, while he was wakeful and restless. His shirt seemed to be alive—crawly.

Quietly he slipped out of bed to ascertain by a light the cause of these strange sensations, and found to his horror that the shirt was indeed alive, having been animated by contact with the Mexican who had ridden with him that day.

"Cooties!" Of all humiliating discoveries, this was the most mortifying. He knew in a flash where they had come from. But would the others know? Had his bed-fellow been inoculated? What should he do? This was Lafe's first experience with parasites and the effect upon him was so utterly mortifying that the next day he quit his job without explanation and went home to get rid of them, walking the two intervening miles. Luckily, due to Lafe's flannel shirt which the little visitors liked too well to leave, his bed-companion escaped contamination.

Before reaching the door of their isolated cabin, Lafe deposited his bedding on the ground and there removed his clothes, stripping to the skin. There were no human eyes within a wide radius to be shocked at this exhibition. Leaving them all there, he went into the cabin and built a fire in the stove, placing upon it a tub partially filled with water. There he sat and fed the fire till the boiling point was reached. Then venturing forth again in his birthday suit, he brought in the contaminated apparel. The hat he promptly put into the firebox under the tub to feed the flames. Then came his shoes. These he thoroughly sterilized by immersion in the boiling water. The outer garments went in next and after boiling them for a few minutes he took them out and put in his bedding and scalded that. Then he went out of the cabin and spread them all abroad in the sun.

By the time he had taken a good hot soap bath, scrubbed his head and dressed in other clothes, the day was well advanced. But the cooties were finished. The thorough work done by the boiling water had settled that problem once and for all.

Again and again he turned his bedding to the sun, but when the time came for "Old Sol" to hide his face, it still was far from dry. There he was at bedtime with nothing else in which to sleep. The late fall nights were growing too chilly to do without covers. But since these were too damp for adequate protection by themselves, after rolling himself up in them he burrowed into the stack of rusty hay, and there essayed to sleep.

In a short time, however, he was steaming all over and wet to the skin. Soon he began to grow cold, then developed a headache. There being nothing else to do, he "stuck it out" till morning, crawling out with the first streak of daylight. This experience fortunately was followed by no disastrous results. But that night stands out in memory as the most wretched of his life.

A Friendly Capture

George obtained his drinking water from a spring located at the foot of great granite rocks embedded in a heap upon the mountainside. This spring was tapped by an iron pipe that brought the cool refreshing water down behind three other mammoth rocks to meet a little wooden trough set on standards into which it trickled musically. The trough extended at a gentle slant a convenient distance out below the rocks and in its end was a stout nail driven, where a bucket might be hung while receiving the slowly dribbling water. About two feet away from the end of this trough, another embedded rock of smaller size made a convenient seat for the watercarrier waiting for his bucket to be filled.

One bright day Lafe, having come to the spring for water, hung his bucket on the nail and took a seat on the rock to wait while it filled. He was soon made aware that he was not the only one who desired water, by the buzzing of a gaily-colored little hummingbird overhead, who seemingly could not make up his mind to venture near enough to the human intruder to quench his thirst at the falling stream.

Over and around he would hum, poising with whirring wings in mid-air, then for an instant alight on the nearby rocks, soon darting away again to repeat the maneuvers. Growing a little bolder, he then alighted on the edge of the trough. But not daring to drink, again flew up and around over Lafe's head, this time closer as if investigating to determine the advisability of gratifying his thirst.

Lafe, encouraged by the bird's increasing bravery, and recalling an account related by Father of the capture of a hummingbird by Grandfather, determined if possible to catch this one himself, just for the fun of it and the joy of accomplishment. He had caught hummingbirds before while on their nests. But that he considered only a "steal." He wanted to get one out in the open as Grandfather had done. How this was to be managed he could not yet determine, but the first thing necessary was to sit so perfectly still as to be taken by the trusting little creature not for a human being, but for a part of the landscape. So, like a statue he sat, not moving head, hand or foot while waiting his opportunity.

Again the beautiful bird alighted on the end of the trough, looked with growing resolve at the water, then at the statue, and flew away. After darting around a little longer as if to finally satisfy himself, he alighted-this time not on a rock or the trough, but on the top of Lafe's hat. It was a thrilling moment. But Lafe knew that it would not do to make the attempt to catch him without being able to see him. So moving not a muscle, he let the bird rest there till ready for flight again. This time he flew over to the iron pipe and from that perch examined the statue with his sharp little eyes, as if to remove the last lingering doubt about its possible danger. Then, darting up into the air, and with a quick movement down again to the point of the flume where the water was falling over its edge into the pail, he paused with wings buzzing and bill-tip in the water till a sip was secured, again darting away. Knowing he would return, Lafe, keenly alert, awaited his chance, deciding that the opportune instant would be just as the bird was diving downward for a sip with its mind all intent on that accomplishment. Again the beautiful timid creature darted down and secured another sip of water. Lafe waited for still a third descent when confidence should have been still more firmly established.

The next time just as the bird came down poising with bill outstretched toward the coveted water, Lafe with a super-quick movement of the hand, climaxed his strategy by covering and making the bird a prisoner. Thrilled with exultation at his achievement, he carried the frightened little captive over to his cabin, closing the door. After a few minutes' fondling, he released the bird to the larger prison. For some time he watched with keen enjoyment the swift and graceful movements of the beautiful little creature darting about in his humble domicile. Then, through a small opening under the eaves, the prisoner escaped out into the wilds again, none the worse for his brief but friendly captivity.

Rat Farmers

George and Lafe were not the only farmers who inhabited that gunnysack shack as a bedroom. The whole country was infested with large Kangaroo Rats, who had their own methods of agriculture.

Though obnoxious to man, these rodentia nevertheless possessed a wisdom superior to many humans in the matter of food qualities. They would gather up kernels of grain, plant them by "hills" in the moist earth, and then wait for them to sprout. When, in the springtime, the little sprouted bunches of grain were riches in vitamins and mineral salts-food essentials at that time unknown to ordinary human beings—the wiser rodent farmers would dig them up to feast upon the fresh life-giving qualities thus developed, becoming fat and sleek thereby.

These little agriculturists carried on their operations after nightfall, and during those hours set apart by nature for sleep, would sally forth and scuttle about unconcerned with the problems their activities created, putting in their crops preliminary to the feasts and keeping their human companions awake hour after hour. They would run a short distance, stop and dig rapidly, noisily throwing out the dirt, run on a little way and dig again, repeating this procedure indefinitely until the boys were desperate for their needed rest.

One late afternoon, when George was gone to town, Lafe decided to "fix" the rats. Hunting about till he found on the hillside an elder tree, he cut a stalk and fashioned it into a bow, shaping the ends with his pocketknife as many a time before he had fashioned other bows when a boy on the farm at home. Then hunting about for some material that could be used for arrows, he found a bunch of cane grass at the foot of the hill and made himself a number of formidable arrows, driving nails into the tips, the blunt heads of which he left for arrow points.

By the time these were finished the dusk of evening had displaced the sunshine and an early moon was visible in the sky. George not being expected home for some time yet, Lafe took up his position outside the sack door to await developments. Soon the unsuspecting rat-farmers began their work, scurrying about from place to place as usual. Then something happened. Twang! Their enemy had begun operations with his bow and arrows. These proved to be deadly in the bright light of the lantern hung out in the sky, and one after another the little victims were laid low never to farm again. When George returned at nine o'clock Lafe exhibited thirteen rats and mice that he had killed with his bow and arrows by the light of the moon. That night they both slept like logs.

A Lesson in Chemistry

The San Jacinto country also supported huge flocks of quail and other game. While George was again away one day, Lafe took a notion to have quail for supper. Sometime previous to this, friends visiting from Santa Ana, after learning that the boys had no fire-arms with which to supply themselves with game, had left them an old muzzle-loading shotgun. Taking this old gun, Lafe started out after quail.

A huge flock had been seen recently near the foothill at the farther side of the valley, and thither the hunter bent his steps. As he approached their feeding grounds an immense number rose with a mighty whirr to take a position farther away from danger. But a shot fired into their midst brought down to earth not a few of the birds, the rest settling down out of range. Gathering up his dead game and stringing them on his game ring—made from the heavy wire-ring-handle of an old kerosene can—and reloading the old "blunder-bus," Lafe followed the flock. Again at his approach they rose in immense numbers, and again he fired into the midst, bringing down more of the game. These he added to his ring each by the gambrel of one leg—that is by the tendon at the knee-joint and again took up the chase. Soon the bevy was startled again, Lafe firing into their midst as they rose and reloading again. This performance was repeated until he had fired five shots—the last one bringing down eleven birds and no previous shot less than three. He had now secured thirty three quail and his game ring was so full it would not hold another bird. The sun was setting, and though still good sport the chase was abandoned, and well satisfied with his success, he carried home the load of game.

The next thing on the program was to dress the birds. This was by no means a small task, and kept him working till nine o'clock that night. After skinning them and removing their internal contents, he took off the breasts and put them aside, deciding to salt them down for preservation till the rest of the meat should have been eaten. The choicest part of the birds was thus saved for the last of the protracted feast.

After putting the remaining parts—backs, legs, and wings—without dismembering into a kettle on the stove to stew, Lafe cast about for a suitable vessel in which to salt down the breasts. He could find nothing but a new zinc bucket. Regarding this as all that could be desired, he salted down the breasts in layers, setting it away in the coolest place he could find. Coming home late that night and hungry, the unexpected feast seemed good to George, who enjoyed it with Lafe before going to bed.

When, after several days the last of the cooked flesh was finished, the bucket of breasts was brought forth. But to their dismay they found that a chemical reaction had taken place between salt, zinc, and meat-juices, and as a result, those delicious quail breasts were all discolored and wholly unfit for food. So, afraid of poisoning, in much disappointment they threw away the sorry looking lot, having learned a valuable though disconcerting lesson.

A Near-Disaster

There were other diversions that fall, one of which came very near being disastrous. The uncultivated land of the whole San Jacinto country was covered with Tar Weed that was grown at the time to a height of about three feet. Some distance from the cabin was a long hill not connected with any mountain range, the top and sides of which were masses of rock and boulders, and so comparatively free from vegetation. But its base was completely surrounded with this tar weed.

At the farther point of this hill in a little cabin lived Billy Jones, the man who had been Lafe's bed-companion while both were working for Frank Clapp earlier in the season. One afternoon, he conceived the idea of burning off the grass that surrounded his cabin. After destroying the grass the fire got out from under his control and jumped over into the field of tar weed. Here it roared gloriously, racing in every direction as if fed with oil—for that is the nature of tar weed.

George and Lafe, armed with wet sacks hurried over to help fight the fire. Lafe was beating along the fire margins with a big wool sack ripped open about the size of a horse-blanket. But so thick and tall was the tar weed that the fire would catch ahead faster than the men could put it out, and because of its exceedingly inflammable nature, the work was unusually dangerous to the fire fighters. Seeing that this method was inadequate, Lafe decided to try something more drastic and hazardous. Handing his wet wool sack to another man—for a number had gathered to the work—he cast about for a big stout stick. Finding a heavy club six or seven feet long, he raced ahead of the fire, shouting to the others, who seeing his plan, followed after; and with this club he struck down the blazing tar weed toward the flaming area away from the standing weeds not yet ablaze. Those following mopped up the fire margin thus made by him, preventing the fire from leaping across the break.

By this method, after a mile or more of territory had been burned over, the fire, which otherwise would have raced through the whole valley burning up everything, was brought under control and finally extinguished. It had been a hot fight for everybody concerned. But Billy Jones had learned his lesson.

Inexperience Loses Opportunity

The following year was as dry as this one had been wet. During the whole winter season not enough rain fell to wet the ground more than five or six inches below the surface. Though a little rain fell during each of the autumn months and in December, yet not enough to be more than an aggravation to farmers, whose prognostications as to crop prospects were discouraging.

It was cold—as dry winters invariably are—and the unbattened cabin was but a flimsy protection against the draughts of wintry weather. George was in desperate straits. In an effort to re-finance himself, he left San Jacinto in the late fall, to see men whom he hoped might help him out. In Santa Ana lived a man of means by the name of Wars Martin who was a horse-trader by profession—a calling usually considered synonymous for crooked shrewdness. This man had taken a partner by the name of Goodwin, and together they had gone into the Real Estate business, though neither was a regular broker. George went to interview Wars Martin. Here, hope was held out to him of possible help. These men promised to come up to the San Jacinto valley and look over the situation, and if satisfactory to make him a proposition. Thus encouraged, George returned home. Soon afterward the men as agreed came up to the valley. Admiring his broad level acres, Martin asked George if his land was for sale, and being told that it was, inquired his price. George replied that he would sell for twelve-fifty an acre. Then Wars Martin wanted an option on it.

Seeing in this an opportunity, George returned answer that he would give him the desired option and half of what he should raise on the land that year provided he would furnish horses, feed, seed and proper implements for him to put in his crop, and have them delivered at the place by the first of January, Eighteen Eighty-Five. To this Martin agreed. In the making of this bargain, which was entirely verbal, the consideration was the promised half crop. As a separate transaction, George then gave him an option to buy, with Lafe and Mr. Goodwin as witnesses. The men then took their departure for Santa Ana, and George, with a lighter heart, began making preparations for putting in his crop, mending his harnesses and getting things in ship-shape for the winter's work.

A few weeks after these events had transpired, a man by the name of Butter got in touch with George and made him a spot-cash offer for his land. Butter did not think the option would hold. For further opinion they went together to see a local merchant by the name of Hewett, himself a large landowner and one of the founders of San Jacinto. Hewett asked George:

"How much cash did Martin pay for the option?"

"Nothing at all," said George.

"Well, that won't hold. Unless he paid you at least one dollar, the option is not worth the paper it is written on," was Hewett's verdict. Whereupon Butter urged that the land be sold to him.

George felt his inexperience. Being only twenty-five, he knew very little about the ways of business. But he did know something about the ways of Wars Martin, and had never known him to be worsted in a contest at law. He felt sure that should Martin hear of such a sale he would immediately instigate a suit to recover damages, and that with his partner Goodwin as a witness, a strong case might be made against him. If this man, cold and calculating to advantage himself, should get a strangle hold on him, he could expect little mercy. So after due reflection, with the greatest reluctance George regretfully turned down Butter's offer, and the sale was lost.

The first of January came around, when Martin was to deliver the implements, stock and feed as agreed upon. But he did not show up. George waited and wrote. But there was no answer and no move on Martin's part to carry out his agreement. Precious time was passing in which the ground should be under cultivation for the crops. George fumed and fretted. January was well advanced when finally a good shower of rain came. George grew desperate. Unless the ground should be worked before drying out, it would be useless to try to do anything with it and too late to put in a crop. But Martin still made no move to communicate with him or fulfill his word.

Finally the information reached George that Wars Martin was in the valley putting in a crop for himself on land he had secured. George went over to see him. He found him in the field plowing with a big gang plow and several teams of horses. When George asked him why he had not carried out his bargain, Martin said he had been too busy. He seemed to be utterly indifferent to his obligation and to George's interests. After a little conversation on the subject, in which George endeavored to set before him his dependence upon the carrying out of the contract, Martin, pointing to a small one-share walking plow, finally said: "You can have that, if you want it, and I'll let you have a mule or two." George turned away in utter disgust. To be told, with January already nearly gone, to plow three hundred and twenty acres with a one-share walking plow, was equivalent to being told by Martin that he had no intention whatever of fulfilling his agreement in any particular—as indeed he had already proved by delinquency.

Sick at heart, George went home. He had been very definitely damaged by the man's defaulting, and could prove it by Lafe. But as Martin was aware, he had no money to fight anyone, much less a man with plenty of money to back him, who knew every crook and turn of the law and would not scruple to use any means to secure his ends. So there was nothing for him to do but make the best of a bad bargain. It was too late to hope for help by appealing to anyone else. His chance with Butter was gone. He was feeling downright blue and bitter, for no crops could he put in that year.

The Last Resort

Close to his own land was a small acreage of what is called self-irrigated land, which being on a lower level, held what moisture it received, and since the owner was not farming it the boys decided to rent this piece and put in a few potatoes. They were able to secure it on the promise of a low rental in the spring out of the crop raised. With the little means at their disposal they bought a sack of seed potatoes and after plowing the ground, cut and planted them. Even on this plot the rains had soaked in barely deep enough to admit of turning the top soil. But the potatoes thrived.

When the time came to dig them about the last of May, it was found that the one sack planted had yielded fifteen sacks of most beautiful potatoes. The price too was good, especially in small lots. So George and Lafe determined to peddle them from house to house.

For this work it was necessary to have a team. But George had only one horse for his wagon. From a neighbor, he borrowed as oft before when using the wagon, a horse to team with club-foot Minnie, and they started peddling these potatoes. Sometimes they went both together and at other times one of them alone.

One evening after sunset Lafe, having peddled all day, was driving home with this ill-matched span of horses when one of the rope traces broke—the harness being a patched-up affair. The parting of the trace freed one end of the singletree to which it was attached. This end flew backward while the opposite end flew forward. At the same time the horses pulling naturally brought the neck yoke off the wagon tongue, since there was then nothing to hold it on, and in falling, the end of it stuck into the earth. This brought the wagon to a standstill with a jerk. Lafe hanging onto the reins, was banged forward against the dashboard. The horses, all excited, whirled "right about face" with heads toward the driver and tails where their heads ought to be. With the harness wrecked completely, Lafe was left stranded a mile from home. Leading one of the horses and riding the other Lafe was obliged to carry home the harness to be repaired before he could return for the wagon with the remaining potatoes. This was just another one of those little diversions that made farm life interesting in the San Jacinto Valley.

CHAPTER 43 NEW ACQUAINTANCES

Having sold their year's harvest—fifteen sacks of potatoes—and out of it paid rent for the land, George and Lafe decided to leave San Jacinto for the time being and seek work on the coast. Loading their blankets and bundles of clothes onto the back of Club-foot Minnie, with something in hand to lunch on, they started out afoot on a "ride-and-tie" jaunt, intending, when they should become tired of walking, to take turns riding the mare and tying her ahead for the other to overtake. They expected by this means to reach their destination within a few days.

However, the first day out, the little mare went lame. They were then worse off than without a horse at all. Not only had they to walk the whole remaining distance, but to lead a limping animal whose increasing infirmity delayed their own progress.

In spite of these difficulties, they at last reached the coast footsore and weary, and stopped for awhile with the Frank Goff family to recuperate. George soon found a little work to do, and before long Lafe also had an opportunity to go to work. Nate Brooks was harvesting his hay and needed help. But Lafe was confronted with a problem. He was now near home, and being still under legal age, Father could, if he chose, collect his wages. Not knowing what Father's attitude would be in the matter, he was not a little disturbed over his unsatisfactory position. But solution of the problem was found by a friend of both.

Frank Goff suggested that he endeavor to secure from Father legal papers setting him free from parental authority and making him responsible for his own support, and offered to become mediator between the two. This greatly appealed to Lafe. So Goff went over to see Father about the matter and succeeded in persuading him to give Lafe the papers asked for. The outcome was that an agreement was drawn up and signed early in August by both interested parties before witnesses, making Lafe a free man to live his own life as he pleased. With a light heart he now resumed his work in the hayfield knowing that what he earned was indeed his own from henceforward, and feeling himself to be a man among men.

While in Nate's hayfield an incident took place that demonstrated the power of intuition, supernatural impression, angelic guidance, or whatever it was, that on a number of occasions was manifested in Lafe's experience. While Nate was driving the team hitched to his hay rack, and with his fork arranging the hay in place as it came up, Lafe was working on the ground pitching up to him on the rack the hay from the shocks—or as Californians say—"hay-cocks."

Always on the lookout for rattlers—for Lafe could never quite get over the effects of his early experience with snakes—he kept thinking about the possibility of there being a rattler concealed under the shock, where he blindly put his toe each time in lifting a fork-full. Every time he came to a fresh shock, the thought would occur to him: "What if there should be a rattler under here!" But thinking of course, it was just his imagination, he kept right on thrusting his toe under, never looking. The danger was indeed small, for snakes were not at that time so numerous as in past years—civilization and fires in the mountains having thinned them out considerably; and he would not allow such a fear actually to lodge in his mind. So, though he had been at work in the field for hours, and had gone through the same procedure of thrusting his toe under the shock times without number, he had never seriously looked for a snake.

Late in the day, as he came to the next shock and was about to put his foot under its base and thrust in his fork, he was suddenly restrained from doing so by a strong impression of danger, which impelled him first to examine the place for a snake. He obeyed the impression, and sure enough, there was a rattler coiled up in the exact spot where he would have put his foot.

Castor Beans

When George and Lafe had been peddling their precious fifteen sacks of potatoes that summer, they had visited Winchester Valley, and there had met a family by the name of Walters, by whom they had been very kindly entreated. After selling them two sacks of potatoes, they had engaged with them in conversation. Learning that they were soon to take their summer's vacation, the boys told them about the beauties and advantages of Aliso Beach as a camping ground. Of this place they had never before heard and were so much interested that they decided then and there on Aliso Beach as the place for their vacation. That summer found them encamped on the strip of sand before the mouth of Aliso Canyon. This was but the first of a series of such trips to Aliso, and the acquaintance grew into a friendship between the two families which lasted a number of years.

The star of the Walters household was a grown daughter, who had been christened the names of family ancestors for generations back; to which she later added another by marriage. Her full name then, when strung out in eight sections, was "Effie Estella Adelphia Philander Gopiter Snapoo Walters Thornton." However, she seemed to thrive under the burden thus imposed upon her, and we thought her as charming as her names were superfluous. Lafe liked Effie and on the beach one day, caught her after an excited chase, and painted her cheeks red with the skins of ripe Beach Apples.

Scattered along the banks of our creek, encouraged by plenty of moisture and sunshine, could be found growing luxuriantly, plants of the native wild Castor Bean. More than a decade before, similar plants had been cultivated extensively all through Southern California to supply material for the castor oil industry centered in San Francisco—the factories supplying seed to growers and guaranteeing to buy their crops. However, after the farmers had learned by experience that these crops greatly depleted their lands, their cultivation had fallen into disrepute, and the industry had gone under.

The Castor Bean is not a true bean at all but resembles the legumes only in the shape of its seed. It is a strikingly beautiful shrub which grows to tree size and is of very rapid development. The leaves are broad and large—often a foot or more in diameter, with many deeply cut, star-like points varying from six to twelve on a single leaf and are of a deep glossy green tinged when immature with red. The large striped maroon-and-white bean-shaped seeds are enclosed in clusters of briary capsules resembling chestnut burrs; which while immature, are of a gorgeous bright red color most attractive in appearance.

At the close of their vacation the Walters family broke camp when nearing time for the noon meal, and drove along up our creek on their way home, passing our place where they stopped for a few moments to bid us goodbye and lay in a supply of fresh fruit and vegetables. After leaving behind barn and gate, they decided to camp for their dinner in the shade of the willows which they found again beyond the second bend.

Here, they beheld with delight, for the first time, these Castor Bean trees, in all their luxuriant beauty of shining green-and-red foliage—their striped beans bursting out of their bright capsules invitingly, as though waiting to be gathered. Charmed with the beautiful sight, and supposing them to be true beans and therefore good for food, they gaily gathered a bucket full and cooked them for supper, finding them agreeable to the taste.

The rest of the story is easily guessed. A sicker family could hardly be imagined. Scarcely could they get home. Though "nearly turned inside out," as they afterward described the harrowing ordeal of purging and vomiting, they all pulled through—weak and exhausted from the experience, but having proved the truth of the old saying: "all is not gold that glitters."

A Monterey-Cypress Timber Claim

After Nate's hay was harvested, Lafe had an opportunity to work for Bert Fuller in San Juan Capistrano, harvesting his walnut and apple crops. So in September he began with Bert and worked through into November, when he became sick with malaise and fever. He lay around for a few days, thinking soon to recover from the attack—the cause of which was a mystery to him. But instead of getting over it as expected, he grew steadily worse, and finally had to quit his job and go home to the folks in Aliso and go to bed. Father, with the family doctor book in hand, by which he had diagnosed and treated every sickness that had yet intruded into the household, soon pronounced the ailment to be typhoid fever, and began treating it accordingly.

Faithfully and tenderly was the boy nursed by Mother and the girls, and at the end of three weeks' time, the fever was broken; though it was many weeks before he gained strength enough to go to work again.

Feeling that he in some way must reimburse Father for this long and enforced imposition upon his support and care, Lafe stayed at home for awhile helping with the farm work. Mr. Mac Mannus had secured a job in the North somewhere, and with his wife and family was leaving the southern part of the state. Desiring still to keep the claim at Three Arches, which his absence for so long a time would forfeit, he commuted it into a Timber claim instead of a homestead, and asked Father to look after the planting of the required forest of trees to enable him to hold it. Father, as a neighborly act, agreed to do this, and Mr. Mac Mannus before leaving brought him a large package of seeds which he told him were Monterey Cypress; both trees and seeds being wholly unfamiliar to Father.

Father then asked Lafe if he would like to take care of the Mac Mannus place and plant the trees. Being willing, Lafe went to work to get the land in shape for the planting. As soon as the ground and weather conditions were right that spring, he opened the package of seeds preparatory to setting out the forest. Somehow, they did not look like tree seeds to Lafe, but so far as he could remember, resembled alfalfa seeds. He showed them to Father, who, having never seen Monterey Cypress seed before, and having no idea what it looked like, assured Lafe that Mac Mannus must have known what he was doing, and he certainly would not have brought him alfalfa seed—though it did bear a resemblance to that which he had planted years before. However, he had not raised alfalfa for a number of years, and was not quite clear as to its exact appearance. So he told Lafe to go ahead and plant, that he guessed it was Monterey Cypress all right. So Lafe set out the trees with a first watering, depending on the rains to keep them supplied, and this job done, since his exchequer was getting low, started out to look for other work.

There was an Englishman—a bachelor up in the mountains near San Juan Hot Springs, who raised bees; and Lafe heard that he wanted help with his extracting. Being familiar with that sort of work, Lafe took the position and went up to Hot Springs to help this man through the bee season. He was not worrying about the trees, for the rains had been ample to keep them in good condition, and he expected to see them all sprouted and thriving upon his return.

When the work with the bees was done, and the hives all ready for new stores, he came back to the Mac Mannus place to see how the trees were progressing. He found them all sprouted and thriving wondrously; but instead of Cypress trees they were just neat little hills of alfalfa.

It was now too late in the season to do anything about it. Father wrote to Mac Mannus and told him how his Monterey Cypress seeds had turned out. The red-headed Irishman wrote back a furious letter, accusing Father of purposely planting alfalfa instead of the seed he had given him, in order to get the land for himself. This made two angry men instead of one. Mac Mannus never showed up again, and the land in time reverted to the government. For many months Father and Lafe expected him to put in an appearance, and Lafe did his best between jobs to look after the place for him. But his job evidently meant more to Mac Mannus than his beach interests.

George, after working for awhile on the coast, and earning a little money, had gone back to San Jacinto to prepare his land for spring crops and was now farming again to the extent of his means, and renting out part of his land to others.

About that time, the summer of Eighty-Six, there was great excitement in the country. A strange wave of prosperity seemed to be sweeping into Southern California. Men were abroad looking for country properties to buy up with a view to sub-dividing. The first thing we knew, Hub Goff Hubbard had sold a portion of his land for this purpose, and was preparing himself to sub-divide that he had left. Though not then sensed, the great Southern California Boom that has passed into history was just beginning.

Harry and Bob

That summer, we made the acquaintance of two British lads, Harry Hughes and his younger brother Bob—then nearing nineteen—who had come with John and Emma Cordell, friends of theirs from Villa Park, and the two Baker girls, Jessie and Jennie, to camp for the summer on Aliso Beach.

Some two years previously, Harry and Bob had left Wigan, Lancashire, of their native England, to seek their fortunes in a foreign land; and in the late fall of Eighty-Four, had first set foot on American soil. Their father, Thomas, and young sister Emma, having preceded them by several years, had settled at Carbondale, a small mining village in Silverado Canyon; where the boys were then working in the silver mines. An older married brother, Tom, was also in this country, and living with his family in Silverado Canyon, a branch of Santiago. These men, in the "old country," had all been miners, and since a very small lad, Harry had spent his life underground in the coal mines.

They had also an older cousin in this country—Robert Hughes—of whom Bob was a namesake. He had been a brick mason in England, and had come to America in the Sixties. In America he made the acquaintance of a fellow brick layer by the name of George A. Ralphs, who had learned the trade when a boy, and enjoyed the distinctive title of "Champion Bricklayer of California." Robert Hughes—always called "Bob"—in the early days when real estate was cheap had bought a lot on the corner of Sixth and Spring Streets in Los Angeles, and had built himself a small grocery store; which he operated for a number of years. He afterward sold out this corner property to his friend George Ralphs, in the boom year of Eighty-Seven; receiving for it what he considered a good price.

For awhile, the store then went by the name of "Ralphs and Francis Grocery," and later, by the name of "Ralphs Brothers." This little store was the beginning of the great chain of stores now known all over the country as "Ralphs Grocery Company."

We did not meet this cousin Bob, however, until about five years after becoming acquainted with his nephews.

Harry and Bob were fine looking young men. Both were slender, but Bob was the taller of the two and well-built. Both were very shy and diffident; and Bob extremely so. Harry was broad of shoulders, with well-developed chest, and rather small hips. He had especially attractive features, with large, speaking eyes, shaded by long lashes, and a small, becoming moustache—then commonly worn by young men. Bob was smooth-shaven and a bit awkward; but well-mannered.

We had never before come in contact with English people fresh from the "Old Country"; and found their English accent and inflection of voice most captivating. Harry played the Concertina expertly—though entirely by ear, and sang beautifully—some of his favorite songs being "The Midshipmite," "Nancy Lee," "Sailing, Sailing," and "I will Take You Home Again Kathleen." He won our hearts completely.

Harry was also very athletic, fearless and daring. He swam in the water like a fish. He would dive through the great combers that rolled mountain high up onto Aliso Beach, where nobody who actually knew the place, ever dared go in bathing because it was so dangerous. But Harry laughed at danger. That which frightened others was to him a challenge.

He got hold of a row boat one day and started to row over to Santa Catalina Island—a distance of twenty-five or thirty miles. But the day being so bright and free from fog that the mountains of the island rose up clear and distinct against the horizon it appeared to him to be only a short distance. However, after rowing for a few miles, and finding himself apparently no nearer to the island than when he started, he very sensibly turned the boat about and came back to shore, laughing at himself for being so deceived.

The boys enjoyed coming up the canyon to the Aliso place, where they were made most welcome. With their advent, the hard-beaten clean-swept front yard was fairly turned into a gymnasium for acrobatic stunts. This was a "picnic" for our own boys—themselves no mean athletes—but Harry, lithe and agile as a cat, could vault the highest, jump the farthest, chin the beam the quickest, turn a handspring the easiest, walk about on his hands with heels up and head down, the most gracefully, perform the slickest tricks in wrestling, swing himself up over the bar stretched temporarily across the end of the porch, the most effortlessly of anyone; while an admiring audience of girls perched about on the steps, provided ample inspiration for the performances.

Figure 31 Joan Thurston, 1882 (Age 11)

After the Hughes boys had gone from the coast, in the late summer, Lafe and Joan—then nearing fifteen, set out in a "single rig" to visit the Walters family in Winchester. They had proceeded no farther than the vicinity of Orange, when they espied ahead the two Hughes boys, who had been to town for supplies and were now returning to the mines in Silverado Canyon. This chance meeting set Joan's heart to fluttering, for Harry, though extremely bashful in the presence of womenfolk, had during their former meetings, looked upon her with admiring eyes, blushing like a schoolboy the while.

When overtaken the two boys halted their horses, climbed out of their wagon, and came over to talk with Lafe and Joan, showing evident pleasure at the meeting and their beach acquaintance was there renewed. The road led alongside vineyards of ripening grapes, and these two venturesome lads from "merry England" made a foray into one of the vineyards and returned with a quantity of grapes, which they put into Lafe's wagon for them to eat on their journey. Though not a party to the raiding, Lafe accepted the grapes, which were really far from being ripe, the grape season being just begun. Resuming their journey, they followed the boys for a number of miles till their ways diverged, when with waved good-byes, each lost sight of the others.

Arriving in Riverside that evening, Lafe engaged a room for Joan at a rooming house, put his horse in a stable belonging to the place, and then took her to an ice-cream parlor for the first such treat of her young life. They had eaten heavily of the half-ripe grapes along the road, and the ice cream had no sooner reached Lafe's stomach than warnings were telegraphed to his central receiving station that there was trouble ahead. Without mentioning to Joan that anything was the matter, he hastened to conduct her upstairs to her room—she supposing that he would take another for himself as he had intended. But instead, he hurried down to the stable where his horse was tied, and rolled in agony on the straw of the floor, until Mother Nature chose to relieve him by emptying the contents of his "dinner basket" sailor-fashion. And there he lay upon the straw till morning light. By that time he felt better and they continued their journey—Joan having been none the worse for her grape and ice-cream combination.

They spent a very enjoyable weekend at the Walters home; and while in the valley Lafe met his old acquaintance of Bear Valley days, Mr. Stripling, who was then farming in the Perris Valley a few miles distant and operating a grain threshing outfit which accommodated all the farmers of the district. He engaged Lafe to return and assist in the threshing soon to begin.

After that the Hughes boys would come occasionally to the coast; often riding up and down past our place on horseback, and stopping to visit at the Aliso farm. I was picking olives one day by the roadside, when Bob having just left the house where he had stopped to chat with the girls, came riding blithely by on his way to the beach, looking so manly and strong on his big fine horse. He slowed up, and after exchange of greeting, stopped for a moment to admire the beautiful black, cherry-like fruit hanging in tempting bunches from the branches. Filled suddenly with the spirit of mischief, I asked innocently, feeling like "the spider to the fly":

"Would you like some?"

"You bet!" was the eager answer in his characteristic English fashion.

Picking a small bunch of the nicest appearing ones, I stepped to the side of his horse and handed them up to him. He must have thought me stingy to offer him so few, but well did I know what would be their fate. Bob took the olives and thanked me, riding away toward the gate, which he dismounted to open. I saw him put one of them into his mouth, but he made no sign, neither looked back at me nor threw any of them away while in my sight. So my laugh I had all to myself, and not without a conviction of meanness at playing such a sly trick on one so unsuspecting and genuinely appreciative.

CHAPTER 44 A CALIFORNIA CYCLONE

Sometime in August, Lafe returned to the Perris Valley to fulfill his engagement with Mr. Stripling. This district, commonly called "Pinacarta Valley," or "Pinacarta Plains," on account of the vast number of black beetles of that name that infested the country—the same beetle that little Hulda, years before, had called a "tint bud"—was about ten or twelve miles wide and thirty miles long. From the east, Winchester Valley opened into it, and a few miles to the west of where the threshing was going on, lay the little town of Perris, some eighteen miles west of San Jacinto. The grain had all been cut and stacked in "settings" before Lafe's arrival, and the threshing was about to begin.

Grain to be threshed is cut quite differently than for hay-making. Instead of including in the cut as much of the stalk as possible, the "header" sickle is "set" at just the right height to clip off the lowest heads of grain in the field; thus retaining a minimum of straw to be handled in the separator. The stubble is thus left standing much taller than when grain has been cut for hay.

The "header" is not drawn, but pushed by four horses, or mules—two on each side of the "tongue" that extends out behind, on the end of which the driver stands, while he drives the team and at the same time operates by means of a lever, the sickle in front of the teams. The rolling wheels revolve the "reel" that moves a broad cleated grain belt inside of a wide spout; one end of which extends upward and outward for emptying the grain as it is elevated, into the "dump rack" or "header bed," a separate vehicle that is driven under the spout to receive the falling grain.

The header bed is built low on the left side next the header, and high on the off side, with ends slanted accordingly, and a second man beside the driver stands inside with a fork and arranges the grain evenly about in the rack as it falls. As fast as one rack is filled, the header pauses while it is driven out, and a second that has been following closely is driven under the spout. The full rack is then driven to the "setting" and there dumped.

A "setting" is an arrangement of two long, low, wide stacks, paralleling each other, and built just far enough apart to admit of the thresher being driven in between them, where it is fed, first from one stack and then from the other. The doubling of stacks saves time and expense required for moving from stack to stack. After the grain has all been cut and stacked in this way, the threshing begins.

A threshing outfit is no small affair. It consists of many parts, and requires from twelve to twenty men to operate, besides a large number of horses or mules. The thresher itself or separator—so called from its function of separating the grain from the straw—being fed from the stacks of the setting, turns the threshed grain out through a spout into the sacks, which are hung, one at a time, on hooks beneath it. As fast as one is filled it is removed and another hung in its place; the full sack being immediately sewed up by another operator, and stacked ready to be hauled from the field. The engine—usually a straw burner—which stands about thirty feet from the separator, runs it by means of a long belt stretched from a revolving wheel of the engine. The derrick wagon carries the feeding table, mast, and derrick fork used to pitch and carry the unthreshed grain from the stack to the feeding table, from which it is fed into the thresher.

This fork in size is something like three feet each way, having a number of curved teeth several feet in length bolted through a heavy framework. To its stout handle a heavy rope is attached. This rope is first passed through a pulley at the top of a mast over the feeding table, and reaches to the ground on its further side. There, a horse, wearing a very simple harness to which the rope is attached by means of a singletree, draws the loaded fork up to position over the table. Then, at a signal, he starts back. At this psychological instant, the forker, with a quick, dexterous movement, releases a catch on the fork and the fork turns over, emptying its load onto the table. The inverted fork is then drawn back tines up, to the stack again, where it is grasped and driven downward into the stack up to the hilt and locked with the catch, ready for another haul. All this forking equipment is transported from stack to stack on the derrick wagon.

There was also a water wagon—a large tank on wheels that kept the outfit supplied with water, a general utility wagon—usually a light general farm wagon—used for errands of all sorts and for hauling supplies, and a "truck wagon" or "trap wagon," as it was also called. This was built upon massive running gears and floored with heavy two-inch planks, underneath which was a large bin full of tools and repair parts. On each side of it was a long partitioned feeding trough, where the animals ate their grain, and on top of the bed, or floor, was built a large rack for carrying rolls of bedding and personal equipment. This heavy truck wagon was drawn by six horses.

The "Cook wagon" was a large, heavy, enclosed house on wheels, built of flooring boards, and furnished with stove, tables and bench seats built against the walls under rows of windows. In this, meals were both cooked and served. This Cook-wagon was placed conveniently near the thresher, and moved only when necessary.

The "straw buck" consisted of a heavy plank shovel about twelve feet long to each end of which was attached one end of a long rope, thus forming a loop, the center of which was loosely connected by a hook to the doubletree behind a team of horses. This contraption was used for dragging away the waste straw that rapidly accumulated under the "tail" of the thresher as the grain was threshed. This plank was dragged up against the pile of straw, and the rope was then unhooked from the doubletree and thrown over to the further side of the pile. The horses wearing canvas hoods to protect their eyes, were driven around to that side and the rope again hooked up to the doubletree. The driver—who also was called the "straw-buck," then stood in the center of the plank to hold it down while he drove the horses, carrying the straw before him against his own body, to a distance from the machine, where it was dumped; the outfit returning to the straw-pile for another load. Someone was usually on hand to build these dumps into a stack for convenience in handling, either for burning in the engine, or for hauling away to farm yards later as stock bedding. This job of straw buck was considered the dirtiest and meanest of the whole set-up.

Working on a thresher was no lazy man's job. The work was hard and steady, the hours long, the weather sweltering. Every man had his special place and must hold it and keep moving fast without let-up, hour after hour. No time for rest or day-dreaming here, and no place for a weakling. To stop the outfit for any reason meant the loss of much money; for every minute was costing the owners a large sum. Should a man for any reason be obliged to drop out, his place must be filled immediately by someone else; hence, only men of endurance were wanted around threshing outfits.

Should any part of the machinery give way, delay for repairs meant much loss; so to avoid this as much as possible, every night, expert men looked over the machine to see that everything was in good order for the next day's strain.

The men usually unrolled their beds on the stacks to sleep at night out under the stars; then at the four-o'clock whistle they were up again and in a few minutes ready for work, putting in two hours or more before breakfast. The cook also would get up at the same time and at six o'clock the whistle would sound again for breakfast, and all hands troop into the cookhouse. Breakfast over, the great machine would start up again and run till ten o'clock, when a hand-out snack lunch—consisting usually of bread and meat—was served the men at their posts, who ate it hastily; after which things hummed steadily till dinner time. A good hour was allowed the men at noon, and sometimes longer; and should the ten-o'clock lunch be omitted, the noon meal was served early. After dinner, the work went on without let-up till dark; when again the whistle blew for supper and quitting time.

After supper, the men usually sat around camp and chatted for a little while before "turning in" for the night. On one of these evening occasions, when the men were "spinning yarns,!' each having something interesting to tell— usually about his own experience in the past, Lafe also told a story-one he had heard Father relate concerning his own father; who had evidently been a man of some prowess.

According to Father's account, Grandfather distinguished himself physically in many ways. Being possessed of remarkable strength and agility, he never missed taking a dare—in fact, was fond of making dares, which he always won. He once demonstrated the strength of his jaws on an oak barrel having within it forty pounds of stone. Grasping in his teeth the top edge of this barrel, he lifted and tossed it backward over his head. At another time, his agility was displayed when walking along one day with another gentleman in the great out-of-doors. The sound of a hummingbird fell upon their ears, and they both stopped to look for the bird. Just at the instant they discerned him, he darted past in front of them—that is, past the other man. But he did not get past Grandfather, who reached out his hand with a super-swift movement, and caught the hummingbird. His astonished and admiring companion confessed that he had not hitherto given credence to the stories of his exploits, but now said that he was ready to believe anything. It was the recollection of this story that had given Lafe the inspiration to try his own hand at catching hummingbirds.

But the main point of the story that Lafe told the men at the thresher that evening, concerned an egg-sucking stunt. Grandfather once made a wager—so the story went—that he could suck more raw eggs than any other man in town. As he expected, his wager was taken up by the champion egg-sucker of the neighborhood, who, at the appointed time and place, came to meet him bringing three dozen eggs.

These, he proceeded to suck and finished them all. Grandfather then displayed three dozen eggs, and did likewise. After getting away with these, he produced a half dozen turkey eggs and sucked also every one of them. After the relation of this story, Lafe's name, so far as that outfit was concerned, became "Turkey."

Lafe Turns Prophet

On the particular day with which my story deals, the thermometer was registering a hundred and seventeen in the shade. For days past, it had been hovering around a hundred and sixteen. The early dinner was over, the hour of rest past, and the crew had just gotten well started on their afternoon's work. They were almost through with the next to the last setting, and were expecting to move to that in a short time. The last setting on this particular job consisted of only a single stack, as there had not been enough grain to build a double.

The men were all working like beavers to get through, when the rumbling sound of distant thunder fell upon their ears. Looking to the south, they beheld a dense cloud of what appeared to be dust about twenty miles away, as though a large band of sheep was being driven across the country; which indeed, some thought was the case. Whatever it was, it was too far away to concern the busy crew overmuch.

Then, it was, that Lafe turned prophet. A lad of only nineteen past, he was utterly inexperienced in things of a cyclonic nature that the Easterners among the crew were more or less familiar with, but he seemed to be given at the first glimpse, a grasp of the true situation. With a comprehension and assurance that could have come only by intuition; he said earnestly:

"That's a storm coming, a terrible storm!" Then with increasing conviction:

"It's something we've never seen before! It's going to be an awful storm!"

"Aw-Turkey!" ejaculated others, with good-natured contempt.

Unabashed by their ridicule, he continued with cumulating emphasis:

"That storm will drench everything it strikes, and there'll be nothing left to thresh after it hits us. It's no use to move to the other setting; there won't be a dry straw in it! When that storm passes, we won't turn another wheel!"

Impressed in spite of themselves with this outspoken earnestness, the crew listened. Lafe proceeded with great detail and definiteness, to outline the course the storm would take in its journey toward them. He told them it would proceed northward till it came opposite Winchester Valley which it would follow to "Rock House" where it would turn north again until it crossed the ridge there and entered a little valley extending east and west, where it would turn to the west and travel straight for the spot where they were working; after which, it would pass right on and strike Perris.

The others laughed at his "presumption," yet, impressed by his seriousness and personal conviction, not without some apprehension. From time to time, they would look up and note the course of the distant dust cloud. Sure enough, it was taking the exact course outlined in the prediction. It was accompanied by thunder that grew louder the nearer it approached.

At one-thirty, about three quarters of an hour from the time the cloud had been first sighted, they finished the setting on which they were working, and started to move to the last single-stack setting. After moving the separator and derrick wagon the men were returning for the rest of the stuff—Lafe and two others by themselves afoot, and the others bringing the horses. The cook wagon and the trap wagon were standing on the firebreak—a strip of plowed land surrounding the setting just finished—and near the latter, a large number of sacks sewed up full of grain lay stacked where they had been placed when taken from the separator.

As Lafe and the two men with him neared the straw stacks, the first scattered drops of the storm struck them, accompanied by deafening peals of thunder, flashes of lightning, and a terrific wind. Each drop, where it struck, penetrated to the skin instantly and wetted a spot as large as a half dollar.

Passing the cook wagon, they saw that it had been twisted as one twists a dishrag half of it still upright, the other half upside down. The cook was under the over-turned part trying to put out the fire in the upset stove. Lafe shouted to him:

"Get out of there! The rain will put out the fire!"

Reaching the trap wagon, they hastily grabbed their rolls of bedding out of the open rack and jammed them underneath the floor boards on top of the running gears—part of the men huddling under there themselves, clinging to the wagon tongue and other parts. The rest of the crew burrowed into the straw stack, as the full force of the storm struck them with a deafening roar.

Almost immediately everything was flooded with water, and the fire break had become deep mud. The fierce wind, coming from the rear end of the heavy, cumbersome trap wagon, moved it forward six feet in this mud, with the men still hanging onto the front end of the running gears. The lightning flashed ceaselessly, and the roar of thunder was indescribable.

Veering this way and that, the wind changed its course with rapid frequency, as though trying to blow in every direction at once, twisting and tearing with cyclonic force.

All this was something wholly foreign to California, and had never before been experienced here by any of the men present. To Lafe, this new experience was indescribably thrilling, and filled him with a strange feeling of elation. He jumped about like a jack-rabbit back and forth from one side of the grain sacks to the other, enjoying the whole occasion immensely, and shouting at the top of his voice—though his voice was lost in the roar of the elements, and the lightning was striking the ground on every side of him. Seemingly, he was the only creature present who found in it anything to enjoy.

After a prolonged deluge of rain, came pelting hail—each hailstone about the size and same general shape of a man's thumb to the first joint, driving even Lafe to seek safe shelter under the trap wagon. So thick and fast these hailstones fell that soon the water on the ground was all frozen. No rain came with the hail, but the lightning never let up for an instant. The thunder remained terrific, like the bombardment of cannon directly overhead—the wind still attempting its strange, impossible gymnastics of sweeping in every direction at once.

The cold then became intense. The men, thinly clad for oven-heat weather, suffered with the cold. Hail piled up on the ground, and for some time continued to fall like a deluge of large white stinging bullets, till the men were almost frozen. Then the order changed again, and a deluge of rain poured down upon the hail, soon melting every stone of it.

After four hours of this cyclonic demonstration, the storm passed on toward the little town of Perris, on the last lap of the route outlined by Lafe in the beginning. At about four-thirty, the men began to look about them for the remnants of their outfit.

The horses, about eighteen of them, nearly crazed, had stampeded, and all but two had disappeared entirely. Mr. Stripling hitched up these two to the general utility wagon, into which they loaded their bedding, and the crew of more than a dozen men climbed into it and started for Perris.

Lafe, like the rest, was thinly clad, and without underwear. His shirt sleeve having been caught on a derrick fork while at work, had been ripped off, leaving one arm entirely bare. Some of the men undid their rolls of bedding and wrapped themselves up to keep warm. One of them had a cheap red quilt, which he tossed to Lafe saying, "Here, Turkey, wrap up in that, or you'll freeze to death!" and Lafe lost no time in doing so. All that could be seen on every side as they drove along, was the tips of the tall stubble sticking up out of the water here and there on the highest elevations. The land was what is called by farming men, "hog-wallow land," full of depressions and elevations, and even the tips could not be seen in the hollows.

Perris was built on a slight slope and besides a few general places of business, and the post office, consisted of about forty houses, for the most part newly constructed. As they drew near to the town, the only way they could distinguish the streets from unoccupied surroundings was by the lanes where no vegetation protruded out of the water. At first, not a person was in sight; all having sought shelter wherever it could be found. But all over town were scattered various articles of household furniture upon which were perched wet and drooping chickens.

As they drew up to the post office, they found the front entirely off and torn to pieces, exposing the mail in the boxes, and the post master and his assistants out in the street hunting for registered mail. Climbing out of the wagon, Lafe threw off the old red quilt, and behold, he was Turkey-red all over. Even Esau would have joined his comrades in laughter at his appearance—a turkey indeed.

Yelling like wild Indians, this hilarious threshing crew waded through the town on a tour of investigation. Over they went to the big department store of "Hook Brothers and Oak," where merchandise of all kinds was carried— furniture, hardware, drygoods, shoes and notions. Here they found the two huge twelve-foot plate-glass fronts had been blown inside and shattered in spite of all human effort to prevent it, and glass scattered all through the store. The clerks and manager had placed ladders inside along the glass fronts, and climbed up onto them to push against the glass with all their strength in an effort to hold it in place against the wind—but all in vain.

Out of the forty houses in town, eight were demolished, twelve off their underpinnings, and another house was standing on its own underpinning, but turned completely about, end for end, with the front door facing the back yard as neatly as though it had been built in that position.

At the upper corner of every house that was standing, unmelted hail was still piled up where it had lodged, in wash-tub quantities.

Lafe hunted up his friends, the Reynolds family who had a home in the town, and spent that night with them there, sleeping with the boys in their upstairs bedroom. The windows were the old-fashioned kind with small panes. And every pane of every window in their house had been knocked out by the hail. On three sides of the house the paint had been chipped off, as though with a sharp instrument. In the yard were some young umbrella trees planted the year before. The bark on these trees was beaten to a pulp and loosened so that it might be taken hold of at one end, and the whole tree stripped of its bark with one pull. They all afterwards died, as was inevitable.

So hot did it become after the storm was over, that at nine o'clock that night, they lay on their beds without covers or clothes and perspired in the sweltering heat.

A day or two later on the twentieth of September, Stripling gathered his crew together and went out to the thresher to pull in the outfit. They found the big separator turned upside-down. But as it had gone over, the front trucks with their two wheels had broken loose and fallen back again as they were, while the rear trucks had continued on over with the separator, and lay wheels up in the mud.

The bags of grain were soaked through and through. In the stack of the last setting there remained not even one dry straw, as had been predicted. After this experience, the crew added to their nickname for Lafe, calling him, "Turkey, the Prophet."

The poor little meadow larks fared badly in this storm. Many of them were killed outright, but large numbers were left crippled by the hail, and for some time afterward, wounded birds might be seen everywhere.

That year there had been a shortage of grain sacks. Most of the farmers had been able to secure just enough sacks to keep the thresher going. They had economized on sacks by digging temporary storage pits in which they would empty them, using the sacks over and over, while waiting for more to come. The grain thus stored in these temporary pits was all flooded with water and practically a total loss.

The End of the "Tail"

Frank, then a lad of twelve, had developed a special fondness for Charlotte, his junior by five years, whom he called his "little Pal." When gathering the eggs of an evening and doing other chores about the place, he always wanted her tagging at his heels.

On this particular morning, he arranged for her company in herding the cattle, which he was to drive as usual to pasture up on the Laguna mountains. For their lunch, he planned as a treat to brew hot coffee over a campfire, and took along an old black coffee pot, with coffee, sugar, and a canteen of water. The milk, he was to extract from one of the cows. The main delicacy of the meal was to be the bag of stale, left-over biscuits he had discovered in the bottom of the bread-box, which had graced the table some days before.

The day was hot and windy. A "Santa Ana" was blowing. Now all Southern Californians know what is meant by a "Santa Ana." But for the benefit of others who are not initiated into the mysteries of our language, and whose ideas as to our climate have been sincerely formulated according to the clever eulogistic advertising of propagandists, who always exercise their right to leave out what they do not want to put in, a word of explanation might be in order.

The "Santa Ana," despised by everybody, is a wind peculiar to the southern part of the state, that derives its name from association with the pass and river valley of that name. It comes down over the Siskiyou ranges from the northeast in the fall or spring and ordinarily blows steadily with varying intensity for a period of three days without let-up. It is accompanied by electrical manifestations—though not of a sensational character. The hair becomes dry and crackling, a comb drawn through often causing electric sparks. The period of duration may vary occasionally.

Being heated by compression in its descent from the mountains, this wind is typically "hot as a furnace," "dry as a bone" and extremely dusty—an "ill wind that blows nobody good," lip-cracking, skin-drying, hair-crackling, nerve-racking, irritating, head-achey, and sand and gravel carrying. The soil dries out, cattle become restless, cows give less milk, houses and furniture become coated with dust that one might as well forget about till the third day has passed. Should weather conditions lower the barometer the typically hot "Santa Ana" may turn cold. This wind usually visits us in the fall, but if it should come in the spring, after the trees have bloomed and the young fruit set, it is very disastrous to crops; both the blossoms and the miniature fruit dropping off within a short time after.

Fortunately, this does not often happen. There is one redeeming feature about these Santa Ana Winds, and that is they are very infrequent.

It was this sort of wind that the two children faced, as they started up the side of the Laguna mountain range driving the cattle, lunch-kit in hand, and anticipating "lots of fun"—for to children, a wind is a wind, and nothing to worry about; though, as it whined lonesomely over the hills, Frank was glad of company. He helped his little sister over the steep places, guided her around the cactus patches, and warned her of snakes and badger holes in true brotherly fashion, until the feeding grounds were reached.

While the cattle browsed, they played; and Charlotte listened in admiration to Frank's stories, as he told about the "big" things he had done, or was planning to do; and after a while, it was time to build a fire and cook their coffee.

But suddenly, without an instant's warning, it turned bitterly cold, then began to rain—big splashing drops that wet to the skin. Soon their clothes were soaked through. They had brought no wraps; for the warm wind had precluded any anticipation of such a need. And now it had switched to a freezing gale that penetrated almost to the marrow of their bones. The ground was soon soaked, and the brush, and everything they had expected to use for fuel. Frank tried to start a fire. He gathered some rocks and built a little fireplace under some bushes; but could not make the wet twigs he had collected, burn. Shivering with the cold, the two kept up a search in every sheltered nook for leaves and twigs that might possibly be found dry enough to light with their matches.

Colder and colder grew the atmosphere, and it began to hail. At last, Frank succeeded in getting a smudge, nursing it with such oily foliage as would burn feebly even though damp, over which they huddled to keep from freezing. Meanwhile the coffeepot was balanced on the rocks, while they coaxed the fire to induce it to steep the coffee which they needed now so desperately to warm their insides.

The cattle too were shivering with the cold, not knowing what to make of this sudden freakish change in the weather. From one of the cows, Frank procured some milk, and at long last, the coffee was warm enough to drink; though it is very doubtful if it ever came near the boiling point. Then the biscuits were brought forth. But these had become so hard in the drying wind that had preceded the present dampness, that not even the hot coffee would soak them through. They remained impenetrable as so many bricks.

After this attempt at a repast they started for home, driving the cattle before them. Hungry, soaked to the skin, their wet clothes whipped by the cold wind until their bodies were almost stiff, the two came down the mountain, the bitter cold continuing until they neared the valley again. Here the wind was as it had been when they left home, warm and dry, and their wet garments were almost dried out by the time they reached home. None of this freakish disturbance had been experienced in the Aliso Canyon.

Afterward, it was learned in a letter from Lafayette, that he had passed through a cyclone in the Perris Valley that same afternoon. It seemed that the Laguna mountains had been touched by its dripping tail, and the two children caught in the outmost fringe of it.

CHAPTER 45 PLOT AND COUNTER-PLOT

Lafe secured a ride back from the Perris Valley as far as Los Angeles, with Mr. Walters who was coming that way. When he reached the coast he found a great stir of activity. Men were subdividing and selling land for townsites. Hub Goff Hubbard and Nate Brooks had gotten their heads together and decided to lay out a townsite of their own. They had entered into a sort of "mutual agreement" in which lands belonging to each—barring certain personal reservations—were to be combined, laid out in town lots and put up for sale to the general public.

Nate, who owned the only water source of any consequence in that part of the country, was to develop water for the townsite by enlarging his tunnel in the mountain above his house, and pipe it onto the lots. Hub Hubbard was to put up a hotel on a portion of Nate's acreage set aside for the purpose just above the ocean bluff. This site gave a beautiful view of the sea and almost overlooked the lone arch that pierced the huge point of rock a little to the north, in commemoration of which the town was to be called "Arch Beach."

Figure 32 Arch Beach Hotel [11]

They planned to float in from freight ships at anchor, the lumber for use in building the hotel and other contemplated dwellings of lot-purchasers. Hub, not having money enough to build this hotel, traded lots for labor and for locally bought materials. As soon as Lafe put in an appearance, Hub, knowing him to be handy with tools, made him a proposition that if he would apprentice himself to work on the hotel and stay with the job from start to finish, he would give him board and room and teach him the carpenter's trade, turning him out a finished mechanic. In addition, he was to give him certain lots in the townsite.

Having long desired to learn carpentry, Lafe accepted this offer. He purchased a set of carpenter tools and began work immediately. During his many months of work on the hotel, he was bound out by Hub Hubbard at intervals to do short jobs for others. At these times he was paid one dollar and fifty cents a day. One of these jobs was to build a little cottage for Ammon Goff and his bride, the former Miss Vina Hildebrand, schoolteacher at Laguna.

The next undertaking of these subdividers was to construct a fishing pier to further attract pleasure seekers. From this pier, a little north of the arch, Nate shipped his hay to the market in San Diego for several years.

Figure 33 Arch Beach Pier [12]

Early in Eighty-Seven, Lafe wrote to George in San Jacinto telling him about the "boom" that was started along the coast, and the opportunity that was open to buy lots and sell at a profit. A man whom we will call Jones—though that name is fictitious—had land to sell that was excellently located, whose advantages he set forth.

George had recently sold a corner of his own land in San Jacinto for five hundred dollars. He had also re-sold Sprowle's, receiving a little commission. With this capital he had paid off all his indebtedness to the government for his own land, and now holding a clear title and having a little cash left over, he was feeling quite satisfied with the world.

Clubfoot Minnie had been traded on the purchase of another outfit, consisting of a buggy and a little gray mare named Dollie. Thus equipped, he decided to make a trip to the coast. Though having no intention of buying lots, he felt the need of a cool vacation, for he had now been three years in the trying climate of the valley. He had learned also that Sister Sadie was expected home on a visit that summer, to which he looked forward with pleasant anticipation.

At the time of the complete crop failure in Eighty-Four, George had promised Lafe by way of remuneration for his labor, since the anticipated crop-division did not materialize, that he would give him a deed to forty acres of his land as soon as he should secure a title to it. That time had now come, and George was happy to be able to fulfill his word. Upon his arrival at the beach, the first thing he did was to hand Lafe a clear deed to forty acres of land in San Jacinto, now much more valuable than when promised.

George found the whole coast country teeming with activity and excitement. Even Father had caught the enthusiasm and had decided to sell the Aliso place. He made a proposition to George that if he would sell the farm for six thousand dollars he would give him a commission of five hundred. George went to work at once on the project. He was at that time putting up at the unfinished hotel, where also was Jones with his family.

George Invests

Though he had left San Jacinto with no intention of buying anything on the coast, George, in spite of resolutions, was swept off his feet. As he beheld townsites being laid out with bustle and activity on every hand, water being developed in the mountains, the hotel steadily nearing completion, town lots staked off and many of them labeled "sold," the main wide street paralleling the coastline already surveyed, graded and named "Pacific Avenue," the new grocery store on the corner partly stocked and open for business—when he gathered with the crowds that springtime in the invigorating coast climate amid the flags and banners, colored streamers and bunting, and listened with the rest to the flowery speeches of the promoters, eloquent and all afire with enthusiasm, it is not to be wondered at that he too succumbed to the charms of speculation. He was persuaded to purchase at a lump price a block of lots, including a frontage on Pacific Avenue.

Lafe was made a partner in this deal, George supposing him to be working for wages and able to carry his end of the burden. The price of this purchase was two thousand eighty dollars. George paid eighty dollars down and contracted to pay the balance of two thousand in one year's time. For promotion purposes, in order to make a big showing on paper that would aid him in selling other lots at a larger price, Jones wrote the price nine hundred and twenty dollars higher, acknowledging receipt of a thousand down a payment.

The ground was covered with brush and weeds. George immediately set himself to grubbing off his land to make it appear attractive to prospective purchasers. He hoped to sell it all soon at a large profit and experience no embarrassment about meeting his payments when due. But when he came to Lafe for his share of the expense, it was revealed that Lafe was not receiving cash wages and had no money to put up. He was expecting his proportion of expense to be deducted from his share of the profits as the lots were sold. So George decided to dissolve partnership with Lafe, and went to Jones to find out how it could be done.

Jones very obligingly told him that if he wanted to divide up the lots, he would give a clear deed to Lafe for two of the lots and George could hold the contract for the rest by himself. To this proposal both George and Lafe readily agreed. So Lafe selected the lots he wanted and Jones gave him a deed outright, making over to George alone the contract for the remainder. This contract was drawn up and signed in April of Eighteen Eighty-Seven.

George worked hard and long in clearing the land, becoming an enthusiastic booster for the townsite. He put his purchase up for sale, intending to remain on the coast until every lot should be disposed of. But sometimes things happen unforeseen for which no provision has been made. And so it was in this case.

An Unexpected Angle

Jones had a daughter, and in his own mind was laying future plans for her. George was an agreeable, industrious young man with a humorous and kindly personality, having besides these qualities, a financial start in life. Jones decided he would make him a suitable son-in-law. But George thought differently. He had his own ideas concerning the sort of girl he wanted for a wife, and this girl did not fit into the pattern. So it was that all overtures made in that direction were met with indifference.

This was most humiliating to Jones. When he saw how things were between them and that the girl was not being appreciated, his friendship for George turned into bitter hatred—kept however, under control and hidden—for he was cunning and suave—and he began to plot revenge.

Whenever George would have a prospective buyer for one of his lots, Jones would secretly "collar" the prospect and sell him one of his own lots instead, at the same time outwardly manifesting regret at the preference shown by the purchaser. This sort of scheming went on all summer. While Jones was selling lots right and left, George had brought to completion only one sale, and that through an agent from Santa Ana who had brought his prospect down to the scene and stuck right to him until the deal was consummated, leaving no opportunity for Jones to get in his underhanded work. This buyer made a fifty dollar down payment, fifteen of which went to the agent and thirty-five to George. Jones suavely professed pleasure at his turn of luck.

George was by nature trusting and unsuspecting, and himself practiced upright dealing; hence was no match for this mature, experienced schemer in whom was coupled an utter lack of principle with a very pleasing personality. But as the time drew near when his contract was to expire and still the remainder of his lots were unsold, he could no longer close his eyes to the fact that something was wrong somewhere.

Jones, for some time, had been carrying on a "whispering campaign" against him, and now George's friends began to drop hints to him of what was going on.

One day George started to town with his horse and buggy. When about a hundred and fifty yards from the hotel, he heard a shot fired. Looking back past the store, he saw a group of men standing in the hotel yard. Thinking little of the incident, he went on his way, soon forgetting all about it.

On his way back from town the day following, he stopped at the store for a few minutes, and was surprised when the storekeeper said to him:

"Did he come very close to you yesterday when he fired that shot?"

"Who? What do you mean?" asked George.

"!Why, Jones," was the reply; "He said he was shooting at you."

"Shooting at ME?" George exclaimed; "I didn't hear any bullet go by. I glanced over my shoulder when I heard the shot."

Then his friend began to unfold what his secret enemy had been saying about him, and how he was bragging of his intention to "bust up George and get everything" he had. Light then began to break. George could see why it was that Jones had secured all the sales. Other "queer" actions of the recent past stood out clearly, for which only one reason could be divined.

George thanked his friend in departing, and began to question others. The story proved to be well corroborated. He felt, however, that the rifle shot had been merely a braggadocio gesture and meant nothing more than an expression of enmity. Being a good shot, Jones could easily have sent the bullet home, had he so intended. It was nevertheless an effective warning of evil designs he had little suspected.

October was closing. More than half of the time of the contract was gone and still he was without means and seemingly at the mercy of his enemy. George said to himself:

"I've got to make a deal of some kind somehow, to save my bacon."

The only way out would be to turn the contract to someone who could handle it. But who should that be? To find a man who would take it over was easier said than done.

Taking with him his contract, he hunted up his old friend Nate Brooks, who, as it happened, was himself getting tired of Jones' actions and wishing he could do something about it. Together they talked the situation over. While carefully perusing the document George had brought with him, they made the interesting discovery that the legal description of the property lines showed glaring inconsistencies.

The avenue on which fronted the lots in question, paralleled the ocean bluff, which at that place extended northeast by southwest. But Jones had described this strip of land as running true to the cardinal points of the compass, north, east, south and west. His legal verbiage: "Thence south to the Pacific Ocean, "to express his real meaning should have read: "Thence southwest at right angles with Pacific Avenue to the Pacific Ocean." A point of land there extended out from the coastline, breaking its general contour, and this, the word "south" took in. By this inaccuracy there was actually included in the plot sold to George about three acres of his best ocean frontage in addition to the lots intentionally sold. Two other mistakes of importance equal if not greater were also revealed. In a blanket description he had included three short ends of cross streets leading to the bluffs, which had already been donated to the State and put on record as public property. As if this were not enough, his bungling description had included government land lying below the high tide limits.

Over this clumsily written document, which effectually "turned the tables" for George and placed his enemy in his power, the two men chuckled gleefully. They saw that Jones had gotten himself into a real mess. Had he been playing the game fair, George would have gone to him immediately regardless of personal feeling and given him a chance to re-write the contract. But in the light of recent disclosures, he felt justified in taking advantage of the blunders.

The first thing they did was to hunt up Lafe and ask to see his deed to the two lots allotted him from the same tract. This document followed the same general method of description, and by so doing confirmed the contract. Lafe was then taken into their confidence, and warned to admit no mistake in the legal description to anyone, but to stick to the description as given. They saw that unless they stood together on this point, neither deed nor contract would be worth the paper on which it was written.

What should be done next? While pondering this, George conceived a happy thought—Wars Martin! They would go to him, the shrewd horse trader and realtor who never had been known to lose out in a deal, and who just loved a thing like this. To get him after Jones would be the quintessence of satisfaction. So George and Nate drove to Santa Ana to interview Wars Martin.

After thoroughly studying with them the contract and deed, Wars Martin said:

> "We'll take the thing over. You turn the contract to me. It's my contract. You retain a third interest in the contract as a silent partner; and you, Brooks," turning to Nate, "will also be a silent partner with a third interest."

Thus Martin assured himself of their full cooperation in whatever followed. Martin agreed to trade for the contract a fine span of horses, harness and light wagon. Nate, for his interest, was to turn over to George a lot, some hay, and a two-year-old heifer. In high spirits the two left Martin's office. George remarked to Nate:

> "It's worth all I've got in the deal to get that scalawag after Jones! "

Not long after this, a hint was let out purposely to the effect that George had sold his contract to Wars Martin. As was intended, others promptly carried the news to Jones. The man was furious. He sought out George and abused him wordily as though he had been a traitor.

> "Well," said George deliberately, "I bought the land and I've sold it."

So Jones could get not even the satisfaction of a quarrel out of him.

After this, Wars Martin let out a hint that he had found "kinks" in the contract. When this report came to the ears of Jones, he declared that any such were mistakes and made accidentally; and that he could "prove it by George himself."

Not long after this Lafe went to town, and on the street happened to meet face to face Jones' lawyer, with whom he was acquainted. This man was effusively glad to see him, and invited him up to his office for a "little friendly chat." After inquiring all about the progress of affairs on the coast in a general way, simulating an interest in everything and everybody concerned, he remarked, as if just remembering the fact:

> "By the way, Lafe, you've got some lots down there, haven't you?"

Lafe replied that he had. Then by adroit questioning the lawyer led him on to describe his lots. Lafe gave the description as it read on the deed. The lawyer then endeavored to entangle him into admissions of error in the descriptions. But Lafe stood his ground consistently. He then asked the question point blank:

> "Is that description correct?"

> "Yes, that's just the way it reads," Lafe answered.

This brought the little "friendly chat" to a close and the boy took his departure. The next time this Attorney saw his client, he said to him: "Jones, you're stuck."

April rolled around, and the contract matured. One day Martin informed Jones that he was ready to pay for the property and invited him up to his office to complete the deal and deliver the deed. They drove to town together in Martin's conveyance, and in his office proceeded to make out the papers. Jones took up his pen to sign the deed, at which he was interrupted by a question from Wars Martin:

> "Jones, are you going to sign that deed?"

> "Why ye-e-s," he replied.

> "Don't you know that it is a state prison offense to deed away those three street portions after putting them on record as public property?"

Jones stopped to consider for a moment, then said:

> "I'll give you a deed to three other lots just as good as those three."

> "No you won't give me a deed to any other lots. You'll PAY for THOSE!"

> "Well, how much do you want?" asked Jones.

> "I want three hundred dollars apiece," replied Martin.

> "They're not worth that!" stormed Jones.

> "That's the price at which you're selling lots," said Martin.

> "Well, they're not worth that!" repeated Jones.

"That's what you'll pay for them," said Martin firmly. "If you want to get out of it that's what it'll cost you."

"We'll leave it to arbitration!" proposed Jones. "You pick out a man and I'll pick out a man. Let them choose another man and we'll abide by what they say."

"Very well," agreed Martin. "We'll leave it to arbitration. Who do you choose to sit on the board?"

"I choose Nate Brooks," promptly replied Jones, sure of his man.

With an inward desire to laugh, Martin then chose for his own representative, Boring, the storekeeper, who had been George's informant of crooked work in the first place. Jones was pleased with this choice, for he considered both of these men his friends. But when Nate was approached to sit on the board, he absolutely refused.

"I'm too busy, and I don't want to sit on any arbitration board."

But Jones begged and pleaded. He simply would not take "no" for an answer. So finally, still under protest, Nate consented:

"All right, if you are bound to have it that way."

The two men then chose for the third member of the board, Lonnie Lumis, who was married to Henry Goff's daughter Clinny, and lived on a corner adjoining the townsite. Jones was elated for he was sure of the friendship of Lonnie.

During the arbitration proceedings, of all three men Nate was the one least inclined to show mercy. The others, though fully agreed that Jones deserved to be "stuck," were in favor of mitigating somewhat the severity of the punishment. Since Jones had actually sold the lots to George for much less than three hundred apiece, Nate yielded, and a blanket price of seven hundred and fifty was put on the three street ends sold as lots; thus saving Jones merely a hundred and fifty from Martin's price, leaving him a cash balance due of twelve hundred and fifty. This balance covered not only the lots originally sold, but the extra three acres of frontage inadvertently included by Jones' wild description, and left him smarting with disappointment; for he had expected more consideration at the hands of friends.

The question of this frontage, over which there was sharp contention, together with the matter of tide lands deeded away, had then to be threshed out in the courts, which upheld the description as given so far as land belonging to Jones was concerned, and awarded to Martin further reimbursements.

George and Nate relinquished to Martin their two thirds' interest as silent partners, and Martin reimbursed Nate for the cow, hay, and lot he had turned over to George. The previous sale of a lot out of the tract offered no difficulty of adjustment it having been described by number only. The thirty-five dollars profit on this sale to George, reduced his total outlay from eighty to forty-five dollars. For this sum, plus his work at grubbing, he received a lot, a cow, two horses, two harnesses, a wagon and a little hay, besides an enjoyable summer's vacation.

A Neighbor Sells

The first unit of Hub Goff's Hubbard hotel was completed, when a group of promoters representing the Whitcomb-Raymond Company, who had built the Hotel Del Coronado at San Diego, approached Frank Goff with an offer to purchase his property. It was their purpose to put up a hotel and lay out a townsite there on Goff Point. Frank was not anxious to sell. He had visions of making some money there himself. But the company agents were insistent. Finally he named his price, setting it so high that he thought surely they would turn it down.

The hundred and twenty-five acres left him after dividing his original hundred and sixty with Hub, had cost him about a hundred and fifty-six dollars. To this initial amount had been added the cost of building the simple cabin. He had lived there a little over eight years, his additional improvements being a barn and cistern and a roadside hedge. In his own mind he set a very modest value on the property. But this estimate was multiplied many times in the price he now named to the Company. Twenty-five thousand dollars was his price, with the added stipulation that if they bought it they would also buy out his brother Lee at fifteen thousand. These men were not eager to secure Lee's property, but they wanted Frank's so much they took him up on his proposition. Frank himself was secretly surprised at their acceptance.

At the time the bargain was made, George was present with the group as they stood near the roadway in Frank's yard. While they were discussing the terms, there carne driving by, old man Bacon on his way from San Juan Capistrano to Laguna. In passing the group, he slowed down, keen to hear what was going on. From floating sentences, he quickly gleaned the astounding news that Goff had sold out for twenty-five thousand. Immediately he wheeled his horse about and went back the way he had come. When he had crossed the sand at the mouth of Aliso, he turned up the canyon to Father's place, that he might be the first to acquaint him with the astonishing news.

Upon consummation of the deal with Goff, George approached these buyers concerning the property in Aliso Canyon, naming to them the price set by Father, of six thousand. They were at once interested, and agreed to accompany him to the place and look the property over. Upon their arrival, as they drew near the house, Hulda, a girl of fourteen, ran out to meet George in great excitement to tell him the news that Frank Goff had "just sold out his place for twenty-five thousand dollars." Bacon had been there and gone.

When George presented to Father the two prospective buyers, behold, he had raised his price from six to fifteen thousand. George was nonplussed, the men cooled in ardor. They looked the property over without enthusiasm. Before leaving they asked Father how much he would take for the pond alone. His answer was, "Three thousand dollars." The men departed, no longer interested.

Father never received another offer for the place. But it was worth the sum he had asked, and perhaps even more by comparison with Goff's property, which was orchard-less and entirely without water except from rain caught in the cistern, its sole advantage being an attractive beach frontage. Our Aliso farm was a bower of green beauty, with a creek for the stock and supplied with domestic water from the spring on the hillside. It too had a smaller beach frontage with the added attraction of an inland pond that might be developed as a place for sports. Had the higher price named been given them at the first, very likely they would have taken the property. But the psychology of Father's selling methods repulsed them. Needless to say, George was himself disgusted and made no further effort to interest buyers in the Aliso place.

CHAPTER 46 AN EVENTFUL YEAR

On July fourteen of that year, Sadie arrived from Phoenix, bringing her little first-born son Lawrence, then a year and three months of age. Artie, who at the time happened to be out of work, met them at the depot in Los Angeles and took them to her room on East First Street for the night. The next day she accompanied them to Aliso.

This visit was a great event to us all. We children had a grand time with our only little nephew, and delighted to call Clara "auntie," who was less than a year and a half his senior. We vied one with another as to which should have possession of him, and would hardly let him alone long enough for his daily nap—a matter in which Sadie was inexorable.

She had been given the girls' room to occupy with her baby, while they had betaken themselves to the honey house to sleep. But still Sadie found the small dwelling with its many inmates too noisy a place for Lawrence to get proper rest in the early evening and his daily nap undisturbed. So the family was persuaded to transport the organ also out to the honey house, and to turn that place into a sort of entertainment room for us all.

Being willing to do anything possible to make her comfortable and prolong her visit, the family gladly acceded to this plan. We tried our best to be quiet in the evenings, but with all our endeavors, poor Sadie had a difficult time trying to preserve the health habits of her little son.

The Cordells too came again to the beach that summer, and this time instead of bringing with them the two Hughes boys, who then were hard at work in the mine with their father, they brought Emma Hughes, their young sister, and we became acquainted with this charming lass of sixteen.

Emma, as well as her brothers, was full of that subtle essence called "charm," possessed in general by our English cousins. It seems to be bred and born into the race. Regardless of character and principle, whether these are good or bad, nature and training combine to make their outward manner agreeable and attractive and their voices soft and pleasing.

An illustration of this inbred politeness is furnished by an incident that took place some twenty years later, as related by this same Emma, then Mrs. Towns. Some years after the turn of the century, she and her husband took a trip back to their native England. With a party of friends and relatives they went into an inn for lunch. The two wandered away by themselves to a table somewhat isolated, and sat down. While waiting for an attendant to take their order, two disreputable looking fellows took seats at the same table. Soon, a fine appearing, well-dressed gentleman walked up to them, and bowing respectfully, said to the two disreputables:

"I beg your pardon, Gentlemen. I am very sorry to have to say this to you, but one of you has stolen my pipe."

To this extremely courteous arraignment, both men listened in silence. Then one of them slowly reached his hand into his trousers' pocket, pulled out the pipe, and laid it on the table. The gentleman thanked him with the utmost courtesy, took up his meerschaum, and walked away.

After Frank and Lee Goff sold out in the spring of Eighty-Seven, they took their families and went East, visiting, for about two months, their friends and relatives in Connecticut, Massachusetts, Rhode Island and New York. Upon their return, they settled in Tustin, and together went into the grocery business in Santa Ana. For this they put up a brick store building on the southeast corner of Fourth and Spurgeon streets.

It was then the custom in both towns and country to keep drinking water cool by means of ollas (pronounced o-yas)—a porous form of Mexican pottery jars, which were wrapped in sacking, dipped in water, and remained moist by means of constant seepage from within. Hung up out-of-doors in shady places, they were kept cool by evaporation, aided by whatever breezes might be stirring. In our cool coast climate they were not needed, and for the first time I saw one of these suspended from the bough of a tree in the yard of the Goff home in Tustin.

Shortly after they located there, Father drove into town one day to do some trading, and Mother went along with him as far as Tustin to visit her old friend Emma Goff. While there she began to suffer strange and violent pain in the first joint of her left forefinger. Once, years before, there had developed on one of her fingers, a felon—a dangerous, deep-seated whitlow, which is an inflammation of the bone sheath, or periosteum, underneath which pus forms that finds no outlet. It soon became evident that this was to be another felon.

While waiting for Father to come from town, she treated the finger with hot applications. But by the time he arrived the pain had increased to an intensity that was almost beyond endurance. Father hastened to get her home. But the journey being so long, poor Mother was almost beside herself with agony before they arrived. The thing he should have done first was to look up a doctor before leaving town. But doctors were outside Father's calculations. He probably did not even think of it. It was his boast that with all their family, he had never had a doctor in the house.

Once at home, they began immediately to treat it as in the former case, which then had proved so successful. Hour after hour Mother held her finger in hot lye—as hot as could be borne. But the time consumed in travelling without treatment had allowed the thing to get such a start that now it was too late to arrest its progress by even the most drastic treatment. Poor Mother! How she did suffer! For days she could neither eat nor sleep, but walked the floor in agony. When at last recovery set in, the poor finger was permanently stiffened and stood out from her hand like a stick. The next finger had to be patiently trained to do double duty. Though by persistent manipulations through long years she became able to bend the joints slightly, yet Mother had a stiff finger for all the rest of her life.

Something like a year previous to this, while working on the McManus place clearing off the ground ready for planting trees, Lafe had run his finger against a ball cactus and one of the spines had stuck in the joint, with the result that inflammation set in, pus formed under the periosteum and a felon began to develop. At Father's direction he had soaked his finger in hot lye. Father had pierced the periosteum with a darning needle to let out the pus, and he recovered without evil after effects—except to the other fingers immersed with it, from which the outer skin had been eaten off, which delayed complete recovery.

Eighteen Eighty-Seven was an eventful year, not only in the history of California and in the experience of neighbors and friends, but also to the family in Aliso; for before that memorable summer ended, Father was gone from us, and Mother was left alone with her children.[13]

In life's varied experiences, there are times that memory shrinks from recalling—strange, sad days, that affect the whole after life. Over these, the heart instinctively draws a merciful curtain of silence. Such were some of those August days.

Sadie was still with us, and lingered on through September, till Arthur was becoming insistent on her return. As the time of separation drew near, an effort was made to get the children of the family all together for a final visit and outing on the beach. Never had the whole family been together all at once, and now that one was missing they would never be. But Mother and her children might still get together for the first time in their history. At every gathering since the birth of the two younger girls, someone had always been absent and too far away to be present. But at last, here we all were near at hand—George still on the coast, Lafe cutting wood in Santa Ana, where he had gone after the hotel was finished, Artie working in a restaurant in Los Angeles.

A Sunday was set when she could be off for the day, and we all gathered for a final reunion and picnic dinner on the dear old beach we had known and loved so long. Thirteen of us children, together with Mother making fourteen, were all together for one day—an event that happened only once again in our lives.

After this happy occasion was over, on the twenty-seventh day of September, we bade goodbye to Sadie—reluctantly and not without tears. She took her departure with little Lawrence, who was not to see California again and his numerous aunts and uncles until he was a lad past sixteen. George drove them to the depot in Santa Ana in his buggy, while Joseph followed with their luggage in the buckboard, taking also Lafe's trunk to him.

It was strangely lonely for those of us who were left behind. Lafe accompanied Sadie as far as Los Angeles, where she intended to stop over and see Artie before leaving the city. They went to her old room at 172 East First Street, but were disappointed to learn that she had just moved from that place, leaving no address. So Sadie was obliged to take her train for Phoenix without the final goodbye she had counted on.

After cutting wood for awhile, Lafe went to work for Mr. Towers of Tustin on a thresher. When this job was finished, he came home to help with the late fall work and take up some of the duties and responsibilities where Father had laid them down. He helped in the disposal of the nuts, the harvesting and sale of the apples, and the making of wines and cider from the grapes and windfall apples, as Father had been doing for a number of years.

Leon Files a Claim

About that time, Leon Goff, having recently attained his majority, came over into Aliso Canyon and filed a timber claim on the strip of land that the survey had taken away from us just north of our true line which we had nevertheless been farming ever since. This took away from us a slice of our barley ground, including the rock wall and pepper row at its upper end. Upon this land that we had used for sixteen years, Leon set out a dense grove of Eucalyptus trees, which grew and flourished, and can still be seen growing on the old "barley ground." Though we knew he had a legal right to do this, it did seem to us unneighborly; and was a pecuniary loss.

This action caused the family to fear that something similar might happen to the Little Hill, which would be even a greater calamity, since this line came so close to the dwelling and cut across our road, taking in also a portion of the creek. There was but one way open to insure its being kept in the family; and that was for Lafe to file on it himself. But Lafe was not yet of legal age, and would not be until the following March. This matter was much discussed and the conclusion finally reached that he should file on it anyway to prevent anyone else from doing so, and if necessary, a second filing could be made after his birthday. So Lafe filed a homestead on the Little Hill three months before he was legally of age; and built himself a tiny cabin in which to sleep, for the law required that he should live upon it, at least half the time.

Shortly after filing on the land, and before the cabin was built, Lafe decided to burn off the brush and poison oak that covered his new claim, and started a fire at the base of the Little Hill, expecting to be able to keep it under control till his purpose should be accomplished. But he reckoned without good judgment. The fire soon escaped from its intended bounds, and became a raging wild fire, racing over the mountains back of our place and burning up everything before it. Miles and miles of mountain pastures were destroyed and hundreds of acres of honey sage; and after several days, when the fire had burned itself out, the beautiful mountains were stark and bare as far as the eye could see, and much farther, and charred to a black cinder—the blackened stems of denuded tree-shrubs standing out like gaunt spectres on the hills.

In the little eight by eight cabin that lay close up against the foot of the hill, we children played during the absence of its owner, and had grand times. It was scarcely larger than a play house, and how we did enjoy it! There we played "family" to our heart's content, sleeping on Lafe's bed when "play-night" came, and in the "play-daytime," eating our meals up under the Eucalyptus trees near the "bone rock"; where we cooked real food with real fire on our real stove made out of the five-gallon kerosene can.

That winter when the heavy rains came, the denuded mountains were unable to absorb the water that fell. And with no vegetation to check its onward rush, it swept in torrential sheets down over the face of the cliff, widely overflowing the little draw above and the gully where it struck below-which normally carried off the surplus water in a little stream during winter rains—and cut a deep gulch all along its course as it rushed past the Eucalyptus trees, between the Honey House and apiary, past the end of the bunch-grass row, through the orchard, across the road, and on down to the creek below the willows.

But in process of cutting this gulch, the little gully above the Honey House being incapable of containing the torrent, it divided in its on-rush, and a portion of it swept down the slope toward our back kitchen door, which being raised only a few inches from the ground, allowed the water to enter the kitchen. Mother and the girls fought it frantically with brooms, endeavoring to sweep it out as fast as it came in, until the boys could dig diverting gutters and bank up soaked dirt enough to turn its course away from the door around the end of the house. There it swept away a pile of lumber that lay in its path, scattering it over the orchard below.

After the rains had ceased and the water in the gulch had subsided to a muddy rivulet, the road was repaired and the lower end of the gulch filled in and broadened to allow the water to spread out across a broader area, where it would flow over the diagonal road without much cutting.

This new gulch, still containing a modicum of water, became a new source of fun to us youngsters. The damage it had done to our property was the least of our concerns. Here was a channel, narrow enough in places for us to jump across, yet wide and deep enough to afford an element of danger; and a brand new "game" was created, called "Jump the Ditch." I would take little Clara by the hand, then about three, leaving Luella for Annie—for of course as the "big boss" I had my choice, and the choice was always the baby. We would take a run and a jump across this big ditch, dragging them after us in a wild leap that was exhilaratingly frightening to them and immensely thrilling to us, repeating this exercise at intervals day after day endlessly, never seeming to tire of the exertion. Sometimes little Charlotte, just turned eight, would plead: "Jump me too!" for there were very few places where she dared try it alone, and then I would give her a turn.

This enlarged gulch became a permanent fixture on the premises; remaining for several years deep and sharp enough to preserve the charm of our game of "Jump the Ditch." Gradually filling in by slides from its banks and by rubbish collected, it was preserved from being re-deepened by a fresh growth of brush on the mountains that held the water in check.

That winter, a very sad event took place, culminating on December Twenty-Seven, shortly before the passing of the old year. Early that fall, Harry and Bob Hughes came to Arch Beach having been engaged by Nate to help him with his water tunnel in the mountain, which he was then enlarging for supplying the townsite. With alacrity they left the mine to spend the fall and perhaps winter on the coast. For they loved the ocean—loved its swimming and its fishing and its rowing, and the bracing salt sea-breezes. There was social life too—parties and dances along the coast, and they loved dancing, being expert at the graceful pleasure. But more than these, Harry liked to spend his evenings over at the Aliso farm house.

One evening not long after their coming, there was a dance at San Juan Capistrano. Bob, chaffing Harry at his evident preference for the canyon society, rode his horse across the southern mesas to the dance. After an enjoyable evening of almost constant dancing, he left the hall late at night while wet with perspiration, and started out toward the beach for the return journey of ten or twelve miles. As he struck the coast mesas, a strong cold breeze swept in from off the water, and it was not long till he was chilled to the bone. Being new on the coast, he had not counted on anything like this, for usually he was not so affected by cold. But this was penetrating and damp and Bob was not sufficiently protected. He took a dreadful cold.

The next day, though sick, he got out of bed and went to work in the cold damp tunnel when he should have remained in bed. His cold turned into pneumonia. He was taken home to his father and sister at Carbondale in Silverado Canyon to be nursed, and placed in the care of Old Doctor Rowan of Santa Ana, who before long had diagnosed his case as "typhoid pneumonia."

Bob did not get any better in Carbondale and his friends in Villa Park begged that he should be brought to them for care. So he was taken down to the Cordells, where he lay very sick for weeks.

Harry was still working for Nate in the tunnel, and spent many of his evenings at our place. But he was restless and uneasy, and all of us were much concerned about Bob. One evening we were out in the Honey House, the girls playing the organ and singing with Harry in an effort to drown his worry, when word was brought to him by a messenger that his brother Bob was dead.

A pall of gloom and sadness fell over all the household, as poor Harry rode away on his horse alone with his grief. Far, far up the canyon, across two ranchos and through several towns he must ride before he could join the rest of the stricken family in Villa Park.

A Child's Blunder

I was just turned ten when we first became acquainted with the Hughes boys; and though by nature romantic to the "nth" degree, as yet had given little if any thought to the sex question. I admired Bob with the simple admiration of childhood, entirely independent of sex, though my preference was really in favor of Harry, who was more openly friendly and talkative. Bob was bashful as a schoolboy—that is, as schoolboys were in those days—but tall, well-built and healthy looking, and to my childish eyes, was almost a giant. I had often heard my elders discuss the tendency of people to marry their opposites in disposition, complexion, form and size—though innocent as a baby concerning marriage relations—and looking at Bob, I wondered if he would marry somebody very small by way of contrast; supposing that to be the proper thing.

One day during their employment on Nate's tunnel, Bob was at our house. I, as children will, was listening to the conversation in which I had no part. The idea occurred to me again what a contrast it would be if Bob should marry a very small woman. During a pause in the conversation, without the least thought in my mind of being myself concerned in any way except merely as an illustration of size, I spoke up suddenly with the astounding suggestion: "Bob, when you marry, you ought to marry somebody little-like me." There was an ominous silence. Joan gave me one withering look. Then it dawned on my consciousness what I had said and how it sounded. I crimsoned to the roots of my hair—and under the roots. Shame and confusion enveloped me. My heart sank like lead. Oh, that the floor would open up and swallow me from sight! Consumed with the necessity of explaining, yet knowing that I never could—that nothing on earth would convince Joan or anyone else, of my perfectly innocent intention, with cheeks burning and tongue tied I slunk from the room feeling forever disgraced beyond all recovery. I felt that never could I look Bob in the face again. The false position in which I had placed myself subjected me to such unmitigated scorn, which, according to the law of motives, I deserved not, yet which there was no possibility of averting, that the situation was unbearable. I was a worm of worms—humiliated to the dust, and under the dust. Fully expecting a scorching reprimand from Joan as soon as Bob should be gone, I felt it could not be endured.

But Joan's scorn was deeper even than I had imagined—so deep that she treated me with silent and utter contempt, not even deigning to mention the matter again—for which I thanked my unlucky stars—as though I had been a hopeless incorrigible on whom words could be but wasted.

But Bob! How could I ever meet him again? No one ever knew the prolonged humiliation I suffered over this blundering mistake, though tight locked within my bosom. Others forgot the incident; I, never. Whenever Bob came to the house after that, I managed to be somewhere else; and am quite sure that I never spoke to him again. When Bob died, there was mingled with my sorrow, a wicked feeling of intense relief that now I would never have to dread meeting him again.

Who can analyze such exaggerated and unnecessary suffering in the heart of a child? Was it the imbibed results of the false and double standards and stupid psychology of the times? What a blessed thing it is to "keep in the middle of the road!"

CHAPTER 47 THE BOOM

The great "boom" within the memory of many still living, that struck Southern California in Eighteen Eighty-Six, reached its highest peak in Eighty-Seven, and climaxed in disaster in the summer of Eighty-Eight, was not sudden in its inception. It came upon the country gradually as the natural result of forces set in operation when the statehood of California was still in its infancy.

At the time of the organization of the first Board of Trade in Los Angeles in Seventy-Three—soon followed by other similar organizations throughout the State—a systematic campaign of advertising was launched with the one avowed object of making California, with its broad unsettled areas its natural resources and advantages, known to the rest of the world; thereby inducing outsiders to locate within its boundaries. This campaign was carried forward with increasing diligence throughout the years that followed.

Agents of these organizations were sent East to distribute descriptive literature, not only in the cities, but all through the rural districts of the Eastern and Middle states, and among the immigrants as they entered the country. In the large cities were maintained regular displays of California products, industries and scenic attractions. This propaganda, in lesser proportions, was carried even to Europe.

At the Centennial Exposition held in Philadelphia in Seventy-Six, celebrating the nation's first century of existence, California was widely advertised, not only by pamphlets and exhibits, but by the extensive circulation of books written by popular authors extolling California.

In Eighty-Two, the "Immigration Association of California" was formed, with headquarters in San Francisco. This organization distributed yearly about a hundred thousand pamphlets and folders eliciting from interested parties at a distance a deluge of inquiring letters. Thus, a general interest and curiosity was awakened in the public mind, which paved the way for the influx of Easterners that took place later.

This association also made a business of conducting into the state and locating immigrant parties. The office of "Commissioner of Immigration" was created by the state and appropriations made for furthering the work. Ever since the "Gold Rush" days of Forty-nine, a magic charm had been connected with the name—"California"—and it had been the unfulfilled dream of thousands to visit the state. Now that dream was made possible of realization.

The railroads and steamship companies cooperated in these advertising schemes by giving excursion rates from important points in the East. A coupon book was sold covering not only train fare, but all expenses incident to the journey; such as boat fare, streetcar fare, stage fare, even mule-back fare into regions beyond the settlements, and sometimes including board and lodging on the journey.

Three thousand families were thus located in Eighty-Three. In Eighty-Four, fifty thousand immigrants came in over the Central Pacific railroad alone. And this was but a prelude to the great, unprecedented in-rush that began to pour into California in the spring of Eighty-Six, culminating in the great total of two hundred thousand in Eighty-Seven— the peak year of the boom, when for a time, they were coming in at the rate of twenty-five thousand a month.

California oranges—the industry having developed since Seventy-Three when the first tree had been introduced into the state—had in Eighty-Four at the New Orleans Exposition taken the prize away from Florida. This also, being widely known, had added impetus to the advertising propaganda. Though already, for three years past, the dreaded black scale had been working havoc in the California orange groves, that fact was not exploited. But a decadence had indeed begun that threatened the near extermination of the industry; which was averted only by the importation of the precious little ladybug from Australia in Eighty-Nine.

In November of Eighty-Five, the Santa Fe Railroad ran its first train into Los Angeles, using by special arrangement from Colton on through, the tracks of the Southern Pacific—its own tracks being not yet finished. Within ten days of the completion of the line, the Santa Fe began cutting fares from eastern points. The Southern Pacific retaliated by cutting a little lower; and this competition, in the spring of Eighty-Six, developed into a protracted "rate war" unparalleled in the history of railroads; becoming the main contributing factor of the Boom.

Passenger fares and freight rates from eastern points to California were so drastically cut as to amount to almost nothing. One could buy a round-trip ticket from Chicago or other equally distant centers to Los Angeles for as little as fifteen dollars, or ten dollars one way, and from New York, a round trip for seventeen dollars. Tales are told of even lower fares than these—of a ticket from St. Louis for five dollars and for one day only, of a give-away of third class tickets for one dollar.

Freight rates fell from three and five dollars per hundred weight, first to one dollar then fifty cents, then thirty-seven cents, and even thirty cents per hundred pounds; and the household goods of emigrants who bought more than one ticket were carried almost free. Since the railroads would benefit equally with others by an increase in population some have advanced the theory that this railroad fight was actually by collusion, and carried on as a pretense merely for purposes of advertising propaganda. This may be doubted. But however that may be, it became a major factor in the Boom.

Taking advantage of these extremely low passenger fares, Easterners flocked into Southern California to see the country and to visit friends already here. Many of them, becoming captivated by the climate and other natural advantages, remained to invest their capital in the West.

Eastern capitalists, watching the trend of things, prepared to reap a harvest. The boom was promoted by Eastern men and Eastern capital. In the early beginnings of these prosperity signs, a man named Moy came out from Chicago or New York and joining forces with a local piano merchant of Santa Ana, a Mr. Gardener, with him went into the real estate business. Mr. Moy was a tall, well-spoken man with a polite, impressive manner; and to all appearances, a very fine character. He was a man who could originate big projects and "put them over"—a man who understood human nature and how to play upon it. Always obliging, he had a very confidential way with him. When talking with a prospective purchaser, he had a manner of putting his arm familiarly across his shoulders in a most brotherly fashion, as if confiding to him something he would not tell anyone else. He was never too busy to devote some time to every individual with whom he came in contact. In short, Moy was one of the slickest promoters this country has ever seen, and became one of the chief figures of the early boom period in our corner of the state.

The method of procedure followed by these first promoters was to get out into the country among the hard-working farmers who had not yet sensed anything unusual in the wind, and quietly take options on their properties, offering prices that to the owners seemed unusually generous—even extravagant. Gladly would they give these options, agreeing to any terms of payment the purchasers desired. As their neighbors would hear of the good news, they too would be eager to sell and give like options on their properties. When a sufficient number of these options had been thus secured, the promoters would then form a syndicate for the purpose of buying and promoting the properties.

The usual terms of sale were one third of the purchase price down, one third more in one year, and the balance in two years—the law allowing still another year before final foreclosure in case of default. In this manner the properties would be tied up for a period of three years, and any advance in prices meanwhile, would go to the purchasers.

Since these contracts carried a penalty of forfeiture for non-payment and were drawing good interest, the sellers, far from worrying about their unpaid principals, rejoiced in a high degree of satisfaction over the "bargains" they had made. Thus was characterized the first stage of the "boom."

The Second Stage

The next stage was the boosting of land prices. As the stream of Easterners kept coming in, urged on by many inducements held out to them, they were met by systematic campaigns of advertising set on foot by the big promoters to strip them of their cash and unload their syndicate purchases.

Land sales were held and flowery speeches made amid flying banners and bands of music. It was then that the native Californians began to wake up to the fact that they had the "garden-spot of the world"—that they had been asleep on the top of an inexhaustible goldmine without knowing it—that everybody in the United States would want their property if they could only see it or hear about it.

When this idea took hold of the people, everybody became enthused over the prospect. Business men were fired with it. New estimates of values began to be put forth. Soon the boom got under way and in a short time had swept over all Southern California like a conflagration. Though the chief focus of the contagion was the southern part of the state, embracing Los Angeles, San Bernardino and San Diego counties, the excitement spread the length and breadth of the state from Oregon on the north to Mexico on the south.

In the first rank of the immigrants were many from Ohio, Indiana and Illinois; followed by thousands of others, bringing their capital to invest. Soon all available living quarters were filled to overflowing, and tent cities began to spring up like mushrooms in many places. Many began to buy and build houses, others to speculate, buying up land and also in anticipation of rising prices purchasing many of these promotion contracts for investments. For these they paid in gold coin at an advance price over face value—the difference being clear profit to the sellers of the contracts.

The syndicates formed for the purpose would promote the sale of the acreages they had bought, by laying out townsites everywhere and anywhere, whether or not any natural demand for a town existed, or any background to support it, and without regard to water supply, communication, or nature of the soil. The sensible laws that govern sub-dividing today, were then unknown. All that was necessary to start a town was to get out a blueprint and drive a few stakes into the ground. Then, with a few loads of brick and lumber unloaded on the tract, to give the appearance of active improvements about to be made, an abundance of colored bunting, and a few dollars spent in clever advertising, the sale of lots was on.

In each such sub-division, a plot of the ground would usually be donated free to some citizen of means who would agree in return to put up a hotel on it without delay. Other plots would be similarly donated for banks, others for parks.

An auction sale would then be held, which had been widely and extravagantly advertised. And flowery speakers, men of vision and imagination, would picture to the assembled crowds the "Garden of Eden" the place was destined to become. Lots would be put up for sale singly or in blocks, to be sold to the highest bidder. Prices would soar beyond all reason. No matter how much had been paid for a lot, a little later someone else would offer an advanced price for the "bargain" that netted a big profit to the former investor.

All sorts of clever advertising schemes were resorted to. In the city of Los Angeles, brass bands playing loudly rode through the streets on cable cars, hay-wagons or carriages, flying promotion banners lettered in gigantic type with impossible promises and descriptions. The single-track cable-car line was in this year—Eighty-Seven—changed to a double-track line to provide increased facilities for travel about the city.

The Third Stage

Thus began a third stage, a wild orgy of speculation developing into a mania. No matter what was offered for sale, it was eagerly snapped up. The crowds were so immense that they had to be served each in his turn. In order to be first on the ground at the opening, lines would be formed by would-be purchasers in advance of the sale. In some instances these lines were formed several days before the sale date, and the weary and hungry bargain-seekers would stand in line day and night rather than lose their place in line. Men of wealth would pay large fees to others to hold these places in line for them until the hour of sale arrived. Such fees were often as large as one hundred dollars. The story is on record that in one instance of a specially advertised sale, beginning the day before a long line was formed in front of the real estate office, the weary and hungry applicants holding their places all through the night. The first one in line clung desperately to the handle of the big front office door. Later arrivals, passing up and down the lines, would offer money in exchange for desirable places. As far down the line as number fifty-four, a man offered to sell out for a hundred dollars. Number three in line was induced to sell out for five hundred dollars. Number two claimed to have refused an offer of one thousand dollars for his place, while number one, deaf to all offers, continued to cling doggedly to the handle of the door, securing at last the coveted prize—first choice. This meant also the paying of an exorbitant price for his purchase. That first day, twenty-eight thousand dollars' worth of lots were sold in that particular townsite.

Real estate offices sprang up like toadstools everywhere. Rents rose so high in the cities that landlords acquired fortunes from the rentals of old buildings. In Los Angeles, they were crowded. An old dilapidated building on Spring Street that in normal times might have brought its owner fifty dollars rental, was divided up into booths and let out to real estate dealers at from seventy-five to one hundred and fifty dollars a month for one booth, thus netting its owner a thousand or more per month.

Real Estate offices remained open far into the night to accommodate buyers and rake in the gold. Fortunes changed hands overnight. Millionaires were created in a day. Often large fortunes were refused in the hope of gaining larger fortunes. The same property might change hands several times in twenty-four hours. It is said that real estate transfers at the crest of the boom averaged two million thirty-two thousand dollars a day.

Fruitful orchards and fields of grain and garden stuffs thus bought up and divided into city lots and auctioned off, were left neglected. Those engaged in this game of speculation were too busy and excited to give any thought or time to the improvement of properties already bought, but were out searching for more on which to make a re-sale profit. So the countrysides were filled with decadent farms, where weeds flourished in former gardens, and orchards no longer productive stood unwatered, unharvested and uncultivated—mute monuments to the insane folly of man.

These inflated values were in the land itself, not in the improvements built up by patient toil and sacrifice through the years. Land that had formerly been valued at fifty dollars an acre, now sold for a thousand; and that valued at ten, now brought four and five hundred. A twenty-acre tract of land that had been bought in Sixty-Nine for one hundred and fifty dollars, sold in Eighty-Six for ten thousand; and two weeks later sold again for fourteen thousand.

As prices sky-rocketed, those who had not yet had a chance at the "picking" would rush pell-mell to get in on the good things before it should be too late, even sturdy old farmers, who had originally sold their land for one third down at figures pitifully lower than the same land was now bringing, had become discontented and uneasy, wishing they had waited for the increased values. They too became inoculated with the fever of speculation. Looking around to find something that could still be bought at less than the prevailing peak prices, they would snap up anything they found and on the strength of their second payments soon to become due, would pay down on the new investment a deposit of one third, with terms similar to those on which they had themselves originally sold, timing the payments to correspond to their expected incomes of total balances in two years. If fortunate enough to re-sell at a profit, instead of clearing off the slate, they would begin a hunt for more property and re-invest in a gamble to make more money.

Statistics show that during this boom, real estate transfers in Los Angeles County alone aggregated more than one hundred million dollars. Between the eastern limits of the city of Los Angeles and the boundary lines of San Bernardino County, a distance of thirty-six miles, there had been started thirty-six towns—twenty-five along the line of the Santa Fe, eight along the paralleling Southern Pacific, and three between the two lines—all in the San Gabriel Valley. A few of these have since grown into thriving cities and towns; but the greater number perished in the "flag and bunting" stage of their existence and have long since been forgotten.

The Fourth Stage

It was a crazy time. But the reckoning day always comes. Such colossal folly could but merit the rebuke it received. In the summer of Eighty-Eight, the banks—who themselves had invested heavily and perilously—stopped loaning on all real estate except that in the heart of the cities—and that, only on the basis of former normal values. Thus was ushered in the fourth and final stage of the boom.

It was like puncturing an inflated balloon. The boom collapsed. When payment on primary sales came due and were defaulted—the fate of most of them, the original seller, having bought again on the same terms, could not meet his own payments on property so bought. Neither could the one who had sold to him meet payments due on property he himself had contracted for. The "vicious cycle" affected nearly all speculators. When no payments that depended on defaulted payments could be met, when those who, in their excited enthusiasm, had borrowed to the limit to deposit on land purchases and could get no more backing from banks, there was begun a wild scramble to get out from under the burden. But nobody could do this for nobody could sell because nobody could collect. The whole scheme reacted like a row of dominoes set up on end two thirds of their length apart. When the first one topples, it strikes the second, that one the third, and so on till the whole row falls like mowed grain flat on the board.

Unprincipled promoters, in an effort to steady things and save their own skins, continued to carry on a persevering campaign enticing unsuspecting persons not yet aware of the true state of affairs, to invest in wild projects. They would plant groves on the tops of mountains and worthless hillsides, and by cunning advertising, sell these as "improved properties" to distant purchasers who had never seen them and knew nothing of what they were buying.

When a realization of the instability of all these inflated values, the worthlessness of reckless investments, defaulted contracts and fraudulent enterprises began to dawn upon the people of the country generally, confidence was utterly destroyed. Rapid as had been the inflation, the deflation was still more swift. And so, from sheer top-heavy overbalancing, the whole structure of financial speculation fell—and "great was the fall of it." The big promoters with the small—the buyers with the sellers, were carried down together. Business became demoralized. Panic followed. Transportation rates went up. The inflow of people and of money ceased. Trains came in empty and went away full. People were leaving at the rate of a hundred a day. Houses became vacant; tourist hotels empty. Work on buildings already begun was halted and they fell into decay. Among them was a great million-dollar hotel on Tenth Street in Los Angeles, the foundation alone of which had already cost eighty-five thousand dollars. Wages shrunk. The unemployed filled the cities. Tramps thronged the highways. Rents fell to zero. Courts became swamped with litigation. Lawyers were working overtime. Insanity increased. A number of suicides took place. People begged from door to door. Jails overflowed. A few prominent rascals decamped to Mexico to escape justice. Land assessments fell to the tune of fifty-one million dollars. Newspapers carried three-page lists of unknown owners whose taxes were delinquent.

Nature herself seemed to frown upon man's folly; for the very climate, that for two years had been ideal, suddenly became the reverse and began to "cut up capers" that astonished the natives. Extreme heat, accompanied by slight earthquake shocks, were followed by wind storms, down-pours and floods.

In the countrysides around, sorry spectacles greeted the eyes. Everywhere were neglected fields, half-dead orchards, lonely abandoned hotels, tattered bunting fluttering from weather-beaten stakes, deserted townsites, plotted parks overgrown with weeds and bordered with dying young trees; incongruous stretches of pavement half buried in the midst of abandoned grain fields. Land that had swallowed up many thousands of dollars given over to the coyotes and jackrabbits.

The whole country was left in a deplorable condition from which it took many long years to recover. Wrecked fortunes, poverty, and wretched regrets were the order of the day.

The young city of Long Beach, incorporated just before the bubble burst, was so hard hit by the deflation of the boom that it was obliged to disincorporate in the fall of Eighty-Eight, remaining disincorporated for several years afterward. Hundreds of "mushroom towns" dying almost before they were born, passed into the limbo of forgotten things; but a few of their sisters, weathering the vicissitudes that followed their birth, are with us still, having made a sturdy and substantial growth. Among these are: Whittier, Burbank, Monrovia, Pomona, Glendora, La Verne (Lordsburg), Sunset, Inglewood, Fullerton, Rivera, Buena Park, El Modena, Olive, Garden Grove, Laguna, now coalesced with Arch Beach, Newport, McPherson, Yorba Linda, and still others. During the boom, the island of Santa Catalina, twenty-five miles out from the shore of San Pedro, was sold to an English syndicate to exploit for minerals. Failing to find the expected mineral wealth, this syndicate let the island revert by default to its former owners in Ninety-Two.

After the boom was over, many of those who had bought city lots were obliged to build on their properties in order to create an income on which to live. Building materials had dropped greatly in price after the boom had "busted," and quite a building boom followed in the wake of the crash. Some of these business properties became in after years, profitable investments.

In the midst of the boom, the first street-paving was begun in Los Angeles; whose streets up to this time had been a "!sea of mud" in the winter and "dust clouds" in the summer—allayed somewhat by spasmodic sprinkling. Besides this street-paving, many miles of paved sidewalks and curbs were put in, becoming permanent investments. In Eighty-Eight Los Angeles passed its first traffic law, prohibiting any conveyance to cross a street intersection faster than a walk.

Cheap sidewalks were laid in many of the sub-divisions throughout the country. The first cement walks ever laid in Santa Ana were of this character, being laid in a sub-division lying to the south of town and soon abandoned, and many years later incorporated into it. Some eighteen years afterward, when men were excavating for the laying of the first real permanent sidewalks in that section, these old forgotten sidewalks were discovered buried under a foot of earth. They were exceedingly thin, like the stability of the times that begat them, being only an inch and a half in thickness.

In the height of the boom, Mr. J. M. Bundy, a business man of Santa Ana, put in a streetcar system from Tustin to El Modena by way of Orange. On the rear end of each car was built a platform on wheels to be used for a very unique and humane purpose. The return trip to Orange was down grade all the way. Before starting down, the mules were unhitched from the car and placed on this platform as passengers, the car returning entirely by gravity. Eighteen years after the crash, still lying about, were piles of old ties and rails left where they had been torn up after the system had been discontinued.

A time of great depression followed the boom, the after effects of which were felt for more than a decade. Five years after the California bubble burst, the whole nation was struck by a terrible economic panic that lasted for several years. Banks failed by the score in every state in the Union. Between the months of May and December of Ninety-Three, six hundred banks failed, only a hundred and sixty-five of which ever opened their doors again. Prices for produce declined. The sheep industry was hard hit. Wool dropped from twenty cents a pound to ten cents. Railroad strikes paralyzed traffic and obstructed the mails so that troops had to be called out to restore order. There was widespread unemployment. Men often worked for board and room. It was a time of great industrial distress and agitation. Rents went down almost to zero. In Santa Ana a five roomed house within walking distance from the center of town would bring only four or five dollars a month, and at that stand vacant for long period. To have one's property under mortgage meant almost certainly to lose it. It was practically impossible to borrow for re-financing.

In the late fall of Eighty-Seven, the buyers of the Frank Goff property wanted to put a road down the side of the bench into Aliso Canyon. Their side of the dividing property line was not a suitable site for the road, a gulch there making it impracticable. They appealed to us to donate the strip of land necessary for the proposed road. Father's deciding voice being now absent, and the boys differing in opinion as to what should or should not be done, the matter was debated pro and con for some time.

Becoming impatient at the delay, the County Road-Master, George Rogers, brought his work outfit and men over to the place and began to build—permission or no permission. However, no obstacle was placed in his way and Joseph went over and worked on the road for wages till it was finished. So far as we were concerned, this road was the greatest improvement made during the boom. Not only was it the end of the old steep, winding footpath we had toilsomely climbed for so many years, but also it ended the hard pull by team up and down the steep end of the bluff and across the strip of beach sand at the end of the pond over which the poor horses had for so long strained with loads of hay from our plot on the bench.

A decade later, a bridge was built from the foot of this county grade directly across the narrow neck of the pond to the Lee Goff side, and the old beach road was abandoned altogether. This bridge did away with the old wagon road across the headwaters of the pond by which for thirteen years the horses had scrambled up the slippery bank to reach the Lee side.

During the boom time, one day I went out to town with George in his buggy. There I saw on the street a man riding along astride the top of a high velocipede—the forerunner of the present-day bicycle. How the man could stay on the thing was more than I could see. Should it become unmanageable, how he was to steady himself and avoid a bad fall was past my comprehension. To me, it appeared like a lone wagon wheel rolling down the street, with a man atop keeping his balance and guiding it by some mysterious magic. A very small wheel followed behind, the use of which was not to me apparent.

With the seat directly over the main wheel, which was about the size of our buggy wheel, and the pedals so high up from the ground, the machine must have been very difficult to control. Should it strike a rut or a stone in the road, and the rider be pitched forward, resulting in a "header"—what could avert a serious accident? Truly it was a dangerous machine to ride. That is why the modern bicycle when it first came out, was called a "safety bicycle." At first the pleasure of this rapid travel was for men only. It was a great day when they first began to dip the top bar and adapt it to the use of ladies also.

Yet, in spite of all the disadvantages of the velocipede, a man by the name of Curtis, mounted upon one of them, rode twenty miles and three hundred yards in one hour. Another man named Thomas Stevens rode all around the world on a velocipede, leaving San Francisco in Eighty-Four and returning to that city in Eighty-Six, thus accomplishing the feat in two years' time.

A Final Word About the Goffs

Soon after the hotel at Arch Beach was finished and in full swing, Henry Goff sold his own hotel at Laguna with his entire holdings to a man named Spencer, and with his family went back to Missouri, where we lost track of them entirely.

Mr. Spencer conducted this hotel, which was named for him the Spencer Hotel, until his death in the late Eighties; after which his widow carried on for a few years alone. Then it stood idle for some time.

After the boom became a thing of the past, Hub Goff Hubbard, having made more or less of a failure of his hotel venture, sold out in a mortgage deal to a man by the name of Ambrose, and went to the deflated boom town of Lordsburg, founded by Mr. Lord, but later known as La Verne.

The Arch Beach hotel was then for a time known as the Ambrose Hotel. Ambrose later lost it to the bank that held the mortgage, and it too stood idle for a time.

In the middle Nineties, an enterprising man by the name of Yoch, becoming interested in the beach town, bought the old Spencer Hotel and opened it up. The following year he bought of the bank the empty Ambrose Hotel., and at great expense and effort that consumed many months of time, he moved it over to Laguna, joining it to the Spencer to form the "Yoch Hotel," which prospered and served the beach resort for many years until it too was demolished to make room for the new "Hotel Laguna" which now occupies the site.

Yoch's hotel in its day was the center of Laguna's social "good times" contributed to by summer residents from far and near, and ably presided over by its amiable hostess, Mrs. Yoch. Here among others, was often heard the sweet voice of Mrs. James Rice of Tustin—Artemisia's former employer—singing at evening entertainments.

The brother of Mrs. Yoch, Mr. Nick Isch, for twenty-five years Laguna's best-loved storekeeper, was a genial soul, kindly, accommodating to a fault, in the old days when everybody knew everybody else, and neighbors borrowed back and forth, sharing with one another anything that was needed. Mr. Isch was not, however, Laguna's first storekeeper. That distinction belongs to Will Brooks, the brother of Nate.

Shortly after the Goff brothers, Frank and Lee, had taken up their abode in Tustin, meanwhile operating their grocery business in Santa Ana, tragedy came—an unexpected guest. One morning Lee and Nettie, his wife, lay for a few minutes in pleasant conversation before rising for the duties of the day. Lee gave a sigh and turned over in bed. Presently his wife spoke to him. He did not reply. She spoke again, thinking it impossible that he should have fallen asleep. Still, there was no answer. She raised up and shook him. But Lee, her husband, had indeed fallen asleep—clasped in that long slumber that knows no waking this side of the resurrection. Suddenly, unpreparedly, painlessly, he had departed without a farewell word to loved ones. Nettie and the children were left alone in their grief—left wholly unprepared and unequipped for the battle of life. A more helpless woman could hardly be found than this poor widow.

In the years that followed, the family soon went through with all the means he had left them, and were thrown penniless into the pitiless maelstrom of life with its many pitfalls, to battle with destitution and want. Poor Nettie, who had never been an efficient housekeeper, was to be seen going from door to door in pitiful raiment, cleaning for a living the houses of other people and washing their clothes. Still she bore her sweet smile and spoke in soft gentle tones.

After being in business about ten years in Santa Ana, Frank Goff sold out his grocery store to a Mr. Christman, and moved to Los Angeles. His son Leon, in Ninety-Five went to Honduras, Central America, joined a year later by his father. They purchased at first a coffee plantation, then a banana plantation in San Pedro Sula, from which they shipped large quantities of bananas to New Orleans and Mobile. Meanwhile, a rubber plantation was being grown between the bananas, whose life-span was comparatively short, with the expectation that it would come into production about the time the bananas failed.

Frank's wife and daughter Lena followed them to Honduras in Ninety-Seven, remaining there three years. At the end of that time, which was also the closing year of the century, Mabel and her husband Fred Bennett set sail to visit them in Honduras, not being aware that they planned to return. The Goffs started back in March to avoid the summer quarantine on the Mississippi. The Bennetts were delayed one day on the trip by the boat's not making its schedule time, and reached Honduras the day after her parents had sailed for home. To their dismay they found Leon the only one there. Their visit with Leon, however, was timely, for it proved to be the last.

For the next two years, Frank went back and forth between Central America and Los Angeles, while Leon, still single, remained on the plantation. In Nineteen Two, while there alone, he was stricken with typhoid fever, the second case ever known in the country, and at the age of thirty-six passed away far from loved ones whose tender care might have saved his life.

Leon's death was a bitter blow to his sorrowing parents and sisters. Three years later the sale of the plantation was effected and Frank Goff retired. He survived his son fifteen years. Nellie followed him three years later, and in another three years, his wife Emma passed away. Mother missed her sorely, and the correspondence they had enjoyed together through the years, for they were close friends. Mabel spent her last years in Arch Beach, passing away in her early sixties. Her son, Leon Bennett, survives her, the only member of the second generation of the family. Lena, now Mrs. Cummings, with her husband lives in the cottage once owned by Nettie Goff, built in Eighty-Nine. She is the sole surviving member of Frank Goff's immediate family.

Her father's property bought for a hotel site, was never so used. The collapse of the boom rendered the investment a total loss. Costing twenty-five thousand, it was afterward twice sold for taxes. The first time to Mr. Ball for four hundred dollars, the second time to Miss. Dolph for eight hundred. For many years the old house stood empty, and about the year Nineteen Ten was torn down. Out of the materials a cottage was built in Arch Beach for Mrs. Chatterway, Emma Goff's mother.

It was about the turn of the century that artists "discovered" Laguna. The foundation was laid then for a real center of culture, rather than for an ordinary beach town of cheap amusements. As a resort city of high class, Laguna is now nationally, and even internationally known through canvas displays of her unsurpassed scenery. The whole coastline above and below Aliso is now generally spoken of as Laguna and South Laguna, especially in artist parlance.

Aside from the natural landscape of ocean, mountains and sky, very few of the old landmarks remain standing. The old Hemenway house would not be recognized today. It has been covered with half-logs to simulate a log cabin, and near it is the subdivision known as Canyon Acres. The dwelling formerly occupied by George Rogers has been turned into the "Woman's Club House," and is the only original farm house yet remaining in the city of Laguna.

The ground once owned by Lee Goff on the southern mesa, is now the beautiful "Coast Royal," and the old McManus claim once owned by George is now known as the "Three Arch Bay Tract."

Goff Point, directly seaward from the old site of Frank Goff's early cabin, is now a large camping ground filled with trailers and summer cottages, and provided with modern utility service.

Adjoining it on the north is the new subdivision of Lagunita, meaning "Little Laguna." The picturesque old sand dunes in the canyonette are gone—devastated to make way for the new growth of man's devising. Somehow I wish they had been spared.

This old cabin site with all the surrounding acreage, rich in association for thousands who in the past have learned to love it, ideally located for a scenic village, lying close to the wide paved coast highway that for hundreds of miles from Santa Monica to San Diego, sweeps along from town to town in graceful curves above the sea, may one day out-rival them all.

CHAPTER 48 MAKING MUSIC

I cannot remember the time when meter and rhythm were not a part of me. Even when very small, the appeal of a rhyming couplet, the music of jingling words set bells a-ringing in my soul. Lured from earliest childhood by the mystic spell of the moon and stars, I would think out short lines that rhymed; sometimes singing them in little original melodies. But my first attempt at making concrete in writing, these poetic imaginings, was when nearing the precocious age of ten.

Though I was woefully lacking in religious instruction and knowledge of the Bible, other than that gleaned from occasional stories in school readers, yet this primeval "poemette," retained still in memory, embodied the heart-longing of the human family for immortality:

HEAVEN SO BRIGHT

Sweet Fairy Bell
And her cousin Nell
Loved each other dearly.

They looked each night
At the stars so bright,
And thought they'd sometime go there.

And they were right,
For Heaven so bright
Became a home to them.

Nell's mother was wild
At the death of her child,
And Fairy's mother too.

But they were lonesome not long,
For soon they were gone
To dwell with their children in Heaven.

You smile, as I, at these childish stanzas, yet, in their appeal, no words are wasted in useless preliminaries. Quickly the theme sweeps on from its inception to the sublime and satisfying climax. But in between, is packed the great love of David and Jonathan, the heart-longing induced by starry vigils and soul-traversings of inter-stellar spaces, the ambition for spiritual attainment, its final accomplishment in the supreme joy of home-going, the sadness of parting and the abandonment to unavailing grief, the loneliness of the broken fireside, the mercy of healing balm in the blessed and final reunion, the natural acceptance of heaven and God with all He means to the human family—all in embryo in the heart of a child.

Another, written at thirteen in the minor strain that characterized all those early productions, reflected the futile heart-longings for educational opportunities that saddened all my youthful days. Having gone down to the creek to fetch water, I wandered, bucket in hand, half forgetful of the errand, and seated myself on a little patch of dry sand islanded among the salt-grass and weeds. There, gazing down into rippling, murmuring water to the pebbly bottom, in the only avenue of expression that came natural to me, was born the following melancholy odelet:

THE STREAM

I was sadly wandering along
When I sat down by a stream
And listened to its murmuring
As if but in a dream.

I could not bear to leave it,
But seemed enchanted there.
As it washed away the pebbles,
It washed away my care.

It seemed to soothe and comfort me
And make my heart feel glad.
And I often sit by the streamlet now
Whene're my heart is sad.

And always, when again I rise
And turn from it away,
I've better hopes than I had before
Of many a brighter day.

While working away at my tasks, whether herding pigs, hoeing weeds, suckering corn, harvesting nuts, carrying water, making beds, washing dishes or whatever assignment the day or hour or season made necessary, my head was always in the clouds—my mind "wool-gathering" far from the homely tasks at hand. In my pocket was usually a pencil and scraps of paper—perhaps the last blank page of an old discarded letter, or an envelope split open to afford more writing surface, or maybe just wrapping paper—anything I could get my hands on that would accommodate a pencil.

Sometimes an inspiration to write would suddenly seize me while in the midst of washing dishes, and out would come dripping hands to be hastily dried on the towel, that by paper and pencil the will-o-the-wisp of inspiration might be caught and imprisoned for future interviews. This subjected me to many jibes, with much ridicule—more or less good natured, yet not without its disparagement. But the urge within me was greater than any counter force without, and little effect did this have by way of cure. Its only effect was to make me secretive. As well try to stop water running through an open tap by pressure of the hand. It may slacken for a moment, but soon the hand itself, with all the manual strength behind it, is forced away, and the dammed-up water pours forth.

Snatches of other songs and poems long since forgotten, come floating scrappily into mind out of those early mists of memory, all in melancholy strain; like this one uttered spontaneously while wandering in the pasture after dusk—the other nine or ten verses forgotten:

"Away down in the meadow
The frogs I faintly hear.
Somehow, they chirp so sadly
Tonight, my heart is drear."

Or the grand finale of a soldier song, sung to an appropriate tune of original composition:

"But all in vain, she waits for him
Who in a soldier's guise did part;
For the very last shot that was fired
Pierced this brave young soldier's heart."

"Spieling" Novels

During the years next preceding my teens, I now and then discovered and sneaked from its hiding-place under the girls' pillow or from a shelf of the closet or some cupboard hidden out of Mother's sight, a novel-rightly considered unfit for the perusal of a child—and read it unbeknown to my elders. Each time after indulging I carefully returned it to the same hiding place, so as not to be suspected of so culpable an act, and also that the way might be left open for future similar discoveries with their forbidden pleasures.

After gorging on these thrilling and exciting adventures, it became my great ambition to write a novel. Then romance began to be manufactured by the yard. However, the labor of committing all this to writing, appeared so stupendous as to dampen ardor in that direction. I wondered why there couldn't have been some invention made whereby one's utterances might automatically be preserved without all the trouble of writing them out by hand. No one had yet heard of a typewriter.

But after all, why be bothered by committing it all to writing, when I had an admiring audience ready to hand? My younger sisters begged me to "say it" to them; and I began to spin these yarns verbally, as a spider spins its web, without laborious effort; while they hung with devouring eagerness upon every sentimental word that fell from romantic lips—all very complimentary, and quite satisfying to the ego; and thus it was that all those wonderful productions went unrecorded at such loss to posterity.

Every story must of course have an interesting title. I had always liked the poetical sound of "Capistrano." But of course it would never do to have a name that all would recognize as a real place. And to borrow from anyone else would be to clip the wings of imagination and dissipate the romance. So, thinking out a modification, I called my "novel" "Capadorno."

Hour after hour, day after day, as we hoed weeds among the potatoes, beans and corn, I would reel off extemporaneously, chapter after chapter of "Capadorno" into the eager, tireless ears of worshipful listeners, whose hoes flew fast to keep up with mine. For no one wanted to miss a word by lagging behind.

It was to my interests to keep the crew busy; for mine was the responsibility to see that the hoeing was done—and well done. If they should fail in this, who but I would have to "finish up"? Charlotte was usually little more than a volunteer anyway, and could quit whenever she pleased. But nothing on earth could keep her away from the job so long as the wonderful story held out.

Whenever I would grow tired of "spieling" or run out of material; or when I had gotten my hero and heroine into some exciting and precarious situation, and was not quite sure in my own mind as to the best and most interesting way to get them out again, I would suddenly close with the announcement:

"To be continued."

Then what a disappointed chorus would assail me!

"Oh, don't 'continue' yet. Tell us some more!"

And all those long even rows of succulent plants with their mingled weeds would immediately degenerate into sordid tasks without charm or interest.

Sometimes two stories were kept going at once, and one being for the time dropped, the thread of the other would be picked up and carried on, with an entirely different set of characters resuming their places on the stage of action—only to be "continued" in their turn when the dinner call sounded.

All summer long "Capadorno" continued to thrill my audience; and so far as memory serves me, was never brought to a finish—chiefly because nobody wanted it to finish, least of all its author. For who would want to end a story when continuing secured the most willing cooperation in every task? To secure these gratifying results, all I ever had to do was announce a "story." Besides, finishing a story is a hard job anyway.

Between these times of story-telling, little Charlotte would entertain herself as she went about her play, by muttering and mumbling in an undertone meaningless gibberish in imitation of this yarn-spinning—getting in some of the emphasis and inflection, if not the sense. It was during this period of our social relationships, that the wheels of domestic machinery ran the most smoothly.

A Text On Reading

When between the years of twelve and thirteen, I wrote a school "Reader." It was modeled after those then in use with covers and pages of similar size. From cover to cover this textbook was original. Each lesson was complete in itself, and the series arranged consecutively, progressing from the simple to the more complex. From each reading lesson, was selected a group of the most difficult or unusual words, to precede it, with syllabic divisions, accents, and diacritical markings; and the pupil was instructed in a "note" to look up the definitions to these words in the dictionary. This was to be the spelling lesson of the day. Sometimes, between lessons, a whole page of spelling was introduced of words that were to be learned and used in sentences. These inserted pages contained selections of "tricky" and "catchy" words and of the most often misspelled words in common use.

At the close of each weighty lesson, a short set of questions served to provoke thought and fix in mind what had been read.

There were stories of nature, animals, plants, the ocean, history, great men, and fiction stories with morals that aimed at character-building. There was no nonsense, no wasted effort, but all was decorous and sober, as becometh a school book. One lesson was devoted to the subject; "How to Read"; and many a modern school product would be a better reader had he but followed instructions similar to those there given. There were helpful instructions concerning proper expression, enunciation, pauses, climaxes, inflection, suspension, and naturalness in reading and how to read poetry without being sing-song and monotonous. One of the rules laid down was this: "When reading, always let your eyes go ahead of your voice and know what is coming before you get to it. Then you will not stumble over words, and you will know whether the sentence should end with a rising, or falling inflection of the voice— whether what you are reading is a simple statement, or a question." Other lessons concerned diacritical markings, accents and punctuation. There were lessons emphasizing the importance of honesty, moral courage, honor, keeping promises, truthfulness, and the rights of others.

All these were no doubt timely, primarily for the author; who after all was the chief beneficiary, and pondered them to herself as an ideal for personal attainment. Very little of all the material in this book comes to mind word for word. The first and last stanzas of a little poem on "The Hummingbird," consisting of five or six stanzas, repeat themselves in memory; though all that is between eludes me:

> *"Oh, there's a pretty hummingbird—*
> *Glossy little fellow-*
> *Sipping honey from the flowers,*
> *Purple, white, and yellow.*
>
> *From the little hummingbird,*
> *Busy all the day,*
> *Let us take a lesson.*
> *There, he darts away!"*

I kept this little book for eighteen or twenty years; though not at the time fully appreciating its unique interest as a memento. Then, during an absence from home, extending over a period of months in which my house was tenanted by others, mischievous boys, finding it, with a host of other things just as personal, from instincts of pure vandalism, destroyed them all. In after years, a destructive fire finished what was left of those early effusions; so that none were preserved except the few that memory could reproduce. With them went also to the flames, several notebooks full of poems that were the fruits of riper years; only a small number of which could ever be reproduced, leaving a lonesome spot that nothing could fill—as though some part of myself had been destroyed.

Primitive Instruments

The Children of Aliso, though deprived of scientific training in the musical arts, all possessed in common with the human race the inborn desire to "make music."

George, when a boy at home, inspired by the example and skill of Hubbard Goff, with only the crudest of tools, made for himself a "fiddle" all complete from "head to tail," carving out the graceful neck and even the bridge, buying only the strings. On this he played by ear all the tunes of the day. In comparing it with Hub's fiddle, he discovered that the neck was a trifle too long. But aside from this it was a very well-made and creditable instrument—a monument to his love for music, as well as skill and ingenuity. This fiddle is still in existence somewhere.

Years later, other fiddles were bought, and the younger boys learned to play them. But such an instrument was then considered unsuitable for girls, and we were discouraged from attempting to learn.

The accordion, invented in Fifty-Six by a man named Anthony Faas, was a very popular musical instrument in our young days. However, it was not then the large, piano-toned, ornamented, complex and elaborate instrument that it is today, but simple, sweet-toned, and having a very limited range of keys. A number of us learned to play it with very pleasing success. At neighborhood dances and other gatherings, the accordion was usually in evidence, as well as the violin; and often they were played together.

The concertina became known to us with the entrance of Harry Hughes into our circle of friends; but though we revelled in the music he brought forth from it, we never possessed one ourselves.

The "mouth organ" or "harmonica," which today is considered suitable only for children to play, was also a popular little music-maker; and our boys handled it with skill—all of us playing it more or less.

Then there was the "Jews Harp," that little instrument of minor importance, whose soft, musical twang greatly resembled the tones of a guitar. These varied in size from two and three to four and five inches in length. Mother played the Jews Harp to perfection; striking its curved tongue with her forefinger while breathing her tune through its single reed; and its mellow notes rose to full capacity under her skillful manipulations. Memory still retains a picture of Mother standing near her open chest where she had gone to look for something, with a large Jews Harp to her lips—having picked it up on the spur of the moment from the till where it lay—and the melodious twang of it still resounds in my ear after half a century has passed.

But the instrument par excellence—so far as we little children were concerned—was the comb. This Mother taught us to play. The teeth of combs were not so wide apart as they are today, and paper itself was more porous. To make a success of comb-music both paper and comb must be just right. We would fold a piece of paper over the teeth of the comb, and pressing our parted lips ever so lightly against it, breathe a song without words through the comb; which produced buzzingly tuneful vibrations, to our great enjoyment.

We would also go about strumming on the wire fences to produce musical tones; singing our songs and using the wires for instrumental accompaniment; imagining them to be pianos, organs, or guitars.

Playing once, with narrow rubber bands—called, not "rubber," but "elastic," and far less common then than now—I made the accidental discovery that by stretching a band and then twanging it, a musical tone was produced. This started me to making experiments; which soon revealed that the tones varied in pitch according to the degree of tautness to which the bands were subjected, and hunting up a small piece of board, I set out to fashion me a musical instrument. Across it near the end about an inch or less apart I drove a row of nails a little way into the wood; then some five or six inches from this, another row, each nail of which stood opposite one of these, but graduated in a slant across the board. I then began stringing my bands between opposite nails from the first row to the second, each thus being a little longer and more taut than the preceding one. Then I would "twang" them in an effort to get the do, re, mi, fa, sol, la, ti, do scale, which I had heard. Success did not come at once, nor easily. The discovery was soon made that notes were modified by the width as well as length of the bands; and the graduated row of nails had to be switched about till they were not a row at all, but a small forest. Besides, my first guess at right distances was not correct, and had to be repeated over and over, and the nails changed accordingly to suit each individual elastic. By patient and persistent effort a series of tones was finally produced that somewhat resembled the musical scale; and with a little imagination, I could play simple tunes on my instrument board. At this, my joy was unbounded. To me, it was the sweetest music ever produced. Sometimes this pleasure would be interrupted by the sudden breaking of a band; which misfortune often caused a prolonged suspension of musical activities. For elastic bands were not so easily replaced then as today.

Pianos, in our western world were then few and far between and confined to families considered well-to-do. But among those of moderate means, the Reed organ was in common use. To possess an organ was to be "up to date." Being so far from social centers, we seldom heard either instrument. Things of this kind were not offered second hand on the markets freely as they are today. A second-hand store of any kind was a novelty. Those who purchased goods usually paid original prices, and retained possession of their property until it was worn out or lost through some calamity.

The Organ

The summer after I was nine years old, something occurred that profoundly affected our musical history. An agent, named Judson, found his way down Aliso Canyon, having in the back of his wagon, a large Reed organ. This he persuaded Father to let him put into the house "without obligation" for the family to try—an old and effective trick common to all agents from time immemorial. The house was so crowded, there seemed to be no place to put it. But the trunks and sewing machine were moved around in Mother's room, and a place made temporarily in the corner near the back window. Mr. Judson sat down on the stool and played and sang for us to demonstrate the wonderful tone qualities of this Story and Clark Reed organ. A snatch of one of the silly songs he sang that day—the racy tune adding a flavor not conveyed in words—comes floating back to me through the long corridors of memory:

"I told her to sit down where she pleased;
She took a seat across my knees,
And there, she seemed quite at her ease;
Oh Rose of Alabama!

Oh my brown Rose, so dear,
Sweet Rose of Alabama,
You're my sweet tobacco posie
And the Rose of Alabama."

Mr. Judson went on his way, giving us time to "think it over" and become attached to the organ. Then he returned to make his sale. Father had no money for an organ. But such a condition cannot daunt an agent. Trading "this for that'! was a common expedient in those days; and after much "dickering," Mr. Judson and Father came to terms, and a trade was made. Then it was, that faithful old Cherry, whose prime was now long past, old Daisy too, and another younger cow left our corral and went away with Mr. Judson, never to return, while the organ remained with us.

A place was then made for it in the far end of the dining room near the window. The big cupboard which had so long occupied that spot, was moved into the far end of the kitchen, and placed against the wall that separated from Mother's room—her door then opening between cupboard and stove.

On this organ, were two circular, lathe-turned ornamental lamp stands, one on either side, attached by screws, for holding the kerosene lamp when playing by night. There was also a very tall, fancifully ornamented removable back to the organ—a concession to the ideas of beauty that then prevailed; whose much carving and open-work made it an excellent dust-catcher, and added materially to the expense of manufacture. In later times, this ornamental back was taken off and discarded. This old organ after more than half a century is still in use.

A large, and very thorough self-instructor came with the organ; which proved a great blessing to us all. There was no money for other instruction; and it is doubtful if a teacher could have been found so far away from the settled districts, even if money had been forthcoming. We were given an instrument, and left to learn how to play it as best we could.

Poetry is but another form of music—the music of words; and both forms touched invisible chords in me. Music I loved—though from lack of proper instruction handicapped in its expression through the fingers—I would "make up tunes" to fit the words of every loved little poem that seemed suitable for a song. Often, I would compose my own songs—words and tunes at the same time, to blend together in mutual expression, each enhancing the other. Soon, after beginning to study the organ instruction book, I learned to write out these tunes in musical notes on the treble staff, and thus preserve them.

As the fiddle was considered a boys' instrument, so was the organ considered a girls' instrument, and none of our boys ever tried to learn to play it. Though from the first we girls began to amuse ourselves by picking out tunes with one finger and later chords by ear, yet, being so young, it was some time before I awoke to the realization that it was really possible for me to learn to play by note. Joan, then about fourteen had begun at once to study the instruction book and soon learned to play "pieces." Her success was an inspiration to me. If Joan could learn, why not I? This realization was the beginning of a new era in my experience. Life took on a new meaning. Once it dawned on my consciousness that I too could understand the book of instructions, all childish fooling around with picking out one-finger tunes ceased; and I began in earnest to study the book; beginning with its first page, and applying with diligence, every principle set forth, as it was mastered. There was the "f-a-c-e, face," and "Every Good Boy Does Finely" of the treble clef, and the "Apples Cure Every Good Boy" and "Good Boys Do Finely Always" of the base clef, which enabled me to figure out the notes, but were not much help in learning to read them at sight. One is sure to get to depending on the jingle instead of the position of the note on the staff. But that is the way they taught in those days, and for lack of proper training here, I never did become a free and ready reader of notes. The time measures in music never bothered me; for time was as natural to me as rhythm in poetry. The difficulty came in the coordination of my two hands to produce the desired results. This could be overcome only by patient practice.

In this book, correct position at the instrument was stressed. The stool, which screwed up and down, must be set to give just the proper height so that the arms from elbows to finger joints were on a level, the wrists and knuckles under control to preserve this line. How diligently did I practice to secure this desirable position, and to maintain it through all the finger exercises, and running of the scales! And how earnestly did I seek to avoid all the bad habits the student was warned against" With what patience did I endeavor to make that recalcitrant "little finger and the one next to it do their honest part in all the exercises!" How meticulously did I observe the numbered fingering—the thumb, indicated by an X, and the others 1, 2, 3, and 4, to produce ease and grace of movement! And soon the exercises developed into simple melodies, and those into real "pieces"; and in a short time I was playing: "Comin' Thro' The Rye," "The Harp That Once Through Tara's Halls," "Ave Maria," "Her Bright Smile Haunts Me Still," and many other old favorites; mostly polkas, twosteps, and waltzes.

But when the book launched out into the deeper science of harmony, it proved inadequate to enable me to obtain a proper grasp of the subject. In vain I racked my brain for power to understand. I seemed to go just so far, but no farther, like one who has come up against a "brick wall"; and this distressed me greatly. It was never my nature to do anything by halves. Thoroughness was my "middle name"; and to be baffled here was most disappointing. But finally, I had to own myself defeated, and skip this part of the book, intending to go back to it again when older; and content myself with "learning pieces." Farther over in the book, were many beautiful compositions—some of them very difficult. Joan was learning them. So I was not afraid to "tackle" them too—skipping around and picking out the easiest ones first. There was one very sweet Waltz, called "Whispering Winds," which I greatly loved, and devoted myself to its practice till mastered. This piece never grew old or ceased to thrill me; for my soul recognized it as real music.

Another, and still more difficult piece, which I learned to play, was "March of the Huguenots"—though what they were, I had not the slightest idea. Still another, less difficult, but more fascinating, and equally mysterious was one called "Feast of the Incas." The weird, minor strains of this were so thrilling and intriguing, that I could not rest till words were written to sing to the music.

Who were the Incas? I did not know—had never heard of them or their country. Incas being a proper name, I could not find it in the big family dictionary. Whether they were a living race or a dead one, I knew not; or whether their home was in the mountains, or on the coast. But the music spoke to me of surging waters and cavernous deeps; of storms and thunderings; and of waves beating on the shores; and so I wrote:

> *"Wild the night,*
> *A storm is on the mountain;*
> *Fierce and white,*
> *The snow is drifting down.*
> *Keen the blast,*
> *Tempest-tossed*
> *Writhe the trees in anguish;*
> *Thunders crash,*
> *Lightnings flash*
>
> *Neath the mountain's frown*
> *Wail and weep*
> *The elements around us;*
> *Where is sleep*
> *Where now her holy rest?*
>
> *Refrain: Here the surges beating, beating,*
> *Beating, beating on the shore;*
> *Now retreating, now repeating;*
> *Thus, forevermore!*
>
> *Hidden in*
> *A cavern wild and gloomy,*
> *Through the din*

The thundering caves among,

Gleams a light

Keen and bright

O'er the slippery pathway

Like Hope's star

Seen afar

In Death's blackness hung.

'Tis the camp

Fire of the Incas, feasting,

This their haunt,

With nature reveling.

Refrain: Hear the surges beating, beating,

Beating, beating on the shore;

Now retreating, now repeating;

Thus forevermore.

The words seemed almost to write themselves, so well did they fit the music. But being anything but sure that they could appropriately be applied to the Incas, I was ashamed to sing the song to any other than myself, considering it merely a lesson in descriptive expression.

The first sheet music—and incidentally first lesson in Spanish—was the old favorite, "Sobre Las Olas." Of this number I was very fond, for "over the waves" it seemed to bear my poetic soul. Being a difficult piece, this required time, but when at last conquered, was a triumph of pleasure.

A Kindly Gentleman

Soon after the boom began, Laguna had a visitor in the person of Judge William A. Cheney, then on the bench of the superior court of Los Angeles, who took a strong liking to the place. He bought two lots on the high point above steep bluffs overlooking the sea, just south of the deep gulch that is afterward called "Sleepy Hollow"; and now doubtless done away in the march of progress. There, commanding a superb view of the ocean and narrow stretch of rocky beach below, he built the second summer cottage ever erected in Laguna. Other cottages there were, of more or less cheap construction, that preceded his, but they were for year-round occupancy, with the exception of one across the hollow to the north and somewhat more elaborate.

This fine gentleman had first come to Southern California in Eighty-Three. For four years just preceding, he had represented Plumas County in the State Senate, following two years of local County Judgeship. With his good wife and only son Harvey, a fine lad about three years my senior, he spent a portion of every summer thereafter at Laguna Beach in their simple cottage overlooking the sea.

From his first discovery of the beautiful little farm in Aliso Canyon, Judge Cheney took a genuine interest in the family. Every summer he would come over once or twice and pay us a visit. In the summer of Eighty-Nine, about the beginning of my teens, he sent over from Laguna a generous box full of wholesome magazines and periodicals that had first been read by his own family. Among them were copies of the Ladies' Home Journal, Youths' Companion, and a whole year's subscription to Saint Nicholas, beginning sometime in Eighty-Five. Besides these, there were some publications bearing names now forgotten, and quite a number of up-to-date issues of Current Literature—dressed then in plain, somber brown covers about twelve by eight inches in size.

Never before had anything like this come into our home. I carted all this literature out to the honey house to feast upon it in my spare time, and there reveled in an orgy of delirious joy. "As desert sand drinks in the rain," my soul drank in this new elixir of life.

No voice was raised to dispute my appropriation of all this treasure. The girls were extra busy that summer. Their thoughts were more or less on their beaux anyway. Joseph was too busy to pay any attention to such things. Frank was not the least bit interested in books or reading matter, and Annie had other things that claimed her attention—

though often I would share with her the stories. These she loved to hear me read, when not occupied with the fascinating task of trying on new clothes—for that was the summer she took her long trip. So there I was left to myself to feast upon the wealth of the literary world, which my soul loved.

In the old copies of Saint Nicholas, I read the charming story by Francis Hodgson Burnett, "Little Lord Fauntleroy," begun as a serial about December of Eighty-Five. This thrilled me to my toes. An entirely new world was opened up to my consciousness, gripping my heart with interest and sympathy.

In one of the other serials was a story called, "The Mill Boy of the Gennessee," a most interesting adventure story—but alas! Some of it was missing, so that I could never finish it; for which I mourned.

But of all the magazines in the collection, I most enjoyed Current Literature. Its pages were crammed with the best of prose and poetry culled from other magazines then current—the cream of the feast. Words can never tell how I reveled in these pages of poetry. James Whitcomb Riley, then a young man making his name in the world, was represented by such poems as "The Elf Child"—now called "Little Orphan Annie"; "Mongst the Hills O' Somerset," "When Bessie Died," "An Old Sweetheart of Mine," and other poems, since become household favorites. Then there were "A Dutch Lullaby" by Eugene Field, "The Song of the Camp," by Bayard Taylor; "The Last Letter," by Frank Dempster Sherman; "The Beggar," by Clara G. Dolliver; "The Church and the World" by Matilda C. Edwards; "The Watch at the Sepulchre" taken from the Edinburgh Herald; and dozens of others by authors not so commonly known.

One exquisitely touching little gem by Mary M'Guire, so appealed to the melancholy strain in my make-up that I memorized it entire. It was called:

THEN AND NOW

I was so small they lifted me to see
Her still white face, lying mid folds of lace
In that hard bed.
They told me she was dead.-
The little friend whom I
Had loved so much.
I shivered at the touch
Of the pale hand—I could not understand,
Not then.
And when again, companionless I strayed
Through sunshine bright, and saw the yellow light
Like billows pass
Across wide fields of grass
Where we had played:
I turned aside and covered up my face-
Remembering that dark space-
And wondered why God made her die,
And let me live.

It rests me now—the memory I keep
Of that hushed face; no bloom in life's dark place
Seems fair to me
As death's white mystery-
That slumber deep.
Oh, little playmate of life's margin years
(Alas these tears)
I wonder why God let you die
And made me live."

Never shall I forget the kindly visits of Judge Cheney to our home. One such visit in the summer of Ninety-One just after we had become settled in our new house (of which another chapter will tell), especially stands out in memory because of a few words of sincere praise from him; which repaid me a thousandfold for all the hard digging into that old Instruction Book. After roaming about over the place in the company of Joseph, enjoying the orchards and gardens, he came into the front room—attracted no doubt, by the sound of the organ. When I would have ceased, he urged me to continue. This I did with some embarrassment—for he was highly cultured, which caused me to feel keenly my limitations. He listened closely. Then, during a pause, asked me with interest:

"Where did you take your lessons?"

"I have never taken any lessons," was my simple answer.

He gave me a look, scrutinizing, then came up close to the instrument, asking me to go on playing; and standing at my side, observed the performance very intently. When the piece was finished, he said to me:

"You have the most perfect hand position of anyone I have ever seen play. Where did you get it?" "Out of the book," I replied, in pleased surprise, "I just practice what it says."

The Judge then encouraged me still more with kindly words of approval, showing that he marveled at the painstaking initiative and perseverance displayed by a girl of fifteen who had not the advantages and inspiration of a teacher. This kindly word of appreciation did me a world of good; spurring me on to attempt greater achievement.

Somewhere in the neighborhood of their beach cottage, on a spot more level, the Cheneys set up a small tennis court, where, with their friends, they racqueted the balls over the net in the invigorating salt sea air. We three girls, Annie, Charlotte, and I, once went down to see them on a summer day; and Harvey, true gentleman that he was, spent some time instructing me—an awkward girl in her early teens—in the art of tennis.

Figure 34 Tennis Court at Laguna [14]

Harvey Cheney afterward studied law at the University of Southern California, being admitted to the bar in October of Eighteen Ninety-Six. Seven years later, he married Miss Emma Alice Patton. Both of them recently passed away suddenly, within a day of each other, on November four and five of Nineteen Thirty-Eight, he of a heart attack, she of grief and shock at her sudden loss. His dear old father already had been laid away in Twenty-Five, having survived his companion by nine years. Harvey and Emma Alice left a son, young William Cheney to carry on the family name and perpetuate its pleasing characteristics.

Through long years, the Cheney cottage stood on the bluff overlooking the sea. But its surroundings grew to be very different. So great became the trees, so closely built the houses all about it, that the cottage could no longer be seen from the highway, though raised to a wide and high concrete boulevard. But its view of the sea was always unobstructed. As long as they lived, the Cheneys continued to spend their summers at Laguna, in the little cottage; preserving with reverent sentiment the spirit of the olden time by using the same old wood stoves and kerosene lamps of former days. It was there they passed away with tragic suddenness.

Great changes had come to the little seaside resort where one once might pitch his tent where he pleased and have the beach all to himself, but still this old landmark stood, and we who loved it fondly supposed it would remain undisturbed. But now it too has succumbed to the pitiless march of commercialism. No longer from its elevated knoll it gazes out to sea as if in quiet meditation. After its owners' passing it was sold. When recently I chanced to pass that way and beheld not a timber of it left—when I watched the graders filling in the picturesque ravine, with plans to level even the beautiful knoll above where once the cottage stood, my heart filled with tears. Never can they put into an auto-court the poetry and sentiment cast ruthlessly aside. But—who will remember save the moaning sea?

CHAPTER 49 LIGHTS AND SHADOWS

After Sadie went back to Arizona, she sent by freight as a gift to the family, a washing machine, which was received with great rejoicing. This was a wooden, hand-turning affair—a real back-breaker, but way ahead of the washboard at that, and the best that was then known.

During the latter part of the following January, announcement was received of the arrival of a tiny girl to join their family. Lawrence was now all taken up with his little new baby sister. In the same letter, Sadie made the astounding proposal to Mother that she take a trip out to Phoenix and make them an extended visit. Not that Sadie felt there was much chance of persuading Mother into such an extraordinary adventure, but she hoped the idea might take root and bear fruit someday, if not very soon.

This letter found Mother in somewhat of a mental turmoil over another unexpected invitation. A letter dated January twenty-eight had been received from her own father in which he urged her either to sell or lease the Aliso property and come to him in Utah, bringing her whole family—those still at home with her—to reside and send them to school.

"We will assist you in raising your children and educating them," he wrote, "and will help them to positions of usefulness and self-reliance if you cannot sell you can leave your place in care of one of the boys to sell or lease, and we will help you bring your family here."

Enclosed in this letter were two Wells Fargo money orders of fifty dollars each, payable to her order at Santa Ana, "to relieve immediate necessities" and expenses already incurred.

Touched by his kind and generous offer, Mother replied to this letter on February nine, writing, however, to the effect that she did not see how she could sell out and make a permanent move. This letter Grandfather acknowledged on March sixth, still pressing his invitation with added inducements. "I still feel more than ever the necessity of educating your children," he wrote, "and if you cannot feel to sell out and remove yourself and children…permanently, I should be much pleased if you would come and bring all the younger ones who ought to be in school, and we will provide for you and them, and give all one year's schooling, and as much longer as any of them may wish to stay; and let you go back again at your pleasure. I have abundance of house room…unoccupied, and the boys and I will make you comfortable, and…all be happy in your society…August or September would be a good time to come, just at the close of summer vacations and in fruit time. Possibly a good team and camp outfit might be cheaper than rail; but we would either send a team or would arrange a cheap emigrant rate with the railroad, for about four hundred miles from Santa Ana, to Thackbury Station on the A. and P. R. R. which is about a hundred and eighty miles southwest of St. George where we would send to meet you…But if you cannot adopt this plan, send me two or three of the children, and we will do the same by them."

This letter, so full of pleading and love, was not immediately answered; as Mother was in a quandary concerning the matter, which she was taking plenty of time to think over. In the meantime, she received a newspaper from her Father containing the announcement of the death on March twenty-two of her own brother Erastus, who for years had been ailing—her father's namesake, as also had been her own little son—news which added its weight of sorrow to Mother's heart.

Then came another letter from Grandfather dated April seventeen and addressed to both Mother and Artemisia to insure a prompt reply from either one or the other, expressing anxiety at the silence, and announcing that he as an overseer, was about to make a tour through the republic of Mexico and wished to arrange with Mother for a visit to Aliso enroute; for which reason he must have an early reply. Dear Grandfather must have entertained hope that by this proposed visit he could accomplish his purpose of inducing Mother to make the move he had suggested, or to accept at least one of his propositions. So much of love and solicitude may be read between the lines of these old letters.

Mother hastened to answer this letter, expressing her pleasure at his intended visit; and began to look daily for further word from him or even for his appearance at Aliso without other announcement. But as time passed she persuaded herself that he might have gone on to Mexico first intending to see her on his way back—a meeting to which she looked forward with more than ordinary eagerness and interest, not unmixed with suspense. Who could tell what might be the outcome of his visit and the effect of it upon the future of all the family? We children were on the tip-toe of expectancy, eager to see dear Grandpa again—though Mother had kept her own counsel about the plans for schooling.

But the weeks passed, even all of May, and still he had not arrived. Then came a letter—not from her dear father, but from others, bringing the shocking news that Grandfather was dead. This sad and bitter blow filled her heart with unspeakable grief, sorrow, and disappointment, saddening the whole household.

Less than two weeks after writing his last letter to Mother, Grandfather had taken a bad cold, which had aggravated the malady—Bright's Disease—from which he had suffered for years, and for almost a month was ill, most of the time confined to his bed, yet hoping to be up again and on his way. But instead of starting May the twentieth for California, exactly a week later he passed away, on May twenty-seven.

With his passing, all those loving plans regarding us children and our education became but a memory and a "might have been." Dear Grandpa had laid down his burdens forever including his burden for us and our education. With a heavy heart, poor Mother took up the thread of life again, and went about her daily duties with falling tears; for life had brought to her heart many sore woundings.

Grandfather Snow had been greatly beloved by all who knew him. On the day of his funeral, May thirtieth, Emily H. Woodmansee wrote in his memory a poem of considerable length, addressed to his friends, from which are taken the following lines:

ERASTUS SNOW

Sorrowing Friends, who drop the tear
Over one so justly dear,
Mourn him not as lost, instead
Count him with the glorious dead.

For his consecrated youth,
For his life-long love of truth,
For his aims that upward led,
Count him with the glorious dead.

For his course so free from guile
In a life beset with trial,
For his scorn of dangers dread,
Count him with the glorious dead.

For domestic graces rare,
For his ever thoughtful care,
For the sunshine that he shed,
Count him with the glorious dead.

Cupid and a Wedding Gift

On February fourteen of that year, a Valentine party given in San Juan Capistrano was attended by the young folks of Aliso, Joseph and the girls driving over in the spring wagon. It was a "wonderful party"—at least Hulda thought so, for a very nice young man, whom we will call Jed Wilde, paid marked attention to her. She was only fourteen and seven months, and this was one of her first parties.

To be singled out as the recipient of attentions by any young man, was a compliment quite thrilling. But this young man was especially good looking and might have had any one of the young ladies present for his partner. He was a few years her senior, tall, slim, well-dressed, with dark wavy hair, smiling features and proper manners.

His presence at the party had been made possible by a temporary position on the farm of a young friend at that place, his own home being some eighty or ninety miles distant. There was one very delightful sister in this family of several brothers, who was soon to be married to this same friend. She also was at the party, and to her the girls took a great liking, as did she to them.

Hulda was a slender, modest girl of medium height, with blue eyes and wavy brown hair, and was dressed very becomingly; for new dresses had been a part of the preparations for this party. Her frank open face radiated with pleasure at the attentions bestowed upon her by this young man. Romantic, trustful and idealistic, she at once made a hero of Jed, and hoped with all her heart that their acquaintance might continue.

What was her delight at the close of the party, when, as goodbyes were being spoken, he asked her permission to call later at her home! After receiving directions for finding the place, he accompanied her out to the wagon. All the way homeward, she smiled, with a song in her heart, in spite of the teasing banter of Joseph and Joan, at which she only laughed. And laughter seemed to come more easily than usual.

Some time after this meeting at the party, the young man rode over on horseback to Aliso, where he spent a pleasant day making the further acquaintance of Hulda and her folks. This adventure was repeated several times before he left the coast town. By that time it had been accepted by the family that Hulda had a beau. Though his manner was a little more formal than that of Harry, we all liked him. He followed up this acquaintance by letters, at the receipt of which Hulda's girlish heart fluttered with ill-concealed delight. This proved to be the beginning of a correspondence that lasted for years, punctuated by occasional visits in person.

Joan and Harry had been "keeping company" ever since they first became acquainted; though his visits to Aliso—there being so many miles between—were necessarily infrequent. On those rare occasions, when he would visit us, he and Joan would slip away by themselves for walks over the more remote parts of the farm. Luella, too young to understand the lovers complex, thinking they would just love to have her with them, would hunt them up and go out to meet them in order to walk home in their company.

That summer something else pleasant happened on the coast that helped to make family history. The Reynolds boys from Perris with their parents came as usual to camp for awhile on Aliso Beach. This time they brought with them their cousin, Minnie Reynolds, who was visiting from the East.

Minnie was tall, large-built, fond of the out-of-doors and an expert horse-woman. Two "fetching" dimples glorified her smile, and there was plenty of sparkle in her eyes that looked out below straight brows and a broad forehead. She dressed plainly, combed her hair simply, yet becomingly, and showed commendable character and individuality by refusing to conform to the prevailing style of wearing a bustle—a style that had become so firmly entrenched that a woman with a "flat back" was almost considered immodest. But Minnie did not think so.

Meeting this young woman, George was immediately captivated. If there was one thing above another that he detested, it was the bustle. He declared that if God had intended a woman to look like a camel, He would have made her with a natural hump and he couldn't for the life of him see why any woman should want to imitate a camel. So when he met this young lady without a bustle, he lost his heart to her.

The attraction was strongly mutual; and it was not long till Minnie had "thrown over" her Eastern beau to become engaged to George. After only a few months' acquaintance and a very short courtship, they were married on the twenty-fifth of the following October, at the home of the bride's uncle in Perris. Upon their return to the coast which they both loved, George having suspended indefinitely his San Jacinto farming, they took up residence in the cabin on Goff Point that, upon the departure of the Frank Goff family, had so recently been left vacant.

At the time of George's marriage, Lafe was still making the Mac Mannus place at Three Arches his part-time headquarters, dividing his time between that and his own claim, which he was obliged to occupy at least six months out of each year until he should have received a title. Having used up his filing rights on the Little Hill claim he could not take up the Mac Mannus place for himself, even though now of legal age—having attained his majority the March previous. But he enjoyed being close to the ocean, and, since there was now no claimant, between jobs of work here and there, and other obligations, he would resort to the cabin at Three Arches.

He had put in a little garden there, and was nursing it along, when deer began to help themselves to the green vegetables. One day, he saw a buck in the neighborhood, and made up his mind to get him as soon as he should have the time. It was on the morning of George's wedding day that he started up the mountain back of the cabin in search of this buck—which coincidence he remembered only after that happy event was over.

It was not long before he had routed the buck, who jumped up out of the brush and began to run—Lafe after him. But soon he was lost to view. Tracking was very difficult on the dry ground of the mountain but now and then a track could be made out, and was sufficient to reveal the general direction taken by the fugitive. At last he caught sight of the deer, and taking aim at his head while he was running through the brush, fired. But the deer went on. All over the mountain for miles around, he trailed him, firing at every opportunity, and being quite sure that some of the bullets had taken effect. Then his ammunition gave out and he was obliged to return to the house for more.

Picking up the trail again, he resumed the chase, and again the deer was sighted. This time the animal stopped and turned his head to take a look at his pursuer, and taking advantage of this opportunity, Lafe fired. The buck fell. He hastened toward him to finish the job, when to his surprise the animal scrambled to his feet and ran on again apparently unhurt.

So again the pursuit was resumed, and the mountains continued to echo with ringing rifle shots. Again the deer was struck, and fell. Lafe hurried over toward his prostrate victim. But when within a few feet of him, the animal showed signs of reviving, and began to scramble to his feet. The last bullet had merely struck his horn and stunned him, nothing more. Lafe stopped to take aim. But when he pulled the trigger, it only snapped. So interested had he been in the chase that the last shell had been fired and ejected without his being aware of it. He felt in his pocket for a shell but not another cartridge did he have upon his person. There was nothing to do about it but to stand foolishly by while the deer, not more than six feet distant, rose, looked him in the face, shook his head as if to get rid of a daze, turned, shook his tail as a final riddance and finally bounded away down the hill—Lafe watching till he plunged into Aliso Canyon.

Determined not to let his prey elude him so near the victorious consummation once again Lafe went home to replenish his ammunition. With plenty now in his pockets, he returned to pick up the trail; which he followed down the mountain to the Aliso creek. Since tracking in the water was not possible, he worked along both banks back and forth like a hound, in search of the trail again. He finally found tracks on the Lee Goff side where the animal having travelled considerable distance down-stream and into the deep water had gone up out of the pond to the highway. Lafe then followed the tracks up the roadway onto the mesa in the general direction of the hills he had just left.

The tracks continued along the road toward the abandoned Lee Goff dwelling. Just before reaching it, the road led down into and crossed a deep ravine that was cut athwart the mesa from the mountain to the ocean bluff. In the bottom of this ravine, below the road-crossing was an old dam that had formerly been built to catch and conserve water that came down in the winter freshets. And here, on the top of this abandoned dam, stood the hunted animal with head erect, silhouetted against the blue of the ocean beyond.

Caught unawares, he was momentarily off his guard, and Lafe, taking deliberate aim, fired the fatal shot. It was then four o'clock in the afternoon, and the hunter had been trailing him since early morning. Thirty-three shots had been fired in the chase, and upon examination he was found to have been struck by eleven bullets.

Having secured this prize on their wedding day, Lafe presented to the bridal couple on their return to the coast, the beautiful antlers, which served them as a hat and coat rack all through their life together and are still to be seen adorning the family wall.

Within a short time after his marriage, at Lafe's suggestion, George decided to file for himself on the claim at Three Arches. And thither, the couple moved from the old Goff house on the Point. We now had someone near of our own to visit, and the Three Arches saw us more often than before.

Mother Goes to Phoenix

Letters kept coming from Sadie at intervals all summer long urging Mother to visit her. Every argument that could be thought of was used to induce her to consent; for well Sadie knew how difficult it would be for Mother to make up her mind to such a complete break in the regular routine of her busy life. Mother was not used to planning any pleasure or spending any money for herself. Her thought had always been for others. She had never been on a trip or had a vacation since settling in Aliso seventeen years before. And now, how was she to begin a change so radical?

But added to Sadie's importunities, were those of the whole family; who felt that Mother was richly entitled to a change. All her objections and arguments were overridden. Sadie had offered to contribute toward the expense of the trip, and here was this gift from her father, not yet all spent. Artie wrote offering to come home and stay during her absence to help take care of everything, and enclosed a twenty-dollar bill to assist in outfitting her for the journey. Then we children promised to help all we could to make things go smoothly at home and be "good" as we could be. So there was really no reason under the sun why she should not go, as everybody assured her. At last, Mother consented, but put it off till after the wedding, for Phoenix was too hot a place to visit until late in the fall.

Mother and Joan went to town to buy her a new outfit. There was a hat, a pair of shoes, stockings, gloves, handkerchieves, goods for several dresses, and muslin for underclothes; until Mother felt that too much money altogether was being spent on her. Then Joan commenced with the sewing. No dresses or underthings were to be had ready-made in those days. Petticoats—and every woman wore at least two at a time, made very full with flounces lace trimmed or embroidered—corset covers, with many buttonholes to be worked, drawers and chemise—commonly called "shimmy"—were always made at home out of muslin, and all lace-trimmed.

Clara, who was to accompany Mother, had also come in for her share of new things from top to toe. Joan sewed steadily for a number of weeks to finish up everything.

Finally the time came for them to start. On the eighteenth of November, at the beginning of the rainy season, loving goodbyes were spoken. Joseph took them to the Southern Pacific depot in Santa Ana, and the train carried them away, on and on, out of California to far away Arizona—an event that made history then.

Soon, word came of their safe arrival. Mother's son-in-law, whom she had never seen till then, was at the depot to welcome them and drive them to his home in his buggy. Letters that followed told of the good times they were all having together. Little Lawrence and his young aunt Clara were having wonderful times between themselves and enjoying each other's company to the full.

Figure 35 Arthur and Sadie Byers Family
Left to Right: Harold, Mildred, Arthur, Lawrence, Hazel, Viola, Sadie

Artie did not get home from Sierra Madre where she was working in the hotel Sierra Madre Villa, until the second of January, but from that time on, stayed with us at Aliso during Mother's two remaining months in Phoenix. She did her best to help us and see that everybody had a good time. Her spare moments were spent in crocheting lace for a dress for Sadie's little new daughter.

When Artie heard me singing the grown-up popular songs of the day, it distressed her. She told me they were not suitable for a child my age, that I should learn some children's songs to sing. Forthwith she began to teach me those she knew.

Just approaching the "teen" age, strange "movings" had begun to surge through my breast. Emotions that distinguished me from the child, yet fell short of the woman, proclaimed me only half-child and made me an enigma to myself, as well as to others. One of the songs sister Artie selected as suited to my age went like this:

"Sitting in the window
In my cloak and hat,
I saw Mother Tabbykins,-
A real old cat,
Very old, very old,
Crumplety and lame,
Teaching kittens how to scold,
Is it not a shame?

Kittens in the garden,
Looking in her face,
Learning how to scratch and bite,
Oh, what a disgrace!
Very wrong, very wrong,
Very wrong and bad,
Such a subject for my song
Makes me all too sad."

Though a very pretty little ditty, and no doubt entertaining to mere babies, this no more satisfied my developing soul than would the rhymes of Mother Goose. Artie's choice for me gave me the feeling of being demoted.

Another one she sang I liked much better, since it had more grown-up appeal. The chorus only, survives in memory:

"Then let us cheer them on;
They can't be with us long.
Don't sneer at them because they're old and gray.
But remember while you're young
That the day to you will come
When you'll be old and only in the way."

When Mother's relatives learned that she was in the neighboring state of Arizona, and therefore very much nearer to them than usual, they began urging her by letter to visit them also before returning to Aliso.

But Mother did not see how she could be spared so long from home. Besides, with her father and mother both gone, a trip to the old home state had but little appeal to her. As the time drew near for her return to California, their letters became more urgent, for they supposed that once at home she would give up the idea entirely.

Sadie also was of this opinion, and tried to talk mother into going while she could. "Come while still you have Joan with you," they all urged. Joan was now going on eighteen and soon would be of an age to break the home ties should she choose. And who could tell whether such an opportunity to make the trip would ever again be Mother's?

Near the close of January, Sadie wrote home to Artie:

"Mother is writing to Uncle now. She says she don't see how she can possibly go to see them. I think she feels quite undecided. I don't see how I can spare Mother at all.

Again in the middle of February:

"Mother calculates to start for home about the twenty-third: may lay over at Colton a day or so...I don't see how I can let her go, but suppose I will have to...I am much obliged to you all for trying to keep Mother with me so long Thanks to you all."

On the twenty-seventh of February, Mother and Clara reached home, after an absence of over three months. Though we were all very glad to see them again, we agreed that she should have gone on to Utah to see her folks. But Mother's reluctance to do so had been due in part to her longing to see her dear father and the fear that his absence would cause her too much sadness. Again she read over his last letters with tears.

They wrote again, strongly urging her to seize the opportunity while circumstances permitted. We all joined in importuning her to go even yet, assuring her that we got along just splendidly during her absence. At last she made up her mind to do so.

Hearing of this decision, Sadie, on March seventeen, wrote to Artie:

> *"I was really surprised that Mother had decided to go and visit her folks. Was afraid she would give it up when she got home, but am glad she did not...Do you think you will stay till she comes back from her visit?...Ever and ever so many thanks for the shell lace. It must have been a big job for you to make so much, and so wide. A thousand thanks."*

About the time Mother went to Phoenix, a strange and terrible vine disease that had recently visited the southland, suddenly struck our vineyard with the rest, and the vines began to die. How distressing it was to watch our lovely vineyard wither away! And we wholly unable to do anything about it! Though everybody in the country was disheartened, none understood it. Even experts were baffled. There wasn't a thing that could be done to stop the spread of this unknown disease.

Not a vineyard in the whole of southern California escaped its ravages. The brewing interests at Anaheim were badly smitten. It seemed almost like a judgement upon the liquor traffic. Eventually, every vineyard in the country had to be dug up.

Shortly after Mother's return from Arizona, on March eleventh, Governor Waterman signed the bill that divided Los Angeles County, and now we found ourselves living in the new Orange County, and Santa Ana so near at hand, made our own new county seat.

Los Angeles County had at one time comprised not only all its present territory, but all of San Bernardino and Orange Counties and parts of the territory now included in Riverside and Kern Counties—an area greater than the combined states of Connecticut, Delaware, Maryland, Massachusetts, New Hampshire, New Jersey, and Rhode Island. The partitioning off of Orange County was the last stage in its dismemberment. The next stage has at this writing already been discussed by civic officials. If their suggested plan materializes, Los Angeles County will be reduced to include only the great city that bears its name.

Mother's Memorable Buggy Ride

During the interval between Mother's first and second absences from home, she started one day to drive over to Three Arches—a distance of about three miles and a half as the roads were then, for a visit with George and Minnie. She was accompanied by Charlotte, then past nine, and Clara, whose fourth birthday had been the day before George's wedding. Mother never went anywhere without Clara, and they sat, three in the seat of the buggy.

She was driving our little mare Sally. Father had bought Sally when a tiny colt of a Mr. Funk, trading for her two cows, and receiving ten dollars to boot. She was at that time in the prime of her life, a beautiful driving animal of a deep cream color with dark brown mane and tail. Sally was high spirited, eager to go, somewhat skittish, shying easily at unfamiliar objects, but withal a favorite on the farm. Everybody liked Sally and petted her. There is quite as much individuality among horses as people, which those who know animals appreciate.

For the first half of the way, all went well. Mother avoided the deep water and slippery bank of the pond-crossing, choosing the long way around over Frank Goff Bench and across the strip of beach sand to the southern mesa. Passing up the steep grade of the Lee Goff side and crossing small intervening gullies, she reached the deep gulch spanned by the dam below the road where Lafe had killed his buck the fall before.

In the bottom of this ravine, kept alive by spring rains, still flowed a little winter stream that after crossing the road and crawling through the broken dam, tumbled down the rocky depths beyond on its way to the sea. The road slanted down the side of this big gulch, making at the bottom a sharp, almost hairpin-like turn, and then rose windingly up again on the farther side.

As they started down this grade, Sally showed a disposition to run, which was anything but safe. Mother cautiously held back on the reins to compel her to go slow. This allowed the traces to slacken, and the singletree in consequence came in contact with Sally's hind quarters. She was just resentful enough, and skittish, to kick up her heels in protest. In doing so, one of her feet got up over the singletree and she couldn't get it back. Thus crippled, she continued erratically down the hill hopping awkwardly on three legs and jerking the other.

The frightened children began to scream, which only increased her fear and excitement. Mother, the reins held firm and steady in hand, and foot on the brake, began to speak gently and soothingly to the befuddled animal while endeavoring to bring her to a standstill. But Sally was not to be stopped. It was a dangerous situation. The screaming children, afraid to attempt an exit from the moving vehicle, and more afraid to stay in, presented another problem.

Just as they reached the bottom, Sally, exasperated, gave a "broncho buck" in an effort to free her foot by kicking the thing loose. But instead of freeing that one, she hooked her other hind foot also over the single tree, and fell with a crash to the ground. The left front wheel rolled off from the axle, letting the hub down to earth and throwing the floor and seat of the buggy suddenly out of line at a perilous angle.

The terrified children hastened to climb out, begging and pleading with Mother to do the same. But Mother had succeeded in keeping her seat, and holding onto the reins, still talked gently and soothingly to the struggling horse;

"Whoa, Sally! Be quiet, Sally! It's all right, Sally, Whoa!"

"Mama! Get out! Oh Mama, Mama, please get out!" yelled the two children in chorus, fairly beside themselves with fear for her safety.

Jumping up and down with wild hysterical screams, Clara, too excited to realize what she was doing, ran up onto a little rise by the side of the road and sat down in a bunch of ball cactus. Charlotte, seeing her plight, rushed up after her and pulled her out of the cactus, raking off some of the spiny balls adhering to her clothes and flesh. Clara then had something real to scream about.

Still, amidst the din, came the same even gentle tones of Mother, wholly unaware of the cactus episode:

"Whoa, Sally. Lie still, that's a good girl, be quiet. It's all right Sally!"

Finally, soothed by her unafraid, even tones, Sally quieted down somewhat. Mother got out and went around to the prostrate animal. Continuing her soft-spoken words, and patting her gently, she began trying to unfasten the traces (tugs, we called them) and loosen the harness in an effort to extricate her from the tangle. But everything was in such a tight strain and so tense that it was impossible to do anything about it. Not a coupling was she able to unhook. Finally she decided to send Charlotte home for help. She hated to do it for it was a long way home afoot, and Charlotte was a very timid little girl.

"You are not afraid to go are you?" she asked.

"No," said the trembling Charlotte, rising to the emergency, "I'm not afraid," and started out on a dead run for home and Joseph, a mile and a quarter away.

Fearful that Sally might become desperate in her uncomfortable position, and floundering about, break the shafts, or worse still, roll off buggy and all, over the embankment into the gulch below, Mother dared not leave her side for a moment. So she still kept talking to her and tugging away at the harness trying to loosen it. But things were still in such a tangle and drawn so taut that all her efforts seemed vain.

Sally lay submissively in her wretched position as if expecting relief, but finally despairing of any help from Mother to alleviate her distress, became restless again and began to flounder and struggle to rise to her feet, only to fall back unsuccessfully. Before Mother, caught by surprise, could get out of her way, her heavy body came down full weight on Mother's foot, inflicting a terrible sprain and nearly breaking the ankle bone. Suffering from the pain of this injury, Mother still kept her post at Sally's side to prevent some worse calamity; working away again at the problem of getting the harness loosened.

Charlotte running till out of breath, trudged on her way homeward, spurred by fear for Mother's safety. As she reached the grade down the side of the bench, she saw a man driving toward her across the sand from the Frank Goff side. In order to make the turn into Aliso Canyon before he should meet her she quickened her steps down the grade, for she was desperately afraid of strangers. It did not occur to her that here was an opportunity to secure help about the distressing situation left behind. Her whole thought was how to avoid meeting him. But, instead of passing her and continuing up the grade on the Lee side, he too turned toward Aliso and overtook Charlotte along the foot of the hill. Then she saw that it was Nate Brooks.

He wondered at seeing her so far from home alone, and stopped to offer a ride. Almost afraid to speak to him or to look into his face, she still accepted the ride; urged on by the knowledge of Mother and Sally in such desperate straits. But in her fear and timidity, she never once thought of telling Nate about the trouble. Tongue-tied and self-conscious at his side she sat on the high spring seat, answering his remarks in monosyllables and thinking only of getting home to Joseph for help as she had been bidden. So Nate, knowing nothing at all of the dangerous situation, drove leisurely along the creek and up to the house with his little passenger who was so eager to see her big brother that she left him immediately, climbing down almost before the wagon stopped, and disappeared to hunt him up. Not till he heard her tell the story of distress to Joseph, did Nate suspect anything wrong.

Joseph immediately hitched up the team to the spring wagon and hastened to the rescue. By the time he reached the scene of the accident, Mother in her perseverance had Sally up on her feet and the harness detached from the buggy; which was blocked with stones to keep it from rolling down the hill. At the time she was closely occupied in trying to get the cruel spines out of poor little Clara's lacerated flesh.

Sally, during the long trying ordeal, had behaved herself with amazing good sense for an animal and Mother had much to say in her praise. Howbeit, the whole trouble had been started by her saucy heel-kick. Mother's poor foot and ankle had turned all black, and was a long time in making a complete recovery.

A Last Sightseeing Trip

Artie was still at Aliso, and realizing that she soon must be about her business of earning a living for herself, desired very much before leaving the coast again, to carry out a long cherished purpose of visiting "Forest of Arden" the beautiful and picturesque mountain home of Madame Helena Modjeska, the Polish actress, which it had never been her privilege to see, and of admiring the large flock of a hundred or so peafowl kept on the place—an added attraction to sightseers. Also she had heard of the wealth of scenic loveliness of Santiago Canyon in which they were located, with its oaks and sycamores, its alder-lined streams, its ferns and vines, its birds and wild life; which she greatly desired to explore for herself.

So one day she and a young man of Arch Beach whose acquaintance she had made that summer, hatched up a plan together to take this trip the following Sunday—his only accommodations being a mangy, woe-begone looking horse, and a two wheeled "sulky," whose seat, originally intended for one only, could seat two by some crowding. She wished regretfully that Hulda might accompany them—for the two liked to be together—but how this was to be accomplished was not then apparent.

Madame Modjeska and her less famous, but most charming husband, Count Charles Bozenta Chlapowski, completing a party of ten, had come from Poland to Southern California to establish a Polish colony, having sent a friend ahead to choose a site. They arrived in July of Seventy-Six, stopping off enroute to visit the Centennial Exposition in Philadelphia. The colonization scheme was not a success and two years later, after she had gone to San Francisco to make her debut as an actress under the pseudonym of Adrienne Lecouvreur, starring with Booth, she had bought the beautiful homesite of J.E. Pleasants in Santiago Canyon. It was after this, when she had become famous on the English speaking stage, that she had built the charming home, "Forest of Arden," near the site of their former rustic cabin. Madame Modjeska passed away long years afterward at Balboa Beach on a little island in the bay.

When Fred came over from Arch Beach to Aliso on that Sunday morning, driving his "sulky" outfit, he was not alone. On the coast, lived an orphaned family by the name of Clark; consisting of three brothers, Billie, who I believe was married, Jim, and Jess, and two twin sisters—Effie, a sweet, modest, pleasant girl, and Allie, a pathetic little hunchback, whom we all tried to make feel as one of us in everything, but who was nevertheless somewhat of an introvert. A married sister lived in the suburbs of Santa Ana. These young people visited back and forth with us, and awakened, besides real liking, a certain feeling of compassion on account of the crippled sister and the motherless home. Jim had an unusual accomplishment which was very mystifying to us children. He would sit unobtrusively tilted back against the wall in his chair, and without the least apparent effort, or attracting any attention to himself, give a ventriloquistic performance that might have put him on the stage had he realized its value. Voices would roll out from any corner of the room, or wherever he elected to throw his voice, and there was no visible way of connecting them with their true source. Moreover, a brotherly sort of chap he was, of the most cheerful disposition, a good mixer who never showed at home or abroad that he possessed such a thing as a temper, and who could administer a needed rebuke in such a pleasant manner as to give no offense to anybody and leave no hard feelings—a rare and enviable quality. But the Clarks were very poor.

This young man, though paying no special attention to either of the girls, often came over to the Aliso place, and was sitting alongside of Fred in the sulky when he drove into the yard that March day. Having no outfit of his own, he was optimistically trusting that arrangements might be made by which he and Hulda could accompany Fred and Artie on their trip, by using Mother's buggy and horse, Birdy.

To the satisfaction of all concerned, this arrangement of a "foursome" was effected, and after the noon meal, at an hour that was rather late for so long a trip, they started out on their sixteen mile excursion to "Forest of Arden" and the peacocks.

Travelling up Aliso Canyon, they crossed at right angles the old stagecoach road, leaving to their right Moulton's ranch house, perched on its distant knoll, and continuing on eastward, passed the town of El Toro; and soon thereafter, struck the mountains, with five miles or so still to go. They were now on a road less frequently travelled and therefore more subject to neglect by the always inefficient road overseeing department of community government. And here their difficulties began.

Across their mountain highway loomed an impassable gulch, the result of recent mountain freshets that had taken soil, road and all with them. The sides of the gulch were steep and slippery entirely without road or wheel tracks, and deep, with a sharp turn at the bottom. It was impossible to drive the horse across with the buggy, even without passengers, without gravely endangering the safety of the vehicle.

Hulda was of the opinion that they ought to turn back and not try to cross it; and for awhile it seemed that this would have to be done, for these inexperienced mountain travellers had brought no shovel along for emergencies. But the boys' ingenuity formulated a plan for negotiating the ditch.

Unhitching the horses they led them across, and while the girls held them, went back and took their places in the shaves, drawing the vehicle across the gulch by hand. Once on the other side, they again hitched up the horses and proceeded on their way; but not without some misgivings as to the return journey.

A mile or so farther on, what was their dismay to find a second of these impassable ditches that had been cut across the road. Hulda was all for turning back, but the majority were against her. Artie being the older, and bent on seeing the "palace and the peacocks," was not inclined to be thwarted so near the coveted goal. This with the neutrality of the young men, who thought they could make it all right, outweighed Hulda's objections, and the former performance was repeated, some time being consumed as before in unhitching and bringing the "cavalcade" over by hand, to be re-hitched and driven on again, their hands not a little soiled and trousers liberally besmattered with canyon mud.

But "the most unkindest cut of all" was when they came to the third one of these road-crossing gulches, if anything worse than those that had gone before. Hulda balked; it was now more than an opinion. She was determined that this foolhardy ditch-crossing should be carried no farther. It was getting very late, and the thought of re-crossing them after dark was beginning to prey upon her mind. But in proportion to her protest, rose Artie's persistence.

What, give it up now so near the goal? Unthinkable! They would now soon be there. This was undoubtedly the last one. What a waste of time and energy and expectation to turn back with the goal in sight just around the bend of the next jutting hill! Let Hulda turn back if she chose, she was going on.

Jim, in an aside to Hulda urged that they keep with the others to see that all reached home in safety, and if Artie and Fred were going on, they must yield their wills and keep together with them, as that was the only right thing to do.

So again Hulda gave in, but ungraciously, and the ditch was crossed in the same manner as before. But by the time they reached "Forest of Arden," it might just as well have been a forest of willow trees for all they could distinguish in the deepening dusk. Count Bozenta came out at the barking of his dogs and met them at the gate. They conversed for a few minutes pleasantly. The peafowls, he said, had all gone to roost and could not be seen. It was rapidly growing dark and there were no electric floodlights to illuminate these beautiful grounds. So all agreed that there was nothing to be done but go home.

Seeing now when too late, her unreasonableness, Artie made the suggestion that they turn around and proceed to attack their job of "ditch-jumping" before it got any later. But Hulda here proved a more formidable obstacle to that procedure than all the ditches. Not one of them would she cross that night.

"Why, we could drive right into one of them in the dark before we knew it and have a terrible accident." This was not at all impossible since no lantern had been brought to shed its light upon the situation. The boys endeavored to assure her that they would "make it all right," but Hulda was obdurate.

"Not with this horse and buggy," she said firmly; and it was apparent to all that she meant it. "How shall we get home then?" asked Artie with a suspicion of meekness.

"We'll go home through Santa Ana Canyon where there's a decent road," said Hulda.

"But that's so far!"

"Well, you <u>would</u> come, "she reminded," and I'm not risking <u>my</u> neck crossing those ditches tonight in this dark," and that was final. The traditional family persistence and determination had met face to face.

This time, Hulda, with her horse and buggy constituted a majority. And obediently they all started on home by way of Santiago Canyon—its many attractions now lost in the growing darkness—to follow it till it should merge into the Santa Ana Canyon that was to lead them to the town of that name. It was eight miles from the Modjeska ranch" to the Santa Ana Camp Ground—now Orange County Park—and seven from there to town, which added to the twenty-five miles from Santa Ana on across the San Joaquin Ranch and down the Aliso, totaled a distance of forty miles that could hardly be accomplished under seventeen or eighteen hours at the rate they must travel in the dark. And they had the night before them.

On and on they went; the road most of the way a mere wagon-wheel track and difficult to follow; the weary and hungry horses doing their best uncomplainingly to cooperate with their erratic masters. A faint moon came up late in the evening, and growing along the roadside could be seen tempting green grass to regale their nostrils.

Finally Fred's horse refused to go another step. He wanted grass, and he wanted it right now. So there was nothing to do but unhitch the horses and let them feed for awhile on the young filaree and clover to renew their strength. Hulda and Jim sat in the seat of the buggy, but poor Artie was so utterly weary from the backless seat of the sulky that she climbed out and spread down the buggy robe between the shaves of the buggy and tried to rest. But the ground was hard and every bone ached.

After awhile when the horses were sufficiently refreshed to resume their journey, the cavalcade started on again. At about four o'clock in the morning, just as the first birds began to twit and wake their fellows, and the redoubtable chanticleers to herald lustily the approaching dawn, they drew rein at the home of Jim Clark's sister in Santa Ana, whom he roused out of bed, explaining their predicament. She dressed and made a fire to warm them—for all were very cold—and prepared them something to eat. Then after this pleasant refreshment and a little rest, the tired adventurers took to the road again for the last twenty-five mile lap of their journey.

At the edge of town another difficulty was encountered. The thrifty mustard growing close to each side of the wagon-wheel tracks from seven to nine feet tall, stretched out for six miles ahead and several miles on either side in one waving field of yellow bloom. Their horses and vehicles were completely buried, crawling along through it like fleas in the thick hair of a dog's back. Had it been dry hair, they would not have minded it so much; but it was as if a shaggy dog, having plunged into the water, was now shaking his dripping coat. The water rained down upon them, and with it, the wet petals of the mustard, flecking the whole ensemble, horses, harness, buggy and cart, robes and clothes and hats of the two who sat uncovered, with the yellow, unmelting snowflakes that stuck where they fell, giving the whole a ludicrous appearance.

This experience soon became unbearable to Artie, who asked to be allowed to ride with Hulda and Jim in the buggy. Jim gallantly exchanged places with her, taking his seat in the uncovered sulky; and when the bedraggled foursome reached home at about half past nine that morning, the girls were together in the buggy and the boys in the cart.

It was well that they came so. The first thing they beheld was Mother, sitting by the front window intently and wearily watching the road, where she had been sitting the whole night long without a wink of sleep.

"Well," she said, with ominous calmness, her voice one great sigh of relief: "You're back are you?"

There was an undercurrent of severity that she made no attempt to conceal; howbeit mollified to some extent to see the girls together and the boys by themselves. And then, knowing nothing of the circumstances except the apparent fact that her two girls had been kept out all night by two young men, thus exceeding the limit of social explanation and parental sufferance, she turned to the two silent "culprits" in the sulky, and, in unmistakable tones of insulted hospitality and confidence, vented her weary and righteous wrath—however unmerited—upon them.

"You two go on home, both of you, and never set foot on this place again!"

This was definite, final, precluding appeal; and none was attempted.

"Alright," said Jimmie cheerfully, and the two drove away; and that was the last time we ever saw either of them at Aliso.

Soon after this, Nellie Fuller was taken sick, and Artie went over to San Juan to take care of her and do her work. She was there at the time Mother left for her visit out of state, and continued on for some time afterward during the summer harvest.

357

Birdie, the old mare they drove that day, had been the foal of old crippled Nellie—long since departed this life—and was herself the mother, grandmother and great-grandmother of many. After she became too old to work, she was turned loose in the pasture to enjoy her old age without labors. One day, sometime afterward, she lay down in the pasture near the corral and died. All the horses and colts that were shut up inside the corral, many of them her own progeny, having witnessed the tragedy of her passing, crowded as close to the spot as was possible, and were found watching with their heads hanging over the fence, where they had evidently been standing ever since her death. The green grass growing all around seemed to have no attraction for them as they mourned in their dumb way for their loved companion.

A Long-Deferred Visit

Having decided to visit her people, Mother began preparations without further loss of time. Joan again bent over the sewing machine, working overtime till Mother and Clara were outfitted. Then the latter part of March, Mother telegraphed her folks that she was coming, requesting an answering wire that they would meet her as arranged. But, due no doubt to lack of coordination in the telegraph service, which was very faulty at that time, she was kept waiting for an answer. However, after some delay it came and Mother and Clara finally got started on their journey. After they were gone, a letter arrived on April two from Sadie, in which she said in part:

"Tell Mother to telegraph again for pitie's sake! I don't believe they ever received the telegram. It is too bad for her to have to wait like this. There have been so many awkward mistakes made here in the telegraph offices; and people not receiving the messages, that Arthur says, he don't believe Mother's message ever reached its destination."

A royal welcome awaited them at the other end, and in spite of the absence of her dear parents, Mother had a good time and enjoyed the visit with her numerous relatives. They went about from one place to another; first with this brother, then with that, and then to her sister Artemisia and husband, Daniel Seegmiller; and to various nieces and nephews—all of whom feted and dined them, and gave them a good time.

Lafe Shoots a Squirrel

Spring had come in Aliso, and with it, the birds began to sing in the orchards, and the little squirrels to scuttle about foraging for spring dainties to supplement their depleted winter stores. One of these little rodents had formed the habit of coming into our immediate yards, and even into our corn cribs and helping himself to stored corn and nuts and other things not meant for squirrels. So Lafe determined to get rid of him at the first opportunity.

Under the row of pepper trees along the lower side of the rock wall, stood a dozen or so empty bee hives in a row where they would be handy when needed for new swarms of bees. The front ends of these hives were raised up from the sloping ground to rest on two-inch cleats, in order to make them level and to provide a circulation of air underneath for evaporation of moisture. Each had a four-inch porch extending out in front; and these were covered with dirt and grit from standing through the winter.

One afternoon about four o'clock, Lafe and Joan, standing half way up the slope, saw this little squirrel running about under the pepper trees. Leaving Joan to watch the squirrel, Lafe slipped over to his cabin to get his gun—an old Cap and Ball Colt revolver that he had picked up somewhere and repaired. It was loaded with black powder and a bullet. Upon his return, the little pest promptly ran under one of the bee hives. Lafe got down and lay with his face close to the ground looking under the box to locate him. In the deep shadow, he could see one little eye gleaming brightly. Holding the muzzle of his pistol about two feet from the hive, with his face still low to the ground, he took careful aim at that one little eye, and fired.

What happened to the squirrel is not recorded. After that shot, nobody was interested enough in him to investigate. The important thing was what happened to Lafe. When that old gun went off, the blast of the concussion blew a large quantity of this fine dirt and grit, mixed together with black, unburned powder, backward into his face and eyes, embedding it deep in the flesh, and in the eyeballs, drawing blood, and causing extreme pain, with immediate blindness. The right eye was filled with black powder, the cheek, nose and upper lip peppered with it, and the whole face more or less affected.

Joan wrung her hands at the sight. Lafe, thinking of other men he had seen whose faces had been marked for life with black powder, in the midst of his pain, asked Joan:

"How does my eye look?"

"Oh, it's ruined! It's ruined!" she exclaimed; "What shall we do? We'll have to have a doctor!" But there was no doctor within twenty-five miles, and night in the offing.

Together they went down to the house, Joan assisting him, for he could scarcely see to walk; and standing up before the little looking glass hanging on the front porch, with thumb and fingers he opened his eyes, one at a time, enough to see the plight he was in.

What should he do? Lafe thought hard. The pain was almost unendurable.

In this extremity, he was vividly impressed what to do. He told Joan to get some fresh milk, scald it and cool it in a basin and bring it to him, with cloths enough for two compresses. This, she did speedily, and helped him out to his cabin by the Little Hill. Drawing a stool up to the bedside on which to set the basin of milk, he lay down and began to put milk compresses on his eyes and face, changing them frequently.

All night long, without sleep, he kept up this treatment, and marvelous were the results. The powder was drawn to the surface and dissolved, and at the same time the dirt and grit were drawn out—the milk acting as a healing agent as well.

At daylight next morning, he stood up before the little three-inch looking glass that hung from a nail on the wall, and taking his open jackknife, placed the sharp blade against the flesh, and scraped his face all over; wiping off the blade frequently. His right eye was still full of the dissolved powder and grit. With his left hand, he held this eye open and gently scraped the ball of it with the open blade. By this delicate operation, he managed to scrape every bit of the foreign matter out of his eye, with the exception of one embedded grain of powder in the outer corner. His face was then free from powder, except for a small amount on his lower lip that had been missed by the compresses.

Within a short time after finishing the job, he had a bandage over the right eye, and was out hoeing weeds in the orchard, entirely free from pain; and within a day or two, his face was entirely healed, and his eyes perfectly normal.

Calamity Comes

During Mother's absence, something dreadful happened at the Aliso farm. A terrible, fatal disease—Bloody Murrain—broke out among our cattle with which we were powerless to cope. Our milk cows began to succumb one after another. Morning after morning, Joseph would come into the house with the solemn announcement:

"Another cow died last night."

We wondered how it would end. Mother was not told; for telling her could not help the situation, and it would have spoiled her visit—perhaps have brought her home before the time, to no purpose.

Milk was the chief article of our diet. We ate "bread and milk" for supper practically every night. But now, what should we do? We continued to use the milk up to the time a cow showed symptoms, then, soon after, she was dead. One by one, they died till finally, one morning Joseph entered the kitchen and said with solemn sadness:

"The last cow died last night." Not a milk cow was left. We had lost a dozen or more.

What should we do for food, with no milk and no butter? Cornmeal bread was poor stuff made without milk or buttermilk and eaten without butter. Potatoes without butter or milk-gravy were flat. It seemed as though milk had been used for most everything, after we had it no more. And what could we get for supper. That was our problem. George and Minnie came over to see us and discovered our plight. They were no better off than we, for the boom had "busted" and everybody everywhere was as poor as the proverbial church mouse. They could give us neither money nor help. But Minnie offered a suggestion:

"Try bread and vinegar together for supper," she said. "I used to eat it, and it tastes good. Put some salt and pepper on the bread and then cover it with diluted vinegar." We did so, and it didn't kill us. But it is a recipe and a substitute we are not recommending.

Then something else happened. This time it was not at Aliso, and not cows that were sick; but our own little sister Clara, who, far away from home, had been taken down with "lung fever"—spelled today, "pneumonia." When we learned of it by the slow process of United States Mails—which though slow, were still much more frequent and regular than formerly—we had no means of knowing for sure that she was even still living. The letter had said that there was grave danger that she would not pull through. We clustered about with scared faces, and spoke to one another as people do at funerals, in low, hushed voices; going about our tasks mechanically, hoping against hope that the "grim reaper" would be defeated and our little baby sister be spared to us.

A great fear gripped my heart that she might die. I wondered how any of us could live after that. She was such a little mite of a thing, so frail, and subject to everything in the way of contagion that came around. So many times before, she had been sick. Would she have the strength to battle this new foe?

In my extremity, I turned instinctively to seek help from a higher power than the human—as many another unbeliever has done—I had heard that some people believed there was a God, and our school books mentioned Him in reverent language. In my world, God was somewhat of a bystander, who had no particular part in our affairs. I didn't know if He did. But I was open to conviction—or thought so. Some people even believed that God would hear and grant their requests. This emergency, I thought, would be a good time to test Him out—to find out whether there really was a God or not. So, stealing away by myself into Mother's empty room, I stood for a moment at the foot of the trundle bed and looked furtively about to make sure that no one was around to see and then, bent my head and my body, and in a low voice, spoke:

"God, if there is a God, make my little sister Clara well, and I will believe in you."

That was all. It was the first prayer of my life. Then, half ashamed of myself, I stole away from the spot.

Only a few days later, a letter came from Mother, saying that Clara was much better. Then "Reason," that necessary power so often used to flout the God who gave it, began to "grin" at me, and to say sardonically: "God, indeed! She was already getting better before you ever prayed!"

And the girl just turned thirteen, who three years before had written of "Sweet Fairy Bell" and "heaven so bright," was once more in the clutches of 'doubt, knowing nothing of the unseen battle between the powers of good and evil that was being waged over her own soul.

After Mother and Clara had returned home, and once again we had our darling safe in our arms, seemingly as well as ever, God, and His possible part in it were entirely forgotten. Things just "happened" that was all.

Making a Parlor

It had always been humiliating to the girls to be obliged to entertain their gentlemen friends and other guests in the common kitchen and eating room, where all the family parties and gatherings had been held in days gone by; but during Mother's absence, they began to visualize the possibility of turning her room into a guest room if only her consent could be obtained. They could vacate their own room, turn that over to her and betake themselves out to the honey house, where some of us had been sleeping ever since Sadie's visit home a year and a half before. The more they thought about it, the more feasible seemed the plan; the greatest drawback being the lack of an outside entrance, which made access through the kitchen still necessary. Here, Lafe, joining in their cogitations, suggested that the little sliding window opening onto the front porch could be taken out and a door put in its place to give a front entrance—a suggestion that was hailed with delight. And they determined to "storm the fort" as soon as Mother should return.

So Mother had scarcely become settled after her return before she was approached with this proposition. Mother was always slow about making changes; but her two recent visits had somehow "broken the ice"; and her consent was gained more easily than was anticipated.

The greatest objection was the expense involved. But she had spent so much on her own pleasure, that it seemed only fair now to look to the pleasure of others; and such a change might mean keeping the girls with her longer. Another objection was the physical impossibility of crowding all her personal belongings into the small room assigned to her. But she was persuaded that those of her belongings not used often would be as safe in the honey house as anywhere. And so again all her objections were overruled; and the young folks lost no time in setting about the task of converting Mother's room into a parlor.

All the beds but Mother's and all other things not needed in the dwelling, were carted out to the honey house; and it was then that the picturesque old swing shelf disappeared forever. Lafe changed the window into a door that opened onto the front porch, which in itself was such a great improvement that all wondered why this scheme had not been thought of before. They tore off the old canvas ceiling from the rafters, and stripped the old worn and faded paper from the walls, and covered both walls and ceiling with white cheesecloth stretched tightly and tacked on closely and neatly. Over all this, was then pasted a beautiful pattern of wallpaper, which had been carefully selected in town; and the transformation was truly wonderful. A cheap carpet which they had bought, was placed over the uneven boards of the worn floor, the best chairs moved in from other parts of the house, and one or two added by purchase, and pictures were transferred from other walls to this one; together with various other wall decorations then in vogue to brighten things up. The organ was then moved into the room, and placed across the corner where Mother's bed had formerly stood and lo, we had a parlor—the pride of all the household. Never did the parlor of any grand mansion afford more satisfaction to its proud possessors than did this simple "front room" to the young folks of Aliso.

Mother settled down in the girls' room, not quite contented—for it was hard to get used to the smallness of it, and the step up into the dining room; but she too enjoyed having a guest room in the house and took pleasure in the thought of others being so pleased. But when evening would fall, the family all would gather still about the big table in the dining room; for Mother said it seemed cozier than to sit in the more formal front room. And at bedtime, we all traipsed up the slope in the dark to the honey house to bed; except Clara, who still slept with Mother, keeping her company in the house alone.

It was wonderful to have the organ in a room by itself, where we could go away from the hubbub to practice; and from this time on, we took an added interest in our daily practice at the keyboard. Joan was becoming quite proficient, and played beautifully many of the more difficult pieces in the book. I was also getting on creditably; and now Hulda began to get the inspiration to learn too; and soon picked out the chords, and began to learn to read the notes.

Long before this, I had begun to teach Annie what I knew, and she too was practicing on the organ and learning to play simple tunes; manifesting a great deal of expression and talent. She was, however, far less painstaking about technique than I, being eager to bridge the gap between exercises and "pieces" without bothering about intermediate steps.

Another Disappointment

After George had lived on the claim at Three Arches for something like six months, the discovery was made that a grave legal flaw existed in his filing papers. He had taken up the claim as government land, whereas it was in reality, state land. So it became necessary to change his filing and begin the period of residency all over again. Upon learning of this discrepancy, he went to the proper office to make the necessary changes, but someone else had been there ahead of him.

The law provided that a veteran who had used his filing rights in taking up government land, but had received less than his quota of one hundred and sixty acres, might at any future time file again on government land to the amount of that lacking to complete his quota—a privilege accorded only to ex-soldiers.

Mr. Whiting of El Toro had secured some of this "soldiers' script" to which he, as a veteran was entitled, and had filed on all the ocean frontage that was left untaken between Aliso Beach and Mussel Cove. This included all the frontage naturally belonging to George's claim on which he had previously made a mis-filing.

Robbed thus of its ocean frontage, in his estimation the rest of the claim was not worth bothering about. So after making a proper recording on the rest, he began to look around for a buyer to take it off his hands, intending to return to San Jacinto to farm his own land, which for two years or more had been let out to others.

Shortly after Mother's return from her last visit, he sold out his claim "for a song." At that time Nate's mother, Mrs. Draper, had recently passed away, and his house was lonely; so Nate invited George and his wife to move in with him and let him board with them till after their expected baby should be born and they be ready to take up residence in San Jacinto. This they were glad to do, moving in the latter part of June. But Minnie, being poorly, was unable to keep up the house, and Artie, who had returned from Fullers in San Juan Capistrano, was invited to come over and help them out for awhile. This she did, staying there with them for about two months.

CHAPTER 50 MAJOR SORROWS

In my early life were two major sorrows; the first, that I had been born a girl instead of a boy. I considered this a most cruel fate. As far back as memory goes, the desire to be a boy was a part of me, and my early childhood was embittered by this futile longing to be a boy.

There were too many girls and not enough boys for the farm work anyhow; and so from the first, Father had appointed me to the outside work. Not that the other girls were exempt from such work. They always helped in emergencies, in times of special need for all hands; but in a special sense it was my job, and always, as a matter of course, took precedence over all other duties. Should only one be needed on the outside, that one was always Harriet.

So my days were spent herding hogs, suckering corn, hoeing weeds, riding the horse in cultivating the garden stuff to guide him between the rows while Joseph managed the cultivator, picking up potatoes, or cutting them for seed, clearing away prunings from orchards, gathering apples and sorting them, harvesting almonds and walnuts—as we all did—picking olives, husking corn, cutting wood when no boys were at hand to do it, carrying water, pulling fodder, and helping with the chores.

When the men would haul hay from the field, sometimes barley, sometimes alfalfa, grown down in the cart-road garden, while Joseph pitched it from the haycocks onto the big rack, and Father drove the team, I would follow with the long-handled, wooden-toothed rake, piling up the leaving for Joseph to pitch up onto the rack.

But this outside work by no means let me off from inside work—no indeed. Like any other girl I had to do my part of the housework from which boys were exempt. There were dishes to wash—which I detested-floors to sweep, beds to make, apples to peel, peas to shell, game to clean, and butter to churn.

To lift that dasher endlessly up and down, up and down, till the lumps of butter would come—and sometimes they took plenty of time about it-wasn't enough. A boy would have been allowed to stop there. But I, being a girl, must also take it up in the wooden bowl, wash and salt it, work it and mould it—unless there should be other more urgent tasks awaiting my performance.

All the things that boys did, I wanted to do—and do by right. Jumping, wrestling, climbing trees, shooting bows and arrows, scaling fences, playing ball, whittling, whistling, and riding horses were activities in which I imitated boys as much as possible, cultivating a lofty independence.

I disdained to be afraid of anything large or small. A mouse fared ill if once cornered; lizards, I delighted to catch—if that could be done without getting hold of their tails; for these would be snapped off and left in my hand, and I wanted to turn them loose again intact. Toads were my playfellows. Horses, cattle, dogs, and even wild animals had no terror for me. Snakes I would pick up by the tail-tips and swing them at arm's length around my head—but I drew the line at rattlers. Of those I was deathly afraid; though when old enough, hesitating not to attack them with proper weapons. The ugly tarantula also, which we were taught was deadly poison, I had no use for; but was not afraid to kill him whenever found.

But all these accomplishments could not avail to make of me a boy, any more than could "the Ethiopian change his skin or the leopard his spots." After earning all the rewards of a boy, I still was compelled to remain "only a girl." It was too cruel.

We all, girls and boys alike, played outside games, such as "Pomp, Pomp Pull-a-way," "Prisoners' Base," "Hide and Seek" and ball throwing games; but the others played as girls—I as a would-be boy. I grew to be a "tom-boy," earning the "name without the game." I think Father too must have wished me a boy; for he very unwisely fostered in me every tomboyish propensity.

It seemed as though I was eternally being corrected for acting natural.

"Harriet, don't do that way, it isn't nice!"

"It isn't lady-like to whistle."

"Why don't you take care of your hands?"

"Why don't you wear your sunbonnet?" "You'll be as speckled as a hen!"

"You mustn't be such a tom-boy!" "Don't storm around so!"

"For pity's sake, don't be so awkward."

They never got after boys about these things. Boys were allowed to do just as they pleased.

To "cap the climax," boys were thought to be—and thought themselves to be—so very much "smarter" than girls, that they put on an attitude of superiority, and treated girls as if they couldn't possibly know anything worth knowing. Really, they seemed to consider themselves as belonging to a superior order of being.

But when the days of adolescent changes came—which they did suddenly out of a clear sky, for Mothers then never talked to girls about themselves—I simply rebelled to tears. A bitter handicap was put on my activities that seemed to me "the last straw that broke the camel's back." Surely, boys had all the best of it, and girls the worst.

I must have been a queer kind of contradiction—a sort of cross between; or, as English Harry might have put it— dropping his "h's"—"A bloody 'alf an' 'alf"; for with all my tom-boy propensities, I had the most inordinate love for dolls; which never lost their charm for me until long after adolescent years began. I could not give them up until actually ashamed of being seen with them. Then it was with great reluctance that I parted with my beloved dolls to distribute them among the younger girls, with many admonitions to be careful and not break them; retaining until the last, the most adored.

The Other Major Sorrow

The other major sorrow—and by far the greater one—was the lack of opportunity to obtain an education. Lack of school privileges was not uncommon in those days. Often families pioneering on the frontiers had no schools within reach. It was considered quite the noble thing in such cases, to do as did Abraham Lincoln before the log fire in his backwoods cabin, dig out their own education for themselves. There were no laws of compulsory schooling in force then, and nobody to interfere in case of children being kept at home.

At first there was no school to attend within sixteen miles of Aliso, in the Mexican settlement of Capistrano; and these miles lengthened out into many more by the hilly, roundabout roads then traveled. But with the coming of neighbors to Laguna, a small school had eventually been started on the hillside near the mouth of Laguna Canyon, about four miles from our place. There were eight or nine reasons—then considered insurmountable, why we children could not attend this school.

Figure 36 Laguna Canyon Schoolhouse, 1889 [15]

In the first place, we were very poor. Out of this poverty grew several of the other reasons. We had no money with which to buy clothes suitable for school attendance. As long as we could be called "children," we went barefoot from necessity most of the year. In order to extract a living for the large family of us from the few acres we possessed, every hand was needed on the place, either inside or outside. There seemed no time for anything but work, work, work, from morning till night. We had no money with which to hire help in order to release members of the family to attend school. The most important work of the farm began about the time of the opening of school, or even earlier, and lasted from August through November without let up. There were the grapes to pick, the almonds to harvest, the apples to gather, the walnuts to harvest and the olives to pick; all of which required every pair of hands; and our very existence depended on these crops. Not the least of our reasons for non-school attendance, was the very real physical barrier of frequent floods and high waters in winter time. Beginning sometimes as early as November, but more frequently after the turn of the year, the creek was often so high as to be unfordable either by horse or team and wagon; and not at all by foot. There were two crossings necessary to be made in reaching Frank Goff's Bench; and much of the time in winter both were impassable. There were seasons when the family was penned in by rains and high water for three months at a time, with only a break now and then between; so that consecutive attendance would have been out of the question in any event.

We did not have horses enough for use on the farm to be able to spare one or more for daily travelling to and from school; nor did we have a conveyance to spare regularly for such purpose. Our wagon must frequently be put to other uses.

In pleasant weather, we could have walked; though that would have necessitated very early starting, and have brought us home after nightfall. But school days are for the most part winter days; and winter days meant rain—and usually much of it; when, for reasons of health, we could not have gone; for it would have meant often the wearing of soaked clothing all through the day.

There was another reason also, in Father's mind. Discussing the school situation with Nate Brooks one day, he was overheard to make the statement:

"I would far rather my children had no schooling at all than to be constantly exposed to such immoral influences."

Whatever it was that Father might have known along this line, he did not impart it to us younger members of the family. So, taking it all in all, we considered it a part of our misfortune to be excluded from school privileges.

The "A, B, Cs" were taught the younger members of the family by those older; and we sat at Mother's knee while she sewed, to study our reading lessons and do our "sums." We had our slates and pencils, and after doing one example, would rub it out and do another. Of "scratch paper" we had none—there were no "scratch tablets" in those days. Paper was something to be handled very economically.

We each had our "copy book," with writing lessons several times a week, in which we strove to imitate the beautiful script at the head of the page. If we showed a disposition to shirk our studies, Father would stand us up on a box in the corner until we were ready to proceed in a proper manner. Father had other methods of punishment for minor offenses, such as boxing or pulling our ears, and pulling hard on a bunch of our forelocks. But the most common was standing on a box in a corner.

As we grew older, we endeavored to learn our lessons around the family table at night after the day's work was done—often falling asleep over our books from sheer fatigue. For who can study well after a hard day's work when both body and mind are weary? And who can get from inexperienced older brothers and sisters, or even parents, the type of help needed, that only regular teachers can give? Studying at home left indeed, much to be desired.

Sometimes, we had opportunity to study during the daytime, for not always was work so pressing, and in our school, there were no summer vacations. Father kept us supplied with school readers and arithmetics, and there was an old grammar that had done duty for many years, available to all who desired to study it. There was also a large old geography up in the attic, which the older ones had studied, but as for me, I could make neither head nor tail to the maps; though sometimes I got it down and pondered over it.

Sitting out on the honey house steps, I struggled over long and short division of which I was then suffering the birth-pangs, and great was my satisfaction when at last the subject became plain to me. There was one advantage in this home school—we were not hurried from one phase of a subject to another with only half an understanding of it. We kept pegging away until the thing was understood and became our own.

Father, according to the standards of those days, had a fair education and a good command of English; and Mother herself was not far behind him, though not of the same literary turn of mind. This was no doubt of great benefit to us children who thus imbibed unconsciously as we grew up, fairly correct grammatical forms of speech. But this haphazard method of education was far from being equal to regular school work. At the most, only the bare essentials could be taught. For arts and sciences aside from mathematics, there was no provision. Laboratory subjects were out of the question; and we were left with hearts and minds unsatisfied.

As for me, it was the grief of my life that I could not go to school. Looking back, it does seem to me as though a way might have been contrived for some of us to get to the school. To me it has always seemed that those four mountainous miles between our home and the little country school could somehow have been bridged, even though there were no horses; even though swirling waters might cut us off for weeks at a time; even though there were no good clothes to wear; and no money for school supplies; even though every pair of hands were needed on the farm; even though-everything!

One day in my early teens, I walked the four long miles over hills and hollows to that little school house—what for? Ostensibly to see if I could borrow a book from the school library to read; actually to see what a schoolhouse looked like inside. I had never before been inside the doors of a schoolhouse. I felt strangely like a little lost pup that has somehow gotten into the other dog's yard, and feels his unwelcomeness. Hungry-oh so hungry for a bone! The bone is there; but the big dog who isn't hungry, guards it. I was an outsider. I was treading upon territory to which I claimed no right. Even if I were with them in school—I would not even know how to act. I would be only a laughing stock to the others who knew so much more than I did. Schools and schooling were not for me. Forever I must stand back and gaze longingly—rebelliously, at the star; but how to hitch my wagon to it, I knew not. The star was so high—so unattainable—so utterly above me—and my wagon in such a hopeless mudhole.

Not that the young school teacher was discourteous; he was not. The cause was all within myself. Feeling my ignorance, I felt inferior; which actually, I was not. My brains were equal to those of anyone there; not even excepting the schoolmaster himself. He discussed with me the books, very courteously; but he did not question as to my educational ambitions-did not ask me if I attended school, and where—did not ask me if I would like to attend—though he knew there was no other school within possible distance. He did not attempt to draw me out.

Had he done so—had he encouraged me ever so little—had he shown a real regard for my future—a genuine interest in me—something might have been started that day that eventually would have drawn me into the school—who knows? There were neighbors in Laguna with whom I might have lived and gone to school, had there been any effort made in that direction—though no such thought occurred to me. A few earnest words of encouragement might have changed the whole course of my life—but they were not spoken. So I went home again with my book under my arm and a bigger grief in my breast.

Had we gone to school like normal children, and rubbed elbows with the child world around us, the contact would have been worth our weight in gold to us. Half of education consists in the social contacts of community school life in early years. Never could any of us be what we might have become had we been privileged to attend school in the formative period of life. However much knowledge might have been acquired in later years, it could never make up for this early lack.

I am sure that Father, while he was with us, never dreamed that any of us ever suffered so poignantly over the longing to go to school. Though it sapped at our very vitals, yet we were reticent with him; and after he was gone, though we could talk more freely with Mother, yet we would not make her miserable with worrying over-much on account of conditions she was powerless to remedy. She was to be shielded not burdened unduly.

During the summer before Mother's visit to Sadie, a letter had come from her in which she asked Mother if she could not send Harriet out to her to help her and go to school. Eagerly, I had caught at this straw that seemed to point the way to the one thing I longed for most; and from that day forward, this star of hope was cherished.

I knew that the matter was discussed between her and Mother, and though nothing more was said to me, yet I never forgot it, and felt that someday the opportunity might materialize. Though Mother in her characteristic way would not say anything to encourage me overmuch I felt that it was because she was guarding me against possible disappointment, and I read even encouragement in her noncommittal manner. Thus my hope was even strengthened.

After her visit to Phoenix, I mentioned the matter to her, trying to be casual, so as not to betray too plainly my great eagerness. Her reply was very guarded, she said that Sadie and she had discussed the matter, that Sadie had asked for either Harriet or Annie, and that she thought Annie could be better spared than I; but that she had not made up her mind yet whether or not she would send either one of us.

Now it was not Annie who was pining for schooling. I knew that, and so did Mother. Annie naturally had her longings for things other than she possessed—longings that were as real to her as mine to me; but among these, schooling was not uppermost. She longed for better clothes, for social advantages, for the things money could buy; but no one ever heard her speak of longing to go to school. Annie was not lying awake at night grieving over her lack of education as was I, and weeping with straining soul that groped for some way out of the darkness. Mother did not know how deep and inconsolable was that longing; for I could not express my innermost thoughts to anyone. She knew that I wanted to go to school; but what she did not know was that the desire burned like a consuming flame that could not be quenched night nor day—a sacred flame to me. It could not be framed into words—I had no words—that was the trouble. I was dammed up and bursting for an outlet—an avenue of self-expression. It was a part of that very education for which I longed, to inculcate the art of self-expression, without which life was a misery. No one knew the real heart of me—all they could see was my faults and failings; of which I was too painfully conscious myself. And how was I ever to improve without opportunity for culture?

The idea that Mother would send Annie instead of me, I did not for a moment seriously entertain. It was like her to withhold the best aspect as a protection should worst come to worst. But surely she could not mean it. The very appropriateness of my being the one to go, my more intense desire, my priority of age, would prevent her from bestowing the prize on one who would be less appreciative of it. So thinking, I said little and waited. But my brain was busy formulating plans, and every plan included my going to Phoenix to school.

The Blow Falls

When Mother returned from her visit to her people, I waited, saying nothing of the subject so near my heart, for a more auspicious moment to approach her. No doubt my silence was interpreted as a diminishing of interest, rather than as it was, a protection against seeming casualty. I hoped she would broach the matter to me, and thus open the way for me to press my case and make her know how vital to me was the matter. Then unexpectedly one day the blow fell.

The family were together in the room, when Mother spoke up in a manner and tone that seemed plainly to imply that of course everything had been settled for the best, and there could be no dissenting voice from my quarter, and said:

"Well, Annie, I have decided to let you go to Phoenix and stay with Sadie a year or so; and maybe she will send you to school. How would you like that?"

Did no one hear that thud of my heart as it fell down, down, down? Could I control myself so that no one should read my feelings by my face? Nobody seemed to notice me. I sat stunned for a while, listening almost in a daze to Annie's reactions. It was plain that she had been taken by surprise. She had expected the choice to fall on me, and had made no such plan for herself. She didn't know whether she would like it or not. There was an utter lack of enthusiasm. Mother had to use a little gentle persuasion to get her to see the advantage it might be to her.

I could stand no more, and stole away from the scene in the throes of the bitterest disappointment that had ever come into my life—away where nobody could see me, to fight it out with myself. I wept till I could weep no more. The Ship of Hope had wrecked upon the rocks of Despair. Its driftwood strewed the shores of the Commonplace. Existence must go on, but the star had set in midnight.

I was proud. Nobody should discover the depths of my wound. I would not give anybody the chance to think that I was jealous of Annie. It was not jealousy. If Annie had appreciated it—if she had leaped at the opportunity, I would not have thought myself more deserving than she; and could have been reconciled to it; for within me there was a trace, at least, of the martyr spirit. I could have borne to be sacrificed in a worthy cause. But somehow, to me, it seemed all wasted and vain. Annie was being coaxed to accept the prize I had so eagerly longed for. That stung incurably. It seemed unfair and unjust.

Mother could see, of course, that I was disappointed. She had known that I would be, but she had expected me to make more of a fuss than I did-perhaps cry a little; and she seemed genuinely relieved that I had taken the matter so quietly. She said a few words intended to comfort me:

"Maybe you can go too some day, Harriet."

Little did she know of the great bitterness that possessed my spirit. Could she have seen me that night sitting alone in the dark grappling with an overmastering rebellion impossible to describe, she might even have reversed her decision; for after all, I think she was not so decided in her own mind as she had tried to appear. It had taken her many months to make up her mind which of us to send. I am sure she really desired to send me, but felt that I could not be spared from the work of the farm. I too recognized that it would have been hard for her to spare me. I did not blame her. Mine was the more responsible position—my hands the more capable for outdoor labor. It was some comfort to know that she appreciated my work on the farm.

Finally, I came out of the fog somewhat, and began to let reason take its place above emotion. "What can't be cured, must be endured"; and Annie must never learn how I felt. I could not endure that she should think me merely jealous over her good fortune. But was it to her, good fortune? She seemed not at all sure of that. The more she thought about going, the more it took on the aspect of sacrifice on her part. She was not elevated over the prospect of leaving home and all of us. She was going to be lonesome.

From the time of this decision to send Annie, she became the important one in the household. Joan's back was again bent to the sewing machine to fashion the new clothes needed for her equipment; which, though simple, were a satisfaction to Annie who loved pretty clothes, and in a great measure compensated her for all she was leaving behind. Hulda worked buttonholes and sewed on buttons, and patched up all her old things that had to go along, and darned her stockings; and finally the ninth of August came, when we all bade her goodbye, and Annie was taken to the depot in the spring wagon and put upon the train at El Toro; which bore her away on the first lap of her journey.

I turned back to the drudgery of the farm routine, now necessarily to be rearranged and made a little heavier by the loss of one pair of hands; and feeling a lonely spot in my heart at the departure of my old playmate and the disruption of the recreative diversions we had shared together. This parting was a landmark in our experience, marking a distinct turning point in life's journey. For never again were we children together on the farm.

A letter soon came from Sadie describing Annie's journey:

"Of course you got our note written the day Annie arrived. She had no trouble whatever or worry on the trip, but had just the very best of care. When she reached Colton (where she was to change lines) the conductor took her and her baggage to the other depot and gave her in charge of the next conductor. Then a man at the depot invited her to his house, as she would have to lay over from two till half past ten at night. So the conductor gave her leave and she had a pleasant time; had lunch with them, and they brought her back at train time. The transfer cost her nothing. Then at Maricopa, the conductor here took her in charge. They had to lay over all night, so she got a good night's sleep; as the landlady was very good and made her a bed out-of-doors beside her own (Arizonans at Phoenix all sleep out-of-doors during warm weather) and got her up in time to dress for train time. Then Arthur met her here with the buggy. So you see, she had not the least bit of worry...Annie says it is not quite so hot as she expected to find it. She sleeps...like a log. The other night we had a terrible sandstorm. We pulled the covers over our faces till it was past, and then I got up and brushed the dirt out of our bed before I could sleep. Annie knew nothing at all of it and next morning wondered how so much dirt got in her bed."

Annie's first letter home, written to Artie at Arch Beach, August sixteen, says:

"I have been here...a week tomorrow. Saidy and I have been cleaning house...and just as we got the floors mopped and windoes, there came a sand storm and sifted dirt and sand all over everything. Then it rained and blew the rest of the night, and of course everything got muddy. Yesterday evening Arthur took us all down town in his carriage; and Saidy bought me a pretty hat. I tell her I like it better every time I see it...The hat is pink and is lined with ribbon of the same kind of which it is trimmed...It cost 3 dollars."

Annie had been gone only two or three weeks when we all came down with the mumps—all except Clara, who for some unaccountable reason escaped; and what a "mumpy" time we had! With towels passed under our swollen and painful jaws and tied up over the tops of our heads, we went around endeavoring to perform our various tasks, unable to take anything but liquids—and those entirely non-acid. To attempt a cup of lemonade was sufficient to cause "conniption fits."

While we were still going through this siege of mumps, into the family of George and Minnie on September nine, came little Pearle Edna; and we could none of us go over to see the baby on account of the danger of carrying mumps.

Something like a week after this event, Artie received a call from the family of Mrs. Poole in Colton to come up there and keep house and care for the mother, who was sick in bed. So Artie sent over for Hulda, who by that time had fully recovered from the mumps, to come and take her place in George's family; and a few days after Hulda's arrival on the scene, took her departure for Colton on the nineteenth of September.

After Mrs. Poole's recovery, Artie secured a position at waiting tables in the Transcontinental, a sixty-room hotel in Colton where once before she had worked for three months in the spring of Eighty-Eight. She took up this work on the first of November and it proved to be the opening of a new chapter in her life.

Our walnuts that year, though plentiful in quantity, were very poor in quality. Unusual heat at the wrong time and dry, hot Santa Ana winds had dried up the hulls on the shells, and many of the nuts, having been blown off the trees before being properly ripened, were blighted. Others, having been arrested in growth, remained small. The crop had previously been sold on contract while on the trees, with the agreement that the nuts should come up to the regular standard. Now it was certain that as a whole the crop would not meet this specification, and since so many nuts were blackened by the adhered hulls, much more time and labor would be required to harvest them.

Lafe came home to see what could be done to remedy the situation, and the boys decided that the crop of nuts would have to be bleached with sulphur. To do this, it was necessary to build a sulphur house. So materials were secured, and Lafe, before going over to Fullers where he had secured a job, put up a small, tightly-built house alongside the drying racks; the walls inside being lined with cleats and supporting arms for the holding of small screen-bottomed racks of nuts. After constructing these racks, he built also a grader, which was used to separate the small nuts from the large; which had formerly been done always by hand-sorting.

As the walnuts were brought in from the orchard, they were placed in these racks on the projecting arms, after first having been dipped in water to facilitate the bleaching process. Down in the center of the dirt floor was set the big brass bucket containing a measured portion of sulphur, after lighting which, the attendant would slip out and shut the door; leaving the nuts exposed to the fumes of the sulphur so long as it burned. Though sulphured, there were still many dark nuts that had to be sorted out by hand.

These helpful additions to the farm equipment were ever afterward used for preparing nuts for the market; for sulphur-bleaching was then commencing to be practiced by growers, and nuts so treated commanded a higher price. But even with all this expense and labor the price received that year was lower than that named in the contract.

Joan had become of age that September; and when Lafe, after finishing the sulphur house and grader went to his job at Fullers, she also, with Mother's consent, went with him, by way of celebrating her legal independence, to work for pay during the fall harvesting of crops similar to our own. So for a number of weeks during our heaviest farm work, the household in Aliso was without her capable hands. But Mother did most of the housework, releasing Hulda part of the time to help with the nuts. Early in November when we were finishing, Joan returned, but only to go away again in a few weeks. She had accepted the invitation of Nellie Fuller to accompany her to Colton for the holidays, which she was to spend at the old home with her mother and numerous brothers, leaving her husband alone on the farm.

During the harvest season we experienced two more of those miserably unpleasant Santa Ana winds, which chapped our hands and faces and caused our hair to snap and crackle. After the last of these had died away about the time of Joan's return from Capistrano, the nights turned sharply cold, for which they compensated by flooding the world with beautiful moonlight.

By this time we were ready to gather the olives, whose ripening clusters betokened a job of several weeks duration. Instead of making pickles that year, Mother had sold the olives on the tree to Lafe, who had paid her twenty-five cents a gallon with the intent of making them into oil as others in the country were beginning to do—a new experiment.

He came home with Joan and assisted in picking the crop and hauling the olives away—for the oil was to be made on presses at Capistrano. The following year he made us a press of our own, setting it up out under the pepper trees, where we made oil for several years.

Though Lafe had filed on the Little Hill as a homestead, he found it very irksome and inconvenient to live out his time there. So after holding it as a homestead for about two years, he decided to have it commuted to a pre-emption claim, which the law allowed, the claimant to pay the government the regular pre-emption fee. He borrowed the necessary money and proved up on the land before the year Eighty-Nine had passed off the calendar.

The Bustle Vanishes

That year witnessed another interesting event. Bustles were dealt their death-blow. Soon after they went out of style—though here and there one persisted for a year or two longer.

The occasion of their discard is said to have been a practical joke played upon the young wife of President Cleveland. The story goes that a group of news-hounds in Washington, while short on news between sessions of Congress, conceived the idea of creating some, and sent a society item to their home papers to the effect that Mrs. Cleveland had decided to outmode the bustle.

When this "bomb" exploded in the papers the next morning, Mrs. Cleveland was as much surprised as the rest of the world. But in her simple graciousness, she decided to treat the report as true rather than embarrass the perpetrators by taking the trouble to contradict it. So she ordered a wardrobe to be made without accommodation for the bustle.

I was about thirteen when the bustle was banished. Hoops had already disappeared, and my youthful dream of soon being able to don grown-up attire was shattered to bits. How abused and cheated I felt! Just as I was approaching womanhood and looking forward with eager anticipation—well, there it is again! Ambitions shattered by an unfeeling world!

Why couldn't they have given me a chance to try it just once? There wasn't a thing left now to mark the difference between a girl and a woman, and I was left as it were, hanging in mid-air, without a chance of showing which I was—Huh! And how flat and unlovely they all looked! It was actually as if a part of them were not there at all!

A Make-Believe Courtship

For many months before Annie went away, thus breaking up our inner circle, we had been playing a continuous game, in which we three girls acted out the characters of Meta, Larry, and Jane—the name "Larry" having been obviously borrowed from "Little Women."

This game had overlapped, rather than interrupted, the culinary and housekeeping activities carried on up under the eucalyptus trees with the old kerosene-can stove. I was Larry, the fond adoring beau of Meta. Annie was said Meta, the charming fiancee. Charlotte was Jane, younger sister of Meta and true friend of Larry.

In this set-up, switched from mother-and-baby scenes, to those of lover-and-sweetheart, is betrayed in its originator the unmistakable beginnings of adolescence.

Our daily duties and other occupations had in no way conflicted with the contemporary pursuance of this "game," but rather had been sweetened by it. Tasks had ceased to be arduous, and disagreeable duties had become pleasures under the soothing influence of this make-believe courtship.

Of course there had been lapses during those times when we happened to be on the "outs" with each other. But always, recovery of harmony had found us back in the same old roles again. Now with Annie so far away, this game closed a chapter. But it was only to re-open with another.

That winter, after the farm work was done up, I began to write ardent "love-letters" to "Meta," signing myself "Larry." These were answered in the same spirit under her own cognomen of "Meta"; and so the game went on by correspondence—my letters keeping her in touch with everyday doings and making romance out of them.

Annie declares that the letters "Larry" used to write her, were the most wonderful love-letters any sweetheart could hope to receive. All the homely doings about the farm were turned into romantic episodes, and there was no lack of warmth and ardor in his courtship. Among other bits of news, interspersed with spicy love-making, he would tell her all about Jane and her doings—how sweet she was, and how she helped to while away the lonely hours. In one such description, he finished by saying: "She is so cheerful! She's laughing now. How I wish I could bottle up some of that laughter and turn it loose on a rainy day!"

All this make-believe was only the last flickering of the lingering candle of childhood; for I was fast growing up into young womanhood, and Annie too, soon lost her appetite for childish things. Gradually, her affections grew away from the Aliso farm and attached themselves, as was natural, to other interests closer at hand. And when once more we were together, everything was different. The canyon home itself had changed, and Annie had changed. From its vital interests she seemed to have grown apart. She had seen a larger world.

CHAPTER 51 VOICES FROM THE PAST

After Mrs. Poole's recovery, Artie secured a position at waiting tables in the Transcontinental, a sixty-room hotel in Colton where once before she had worked for three months in the spring of Eighty-Eight. She took up this work on the first of November and it proved to be the opening of a new chapter in her life.

A number of old family letters recently unearthed, that were written to Artie in Colton that fall and winter, and preserved by her through all the intervening years, furnish such a vivid picture of home life as we lived it from day to day in the canyon, that I am constrained to believe extracts from them will be found of interest to our readers. To me, at least, they have been a most thrilling discovery. It is indeed a unique sensation to learn by such means exactly where one was and what doing at a certain hour of a certain day fifty years ago; and actually to see the childish script of one's own hand and that of playmates, and of other dear hands now folded.

Artie had gone away from George's rather suddenly, on September nineteen—a Saturday—without going around by Aliso to tell Mother goodbye. Getting a late start, George had taken her the shorter way up Laguna Canyon to meet her train at El Toro; but on his return, drove the longer way round through Aliso Canyon to see Mother and explain the omission. He persuaded her to go with him over to Arch Beach for the weekend, and on Monday George took her to town on a long desired shopping trip, returning by way of Aliso to leave her at home.

Soon afterward, George and Minnie, running out of hay for their horses, packed up their belongings and came to Aliso, bringing Hulda home with them; and here they stayed two weeks before starting for San Jacinto. From Colton, Artie had written to Hulda at Arch Beach and these old letters begin with Hulda's answer:

"Thursday, October 10, 1889

Dear Sister Artie: Here I am at last. Don't you think I am awful naughty to delay writing so long after receiving your kind letter? Well, I'll tell you what—I have been pretty busy at work ever since I came home from Minnie's, which is two weeks next Monday, and have hardly found time to even scratch a few lines. We girls have been washing clothes almost all day—got the last of them hung out at dark. Hung the line full of white ones, and while waiting for them to dry, I helped in the house; then brought in the white ones and hung out the colored ones; which are now on the line. We all have very bad colds and Joan is feeling quite badly this evening. Minnie and George packed up and came down here to stay a week or two when I came home...on account of their horses which they wanted to feed well to prepare them for their journey to San Jacinto; and it was very inconvenient to haul feed for so many horses. You can imagine it makes a little more work with them here...We are busy now with the walnuts. I helped a little two days, just enough to get my hands good and black. I don't mind the work a bit—rather like it as a change from housework.

Well, Artie, I guess you did find everything pretty well tumbled up when you got there, but not much wonder after the boys had been keeping house so long. But I presume everything is right side up 'ere this, and each separate piece tucked in its own little corner cosy as can be. Well, I should think you did have quite a crowd there to cook for! Weren't you rather relieved when some of them left! How is Mrs. Poole getting along now? Does she get up in time to breakfast with the rest of you?

And how about the widower with the three children? I should think you did make a "crush"! Was it "love at first sight"? No wonder you enjoyed the dance! Well, I am glad you did. Artie, I promise not to make public any of the little secrets you may write me if you will promise not to quoat anything that I may write in the way of noncence.

Minnie and Baby are not very well just now. Along with the rest, they have some what of a cold. She says tell you she will be very glad to have you write to her, and she will do the same. After you went away I was pretty busy all the time; did not get a chance to touch the stockings that were to mend and didn't even cast a bird's eye glance at the box of fancy scraps Mother brought up. (She came and stayed from Saturday till Monday morning)...I had one bath—wore Annie's bathing dress. Went up the coast shell hunting and picnicing with Nate and Will's folks the Sunday before I came home...I did not enjoy the shell hunting very well—and you know why. Oh Nate is just "too utterly utter" for any use though he did come in and wipe dishes for me twice, and did the churning for me once. Wasn't he kind? Says he would like to have a little girl about sixteen come and keep house for him. (Poor man! Think I shall take pity on him!) Oh, Yes! I had the pleasure of getting acquainted with the honorable Mr. Arthur Bradshaw. He came over and stayed all night with Nate. We played cards and dominoes all the evening. He and I were partners, but we didn't get a game. Mr. B. came out and wiped the supper dishes for me. Wasn't he a little dandy? I think he is real nice. He is studying to become a doctor—will work at his profession this winter. Well, enough of beaux and fellows, or you will think I'm crazy. Lafay has come home for a short time to build a sulphur house for the nuts; which are already sold. The apples are all picked, and such a nice large bin full they make! I helped to pick them. We had a shower of rain the other night—just enough to half spoil some apples that were drying which were left out by mistake...Jess Clark is going to work out a little bill here that he owes George, and in return, Joseph is going to take a load up to San Jacinto for them when they go. Oh, yes! Did you hear about the recent fire? Over a hundred miles in length. The beautiful Sandiargus (Santiago) Canyon is now devoid of all its loveliness. We went up to see it just in time, didn't we? Harry and Tom lost their blacksmith shop, and one of their neighbors lost everything he possessed...Well, I think I have written about all the news of this little valley, so will say goodnight. It has just struck ten o'clock. You must excuse the writing and spelling; for I have just scratched away taking little notice of either.

Your loving sister Hulda

P. S. What wages do you get, if you don't mind my asking?"

Hulda's second letter to Artie was dated:

"November 2, 1889

Dear Sister:

"Your long and interesting letter was received last Wednesday. It came early in the morning but I didn't get time to read it until after breakfast, when I snatched time; and the others went down to work in the nuts without me and left me to follow in the rear. Your letter was so nice. I went and delivered that kiss to Mother as soon as I read it...I am sure it would have been just as well appreciated—and perhaps a little more—if it had have come first handed instead of seckoned. No, I don't think she felt really hurt or hard, that you did not come home before going away; as I had told her how everything was, and that you got such a late start. But she was real disappointed, and wanted to see you before you went. I wonder if you are still at Mrs. Poole's? I'll bet you didn't get off as soon as you expected to. (Artie had gone from there the day before this was penned to begin her work at the Trans-Continental Hotel) I was more than sorry to hear of your great misfortune— that your "Dane" was married. So sad to think that all your bright hopes were blighted! I could have cried, but then as...that wouldn't do any good, I laughed. But don't lose heart, Artie. Just keep a sharp lookout for that widower.

...I have been helping with the walnuts almost all of the last week (they are about all gathered now). Joseph and I sulphuring and sorting the nuts yesterday and today. We sort the black—or darkest nuts from the light ones...There has been a miserable old Santa Ana wind blowing for several days; and it is, oh, so disagreeable to work in. My hands and face are chapped and sore as can be. When I started this letter, I had just got through making the children some honey candy; but I got it a little burned, so it was not very good. Joan and Lafay are still at San Juan at work for the Fullers. We are looking for them home tomorrow, which is Sunday. George and Minnie started on their trip the fourteenth of October. Joseph went with them and got back the twenty-third. He intended to call around and see you all on his return but the rain hindered him from so doing...

(Joseph was gone on this trip nine days. Scarcely had they reached their destination and gotten inside the cabin with their goods, when a big storm broke; for which they were wholly unprepared, having no wood on hand or other necessities for comfort. But they were thankful to be inside under shelter; though it was very hard on the mother and young babe.)

"Yes, we have heard once from Sadie; but that was some time ago. Have not heard from Annie. Isn't she a great correspondent?

I think that by the time Jed comes down, we will be over the greatest of our hurry so that we can enjoy his visit. I hope so anyway. Yes, the mumps are all gone long ago. We are having lovely weather for the nuts. The children all send their love to Artie...Mother is writing some, so I guess you will get all the news...It is lovely moonlight nights; but is so cold that I am almost frozen.

Much love, Hulda"

Mother's enclosure, dated November 2, follows:

"Dear Artie:

I have been intending to write you a few lines ever since you went away, but still kept waiting for a better opportunity, for one cause or another; and did not get to send a word in Hulda's either, as intended; and now, am rather nervous; and it is nearly nine. Yes, I was somewhat disappointed at not seeing you again, but can not blame you altogether; for I knew you were all so slow getting off anywhere that I did not much look for you around this way. George came around and made me go back and stay until Monday. I fully expected to come down a-while...and bring the family to see you; but then thought of the mumps; and Joan was so busy putting up fruit she could not come, and Joseph and Frank were too busy to drive me over. So all I could do was to send the word I did. I hated to, as you had not been home for so long, and I didn't know when you would ever come again; as it is so expensive and inconvenient...I hope that you will sometime not very far distant be ready to come home again for a-while. If at any time you find work too hard, or times dull write and let me know. We can get you home, and will be glad to see you.

George felt kind of bad when the time came to leave. It will be a long time before we will all be together so long a time again. They were here two weeks and then got caught in a big rain before they got one comfort around them. They have moved onto a new place, desolate of everything, to encounter many difficulties unforeseen—like many other new beginners. I feel very sorry for them...The little baby is a jewel...We had such cold damp weather...they took such colds...Oh, we had two spells of Santa Anas, some fog, and now very cold nights.

We have just had to keep right at it all the time steady; for we have had so much more to do than usual to our walnuts to get them in the market presentable. The heat and wind dried and blew them off before they were ready. We have to sort, wash and handle them so much, and shuck so many this year.

We haven't commenced our olives yet; getting winter wood, fixing fences, etc. and the grass is most ready to cultivate under. All our grapevines will be dug up this year. Have only made one barrel of claret. Have got a fine crib of corn, but not enough hay. Four nice looking pigs are running loose yet. If we only had a house and it was even half furnished, and we were not in debt for it, the income might afford us a comfortable living. I sometimes think that if I do not get one soon, something will happen and I will never have one, now the boys are scattering; besides, the extras we have to have on the place. Soon, it will be a new wagon, and a stove. Sometimes I feel rather blue; and then again, I feel quite well satisfied the way everything is going. But if only I were stronger and able to do more, there would be some fun in trying to work. Now I am rather nervous, and every little excitement or worry takes all of my strength and makes me almost sick. I sometimes wonder what I would do with myself if anything very serious should happen. I do not know just how I do feel tonight. I am so cold and sleepy.

Your loving Mother, S. L. Thurston

Hulda's next letter to Artie was written:

"November 19, '89

Dear little Girl:

"Yours was happily received last Saturday. Was glad to hear from you, Artie. No, I did not know where you were working I only knew it was somewhere near San Bernardino. And how does dining-room work go once more? Artie, I do hope that your feet are better now; I was so sorry to hear that they were troubling you again. I know it must be a painful drawback to have corns on one's feet—judging from the trouble my in-growing toenails give me at times. Artie, you see I am following your advice; but I want you to do the same. Don't use your note-paper to write to me on, for cheap paper will do just as well—besides I never look at anything but the writing anyway. I am having some trouble with my teeth of late—was awake almost all of last Sunday night with the toothache. Think about the next time Harry comes down, I will give him the task of drawing them for me, one on either side. And I have to be so careful about taking cold or I have the neuralgia in my face. Have a touch of it now.

I was disappointed a week from last Sunday. Was expecting Jed over, as he had written that he would be here. So we got everything ready and planned what we would do and what a fine time we would have. But he did not come until next day. Said he could not get a horse. Of course everyone knew that I was looking for him, and so they all had the laugh on me—Mother especially. I didn't care for that, but I did feel disappointed. I was sick Monday when he did come—had neuralgia and just the worst kind of a headache; in fact most everything was ailing me. Altogether, I felt thoroughly miserable; so did not enjoy the day very well...He was over again last Sunday; and Nate was here too. We had a real jolly time; played croquet, went walking on the beach in the afternoon, and had singing and music on the organ in the evening. Oh, everything was just exquisite! Joan is improving very fast in her music; can play lots of tunes real nice. Mother and I have been patching all day, and have yet another day or two of it on hand. Mother, Joan, and Joseph are all going to town one day this week...We are still rushed with work, Christmas is near at hand, and there is such a lot that we would like to get done before...I wish it were two or three weeks further off. I am "dead broke," as the saying goes, haven't a cent of money to my name...Joan is going up to Colton with Nellie Fuller to spend Christmas and perhaps New Years. I know it will be dull and stupid down here...We are having rainy weather now—had quite a rain day before yesterday...Oh, we just had the best laugh the other evening—laughed till our sides ached, the best laugh I've had for—I can't tell when. Frank came up to the door and knocked very timidly. Mother went and opened it, and he walked in with a long coat and a hideous old mask on. He that day had his hair shingled, and we didn't any of us know who it was for some time. I tell you, he was a comical picture to look at. He scared the children almost to death. Clara screamed, and scrambled over the chairs; and when she found out who it was, almost went into hysterics...Lafay has just come in with some quails to clean. Oh yes! I was told that you had made quite an impression on a nice young man up there; and since you won't tell me his name, I'll have to ask, won't I?

26th Well, good evening! Here I am again! Have waited just a week for Mother's letter, and now she has finished it, will send this off tonight. Artie, I have not forgotten that tomorrow is your birthday. Wish I had something nice to send you but since I have not, will send you the next best—a nice ripe "cherry" and a good squeeze—the very best to be had."

(Cherry was the name for a kiss then going the round.) Though Hulda did not mention it, the very day on which she was penning these lines was Joseph's twenty-first birthday when, before the law, he became indeed a man.

Mother's letter to Artie which was sent in the same envelope with Hulda's was begun on November 20th and finished on the 26th:

"Dear Artie:

This afternoon the two girls and I went with Joseph over to Will Brooks' to get our spring wagon mended. I have only been down to the store once since George went away. Nettie Goff has a nice little house in Arch Beach and has moved down to live. I have not seen her yet. But I do not know how neighborly we shall be, as our team will be in use so much of the time. We have so much to do that it seems as though we can never get done the things that need doing. We may have to let some things go that have been contemplated. We talk some of cutting down the gum trees; as they are injuring the walnuts by taking the moisture from them. We have to rush to get the ground on the bench prepared for crops before the next rains. We want to put in more olives, as we think there is going to be money in them...Yes, we have concluded that the grape vines will never be worth anything more to us, and the trees planted between them will do better when they are out. Oh, did any one tell you that I sold the geese, the ducks, the two dozen chickens, and Joseph's old boat for a very good little riding horse? I went to town next Monday after you left, and must soon go again. We now will have to buy potatoes, meat, lard, flour, sugar, and so forth. I dread to think of the bill. Schomodore has the store here now, and is selling things at Santa Ana prices. I do not know whether I can afford to get my bedstead or not yet. Sometimes I think I might as well live half comfortable whether I save up or not; but again, I know that we must have a little on hand in case of emergencies. We are getting on very well indoors; it is outside that troubles. Joan has made Harriet's new dress and some other sewing. The girls have lots they wish to do before the holidays...Just received a letter from George tonight. They have had dreadful wind storms and rain and a little ice. Are now in their own house ten by fourteen, and very well satisfied with the outlook; but have had very bad colds, and had some of their things mildewed. George has rented a little of his land, and sold some; which will help him...Harriet is getting so big, folks think I have three young ladies yet at home. Oh my! They all get old and big too fast...Lately, our Sundays seem to be devoted to fixing up and entertaining some kind of company and getting something to eat...but if it is pleasant for the rest, I guess we will get along. No, to be sure, we are not much scattered yet; but I do not believe that George will ever move down here again; and Lafay is liable to go off somewhere if he can make it pay...and Joseph is beginning to think he is old enough to be a man, and look out some for his own interests...and Joan, like all other girls, is looking out for the right fellow—but I am borrowing trouble, and am going to stop. But I can not help looking ahead and thinking what a few short years may bring about.

Nov. 24

Joan, Joseph, and I have been to town; done a little business, made some purchases, stood around and traveled until we have come home almost used up...and not half satisfied; for I never got half I needed, and spent so much. The girls each have a dress and fixings, Frank a suit and shoes, bought quite a costly tool for the farm and some other articles, and paid a standing bill and some other expenses. Spent about forty-five dollars, and glad to get out of town. As it was, I never got meat, potatoes or flour either...Well, we had a letter from Sadie and Annie. She says she likes it there and doesn't want to come home; says she has lots of work to do. But Sadie says she will send her home any time she wants to come (as though she might never have to unless she liked) but says she doesn't know how she could ever get along without her; and that Annie thinks so much of the baby...Lafay has not started at the olives yet; been delayed. I must close; it is late; and if I am as long at my other letters, I will never get through. So goodnight, and kisses from a loving Mother."

Another from Hulda to Artie is dated:

"Dec. 21, '89

Dear Sister Artie:

Here I am again going to answer your nice long letter. It was nice as it could be, though I thought it sounded as if you felt a little gloomy. Dear little Sister (I can call you little <u>sister</u> now for Jed says I am getting fatter every day, and he says he doesn't think you would weigh one bit more than you did last Fourth of July) wish I could see you for a-while and have a nice little talk and a good laugh with you; think I could cheer you up a bit. I wish you could be here Christmas; I think we would have a real nice time.

Joan started off on her two weeks' vacation day before yesterday. We have had so much rain in the last few weeks, the roads were pretty badly washed away. We began to think she wouldn't be able to get out of the canyon. But the boys fixed the roads a little so they are just barely passable. The boys killed a pig today—a large one that we lately bought from Bert Fuller. Mother and I have just got through cleaning the fat off. We had good luck and finished real quick. Harriet is now frying the liver. I must go. They are calling me to come and get some before it is all gone. I'll eat a piece for you. Clara just came in and asked who I am writing to. I said it was Artie. She said: "Oh, it's Artie, is it? Well then, send her my love and three kisses. Harriet sends "best love and a merry Christmas."

I have not had any (or much) trouble with my teeth of late, though they are not drawn...yet. Harry was down here and spent Thanksgiving with us, but of course they didn't ache any while he was here; so didn't have the courage to have them pulled out.

Harry and Jed are well acquainted now...they get along fine together; though Jed hasn't got over calling Harry "Mr. Hughes" yet Don't they make a cute span though? He called Harry the "clown." With all his antics and tricks, I think it is quite appropriate, don't you?...Artie, I got the dearest little letter from Jed the other evening...It was just as nice and friendly as could be...No, I will frankly say, his friendship for me has not diminished in the least. He is just the same dear boy, and I like him better than ever. No, Jed has never yet attempted to kiss me; but I am fully resolved that when he does (if that time ever is) he shall have the little token. No, I do not think there is any harm in a little goodbye kiss, now that we know and care for each other so well. Now Artie, don't you mention this subject to any one; for it is strictly private, you know...The little Thanksgiving menu card is real cute. You had quite a feast, didn't you?

I guess you were pretty busy...Yes, I got all those stockings darned, and darned nine pairs more just the other day—aside from my two dresses. I just gave them a good old patching. Took all my spare time for two days. Yes, Sister, I will be over there and help you some day with your patching...Did I tell you about our black dresses in my last? Well, Joan has got them made up. They just fit to a "tee"...are made just alike and are nice as can be. Joseph says 'Tell Artie I would like to send her some word, but don't know what—unless it be a Merry Christmas; and I guess you'll have so many of them all ready you won't know what to do with them'. I have been making a number of little presents for the little children, and think they will be real pleased with them. I made and worked a white apron for Harriet. No, I don't think it will be such a dull Christmas after all. I am not going anywhere, but will stay home and help the children to have a good time. I am as happy as though I was going to a grand ball; for I don't care a snap about going to any. Dancing, for me, is losing its charm...Artie, Mother and I were going to send some apples up to you by Joan; but she went off in such a hurry that we forgot all about them. No, all the children wear their shoes regularly now. Lafay has made us a cupboard; it's just fine. No, Artie, we havn't got the little stove put up in the front room, and I guess we won't put it up this winter. We sit out in the kitchen as usual at the big table. Mother says it isn't half so nice in the front room.

We have had to patch the carpet all over. It did not wear worth a cent. I will give you George's address: San Jacinto, San Diego County...Don't worry about those old cliffs. If they should fall there is one consolation, we could get out of the way even if everything else went to ruin. But there is not the slightest danger of their falling...Yes, we have lots of neighbors; but we havn't seen any of them, since they came, and don't know when we can see them; can't get down on the coast with the wagon...It has just started to rain again. We have rain one day and sunshine the next. No, we havn't heard how Nettie Goff's property is settled, don't think it is settled yet. We don't know for sure yet as we will cut the gum trees down; we would all hate to see them go...Lafay has made a settlement with that bee man, but did not get his pay all in money. Joseph is waiting, so goodbye, much love from all.

Hulda"

A letter from Annie in Phoenix to Artie in Colton is dated:

"January 5, 1890
Dear Artie:

"Here I am trying to write you a letter. It is so dark and gloomy I have been thinking of home all day. I am not real homesick but oh, how I would like to see them all! We received the cards you sent us. They were very pretty, but you had promised you would not send us anything this Christmas. You brook your promise, so I do not like you. Little Mildred has been sick all the week with a high fever. We think she has the mumps. The rest of us are pretty well. The baby has been in short clothes for about a month; and she is getting sweeter every day; is cute as she can be.

Christmas eve we all went down to Grandma's to a Christmas tree. There was quite a crowd there besides us. Lawrence got a ball and a drum. He was just as happy as he could be. All the evening he went marching around beating his drum and when he went to bed he took it with him. And Mildred got a doll. And now for my presents for I was not forgotten eather. A string of white beads like yours; three bunches of ribbon, a pair of gloves, and a little glass jewel chest that will almost hold my beads, also 50 cts. to say nothing of the candy etc. We had dinner there Christmas day and supper Christmas eve. On my birthday (three days later) I got a gingham dress and 25 cts. all from Grandma B. Now don't you think I faird pretty well? I do. We would have been very glad could we have got something for you and the rest of the folks. You remember the $1.25 you gave me to pay my transfer at Colton. It did not cost me anything. I intended to send it to you long ago but forgot about it. I will send it the first chance I get for I know you must have kneeded it a dozen times.

Your loving sister Annie.

In the same envelope with this was a note from Sadie; in which she says:

"My worry now is about you. I fear for you if that new disease reaches Colton, as I hope it will not. Annie and I have been thinking of you ever since we heard of it."

The "New Disease" was the "Influenza," or "La Grippe," which that year swept the whole country. At Aliso we all had it in January, finishing up in the forepart of February; and about the same time Artie also had it in Colton.

A letter from Mother to Artie is dated:

"Jan. 7, 1890
Dear Artie:

The rain is such that we can hardly get along with anything. I am getting even with my correspondence (no less than seven letters and the oldest, one and a half months) while waiting for back mail (can't get to the post office to get). I received a note from Arthur. Am going to send them the last apples I have...if I can find a hundred pounds. Many have spoiled. We couldn't get out with them, nor others come in for them...but we have realized lots of benefit from them ourselves. I felt so provoked that we did not send a few to you by Joan—thought of it the night before...I might have sent you some nuts too. But we always have such a time to get off anywhere and it was a bad morning.

This year is terrible. The floods came so early. Down at the pond they have washed out the road to the last wagon track, and have cut bad above the gate in the pasture. The boys have been working for three or four days fixing it, and now it is raining and the water is up again. I spent one night in a state of worry. But I am not going to again this winter. We cannot plow or do anything that should be done first, it keeps so wet. The weeds are waist high. We are digging up fig trees the other side of the walnut orchard to put in olives. I havn't been on the coast but once since George went away, and will not be able to this winter. I have not seen Nettie.

Oh, that cute little present was so appropriate and admired—Thanks. I was so sorry I didn't know Joan would stop in Santa Ana before coming up there; but that is the luck. I haven't been to town for so long. (Mother means that had she known, she would have had Joan buy a present to take to Artie) Lafay has just been to town. Had a terrible trip; brought home three hundred pounds of flour (six sacks) and one of potatoes at two cents a pound...Just had a letter from George. I think it is rather poor times with them. Everything is so high and scarce, no money, and it's so dangerous to go in debt these dull times. He can't work much it's so rainy; and he must get seed and things to put in crops; and if he borrows, interest is eighteen to twenty per cent on ninety days' time, and he would have to mortgage his team. He broached the subject of borrowing a little from me—says he would rather pay the interest to me than somebody else. I feel sorry for him for I have been through the mill several times. He seems to be hopeful, and wrote a nonsensical letter that kept us all laughing. Minnie said they had only had two and a half rolls of butter since they went up there; and no chickens—get milk of a neighbor. Lafay brought your letter home yesterday. I am having by way of variety, the tooth-ache, and cold in the whole side of my head. But on the whole, I feel very well satisfied and quite comfortable, if I never see any worse time. We have meat and butter a-plenty now. A little heifer not quite two years old, has come in. Her mate a little older, died just before I came home. Have no apples of course; sold the last for three cents. Good, wasn't it?

From your loving Mother, S. L. T.

Another letter from Hulda to Artie, bears the date:

"February 14, 1890

Dear Artie: Here I am at 8 P. M. Valentine's evening. This letter is my valentine to you. Please do tell me how to answer that nice long newsy letter of yours. It is so good. When it was handed to me, I was just beginning a big five-weeks' washing, and didn't get a chance to read it until I went to bed at night...You will wonder how we came to have such a large washing on hand. It was on account of the sickness and rainy, foggy weather. We all had a turn at the "influenza," commonly known as "La Grippe." Well, we got the washing and starching all out in one day. That was Friday; and a bigger pile of dirty clothes I never wish to see—that is, if I have to wash them. We scrubbed floors, washed windows and blackened stove the next day...took Sunday for resting, and ironed on Monday. We both ironed together and got everything ready to put away in four and a half hours. Weren't we lame though, the day after we washed! I got a letter from George the other day. They have all been sick too, but are getting better. He says he has been blowing his nose for the last two weeks. Lafe has just got a job at mining up in Trabuco (Silverado) Canyon. Joseph took him up there this morning; will be back tomorrow. I was glad to hear from you, and doubly glad to hear that you are well and happy—with such a cozy little room too...and a room mate that you like...You say "if" you "each just had a beau now"—that won't do at all. You said some one called; but didn't give any name. You needn't be such a "sly puss" about it...I have just started to practise on the organ—can play the chords quite well, and now I am going to learn the notes. I like it real well. Jed has been over once since he has been in this part of the country—that was Sunday before last, and he will be over next Sunday. The little rogue! Didn't he give me a good surprise though? I did not know he was within eighty miles of here till I saw him. Joan said to me: "Come out on the porch where it is cool"; I walked out, and there he stood talking with Joseph; and you can judge of my surprise. I looked at him half a minute before saying a word; and then told him I didn't know him. That was the best surprise I have had in a long time. He and Joan arranged it between them when she met him in Colton, to give me the surprise; and I gave them both a good whipping. Don't you think they deserved it? I and some of the rest were about sick with the grippe, though; but I had a good old time. The boys played a game of croquet, and then we took a walk—walked almost from one end of the farm to the other; and finally, finding a nice seat, sat down and talked. Don't you think I am crazy to write so much on one subject?...I forgot to say that Harriet is practising too on the organ. The last floods that we had washed the end of the apple orchard off—ten feet or more; and fifty feet of the pepper trees away. And up at the old second gate, it has washed a long way inland and left a bank about twenty feet high. The road down to the pond is also badly cut out clear up to the hill. One can not pass that point of rock even on horseback. Joan and I have been cutting out and making dresses for the last four or five days, and Harriet and Charlotte have been working out of doors helping to haul tree-trimmings; but they are through with that now. I made me a dress yesterday...It looks real pretty. Joan cut it out and together we basted it the afternoon before. She also cut out and made one each for Harriet and Charlotte, and cut out one for Mother which is not made yet. I have been making buttonholes and sewing on buttons today. Don't dread answering this just because it's long....Jed says it's nice to get a long letter because one can leave out all he doesn't care to answer and still have enough left to make a good-sized letter...Frank scared me the other day with a dead wild-cat, so that I just screamed with fright. It struck eleven some time ago, and everyone else is in bed and asleep so goodnight.

Eleven A.M. next day. Morning work done and almost time to get dinner. Joan is sewing on Mother's dress. Harriet and Charlotte have gone down to Arch Beach to wear their new dresses and spend the day; so I had most of the work to do. I am baking bread now. Joseph has just come back and every one at the mines is sick with La Grippe...(Luella says to tell Artie she wants to say something, but don't know what to say.) Oh, those poor chapped hands! I do hope they are well by now. It is a shame to have to work when you are sick. Yes, it is a good plan to wear something on the hands when at work out of doors. The children say that hereafter they are going to wear old stocking legs when they hoe. Harriet says she will write you; but I doubt if she could find much to say at present that is not already said. I suppose you know that Jed has engaged to work at San Juan Capistrano for a year.

Five P.M. I have just got through making pumpkin pies. They're good; come and get a piece. Mother says you wouldn't know me, I have such a round face and—oh yes, I forgot to tell you that Joan and I have got our hair banged. It is real becoming; and mine are wavy—only curl them once or twice a week. But after all, I guess I am not much changed; for Jed said he thought I always did have bangs. Isn't he observing?...You dear little sister! I'd like to play "aunty" for a while and give your stockings and everything else that needed mending a regular good old overhauling. Yes, it was kind of George to send Mother that set of bedroom furniture. It was such a nice surprise; and Mother was real pleased with it. No, bless your heart, Harriet nor I have not had a chance to wear our worsted dresses yet. Oh yes, Harriet has worn her dress once—and that to the last Thanksgiving dance. It is very becoming. I have not been out of this canyon since that time. No Harry has not been down here since Thanksgiving. Well Artie, I will have to finish this and close; for Frank is sitting here waiting to take it to the post...Love from all, Your sister

Hulda."

A note from Mother enclosed in the same envelope, reads:

"Feb. 14, 1890
Dear Artie: Your nice long "proxy" letter came to hand. I am always glad to hear of all the changes, and good news.

I should like to drop in now that you have a fire in your little sitting room. It must be quite cozy. I'm not so sure about knocking though. I might look in at the keyhole first. Too bad about your not having a Mother "around to watch you" and being able to do "as you please." I suppose 'ere this you have...got him well initiated in the art of choring. If you only had some of our wood to bring in now, you would think you might be done with it. Oh dear, how bad you must have felt to be dragging around sick and trying to work! The Grippe leaves a person's system so bad...I escaped with only a cold—was surprised that Clara had it so light. I think we are in a good place in time of epidemics. The atmosphere is pure, and I have heard it is more healthful in the region of blue gums. Well, I'm better satisfied with my home than I used to be. If we can only keep from being washed out, and can get along with our work. But there are four or more months, commencing in the fall, when we do have lots to do. I don't know what we should have done the past months if Lafay had not been here. He could go to town (when the teams could go) and rustle up trade—dispose of nuts, apples, and so forth, so that we made more off of them, and got in supplies. We have disposed of most everything we had; and now our scant butter and eggs do not bring in more than "pin-money" but we have all we need to use. On the whole, I have enjoyed myself at home with my family very well. It is almost three months since I have been away from the house; penned up worse than ever before...The last six months have gone by quick. I hope time will never drag.

With love and kisses to you,
Mother"

The last of these old-time family letters to Artie, is one from Harriet, written on Sunday, March nine, Eighteen Ninety, the day after her fourteenth birthday. For some time previously, Artie had been urging her to send some of her poetic attempts.

Between them, some former joke has given Artie the sobriquet of "Toughie Kellie"; and thus, does Harriet, still in the age of "make-believe," address her:

"Toughie Kellie:

My Dearest Old Friend: I have just finished washing dishes, and thought I would call around and have a chat. Everything is quiet now; I have no fear of being disturbed. How are you prospering? We are all well and happy. Joan and Hulda are in sewing fancy work; and Mother is reading to them. I suppose you know what I am doing just now. Let me see, what is the latest news? Oh, this is. I am bigger (I mean taller) than Joan, Ma, Hulda or Frank; and you must measure yourself to see if I'm not bigger than all of you. I'll be boss of the situation then, won't I? Our heights are as follows: Ma 5—1 1/2; Joan 5—1 2/12; Hulda 5—1 3/4; Me 5—3 7/12. (Evidently Frank objected to being measured). It is rather late to thank you for those nice New Years cards you sent, but all the same we are much obliged for them, and thought them real cute. The children were just tickled with the, and are going to keep them as long as they can. Friday, we children were working out; Saturday it rained; and it is Sunday today.

Last Sunday "Jeddie" and Mr. Brumbly were over. Duke is down to Arch; was here the other day. Really, Artie, there isn't much news to tell, only gossip. Ma, Joseph, and perhaps Hulda are going to town before long. We girls went down to the ocean last Wensday, and had a "way up time," and a bath. It's kind of lonesome lately. I've been wishing you were home; but 'if wishes ware horses, beggars might ride. ' We would have some nice moonlight strowles, wouldn't we? "If."

How did you pass Valentine's day? It was rather dry here; we stayed to home and worked the same as usual. I was fourteen years old yesterday; but didn't have any fun. Though I was glad it rained so I wouldn't have to work out doors. Hulda and I are learning to play on the organ; we practise every day that we have time; and are quite a long way over in the book.

A little "bird" told me that you wished to see some of my g-r-a-n-d poetry; but I am afraid you won't have a good opinion of me or it, after you have read it; so I hardly dare send any. But if you promise not to show it to any one, I'll send you one or two pieces...When you write, you must tell all the news you can find. I can't think of any questions to ask, but you must ask lots, so I can think of something to write next time...I guess the influenza or La Grip, as some call it, went the rounds; everyone all over the world has had it more or less; and some very severly. We had it long ago, and every one down here. Without any exageration, I am perfectly ashamed of my writing; but I am all out of practise and need some one to correspond with to keep me in time. I didn't feel just like it today, or I could have written a better and longer letter. But you must excuse me this time and write soon. With best wishes and many kisses, I remain your loving 'friend' Harriet."

The "poetry" was on a separate sheet; but that I spare you, except only the titles preceded by the heading.

"Here is a sample of my famous 'poims'

"Think Twice" (a dissertation on temperance), "His Last Words," and "Sad Thoughts."

Then followed an appended list of others:

"Titles to the 'poims' I have no space to copy":

"The Old Story	*Neighbor Judy*
As In Childhood	*Words Lie, But Not Tears*
A Memorial	*The Reason Why*
Forget-me-nots	*A Last And Long Goodbye*
A Soldier	*Farewell*
Time And Patience	*The Mitten*
That Handkerchief	*Contentment Wins*
Long Ago	*Law And Justice"*

"Now you can just criticise if you want to; and if you have any suggestions to make, make them. You will get sick before you read them all.

There, I hope your whim is gratified.

H.E.T."

CHAPTER 52 A TRIP TO MARKET

From the foregoing correspondence, it has been derived that the rainy season of Eighteen Eighty-Nine and Ninety was unusually wet, the family being penned in more or less all winter. On their last trip to town in late November they came away without getting flour or potatoes. So it came about that sometime in December they ran out of these commodities completely; and it became necessary that someone take into town a load of farm produce and bring back a load of flour, potatoes and other provisions.

This trip to Santa Ana, whose healthy growth during the past decade had made of it a fairly respectable market for the produce of surrounding farms, was undertaken on the third of January, by Lafe—then acting as "handy man" about the place; who packed the lumber wagon carefully for the journey.

First, he spread down loose hay in the bed of the wagon to serve the double purpose of "shock absorber" and provender for the team of horses. On the top of this hay, he placed sacks of almonds, boxes of apples, and cases of eggs; covering the boxes over with a few boards nailed loosely in place. On top of these boxes of apples and eggs, he spread "gunny sacks," and upon these, set in place a bottomless flat-topped coop full of young cockerels. Then, tucking in some farm implements for possible—and very probably—emergencies, he mounted the high spring seat and set out on his uncertain journey.

The Aliso Canyon road crossed the winding creek eight times between our place and the old stagecoach road that intersected it at right angles ten miles up the canyon. It was our custom to leave the Aliso road at this intersection, and turning northward to the left follow the old stage road into town.

The first crossing, between our filaree pasture and the mustard patch, Lafe found to be full of quicksands brought down by the recent floods; and to make it fordable by wagon, it was necessary to pack down the sands by much trampling until reasonably firm; otherwise, the wagon, with its load, would sink down into the quicksands and become hopelessly stuck. So Lafe unhitched the horses, took off his own shoes and breeches, and drove the team back and forth across the creek till the sand in the roadway was settled; after which he dressed himself, hitched the team to the wagon again, and proceeded on up the canyon.

The second crossing, he found to be much worse. Besides being full of quicksand, the flood waters had cut away the road itself, leaving the bed of the creek deeper than it had heretofore been, with a low, sharp bank on the farther side that had to be worked down with his shovel. After repairing the road, and trampling the quicksand as before, Lafe again hitched up the team, dressed himself, and resumed his journey.

In this manner, he passed all eight of the crossings, with more or less repair work along the line; and finally reached the old stagecoach road. Here, meeting up with other men, he learned that the old road to Santa Ana was utterly impassable, due to deeply washed-out gullies that crossed the highway at various places. These had not as yet been repaired; although work on the road was in progress.

So there was nothing left for Lafe to do but continue on the Aliso road that passed through El Toro—a mile further on—crossed the Whiting ranch, and made connections with the old Trabuco Canyon road into Tustin and Santa Ana.

El Toro was a mile behind him when the slanting sun warned him that darkness was not far in the offing. He had covered that day all told, a distance of about twelve miles. A deep gulch lay before him which had to be crossed, and as he approached this, slowing down the team accordingly, he heard some distance behind him, the sound of a rooster crowing. Stopping the team, he looked back. There in the road, about a quarter of a mile to the rear, stood one of his own cockerels, crowing as if he owned the world.

Examination of his load revealed the cause of the culprit's escape. One corner of the coop had slipped past the corner of the egg-case on which it rested; and the rooster had simply dropped out of the bottom by the natural law of gravity. And there he stood, unfettered in the middle of the road, decidedly master of the situation. The question now was how to get him back into the coop. A rooster loose on an open plain is somewhat more of a problem than the same perched on the roost of a hen-house.

Lafe tied up his reins to the iron arm of the seat, and went back to try his powers of persuasion on the young cockerel. But the cockerel was not to be persuaded. Lafe was pretty good at running, but the cockerel was a little better. Lafe could also play the game of dodge fairly well; but the cockerel was past master of the art. After both man and bird had run till they were well-nigh exhausted, the bird could still not be caught because of his ability to out-dodge every movement of his pursuer.

Lafe then reasoned that if he could get the rooster over to the wagon, he might fly up onto it and there give him his chance to grab him by the legs. So he herded the weary, panting bird over to the vicinity of the wagon. But so exhausted was the bird that he could not lift his wings, and simply went under the wagon for a breathing spell. It would not do to let him rest and recuperate, so under the wagon, went Lafe after him, and out on the other side, went the rooster, and took refuge under the horse's belly. Out from under the wagon and under the horse's belly went Lafe; and out from under the horse's belly and under the wagon went the rooster.

After playing this game of tag for awhile to no definite conclusion, Lafe thought of the horse whip. By using the long lash of this whip, he got the rooster into the notion of leaving the neighborhood of the wagon, and once more in the open pursued him with the whip. After a few passes, he succeeded in wrapping the lash around the neck of the wabbling bird, and drew him into his loving embrace—a sadder and wiser cockerel, glad to return to the lesser world of his own protecting coop.

All this diversion had consumed precious time. Anxious to get onto the Trabuco road before dark, Lafe hastened forward, crossing the deep gulch without mishap. A little further on, the road led down a muddy slope where the horses almost floundered; and there, in the midst of the mud, the wagon bogged hopelessly—three wheels sinking down into the mud up to their axles. Here was a "pretty mess!" Lafe unhitched the horses from the wagon and drove them on across the miry area to firm ground beyond; then rolling up his pants, went back to see what he could do about getting the wheels up out of the bog.

Putting his weight to one of the wheels, he sank knee-deep into the mud. It was no use for him to try to lift it out; the weight of the load was more than he could budge. So he began to unload the wagon, taking out a portion of the heaviest stuff; the biggest problem being the shifting of the coop without freeing the fowls. He then took some of the hay and stuffed it under the wheels; and taking out the three end-gate boards, put them one before each of the three bogged wheels. Then, with much heavy straining, he succeeded in lifting one of the rear wheels out of its hole and onto one of these boards. He then went to another wheel and tried his prowess on that one. It likewise yielded, and he raised it up onto another board. The last, and left front wheel on the down-hill side, was thus left to bear the brunt of the load while still deeply buried in its muddy rut. This one refused to respond to his strenuous efforts. Though by this time almost too fatigued to keep his feet, he struggled and strained to lift that wheel high enough to shove the board under it; but every time failed to "make the grade," and the wheel would sink back into the muddy depths again, till finally he was obliged to give it up.

By this time, the sun was setting, and Lafe realized that he could not go farther that night; but must return to El Toro and find a place to stay till morning. He re-loaded the wagon to protect the goods from possible depredations, and covered the chickens to secure them as far as possible from the prowling coyotes, then bringing his horses back across the bog, re-traced his way to El Toro.

On his way up, earlier in the day, he had passed the wreckage of a small cabin that had tumbled down. He purposed to secure some of these boards next morning with which to build a road in front of his wagon across the bog. Hunting up the owner of the wreckage, he made arrangements to do this, and stayed with him that night.

Early the following morning, this young man loaded the lumber into his own conveyance and hauled it up to the scene of distress. Together, he and Lafe lifted the sunken wheel out of the mud onto the board. After this they built a temporary crossing out of the boards brought along for the purpose, and succeeded in rolling the wagon over them to firm ground beyond. Lafe then paid off his assistant and host with a part of his apples and many expressions of gratitude, and went merrily on his way.

The Trabuco road joined the old stage road several miles short of Tustin, thus completing the triangle detour taken by our hero. Having had a fairly early start, he made good time until he reached the slough where Father had camped sixteen years before. Here, he found a muddy tract about two hundred yards wide, full of deep ruts where wagon wheels had dug down to the axles in mire, and had crossed and re-crossed each other, this way and that, crisscross fashion, at right angles and diagonally, in an effort to straddle the previous ruts. It took some time to get across this bog, but the feat was finally accomplished; leaving more straddling ruts behind.

When Lafe finally reached Santa Ana, it was too late to do much business that day. So he drove out to the house of a friend—a Mr. Holcomb who had a five-acre farm to the Northwest, just out of town, and spent the night there. In order to get Lafe's load under shelter—for the weather appeared threatening, as if more rain were imminent—Mr.

Holcomb took his own single "rig" out of the barn to make room for him to drive inside. Lafe unhitched and unharnessed his horses, and after watering and feeding, tied them to the back of the wagon for the night, and went out of the barn, closing the door after him.

In the morning, Lafe went out to the barn, unfastened the door, and untied the halter of one of the horses to back him out. This was necessary to make room in the narrow space for him to reach and untie the halter of the other. In doing this, he accidentally lost his hold of the halter rope of the first horse. This caused him no concern, as both animals were very gentle and easily handled.

He led the second horse to the watering trough, expecting the first one to follow. But instead of doing so, the horse stepped to one side and began to browse on the green growing barley nearby. Lafe, leaving the one at the trough drinking, stepped over to pick up the halter rope of the one that was browsing. But the horse sidled away out of his reach. So he returned to the drinking horse to tie him up while catching the first one. But, behold, the other horse, having finished his drinking, had left the trough and was also browsing on the green barley. Lafe reached for his rope, and he too sidled away from him.

It seemed that both animals felt just frisky enough that they preferred not to be caught, and kept moving on just out of his reach, as he would approach them with coaxing words. Their halter ropes were only about six or eight feet long; and they kept far enough ahead of him that he could not pick up either of the ropes. In this way, he followed them clear across the barley field, endeavoring to coax them into being caught; but to no avail. When the two horses reached the other side of the field, they suddenly decided to make a spree out of the occasion, and kicking up their heels, bolted as fast as they could toward town.

Lafe was in for it now, and no mistake. Mr. Holcomb hitched up his mare in the single "rig," and together they drove toward town looking for the horses. They made inquiries along the way, and it seemed that plenty of people had seen a pair answering to their description, "one black and one bay," and could point out the direction in which they had gone. But no horses did they find.

Clear through the town of Santa Ana, and on through Tustin, they passed, looking everywhere and inquiring.

"Yes, we saw them. They went on down the highway—one black and one bay" was the usual answer they received; which encouraged the two hunters to go on and on.

Finally, they came to the wide stretch of muddy wheel tracks at the slough. From there they could see, several miles farther on in the distance, some horses, which appeared to be those they were seeking. Thus encouraged, they wallowed through this bog and went on. As they drew nearer, it was disclosed that these horses were on the other side of a pasture fence, and so could not possibly be those they were after; which closer inspection confirmed. So, turning about, they straddled back through the bog again.

Much time had been consumed in following this false scent; and still nothing had been accomplished. There was another road—a shortcut, that led down past Sycamore gulch, also in the general direction of home—and Lafe was convinced that the animals had started for home. So they made for this shortcut. As before, inquiries brought out the information that two horses had been seen on that road—"a black and a bay," running. They turned now, feeling sure of being on the right track, and kept on in a direction southwest of Tustin, till the road turned at right angles, cutting around the corner of a young barley field.

Here, they saw fresh tracks of two horses, who had cut across the corner of the field instead of turning with the road. Lafe got out of the rig to investigate. A close examination of these tracks might reveal to him some familiar mark on the hoof of the horse that made it, or, such being absent, eliminate them as the horses in which they were interested. What he found was this: a fine, gauzy spider web stretched across one of the tracks all covered with dew.

"These are not our horses," he said, getting up from his knees. "These tracks were made last night."

Thus baffled, they hardly knew what to do; but decided to turn around and go back to town. Reaching town, they again inquired concerning the missing team. Someone told them that a pair of horses had been taken up that morning by the Smithwick Livery Stables. Now Smithwick was an old friend of Lafe's; and thither he went without delay. Sure enough! There he found the miscreants, where they had been stabled for hours; having been taken into custody very shortly after bolting. By this, Lafe and Holcomb knew that not one of their voluble informants had seen a hair of them.

The day was by this time so far advanced that Lafe had barely time to dispose of his produce, buy some general provisions, and engage a load of flour at the mill to be called for the next day; after which he returned to Holcomb's and passed another night with him.

Before morning, it was pouring down rain and another storm was upon them, blowing heavily from the south. This situation presented an unpleasant difficulty to Lafe, with a load of several hundred pounds of flour to haul home in an uncovered wagon. How to manage it was a question he must solve; for that flour simply must not get wet. Out to the mill he went in the downpour. Here the miller helped him to solve his problem. Over each sack of flour, they slipped a waterproof jute bag, as they loaded them onto the wagon, for which Lafe paid extra, and with his load thus protected started for home in the black storm.

He decided to take the shortcut, depending upon the road men to have finished repairs during the past three days of sunshine, and thus avoid the spraddling bog at the s lough and the other bog above El Toro, which he had crossed on boards. This road down past Sycamore Gulch ultimately connected with the old stagecoach road; and if he made it home before the present storm had brought other wash-outs, he was reasonably sure of a safe trip. And so it proved. No more difficulty was experienced on account of road washouts. But there were swollen crossings to ford. Lafe drove all the way in the teeth of the storm reaching home on the night of the fourth day of his trip to market twenty-five miles distant.

The Birth of a Pageant

Two days before this trip was undertaken, on New Year's Day of Eighteen Ninety, an event of purely local interest and seemingly insignificant, took place about fifteen miles northeast of Los Angeles in the small town of Pasadena, known until five years previously as "The Indiana Colony."

Here was held a "Rose Parade," the first of its series, sponsored by the "Valley Hunt Club," founded more than a year before. This first parade was a very simple affair, privately financed by the participants, all of whom were residents of Pasadena and vicinity. The citizens entered their own carriages, surreys, buggies, coaches, spring wagons and other conveyances then in use, gorgeously decorated with flowers from their own ,gardens and those of friends. This artistic celebration was intended as "a greeting of flora to fruits," and given in honor of the ripening orange.

Its founders little dreamed of the proportions to which in the future would grow this annual celebration. They could not visualize either the magnitude of the pageant or the phenomenal growth of the small town to a great city, and that forty-nine years later, the fiftieth repetition of their simple celebration would have become the great Tournament of Roses with entrants from all over California, calling together hundreds of thousands of sightseers from all over the nation, to become a major traffic problem of the Southland.

Lafe's Eyes Again

Lafe had gone to the mines to work as mentioned by Hulda in her letter of February fourteen—however, not in Trabuco as she stated, but in Silverado Canyon. But it was not long until he was home again with very badly infected eyes. The symptoms resembled those of erysipelas, with which the family was familiar, since Mother had formerly been subject to its attacks.

For several weeks he was patiently treated as for that malady. The symptoms gradually subsided, and when it appeared that he was well again, he returned to the mines to work. But within three days he was as bad as ever.

He then went to Santa Ana to consult a doctor. In this town there was a travelling eye-specialist of whom he was told, and to him he took his problem. The doctor informed him that his trouble was not at all erysipelas, but that his eyes had been poisoned, probably from the fumes of sulphur used in the mining processes. So Lafe quit the mine for good and went home again to recover.

After this he became acquainted with a young woman of Santa Ana named Lulu Wheeler, who taught Crayon Portraiture. He decided to take lessons of her in portrait making. For some months he studied this art during his spare time from other occasional jobs, learning to do very creditable work. Among his pictures was a life-size portrait of Mother and another of himself, which displayed not a little artistic talent.

This was of course nothing at which he could earn a living, and the first of the following January found him cutting wood in Santa Ana—a calling more prosaic but more remunerative. Toward the last of the month he went to work for Mr. Wheeler, the father of his fair teacher, in Redlands, and when this work gave out, found a job with Mr. Saunders, at which place he was working when next brought into my story.

CHAPTER 53 A LAMPLIGHT ESCAPADE AND AN ALISO WEDDING

Annie's stay in Phoenix lengthened into three years. During that time, many changes took place at the Aliso Farm and in the lives of different members of the family.

One of the first of these changes, was the sorrowful digging up of our now dead and dying vineyard, in December of Eighty-Nine, four months after her departure. All over the country it was the same. Beautiful vineyards had succumbed to the strange and devastating disease that nobody understood and nobody could check. Fourteen years before, the little cuttings had been set out and nursed with tender care; and for ten years had borne their luscious fruit. Now all that was but a memory. We had been obliged to stand by helplessly and see them slowly die, and the vintage cut down to a few paltry pounds; and then to see them dug up and hauled to the woodpiles to be cut up for firewood. It was saddening. How could we get along without our grapes? Always, we had feasted on them from the time they first began to change color in the summer till the last grape was gone in the late fall. Nothing could ever take their place. It seemed as though half the farm was gone, and that a familiar friend had been laid to rest. We missed the income too of course. But the wine-making itself had never had the approval of the family. None of us ever used the wine, nor did it ever appear on our table. Making it had been from the first an expedient in order to realize financial benefit from the crop otherwise unmarketable. The young apple trees that had been set out between the vines, were of good size, but not many of them yet in bearing; and now other trees were planted here and there to fill out the rows.

Soon after these stumps lay piled in a great heap, between road and orchard in the woodpile area, the trail of a snake was discovered one day leading to the edge of the heap. As days went by, fresh trails would appear to and from the place crossing the roadway, by which we knew that a snake of some kind had taken up his abode there. But what kind could not be determined though by the size of the track it was certain that he was a big one.

One day that February, Joseph and Joan went into town—Mother having decided not to accompany them; for a day's "running around town" was harder on her than a day's work. That afternoon, however, she decided to go over to Arch Beach to visit Nettie Goff; whom she had not seen since she had come to occupy her cottage there. Secretly, Mother had been cherishing a desire to ride the little saddle horse she had traded for in the fall, whose gentleness and dependability had now been proven. With the older young folks gone, who might have protested against this unusual proceeding—for though Mother may have been a horse-woman at one time, she most certainly was out of practice, this being the only time I ever knew her to mount a horse—she asserted her independence, and had Frank saddle up the horse for her, and assist her to mount, sitting sideways on the man's saddle. We all watched her ride out of the yard encouraged at seeing how well she sat, and devoutly hoping that nothing would happen to her. Then we went to our various tasks.

Joseph and Joan were not expected home from town till late at night, and when dusk fell, Mother had not yet returned either. Frank and I did up the chores, and then he slipped away up the canyon to spend the evening-as was becoming quite a habit with him, in spite of Mother's oft expressed disapproval—at the cabin of one of the sheepherders, with whom he was friendly. The kerosene lamp had been lighted in the kitchen. Hulda, who had been left in charge of the household, was reading a story by its light to the three youngest children—Charlotte, Luella and Clara, all seated around the table; while I, in the deepening darkness, was returning on my way up to the house from the barn.

As I came opposite the woodpile—thoughts in the clouds as usual-I was startled "out of a year's growth" by the sudden, blood-chilling sound of a rattler, so close under me it might have issued from my own pocket. And there at my feet just leaving the woodpile lay the dim outlines of a snake stretched across the road.

With a piercing shriek that splintered the silence of that quiet evening into shreds, I bounded on over the horrible creature and up the steps onto the porch, "white as a sheet," shaking from the shock, and shouting at the top of my voice, as I burst through the door into the room:

"There's a big rattlesnake out here! I nearly stepped on him! I nearly stepped on him! I NEARLY STEPPED ON HIM!"

Hulda had jumped up at the sound of that first terrified yell, and met me at the door. First satisfying herself that I had not been bitten, she demanded where I had seen the snake, then commanding:

"Get the hoe!", grabbed up the lamp.

We got two hoes—Hulda taking one and I the other—and with the lamp held high, flickering its feeble gleam around us in the outer air, we sallied forth; grim vengeance determined in our faces against the deadly foe. Hulda tried to induce the younger members of the company to stay in the house. But with the lamp gone, they utterly refused to be left in the dark, so trailed after us as we formed in battle array.

It did not for a moment occur to any of us that we should leave the snake alone and not attempt to hunt him after nightfall. Our mental operations did not admit of such a thing. There was that "law of the Medes and Persians" ingrained too deeply for such compromise—besides, who could tell in that event, if we should ever again have the opportunity to rid ourselves of his lurking terror?

So, in the flickering light of the kerosene lamp, we cautiously made our way to the spot where the snake had been seen. He was not there. But his trail was easily traced slantwise across the soft dust of the road to the further side. Here, it was different. A thick growth of weeds made tracking impossible. But, reasoning that he would likely continue in the same general direction in which he had been headed we began cautiously to explore from that point of entry.

Having transferred the lamp to the hands of Charlotte, and bidden the younger children to remain in the road, we began chopping around with our hoes fan-like, keeping the length of a hoe-handle between us and the unexamined area on every side. Slowly and cautiously we proceeded in the general direction of the sulphur house and the empty drying racks beyond, daring not to set our foot on any spot that had not first been proven safe. Finally, reaching the racks, we were rewarded.

"There he is!" "There he is!" we shouted in exultant and unanimous excitement. And there he was still crawling on his way toward the hillside.

Then, while Charlotte held the lamp in proper position, Hulda and I went after him. Whacking in a region near his head, the hoe of one finally pinioned and held him by the exertion of every ounce of strength, his body coiling and lashing about. Then the other hoe came down nearer the middle of his writhing, muscular body and held him while the first hacked at his head, sometimes striking and sometimes missing it, but at last succeeding in severing it from his writhing body. Then we could breathe more easily. This head, we buried to prevent any cat or dog from finding it, but the rattles we cut off to preserve as a trophy and evidence of the vanquishment of our foe. Then back to the house, filed the triumphant lamplight brigade, thrilled with their success, and rejoicing in the possession of a snake-free woodpile.

All was quiet again before Mother arrived home in safety; but when she heard of our exploit, though relieved to know the rattler was dead, she yet chided us for being so foolhardy as to go after him in the dark. Poor Mother had plenty to worry about, with her numerous brood, and somebody always up to something.

Joan's Wedding

Another family event which Annie missed by being absent from the fireside, was Joan's birthday wedding on the second of September, Eighteen Ninety. This was the first and only family wedding that ever took place at home in Aliso.

The house had been scrubbed till it shone. Every unsightly thing had been hidden away. The windows and wall pictures were decorated with evergreen boughs from the pepper trees, then hanging full of their red berries. Such flowers as could be procured decorated shelves and tables; and the front room where the event was to take place, looked its best; with a bower of green arched across the corner where the couple was to stand.

The bride looked lovely in the beautiful, but simple, white dress that her own hands had fashioned; howbeit somewhat tired; for she had worked day and night to get ready for the event. New dresses for the occasion had been made for all six of the others and a number for herself.

The proud and happy bridegroom stood in his place by her side, handsome as ever, but visibly embarrassed at the new role in which he found himself.

After the solemn words had been spoken, the bride been kissed all round the circle, and congratulations offered by everyone present, all the crowd trooped out into the other room where the big extension table, stretched out to its fullest length, was covered with its snowy cloth and laden with all good things ready for the wedding repast.

Then up to the open back door majestically walked a big old rooster, and standing half way in for a moment on the threshold, looked about, lifted his wings slightly from his body, stretched out and crooked his neck, and gave one rousing crow with all the flourishes. It was quite funny. But to make it funnier, Clara, the little minx, then about six, and the family imitator—as has been mentioned—stood up before the room full of people and immediately went through a pantomime of all the bird's motions; meanwhile giving her own interpretation of his greeting:

"He says, 'Oó, oo oó, oó-oo-oo! I 'gratulate you!'"

This unexpected entertainment was followed by much merry laughter and looked upon as a good omen.

Harry took our Jonie—the mainstay of the inside working force, far away to live with him in his little unpainted cabin home perched on a level elevation of the hillside under the beautiful spreading oak trees in Ladd's Canyon—a branch of the Santiago, and only a little way from the Silverado mines where he worked. The mantle of her labors then fell upon other less capable shoulders.

Some time after Joan and Harry were married, they came down Aliso Canyon on a visit, to see us all; and when they returned home, they took me with them to spend a week or two. It was lovely up there under the big oak trees, with the wild things chattering about, and the acorns falling onto carpets of dead leaves.

Figure 37 Joan and Her Children
Left to Right: Henry, Florence, Joan, Jessica, Henrietta, Elma

Out in the yard under one of the great oaks in a screened-over box, Harry had a big rattlesnake confined, which he had caught alive. He was contemplating the extraction of its poison fangs—which he thought he knew how to accomplish—in order to make a pet of it. I shuddered at the thought of such a ticklish operation, and wondered if the fangs would not grow in again some day without his noticing the fact, and the creature become again dangerous and deadly even while he was thought to be safe.

I slept in a tiny bedroom hardly bigger than a drygoods box, at the end of the cabin house. Here I listened to the night-birds vocalize, and to stealthy footfalls crunching the dry oak leaves. I could hear the acorns drop onto the roof and go rolling down to the edge of the eaves, and then fall off onto the ground below.

But meditating there in the dark alone, my reflections were very unhappy. Neither birds nor acorns, nor the refreshing mountain air that came into my small window, had power to comfort me, or win more than a momentary interest. I was fourteen past, and not a day of the coveted schooling had yet been granted me. I lay there thinking, thinking, thinking; worried over my lack of education, and longing for the same opportunity that had fallen to Annie; wondering what was to become of me, and if it was to be my fate to grow up an ignoramus. How could I bear it? I buried my face in the pillow, so that others would not hear the bitter sobs that shook me.

"Oh, give me an education" was the cry of my heart; "Let me go to school and learn." For hours, I wept in an inward agony of desperation, before exhausted nature drew me into the embrace of slumber. This was only one of many nights that had been spent in this fruitless manner. For the longing desire to obtain an education, had grown into an obsession.

How often, since those days, have I been pained by observing young people who do not appreciate the marvelous educational advantages that are theirs—who think of school as a bugbear to be evaded whenever possible, or suffered with grumbling! Or who without any real love for study and the acquirement of worthwhile knowledge use their opportunities merely as a means of obtaining grades for the sake of promotion and its temporal advantages. Or who fritter away the days in sport and mental idleness, neglecting the precious privileges that are provided at so great cost to the community, to make of themselves useful citizens. Or who rebel altogether, utterly refusing to attend school a day longer than the law compels; and contrive to get out of school by one means or another before finishing even the grades.

At such times, I recall the words of brother George—who himself had known the same great bitterness, spoken to me in consolation so long ago as we talked over the situation:

> "I would rather have the ability and not the chance, than the chance and not the ability." And perhaps he was right.

CHAPTER 54 AN OLD LOVE STORY

In those days of old, the idea prevailed that marriage was the aim and object of life, so far as women were concerned. Careers were not then considered the proper thing for women as they are today, nor were they generally open to women, aside from teaching.

Avocations except those of a menial nature were very few. To do housework, wait table, take in washing, or do sewing were about the gamut. To be sure, there were women now and then who defied all custom and claimed their natural right of equality with men in all things—who pioneered the way and fought for standing in colleges of medicine and law. Strident voices were raised demanding equal rights in political matters, even demanding the ballot.

But these suffragists were considered "peculiar" and regarded more or less as a "joke." Such militant women were not to be endorsed by orderly "society" that could not brook those who dared to be "different."

So the conservative housewives, mothers and maidens continued on in the approved and orderly slavery of their conventions, to which they had been committed by their forebears.

For a woman to remain single past the age of twenty-five was to earn the cruel and opprobrious title, abhorrent to all women, of "old maid"; and to have reached the age of thirty without having taken on the yoke of matrimony, was equivalent to a public confession that she had been unable to find any man who wanted her; which called forth the pity of her sex. She might in her youth have turned down a dozen offers of marriage—in fact not to have rejected some suiter, was to be classed as ordinary, but to have done so once too often and been at last "left on the shelf" was a tragedy for which life held no compensation.

On the other hand, an "old bachelor" was held somewhat in honor for being shrewd enough to have escaped so long the "wiles of women"; and at any reasonable time of life, might still be considered a "catch."

Social etiquette forbade the exchange of gifts or photographs between any but engaged couples. A man might give his "likeness" to a girl, and she might accept it; but unless they were engaged to be married, she must not on any account allow him to have her likeness in possession; for that was tantamount to an unmaidenly acknowledgment of a desire to become engaged to him, or even of assuming a claim which did not exist, and which he might not desire. To defy these proprieties, was to challenge the whispering gossip and "ohs" and "ahs" of "old Mother Grundy."

Since, for a lady to make any initiative advances toward the object of her admiration was considered impossibly bold and coarse, cheapening her value and lessening her prospects of a legitimate proposal of marriage, there was nothing that a "nice girl" could do but wait demurely for some man to discover her charms.

However observation demonstrated that the girl who followed most conscientiously these rules of propriety, was often strangely enough, the one to be left a "wall flower"; while the girl who was artful, clever, and unscrupulous enough to slyly disregard the "rules of the game," and lead men on by means the proper girl must frown upon, was the type most often sought after by young eligibles. Men are like that—encouraging the disregard of rules they have themselves sponsored. So, all in all, the poor "nice" girls found themselves "between the devil and the deep blue sea."

It is little wonder that with such one-sided social standards, old maid bugaboos and unfair distinctions, often a good girl not of the coquettish or brilliant type, who really desired a domestic career and would have made an excellent wife for the right man, finding herself slighted and fearful of never having another chance to marry, would be led to accept the first man who proposed to her regardless of love-lack and fundamental differences between them, which inexperience is prone to minimize. But these more than likely would make the marriage unsuitable and unhappy for both of them; when had the bugbear of "old maid" been out of the way she might have been glad to wait till love itself had brought her at least a chance for happiness.

And since divorces were a very real disgrace, wives often put up with intolerable abuse through drunkenness, neglect, violence of temper, overbearing disposition, or incurable incompatibility, without seeking redress; choosing domestic martyrdom rather than disgrace, for it is a sad fact that men, given the upper hand by social custom, have not been slow to use and abuse it.

After exercising their exclusive privilege of "picking and choosing," that men should be able to hold in such unhappy thralldom, wives worthy of a better fate is enough to make "single blessedness" appear very blessed indeed to women. While it is true without question that women themselves, then as now are sometimes the cause of domestic unhappiness, still observation teaches the preponderance has always been on the other side of the scales.

Observing these things from.my youth up, there was added to my list of irreconcilables another real grudge against the fate that had "borned" me a girl. Yet being a girl, I was the most conservative of the conservatives; and not all the "gold of Ophir" could have hired me to appear even remotely to invite a man's attention, no matter what my own heart might have to say, for hearts must be silenced where social principle is at stake.

And who has wisdom enough to distinguish between absolute right and wrong in social matters? Ideas that have been grammared into us from early years, may cause us to grow up with an attitude that unfits us to make the most out of life for ourselves, or to accord the privilege to others.

Sometimes I wonder if the extreme and regrettable laxity of today is not a natural repercussion of the over-strictness of yesterday; since it is human nature to swing from one extreme to the other.

By remaining single past the age of twenty-five, Artie had automatically acquired the undesirable title of "Old Maid." Yet she was still young, and her single state was due to choice. She had received a number of offers of marriage. But jokes must be made, and there must be subjects to suffer them no matter how cruel in principle they may be.

Artie was particular concerning the bestowal of her heart's affections, as befitting any woman. Realizing that her feeling for another was not deeply enough rooted to sanctify marriage, she would very sensibly say so and reject the offer. Her standard was high—high enough that it was in danger of suffering a rude shock when subjected to the prosaic realities of married life. Only the deepest love would ever enable her to readjust her ideals sufficiently to weather the disillusionments of matrimony.

After Mrs. Poole's recovery, Artie secured a position at waiting table in the Transcontinental, a sixty-room hotel in Colton where once before she had worked for three months in the spring of Eighty-Eight. She took up this work on the first of November and it proved to be the opening of a new chapter in her life.

For the most part, the hotels scattered over the towns of Southern California were those that had been put up on a grand scale during the late boom, and were little more than "white elephants" on the hands of their builders. Times were very dull, and many hotels could scarcely get patronage enough to keep going. So their managers and owners economized by hiring as few helpers as possible, most of whom were obliged to carry far more work than would be allowed today.

Work was very hard at the Transcontinental—or "Trans" as its guests and helpers called the hotel for short. Being near the depot, this particular hotel catered to the railroad patronage, which made night meals a frequent necessity. For this no extra help was employed.

There were then no restrictions regarding hours of labor. The girls worked from five o'clock in the morning, with one short intermission after lunch, until ten or eleven at night. There were no days off, except by special request, the granting of which depended upon the availability and willingness of other helpers to shoulder the additional load, with the understanding always that the favor was to be returned by the recipient. So it was that Artie and the other girls were heavily overloaded with work.

The Trans was owned and operated by Mr. and Mrs. White, who were very agreeable people and not unpleasant to work for. In the matter of labor exactions, they were no worse than others of the time. They liked Artie who had been with them once before in Eighty-Eight for four months, which was about as long a time as any girl could stand up under the steady grind without taking a lay-off and seeking other lighter employment.

Shortly after Artie returned to the Trans, a Madam Somebody who claimed the power of second sight, in other words a Spiritist medium and clairvoyant, established herself for a time in one of the hotel rooms, where she carried on her business, considered more or less of a joke. Nevertheless many were going to her to have their fortunes told—at a dollar apiece—which she was reported to accomplish with supernatural and spectacular demonstrations.

Hearing from others these reports and curious to observe the supernatural manifestations, Artie herself on the sly slipped up to Madame's room to have her fortune told. Expecting the woman to go through some great contortions and perhaps fall into a trance, Artie was distinctly disappointed when she simply drew in a deep mouth-breath, folded her hands, closed her eyes, and sat perfectly quiet in her chair without the least visible sign of supernatural powers.

After some little time during which Artie's dissatisfaction increased, a shudder passed over the medium's form and she announced:

"Midgie is here."

"Who do you mean?" asked Artie.

"Midgie is a little Indian girl who comes to talk with me. She will answer any question you have a mind to ask."

"I don't know of anything I want to ask," said Artie, who had not come expecting to assume the role of interrogator.

Madam being well aware that to the usual unattached young person, having the fortune told meant the securing of some information concerning the future mate in life, immediately supplied material for the desired questioning.

"I see a man—a tall, dark man coming toward you."

"Is he anyone I know?" asked Artie, recalling several men of that description who had come into her life in the past.

"No, I don't think so."

"Have I ever met him?"

"So far as either of you know, you have never met."

"Will I ever meet him?"

"Well, I don't think he is very far distant. Y-e-s, you will meet him, and will marry him. You will live in the country and keep chickens and a cow. You will have a family of several children."

"How shall I know him when I see him?"

"When you see him first he will be leading a little dog."

After a few more details, to which Artie paid scant attention, for the chagrin she felt at having wasted her precious dollar over such trash as this, the interview was terminated. Passing down the stairs, Artie met coming up to Madame's room, a young society girl, a guest at the hotel, who asked her:

"Have you been having your fortune told?"

"Yes, I went up on purpose to see her go into a trance, and all she did was to sit there and tell me about a man."

"Well, what do you think of your fortune?"

"It didn't amount to a 'hill of beans.' It certainly wasn't worth a dollar!"

"Well, I think I'll try it anyway," said the young lady, and passed on up the stairs.

Artie came down and, entering the dining room, related to the girls her disappointing experience, expatiating in detail upon her "wonderful fortune" and the "man leading a little dog," ending with:

"I only wish I had my dollar back! "

"Well, I think I'll stay away and save my hard-earned dollar," decided Maggie Daugherty, who had been intending to visit madame also.

There is no question but that such necromancers, or spirit mediums, are often able to disclose secrets and forecast events. Sometimes the things prognosticated come true. Sometimes, they very definitely do not. The fact that they sometimes fail is proof sufficient that they do not come from a divine source; for divinity is infallible. That they do sometimes come true proves only that there are occult powers apart from divinity. Dabbling in these occult manifestations has been appropriately called "the black art," and so known from ancient times.

Practically every medium in America professes to be guided by some Indian control, a deception in which even the medium herself is deceived. The Bible, while recognizing such occult powers as actually existing, ascribes them to an evil source, sternly denouncing their practice and strictly forbidding the ancient Hebrew people to hold any communications with "familiar spirits." Artie, being ignorant of this, the interview to her had no particular religious significance. The incident was soon out of mind and apparently forgotten.

A few days later, during the after-breakfast cleaning-up hour, Artie started from the dining room to go into the kitchen. As she opened the swinging door between, her eyes were arrested by the sight of a small group of the kitchen helpers at the opposite end of the long room, in the midst of which stood a beautiful little Italian Greyhound, timidly receiving little scraps of left-overs dispensed by the Chinese cook.

"Oh, what a cunning little dog!" was her first thought as she gazed, fascinated by the dainty creature. Then raising her eyes upward, she beheld the leading-cord that was fastened to the dog's neck, suspended from the hand of a man who was bending over with pats and soothing words, assisting in the repast while answering questions concerning the dog of the admiring audience whose eyes were fastened upon her.

Instantly, into Artie's mind flashed the remembrance of her "fortune." Suppressing a snicker, she released the door, which swung to, and running back into the dining room to her friend, exclaimed in suppressed pseudo-excitement:

"Oh Maggie! I've seen him! I've seen him!"

"Seen who?" asked Maggie, pausing in her work.

"My future husband!" laughed Artie, sotto-voice, in the same simulated excitement. "The man leading a little dog!" "Where is he?"

"In the kitchen! Look yourself!"

Cautiously opening the door, Maggie peered in, but upon glimpsing the scene, turned away with disappointment, exclaiming in a tone that relegated romance to the discard:

"Aw! That's only Mr. Ward!"

"Oh-o-o, is _that_ who it is," murmured Artie, who had heard of Mr. Ward but had never met him.

For several years past Mr. Ward had been an intermittent guest at the Trans, frequently gone, but sometimes remaining for long stretches, always when in town dropping in as if coming home. He had been away on one of these periodical absences and had just returned to the hotel. Connected with the sporting world, among other activities he engineered baseball teams, managing, directing and booking for appointments, though not a player himself. One of his "boys" was the well-known player Frank Graves.

Mr. Ward had long been considered a confidential helper about the place. Sometimes when Mr. White, short of a cook, would be obliged for a brief period to take over in person the culinary end of the establishment, or when business called him out of town, Mr. Ward would be engaged for the emergency to look after the office; receiving there for meal tickets or other remuneration.

He was now appointed a seat at the "transient table" along with other temporary guests, whom the girls waited on as best they could between times from their "regulars." Here Artie saw him again at noon, and often thereafter. He was well acquainted with all the old hands, but Artie, being a "new girl," attracted his attention. Often it fell to her lot to wait on the transients, and this opportunity to make her acquaintance he was not slow to improve.

Artie, naturally diffident and cautious, though not ignorant of the ways of the world, at first sought to avoid social contact, exchanging words with him only when duty required it. Every time her eyes rested upon him, the thought of that "fortune" intruded itself into her consciousness, with the result that she studied him secretly with a peculiar interest mingled with amusement.

Mr. Ward was a tall thin man, with large expressive green-gray eyes, dark hair, and short moustache decorating a rather long, narrow face. His hands and fingers were slender, on one of which flashed a large set ring. Dressing meticulously, he carried himself with an easy sophisticated air, chatting in a quiet voice that was low and pleasant, with whomsoever he pleased, devoid of embarrassment. Before Artie realized it, they were chatting together like old acquaintances—though with much more volubility on his part than hers.

This meeting at the hotel was not the first time they had talked with each other, though neither of them remembered the incident until later on in their friendship. The previous March, Artie had called up the Trans by long distance telephone from Los Angeles to apply for work. The proprietor being absent, Mr. Ward had answered the call, and on his behalf, engaged her for the position. Before she arrived, however, he had left town again, remaining absent during her stay from March to June, consequently they had at that time missed meeting each other.

Often Mr. Ward came in late for breakfast, which left the two alone for a time in the dining room. This provided a further opportunity for getting better acquainted. Of a humorous turn, he had always some interesting story or incident to relate, and showed himself a charming conversationalist.

His fair acquaintance soon discovered that he was the owner of _two_ little dogs instead of one, to both of whom he was much attached and before long she was listening to their history. Belle, the one she had seen in the kitchen, and

Flossie had been raised from puppyhood without a mother, having been born in the state of Texas where he then lived. Their mother, a pet and favorite with him, soon after their birth had been ruthlessly poisoned by an unscrupulous dog-hater in the neighborhood, who had set out to poison every dog he could find, and being very sly in his work, could not be apprehended.

What to do with the two tiny orphans who as yet did not have their eyes open, was a problem. Their master, grieving over the loss of the mother, had solved it by feeding them with a bottle, giving them particular attention and tender care. Under these kindly ministrations, they thrived and grew.

While the puppies were still very small, he decided to leave the state of Texas and come to California. Not being able to take them with him, he committed them to the care of friends until such time as he should send for them, which he did almost a year later. He supposed they would have entirely forgotten him. But when the crate was opened, to his amazement the two little doggies gave every evidence of recognition and affection. They jumped all over him with demonstrations of delight and joyous welcome. This so endeared them to his heart that ever after they were inseparable friends. Wherever he went, except when distant travels forbade, the dogs, one or the other or both, were to be seen with him, being left when separated with his parents who also lived in Colton.

When, some time later, Artie's autograph album was presented to Mr. Ward for his contribution, he wrote on one of its blank pages the old quotation:

> *"Merry witching little Elf,*
> *Stealing hearts to throw away,*
> *Some day you'll be caught yourself—*
> *That will be a lucky day.*
> *C.F.W."*

Soon after this Mr. Ward made the annoying discovery that some evenings the "witching Elf" had other company, in the person of a young man from the country place where she had worked before coming to the Trans. Others of the girls he knew there had their company, but this he had never found annoying.

One evening a few days before Christmas, as Mr. Ward was passing down the hall, he saw Artie in her room framed by the open door seated at a table writing, and came to a halt in the doorway with the query:

"What are you doing?"

"Addressing Christmas cards," she said looking up with a smile.

"Let me help you," he offered.

"All right."

He walked in, taking the proffered seat.

As if to relinquish the task, Artie drew her chair away somewhat from the table. Her caller, reaching over, picked up the cards with their messages of greeting to the home folks and began to examine the script of her rather stiff and formal hand.

With the air of being perfectly at home, he tilted back his chair on two legs, and soon, yielding to unconscious habit, lifted his feet and rested them crossed on the table as comfortably and complacently as if in his own private quarters.

At her dictation he addressed a few of the cards in his smooth flowing handwriting, holding them on a book against his knee. As they sat thus conversing a step was heard in the hall. Who should it be at that inopportune time, but her country beau coming to spend the evening with her.

Artie arose to greet him. But before she had time to advance a step or speak a word, that audacious Mr. Ward, as coolly bold as if he owned the premises, spoke up with a hearty:

"Come in! Come in!"

As the boy entered, he commanded cordially:

"Have a seat!"

Vexed and speechless at the effrontery, Artie stood in awkward embarrassment. The situation was one to be easily misinterpreted. When at last she found her voice, it was somewhat strained and unnatural. After a few minutes' pointless conversation, the young man took his departure, leaving his supposed rival in full possession and decidedly master of the situation.

To Artie, the attentions of this young man had meant no more than passing the time pleasantly, but to him it had been more of a serious matter, and both his pride and his feelings were hurt. At Christmas time, he came around once more for a few moments. Artie had previously bought for him a little gift, and took advantage of the opportunity to give it to him. He took the handkerchief, saying:

"Artie, you're a funny girl."

"How so?"

"Why don't you give this to the other fellow?"

"Because I got it for you," she told him.

He left her, went to the store, bought a lovely gift, and returning, presented it to her. After this he took his departure, and never came to see her again.

The "other man in the case," having accomplished his object, was secretly both amused and gratified. The way was now open to enjoy his own fun. He liked a flirtation with a pretty girl. His own gift to her was a dainty embroidered blue silk handkerchief.

Not long after this incident, Mr. White was called away on business and again left Mr. Ward in charge of the office. This work included the making out of the menus. He would bring these into the dining room every day just as Artie was finishing up her work, to write out while visiting with his new friend. Artie would watch him at this task, the two conversing pleasantly meanwhile, and the acquaintance made a natural and wholesome growth.

Some weeks after this, Mr. Ward became ill, and was confined to his room with one of the severe and protracted sick headaches with which he was periodically afflicted. Missing him from the dining room, Mrs. White, accompanied by Artie, went upstairs to see him. They found him stretched out upon his bed in abject misery, wishing only to be let alone. He seemed to be almost in a stupor from suffering, responding but feebly to their solicitations and refusing all offers of food, lying with eyes closed like one hardly alive.

Artie's tender heart was deeply touched and filled with commiseration. When, unable to do anything to relieve his suffering, his callers took their departure. Mrs. White preceded Artie through the door and down the hall. In following her out, as she passed by his prostrate form, involuntarily as might a mother with a sick child, Artie rested her hand for an instant gently on the aching brow. Then overcome with sympathy and compassion, she stooped on the impulse and just touched his forehead with her lips lightly as the brush of a butterfly's wing, supposing him too sick to notice anything or care. Not by so much as the flutter of an eyelid did he seem to recognize the touch.

After breakfast the following morning, Artie sought out Mrs. White and asked her if it would be all right for her to carry a tray up to Mr. Ward. Mrs. White answered in the affirmative. So Artie spread an attractive tray and took it up to his room, knocking gently on his door.

Supposing it to be the maid come to tidy up his room, he answered with a feeble and reluctant:

"Come in."

Seeing her, his `eyes lighted with pleased surprise. While he toyed with his breakfast, she waited, now and then making a solicitous inquiry or remark. Though still unable to enjoy food, he lingered over the repast in order to keep her there as long as possible. When she rose to go, picking up the unfinished tray, he said to her mischievously:

"Are you going to bid me goodbye again as you did yesterday?"

Taken aback, Artie blushed furiously. Saying in reply the first thing she thought of:

"How was that?"

"You kissed me yesterday," he reminded.

"That wasn't a kiss. I-It was only a half-kiss—because I felt sorry for you," she stammered.

"Well," he said persuasively, "I'll take the other half now, please."

"You don't need it now."

"But I do need it—to make me get well faster," he insisted.

"You're better today," said Artie in confusion, and went out quickly.

Soon after this, one afternoon they met in the hall. Artie said kindly:

"I'm glad you're better and can be up again."

"I'm sorry."

"Why?"

"Because you won't be bringing me a tray any more."

"You didn't eat anything when I did bring it."

As Artie started to pass, he asked teasingly:

"When are you going to give me the rest of that kiss?"

"I didn't think you would notice that. It was only because you were sick."

"But I'm still sick," he said whimsically.

"You'll soon be well," Artie managed to say, and went on into her room.

She was greatly disconcerted at the evident effect of her impulsive act. It had been merely a spontaneous overflowing of compassion and sympathy. She really had meant nothing by it, supposing he would scarcely notice it in his stupor-like misery. Now that he was making so much out of it, she sought so far as possible to avoid meeting him.

But his own reaction was exactly the reverse. A subtle change had come over him. Whereas before, he had been merely entertained by their occasional informal contacts, his manner now was distinctly that of pursuit. He desired to meet her on every possible occasion. In his eyes shown a new appreciation, a conscious interest, a deference mingled with compelling appeal. In the dining room, there were little considerate acts, and words suggestive of something confidential between them. Artie was modestly reserved, shrinking from anything approaching familiarity, yet conscious of his admiring eyes, low soft voice, gentle touch, and magnetic personality. These drew her, but there were other ways that repelled. A certain imperious force about him she resented as akin to domineering. And she did not like the way he made his living in the world of sports.

The hotel cornered on Eighth and J Streets, facing south. Just to the east of it on the same street, was a rooming house called the "Palace," under the same ownership and used as an adjunct of the hotel. For that reason, though entirely a separate building, it usually went by the name of "The Annex." In this building the girls had their rooms, and here the overflow guests were located.

Emma Reed, an old chum of Artie's had recently joined the force of dining room girls, and was now Artie's roommate. She was keeping company with a young man named Jimmie Lloyd, who came frequently to see her. But the girls had no proper place in which to receive their company. Comforts and conveniences were not then provided for working girls as they are today.

The rooms of the hotel guests were provided with heating stoves, but in their room there was no stove and the weather was distressingly cold. One raw January evening as the two girls came upstairs earlier than usual, they were discussing the lack of heating facilities, and the uncomfortable prospect of an evening without heat in their room. Mr. Ward, whose room was on the same floor down the hall, overheard snatches of this conversation.

"Why don't you girls come and sit in my room where it is warm?" he invited.

"Thank you, the fire does look good," replied Artie. But the two went on to their room.

The next day she approached Mrs. White and asked her:

"Do you think it would be proper for Emma and me to spend an evening sitting in Mr. Ward's room? He asked us to. It is so cold in our room."

"I guess it would be all right, Artie," returned Mrs. White.

So the next evening the two girls accepted his invitation and went in to sit with him before the fire.

Mr. Ward was reading the new book "Peck's Bad Boy," which he handed to Artie asking her to read from it aloud. Mr. White, passing down the hall, looked in at the open door, chatted for a few minutes, and passed on. In that brief interval, he had conceived a helpful idea. It was not long until he had fixed up a vacant room near the girls' with a heating stove as a little sitting room in which they might receive and entertain their company. This was a godsend to the girls. Mr. Ward then began to drop in there occasionally for an evening, and took it upon himself to see that there was wood on hand for the fire. In this pleasant environment they soon became better acquainted. Then came an absence from the Trans of several weeks. Upon his return, he sought the little sitting room. Looking in, his face beamed at finding Artie there alone. Making the most of his opportunity, he came up close to her, and with the air of a man who is not to be put off longer, inquired:

"When are you going to give me that kiss?"

"Oh, I told you I only did that because you were sick," explained Artie once more.

"Well, I'm not well yet," he said.

With a strong compelling arm, he encircled and drew her to him. Then with one firm, gentle hand lifting her chin, pressed a kiss upon her mouth. Artie, covered with confusion, made a move to draw away.

"Aren't you going to kiss me?" he coaxed, refusing to let her out of his embrace. Still she made no move.

"What are you waiting for?" This was almost a command. Another ominous pause, then:

"Nothing," she said, and kissed him.

After this, the courtship grew apace. To win this "little elf" became his consuming ambition., He seemed not to be happy a moment away from her presence. One day, picking up her album, he turned to the page on which was the verse he had written, and below it, jotted down the date of their first meeting, which now meant so much to him, "Nov. 15, 1889."

Soon after this Artie became sick with "La Grippe," the "new disease" that had become an epidemic. Fearing to lose her position should she give up and go to bed, she still kept on her feet and worked, sick as she was, till the malady wore off, leaving her weak and listless.

Charles had been very solicitous during her illness, imploring her to take a lay-off. But finally she recovered and was her old self. When Saint Valentine's Day came around, he presented her with a lovely white fringed Cashmere shawl-'scarf, which she admired tremendously and wore with the greatest pleasure.

One day, happening along when Artie was writing a letter to Mother, he offered to write it himself for her, so she let him do it, dictating her message. This, Mother refers to in her letter to Artie of Feb. 14 as a "proxy" letter.

Very early in their acquaintance, he had dropped the formal "Miss" from before her name. For mere formality as such, he had little use, but Artie still persisted in calling him "Mr. Ward," which irked him. Informally free and easy himself he could hardly understand such reserve.

They had never been out anywhere together. Her work was so exacting there had been no opportunity. As a result, even their closest associates did not as yet suspect the intimate nature of their friendship. Outwardly formal before others, they kept their secret, neither of them wishing to draw the banter and inquisitive attention attendant upon such disclosures. They had set sail all by themselves upon a sea of exploration and adventure which seemed too personally sacred to share with any other.

One day in March, Mr. White made the announcement that he had sold the Palace, and all within the building would have to move over into the hotel. So there was great bustle and stir as the guests selected their rooms and began to vacate. Artie and the other girls packed their trunks, and Mr. Ward went for awhile to stay with his parents on the other side of town.

On the first floor of the Trans at the side next the Palace, were two unused "sample rooms" where various odds and ends of furniture were stored. Mr. White piled all this stuff into one room and fixed up the other nice and cozy for Artie and Emma to occupy. They enjoyed this room, which was more convenient and comfortable than the other. Though they missed the little sitting room.

Artie was disturbed by the news, brought to the Trans, that Mr. Ward was sick, having succumbed to the Grippe at his father's home. One day after this Mr. White employed a carpenter to do some yard construction work, and it was told Artie that the man was Mr. Ward's father. She stepped out-of-doors where he was working and spoke to him:

"Good morning."

"Good morning."

"Are you Mr. Ward's father?"

"Yes, my name-is Ward," he replied, giving her a searching look.

"How is young Mr. Ward? I heard he was sick."

"He has been sick, but he is better now."

"Thank you," said Artie, and went in to her duties.

The carpenter resumed his own work. But that brief interview had put ideas into his head. As he hammered and sawed, he kept thinking:

"I wish Charlie would marry that young girl."

After a time, Mr. Ward showed up again at the Trans, taking some of his meals there but rooming still with his folks. He found some occasions when he could be with his sweetheart, calling upon her when off duty in her new room downstairs. And so March passed away.

About this time, a lady of means, making an agreement with Mr. White, started a hotel in the northern part of the country, which he was to establish and oversee. He was taking north with him some of his most experienced girls to help get the enterprise under way and invited Artie to go. But Artie was tired of hotel work.

Patronage at the Trans was falling off and would be slim during the coming summer months, which always meant a slack time, and a very small force would be required to run it. Mrs. White came to Artie urging:

"Won't you go with them Artie? "

"No, I don't think I want to," replied Artie.

"Work will be slow here this summer. But we need you up there."

"I want a change from hotel work, Mrs. White. When my month is up, I think I'll go to, Los Angeles and work for awhile at something else."

Artie wanted to get away from her present environment and from all her old associates for awhile, and from her lover, and lose herself in the big city among strangers where she could think things over. She was not satisfied to allow her friendship with Mr. Ward to go on as it was, drifting toward matrimony. He was not the kind of man she had always supposed she would marry.

Though his masterful wooing and magnetic personality drew powerfully upon her heart-strings, there was danger that these very qualities would over influence her. He had tastes and traits with which her nature clashed. His imperious disposition chafed her at times. Besides this, his connection with the sporting world as a profession was out of harmony with all her life-long ideals. It would bring her, she felt into a social environment that would be utterly opposite from that she was used to and could approve. She was doubtful of loving him enough to overlook all these objections. Perhaps, back of all these reasons, and more deeply hidden, was that of an image in her "sealed room" of a face loved and lost that had never been entirely forgotten.

So, mentally speaking, she swayed from one extreme to the other. When in his company, she would forget her fears, but when alone, they haunted her. She was miserable over the internal controversy. She hated to hurt him. They had already gone so far that a break would mean much pain on both sides. Yet she must not make a mistake for life on that account. Finally she determined to end it by dismissing him from her life, and to tell him so definitely at the first opportunity. Since it had to be done, the sooner the better. She would steel her heart against yielding to his importunities, even though he was so dear to her—even though his ardent wooing and gentle touch were so irresistible. But there was one quality in her own make-up that Artie had not reckoned with.

Knowing that she was planning to go away from the Trans, Charles had been unusually tender and attentive to her, timing his visits to the hotel when he knew she would be off duty and coming with informal frequency to that little room she was so soon to vacate. A week or so before her departure, and soon after her momentous decision had been reached, as she sat writing a letter at her table one afternoon, in through the open door he walked unannounced and stood for a silent moment or two before she looked up.

Then, anxious to get the unhappy subject off her chest, with her characteristic frankness and without waste of words, she said to him:

"Do you know, Mr. Ward, I've made up my mind that we had better play 'quits.' I'm never going to marry at all."

His face went chalk white. For a full minute he stood unable to speak. Then in a halting voice, full of anguish, he said:

"I was afraid—of that. I guess—the best thing I can do—is to leave you alone."

Artie felt like a murderer. His tone was so hopeless, his suffering so evident, his white face so piteous, she simply could not endure it. She had not counted on her own "chicken-heartedness." She rose to her feet and went to him, her resolves vanishing like ropes of sand. The same tender, compassionate heart that had drawn from her lips that first fleeting kiss, now surged with the irresistible urge to comfort him regardless of consequences.

She put her arms around his neck. He hugged her tight and covered her face with eager kisses, whispering joyously:

"You didn't mean it after all, did you?"

At parting, he asked:

"Sweetheart, will you save all your kisses for me?"

"Yes," she promised. Then he went out and left her to finish her letter.

Charles could hardly believe his good fortune. Knowing that her objections to the union, of which he was not ignorant, had not been eliminated but only subordinated, and fearful that when away from him they would return to torment her again, and that she might even yet change her mind, he hastened to do what he could to bind the bargain more firmly while she was in the mood. That evening when they were alone together, he said to her:

"I'll get you a ring tomorrow."

"You don't need to buy me a ring."

"But I want to. It will bind our friendship."

"Well, just for friendship, then. But I won't wear it around here."

"What kind of a ring does my little girl prefer?"

"Just a plain gold band. That's the only kind I like."

At the moment, Artie failed to realize that this choice actually designated a wedding ring. The next day he slipped it onto her finger. But no one else saw it. Only for brief moments in secret would she wear it while at the Trans, determined to keep the new relationship from becoming a matter of common hotel gossip.

In Los Angeles, Artie had a very dear friend, Mrs. John Buster, with whom she planned to remain for a few days before seeking another position. After last goodbyes, she took the train and went to this friend's house to rest up a bit, still keeping her secret, with Charles' promise to do the same.

When completely away from the presence and magnetic influence of her fiancee, sure enough, the old doubts began to trouble her. In a short time the problem returned with renewed force, until she was again utterly miserable—this time more so than before. Why had she been so "chickenhearted"? Why had she actually promised, and accepted his ring. She did not want to marry. He was dearer to her than ever, she loved the ring. But that sporting life. How could she endure that?

Charles waited impatiently for a letter. Not having her` new address, he could do nothing but wait. Though he fumed and fretted and conjectured, none came, leaving him in suspense and uncertainty. A week went by and longer. Not being able to write him the happy letter that should come naturally from a newly engaged girl, Artie, for some time did not write at all. How could she hurt him again? How be honest and keep from it? It was only fair to tell him how she felt. So her lover waited and worried.

Finally the letter came, written in her characteristic candidness.

The remainder of this old love story can best be gleaned by the reader from excerpts taken entirely from letters written by this ardent lover, and preserved by their recipient through all the years that followed. Her own letters unfortunately for this narrative, when opportunity afforded, Artie destroyed as "uninteresting." But their tenor in a measure, is revealingly preserved by the frequent mention of their contents in his answers.

Letters of a Lover

"April 18, 1890
Dear Artie:

After waiting day after day, I finally received a letter from you.

It seems that this week has been one continual round of disappointments. Monday was election day, and one of my warmest friends was defeated for city marshall. Then I was looking every day for a letter from you and was disappointed until today—and when it came, was sadly disappointed.

Artie, I hardly know how to write or what to say. I probably misunderstood you, or expected too much. You say you do not like to hurt; but your letter hurts very much. I thank you for being so candid with me, so there can be no more mistakes made...You know well you ask an impossibility. No Artie, it is too late; I probably can never be anything else. All my life has been one grand mistake; and I suppose will continue so till the end of the chapter. Do not think I am writing this to try and persuade you to change your mind, for I am not. Not for anything in this world would I have you marry me prejudiced as you are...I write simply to show you how impossible it is for me...to make a living at anything else. Do not think that I do not care enough for you to try...for your sake; for if any thing or person between earth and heaven could persuade me, you could; but Artie, it is useless and I will have to give you up. I have often pictured to myself a nice little home with you by my side of evenings, helping me, as I know you could one you cared for; but those pictures were only pictures, after all.

Keep, and wear the ring; (it was only 'friendship') until some other places another on your finger; then, if you know where I am, and our friendship ceases, send it to me; or take it to Santa Monica or some place else, and drop it into the ocean in deep water where none can find it. I know not how long I shall stay here, nor where I will go when I leave. Think of me sometimes, and think kindly...We may not meet again, still, we may. Anyway, I shall never regret having known my 'Little Girl.'

Goodbye, Chas."

It was natural that Artie should cry a little over this letter from the man she loved—from whom she had thought to run away; but that was not so easy as it had seemed. Love seeks to find a way. Artie wrote again, urging him to give up his old life entirely, and find occupation along lines she could approve; assuring him that she was willing to wait for him, and promising the reward if he should succeed. Whereupon, he took courage and promised to "try":

"My Dear Little Girl": he wrote: "The best and most welcome letter I ever received reached me yesterday...Do not ever say again that you cannot write, for if any one can write a better letter than you, I have never seen it. Your last was full of good advice and a man would not be much of a man if he did not at least try to follow it, when such reward awaited him did he succeed. I have had plenty of advice before, but no reward was ever promised me should I succeed. I will try to do so. But Artie...you have taken just a little the advantage of me, don't you think so? In your former letter you requested me not to try to persuade you from your way of thinking. Then you do your utmost to persuade me from my way to yours. Now no gentleman would ever do that which a lady requests him not to do, so if I am such, I cannot say a word...I am glad you have grown attached to the ring, and sincerely hope you will wear it as long as you live. I am very much afraid though, that as a 'friendship ring,' it is not a success; for I think you and I have passed the 'friendship' stage and gone into something deeper—whether for better or for worse, time alone can tell. We can only hope for the best.

When first we became acquainted, I am sure neither of us had any idea where we were drifting, or thought of the old saying: 'Play with fire, and you are likely to get burned'...Your plan is a good one, only how long it would take me to carry it out, is impossible to say...Wait for me a reasonable time, is all I ask...and if I succeed, well and good, if not, there are others more worthy of you than I.

Thanking you for all your well wishes, and wishing you all the happiness you deserve (I can wish you no more, for you deserve all) I will close for this time.

Ever yours, Chas.

"April 27, 1890
Little Sweetheart:

Your letters came on time...I do not know what I've ever done that I should have such a nice little girl to write such nice letters. I was in a good humor and enjoyed them very much, and especially the last one.

As I have often told you, I am not infatuated with my calling in any way. The only thing I care for is the few dollars it brings. Nor do I care so much for the dollars so long as I have the necessities of life. If I knew exactly what to do, or how to start into something else, I would start immediately. But

I do not, and will have to wait for something to turn up. I shall embrace the first opportunity that offers, and will succeed or turn to the dust from whence I came. For I never take the back track.

It seems ages since I saw you last...Mrs. White sent for me yesterday, and as I passed through the hall, the door to the little room was open. How I wished I might, as often before, go in and take my girl in my arms...But...the room was empty.

Mr. White has two "sawed-off" girls here now...One of them is cross-eyed...Do not write a 'short and sweet' letter. Write a long and sweet one, and soon.

Yours with love, Chas.

P.S. No, we never write 'love letters'—that is <u>hardly</u> ever. If I had hold of you, I would kiss you right square on the mouth for that. You little minx. You are too sarcastic."

"May 16
Little Sweetheart:

Your note reached me this morning, and very glad I was to get it, for I was afraid I would have to go away without hearing from you or seeing you again. I shall leave here Sunday morning for San Diego, and stop off in Los Angeles to see you; for I want to see you 'awful' bad and have lots to tell you. I shall not answer your letters, but will tell you what I think of them Sunday...I have kept each and every one of yours and have enjoyed all of them...Two of them were just a 'little bit cross' and Sunday you will have to pay penalty for the 'cross' ones.

I am going to San Diego to work, and from present prospects expect to stay all summer, and if I do, well, will tell you all about it Sunday. Goodbye until then.

Yours with best love. Chas."

That Sunday, Charles told her not only about his San Diego prospects, but asked her to promise to join him as his wife in that southern city just as soon as he should become established in his new work. She was persuaded, and at last gave her unqualified promise to become his wife. Artie had sat for her photograph, and showed him the proofs, in which he delighted.

Charles did not go that day to San Diego as intended, for he had received word of a delay in the plans. Upon reaching home, he wrote:

"May 24
My Darling Little Girl:

You have today made me one of the happiest men in the town of Colton. I think like the Irish boy said to his lassie: 'You are the natest and the swatest, most complatest little gurrul in the land.' I am in an 'awful' hurry today and have only time to write a word or two, but will write you tomorrow a long letter. I am in a 'peck of trouble,' as you say, trying to get some of these 'doggoned' rascals here in Colton to pay up. If I go away and leave them, they may never pay. Still I am happy. I would like to take you in my arms and kiss you, oh so much. I may not get away from here for four or five days yet.

Yours with best love Chas.

P.S. Tell Mrs. Buster for me that outside of 'my Artie,' she is the best lady in Los Angeles, for I think I have to thank her for helping me just a little, don't I Sweetheart?

Ever yours, Chas.
Tomorrow XX 00

"May 25,

I was in a hurry yesterday, but really had to write a little to you, I felt so good. I thought last night when going to bed, I would get up early this morning and go down to Los Angeles and see my promised wife. I took your advice and went to bed and got a good night's sleep; and when I woke up this morning, it was nine o'clock and all trains for Los Angeles, gone; so I got left. Anyway, I shall try and see you again before I leave; which I hope will be shortly; for I want to get, things ready for my girl as soon as possible. I am getting anxious to have her all my own. But I want to fix a home for her first. You know, Dear, I have not been doing much here for some time past, and have not laid up any money for our future; so you know it will be better for me to see exactly how things are in San Diego before I take you there...When I get you I want a place to keep you well, for my poor girl has worked too hard already in her life and shall work no more—only for me...keeping house for two. If I could not work and keep us both, I would be a very poor man indeed; and as you say, there is always something *a man can do.*

I shall do as you desire about keeping ours a secret until you say so...Still, I am sure my sister would like you very much. I told her once of a little girl who was so kind to me when I was sick, and for whom I would lay awake and watch, hoping she would hurry up and get out of that old dining room; and she asked me why I never brought her up to the house...Then I went out and got a bouquet for the little girl who waited on me and if that little girl was as near me now as she was then, she would probably be in my arms with her head on my shoulder where it belongs, and we would both be 'foolish.' Well, Dearest, if I keep on...you will get tired of nonsense and long letters...Think I shall go by Los Angeles and see you unless I should get a telegram...'Come at once'...Mr. White has gone back up north, and the 'Orange Boys' have gone away too. There is a man stopping at the Trans who has thirty dogs—he hasn't got them in the hotel though; they are in the livery stable. Mrs. White was in the stable this morning when I saw her, and she wanted all the dogs.

Ever yours, Chas."

The San Diego proposition turned out to be rather unreliable—merely a prospect, about which there was nothing definite as yet; and Charles was kept in "hot water" over it for some time without actually landing any job. Those post-boom days were terribly difficult for everybody; jobs as "scarce as hens' teeth" and wages down to the vanishing point. Rents were so low that eight dollars a month for a five-roomed house seemed a good price; and people would look farther for something cheaper. It was almost a hopeless time for a man in his position, who was endeavoring to change his whole manner of life and labor. Manual work, when it could be had paid only a dollar and a half a day; but he was not used to hard manual labor, and could not have succeeded in that at any wage. His father being a carpenter, occasionally could give him a few days work with hammer and saw; but building itself was at a low ebb. He thought of running some hotel.

After another trip to Los Angeles to see his sweetheart, he writes on June 2:

"Dear Little Girl: After having quite a time getting away from Los Angeles, I finally got home again. I came very near getting off at Pomona; for the boys pulled me off the train and said I had to stay in Pomona all night. I told them I had *to get home: so they let me go... The boys all want me to come to Pomona, and as they all live there, and have a great deal of influence, they would be a help to me. If I can make a deal with the parties who own the hotel...it will be much better and pleasanter for me, and maybe I won't have to wait for my girl. She said that as soon as I got well started into something else, she would be mine...I want you to hurry up that photograph and send it; for I want either you or your likeness near me all the time...Yours ever, Chas."*

This was followed by another on June 6:

"...How is it down there? I don't think I ever saw such hot weather in my life. I have been in San Bernardino all forenoon and until two o'clock, and it was 'hotter'n blazes' over there. I have given up the idea of taking the hotel in Pomona...It is too large ever to pay in a place like Pomona, and...times are too dull. There are two dining rooms in the house. One of them is four times as large as the dining room of the Trans. The Gentleman from San Diego I told you I wanted to meet here, came yesterday—he and his brother. They are the parties I expected to work for...They may come to San Bernardino. Then I shall go there and work. He and I were in San Bdno. this forenoon looking up a location; I may have to stay in San B. this summer instead of San Diego. I will know by Monday...Dear, please do send that photo soon—the one with the hair down; for I like you best that way...Mr. White has returned from up north. He says he thinks the hotel up there will be a failure; so it was best that you did not go.

With best love, Chas."

"June 12

I am afraid San Diego is no go...One thing, I will be able to see my little girl oftener if I am here. And times do seem to be picking up considerably now, and money is getting more plentiful...Say Artie, What's the matter with that old fellow of yours? He don't seem to take very kindly to me—does not desire to speak to me as we pass by...Miss Lang was very angry last evening when I went into dinner. The census taker was around and took her census from Mr. White. You know Miss Lang will never tell her age to anyone; so Mr. White told him she was thirty-five...She says she is going to propose to some young man and get out a marriage license just to show people she is not thirty-five...I expect to go and see my little girl on the Fourth of July.

Yours ever with best love, Chas."

"June 15,

I got a letter from the base-ball boys in San Diego yesterday requesting me to take a team down to play there shortly, and asking what terms we would come on. I wrote them, and if they are satisfied with the terms, we will go there soon; and if I can find anything to do there, I may stay awhile. I will have about four or five days to look around in anyway. Two and one half dollar gold pieces are getting scarce, I just happened to run across that one. I have something else for you and will bring it down the next time I come to Los Angeles...You must have been very busy not to get a chance to read my letter till nine o'clock next day...I am very glad to hear you have a situation, and hope it will be a pleasant one and you will not have to hunt another. I do not know where Grand Ave. is situated; it must be quite a ways out of town.

Ever Yours, Chas."

The next is addressed to Melrose Hotel, Cor. Second and Grand; and dated June 16:

"I've got 'em—I mean the photos. and they are nice as can be. look just like my little girl. One is in a frame standing just before me as I am scribbling, and I can almost see it smile—looks so natural...I've been out in the country the last few days for a little recreation and hunting horse thieves—been out with the constables. They have stirred up one of the greatest thieving dens here during the past week you ever heard of. A fellow came here about the first of last year and rented a place of George Tyler (you know him) and he had about twenty horses—every one of them was stolen. How he managed to keep it up and not get caught before, is more than any of us can tell. Most of the horses were stolen around El Monte in Los Angeles County, and their owners are here getting them back. The thieves are not caught yet, and I guess they never will be. They have 'vamoosed' entirely and can not be found...

Yours forever, Chas."

Figure 38 Artemisia Thurston Photo, 1890

Charles had planned to spend the Fourth with Artie in Los Angeles, but that was not to be. After working around at various places while rooming at Mrs. Buster's Artie accepted a position with the Hotel Metropole at Santa Catalina Island, run by Craig and Blinn, and sailed across the twenty-five miles of ocean that lay between it and the mainland; from which place, she wrote to her ardent lover of her whereabouts; and then comes this one in answer dated June 20:

...Why have you gone away out there in the Pacific Ocean to work?

...How in the world am I to get out there? I can not walk there... It is too far to swim; so I can not see my girl probably for a long time...I don't like that. But I guess it will be pleasanter for you there this summer...Artie, I do wish you would stop that formal heading of 'Mr. C.F. Ward' to all of your letters. If we were writing business letters, it would be all right, but ours are not business letters; so 'let it slide' (that's slang)...There is about one hundred and fifty miles of land, and I don't know how many of water, and some months of weary waiting between me and all I want. Things are getting better around here. The S.P. Rail Road is building a line to San Bernardino and the place where the asylum is to be built beyond S.B.; and they will put to work a great many men. The canneries are opening and a good many going to work there. So altogether, times are picking up considerable...Say Artie, do you think a fellow would get seasick if he tried to go over to Catalina Island? You know, I never was on a boat, except a ferry boat—and they say a fellow...who is not used to the sea, if he goes out on the water on a large vessel, always wants to feed the fishes. Now I always hate to lose my dinner-especially that way—and with all the people looking at you and laughing at you—I don't know whether I want to try it or not...Tell me all about the Island. From what I have heard people say, it is not a very pleasant place to stay. They say it is hot, and nothing there but sand and sage brush. I do not know why any one would want to go to such a place to spend a summer's vacation...What days does the mail leave the island? Write to me every mail if you can spare the time for I do not like to wait four days for a letter.

A familiar proverb says: "The course of true love never runs smooth." Whether true or not as a generalization, it proved so in this case; for the next thing was a rift occasioned by the coming to Catalina of a girl named Sophie, somewhat older than Artie, who had kept company with Charles before he and Artie had met each other.

This girl came to the island expecting to get work, but did not obtain a position, so stayed at the island only one night; Artie inviting her to share her bed, though the two had never before met.

Having lived in Colton formerly, when she found out that Artie was from that place, she began to talk about the people both knew; and it was not long before she was asking about Mr. Ward, and whether he was still there or not. Artie, who had formerly heard of this girl and had discussed with Charles their relationship, while giving out no information concerning herself and Charles, listened with ears pricked up to everything the girl had to say about him. It was not long before she discovered that the girl was very much in love with him; and that according to her version, he had encouraged her to expect marriage, and had been corresponding with her since she left Colton.

Artie, by adroit questioning, led her on to tell all she would, and some of it looked black for Charles. The girl even told her some of the things contained in his letters. Artie was inwardly indignant, and made up her mind to get at the bottom of it immediately. It was two or three o'clock in the morning before the two dropped off to sleep; and that forenoon, Sophie took the boat for the mainland.

Artie, at the first opportunity wrote a letter to Charles that she thought would very likely fill him with confusion, and cause him to inquire what she had been told by his "other girl." Jealousy and imagination added their quota to what had been divulged. Her wording implied that she knew much more than the bare facts presented in her letter—that she and Sophie had spent the night together, and that he had been the subject of their conversation. But Charles himself did not take this letter too seriously upon receiving it. He wrote:

June 23
"My Little Girl:

You are the greatest rogue in the country. What a time you must have had 'pumping' (slang) poor Sophie! Well, I hope you found out all you wanted to. So she said I told her lots of 'stories' did she? Well, if she says so, I must have done so; but I do not remember of doing so. It was very hard for her to have to go way over there and not get a situation, and I feel very sorry for her. I think she is a very good girl to work, only a little aged to suit most people. I really did feel my ears burning the other night, but did not think for a moment that you two were the cause of it. Well, I guess I caught 'Hail Columbia,' but no matter. I supposed she had gone back to 'Bosting' long before this, as she said she was going back. So you have not gone in bathing there yet! You ought to do so soon. But Artie, keep away from the skating rink...I think your Chinese laundryman is altogether too high. You had ought to import one from somewhere else in California; then he would have to come down on his prices. You can have some from Colton if you want them. There is one tall, thin, long-eared, sunken-cheeked, pig-tailed Celestial here that we can get along without just as well as not—and for my part, a great deal better. And if you want him there, you can have him free, gratis, for nothing, so long as you get him away...I like the way your last letter was headed...
Goodnight,
Ever yours, Chas."

This letter was followed by another written before Artie's answer came:

"July 7,

I hope you had a pleasant time the Fourth, but don't suppose you did, over there away from everybody. I stayed in Colton all day. It was too hot to go anywhere. They had a great time in Los Angeles, so everyone says; and the fireworks were something grand...Had my little girl been in Los Angeles, I should have gone. At Colton everything seemed like Sunday except for the continual 'pop' of the firecrackers. All the small boys and some of the large ones that stayed at home, celebrated as usual by scaring horses and setting fire to buildings and so forth. There were four houses burned down in San Bernardino. Cause, firecrackers. Mrs. White is having a time with her girls again, and Mr. White is waiting on table. One of the girls has gone, and the other is only waiting till they can get some one to take her place. Emma is coming back the fifteenth. And from what they say, I guess Maggie will return also...I often wish my girl was nearer than she is, but do not want her at the

Trans again, stuck in that little back room...Say Artie, I've got another dog—or rather, a 'purp'...It will be...a good hunting dog ...I was out hunting yesterday and got lots of game, and took the purp along. He hunted fine; but wanted to catch all the ground squirrels in the country-but got left. The squirrels would go into the ground, and poor doggy would look sad. We have moved, and I have a new room much pleasanter than the one I had. While we were moving, Mother saw your photo, and said: 'Who is that pretty little girl with such nice hair all down her shoulders?' I told her that was 'my girl.' She laughed, but didn't believe me. She will find out one of these days, I hope, that she really is 'my girl'; for even when she is my own little wife, she will never cease to be 'my girl'...I am getting awfully tired of waiting, and am afraid I can not get sufficient money ahead here, or anywhere else in California to go into any business with, as times are too dull...Goodbye, God bless you my little girl.

Ever yours, Chas."

Artie's next letter, written before this one reached her, caused him more concern:

"July 10:

...You seem to have your mind made up that I have been deceiving you. I never lie in matters of importance; and when you asked me questions concerning Sophie, I considered them matters of importance, and answered them truthfully. I say once more, I have never seen Sophie's face since the day she left Colton to go to Los Angeles before I knew you. You say I was deceiving you all along, and corresponding with her after I asked you, and carne in every evening and spent my evenings with you. I tell you Artie, I never wrote but three letters to Sophie—I think, anyway not more than four—that, I will swear to upon my honor...and all those within a month after she left Colton. Now, I do not think I spent very many evenings with you during the first month you were at the Trans...Not the second either, for that matter. And you know yourself, it was a long time before we either of us thought of the other more than as a simple friend...You take her word—one you have only known for one night—in preference to mine. I think that you want to know too much, Artie; and you did none of the three of us concerned in your conversation any good when you lay awake until two or three o'clock, investigating. You say you may 'fool' me, where I said I would not have a 'rival. ' Artie, I do not exactly understand your meaning. But what I said then, I say again, and I do surely mean it: that I will never compete with any man for the love of any woman—no, Little One, not even for your love. If ever I find that any other has taken any part of my place toward you, I shall surely step down and out and give him a clear field. I do not think you meant what you wrote, and do not think you have any idea of trying to 'fool' me. If you have, you are at liberty to do so. I was only joking about the skating rink, but Artie, I do not think you would go anywhere if I requested you not to. I shall never ask you not to go or do anything unless I have good reasons...I want you to answer this at once; tell me whether you believe my story or the other. If you feel that I have been deceiving you all along, just write a few words telling me so. That's all I want, Artie. I would never marry anyone who had deceived me, and would not expect it from anyone else. Trust me 'all in all' or 'not at all.' Artie do not take this letter to mean anything but just exactly what it says. There is no 'reading between the lines'...I am not angry with you, no, not at all, Little One, I only feel bad and hurt that you can not believe me when I tell you the truth.

As ever yours, Chas."

His next letter followed before receiving an answer to this one, after getting her reply to his previous one; and it must have made everything all right.

"July 12 My Darling Little Sweetheart:

Your very welcome letter reached me last evening...I am very glad that the steamer has taken the mail again, so I can hear from you oftener. I do not like to wait eleven days for a letter from my little one. Artie Darling, you will get a letter from me today probably, that I am very much afraid will be a cross one. I'll tell you why. In the first place, I was vexed with you for believing what Sophie told you in the place of believing me...Then I was awful sick and really ought not to have tried to write...working every day in the hot sun. Mother moved chickens and flowers...had to build chicken houses, replant flowers, dig trenches, lay about 150 feet of water pipe, and so many other things to do; and it was real hard work, especially digging trenches and laying the pipe; for the 'dog-blamed' pipe did not want to go together. I am very glad you were not here to hear me swear...Mother and Sister sneaked up on me once, and heard me swearing, and one of them said: 'Charlie! Charlie! Where do you expect to go when you die?' I told them I expected to go where I would have the most company...and where there were no water pipes. They looked very solemn for a minute; then had to laugh..."

Artie's next letter was more explanatory, and showed a much mollified spirit; in answer to which he wrote:

"I know now, Dear what you allude to and understand you; and will say this once for all: I did not intentionally deceive you; for I had forgotten of ever saying anything to anyone that would cause them to think things were different than most people thought (you understand me). But I do now remember of saying it to the party you met. Once she was asking me some questions, and I spoke before I thought. Well, as you say, 'let it drop.' But Dear, if you can believe me, I had no intention of ever being anything more to her than what I was—or to anyone else. Nor did I ever think of meeting little Artie, my Sweetheart. Do you know her? The nicest, the—oh pshaw! I can't tell you half how nice she is; so won't try. I thank you Dear, very much for your confidence in me, and will try not to betray that confidence—no never! Some day we will have a good long talk and get these things straight. So one of the girls got after a shark, did she?—Oh what did I say—I mean a shark got after a girl, did it? My goodness! Little one, don't go in bathing any more. For those water sharks are awful! Why, you wouldn't be half a meal for one of them...Water sharks are worse than land sharks...they don't eat you all up, but water sharks do. Don't go in any more, please—anyway, don't go only a few feet from the shore...I did not know there were sharks along the beach. It must be dangerous to go in bathing—really, it must...Sweetheart, you have asked forgiveness for your cross letter. It is given fully and freely. It probably was not so cross, and I know it was not intended to be...Do you know Dear, the reason I learned to love you?...It was for being so good to me when I had those sick headaches...Well, Darling, Goodnight...I can kiss the photo anyway; it wants to be kissed, I know...Bobby Burns says:

> *'Ask why God made the gem so small,*
>
> *And why so huge, the granite?*
>
> *Because He meant mankind should set*
>
> *The higher value on it!'*

And he knew what he was talking about if he meant my little girl; for the value I set on her is very high.

Goodnight, Love, Sweet dreams. Chas."

In Artie's reply, she gently corrected his poetic authority, ascribing the quotation to Tom Moore instead of Bobbie Burns; for which he thanked her.

Charles soon wrote again on July 25:

"Say, Dear, what do you suppose I heard yesterday? It was the greatest surprise to me. I heard you were married; what do you think of that? Emma told me you were married in Los Angeles, some time after you left the Trans...Imagine my surprise...I could not find out who the lucky man was, but you were married sure and fast. Now Artie, I think that real mean in you, to go and get married and not even tell me...Say Dear, if a candy drummer comes over there, I don't want you to talk to him. He's nice looking, and a good friend of mine, and often has stopped at the Trans. Last evening he wanted to know where that 'little black-eyed girl' was 'that used to be here'; and I, like a fool, told him; 'She went to Catalina.' Now look out for him, and if he wants to talk to you, just tell him to give his 'order please,' you are too busy to talk. What I meant by 'going up North' Dear, was the northern part of the state, or Oregon, or probably Washington Territory—anywhere I can find work. So your sister is going to be married is she? Who to? Well, if your sister is half as sweet as her sister, I don't blame anyone for marrying her. September two, you say, and you think she will beat you, do you?

Perhaps so, perhaps not. You don't know what may happen between this and September two. There may be 'orange blossoms' for you too.

Ever yours with love, Chas."

A snatch from another letter dated Wednesday, July 30, says:

"I am very glad you are coming back from that old island where they are trying to work my girl to death...I shall go to Los Angeles Saturday and meet you at the depot...If you do not come on Saturday's steamer, write me at Colton."

But Artie did not come back from Santa Catalina the following Saturday as expected. Several more letters were exchanged before her return. On Sunday, August 5, Charles wrote:

"My Little Girl: I got left. I went clear to Los Angeles to meet a young lady and she did not show up...I returned to Colton last night...Well, it is all right anyway Dear. I was very much disappointed, for I wanted to see you. But I am sure you could not help it...I was at a banquet the other evening. Old Mr. and Mrs. Earp celebrated their golden wedding day; and such a lot of nice old people, I never met before. Old forty-niners—gray-haired men and women; some young folks, but not many. I have a small piece of the cake left to give you. They were married fifty years ago in Kentucky by a great uncle of mine, as near as we can learn; the Rev. Thomas Ward. My father had an uncle of the same name, and a preacher, in Kentucky, but what became of him, we can not find out now...I shall be in Los Angeles again this week—exactly what day, I do not know. I attended to some matters yesterday, but will have to go down again soon. If you are sure when you are going to come away, let me know, and I will meet you at the depot. (But I want to <u>meet</u> you this time, you little Rogue.)

Goodbye, Dear, Yours with best love, Chas."

From Catalina, Artie wrote to Mother, telling her of her coming plans for marriage, and Mother, answering, offered to give her a home wedding. In her next letter to Charles, Artie told him of what she had done, enclosing Mother's letter and also one from Joan. Which he acknowledges in his next:

"Aug. 6,

Dear Little One:

Your kind letter and those enclosed reached me today. So you have 'done gone' and 'let the cat out of the bag' yourself, have you? Well Dear, I am glad of it. Tell your good kind mother that he is no 'tony gent,' and thank her very much for her kind offer; and when the time comes, she may be called upon. That will be just as you desire, Dear. I do not care where I get my girl so long as I get her. I wonder if your mother remembers the 'proxy' letter she got several months ago?. We had quite a storm here yesterday, and some rain today. The rain is spoiling fruit and doing a great deal of damage to the grapes."

Another misunderstanding arose between our lovers, and several letters were exchanged before it was straightened out; after which, things went smoothly again.

"Aug. 17

Dear Artie...I was very glad to hear from you, and so kindly; it was more than I deserved. I shall be very glad to meet you at Los Angeles when you come back; for I want to have a good long talk with you...I am going to build a house on my land in two or three weeks. It has to be completed by the fifteenth of September according to my contract. It will not be much of a house, though—only enough for Mother... to live in. What do you think happened? You couldn't guess if you tried a week. Ed Rose and Maggie were married last Friday; so report says, and I guess it is true. They have a new girl at the Trans...When you are sure of coming, let me know, and you will have help to get off the cars at Los Angeles, and it won't be the brakeman, either.

"Aug. 20

Dear Little One;

Your little letter reached me this morning, and I am very glad to hear you are coming for sure...It seems to me as if I have not seen my girl for years. I guess I must surely be in love, for they say 'love reckons days for months and weeks for years.' Well, in a week I guess, I will get one more chance to see her...I want to give her some thing I have had lying in my trunk for quite a while now, if she will take it. You say it is getting hot over there...It has not been very hot here yet this year—only for a day or two at least. (He must have referred to the few days early the previous June when he complained of the heat.) It has been a very pleasant summer...one of the most agreeable ones I have seen here. Your train gets in at 4:33 o'clock. I think you had better stay on the train and ride up to the stopping place above Commercial Street (I do not know the name of the depot). It is near the cable cars, and we can get on there and go up town. I will get on the train at the depot and find you that way better than if you got off; for there is always such a crowd there.

Goodbye, Love from Chas."

But Charles did not meet her at the depot as arranged, on that twenty-seventh day of August. Instead of that, he took the San Pedro train and went down to the docks where her boat came in from Catalina, and met her there, to her great surprise and delight. Here, he presented her with the gift he had brought from its long hiding place in his trunk—a little oxidized silver watch, which she still has in possession among her treasures. Together they rode to Los Angeles, and from there to Santa Ana—there being no shorter route then—enjoying every mile of the journey as only lovers can, and getting all their little misunderstandings cleared up and brushed like cobwebs out of the way. At Santa Ana, they separated; he returning direct to Colton, and she going on to El Toro, where she was to be met by some of the folks from the farm; arriving there six days before Joan's wedding. Her first letter to Charles from Aliso contained an invitation from Joan to be present at her wedding. This, he answered on September one, declining the invitation:

"Yours from home reached me this morning. I was very sorry to hear you had to wait at El Toro so long...I had to wait two hours at Orange, and was thinking all the time: 'Now Artie will get home before I do.' But I got home about one o'clock. I do not think I had better come to your sister's wedding, Dear, as I told you in Los Angeles; not but that I feel I should be welcome; but for a stranger to be amongst them at such a time, they might feel that they were neglecting him and not enjoy themselves as they would otherwise—or something of that sort. Tell your sister I thank her very much for her kind invitation, and I hope to make the acquaintance of both her and her husband soon. I may come and see you the latter part of this week or the first of next if I can...but I may not be able to get away.

Do not let any of those young fellows down there make love to you; for I am not ready to lose my girl just yet. Which of the places is nearest to your home Artie, Laguna, or Arch Beach? I want to go to the nearest place...Love to you and your mother, and all of you. Chas."

After Joan's wedding, Charles came down to Aliso and stayed a few days with us; which provided an opportunity for becoming acquainted. We liked him very much, and the regard was mutual. He seemed only too eager to fit into the family of whom he was to become a member; and greatly appreciated his visit with us and our welcome so freely accorded. I thought him very nice indeed for a big brother, and we became pals immediately.

Charlie had brought with him a bag of candy for Artie's baby sister, Clara, then just coming six. Luella, who was less than a year and a half her senior, felt keenly the partiality shown; but was determined not to expose the fact. Artie, however, sensing the situation, gave Clara a good strong hint to divide the candy with Luella. This, she seemed reluctant to do. Seeing her attitude, and being buoyed up by her large bump of native pride, Luella, very bravely and courteously said: "Let Clara have it; she's only a little girl, and she likes candy."

In his next letter, addressed to Artie at the Lincoln Hotel in Los Angeles, Charles wrote: "Sept. 24:

I have had no chance to thank you for that kind invitation to your home, and hoped to do so by speech and not by letter; but anyway, I am very thankful to you; for I enjoyed myself very much. They were all very kind to me; and I hope some day to be able to return the favor." (And again in another letter, he said:) "I liked them all. They all tried to make my visit a pleasant one; and they did so; for that was one of the most pleasant times I ever spent, and I shall long remember it. Let me say this, Dear: I like and respect them all as much as any I ever met."

On Oct. 5, he wrote:

"Mr. and Mrs. White have to do the cooking now, as they discharged Sam and cannot find another cook to suit them. Day before yesterday, Mr. White came and woke me up and asked me if I would go to San Berdoo (Bernardino) for him, and find him a cook and a waiter girl. I told him I would try. I went, but could get no cook; but a girl who promised to come Monday. When I got back, Mr. White asked me if I would do the office work while he cooked; and I said I would. Then Mrs. White told me lots of things. She said she thought she was going to get Artie back, as Emma had said something to her about it; but Artie did not come. She said Artie was not at the Lincoln Hotel in Los Angeles; she had asked the employment agency and found out where she was. I let her talk on; for she thought she was telling me news…She said she liked Artie very much. I didn't tell her that I did too; but I do."

Soon after this letter was written, Artie came to Colton to work at the Trans again; and so the sweethearts were once more together for awhile. But it proved to be only for a few weeks; for George wrote and invited Artie to come and work for him in San Jacinto; as Minnie was not well, and another addition was expected in their family. Artie accepted this invitation; at which Mrs. White was very much put out; and allowed Artie to go away without receiving what was due her for labor at the Trans; giving, however a promise of future pay. So Charles' next letter to her was addressed to San Jacinto, and dated Nov. 30, 1890:

"Dear Little Artie:

Your letter reached me last Friday, and I had to put off answering it for two days I was so busy. I was very glad to hear from you, and that you arrived at your brother's safely; for I was afraid that the cars would run off the track, or the wagon upset, or something happen, after all the talk you made…I took your trunk over to the warehouse and got a receipt for it, which I will send to you, and you must be very careful not to lose it, for the man said if you did not bring the receipt, you could not get any trunk …How did you spend your birthday and Thanksgiving? I hope you enjoyed yourself. I had turkey at the Trans. I won a turkey at a raffle, but sold it, as Father was in Redlands, and Mother did not care to cook it for two…I have often wanted to go to San Jacinto and see the town, and I want to go now more than ever; and if I have time, I may come some day soon…"

A snatch from another letter of Dec. 5, '90, runs as follows:

"…I had a strange dream last night. I dreampt that I was walking along the bank of some stream, and I saw far ahead of me, some little girl. As I approached nearer, it turned out to be Artie. I was of course delighted to see her, but wondered what brought her there. We walked along by the stream, and all at once we came to a place where all the brush had been cut off by a machine of some sort, and a field of stubbles left, very thick and hard to cross. Artie turned to me and said: 'Charlie, I can't cross this field.' I looked down at her feet and saw that she was barefooted. Then I looked at my own feet and was barefooted also. I said: 'Come here, I will take you across.' Then I took her in my arms and told her to wind her arms tight around my neck; and took her across all right, and the stubbles did not hurt at all. As soon as the field was crossed, I woke up…I thought over the dream a long time, and wondered if there was any meaning in it for us; it was so strange. Don't you think it was, Dear?…I have quit using tobacco; have not used any for over a week now, and do not seem to have much of an appetite for it. It was a little hard for the first two or three days. I wanted a cigar after my meals; but I made up my mind to quit, and am going to do so. The boys say: 'Have a cigar, Charles'; I say: 'No.' They say: 'What's getting the matter with you? All you need now is a pair of wings, and you will be an angel'…But I am a long way from being an angel…My head is giving me fits. I have a severe headache today, and can not write you a very good letter."

Charles was going through what everyone must who will break from the habit of using the noxious weed. There is a struggle—a clamorous demand of the nerves for their accustomed stimulant; which is bound to last until the effect of tobacco is eliminated from the system; but its disuse persisted in without gratification, will allow nature to throw off the accumulated poisons out of the body cells; and with these, will also go the unnatural craving for its use. After this, the nerves will gradually recover their equilibrium. And the victor may then enjoy the reward of physical betterment and increased character strength.

It was getting very cold in San Jacinto, and Artie had not gone properly prepared having left her warm winter clothes locked in her trunk in Colton. Charles wrote to her on Dec. 8:

"...I am very sorry you are in need of your flannels...If it is very cold there you might get sick. There is considerable sickness through the country now. We are having disagreeable weather here now— very cold and the wind blowing 'rocks and brickbats' and the stove smoking, till I am sure I shall write a disagreeable letter...I did not expect to go to your brother's and stop. I expected to go to San Jacinto and drive over to see you, and return the same day. But as things have turned out, I probably will not be able to spare the time just now...Emma is mad as a hare, and what at, I can not for the life of me make out...She won't speak to me when I go into the dining room, and looks cross, and it makes me feel so bad. It can not be that she and Jimmie are having a falling out, for I noticed Jimmie going in to see her yesterday. I feel sad about it and hardly know what to do...I have not smoked or used tobacco for over two weeks now. What do you think of that? Don't you think I am doing pretty well? The money I save on cigars will help buy the black suit or afterward, we might need a buggy...hold on there! I am getting off, I guess. The wind is blowing so I don't know what I am saying...The room is full of smoke...So I will say goodbye for this time."

Charles wrote again on Dec. 10:

"Your pleasant little letter reached me yesterday, as I was at home on account of the weather—it being so disagreeable I could do nothing at Redlands all this week. It is clearing up, and if the rain stops, I shall go out there and stay the balance of the week. I am sure you do need your flannels, and you had better send me your receipts and let me bring your trunk to you...I did think of coming up there about Christmas, but I guess you had better have your trunk before. I do not know whether it was quitting the use of tobacco that gave me such a headache or not; but I had it for two or three days; but just the same, I did not use any more tobacco; and I feel all O. K. now, I really am getting fat...I remember of some remarks you made once of a drunkard trying to quit drinking, and...you said he had to quit 'short off' or he would never break the habit. So it is with using tobacco. A person has to stop at once or the habit is never broken...I am sure if I tried a cigar now, in a few days I would be smoking as many as ever..."

I quote from another letter on Dec. 13:

"... This has been a very eventful week for Colton. First, a little baby of John Hust died. I don't know whether you know him or not. He is an engineer of the S.P. road. Next, Colo. Stephenson died—you know Frank Miner, and Miner shot him not knowing he was shooting toward him. That seemed the saddest of all. I will send you a Colton paper this evening...A sister of Mrs. Fuller died here last week. Your folks know Mrs. Fuller. She lives at San Juan, I believe. I know I heard your mother speak of them. Emma has gotten in a better humor and is more pleasant..."

"Monday, Dec. 15:

I think after this week I will take a lay-off until after the holidays. Work is slackening up a little and we have the most of our jobs pretty well completed...When I get your receipts I will bring your trunk to you...I really do not know what to say about the money that Mrs. White owes you; but I think you should write to them and have them send it to you. They can hardly refuse to do so. I thought they had paid you before this...Well, Artie-girl, I must go to bed for I have a headache again tonight. I hardly know what ails me of late. Got something wrong most of the time and crosser than a bear. I guess its from the stopping off tobacco. I don't know what else. Oh, my cigars from Mexico have not come yet. Mr. Easton has not returned...Anyway, I won't smoke them when they do come. I will save them as relics...Write me soon and send me the receipt for your baggage."

His last letter before vacation for the holidays is dated Dec. 21, 1890, in which he says:

"...Emma and Jimmie Lloyd are going to get married next Wednesday. Emma wanted me to telegraph you and have you come to her wedding. I told her it would be of no use, as you could not get a telegram any sooner than you would a letter, since the telegram would have to be put into the office...They are going to San Diego on their wedding trip, and are to settle in San Bernardino...Last evening when I went into the dining room of the Trans, there were two new girls there, and the first thing one of them said was: 'Please take this seat over here, as that one is taken.' I asked who had been here since I'd been gone, as I had sat in that seat most of the time for the past three years.

'Well,' she says: 'It's taken, and you will have to vacate.' So I vacated. Now don't you think that's real mean? I am having lots of trouble lately. When I came home from Redlands, my ferrets that Mrs. White gave me were dead—both of them; and my dog Flossie was gone. Some one has stolen her I am sure. I wrote you the old folks were going to move to Redlands, but the question is not settled yet. I find out that Pa is not the boss around our household; and Ma does not like to leave her plants, and so forth. I hardly know how the thing will turn out...it is about an even bet either way, still, I think the chances are slightly in favor of Dad."

Here, the correspondence is broken by Charles' visit to San Jacinto for the holidays where he stayed something over a week; being made more than welcome by everyone. While visiting here, he watched a neighbor, young Mr. Blair, put a harness on his broncho mules by the help of a pitchfork; not daring to approach closer to their vicious heels than the length of the handle. Charles thought this procedure exceedingly funny, and often chuckled over the memory of it. While there, he assisted George in putting up a shed-roofed outbuilding; and the two struck up quite a friendship.

After the turn of the year, Charles took the train home again and his friends who had been looking for him, could not make out where he had been, but nobody found out from him. The correspondence is resumed on Jan. 4, 1891:

"My Little Darling:

It is almost ten o'clock, but if I don't write tonight, I may not get time for a week as I have to go to Chino tomorrow. My father got a couple of houses to build there and left word for me to come over if I ever got back...They are having quite a boom at Chino. A sugar factory is going up there and a new town starting; and there is going to be lots of building going on there. We are putting up a boarding house first. There is nothing of the kind there yet; and we may have to sleep out in a tent till they get it done...Everyone was wondering where I had gone. They thought I had run away. Pa wanted to know where in the 'D——' I had been. He couldn't find out by anybody where I was...Well Darling, I was very much pleased with my visit, and the way I was received...Your brother and his wife treated me very kindly, and I am very glad I got acquainted with them...Give my kindest regards to George and his wife, and kiss little Pearlie for me...Ta, ta, I am sound asleep".

On the eleventh, he writes:

"...We got nearly through at Chino with the work we have on hand there...Dad did very well on these two jobs. Will clear over a hundred dollars on the boarding house alone—a little over a week's work. That's pretty good, 'aind id?' We have had five men on the job besides ourselves. No, I will not try to run the boarding house. Frank Graves' father has leased it. I do not think I would like to stay at Chino. They are improving there a great deal, and are going to work probably three hundred men all the time after they get started. You ought to see a steam plow they have working now. Plows forty acres a day, twelve furrows at a time. If George could see it he would think plowing with a walking plow slow indeed. It only takes three men to run it. They are going to put in five thousand acres in sugar beets. We did not have to sleep in a tent, as Pa got to work and put up a shed house (something like the one George and I built) the first day he got there. But it was cold...as Jerusalem...So you called me the 'crooked Stick'! - - - I'll get even for that...Say, Dear, I wish you could come this way when you go down home, and spend a day anyway, and as much longer as you like...Here it is only a little over a week since I last saw you, and I want to see you as bad as ever. What's the matter with me anyway?...Goodbye, with love and best wishes from your 'Crooked Stick'"

Charles has his photograph taken for his "best girl," and writes her as follows:

"Jan. 13, 1891

My Little Sweetheart:

Of these two photo proofs, which style do you like the best? Or do you like both the best? Or, do you like the original the best?—But I know you do, 'bester' than anybody else...I told the photographer they would do...I guessed, but as I was having them taken to give to my girl, I asked her if she could not make me look a little better. She said: 'Impossible! No one could do that no matter how good a

411

photographer.' So, if you are not satisfied, you will have to get some better looking fellow than your
'Crooked Stick'"

At last, this hopeful lover secured a steady job—and a good one, in the town of Ontario, working for a business man, "O. E. Hardy, Notary Public and Collection Agent, Also Dealer in Carriages, Wagons, and Farm Implements." Through the influence of friends in local political circles, he was also made deputy constable of Ontario; to which place he moved "bag and baggage," securing a room at the home of his employer, a young man recently married. Between the two jobs, which most conveniently supplemented each other, was a suitable competence assured by which to look forward with hope to a union with the lady of his choice. So he writes with manifest elation on Jan. 21, 1891.

"My Little Girl:

Henceforth and forever, please address your letters (those you write to C.F.W.) to Ontario, California, Box 172. I have located at this place I think, for good—that is, if it suits my Little One— and I think it will, for it is a pretty little village—one of the prettiest in the state...I have a good job, and one that will last until I get tired-which will be a long time...I went over and saw a little house this morning a man wanted to rent me. I told him if he did not rent it within a month, I would take it. He said if I would be permanent, he would save it for me. I did not like to promise until you saw the town. I will write Sunday along letter and tell you all about it."

Before this letter reached Artie, a letter arrived from her, forwarded from Colton, in which she tells him of the new baby that has come into George's home—a little son, born on the seventeenth of January, and later named Archie Roy.

Charles' next letter was written on paper secured in Ontario, decorated with the woodcut of Euclid, the seven-mile double Avenue extending from Ontario to Uplands, with corresponding envelope showing the fine new Central School House; and used by all public-spirited citizens. On Jan. 24, he writes

"...What do you think of the pictures on this paper and envelope? You can not buy any writing paper in town but what has these pictures on. The Avenue is seven miles long. I was clear to the end of it last evening, and when I got there, turned to the left and went about five miles farther up the canyon. You can see on the cut where the mountains come down. It was a very nice drive, and I was wishing you were along. When you come to live with me, we will go up there, stay all day and have a picnic...I get up every morning at half past five; don't you think I'm getting industrious?"

In the next few letters, arrangements are made for Artie to stop over at Ontario on her way home to Aliso. She left San Jacinto on the tenth of February, and was met in Colton by her intended. From there to Ontario they came, and Artie spent one night there at the home of hospitable Mrs. Hardy, who took a great liking to her. Before leaving, she and Charles spent some time looking at houses for rent; and he accompanied her back to Colton to take the train for El Toro—this time late, having missed the early one Joseph was to meet—reaching Aliso and home very late that night, never to "work out" again. The remaining nine of Charles' letters were addressed to her at Arch Beach, and chiefly concerned their coming nuptials and plans for the future.

"Feb. 29:

My Little Girl:

I have been longing for a letter for a week; and this morning, I got not only one, but three in one; and very glad too I was to get them. Yours was very short, but I will excuse you as you were 'busy'; but the next will be longer, I know. When I saw Joseph's handwriting on the envelope, I was afraid that you were sick from riding down the canyon so late. No Artie, you did not 'spoil the letter' by that 'heavy handwriting. ' That heavy handwriting has grown very dear to me. I don't know what I would do if I did not see it often—or the one who writes it. Harriet writes very prettily. Her handwriting is much like your married sister Joan's. (Joseph and I had written letters to Charles, and Artie had put in a note only.) We have had plenty of rain here lately, but I guess it is over now. The sun is shining brightly and the clouds rolled away. Mr. and Mrs. Hardy were pleased to be remembered by you. Mrs. Hardy's mother was here on a visit for three or four days. She gave me an invitation to 'come and visit' her 'when your girl comes.' I was over to San B'dino yesterday, and on the way home, stopped in Colton and saw Sister and her husband. They all told me when I wrote to send you their regards...I guess we had better take the little house down near Hardies' where those trees are, you know, the ones we were talking about. It is a very pleasant little place, lathed and plastered and fixed up pretty good. The old fellow has some furniture there, and he says he will furnish it good and rent it for eight dollars a month, or without furniture, for five. I asked him what he would take for the furniture, and he said he would have to see his wife and would let me know in a day or two. I have not seen him since. He asked me lots of questions; and at some of them, I guess I blushed. He asked if I had any children. I told him 'No.' He says: 'Will there be just you and your wife?' I says: 'Yes.' 'Where is your wife now?' says the old duffer. 'Oh,' I said, 'she is not here now.' It is a good thing there was nobody else there...

Goodbye Darling; write often."

The day after St. Valentine's Day, rain began to fall, breaking a long dry season; which made all the farmers glad. But the 'sunshine' mentioned by Charles in his letters did not prove to be of long duration; for, starting in again to rain within a few days, it was loath to stop; and soon the excess of rain was the cause of much damage and loss of life.

On February 24, he wrote

"My Little Girl:

I do not know when you will get this, as everything is washed away, and no trains running at all...It has been raining awfully here for the past week, or since last Saturday, and looks like it will still keep raining."

And on March Three, he wrote

"I wrote you just about a week ago, and I do not expect you have got it yet on account of the wash-outs...How did your folks get along...(I am very anxious to hear from you). I hope it did not get so high as your house; I am afraid of that canyon; but I hardly think the water would get up so far. Anyway, the honey house would be safe. That could never wash away. There was a lot of old religious fanatics praying for rain around through the country, and they overdid the thing—just like they overdo everything else. We did not have any trains for five or six days. I went to San Berdoo one day and when I got back to Colton, there was no train to come home on, so I had to stay there for two days. Finally an engine that was here, went to Colton to get some coal, and I saw the conductor, and he said I could come home if I could ride in a cattle car. I told him I could ride anywhere. So I got in along with a lot of Dagos (Italians) who were going to fix the roads. Oh Henry! How they smelled! The car smelled, and I guess I smelled too by the time I reached home...It was the greatest ride I ever had...The road is now fixed from here to Colton, and they just got the bridge in below Colton this morning; so trains can now go almost to Yuma. But they will not be able to get any further for a week yet. The whole town of Yuma was washed away, leaving only two buildings standing. One of them was a hotel and the other the Territory prison. Several miles from there was an Indian village, with about five thousand Indians. The whole place was washed away, and half of the Indians drowned. Lots of persons were drowned all through Arizona and California. There were five persons drowned near Los Angeles, and I guess, lots we have not heard of yet. Well, I guess you will have the news there by the time you get this, anyway...I gave twenty five cents for this pen. How do you like it? It's a fountain pen-one of those that you don't have to dip in the ink. You just put the ink in the handle and keep writing. They say: 'Never buy anything from a peddler'...but I guess this one is worth 'two bits' anyway."

By this it will be inferred that fountain pens were then a new thing and not generally known or used. Gold pen-points could not have been in use at the low price of twenty-five cents.

"March 14:

My own little Sweetheart:

Were it not for the fact that I got one of the nicest little letters yesterday, and that on the thirty-first of this month, I am going to wed one of the best and sweetest little girls, I hardly think I could write at all today. But those two facts being the case, I must write...just a little Dear, if only to thank you. I have been very sick during the last two days. Thursday I went to San Berdoo; and when I came back to Colton, I went to Mother's and lay down; I was feeling so bad. I kept getting worse till I was awfully sick—one of those old headaches. Yesterday I felt better and came home to Ontario, but last night did not feel so good, and slept not a wink all night long. But this morning I dropped off...and feel better now...All the time I was wishing you were here, Dear, and I know you would like to have been here, too, had you known I needed you. Well, Little One, the thirty-first suits me, and I will be there and make you mine...You—together with all your goodness, and all those little 'moods' of yours will belong to 'your boy.' Well, Artie Darling, I will try to be worthy of you and make you happy...I have spoken to the owner of the little house, and he is going to fix it up ready for housekeeping for us by the first of next month...So you do not like to beg even my pardon, Eh? Well, that's too bad. When I hurt anyone's feelings, I am only too glad to beg forgiveness if I care anything about them. But I know you better than you know yourself...You would not wound anyone's feelings without yourself feeling as bad about it as the other party in a short time afterward. I know very well you sometimes feel blue and downhearted, and have spells when you say you don't care for 'nuthin' an' nobody'; but those spells don't last long, and one good squeeze and a kiss will cure them all. I really ought not to have paid any attention to that letter, but it struck me just as I had a blue spell too. Well, we will let all those little things go now for good and try to be good to each other, won't we, Dear?...Oh dear! I guess I will have to close, Artie, I feel 'sorter old' today. I wish you were here...Anyway, I had a kiss this morning. I looked up and saw the photo of a little girl with her hair down over her shoulder, and she looked as though she wanted to be kissed...Foolish? Oh, no! As for your arrangement concerning your sister as your bridesmaid, nothing would suit me better. And I want Joseph to stand up too, for I know of no one I like any better...I guess you had better tell Hulda and Joseph and see if they will help us out...So your mother took your letter from you, did she? Well, you must look out. They will laugh at us if they get hold of some of our letters...Oh My! What a pile of letters you must have if you have kept them all! There will be enough to start the fire in the mornings for six months.

Yours with best love, Charlie"

But Artie did not start morning fires with those letters; if she had, this little love chapter would not have been written. Had she not burned her own, the story would have been less one-sided.

On March 16, he wrote:

"...So you are bothering that little head of yours planning how to get several grown-up people, two trunks, and two valises...in one small buggy, are you? Well Dear...I'll tell you what we'll do. You write to your brother Lafayette and tell him if he wishes to go to see his sister married to a 'crooked stick,' to be at Colton on the thirtieth of March, and there to keep an eye on the lookout for the aforesaid 'crooked stick,' and when he spies him (you will have to describe him as near as you can) to walk up to him and make himself known. I guess though, I will know him by the family likeness. We can go to Santa Ana together, and there I can get the license. Then we can get a livery team and go down the canyon. The next day we can all come back to Santa Ana and...when I leave Santa Ana, I won't leave alone...I would like very much to pay the folks a long visit, but I can stay only a short time, not more than two days if I can help it; for I want to make all I can now, and every day I am away, I lose considerable...During the summer months we'll go back, and you and Hulda and I will go down and have a run along the coast and have another clam bake, and lots of fun...I am thankful to be getting such a nice little wife...You are really too good for me. But I guess I had better not say that any more or you might think so too; and that would be too bad...You say: 'A more ardent lover never could be wished for.' Well, I don't think you could have a more sincere one, Dear...Thank Joseph and Hulda for me for helping us out. Make any arrangements you care to about getting to Santa Ana, if you want to change from my plans. Of course you folks know the best and easiest way. Tell Lafayette the train leaves Colton at 7:30 A. M., and we can get to Santa Ana before ten o'clock, and get down to your place about four, I guess...Well, Little One, I am going to let this letter go now. Very few more letters will we have to write to each other. Were it not for the fact that I shall be getting the writer of these pleasant little messages, it would be with the greatest regret I should see them stopped. They have helped pass many a weary hour away, even when I hardly thought the time would come when the writer would be half so dear to me; or ever be mine alone. Now, I could not live without her...Do not try to go to town and get any fine clothes. I do not care for them. Of course you want to look neat, but you have plenty of clothes neat enough. Come to me any way you like—I am satisfied. Give my kindest regards to all at home.

C."

Lafe had never met his prospective brother-in-law until that early Monday morning when they met at the Colton Depot to be travelling companions on the way to the wedding. Also, it had been only within a very short time that he had even heard of him; and in his characteristic fashion he plied Charles with personal questions all the way down, seeking to learn all he could about him in the short time allotted; for he felt just a little bit disturbed to think of his sister's marrying someone he had never known at all and of his being thus deprived of the privilege of acting the brother's part. However he made up his mind to like and accept him; for there was nothing else left to do now.

Since most of Artie's personal friends were widely scattered over the country, and therefore, few if any of them could have absented themselves from their respective positions and found their way down to the isolated farm at Aliso, she thought it best to spare Mother the expense and confusion of a home wedding; deciding to be married in Santa Ana. So her plan to be married at the court house by the Justice of the Peace and afterward to partake of a specially prepared dinner at the Richelieu Hotel on the corner of Fourth and Sycamore, was carried out, with no one present but the "home folks." Joseph and Hulda stood up with the couple, while Mother and Lafayette were the guest witnesses. But Lafe was obliged to forego the wedding dinner, as the train which he was obliged to take in order to be at his work again on time, left too early for such festivities.

The rest of the party took their time about enjoying the sumptuous dinner, and after a few pleasant hours together, parted at the depot; where the bride and groom took a late train to their new home and life together.

So the family "Old Maid" was no more; having, at the extremely ancient age of twenty-seven, exchanged her "single blessedness" for the cares and joys of married life and motherhood.

Figure 39 Charles Ward and Artemisia Thurston Marriage, 1894

Figure 40 Charles and Artemisia Ward Family, ~1910
Left to Right: Lorena, Winona, Charles, Gilmore, Merree, Vera, Violet, Artemisia

CHAPTER 55 THE NEW HOUSE

Because it was my birth month and also because it was my lot to remain away from the wedding, and care for the younger members of the family during the absence of the bridal party, Charles, upon his arrival at Aliso before the festivities, presented me with a delightful gift—a large, well-bound, beautifully illustrated book of travels and explorations, featuring special places of interest in all countries, but with special stress on those of our own land. This was a volume to whet the appetite of anyone for travel and sightseeing. And its profound effect upon me has never been effaced. One of the wonders described was the Mammoth Cave of Kentucky, which from that day to this I have desired to visit. I loved that book from cover to cover never tiring of poring over its pages and feasting upon its pictures. That new brother-in-law of mine seemed especially endowed with the faculty of choosing the nicest and most appropriate gifts. This one surely provided me with many hours of unalloyed pleasure and profit. I thought him the best of pals.

Soon after this, I was invited to take a trip to San Jacinto to live for awhile at George's place and help Minnie with her work and babies-for she seemed unable to manage both. This was the first time I had ever been farther from home than a day's journey by team, and was my first experience in riding on the "iron horse."

It was this year, Ninety-One, that saw the very first auto-car invented, and it was run by an electric storage battery. Its inventor was William Morrison, who sold it the following year to J. B. McDonald; but it was many years before this new invention was considered at all practical for use. Not in the wildest imagination of the most speculative minds was the idea conceived that this machine would ever supersede the horse. Only the most intrepid would risk their lives by a trial ride at the exciting pace of fifteen miles an hour; and when the first fatality occurred, by the breaking of a steering device, which hurtled the driver into a ditch by the side of the road, the thing was dubbed an "infernal machine." That the day would ever come when I myself would ever drive or own one of these infernal machines seemed as impossibly remote as that I should acquire a fortune by rubbing Aladdin's lamp. Yet I now count ten that I have owned at different times, all within nineteen years.

When I arrived in San Jacinto that April, the weather was delightful; warm, sunny, but not yet hot, as it would later become—for its summers are among the hottest of all Southern California—and though there was plenty of work for me to do, yet I found time to enjoy myself. Being very fond of Brother George, I spent some time with him out at his work on the farm, and enjoyed fixing his dinners for him.

The coming World's Fair at Chicago, celebrating the four hundredth anniversary of the discovery of America by Christopher Columbus in Fourteen Ninety-Two, was the talk of the valley—as doubtless it was of the whole nation—and the question was up before the World's Fair Planning Commission as to whether the gates of the fair should be kept open or closed to the public on Sundays. Feeling on the subject was strong. The "for" and "against" were divided into two opposing camps, and though its opening date was still two years in the future, and work only just begun, petitions to Congress were being circulated pro and con everywhere.

So, with the enthusiasm of youth, I too took part in this campaign, going from door to door and from farm to farm on foot all over that part of the valley that could be reached from my brother's place. In carrying my petition and presenting it for signatures, besides making the acquaintance of many families in the valley, I gained quite a valuable experience in meeting people out in the world, for which our secluded home in Aliso Canyon provided no opportunity. The fair was at first closed on Sunday, but opened after an injunction suit had been brought and decided in favor of opening.

The bill introduced into the legislature in Eighty-Nine providing for such a fair had been passed in Ninety, too late even for hope that the fair could be opened at the time of the actual anniversary on October Twenty One of Ninety-Two, so the date had been set ahead to May first of Ninety Three, and only the dedication itself was set to take place on the actual anniversary. Then the World's Columbian Commission was formed to undertake the gigantic task of preparing for the mammoth event. The best architects from New York and Boston joined with those of Chicago to erect one hundred and fifty buildings on six hundred and sixty-six acres of land fronting for two miles on Lake Michigan and lying in Chicago's half developed Jackson Park.

The whole Fair city was to be made of jute fibre and plaster of Paris to represent white marble, and when finished, was called "The White City"—a most magnificent sight. One building alone, the Manufacturers and Liberal Arts, covered thirty-one acres, being the largest building ever yet constructed for an exposition. For more than two years the hundreds of mechanics and artisans worked tirelessly almost day and night; and on the dedication date, October

21, '92, while everything was yet unfinished, before immense crowds, the buildings and grounds were formally dedicated. One of the orators on that occasion was Chauncy Depew; and music for the occasion was furnished by a great chorus and orchestra. There were no "loud-speakers" to assist the hearing in that spacious building of thirty-one acres; for such conveniences had never yet been thought of.

More than six months later, in the midst of a financial panic that, starting in the east, swept westward threatening to delay the opening date, the World's Fair was formally opened by Mayor Carter Harrison on schedule time; and the newly re-elected Grover Cleveland, after delivering an eloquent address, touched the button that set in motion all the machinery of the "White City."

Several other cities of the nation had contended most bitterly for the honor of having the World's Fair in their midst. New York, Saint Louis and Boston had lost after a long fight, during which the Editor of the New York Sun had dubbed Chicago a "windy city." The name, "Windy City" has ever since clung to that metropolis.

This first World's Fair, opening on the first of May Eighteen Ninety-Three and lasting through to November, was followed in Ninety-Four by the Midwinter Fair in San Francisco, covering a hundred and sixty acres of Golden Gate Park.

A Dream Come True

After a visit of nearly two months in San Jacinto, upon my return home I found the family all "keyed up" over plans for the building of a new house on the Aliso farm. This was the event for which Mother had secretly longed but had hardly dared to hope for.

From Saunder's place in Redlands where Lafe was working he had entered into correspondence with Mother concerning the matter of tearing down the old cabin where we had lived so long and erecting in its place a new building of suitable size to house the whole family. Now he was through with his work there and could devote himself to the project, an opportunity that might not come again. Mother had received a few hundred dollars from her dear father's estate, and besides that, the walnut crop of the previous fall had been abundant and the nuts of the finest quality. Fortunately they had been sold at the unusually high figure of five cents a pound. This, too, had much of it been laid by to swell the treasury, so that the time seemed most auspicious for the momentous undertaking.

Lafe had himself drawn the plans for the proposed new house, and had spent some time in Ontario going over them with Charles before figuring out the material bill to the last stick. Charles had promised to come down and help a while on the construction during his summer vacation time.

Lafe secured the prices of competing lumber companies both local and at a distance, and finally ordered his lumber from the McFadden Company of Santa Ana, who owned not only the lumber yard but the pier at Newport to which the lumber was shipped from the North, the ship on which it was transported, and the private car line which now freighted it from Newport to Santa Ana. With all these facilities under his control, he was naturally in a position to make the best prices on materials. From Santa Ana, the lumber was shipped by way of the Santa Fe to El Toro, from which place the boys hauled it down Aliso Canyon to the place of operations.

The question now up for discussion, was just where the family were to live during the building operations. It was unanimously decided to use the croquet ground for the purpose, and thus save the labor of preparing some other location, this spot being already leveled. So the croquet wickets were pulled up by our willing hands, and the set boxed and laid away for the summer. The honey house, already being used for sleeping quarters, was crowded to the limit after the organ and trunks were packed in there, so another bed was set up out under the stars behind it, and here slept Hulda and eight-year-old Luella.

The house being emptied of all its old familiar contents, wrecking was begun. The little cabin that with its subsequent additions had served the family so well for almost twenty years, loudly groaning out its protest with every squeaking nail drawn or hammered from its socket, and every splitting board and failing timber, was ruthlessly torn down to make way for its successor. It was with queer sensations and tuggings at the heart that we watched the demolition of the only home we had ever known. Yet the glad anticipation of something better to take its place was uppermost in every breast.

All hands contributed their help in carrying and piling materials. Housework was necessarily suspended, or diminished to the bare cooking of meals and making of beds, washing of dishes and laundering. Tables and cupboards had been set up on the croquet ground, where chairs and other things had been conveyed, and the roof of the cabin was lifted off with as few separations as possible and transported to the campsite where it was erected as a roof over the whole camp, coming down to the ground in places and resting upon beams to make a wide high canopy with a wide opening toward the big green fig tree on the north.

To us young folks, every day in this camp was like a picnic, until the "new" had worn off. And it might have continued to be so all through the summer had it not been for the daily nuisance of flies, which there was no way under the sun to exclude. But for this one trial, we would all have greatly enjoyed the experience of prolonged outdoor camp life.

Day by day we all watched the progress of our new house, and lent what help we could to the boys in their work. Joseph and Frank had as much farm work as ever to occupy their hands, and of course we had our outside tasks as usual. But inside duties being reduced to a minimum, we found much time to spend around the scene of operations. The boys worked overtime to help what little they could. But the actual carpenter work was all done by Lafe himself.

Meanwhile, the routine of life was not without its usual variations and quasi-tragedies to break the monotony. One evening Luella, having been punished for some supposed misdemeanor, felt herself to have been greatly abused, and decided to run away. When we looked for her at bedtime, she was nowhere to be found. Her bed had not been disturbed, and every available hiding place was then searched without results. Of course there was no place to run to, as all well knew; but we hunted nevertheless until ten o'clock at night—all to no avail. Finally Hulda, sure that Luella would come out of her hiding place before the night was very far advanced, decided to retire, and went out to her bed under the stars which the two shared together, and there she found the "runaway" tucked snugly in bed and sound asleep.

Having gone as far as the apple orchard, there she had remained until the surplus indignation was dissipated. During this time her outdoor bedroom had been visited in the search, and of course found empty. But later, she had sneaked back unseen and gone to bed, while the family kept on hunting. Of course there was nothing in this that she could be chided for, not even having been out late. So the anxiety and inconvenience suffered by the rest of the family served only to afford her much inward satisfaction as being properly avenged for her "wrongs."

This building of the new house, and destruction of the old cabin home Annie had left was another of the changes— and the major one—that took place during her absence. Little had she dreamed when bidding us all goodbye that August morning nearly two years before, that never again would her eyes behold the little old house in which she was born, where all her childhood days had been spent and with which all her memories were associated. But life is like that.

The new house was of two-story construction, having seven rooms; four of which were bedrooms, with Mother's downstairs and three upstairs. There was a long, rather narrow dining and living room, a smaller front room, a small kitchen and a bathroom also on the first floor.

For the first time in our history, we had a bathroom and a regular bathtub in which to bathe, and a sink also in which to wash our dishes. To be sure, these were not exactly the kind of fixtures that would be selected today by home-builders; for both sink and bathtub were of galvanized iron, such as were in common use in those days. There was no beautiful tile in connection with either of them, and not even a lavatory or a flush bowl in the bathroom—just the tub. That was luxury enough, and all that could be desired then.

No hot water from an automatic heating tank could be drawn into this tub, for there was no water-heating device of any kind in the house. Water for bathing must be heated in a wash boiler on the stove in the adjoining kitchen and conveyed by hand to the tub. To be able to draw even cold water from a faucet inside the kitchen was considered almost the acme of convenience.

This was made possible by the removal of the outside water tank that received water from the spring, from its location below the house, to a position a rod or two above the back door where it was set up on a newly built high standard to give it fall enough to flow by gravity into the house.

The sink had a small wooden drainboard at one end, and a sheer drop at the other. But it was at least a sink. Most country people had none at all, but washed their dishes on their kitchen tables, as we had done for so many years. As for drainboards, scarcely a carpenter knew how to make them convenient in those days.

There was a little galvanized wash tray and faucet on the back porch for outside workers to use before coming in to dinner, and this took the place of the old bench and hand basin. These three fixtures drained through one outlet pipe into the yard where the waste water could be utilized in growing flowers.

In those days, carpenters and builders knew very little about the beauty and symmetry that today is expressed in our modern architecture. All the closets upstairs stuck out into the rooms from corners, instead of being enclosed between side walls as closets are today. Such were those in the hotel at Arch Beach where Lafe had learned his trade. And such were those in hotels and private homes built everywhere in the country. In all these closets, there were neither rods nor hangers for rods; for none of us had ever heard of such conveniences.

Against the south side wall, opening into the dining room, was built a plain brick fireplace, with a narrow mantle shelf above it—none of your beautiful tile or polished hardwood, but still a place to set flowers and ornaments. And around the room several feet up from the floor, ran a wainscoting, the walls being panelled below by finished battens, and above, boarded up with tongue-and-groove ceiling lumber; with which also the room was ceiled overhead. The three double windows all of a size, featured two panes to a sash, and were held open, as were all the windows of the house, by two spring catches, one to a side of each sash, set in holes bored through the sash into the frame, for we knew nothing then of window weights, and easy gliding windows. The doors were the old-fashioned kind with four upright panels—two shorter below and two longer above. There were no built-in features such as moderns now enjoy; but we do not miss that of which we have never heard.

The kitchen was rather small, but it was thought when planned, to be sufficient since we were always to eat in the dining room; however, there was not a corner to be found in it that would contain the big Charter Oak stove with its convenient reservoir. It was getting rather worn anyway after thirteen years or more of continual use as both cookstove and heating stove. So the dear old thing was discarded, and a new and smaller stove was set up, that could never equal it in any respect.

The "parlor" also featured a wainscoting, but the walls were papered, below it with a darker pattern, and above it with a light pattern, and ceiled with lighter still overhead.

Mother's room was very small and cut up with too many doors; one of which might better have been eliminated, together with the tiny porch that led off from it. Had this been done, the kitchen might have been made that much larger with advantage to both rooms; but we all live and learn by experience. Her closet was the only one in the house that did not jut out from a corner. It lay between this little porch and the bathroom, making three doors in a row. The fourth door opened at the foot of the stairway into a diminutive hall just large enough for this door on one side and another opposite leading into the dining room, between which rose the ascending stairway.

The staircase bent with a landing about midway, and near its upper end passed a short window that opened out over the shed roofs of the kitchen and its porch. At the top, the stairs faced a set of six-foot-long shelves for books across the head of stairway and hall. There the first door, directly opposite the window, opened into the girls' front bedroom cornering on the southwest. The hall then doubled back along the railing of the stairway till opposite the lower landing, where it faced another door that opened into the rear girls' bedroom on the northeast. There the hall turned in an ell that led to the door of the boys' room between those two fronting north and west.

Though this house, which was practically square, occupied the original site of the old cabin house, it covered much more ground from back to front. This necessarily raised the floor of the added front porch to a much greater height from the sloping ground than was the old, so that seven steps instead of five were required, a flight being placed at either end. The distance from the back door to the two sycamores was also much shortened.

When Lafe came to the finishing touches of his new creation, he was in a decorative mood that leaned somewhat toward the "Apache Style." He carved eight sets of bows and arrows—one arrow crossing each bow as if ready for a shot—and arranged a set in each of the eight upper angles made by the junction of the porch roof with walls and with the three upright posts at the front. On the top of the main roof of the house, he fashioned a little fence of short pickets about the size and appearance of a grave mound fence about its center peak. Later, when it came to the painting of the house a wave of patriotism swept his soul, and he had these decorations of fence and bow-sets all done in red, white and blue.

Just as Lafe's labor on the building was a "freewill offering," so also was the painting of this house inside and out— so far as labor was concerned—and it came about in a seemingly providential manner.

An old painter by the name of Peterson from San Juan Capistrano, though a stranger to the family, strayed into the yard one evening on his way through the canyon, and asked for a place to stay all night. He was kindly treated and given food and lodging, his eyes kindling with interest at sight of the new, brush-challenging edifice now nearing its completion. All his painting instincts were aroused, and upon learning that no painter had been engaged, and that the family were too poor to let out the job, and were expecting to get it done somehow themselves, though none of them had ever handled a brush, he offered to do it himself for nothing but his board and lodging.

This was like a windfall from the skies. We could hardly realize our good fortune. By way of explanation, he said that money never did him any good anyway because he drank it up as fast as he got it, and would always be penniless. All he wanted was a drink once in a while and a place to sleep and food to eat. And so it proved. Though one of the best painters that ever wielded a brush, he was a pitiful slave to drink.

So Mr. Peterson became a member of our household for several weeks. The man was an artist, and took an artist's pride and delight in doing his best. The outside was given several coats of a soft gray. When it came to the inside, everything downstairs was done in harmonizing colors and made to resemble expensive woods. In the wet paint, blending together brown and yellow, with a little piece of leather he formed twisted knots and wonderful graining in imitation of the finest hardwood. All the door panels and the upper walls of our dining room were done in this manner. The ceilings were painted sky blue.

Upstairs he would have done the same could Mother have afforded the materials. But the money was not forthcoming, so these rooms were simply stained a brown color, as also were all the floors, and afterward the walls and ceilings were appropriately papered.

When the job was completed, Mr. Peterson was given by way of thanks, a small amount of "booze money." This he accepted as a surprise and was even pleased with the small gift. He had enjoyed his work, and especially his stay with the family.

No painter could possibly have done a better and more conscientious job than did he. Though the house stood for forty years or more it was never repainted; nor during the time it was inhabited did it ever seem in desperate need of repainting.

Of all the floors in the house, only that of the front room was given a covering. This was a sort of grass matting then in use, that came in yard width and was cut into strips to fit the room. The selvage edges of adjoining strips were caught together by small staples a few inches apart that were driven down through them into the floor; while the ends were folded under and similarly tacked.

A sturdy fence enclosing its immediate yards was built all around this house; being made of pickets about three feet in height, with points upward. These were fastened by posts at intervals to the top of a heavy concrete retaining wall for a foundation, that was built step-like to shape it to the slope. Outside in front, stood a concrete horse block and a hitching post.

The builder of this concrete wall was none other than Harry's cousin Robert Hughes, the brickmason who had sold out his little store in Los Angeles to the Ralph brothers of chain-store fame.

The services of this excellent brickmason were rendered at a very low wage by way of accommodation to the family into which his cousin had married. As a testimony to his thoroughness and pride in his workmanship, it stood without fault or flaw through all the years.

This man was an interesting character. He was wont to sing as he wielded the trowel, and floating back into memory comes the chorus of one of his little songs, with its pleasing melody and the peculiar pronunciation given to certain words by this Cornishman.

"Oh I hate to tell, but then I must;
Within her heart I placed my trust.
She was sitting in the garden
Where the little butterfly reposes;
And how we met, I'll ne'r forget
'Twas love amongst the roses."

There was another song that he sang of a humorous character and non-sentimental, in which were related a series of amusing episodes. Each stanza ended with the same words: "The blow almost killed Father," which also furnished the title to the song. One stanza of this comic is still recalled:

"Our old gray mare had the 'epizutics'
Away down in her thorax.

Dad stuck a gas pipe down her throat
Filled up with powdered borax.
Says he, 'You hold this end in her mouth
While I blow in the other';
He blew in the pipe—the horse, she coughed;
And the blow almost killed Father."

After the house was all finished, Lafe built also above the backyard fence, under the northern one of the two twin sycamores, a "milk house" for Mother. Rows of shelves filled one side and end, to hold the many pans of milk—the churns standing against the opposite wall near the window.

Within the light that fell through this window, he built also a "butter table" of original design; whose top of white pine sloped toward the front and right end, where at the lowest corner was hung on a hook, a receptacle for catching the drippings that trickled out of the butter as it was being "worked." These were conveyed thither by means of a continuous groove down both ends and across the front. A strong wooden lever was attached at the center of the upper edge that moved in any direction for "working" the butter—a device that saved much hand labor, as well as doing more thorough work in a shorter time.

This little milk house had one door with two lifts before it, that opened toward the kitchen, and saved many steps for Mother, as well as providing a more convenient place and more sanitary facilities for taking care of the milk and butter industry than had been furnished by the cellar. From this time on, the cellar degenerated into a mere store room.

As soon as the inside of the house was finished, before the front steps had been built to the porch, or the fence and retaining wall constructed, while we were still doing our cooking out under the camp roof on the croquet ground, we gave a dedicatory party and dance; inviting the neighbors from the coast. Artie and Charlie were already there; for it was Charlie's vacation time and he had been helping on the house for a week or more. With them was also Judge L.M. Sprecher, from Colton, who had accompanied them to enjoy a country vacation. He it was who had been partially instrumental in getting Charles the deputy constable ship at Ontario.

This Jurist was another addict of the "liquid fire" by which he was dulling his brilliant mind. The ten days spent at Aliso, he told Charles afterward, was the longest time he ever went without a drink—and to him it had seemed like a month, so insistent had been his craving for alcohol. Long before his vacation was over, he was begging Charles to go home.

Joan was playing the organ that evening for the dance, and had left little Florence, her infant of two months, asleep out in the camp on the croquet ground. While the dance was in progress, Artie, who was not on the floor at the time, heard Frank outside give a great war-whoop, and ran out to learn the cause of the uproar; which the noise of music and dancing completely drowned for those engaged in it. As she reached the porch, another yell from Frank indicated something about the baby. Forgetting that there were no steps to the porch, she got to the edge before remembering. Finding herself unable to get down to the ground by any other means, she took a jump and landed on the hard ground badly shaken and sprained. The baby had awakened and was crying, and Frank had been trying to make someone hear so the infant could be attended to; that was all. But Artie was hurt; and added to physical discomfort, was a heartbreak because Charlie, finding it out, instead of sympathizing with her, scolded her soundly for jumping in her delicate condition.

During this visit of Artie and her husband, I attempted to perform my old "stunt" in the presence of my new brother-in-law; who gave me as great a surprise, perhaps, as I did him. One day several of us were walking down the road below the house toward the cart-road gate, when we beheld, stretched out across the road, a large snake of the harmless variety.

"Look out! There's a snake!" Charles shouted.

Calmly I walked over to it, and to his horrified amazement, picked it up by the tail—its writhing body suspended in mid-air. I thought the man would have a "conniption fit." Cold shivers chased up and down my spine at his yell of concentrated horror:

"HARRIET!"

His face livid from fright, he grabbed my arm in a vice-like grip, and as I dropped the snake, jerked me away as if from certain death, while he gave me a scolding such as I could never forget.

"Why," I said to my "rescuer," "That's only a gopher snake, he won't hurt anybody."

Charles gazed at me as at a specimen he did not know how to classify. To his city-bred mind, I must have been an enigma of the first magnitude.

We were all glad when the time came to move into the new house; which took place early in September, during the harvesting of crops, and before the outside painting was done and the retaining wall built; for we were getting exceedingly tired of the long period of open camp life with its inconveniences and flies. How happy we were to have a real home, a "parlor" and real bedrooms, with plenty of room for everybody in the family! The cistern then fell into disuse as sleeping quarters, and the new-mown hay was left to "waste its sweetness on the desert air"; while the honey house became a storeroom and a place to keep odds and ends.

The family finances were again depleted, and there was little to "go on" till the fall crops should be harvested and sold; but at this there was no complaint from any quarter; for we all felt that what money we had been able to save had been well spent. Mother seemed well satisfied and happy, and hummed as she went about her work—rejoicing in the new milk house even more than in the new kitchen.

Figure 41 The New House in 1891

Figure 42 Aliso Farm with New House

A Heartbreaking Tragedy

Before the end of that summer, a very sad and tragic event took place, which cast a gloom over us all. Our old friends, Annie and Dick Thompson, with their little family and a few friends, were camped as usual on the Aliso Beach, of which they had always been very fond. Scarcely had they missed a season since we had known them even before their marriage without this annual camping trip to Aliso; and their oldest son Johnnie, was now twelve years of age, the pride and joy of his mother's heart. He was a handsome, bright lad, strong and healthy, and a favorite with all who knew him.

They had brought with them to the beach, a young man—a friend of the family, several years older than Johnnie, and all were having a good time. One day when some of us were with them at their camp on the beach, the boys went out around the pond hunting ducks. We heard several shots fired, which indicated that ducks were being secured. But after the last shot, someone came running to camp with the dreadful news of a terrible accident. Little Johnnie had been accidentally shot by this young man, his friend, only a short distance from camp.

Never shall I forget poor Annie's terrible anguish at the news. They brought her boy in on an improvised blanket stretcher and laid him on the ground at the feet of his stricken mother, who knelt over him with indescribable grief to investigate. He had been shot in the abdomen—a discovery that must have forbidden hope in her breast from the first.

Never can be erased from memory that pathetic scene—the sweet pallid face of the boy as he lay there slowly dying, his agonized mother kneeling in her suffering beside him, pleading in hopeless anguish for a doctor—a doctor that was twenty-five miles distant, that a fast team of horses could not bring to her inside of many hours.

Joseph had started immediately for Santa Ana on a race for a doctor—for there was none nearer—a doctor who could not possibly get there to see the boy alive, much less to help him—had that been possible. It was hopeless from the first, and poor Annie must have known it, though desperately clinging to hope till the last.

Poor Johnnie died in his mother's arms before Joseph could even reach town; and they were gone from the beach with their lifeless treasure—their inconsolable grief—their futile blame for the silent suffering boy with bowed head, who had been the cause of the cruel tragedy—gone long before Joseph returned with the doctor—gone forever. We had helped get her things together—helped to load them into their wagon, tried to minister as best we could to the helpless stricken mother, helped to lift into the wagon the lifeless body of their precious son—saw them through our tears drive away from the beach up Aliso Canyon past our home—and that was the last time we ever saw them. For never afterward could Annie bear the sight of the beach where her darling had been so uselessly sacrificed. Poor, poor Annie Thompson! Her grief was too heartrending to describe. We missed them every summer; but they never came again.

When The Bounty Was On

Before Charles and Judge Sprecher left, they talked with Lafe about the possibility, through the influence they might bring to bear, of his becoming deputized to the constableship of Uplands. As he was now without a job, this proposal looked good to him and quite opportune. So the attempt was made, and with success. Soon after finishing the house, Lafe left and went to Uplands to take over his new and unfamiliar job.

A bounty had been placed on the destructive coyote that year, and the government was paying five dollars apiece for scalps. Every farmer and hunter in the country had turned out to make war on the fugitive coyote. At the same time, there had been a bounty of twenty-five cents placed upon jack rabbits; and a pair of their long ears brought a quarter from Uncle Sam.

Lafe was anxious to get some of these remunerative scalps himself; and since the job of deputy did not keep him very busy, he combined with it the hunting and trapping of these marauders as a side line; which seemed to work admirably.

In his one-horse cart, or sulky, having a seat for one, around the ends and back of which was a heavy iron rail, he would drive all over that part of the country with his gun across his knees ready for any fleeing coyote that might be spied, and setting his traps for them in every likely place he could find.

For the rabbits, he would drive into the ground, stakes to protrude about eighteen inches and sharpened on the ends; on which were then impaled sections of poisoned apple. Of these the jackrabbits would partake, and fall before getting very far away. Then he would come around again and pick them up, saving the ears for the bounty, and using the carcasses to bait coyote traps. In this way, not a little was earned to supplement the modest salary received for constable service.

One day while driving thus, the barrel-end of his gun, which he had inserted under the end of the seat-brace to steady it, kept slipping unnoticed by him toward the wheel. Suddenly the muzzle caught between the moving spokes. Lafe made a grab for the gun, and somehow, his finger was jammed between the gun-stock and the iron brace; injuring the joint and causing great pain.

Having had a felon before, he had no desire to experience another; and realizing the seriousness of the injury, went home and began to treat it without delay with hot salt and vinegar solution. But this proved not drastic enough. His finger swelled and throbbed as in the former instance. He had some lemons in the room where he was batching, and cutting open one of these, he slashed the pulp and filled it with salt; then bound it onto the wound. The felon was arrested, the pain subsided in a short time, and soon the finger was well again. Thus he learned how to avert insipient felons.

This bounty lasted for four years; at the end of which time the coyotes and jackrabbits were pretty well killed off; and never afterward were the pests they had formerly been.

After the turn of the year, while Lafe was still at Uplands, Hulda was invited up to Ontario to be with Artie at the birth of her first little daughter on January 19; for both she and Joan following in Mother's steps, had early begun to raise their families.

Lafe would come down the long avenue from Uplands to visit them, and would take Hulda out to the theater of an evening, which to the country-raised girl was a treat. There were then no such things as "picture shows," but only plays on the legitimate stage. She and her sweetheart Jed Wilde had broken up, and the happy little romance being now at an end, any little diversion that would take her mind off herself was welcomed. She had been deeply hurt and grieved at discovering him to be unworthy of all the innocent love she had lavished upon him.

Before leaving Ontario, Hulda spent about six weeks in a dressmaker's shop as an apprentice, learning to cut and fit and make her own patterns by a chart, which was sold her at the end of her period of apprenticeship. This was to stand her in good stead now that Joan was no longer the family dressmaker.

Lafe did not keep his job of deputy constable very long. Having been raised a farmer and being without experience in handling "tough characters" such as an officer has to deal with, he "pulled off" several rather dangerous stunts, and Charlie, afraid he would get killed, persuaded him to relinquish the work. So in the spring, upon hearing that Oscar Rosenbaum wanted to let out his ranch that lay down toward San Juan Capistrano, he gave up his constableship and took over the ranch to run for a year.

THE NEW HOUSE

They tore it down—the cabin of the past—
Built in its place, a grand two-story home.
A bumper crop had paved the way at last.
But that was nearly fifty years a-gone.

A half a hundred years! A long, long day
For buildings made of lumber, to endure,
Where sun and wind and termites have their way.
I never go to see it any more.

The concrete curb in steps, the yard could boast,
Topped by its picket fence, no more is seen;
Nor yet the horse-block nor the hitching-post—
They tell me that the walls have tumbled in!

Wainscoted walls, grained yellow, made to seem
Like maple-knots, above; four-paneled doors
And two-paned sashes, double-hung, between
The sky-blue ceiling and the bare brown floors.

The bathroom, with its long, low tub of zinc,
And water heated on the kitchen range
Brought in by buckets; the same metalled sink,
Boardless, but watering yard-flowers from its drain.

The room I slept in isn't even there;
Nor shelves of books across the hallway end;
Nor the small landing half way down the stair
Where, stumbling oft, we caught ourselves again.

Nor the old fireplace with its chimney dome,
Which once I stood before, in gay attire,
As often, when at night returning home,
To warm my back, and caught my clothes afire.

The stairway closet, that in crooking, stooped
To far dark depths—for castaways a tomb—
Whose angled ceiling brained us as we joked,
Is turned into a bat's nest, I presume.

These all, are tumbled in. And now, they say,
The parlor is a stable, without floor,
Where riding ponies munch, and lizards play—
I never want to see it any more.

CHAPTER 56 SCHOOL AT LAST

The building of the new house had drained our financial resources to the dregs; and to make matters more difficult, the crops that fall had been disappointing. It is often the case that a heavy crop is followed by an exceptionally light one—the trees seeming to feel the need of a vacation, as it were, to recuperate from the extra work. So the following spring and summer found us endeavoring in every way possible to make both ends meet. By going without new clothes and curtailing all unnecessary expenses we were managing to get along; living almost wholly on what the farm produced.

Joseph was making his regular tri-weekly trips to Laguna to dispose of whatever produce we had in the way of garden stuff, early fruits, honey, eggs, and butter; while Frank and I, with Charlotte's help, assisted with the outside work and chores. Mother was now devoting the major portion of her time and activities to the dairy and poultry industries; while Hulda, having returned from Ontario in the March previous, with the help of Luella, then nine, and Clara, seven, kept the house going and meals on the table.

The Exile Returns

Into the midst of this domestic regime, from her three years' exile in Arizona, home came Annie, having first stopped over at Ontario to visit with Artie for several weeks. Dressed in well-fitting clothes, her neck tastefully decorated with a string of pretty beads, wearing travelling gloves and a most becoming hat and coat, and with her hair banged and curled in approved style, Annie, at the consciously grown-up age of fourteen and a half, seemed to the rest of us like a stranger from a different world.

Three years utterly removed from the old environment, spent in the very different association provided by the town and school life of Phoenix, had not only taken away from Annie's demeanor the farm "rawness," together with whatever appetite for its varied duties she may once have had, but had added that undefinable something, sensed, but not to be described, that seemed to lift her out of our class into the atmosphere of "society," where unconsciously she carried herself with an air of superiority.

Having been out of touch with us all for so long, the vividness of memory as to her own past life on the farm dimmed by time and absence, Annie must have found us seemingly crude and uncouth—self-conscious as we were of our chapped and roughened hands, freckled, sunburned faces, old clothes, and general rustic country appearance.

There was no exuberance of joy at seeing us all, nor raptures such as we had anticipated over the new house with its sufficiency of sleeping quarters, nor was anything said about missing the old. These changes all were accepted by her quite philosophically—the bare uncarpeted floors, in her eyes, leaving much to be desired.

For awhile, she seemed like "company." Not at once feeling herself to be a cog in the wheel of our domestic machinery, her assistance with this or that seemed more by way of gratuitous favor than as a matter of course; a period of time being naturally required for such adjustments.

Annie's wardrobe, however familiar and "old' it might have been to her, to us seemed new and altogether stylish and becoming. But our admiring remarks she discountenanced as inappropriate, dubbing her clothes "old things," "old fashioned," and inadequate for a girl of her age.

"That is only 'made over,'" she would say of a dress I admired.

But no one would have suspected such to be the case. Sadie was an expert seamstress and had put style into everything she had made for Annie. From earliest childhood we had all been used to "made-over" clothes. As for myself, only my rapid physical growth had even now written "finis" to that. But so far as I was concerned, if a dress was becoming, being "made over" or "handed down" did not in the least detract from it. With Annie, it was different. Though her clothes were unquestionably much nicer than mine, to that she seemed oblivious, as though she were naturally entitled to more than the rest of us could have.

But the thing that irked me most was the idea, so irreconcilable with my own viewpoint, which Annie still cherished that in going away from home she had been the one who made the real sacrifice and had been having the hard time, while we who had remained at home on the farm were the fortunate ones.

Annie had chafed under the firm discipline that had wrought in her a work of education and womanizing development that twice as many years on the farm where the actual responsibilities were all borne by others, could not have accomplished. Thus impossible is it for youth to appreciate the moulding process by which alone that maturity is to be attained which it desires to reach at a bound.

Annie brought home from Arizona a number of popular songs that were new to us. These she sang very well, with a mellowness and expressive quality that I greatly admired and sought to attain. One of these, "Dearest Believe," the romantic and melancholy sentiment of which appealed to me, I would ask her to sing over and over again, that I too might memorize the words.

> *"How can I leave thee?*
> *How can I from thee part?*
> *Thou only hast my heart,*
> *Dearest believe.*
> *Thou hast this soul of mine*
> *So closely bound to thine;*
> *No other can I love,*
>
> *Dearest believe.*
>
> *Blue is the flow'ret*
> *Called the forget-me-not;*
> *Wear it upon thy heart*
> *And think of me.*
> *Flow'ret and hope may die,*
> *Yet love with us shall stay*
> *That cannot pass away,*
>
> *Dearest believe.*
>
> *Would I a bird were,*
> *Soon at thy side to be!*
> *Falcon nor hawk would fear,*
> *Speeding to thee.*
> *But if by fowler slain,*
> *I at thy feet should lie,*
> *Thou sadly shouldst complain*
>
> *Joyful I'd die."*

Harriet's Turn at Last

It had been tacitly understood ever since the time of Annie's departure that upon her return I should be sent to school. For three years I had been awaiting the fulfillment of this expectation. The details of its accomplishment were wholly indefinite. But it was supposed that when the time should come a way would open up. And thus it came to pass.

Artie, who was not ignorant of my desire for an education, wrote to Mother with the proposal that, since Annie was now at home to take my place on the farm, I be sent to Ontario to live with her for a year and attend school.

Mother, though forced to smile at the thought of Annie's actually taking my place on the farm, pondered the matter for some time before saying anything to me about it. Even though she sensed the justice of it, she could hardly see how an absence for me could be arranged that fall. The work was so heavy that she and Joseph had already found it necessary to hire an extra hand—the first time that had ever happened—and Joel Anderson, a boy a little Frank's senior, had joined our family circle for the harvesting of the fall crops. With this added drain on the family purse, where was the money coming from for new clothes, books, and train fare. Mother's problem was a real one.

But I was so eager and determined to go that the matter of clothes seemed quite secondary. If we could manage one or two dresses, I told her, and the fare to Ontario, that was all I would ask, and would get along somehow, and stay at home till the last minute to help with the harvesting of the nuts. There was nothing I was not willing to do if only my longed for schooling might be secured.

Mother wrote to Artie giving her consent provided the fare could be somehow "scraped together." Artie wrote back that they would drive down before school should open and take me back with them. So, that problem being solved, I was happy. All the rest of that summer, work to me was a song of joy.

Mother and Hulda went to town and bought a little material, and Hulda fashioned me a dress for school—a very simple affair of calico-and another for best of worsted. This was a funny affair having a bolero effect, which made me appear years older than my actual age, and it didn't fit any too well. Hulda, as a cutter and fitter, was not as yet experienced. Since she had taken her six-weeks' course there had not been enough of such work going on to give her much practice. She had some trouble in fitting the sleeves, and took them out several times to remedy the defect. But always, they remained "slightly twisted."

They had bought me a hat too, an inexpensive straw, brown like the dress with a plain band of brown ribbon around the crown ending in a little bow, and having one side of the brim rolled, as then worn by ladies; all of which enhanced the effect of age. In this outfit, I appeared to be at least twenty—until one had a look at my face.

But I made no complaint or criticism, thankful to have a dress of any kind. Yet instinctively I sensed its inappropriateness, and felt decidedly eclipsed by Annie in her becoming little dresses, consoling myself, however, with the thought that when wearing the outfit I would be far away from her and these uncomplimentary comparisons. School to me, seemed so much bigger than clothes anyway, that I simply refused to be daunted or downhearted over anything.

A Poetic Race

We were hard at the nut-picking. The almonds had been gathered and brought up to the house in sacks to be shucked. This was an unusual proceeding. But that year they were closely adherent to the hulls, and by this means, we hoped to have more help than usual with the shucking, especially of evenings. So they were emptied by portions out in a big tub on the floor in the center of the dining room. Around this tub we gathered kneeling with buckets between, day by day. To while away the time, we would play word games, or talk of various things of immediate interest.

One day Joel made the unexpected announcement that he was a "poet." At this, we all pricked up our ears, and wanted to hear some of his poetry. He said he could not remember any of it "by heart, "but would "make up" some for us when he had time. One of the others then informed him:

"Harriet is a poet, too."

"I'll bet I can write better poetry than she can," said Joel.

Now in all my past experience with rhyming I had never thought of telling anybody that I was a "poet." True, I felt that I had in me the gift undeveloped, and I had the poet's longings. But my woeful lack in that direction was so painfully apparent to me that I was afraid my elders might accidentally get the idea that I considered myself a poet. So I seldom read any of my productions to them, but poured them out only upon those too young to know the difference.

Hearing Joel make such a boast, I immediately decided that he must know very little about real poetry such as came from the pens of those truly gifted, whose writings so stirred my soul as to make my own shrink into insignificance. He needed a lesson.

"Let's run a race," I suggested. "You write a poem and I'll write one."

"All right," said Joel with alacrity, as sure of his superiority as though it were already so adjudged. "Let's write about the same thing," said I, "then we'll read them out loud, and let the rest decide which is the best."

"That's fine. What shall we write about?"

"You can choose the subject," I said. "What shall it be?"

"The ocean. We'll both write about the ocean. But neither can get any help from anybody else." "Oh, sure," I agreed, and the test was on.

About the end of the second day I announced that mine was finished. Joel had left just a little yet to complete his, which he said was a "long" one.

The next day we both brought our poems to the shucking tub. I invited Joel to read his first, which he did. This being the only time I ever heard Joel's versification, it is impossible to recall more than its general features. It is remembered as very commonplace, and its rendition equally so, being a composition of simple four-line stanzas, the second and last lines of which rhymed. It was indeed long as he had said-interminably long, and put together in scatter-brain fashion, jumping about from one subject to another like a jack-rabbit nibbling grass here and there and coming often back to the same place for a little more, which made it the antithesis of logical and consecutive. Its subject-matter was almost everything else except the ocean, which was mentioned casually a few times.

When he had finished, nobody applauded. All they could say was:

"Now Harriet, let's hear yours."

There was within me a natural shrinking from the unpleasant and unavoidable result of humiliating Joel; for with all my bravado, within my breast beat a tender heart that never did experience any satisfaction at making others uncomfortable. Well I knew that my verses—so thoroughly memorized that they needed not to be read—declaimed in the eloquent style of oratory I had practiced in secret, would be a rebuke to his boasting, a trait to my mind particularly obnoxious. But he had invited the lesson, so in the presence of a rapt audience, it came:

THE OCEAN

The Ocean, fathomless, before me lies.
From the horizon dim where sunset skies
Touch her broad bosom, streams athwart the expanse,
A glittering path of lights that glint and dance,
Beckoning my feet to follow in their gleams
And glide away to some fair land of dreams.
So restful now, the soothing Ocean lures,
Murmuring her lullabyes along the shores.

Dark forms beneath her surface sport and play-
A moment lie to breathe, then whisk away;
Or travelling schools, with intermittent fin,
Traverse the main, the waters darkening.
Within her depths, the wondrous creatures grow
That build the beauteous shells her beaches know.
Land-dwellers, to forget their discontents,
Play on her sands that gird the continents.

The mighty ship in majesty sails by
With proud masts towering grandly to the sky;
Serenely rides, while peaceful waters sleep,
And seems to be the mistress of the deep.
But should those angry waters be aroused
And all the demons of the deep unhoused,
And tempests bursting, send their fury down,
Lo, 'tis a toy—a plaything of their own.

431

They seize their prey, in awful vengeance rave,
And rock it madly in the treacherous wave;
They snap its masts, they crush its heaving sides
With one vast sweep, filling the huge divides.
Then, battering still, they lift the ruined deck
And cast it from their arms a hopeless wreck.
It sinks, 'mid groaning curse and shrieking voice,
And in its driftwood shall the waves rejoice.

Oh Ocean, thou art cruel—thou'rt sublime!
Monarch of worlds, defier even of time;
Changeless, yet ever changing, as thy tide
Retreats far out, leaving the white beach wide,
Or, rising high, thy billows inland roll,
Tumbling in quick succession to the shoals.
What is not hidden within thy density?
What worlds estranged by thy immensity?

That fall, at the age of sixteen past, I went to school for the first time in my life—went hopefully with as little preparation as it would be possible to imagine. It was "go thus, or go not at all"; and I went "thus"; ready to face whatever lay before me.

In order to be there on time for the opening date of school, I hastened away to Ontario before the harvesting of the nuts was entirely over; thereby forfeiting the privilege to be enjoyed by the others, of having a part in the gleaning. This was regretted especially because I needed more than ever before the financial uplift it would have provided.

The Prize Watch

After my departure, when the fall work was well over, Hulda, tired of the family poverty and longing to replenish her wardrobe, decided to find herself a position, and went to Santa Monica to cook in the home of the married son of Senator John P. Jones, founder of that city. This left Annie the eldest young lady at home, and she and Charlotte for the first time had complete charge of the housework.

One day in looking over a copy of some cheap periodical, they came across an advertisement by the generous terms of which they might become possessors of a "beautiful ladies' gold watch of fine workmanship guaranteed to be a perfect timekeeper," and this, "absolutely free of charge."

To secure this prize, all they had to do was send to the "perfectly reliable publisher" of the "Con-sul-lid-i-a-ted Library," the "small sum of one dollar" as the purchase price of a "valuable literary collection," any one volume of which was "worth many times the amount asked for the whole set." By return mail the library and the prize would be sent post-paid.

The girls were so thrilled and intrigued by this "most amazing offer," that immediately they decided to take advantage of it. True, a dollar to them was almost a small fortune, but—a ladies' gold watch! How could they afford to turn that down? The "valuable literary collection" occupied a very insignificant place in their thoughts, being overshadowed completely by the more dazzling prize.

Neither alone possessed a dollar. But enough of their gleaning money still remained to invest fifty cents apiece and have a little left over. So they agreed to pool their resources and send for the prize.

But that brought up another question. To whom should the watch belong? If community property, which one of them should wear it? Such a partnership would undoubtedly lead to difficulties. To solve the problem, Annie diplomatically suggested that just as soon as another dollar should be accumulated they send for a second watch, and that the first should belong to her and the other to Charlotte. To this her sister agreed. So, without consultation with wiser heads, they sent away the precious dollar according to instructions, to the Consolidated Library in an eastern state.

In due time the "valuable literary collection" arrived. It was found to consist of half a dozen cheaply printed, trashy, demoralizing novels. No ladies' gold watch, however, was enclosed.

"That will come in a separate package, I suppose," they said, bolstering up their sinking hopes in spite of ill-disguised disappointment in the volumes. Long they waited for the "separate package," meanwhile consoling themselves so far as possible by the surreptitious reading of their "Con-sul-lid-i-a-ted" library. But that "ladies' fine gold watch guaranteed to keep perfect time," though doubtless all it was represented to be, failed utterly to keep the time appointed by its sponsors, and never did put in appearance.

The "Merry" of Christmas

Christmas was approaching, and that too, with the exchequer depleted—a combination of circumstances very distressing but by no means unique. In view of this, our two young heroines, imitating their older sisters of Santa Claus memories, felt that they should do something by way of providing a home-made Christmas for the two younger children.

Could anything please them more than to gather up their old dolls and make for them complete new wardrobes? They thought not. But this of course must be done under lock and key; for the one thing indispensable to a successful Christmas was the element of surprise.

So it became necessary to isolate some room and dedicate it to the noble enterprise. Not the parlor; that must be left clean and tidy for possible company. All other rooms on the first floor being open to everybody and in constant use, were out of the question. So they decided to "cart" the sewing machine upstairs and set up their doll dressmaking shop in one of the bedrooms.

Annie and Clara were occupying the southwest room, whose door, opposite the head of the stairs faced the hall window that opened out onto the shed roof of the kitchen. Charlotte and Luella occupied the northeast room, which had a duplicate window that also opened out onto the same shed roof, its door being at the bend in the hall.

This room, by some impish trick of so-called Fate, was selected by the girls to be their dressmaking headquarters. How innocently do we sometimes make apparently inconsequential decisions that afterward lead to unfortunate results we would have avoided at any cost! They might just as well have settled upon the other room, and all that followed been left in the land of the "was nots." But as they made their preparations, the idea never occurred to them that such arbitrary selection of the room occupied not only by Charlotte, but also by Luella, might strike that young lady as an invasion of her "rights" and set up a reaction unfavorable to the whole undertaking.

So, after informing the children that if they were "good girls," there would be something "nice" for them on Christmas morning, they locked themselves in and proceeded to the business of manufacturing a "Merry Christmas."

So far as Luella was concerned, the moment she learned that they considered it necessary to bribe her to be "good," the "Merry" received a distinct shock. Then, the first time she tried the handle of her door to get inside for something she wanted and found it locked, the "shock" developed into "apoplexy," and the pleasant little gnome gave up the ghost without a struggle.

With wrathful dignity and firm-set lips that boded no good to the whole scheme, Luella marched away unseen. But by the two would-be Santa Clauses within, her manipulations of the door-handle were interpreted as an attempt at "peeping"—a thing far beneath the lofty ideals of one who disdained vulgar curiosity. Clara, however, was a living bundle of curiosity, and the "vulgar" part of it didn't bother her a bit. If she could see anything by peeping, peep she would at every opportunity.

Not being exactly sure which of the two was the guilty party, but strongly suspecting Clara, as more in keeping with her nature, Annie, at the first opportunity gave them both the ultimatum that the first one caught trying to find out what they were doing would not get a thing for Christmas.

To the flame of resentment that had been kindled in the breast of Luella, this only added fuel. She didn't want any of their "old Christmas," and but for one thing would have told them so then and there. Worse than a scourge she dreaded to have them point at her the finger of ridicule and while bending and unbending it with facial grimaces, repeat:

"Curley-cue, curley-cue, curley-cue!"

Anything but that. So she kept her own counsel, and no one suspected the state of her feelings.

One day as the two seamstresses, coming up to their work, entered the locked bedroom, they found the window above the shed roof wide open, whereas before leaving they had been particular to shut it. Across the roof to the hall window was but a short distance, and upstairs there were no locks on windows.

"Somebody's been in here!" said one of them wrathfully.

"It must be Clara, the little scamp, and she's seen everything we're making," finished the other.

"We'll find out who did it, and she'll never want to do it again."

So at the first opportunity, they cornered Luella and asked her who did it.

"I don't know anything about it," said Luella calmly.

As her reputation for truthfulness was above reproach, this was considered final evidence that Clara, the one they had all along suspected, was the culprit. Under this preconceived conviction, they went to her with the same question. But Clara likewise denied knowing anything about the circumstance. They had expected this. A lie was only natural to cover up misdeeds. So they told her flatly they did not believe her, and tried to induce her to "own up." This she utterly refused to do, sticking tearfully but stoutly to her first denial.

The whole family of grown-ups was convinced that Clara was lying-a crime far more heinous than that of yielding to natural curiosity. So by words, looks and actions, the girls showed her that she was under condemnation. This attitude was maintained day after day, while Clara went about with tear-wet face and woe-begone appearance. Every time the subject was broached to her, however, she still denied with sobs that she had done it.

Annie, thinking that if no others were present, she might be induced to make a clean breast of it, took her apart by herself one day and repeated her efforts to draw out an admission of guilt.

"It isn't so much your doing it, Clara, its telling a lie about it."

"I didn't do it," persisted Clara, weeping, "I didn't do it."

"Who did do it then?"

"I don't know."

"You do too know," said Annie severely.

"I don't either," wailed Clara with a fresh burst of tears.

"If you hadn't done it you wouldn't be bawling about it all the time," declared Annie with final impatience. But this only made Clara bawl the harder.

In abject misery, Clara wished she might die and escape it all. She thought:

"If they could only look on my dead face, they'd be sorry for what they've done."

But Clara didn't die. However, after this persecution had gone on for a week or more, something happened that cleared up the matter. Luella stood it just as long as she possibly could. Then she went to Annie and confessed that she herself had gone in through the window—not that she wanted to see anything, but just to show them that they couldn't lock her out of her own room. She said that she wasn't sorry a bit that she went in, but she was sorry she had not told the truth in the first place and that she had let Clara bear the blame.

The thing that had kept her tongue-tied so long was more than pride of reputation—though that no doubt cut a large figure—but it was the same fear that had caused her to lie in the first place, the fear of that curling finger of ridicule and scorn, more dreadful than any drubbing:

"Curley-cue, curley-cue, curley-cue!" and "Shame, shame, double-shame!"

How repentant were the girls for having treated Clara so unjustly! They could not do enough for her to show their self-reproach. She was feted and dined and made a heroine. And after all, a little of the "merry" finally revived and came back to reside in that Christmas.

Cremation As One Way

One day during the following spring, Annie, Charlotte and Luella, finding themselves alone on the farm, spent a few care-free hours wandering about together here and there in aimless fashion over the premises, enjoying the pleasant recreation afforded by this release from their usual duties. Presently they found themselves down in the cart-road garden, and there they walked about up and down its length, busy with interesting conversation and reminiscences.

Desiring to get down into the creek bottom without taking the long way back around by the little hill point, they cast about for a short cut through the dense willows that bordered the banks in a thick hedge. Not only was it necessary to pass through this thicket of willows and undergrowth, but also to crawl under a three-strand barbed wire fence, the bottom wire of which two together would lift for the other to get under, that there might be no snagging of clothes.

Having decided upon an appropriate spot to attempt the passage, Charlotte who was in the lead, was just in the act of lifting the wire that they might negotiate the crawl under, when she was transfixed by the blood-chilling sight of a coiled rattlesnake directly in front of them on the other side of the fence. Startled by her warning ejaculation, Annie and Luella halted in their tracks and stood with her gazing on the arch-enemy only a few feet away, whose beady eyes blinked at them in the flickering lights that filtered through the willow leaves.

Their primary object of getting to the creek was immediately forgotten in the concern awakened at this new responsibility so suddenly thrust upon them of disposing of the scaly foe. No rattler on the Aliso farm was to be allowed to escape unharmed; therefore, he must be put to death. But how was this to be accomplished? They looked about for some possible weapon. Thanks to the thorough work of their forebears in deporting stones from off the land, not even one was to be found.

There was no one they could call upon for help. Joseph had gone to town that day, taking with him Mother and Clara. Frank was gone from home and Hulda was still at Santa Monica. With their old-time leader, Harriet the snake-killer, also gone, they were for the first time thrown upon their own resources entirely, face to face with the disagreeable and inescapable duty of dispatching with their own inexperienced hands, the execrable creature coiled before them.

Not one of them felt particularly brave just then. Yet something must be done. Would he continue to lie there quietly while they should go to the house for an implement of some kind? And what should they get? Not a hoe—the usual method of attack—for who could use a hoe to advantage while reaching through three strands of barbed wire? After some discussion as to the most practical and effective weapon to be employed, they finally decided upon a pitchfork. So Luella, being bidden to "hurry," was sent to the barn, almost a quarter of a mile away, to get the pitchfork, while the others remained to keep an eye on the snake.

Apparently unaware of the concern and danger his presence had invoked, the snake had not yet budged from his position when she returned, with the formidable weapon. Annie begged Charlotte to make the attack:

"You do it," she said, "I can't."

So Charlotte, receiving the fork from her sister, and lifting it up over the top of the fence to the other side, summoned all the courage and "grit" she possessed, grasped it firmly in both hands, and after a moment's steadying aim, plunged the fork with a heavy thrust into the snaky coil, determinedly forcing it through the now writhing, contorting creature down into the ground, pushing it even to the hilt and pinning the victim there inexorably. Then letting go the fork-handle, she stepped back from the fence weak and shaking from the exertion and reaction of consciously inflicted torture.

The sight of the poor suffering creature writhing in its agony, futilely struggling to free itself from the torturing impalement, was sickening and almost more than they could endure to witness. But how should they finish the job? They had not thought that far. If he were only on the near side of the fence, a hoe would do it. But to attempt his removal by heaving him over the fence, they feared would cause his releasement from the fork.

Who could tell how long it might take a snake to die? Would evening still find him enduring his unspeakable tortures? The thought was unendurable. So, growing sicker every moment over the visible effects of their most successful coup, they pondered what to do. Annie was thinking hard. She had a scheme that undoubtedly would work. Finally, turning to the others she bade them watch while she went to the house, but would not tell what was in her mind.

In their nerve-racking vigil, it seemed an eternity before she returned. But at last she came in sight bearing a long stick with a tin can tied across the end of it. This she balanced gingerly in one hand to keep it upright, while the other grasped a nameless wad of something. Arriving upon the scene, the tin can proved to be filled with kerosene and the other hand with crumpled paper and matches.

Intruding the end of this long stick, with its inflammable burden, through the fence, Annie emptied the contents of the can over the tortured, writhing serpent—which, let us hope, anesthetized some of its pain—then, withdrawing it, stuffed her wad of paper into the can, lighting it with a match. This flaming torch she now inserted between the fence-wires, bringing it in contact with the kerosene-drenched area, quickly igniting snake and all.

It was a scheme most effective indeed in its operation. But to watch the poor creature being roasted alive was such a harrowing experience that its impression never left them through the after years. To this day they speak of it only with shudders of self-reproach. After the snake was dead, they pulled it through the fence with the fork, and cut off its head to bury. But the whole dreadful experience they kept to themselves as being too cruel to tell about.

A Country "Gink" in School

How shall I relate the experience of my first year at school? One has to live many years after a great humiliation before it becomes "funny" enough to be told to others for their amusement. Time must first put upon it the stamp of impersonality, then surround it with an encircling vacuum that halts all sensory communication. The searching telescope then focused upon it for the discovery of actual values, in the light of which the artificial fade away, becomes, by the charm of distance, a magic wand that turns the whole into a prism, breaking up its qualities into a spectrum of many colors, seen in their elemental parts as amusing, instructive, inspirational, entertaining, tragic, pathetic, and humorous-all blending together to form the white light of human interest.

A gawky girl of sixteen dressed rurally to conspicuousness, appearing on the opening day of school among hundreds of others whose appropriate attire, armloads of books, necessary grade cards, and evident familiarity with the place, proclaim them properly credentialed, who after awkwardly taking her place in line and inching along to the desk of the registrar, and having reached the goal, has then no admission document to present, is some problem on a busy day. Then to be told to step out of line and wait until all the others have been assigned to classes, is to experience the first hint of the patience required to obtain an education.

At last there was an interview, a time of questioning, then of consultation with others. The experience was as new to them as to me. They knew not how to classify or where to put me. Finally it was decided to try the fourth grade. So I was put into a class and assigned a seat along with children from nine to eleven years of age, in the room where Miss Cotton presided over grades four and five.

I had brought along with me two very precious books from the attic library of my father. These books I had longed to master and hoped now to secure help in their understanding. One was a treatise on double entry bookkeeping written about forty years before, and the other an old geography of similar date.

Miss Cotton took one look at these books placed reverently before her, then bent her head for a moment. After she had gained full control of facial muscles, she told me in a very kind and quiet way that we were not using those books now in schools and that I might take them home again with me.

How she must have struggled inwardly to keep her face a mask! In what laughter joined as she later shared the joke with her fellow faculty members! But not so much as a whisper of this reached my ears. She was kindness itself, endeavoring to shield me as much as possible from what she knew was coming—the jibes of amused and unthinking schoolmates. This, I could sense. And how I loved her for it!

When they saw me take a seat in the fourth grade, my roommates snickered. As big as any two of them, size alone made me a curiosity-a target for merciless shafts. Every countenance said plainly: "What must she be—a moron?"

But they soon discovered that I was not there because of inability to learn. However, they set themselves to discover my vulnerable points and make the most of them, watching to trip me as though that had been a special virtue.

After school was out, half a dozen or so of the boys would congregate outside and wait for me to come out of the classroom and start along the cross-lots footpath toward home. Then a chorus of shouts would greet my ears.

"Hair- ry-rat, tat, tat, tat!"

"Hair- ry-rat, tat, tat, tat!"

As long as I was within earshot they would never let up, hoping to elicit some response from me. But though keenly sensitive to every jibe, neither backward glance nor quickening or slackening of pace betokened the tingling of ears and beating of heart. With not the slightest outward sign, I marched along in seeming unconcern, ignoring their very existence. This attitude of course took all the fun out of that particular form of persecution, and after a season it ceased.

Though I knew so very little about some things with which they were all familiar, such as a geographical map and the ordinary procedures of the classroom, it soon became manifest that I knew a great deal about some other things of which they knew very little. Reading, writing, spelling, and "sums," subjects stressed in the fourth grade, were my meat and drink. When it came to reading, they were left far behind. The girl who herself had written unaided a "school text" on reading, needed not to be taught how to read with expression, or to recite "pieces."

The penalty for making a mistake in reading was to take one's seat. So it became the ambition of those in the class who were jealous of this ability to somehow "catch" me that I might have to suffer that humiliation.

Our lesson one morning was Longfellow's "Day Is Done." It was my turn to read, and that to the most critical audience ever faced by a performer. Putting into it all the expression of which I was capable, when I came to the last line but one and read, "Shall fold their tents like the Arabs," hands shot up everywhere and fingers snapped.

"What can be the matter now," I wondered, and paused.

The teacher nodded to one little imp of a boy, who immediately shouted:

"She said 'Á-rabs,' when it's 'Ar´-abs' !"

So I too "folded" my "tents" and silently stole away to my seat in confusion and humiliation. But never again did I have to be corrected on that word.

Now had begun for me the process of organizing and stabilizing book knowledge—much of it still future to the fourth-graders—that up to this time had been spasmodic and fragmentary. Aside from "the three R's," there were bits of this and bits of that gleaned from various meager sources: School readers that contained stories of the Civil War, and set forth the lives of great men and their achievements; from Father's attic library, "Heroines of History" that did the same for women, and volumes of poetry by Moore and Byron; books of travel and romance, borrowed or purloined, that played upon great historical periods such as the "Reign of Terror"; Classics by Dickens, Scott, and others; and my best friend, Webster's big Unabridged, to me, not merely a reference and final court of appeal, but a text to be studied page by page for valuable information. Now as always, I gobbled up book knowledge as fast as set before me, and within a month was leading the fourth grade in everything.

The teacher soon saw that this was not the place for me, and promoted me to the fifth grade. Here they were studying South America, and soon I too was modeling the continent in clay and learning to interpret maps.

In arithmetic, those tricky "A and B" problems that so test the reasoning powers, my classmates found altogether baffling. But my more mature mind soon mastered these with their underlying principles, and each day I was chosen to put on the board the day's most difficult problem, working it before them and giving a thorough analysis of each step.

The faculty of explaining and making clear and plain to others that which I myself understood, was with me a natural gift. This brought me into favor with the whole class as the acknowledged leader of the fifth grade. For this, Miss Cotton, by her tact and kindness in openly recognizing my ability, was largely responsible.

By the teacher's beautiful handwriting, I was fascinated. It was a script to decorate the blackboard of any classroom. I wondered why her "h" was so slim and graceful in contrast to mine so squatty and sprawley, and began to study her writing to find out. I discovered that the curve of her loops were all made on the up-stroke, and that in making the "h" she brought her chalk without curving clear down to the line of writing before beginning to make the hump. This was the secret of their beauty and grace. I began to imitate her handwriting, thereby improving my own very perceptibly.

Everything about Miss Cotton I admired. Never before had I known any woman so perfect. The emotional admiration that youth is wont to bestow upon the opposite sex, I lavished upon her. Yes, I had "fallen in love" with my first schoolteacher, worshipping at her shrine with an abandon of devotion. To win her approbation was my highest ambition. About her, I wrote poems that came from the depths of my soul, though enveloping them as usual in a strange and lonely reticence. Always some haunting fear of seeming over bold restrained me from exhibiting my productions.

Upon the one occasion during the four months under her tutelage when she found it necessary to rebuke me for faulty behavior—and that due not to wrong intention but to lack of ethical knowledge and country awkwardness—it almost broke my heart.

How I did study that year! I literally drank in knowledge "as thirsty sand drinks in the rain," never satisfied with anything short of a hundred in grade marks. There was no subject that I disliked; but every branch of learning brought into the class curriculum I "gobbled up" greedily with a starved eagerness that knew no satiety.

After school I worked for Artie—did the day's dishes, helped with cooking, baby-tending, washing, cleaning and what-not, and as soon as supper was over and the last dishes and chores done would get out my books and sit down at the kitchen table to begin my homework. Long after the others had retired, would I "burn the midnight oil," meticulously working every problem and studying every lesson of the assignment till it was mine practically "by heart."

Quite frequently, Charles would waken after his first "forty winks," and seeing the lamplight still gleaming brightly, would call out in a rather gruff voice:

"Harriet, ain't-cha going to bed tonight?"

"Pretty soon," I would answer, "I'm nearly through."

"Well, you better leave the rest till morning," would be the final rejoinder; and soon thereafter, fearful of disturbing him further, I would put out the light and slip away to bed.

A school exhibit was to be held just before school should close for the Christmas holiday vacation. In preparation for it, Miss Cotton had the class in geography—which was at that time studying about the different races of men that inhabit the earth—to model in clay from pictures in the book, human heads as representatives of the yellow, brown, black and white races. I was assigned the Negro.

With a lump of gray clay at each seat and books propped open at the respective pictures, we went to work. Since those days of childhood when I made "mud dolls" on the banks of our creek, this, barring the recent continent of Africa, was the first clay-modeling I had done.

When Miss Cotton examined my finished "head," she was filled with pleasure and surprise and complimented me before the class. As soon as the clay had properly "set,"" she took it on a tour of exhibition around to the other members of the staff. They likewise were lavish in their praises, and held it up before the pupils of the higher grades as an example of superior workmanship. Many compliments came my way.

This was all somewhat embarrassing to me, for I felt that my success was only an accident. Nevertheless it gave me prestige with my schoolmates and no little reputation with the faculty. When the public exhibit was over, Mr. Lucky, the principal put this model among the permanent collections of the school.

Upon returning to class at the end of Christmas vacation, I found myself promoted to the sixth grade and placed in another room under Mrs. Powers who taught the sixth and seventh. The loss of my beloved Miss Cotton took almost all the joy out of being promoted.

Mrs. Powers was a different type of teacher entirely. There was not that innate kindness and understanding sympathy about her that was natural to the dear teacher I had left behind; and this was disappointing. In my experience, there had been such a woeful lack of association with others and such ignorance of schoolroom ethics, that I was blundering along self-consciously making all manner of minor mistakes in my attempts at orientation, and I needed most of all to be understood. In this room hung large pictures of America's great men; among them Abraham Lincoln, to whom my heart rendered devout homage, taking it for granted that all Americans felt the same. That this was a mistaken idea, I was soon to learn. Mrs. Powers was a Southerner; though that was not then known to me. But had it been so known, I was unaware of the strong feeling that still existed between the north and the south, and could not have interpreted her dislike for such a prince as Lincoln, who loved everybody. One day in her presence, looking at his life-like picture, I expressed in no stinted terms my great admiration for him. Scarcely had the words left my lips than she spoke with asperity: "Lincoln was no better than any other man!"

I was filled with amazement at such sentiments, and with chagrin and regret at having displeased my new teacher. But she had fallen in my estimation. Then someone whispered to me that she was a "Southerner," and I began to learn what that meant.

In this room the two classes conducted a "newspaper," similar, I suppose, to that of which Sadie had written, in Phoenix; and in course of time I became the editor for a short term. We were studying about ants, and especially about the great white ants and army ants of Africa. Every member of my class had to write a composition afterward about ants and read it aloud in class. These compositions were simply amazing—that is, some of them were. Of all the exploits that class had ants performing, and of all the hazy wordings in which they mixed up ants and elephants together in a hopeless conglomeration. I can now recall nothing clearly, except that the compositions were some of them greeted with roars of laugher. After they had all been read, I went in the capacity of an editor to Mrs. Powers and asked for the privilege of looking them all over and turning out something for the paper next week. She gave them all into my hands, and joyfully I took them home with me to work on. The result was a comical medley composed of the "rarest" thoughts and expressions gleaned from all the manuscripts; which when read, gave an uproariously funny contortion of the "ant" subject that filled several columns in the editor's longhand; and after amusing the classes in our own room, went the rounds of the school.

Every day, we had a written spelling lesson in which the teacher from her desk would pronounce the words for us all to write at our seats. It was her custom to have us pass our papers to the one next in front of us to be corrected as she spelled the words one by one. Always my mark was a hundred. I would have considered it a disgrace to get anything less. From the first day of school to its close I never missed a word. Not only was spelling natural to me, but I made very careful preparation for every lesson; and was leading the class in spelling—as indeed in some other subjects. Some of the others also received hundreds often, but would miss a word once in a while; and still others had no knack at all for spelling, and were satisfied if they could get a mark of eighty, or even less, just so it was a "passing" grade.

Of this class was the boy who sat just ahead of me and daily corrected my papers. He was a mischievous scamp named Moore, turning out poor lessons himself, always whispering and hindering those who sat near him from doing their best. He hated like "pizen" to be continually giving me hundreds on my papers; and made up his mind one day to change the order. So when the words were spelled out by Mrs. Powers, he suddenly gave an explosive "Huh" under his breath and marked one of my words wrong which I knew was not misspelled. When our papers were handed back to us, there this word on my paper was marked wrong, though spelled absolutely right, and the total given me as a mark to "turn in" was less than a hundred.

It is always easy afterward to see what we should have done to avoid our troublesome blunders. Happy are those who can see beforehand. My inexperience in ethical behavior placed me in the first rank of the blunderers. Mrs. Powers began to call one by one the names of the class, who responded as usual with the number they had received on their papers; but I, when my name was called, at a loss to know how to handle the situation and not to be outdone by that imp of a boy, answered with the usual:

"One hundred."

Immediately Moore shot up his hand as if in great indignation, and could hardly wait for the teacher's nod, to shout:

"She didn't either get a hundred, she got ninety-three!"

Mrs. Powers was furious. The way she "roasted" me before that schoolroom full of pupils was something to be remembered forever, and furnished ample revenge to my mischievous enemy who had caused my downfall. In vain were all attempted explanations. My guilt was in her estimation unforgivable. I not only lost my record for perfect spelling, but was made to appear as a "cheat" when actually I was the one cheated.

The injustice of it rankled for many a day. I never did know whether or not she righted the matter as to her books; though having before her all of our papers to re-examine if she chose, she could see for herself that the word was correctly spelled. I do know, however, that this dishonest boy was never publicly reprimanded for his part in the affair, and that ever after, he openly gloated over my frustration. Yet I had to continue to sit behind him and submit, with inward disgust, to his daily correction of my papers.

Some time after this, Mrs. Powers, wishing to demonstrate to the seventh grade something in regard to the Negro race, thought of the model I had made in Miss Cotton's class, and sent to the Library to have it brought to her. While holding it up before the roomful of students and discussing from it certain Negro characteristics, she accidentally let it slip from her fingers and down it went smashing to bits on the floor. Mrs. Powers was genuinely distressed. Somehow, that model was the pride of the faculty. Everybody felt pretty bad about it. And of course I did—though saying nothing at all. After class, Mrs. Powers came to me and asked me to make another head like it. Imagine my dismay!

"Oh, I couldn't do it again," I said; "I'm sure it wouldn't be as good."

"Well, you will try, won't you? I feel so bad about breaking it."

With many misgivings, I consented to "try." So she brought me a special table with a modeling board and set it where the light was good, and brought me the clay and the same picture, and I went to work. When the work was done no one was more surprised than I to find that the whole faculty considered it better even than the one that had been broken. Everybody was more than pleased. This one also, they very carefully preserved in the school art collection.

The question of clothes was getting to be exceedingly urgent with me. I had worn that same dress till I was ashamed any longer to come onto the school ground in it. Every weekend I would wash and iron it, and put it on clean again Monday morning. On special occasions I wore my best dress; but it would never do for me to take that one for everyday school wear. I had once or twice worn an old common dress for a change, but it was so unsuitable that I felt worse in it than in my regular dress. But now even that was wearing out, and I simply had to have another or quit school.

For a Christmas present Mother had sent me sixty-five cents, which I was carefully hoarding against just such an emergency. I had never made a dress in my life. Being always an outside farm girl, I had never seemed to have the time to learn to sew. There had been little need for it heretofore since older girls had made our dresses; but now, how I wished to be able to cut and fit a dress! In those days one could not go to a store and buy a ready-made dress. We knew nothing even of ready-made patterns. I do not remember ever seeing such a thing up to that time. They cut and fitted by chart, and a well-fitting pattern, once made, was carefully preserved for years, to be the foundation of every dress that was made, no matter what the style. This foundation, experienced hands might vary as they chose. Artie could not sew at all—not even to make her own baby clothes, though she was trying to learn. So she could be no help to me. I knew how to sew up seams and make hems, but had never fitted a sleeve, neck or shoulder seam, or cut out a garment. My experience in sewing was confined to underthings and children's garments, at which I had occasionally assisted, and of course as a child I had made my own doll clothes, learning thus to use a needle. I had learned to operate a sewing machine; but Artie had no sewing machine. What should I do? I had brought along an old close-fitting basque pattern which had been used as a foundation for my present dresses, but I knew not the first thing about how to vary the style of it.

In the late winter or early spring, we had a few days of vacation. Knowing that this was the only opportunity I should have to get a dress of some kind ready to wear at the resumption of classes, urged on by dire necessity, and with a great determination, I went shopping with my precious sixty-five cents. I found many pretty patterns of goods; but alas, none that could be bought with my slender purse. Store after store was visited with the same result. The only thing in that small town that could be purchased with sixty-five cents, was a remnant of blue striped outing-flannel. So reluctantly, I made the purchase. There were thread and buttons to be bought too; and I went home with my bundle—not exactly happy, but courageous.

Artie expressed disappointment when she saw the goods. But it was then too late to do anything about it. Had I first appealed to her for a bit of help, doubtless she would have managed to add a little to my store, but I knew that she and Charles were hard-pressed no less than I for means; and it had not entered my head to call upon them for clothes. It seemed to me quite enough that they should provide me room and board, and kerosene for my night work; as for clothes, they had not been included in the bargain.

That was a year of great financial distress when panic had closed nearly every bank in the country—in Los Angeles, only two remaining open, and gloom was everywhere.

Perhaps I was too independent for my own good. But not counting my help as being of any monetary value to them, I was of all things determined not to be a burden. So I spread out my yardage on the big table, measuring it with a tape and the basque pattern. Yes, there was just enough of it if I cut the goods carefully.

I cut out my tight-fitting basque, plain sleeves, and plain neckband, and got them sewed together in pretty fair shape. Having no pattern for the skirt, all I could do was tear straight strips for that. Then I sewed up the seams, hemmed one end and gathered the other, and attached it to the bottom of the basque, which came a little below the waistline, finishing all in the "jersey" style worn frequently then.

Ye gods! What a dress! Down the front I sewed big pearl buttons several inches apart, and made my first buttonholes—that is, my first in outside wearing apparel-and not having any buttonhole scissors, folded the goods to cut them. Some turned out to be straight, others would not bear close scrutiny.

I had not thought of asking help from the neighbors. Perhaps it was shame that held me back. So this garment when completed, was all my own handiwork, and except for the kind of material, it was not so bad as it might have been. One thing at least was in its favor—it would wear, and last me till school should be out. But for all my bravado, I dreaded to appear in school with this singular outfit. Never did I cease to feel painfully conspicuous in it.

No one discovered from my actions the inward trepidations that filled my breast, and the ordeal was less embarrassing than I had anticipated. If any made fun, it was behind my back; and one or two even complimented me on my appearance. They must have welcomed a change of some sort even if bordering on the grotesque—or was it simple kindness in those who were now able to see the real worth beneath the surface. For my achievements had won their respect regardless of oddities.

If only I could have dressed like other girls, even with all my country awkwardness I should doubtless have made many more friends that year in school; but in spite of these drawbacks, I did find a few good friends among my classmates, who stood by me loyally and there were others who were glad to have my help with their studies. Among these classmates, two especially stand out in memory, whose friendship persisted for years until we wholly lost track of each other in the mazes of life.

There was dear little Ethel Leake of Uplands, dark complexioned with a sweet oval face and beautiful expression, four years my junior, quiet, modest, and a devout Methodist. She combed her dark hair back as plainly as I had always worn mine, only with her head so well rounded on top that style of headdress was more becoming to her than it had been to me with my flattened top, so long bewailed.

This dear girl of twelve, in many ways my own age, took me home with her on several occasions—a motherless home, having only father and brothers, in which Ethel herself was the little house-mother, which no doubt accounted for her grown-up ways. These occasions I greatly enjoyed. They were little oases in the desert of life.

She invited me to her church one Sunday. As I watched her bow her head in solemn reverence, though not sharing the same feeling, I vaguely wished that I could, and admired her all the more.

Long years after this, when wrinkles were beginning to appear in our faces, Ethel and I met by chance in a vegetarian restaurant in Los Angeles, and recognized each other. We had only a few minutes for conversation, but that brief interval was sufficient to disclose how the tables had turned. Ethel, still unmarried, had long before given up her faith in the Bible and turned to the shifting sands of "higher criticism," while I, on the other hand, having given up the attitude of the critic, had become a Christian and planted my feet on the solid rock of God's Word. She was still a sweet girl. I have not seen her since. But the discovery of her defection has never ceased to pain me.

Then there was Lulu Powers—no kin to the teacher—a slim girl with freckled face and fiery red hair, who though she could lay no claim to beauty, had a friendly heart, and liked to be in my company. Perhaps she too was lonely; for a keenly critical mind and sharp tongue—that might have been overlooked in one having a beautiful face—rather militated against popularity; and we chummed together quite a bit. Years later, I met her again by chance in San Diego, still single and still keen of tongue; and she took me to the Onyx works, showed me around and gave me a "good time." Through her, I heard again of Miss Cotton; who, it seemed had married and was not very happy. This too pained me. But these reminiscences are really outside of my story.

Near the close of school, a distressed letter came from Mother containing the news that Frank had gone away from home on May nineteenth; having been secretly taken to the train by Joel Anderson after night. He had bidden nobody goodbye, and she did not know where he was. She said she did not know how they were going to get along without him, that I was needed very badly and that she was glad school would soon be out so I could come home.

Mother did not state any reason for his leaving home; but afterward I learned from Charlotte that he and Joseph had not been getting along well for some time. Joseph, upon whose shoulders rested the farm management, was dissatisfied with the way Frank did his work, and Frank, who was six years his junior, resented his older brother's authority over him. So when the situation had become acute, Frank had simply picked up his baggage, as had Lafe before him, and "pulled out." He soon wrote to Charlotte, his "little pal," telling her why he left, where he was then, and what he was doing; sending a "proxy" message to Mother.

He had gone first to San Juan Capistrano, where he worked for awhile before going on to San Diego; and was at the latter place when the Sweetwater dam broke. His surplus earnings, he would send to his sister to put into the bank in Santa Ana for him. After he was gone, it became necessary to keep Joel on the farm force regularly during heavy work.

There was to be another school exhibition on the last day of school, and the teachers were having the pupils in their respective rooms decorate the blackboards with the best of their own drawings, that visiting parents might see the type of handiwork their offspring were capable of doing.

Some of us were practicing on the board to see what we could do, and I drew a frog; which immediately attracted Mrs. Power's attention. She liked it so well that she had me drawing frogs at various locations all over the board, amongst pictures drawn by others; so my many humiliations were not without compensations. At the close of school, I received a card promoting me into the seventh grade.

Often I would slip in to see Miss Cotton after dismissal of classes, and on one of these occasions, as final goodbyes were drawing near, she made a proposition to me which could I have accepted, would no doubt have changed my whole career in life. She invited me to go home with her after school and live with her. She said that I could help her with her work and she would provide my clothes and living expenses, and put me through school and "make something out of me."

I was thrilled with hope and joy—but only for a moment. I thought of Mother's letter, of their great need of me on the farm, of my younger sisters who must somehow be put into school, of my obligation to help them also to get an education. My heart sank. It could never be.

Hiding in my own breast the most of all this, I told her they needed me at home, and refused the offer that would have meant the gateway to success in life. Though I felt that merely to associate with Miss Cotton would mean untold benefit to me, there seemed nothing else to do but say no. Such rare good fortune was not for me. To accept I thought would be supreme selfishness. So I said goodbye to Miss Cotton on that last day of school, and never saw her again.

And now the time had come when I must leave Ontario and the babies; of whom I was very fond. Yes there were now two of them; for in March, infant Charles Gilmore had come to join his little sister Winona—called respectively, "Dottie" and "Mannie" by their doting parents—and the two of them made a houseful of work; which their mother was to be left to cope with alone. Charlie himself was a handful without any baby. For with all his pleasing personality, he had very disorderly habits, leaving everything he used just where he happened to be when he got through with it—newspaper scattered over the floor, shoes kicked into a corner, hat thrown down onto a chair, shaving-brush and mug left anywhere but in the right place, towel tossed across the back of a chair instead of being hung up, and clothes lying anywhere just as he stepped out of them.

Artie, who was the very soul of neatness, had never counted on this, and was distressed beyond measure. To her, it seemed a major calamity, and in her efforts to correct this fault, nagged him almost to death and narrowly missed wrecking the domestic ship. But being truly fond of each other, in spite of stormy times, they weathered the gale and spent a long life together. Should both of them live to the Thirty-First day of March, Nineteen Forty-One, a Golden wedding will be in order.

Mother had sent me money for my fare home, and I took the train for El Toro, where Joseph met me with the spring wagon. When we reached home, Joseph drove around into the back yard above the fence with its concrete foundation, stopping on the slope about midway between that and the milk-house under the sycamore. He then stepped to the right wheel of the wagon to lift me out over it on the downhill side. He had raised me into mid-air and was setting me down, when our big shaggy dog, in his joy at seeing me again, with tail wagging, ran suddenly up and stopped directly under me, and down I came full force with both feet on his back; which nearly broke both my ankles. So my home-coming was turned into a near-tragedy, and heralded with pain, inconvenience, and disappointment; for it was several weeks before I could bear my weight on my feet. I could not run about over the farm as I had anticipated, or assist with any of the work that could not be done from a chair; and even when recovered sufficiently to take my place in the routine, my ankles still were not strong, but subject to spraining easily over the least provocation. In fact, they never were normally strong again.

Some time during that autumn following my return from school, I met for the first time, the young man who four years afterward, was to lead me to the marriage altar at the age of twenty-one and a half.

CHAPTER 57 THE "COOK" AND THE "TINKER"

After Lafe had put in a year at the Rosenbaum place, he was called to the little town of El Toro to begin work on a group of dwellings that were being erected by a small colony of Englishmen. These subjects of Great Britain, for the most part wealthy landowners, had settled in the suburbs at the margin of a rich farming district.

About this time a literary society, doubtless headed up by the local school teacher, was organized in the community, and dignified with the name of Lyceum. Once a week from far and near, the greater part of the population, rich and poor alike, would turn out to spend a pleasant and profitable evening at the schoolhouse either listening to or taking part in a program of recitations, musical selections and debates.

It was not long before they had added to this a neighborhood "newspaper" similar to those "published" by the schools of Phoenix, Ontario and other places. Suitably arranged columns copied in the Editor's longhand on news-size sheets of paper, were read aloud by him to the assembled audiences at their weekly meetings.

Voluntary contributors rendered cooperation by scouring the neighborhood for interesting bits of news, jokes and funny things to supplement those collected and devised by the Editor, himself constantly on the lookout for such material. They called this sheet "The El Toro Squib," and it soon became a leading feature of the evening's entertainment.

The first Editor was Mr. Coleman the station master, who held the office for the prescribed term of one month, followed by Lafe and others. We of Aliso attended these lyceum meetings whenever possible, though often obliged to miss them; for twenty-two miles by team there and back was a long way to travel for a bit of fun.

The only store in the place was a grocery run by Mr. Squires in connection with an unpretentious and often guestless hotel. Lafe went in one day to buy a loaf of bread, and was waited upon by Ella Cox, the new cook, who also served upon occasion as clerk in the store. After meeting her, he took to sauntering in daily whether or not he needed anything from the shelves.

Ella was a widow with a beautiful little four-year-old daughter who lived with her grandparents in Los Angeles. Very slender of build, with dark hair, brown eyes, soft well-modulated voice and pleasant engaging manners, she was sweet as could be, and lacked one day of being Lafe's own age. She came to be known in the community as "the cook," and her delicious meals soon brought her local fame.

After finishing his carpentry work, Lafe still lingered on, living in a tent which he had pitched. Being an accommodating fellow, he was sought for odd jobs of repair work by those of the community in need of such services, and before long had acquired the title of "The Tinker." This went on until his real name was hardly ever spoken. It was always:

"Here Tinker, can you fix this?" or:

"Take it to the Tinker. He can fix it if anybody can."

Meanwhile, Lafe had been hunting and trapping coyotes as opportunity afforded, but now began to find other and more interesting occupation for his Sundays. When the store was closed and Ella, as occasionally happened, was off duty for the day, he would bring her down to our home in Aliso, or take her to the beach. Sometimes we all together would go to the beach, taking our dinner along. We liked Ella and she liked us. It was also very evident that she and Lafe liked each other exceedingly well.

It is not to be supposed that these activities and Lafe's predilection for the store could long escape the eagle eye of the "Squib." So "The Tinker" and "The Cook" were making front-page news. But that didn't seem to stop the association in the least.

For some time I had been secretly sending in anonymous contributions to the "Squib" based on "Mother Goose" rhymes. In this form were played up the funny things I heard, individual idiosyncrasies, and interesting and embarrassing bits of information that came my way.

A young man, just to be "different," began to let his beard grow. When it had reached the long and silky stage, to the annoyance of his personal friends, he found himself one evening the subject of a "Mother Goose" in the "public press" and all the roomful enjoying a laugh at his expense.

"One misty moisty morning
When cloudy was the weather,
I chanced to meet a young man
With face wreathed in feathers.
He began to curt'sy
And I began to grin,
Saying: 'How day do?
And how are too
The whiskers on your chin?"

Someone named Jimmie had killed a wildcat and never got through telling others about it. Always he ended his account with:

"And I shot him right through the eye!"

His listeners naturally found this a bit tiresome, and though he seemed not to sense it, the thing became a neighborhood joke. After I got hold of it, this came out:

"Sing a song of sixpence,
A pocket full of rye,
Jimmie killed a wildcat
And shot it through the eye.
When the cat was buried
He wouldn't let it be,
But every day he dug it up
To let the neighbors see.!'

The reading of this was greeted with roars of laughter. And after that they heard no more of his exploit from Jimmie. But to the chief subjects, neither of whom even once suspected the true culprit, the source of the following always remained a mystery:

THE TINKER
"'If ifs and ands
Were pots and pans,
We'd have no use for tinkers'-
For pans and pots
Are mended not
By sages or by thinkers—

But since our 'ands'
Can join no pans,
Although they are conjunctions,
We welcome here
The 'Tinker' dear,
Fulfilling all his functions.

Upon this friend
No doubt depends
The peace of all our thinkers;
But upon the 'Cook'
Depends no doubt,

The welfare of our 'Tinker.'
His own, he shirks,
To do our work
With hammer, nails, and solder;
So let us look
To find a 'Cook'
To keep his house in order.

Then with the Squib
With plans so big
To help him in his wooing,
Its readers guess
He'll have success,
And wish him all that's due him.

When March of Ninety-Four came around, Lafe and Ella, wishing to celebrate on a Sunday their double birthdays, which fell on the twenty-third and twenty-fourth respectively, planned a picnic dinner on the beach in which all the family then at home joined.

We drove down to "Shell Beach," a point below Three Arches, and spent a care-free day visiting, bathing, gathering shells, and enjoying ourselves generally.

Ella had prepared most of the good things served that day on the long white cloth spread out on the clean ocean sand. And all being wholesomely hungry—for there is no place like the ocean beach to whet the appetite—we gathered about the picnic dinner with hearty enjoyment.

When the time came for dessert, Ella explained to us that in stirring up the cake, she had dropped into the batter a penny for prosperity and a ring for a wedding, and that whoever received one of these in the piece of cake served, would be blessed accordingly. The cake was parcelled out to us impartially and we bit into it rather gingerly, watching out for the penny and the ring. Pretty soon, Lafe exclaimed:

"I've found the penny!"

Sure enough there it was, symbol for him of a prosperous year. Soon Ella, much to her surprise and the pleasure of us all, announced with a laugh that she had found the ring. This meant that she was slated for a wedding. Thus by two coincidences, the tokens were appropriately distributed as to the persons selected and the most fitting symbol for each.

It was then that they announced to the family their recent engagement, and received our pleased congratulations.

On the twentieth day of the following November, Lafe and Ella were married and went to Los Angeles to establish a home of their own.

A Night in the "Black Star"

In this settlement of English families lived Mrs. Cope; who was desirous of having a young girl to live with her and work for board and school privileges. Hearing of this, I immediately began to interest Mother in sending Charlotte there for the coming school term. This arrangement was effected. And so another of the children of Aliso, at the age of nearly fourteen, started to school, attending at the little country schoolhouse in El Toro.

Figure 43 Charlotte Thurston, 1890s

At the same time urged on by burning enthusiasm for education, I pleaded for Luella, then nearing eleven to be sent to live with Joan and Harry up in Ladd's Canyon and attend the little mountain school in Silverado. Joan was not in very good health, and Luella's help with dishes and the babies after school hours, would more than compensate them for the expense incurred. So arrangements were made and we got her ready. I was to take her up there in the spring wagon.

I was now seventeen and a half and Annie nearing sixteen. We had not seen much of each other since her return home, and it was a treat to be together. We were really getting acquainted all over again, feeling now quite on a par with each other as to schooling, and able to discourse on kindred topics. She went along with me both for company on the return journey, and also for the enjoyment it would afford her to visit Joan's mountain home.

It was, however, a very dismal day for such a trip. The Santa Ana wind was blowing lonesomely; having only that morning begun its customary three-day's "jamboree." could not put off going until it was over and be tardy for the opening of school, so after a late breakfast, started out.

The back seat of the wagon had been removed to make room for the box containing Luella's belongings and a small roll of quilts we were taking along to help out with bed-covers in her new home. So the three of us sat together on the front seat.

Several miles up the canyon, as we drove along conversing, a large rattlesnake made himself seen crossing the road in front of us. Stopping the team, we all climbed out of the wagon. Finding no stones we gathered up a heap of hard clods as ammunition before beginning the inevitable battle. With these I pelted him, the girls supplying me and replenishing the pile as depleted, meanwhile preserving a very respectful distance from the now infuriated reptile. After a long offensive in which the horsewhip played a prominent part, he was at last conquered and lay quite dead upon the ground. Twisting off his rattles to exhibit as a trophy, we resumed our journey. But this little diversion had consumed considerable time.

On several past occasions I had been to visit Joan and Harry in their mountain home, and took it for granted that I knew the way perfectly. Leaving the old stage road at Tustin and missing Santa Ana by passing to the east, the road led through Orange into Santiago Canyon, following that until Silverado branched off from it to the left.

After this, the alder-lined creek in Silverado Canyon was crossed several times, and now and then a beautiful evergreen oak tree passed before reaching the little unpainted schoolhouse by the roadside and Tom Hughes' place a short distance farther on. Then came the smaller Ladd's Canyon opening into Silverado from the west, in which Joan and Harry lived. Here the road ascended the side of a hill to the small nearly level bench on which stood their little cabin among the great oak trees.

This all seemed very simple indeed. But always before I had ridden merely as a passenger while Joseph or Harry drove the team. The passenger never pays such careful attention to roads as does the driver. Small deviations and landmarks are likely to escape the notice of one not handling the reins—or in modern parlance, the wheel. Lapse of time also—in this case two years or more—may dim the memory of a supposedly familiar road, or even suffice to change its appearance.

All went well until we got beyond the settlements and were following up the Santiago where less travelled roads degenerated into mere wagon tracks. Suddenly I found myself puzzled. Here was a branch road to the left. It had a rather unfamiliar aspect, but then all such roads into smaller canyons appeared much alike. I knew of only one branch road in that locality. The horses travelled up the canyon so seldom that they could not be relied upon to choose the way. There was no farmhouse within miles where inquiry might be made. The girls with me knew nothing about the roads. So the decision was left entirely to me.

Saying nothing to them about my momentary doubts, I turned off into this branch canyon just as the afternoon sun was sinking low in the heavens.

The wind had blown all day a very disagreeable dusty gale, which made the journey anything but the pleasant drive we had at first planned.

Breakfast, though very late, was now long in the past, and we were all getting hungry. The horses too were hungry, thirsty and tired. Some time before, they had slaked their thirst while crossing a little stream, but no more watering places had been found, being at that time of year almost all dried up. We travelled on and on, never seeming to get anywhere. Secretly, I began to grow anxious. By this time we should have come to some familiar landmark and the running water of Silverado creek, whose rocky bed was never entirely dry.

But the low scrubby shrubbery persisted in place of the great oak trees that should have come to view. What had become of them? Where was the little schoolhouse? And Tom's place? Where were we? It then dawned upon me that we were lost. Evidently we were somewhere else than in Silverado Canyon but where, I had not the slightest idea.

Darkness was falling, the wind whining dismally. Reluctantly now I disclosed to the others our predicament, becoming the object of their censure. Weary miles lay between us and the spot where we had turned off the main road up the Santiago. To retrace our steps and find it was an impossibility in the darkness. There were no "headlights" on wagons. The word itself had never yet been coined. "Flashlights" likewise had never been invented. We had brought no lantern with us, expecting to have reached our destination before dark. Without the light of day, we would not be able to recognize the road when reached, and the horses would keep going on homeward. What should we do? There was but one thing we could do, pass the night just where we were without a bed, with neither food nor water for the poor weary horses or for ourselves.

A small spreading oak tree, one of the few we had seen, stood a little distance from the road. Up to the edge of its branching circumference we drove the wagon, and there got out and unhitched the horses, removing the harnesses from their weary backs. The only ropes we had were the short pieces attached to their halters. These we fastened to boughs high overhead, for no branches grew low that were stout enough to hold them. This made it impossible for them to lie down or even lower their noses to the ground to munch the dry oak leaves that dropped, reeling giddily under their feet.

All the loose sand had been blown away from the spot, exposing the bare embedded rocks, and on this rough surface the horses were obliged to stand without food or water through that long dreary windy night, a more distressing situation than our own plight.

We untied the roll and spread down a quilt in the bed of the wagon, enclosed by end and side boards about a foot high. Into this short and narrow bed we squeezed ourselves, lay down with heads under the seat and feet against the end-gate, packed literally "like sardines in a can," or spoons fitted together. No one could move independently of the others. If one wished to turn over, all three had to do likewise.

The hard floor of the wagon grew every moment harder, and our pillow-less heads received more than their normal allotment of red corpuscles. Sleep was utterly out of the question. The wind howled and whined dismally, rising and falling with weird, lonesome noises. The boughs overhead creaked as they were shaken by the poor uncomfortable horses endeavoring to lower their heads to the earth, and restlessly shuffling their feet about on the rough stones.

And thus the night wore away. Toward daybreak it became uncomfortably cool. We were up the next morning in time to catch all the "worms" before the "early birds" had even thought about it. Stiff and unrested, but filled with the hope of a new day, we soon had the horses in harness again and headed down the canyon.

The true turn-off into Silverado, when at last we reached it, seemed familiar enough, and we arrived at the home of Harry and Joan before they were out of bed. How great was their surprise to see us so early in the day! And how those two horses appreciated a good breakfast and a long drink of water, with plenty of rest before starting home again!

Harry informed us that the canyon in which we had been lost was the "Black Star," and that I was not by any means the first one to mistake it for Silverado.

Reality Versus Fiction

That year Annie and I stayed at home and worked hard, for our number was considerably decreased. The bees had been disposed of, since Joseph, with so much other work to do, and the rest of us so frequently absent, could not give them the necessary care.

Whenever Hulda happened to be at home, she, with Clara slept in the southwest bedroom, while Annie and I occupied the northeast. Joseph, in his room at the end of the bent hallway, had company one night, none other than Bob Hughes, Harry's cousin who two years before had built our retaining wall. The two had gone to bed and to sleep. Hulda and Clara had done the same. Mother was in her room downstairs puttering about as usual getting ready to retire. Annie and I had also gone to bed—but not to sleep. At that time I was reading to her in nightly installments, one of the forbidden "thrillers" by H. Rider Haggard—whether "He," "She," or "It," I cannot now remember—and, to preclude any surprise intrusion, which might lead to the unwelcome discovery of our depravity, had locked the door. This would give us time to hide the "yellow-back" before admitting any over-critical visitor.

On the stand at the head of the bed, the kerosene lamp stood lighted, by whose feeble beams, we were living over the thrills of Haggard's hero and heroine. Suspecting that Annie was beginning to drowse, I would occasionally pause in my reading to inquire:

"Are you listening?"

So long as there was a ready reply, I would resume my story. But as she grew less responsive to this stimulus, to avoid repetition on the following night, I decided it was time to fold down the corner of the page, blow out the light, and close my own eyes for the night. It was no fun to read without a listener.

So I reached over and laid my book on the stand preparatory to extinguishing the light. As I raised my hand above the chimney, cupping it to catch the blast of breath and turn it downward onto a protesting flame, by some awkward movement—one of those inexplicable and abominable abortions that have dogged my steps all through life—instead of blowing out the light, I knocked the scalloped rim of its transparent tower, and overboard tumbled the lamp with a crash of splintered chimney onto the floor.

A wild yell shattered into smithereens the castles of dreamland and sent the sandman scuttling to safety, as I leaped out of bed onto my knees before the flaming symbol of Aladdin now wallowing in its own life-blood-the thrill of fiction having given way completely to the more absorbing excitement of real life.

The oil pouring out through the wick-slot of the burner, formed a rapidly spreading inflammable lake. I made a grab for the prostrate lamp, but only succeeded in rolling it around in a circular track through the oil, which caused the flame to envelop its glassy bowl.

My hideous shrieks had brought Joseph, Bob Hughes, Hulda, Clara, and Mother running—not to the scene, but to the locked door, on which they were pounding for admittance.

Every grain of commonsense I had ever boasted of possessing, like "fair-weather friends" had now deserted me. All I seemed capable of doing was to continue the frantic screams for help and to poke wildly at the rolling, blazing lamp in its oily lake that was every instant expected to become a "lake of fire" by some terrific explosion of that diabolical fugitive lamp-bowl that refused to be captured.

Annie, having rallied from her first shock, after watching me for a few seconds that seemed like hours, remembered having read somewhere that flames could be smothered with a blanket. So, seizing some of the bedcovers, she threw them over the whole imperiled area—lamp, flames, oil and all; and then went to the door and unlocked it just as Bob Hughes was on the point of going to fetch an ax to break it down.

When, in various scarecrow garbs, male and female, they burst into the room, excited, wild-eyed, vociferously clamoring to find out what was the matter, there they found me—Harriet, the bold, the fearless, the leader—a floundering lunatic in flowing nightrobe, humped over the now extinguished and buried wreckage of my own colossal awkwardness, saved, rescued, delivered by the simple "first aid" of a younger and supposedly less efficient sister.

CHAPTER 58 IN THE THROES OF DEPRESSION

With the "bug" of "Education fever" buzzing in the air—the different ones going away from home to obtain here and there such snatches of schooling as they could, and with Frank completely out from under the burden, Joseph himself became infected with the general discontent, and decided that he too was entitled to a change from the farm responsibilities. He felt the injustice of its being taken for granted that he was always to carry the burden of the farm while the rest of us could shift ours in this manner.

At that time Frank too was living with Harry and Joan and attending school in Silverado Canyon along with Luella. He had just gotten nicely started and interested in his school work when word reached him that Joseph had decided to leave home.

Figure 44 Frank Thurston

Frank had previously sent a reassuring message to Mother that any time Joseph should make up his mind to go away, he would come back and take charge of the farm. So when these tidings were brought him about the last of January, he immediately got his belongings together after five months of school, and returned to Aliso at the age of nineteen to take over the farm responsibilities, having been gone eight and a half months. And that was the end of his schooling.

Though Frank, in running the farm, did not do so well as our more efficient Joseph, yet he did better than any of us had expected, and much better in full charge than as an underling. The Laguna peddling of produce was suspended, being carried on only intermittently during Joseph's absence. But we somehow managed to make a living and to get the necessary work done by hiring help occasionally. Labor was cheap and with so many of us gone, there were fewer mouths to feed and less clothing to buy.

A few weeks after Frank's return, Artie came down to Aliso, about the middle of February, to visit us, and stayed for something like two months. During this time, little Lorena, her third child was born on March eleven.

From an old letter written to her by Charles, then Constable of Ontario, Cucamonga Township, on February twenty-two, Eighteen Ninety-Four, I take the following:

"Washington's Birthday
Dear Little Wife:

I have not received any word from you yet, and am somewhat disappointed...The mail only leaves there three times a week, I believe, but we can not remedy that unless you get a chance once in a while to send a letter to post up to El Toro...I went and saw Mrs. White in Colton. The first thing she said was: 'Where's Artie? I want her.' Poor Mrs. White! I feel sorry for her. We had a long talk and she told me everything. She said, had John only taken sick and died, she could have stood it better; but to have him take himself away and leave her and the little babe, she felt that she could not stand it...Mr. White tried to kill himself while up at Hemet working last summer. The boys worked for four or five hours getting him around. He took poison; so it seems that he was determined to get himself out of the way. The only pity is that he did not succeed the first time...so that Mrs. White would not have her hands tied with that poor little babe. I thought John White a braver man than I now do. I think his last act a cowardly one. Katy Lang was there with her. She came down Sunday on the ten o'clock train. She had been at Colonel Maybury's at Alhambra. Mrs. White...does not know which way to turn. She has no money at all and no property, and that little babe on her hands. She thinks of doing first one thing and then another. Sometimes thinks she will try to get a hotel to run; then she thinks of going home; then something else. Her last plan was to try and get some place to work for her board until her babe gets larger. She says John left her with a dollar. She has her horse and surrey, a cow, and five or six dozen chickens, and the furniture in the house; which she proposes to sell, and which will bring her in quite a little sum; for I think under the circumstances, she can dispose of them for a good price. Miss Lang will stay with her until she gets settled.

Pa is here with me...and he does the cooking and washing dishes—in fact, all the housework that is done. Mrs. Cooper got the stale cream and sent us some cookies. She does not get much milk, for Pa and I drink most all we get. She came over and invited us to supper the other evening...Our social and speaking entertainment turned out nicely considering the weather. It was cloudy and disagreeable, and started to rain; but a great many came, and enjoyed themselves. I did not get to dance at all—got disgusted—asked three ladies to dance the first quadrille, and all refused; said, 'Oh yes, your wife is away, and you think you will have a nice time—not much!' and so on. So I quit trying to dance and went to attending to the wants of...the company....

It is blowing today a perfect hurricane of dust, so one can hardly see ten yards. About the worst I have seen in Ontario...Tell everybody to forgive for my neglect of them. Make any excuse for me that you can trump up. I can find none good enough...Well, Little One, that's all for this time. Love and kisses for yourself and babies, and all the rest.

Popa."

On the twenty-sixth, he wrote:

"The little house is lonesome now. I never thought it would make so much difference to take a wife and babies away. Pa is no company at all. He is like me—comes in and takes a paper and sits down to read, or goes to bed, and is not a bit sociable. But he does what cooking and dishwashing is done, and so forth. Things do not look nice and bright as they do when you are here. We had some hotcakes for breakfast-and the saddest lot of cakes I ever ate; pale and thin. I said: 'Pa, your cakes are not baked.' He said: 'No, the fire went out,' and I guess it did...I had a turn-over yesterday; went out to water the colts, and in taking Dandy and Dude back to picket them, they got to cutting up; (had them tied to the cart). They jerked back and sidewise and upset the cart. I fell square under and the cart on top of me. One of the shafts struck Billy in the side; and how I got out, I can never be able to tell; but I did, without a scratch; except on the end of one of my fingers. Billy started, and around and around they went, I looking on, until he had broke the harness all off and got loose from the cart-all except the lines, which were fast, and he had his head where his tail should be, and vice versa. Then I went to him and led him away. The colts got loose and I had a time catching them, but finally at noon had everything as good as ever—except the harness—Everything is getting on nicely except

451

the house, which I would not like you to see. Will have two or three people to clean it up before you come home. Kiss Dot and Manny for Popa every night and morn. Love and kisses for yourself and everybody.

Chas.

For Dot.

Dot, Popa is lonesome, and wants to see Mama, Dot, and Manny. You must take care of Mama and Manny for Popa while you are at Grandma's, and give your Mama a great big kiss for Popa. Dot's colt is a rascal. He turned Popa over and spilled him on the ground.

Popa."

On February twenty-seven, Charles wrote:

"I would like to see Joseph come up to Chino; but if he has a job down there and can get fair wages, he had better not quit it now, for times are dull, and many idle men through here hunting for work. A man came to me tonight and wanted to sleep in the jail. Said he had been working for two months for his board, and could get nothing more. He was a big strong fellow and had the appearance of being a good worker."

By this, it may be seen that it was a very inauspicious time for Joseph to strike out for himself. The financial outlook could hardly have been any blacker than it was at that time.

After the baby came, Charles drove down to Aliso to see his wife and babies, including the new arrival, and stayed a few days. When he went back, Joseph quit whatever he may have been doing on the coast, and went back with him to the San Bernardino country.

On the nineteenth of March, Charles wrote:

"We drove through the same day we left; got home a little after five o'clock. Pa had just started to get supper; and as soon as Joseph and I got the horses put up, supper was ready; and we enjoyed it too; for we were hungry...Joseph stayed with us until yesterday, then he went to San Bernardino...Pa went to Colton yesterday to get his tool chest and fix for building our cottage. I made preparations for the lumber Saturday. It will cost a hundred thirteen dollars and fifty cents for the lumber and probably about one hundred fifty in all by the time it is finished. So the whole house, land and all, will cost us about five hundred dollars; and it will be a pretty neat little place. Pa and I were talking about the ceiling in the kitchen, the other day, and we came to the conclusion that it would be very warm in the summer time and not look quite so neat, as to plaster. If you have no objection to plaster other than as to the driving of nails in the walls, we can put some casing boards across the walls and then wainscote up two and a half or three feet, and it will look neat and not be so warm. The cost will be about the same. So let me know which you prefer.

I am tired out today; was in the saddle all the night. Yesterday about half past three, six hundred men marched in here and camped in the outskirts of our town. They were the advance regiment of a body of men calling themselves the United States Industrial Army. Their object is to march to Washington and present in person, their grievances to President Cleveland and the United States Congress.

They were in fact, a large body of tramps and 'hobos' taking that course to get through the country and get a living off the people. At Pomona, they fed them, and here, we had to do the same. Many of them were tramps that had lodged in my lodging-house (the jail) over night, and many were taken to serve sentences in San Bernardino. Well, they came; and I never left them—except to feed and water the horses and cow—until they left this morning on a freight train for Colton; where they are now. Pa just got in and says they are now in Colton.

I had just got the cow milked when George Hall fell in and says: 'For God's sake, get up town. They have all broke loose and are taking in the town!' I grabbed my rifle and jumped on Dick and was in amongst them in a few minutes. Things were not quite so bad as I expected. They had made a break for a freight train, and the engineer saw them and did not stop. They finally got quiet, and I did not leave them again. I had twenty deputies sworn in, and they stayed with me.

So I am sleepy and tired. I laid down for a couple of hours this morning. So ended along tiresome night; and very glad I was when the train pulled out this morning with them all on board the box cars."

In the popular hope that his election would alleviate the suffering caused by unemployment, Cleveland, after a lapse of four years in private life, by an overwhelming majority, was sent to the White House for the second term. Before his administration was more than begun, in March of Ninety-Four, laboring men everywhere had begun to organize into "Industrial Armies," and frame documents of demanded reforms. Among these were a "Good Roads Bill" and a "Non-interest-bearing Bond Bill" both intended to provide employment, and calling for unbacked paper currency by the government.

The preamble to the constitution of their organization contained articles setting forth their reasons for organizing. From an old copy of the "Arena," published in Ninety-Four, is taken the following extract.

"Why is it that those who produce food are hungry? Why is it that those who make clothes are ragged? Why is it that those who build palaces are houseless? Why is it that those who do the nation's work are forced to choose between beggary, crime, or suicide in a nation that has fertile soil enough to produce plenty to feed and clothe the world; material enough to build palaces for them all, and productive capacity through labor-saving machinery, of forty thousand million man-power, and only sixty-five million souls to feed, clothe and shelter?

Recognizing the fact that if we wish to escape the doom of past civilizations, something must be done, and done quickly:

Therefore, we, as patriotic citizens, have organized ourselves into an industrial army for the purpose of centralizing all the unemployed American citizens at the seat of government 'Washington D. C.' and tender our services to feed, clothe and shelter the nation's needy; and to accomplish this end, we make the following demands: First: government employment for all her unemployed citizens; Second: the prohibition of foreign immigration for ten years; Third: that no alien be allowed to own real estate in the United States."

The leader of this movement, Jacob Selcher Coxey, led an army of some five hundred men, starting on Easter Sunday, March twenty-five, Eighteen Ninety-Four, from his home town of Massillon, Ohio, to Washington; intending to reach there by May Day.

But Coxey was only one of many who led regiments of these unemployed men from many sections of the country, nor was he the first to start marching. Louis Frye led seven hundred from California to Missouri; Josiah Ross headed a band of five hundred in Buffalo, New York; Kelly, with one thousand two hundred, moved through Indiana; and others from other parts of the country. Randall, with a contingent, marched out of Chicago, bearing banners inscribed: "No Charity, But Work and Fair Wages," "An Injury To One Is An Injury To All."

They were organized after military form, with "generals," "colonels," "lieutenants," and "corporals." This movement caused great excitement throughout the nation and in every city through which the men marched drew demonstrations of popular approval.

The movement also called down upon their heads, bitter vituperation and denunciation from law officers and others unsympathetic with their methods. Much of this was unfeeling and extreme; though some of it was no doubt justified; for among such gatherings are always extremists and unlawful agitators, who bring disrepute upon the whole body by incendiary speeches and deeds of violence.

These men were accused of being unwilling to work. Though there were among them some of that stamp, yet, in the main they were doubtless composed of honest men who wanted work and a chance to earn a livelihood for their families, but could not find it. Wise or unwise, the method of organization, the military usages, the demands upon congress, brought them into disrepute, and Coxey and others were arrested in the Capitol grounds.

Joseph worked at various places during the two years and a half he was away from the farm. For awhile he sold beans in San Bernardino County; and in the late summer secured a job on a threshing machine. The San Joaquin had now become the Irvine Ranch; and all the sheep of the country had disappeared and their broad pasture lands been turned into grain fields. When the great threshing machine with its outfit came onto this ranch to thresh the grain, Joseph became a member of the crew.

For this strenuous work, which only strong men could endure day after day, the men received—if unskilled hands—one dollar and fifty cents a day with board. Those with special experience in the technical positions received more. Joseph was of course, counted among the unskilled; this being his first experience on a thresher.

After threshing was over, he went to work on a farm at Los Nietos near Whittier for a man who had a large walnut orchard. On this farm was a big bay horse—a very fine animal, full of life—but also full of tricks. After working him in the harness for several days, Joseph led him out one afternoon to turn him loose in the corral, having only the halter-rope about his neck. He opened the heavy gate, which lifted out of its socket to swing around, and turned the horse loose to go inside the corral, slipping the halter rope off his neck just as his head and shoulders were within. Then he stepped back to shut the gate. But the horse, instead of going on in as expected, backed out quickly before Joseph could send him forward with a slap on the rump, and turned to run. Quickly reaching up, Joseph caught hold of his neck as he passed, to put on the rope again. But the horse suddenly lifted his head so high that he was raised off his feet. Just at that instant, the horse tripped and fell, turning a complete summersault and landing in the manure pile beyond. As he went over, taking Joseph with him and under him, his sharp hoof struck him a terrific blow on the side, cutting a hole through jacket, shirt and undershirt.

The first to extricate himself from the melee, Joseph arose painfully and while the horse was struggling to get on his feet, put the rope around his neck; then led him back into the corral and turned him loose apparently none the worse from the fracas. But he himself was badly hurt. No doubt an X-ray—had there been such a thing then known—would have revealed fractured ribs. He could work no more that season, but quit his job and went to George's home in San Jacinto where he stayed for several months to recuperate.

CHAPTER 59 AT THE FOUNTAIN IN THE MOUNTAINS

With Luella's return to Aliso for the summer at the close of her first school year, word was brought to us that the young schoolteacher, Clara Mason, having homesteaded a piece of land in Silverado Canyon, was desirous of finding someone who, for board and school privileges, would live with her as companion in her mountain cabin on the claim. My name had been mentioned to her by Joan and Harry, and through them she had extended to me the invitation.

I was only too eager to accept. As Mother seemed to be favorable, and there were no objections raised from any other quarter, I went up to Silverado Canyon before the opening day, to begin another school year under circumstances the most pleasant. Luella had already gone back to Joan's for her second term; so we were to be together in the same school. Charlotte also had returned to El Toro to school—this time living with Mrs. Squires; where she was to work for her board and room.

Miss Mason, driving a single horse hitched to an open conveyance, met me in Orange, and together we drove up through the valley to her two roomed rustic cabin far up in Silverado Canyon, about a mile and a half beyond the schoolhouse.

Dispensing with formalities, we began at once to get acquainted with each other. From the first she took an interest in me, giving most practical advice. There being no other pupil in my class—for again I was amongst children years younger than I—an intensive program of individual study was possible. She mapped out a course composed of wise selections from seventh, eighth, and ninth grade work that filled up gaps in previous subjects and would put me through the ninth grade at the end of school, stressing those subjects most practical for me as a preparation for future advancement. This intensive course, included private recitations at home of evenings with freely proffered extra help from her.

Clara Mason was my senior by eight or ten years; but notwithstanding this disparity we became fast friends and pals. She was a little mite of a thing, with dark hair, firm mouth and brown eyes that were full and round. In very poor health, she nevertheless possessed an exuberance of energy, and kept going by the force of her indomitable will.

We hunted up and gathered our own wood, dragging it down from the hillside, and chopping it ourselves ready for the stove. Not one thought was ever given to the vanities women are supposed to love and require. Lipstick, rouge, powder and permanents were not a part of our toiletries.

The spot was exceedingly beautiful; the mountain air and scenery most invigorating to physical life, and conducive to quiet study and contemplation. Great oaks and other mountain trees surrounded the cabin. Gray squirrels, with their black stripes and long bushy tails played about in our yard among the oak leaves and acorns. Birds of every description sang overhead and all about us. Alders bordered the banks of the mountain stream that flowed past, a few rods distant from our door. In the little still pools and eddies among the slimy rocks along its margins shaded by low branches, Water Newts, or Salamanders, the first I had ever seen, floated and played about. The constant murmuring and singing of the stream, tumbling downward over rocks and waterfalls in its hurry to get out of the canyon, could be heard above the other sounds of the wood; its soothing lullaby comforting to daytime nerves, and wooing one to sleep at night.

Clara did much for me aside from regular class work, giving bits of instruction on various subjects as we busied ourselves about the cabin and grounds.

Our early morning walks to school and back again in the evening were in themselves poems of delight; especially in the springtime when all the flowers were out. Clara was always dissecting and classifying plants and flowers. I hungered for this knowledge and in listening to her and learning the names of many flowers, birds, and insects, was developing a great desire to study into these subjects myself. This at a later time was to be gratified to some extent. There seemed to be nothing I could ask about but that Clara was able to give me some information. I learned much about the common every-day familiar things seen, heard and handled, that had not before been understood. This was education in an ideal setting.

Clara's widowed mother and older brother Charles lived in the mountain home farther up the canyon where she herself had grown up, and on Sundays we would invariably go to this home for dinner. Never will I forget the kind hospitality of her mother and those good dinners she served. Always she had "lemon sauce" a favorite dish with her family; made something like the filling for a lemon pie. I learned to make it too and often served it to others afterward.

In this home was an organ; in which I took great pleasure when there, playing from memory "pieces" from our "Self-Instructor," and learning others from Clara's sheets. One of her beautiful little Reveries, I copied note by note to take home and reproduce on our own organ.

Clara was not only a teacher and musician, but also an artist of no mean ability; always sketching this and that—especially the funny things. Both of us could see the humorous side of everything; and many a laugh echoed through the canyon as we went to and fro. She made two little sketch-books just alike; one for me and the other for herself; and in these she made permanent in pictures all the funny incidents that happened, duplicating them so that both books would contain the same. There were tiny sketches in corners and around margins to remind of innumerable interesting things we had seen or laughed at, as well as larger pictures of page or half-page size. There was the bee that entered under the eaves and couldn't get out but "mumbled and grumbled among the rafters" and kept us awake at night, the "new kind" of flower I had called her attention to in our journeyings that had turned out to be an old familiar flower with a spot of dirt on it, and the bat that wheeled about in the dusk catching insects and then hung himself up under our eaves at midday, the friendly squirrel that ate near our kitchen door the trifles we threw out to him. There were jagged bars of little black notes on short sections of the treble staff to remind of the snatches of songs we had sung, and ever so many other things of humorous character.

Then there was "Drum," her big hound dog, so named because, on account of his endless capacity to gormandize, he was supposed to be hollow inside. A life-like picture of Drum occupied a full page in this sketch-book.

Winter downpours turned the quiet, murmuring creek into a raging torrent, fearsome and awe-inspiring—a real Jordan that must be twice crossed in reaching the little schoolhouse and returning. There were no bridges, other than a natural one. Some distance farther down the stream than our beaten path, a great tree had fallen from its position on the near bank and lay stretched across the water, its top resting on the other side. This was our bridge—its approaches rather difficult, but alluring, its rounded surface testing our powers of equilibrium. At times of high water we would start earlier than usual to school to make up for the extra time consumed in crossing the creek. I was afraid to attempt to walk across the curving bole over that swift, treacherous current; so sitting astride of the trunk I crossed by the slow process of "inching" along its length; and Clara, though much more sure-footed than I—being a mountain-raised girl and slim—followed in the same manner. Nothing so funny as this could escape caricature in that sketch-book. So there I appeared "in situ," bearing enough individualisms to insure identification, astride of the log above the billowy torrent, with my dress stretched tightly far out behind where it had caught in passing on a knot left by a missing branch.

Sometimes our shoes would wear out. We were far from town-much too far for any mere afternoon shopping. Moreover, we had no conveyance of our own and were under the necessity of depending upon borrowed facilities, or to await a time convenient for both ourselves and her brother, when he could drive us in, not overlooking the possibilities of inclement weather interfering with our plans.

In the meantime, it often became necessary to do some original patching to make our old shoes hang together. Lack of means, made my own problem more acute than Clara's. In order to make my shoes last, I would change from one old pair to another, selecting the best to wear till it ceased to be any longer the "best," then going over them all again to find another "best" pair, till finally I had but a disreputable assortment that were both "best" and "worst."

So Clara one day gathered up these old shoes and piling them in an indiscriminate heap on the top of a box in the light of the window, sketched them in the books, emphasizing with a few exaggerations of her own, such things as hairpins sticking through the soles of some and strings tied around others to hold them together, adding underneath an appropriate title. This page never failed to cause a laugh.

Thus, were all our misfortunes and experiences turned into jokes, pleasantries, fun, frolic, and laughter. A few of the pictures I drew myself with much less facility than she, and both of us wrote snatches of verse on these pages, for not one whit behind her other accomplishments was her ability to write versifications. These had about them more finish and maturity than my own. So, accompanying a sketch would often be a few humorous verses by way of amplification or further reminder.

That year spent in the mountains of Silverado Canyon—spent with Clara Mason, that friend of so many talents, did wonders for me. Though after that year our paths led in different directions, and except for an occasional brief meeting at long intervals through the years that followed, we were never together again, yet she left an impression upon her nineteen year-old friend and admirer such as few others have left. What a wonderful thing is education rightly used! How much it may be made to bless others besides ourselves! And what a marvelously potent power for good it is when yoked up with human kindness!

A Gift From Old Saddleback

Along the eastern boundary of Orange County, lies the high range of mountains known in the days of the padres by various names, Sierra Trabuco, Sierra Temescal, and Sierra de Santa Ana; but to us as the Santa Ana Mountains. From the crest rise two high peaks having a dip between, the formation resembling a saddle and called locally "Old Saddleback." The higher, rising to the southeast was named Santiago Peak, and the other to the northwest, Modjeska Peak, the home of Madam Modjeska" being in the valley on the other side.

Before those happy days ended, Clara invited Lydia Killifer, an old classmate of hers to spend a weekend with us in the Canyon. Clara, with her brother, planned for the party a climb to the top of old Mount Saddleback that loomed above the horizon to the northeast. A young man by the name of George—Somebody—also joined the group, and in order to get an early start we all spent the night preceding the outing at the home of Clara's mother.

At early dawn our hiking party was on its way. We carried with us knapsacks, staves, canteens, and rolls of blankets, for it was to be an overnight trip.

The mountain, though it appeared to be very close, was actually several miles away, and to reach its foot was quite a hike in itself. Then we started up. The men had brought with them hatchets with which to cut paths through the chaparral wherever necessary, for the foot-trails were so seldom used they were much overgrown. Up and up, we went through brush, weeds, thorns and manzanita, crossing ravines, stopping frequently to rest in the rarified atmosphere, till finally, late in the day, we reached a level, wooded, bench-like area of several acres. This, but for its inaccessibility, would have been an ideal homesite. Here we found, a little apart from other trees scattered about, a beautiful, low-branched, spreading, symmetrical tree, which we immediately adopted as our camping place, and deposited our various burdens underneath it in the shade.

We seemed to be almost at the summit which it was our purpose to reach before dark. It rose above us, a steep, rocky declivity, devoid of trees and shrubbery and supporting very little vegetation. After welcome refreshment and a good rest, we went on—this time without burdens. But though seeming so near, this last lap to the summit proved a good stiff climb, and the roughest part of our journey.

The sun was setting as we stood at last on the windy top of Mount Santiago—the horn of the saddle—which seemed indeed to be the top of the world; for nothing so high was visible in all our range of vision. The surrounding mountains that stretched away on every side seemed far below us. From our vantage point, we had a magnificent view of three counties—Orange, Los Angeles, and San Bernardino. Away to the north lay the Sierra Madre Range, rising from behind the town of that name to the northwest of Pasadena. The immensity of the unobstructed view was almost frightening, for the top of the peak was small of area, and the wind strong and masterful. We could not help wondering where we would alight miles below if the wind should blow us off the summit.

In the center of this wind-swept, rocky area, stood a monument of concrete, the boundary meeting-place of the three counties. A receptacle underneath its base contained a corked bottle in which names of former visitors to the spot had been deposited. So we added our own on bits of paper, and returned the bottle to its resting place. Perhaps they still are there. Then we came down off the summit to our tree-camp, reaching it before dark. After another repast, we spread out our blankets—the men on one side of the tree, and we three on the other side; the branches sweeping the ground between making a natural partition so dense that objects on opposite sides could not be distinguished, and without removal of clothes lay down to rest.

We slept too in that wonderful mountain air with its piney odors-slept in spite of hard beds. Weary as we had been with our long exertion we were up again with the first streak of dawn—which meant bright sunlight on the mountain hours earlier than in the valley below.

And now, a most glorious surprise and vision awaited us—the crowning delight of that unforgettable trip. Walking to the verge of the green bench to gaze westward over the valley we had left the day before, our eyes were greeted with one vast, snow-white, billowy sea that seemed to cover all the world except the higher spot on which we stood.

The world was covered from view by interminable banks of fog stretching out to the far horizon like a great ocean, whose billows rose and fell, folding and unfolding as if forming to break—only with creeping slowness—and in the unintercepted beams of the glorious sun, glittering and sparkling with a luster indescribable, breathtaking—a scene to feast upon and hold in memory forever.

We were gazing down from the upper side upon a canopy of fog that our eyes had been accustomed to behold only from underneath, where all this radiance and light were shut away from view. In fancy, we seemed to be looking from behind the veil of heaven—seeing what God sees beyond the shadows of this world—not merely a "silver lining" which itself requires the eye of faith to discern, but a whole great background of diamond-studded length and breadth, holding the promised riches of eternal glory.

CHAPTER 60 GOODBYE OLD HOME

Little sister Luella and I went home together at the close of school to resume the usual summer's work. Soon, however, though we knew it not, momentous changes were to come into our lives; for Aliso days were drawing to a close.

As one event is contingent upon another in the scheme of life, so this change came about in a very natural manner. For most individuals the very warm climate of the San Jacinto Valley, in spite of the heat was healthful, but it had never agreed with Minnie. This, together with a chronic affliction that had developed coincidently with the birth of her third child, made a move to other parts seem advisable.

In looking about for an opportunity to effect a property exchange of some kind, George found in the city of Santa Ana a fairly well located group of houses that fronted on two streets consisting of a large building that had been originally intended for a rooming house, four cottages, each having five rooms and bath, a barn and store building, and other unimproved lots making twelve in all; with liabilities to assume of twenty-eight hundred dollars.

In December of Ninety-Four he traded the south hundred and sixty acres of his original two hundred and forty for this mortgaged property, moving his family onto it the following April. They took up their residence in the large house, planning to let out rooms and to rent the four cottages, expecting that the income derived added to that he might earn by working for others, would support the family and in time pay off the mortgage.

George had been settled in Santa Ana only a short time when he began to use persuasion upon Mother to induce her to move out to town for a year, where she might place the younger children in school without having to send them away from home, and at the same time herself enjoy a complete change and rest from the farm work.

Every one of us backed him up in this proposition, even Frank, who was willing to remain on the place alone and do his own cooking, hiring whatever help was necessary and sending to Mother all profits from the crops for the support of herself and the three younger girls. As for us who were older, we proposed to secure jobs for ourselves and assume the responsibility of our own support.

Figure 45 Charlotte, Frank, Annie, Harriet and Family Friend

Mother was "poo-poohed" out of her objection that with her absent from the Aliso farm, everything was sure to go to "rack and ruin," and finally allowed herself to be persuaded into making the greatest change that had come into her life since the day when she first stepped foot upon Aliso soil.

George, soon after his move, had discovered that depending upon income from renting houses was a far greater risk than farming. The prevailing rental of a cottage such as his was then five dollars a month-some even renting for four. He offered Mother a reduction of twenty dollars on a year's rent if paid in advance. So for the sum of forty dollars Mother secured the house for a year, paying this in two installments.

Then followed much packing and sorting. We had accumulated a great deal of stuff through the years and moving was a tremendous job, even though it was for one year only.

Late in August I went out to town, and with George, papered and painted inside the cottage that was to house our family, until everything was in "ship-shape." Then one day early in September we bade goodbye to the old home with its life-long reminiscences, and to the new house occupied but four years, and removed, "bag and baggage" out to Santa Ana and into the cottage.

Harry and Joan too decided to do the same thing—move from their mountain cabin for a season of change down into town while Mother was there. This was soon effected, and they took up their abode in the old store building, which Harry first cleaned and papered and fixed up to receive his family. Within a very few months they had exchanged this for one of the cottages, and remained in town from the middle of September until May of the following year, when they again returned to their mountain home.

Annie and I secured work in Los Angeles in a peach and tomato cannery—a place our present sanitary canneries would blush to own as a predecessor. From this time forward we were home only "off and on."

Sometime during this period, I attended a business college in Los Angeles, working in the home of its principal for board, room and tuition; an arrangement anything but ideal. Charlotte later took a business course in the same city in Nineteen Three. Annie, in Nineteen Six was invited to visit Salt Lake City and there took an apprenticeship in office work, with the Salt Lake Hardware Company.

Figure 46 Hulda and Annie Thurston, 1911

At the time of our removal from Aliso Canyon, Mother could never have been induced to completely abandon her home there. Nor did one of the rest of us even think of such an outcome. We all considered that the change was to be for a year only. That first year, however, proved so advantageous in every way, both as to school privileges for the girls, and associations for Mother, that the allotted twelve months slipped into eternity all too soon, and none of the family wanted to go back. Even Mother herself preferred town life. She was happy now to be near some of her married children, and closer to others, as well as enjoying new friendships made.

The farm yielded as formerly its meager support in spite of its income being diminished by the hiring of help, and showed no indication of going to "rack and ruin." Thus it was that never again did the family return to live on the farm—that its leave-taking was final, and proved to be indeed "Goodbye Old Home."

In late June or early July of Ninety-Six, Joseph had taken over the place, and Frank had gone out onto the Irvine Ranch to farm for himself a piece of ground he had rented a few miles out from town.

Joseph later leased the Aliso farm with all its appurtenances, and for a time, paid Mother a rental. Eventually he bought the Aliso Canyon home, and farmed it for himself. It remained in his possession until the unfortunate Wall Street crash and dark depression beginning in Twenty-Nine, when it passed out of his control into the hands of strangers.

Before the close of the century, Mother had purchased a lot and established another home of her own in town, which then became to the scattered family a "Mecca" for their pilgrimages.

Figure 47 Mother at Her Home in Santa Ana, ~1911 and 80th Birthday 1921

Luella in due time graduated from the high school in Santa Ana with valedictorian honors, afterward attending Berkeley College to fit herself for teaching. For a number of years thereafter, she taught in the high schools of California.

While serving in this capacity on the staff of the high school at Monterey, Luella, for a summer vacation, took a trip into Alaska. Of this experience she writes:

"I visited friends for three weeks in Juneau, and went west to Seward Bay and up the Copper River Railway as far as it was then built. Saw icebergs born from glaciers and heard their thunderous fall, visited some great goldmines, picked the largest violets I have ever seen, and enjoyed the novel experience of twilight without real nighttime. Had some interesting personal experiences, lots of fun, and stayed two months. I met some interesting people, the editors of the woman's page of the Chicago Tribune, who later entertained me when I passed through Chicago."

Figure 48 Luella Thurston Little

In Nineteen Eight, Frank went to South America and was in that country for a year or two. He wrote to his "Pal" in Colton, who after enjoying the letter himself, handed it to the Editor of the local paper. It appeared in print under the caption: "A LETTER FROM SOUTH AMERICA"

"Tuquerres, Guachavace

Columbia, South America "Dear Bud:

I have just had supper, and as my best girl has gone to spark another fellow, I made up my mind that instead of crying my eyes out, I would write you the long-looked-for letter I promised to send you.

In the first place, you wanted me to describe to you this country. Well, well! It is a hard thing to do, there is so much of it. And such a funny one! It is 250 years behind North America. In the first place, there are only two pairs of shoes in this state, and one of these belongs to me and the other one to my best girl. She only wears hers on Sunday when she goes to church. On week days she does look so cute walking about in the mud—for there is plenty of mud here. It rains nine days a week for eight months in a year. Six months more, and the rainy season will be over for four months. Just think of it! There isn't enough level ground in this whole United States of Columbia to make a Colton lot. Some of the small hills are 13,000 feet high. I walked up one for 8, 000 feet the other day just to get on the other side, and I was 5,000 feet when I started.

Everything is just as green as it can be, and there are hundreds of different kinds of ferns, vines, grasses, monstrous thorn bushes, wild roses, blackberries, and even wild potatoes. There are turkeys, wild pigeons, and rattlesnakes; and crocodiles in the rivers; monkeys galore in some parts, and parrots. And don't say "banana" to me; for I saw 85, 000 bunches in one boat. And cocoanuts? Great goodness!

I saw the Panama Canal from one end to the other. It will be finished in twenty years from now. There is only one stove in this country; and an English mining company owns it.

The people build houses here without lumber, nails, or shingles. They have lots of dirty-nosed kids, and one of the sweetest schoolmarms you ever saw. The children go to school three days a week from six to three o'clock. They change about, but the pretty little schoolmarm goes six days.

They have a cup of coffee at six, dinner at ten, and supper at 5:30. They have from three to four courses of potatoes for every meal, parched field corn, meat, mortar-ground wheat soup, and very little bread.

Men, women and children—as well as horses, mules, and bullocks—pack heavy loads on their backs. Some of the children wear hats, some wear skirts, and some of them don't wear anything but a shiny skin that the good God gave them...They go to church in the forenoon and get drunk in the afternoon, and have rooster fights and scraps.

There are two missionaries in Columbia. They are sorry-looking human beings. They look quite God-forsaken.

Everyone has from ten to fifty guinea pigs in the house, and some a cat, and some a dog. They don't eat at a table, but sit on the ground and eat out of gourd shells. Some of them have a few plates. But none of them have stovepipes for the smoke. Have one or two doors, and no windows. They have a few rocks to cook on, and the wood is either green or wet. I can tell you it is great.

B. F. T."

After Sadie and her family had removed from Arizona and come to California to live, and Frank, having enjoyed for a while a foreign residence, was back from South America, then on July eleven, Nineteen Eleven, we held our second and last family reunion—complete but for the absence of Father—as described in the following clipping taken from the Santa Ana Register:

"A FAMILY REUNION

MRS. THURSTON AND HER THIRTEEN CHILDREN ASSEMBLE IN HAPPY GATHERING"

"Yesterday, for the second time in the history of her family, Mrs. S. L. Thurston and her thirteen children were all together at the same time. The family party met at Mrs. Thurston's newly remodeled home on Third Street.

Not since the thirteen sons and daughters left the family home to go out into the world to make homes for themselves, have the entire family assembled before; and the reunion is all the more remarkable for the fact that the children range from twenty-seven to fifty-two years of age. Their homes are scattered over a large section of the country, and it was no small undertaking for them to get together.

After a visit to the Hickox studio for a family photograph, the party, enlarged by sons and daughters in law and grandchildren, spent the remainder of the day most enjoyably at Newport Beach, experiencing all the pleasures of an old-fashioned reunion.

Mrs. Thurston is well known here as a pioneer citizen, she having come to this country when Santa Ana was a "mustard patch." A large number of her creditable family are native Californians.

Such affairs as this reunion are real events in the history of the valley. Much interesting material to a record of the past thirty-nine years of Santa Ana could doubtless be contributed by the various members of the Thurston family who met together yesterday."

Figure 49 Thurston Family Reunion, 1911
Standing (Left to Right): Artemisia, Harriet, Hulda, Lafe, Charlotte, Clara, Annie, Joseph
Sitting (Left to Right): Sadie, George Jr, Joan, Mother, Luella, Frank

And so must end my story of the Children of Aliso, who were of Aliso now no longer.

But first I must tell you about my being cured of that rankling bitterness, conceived in early childhood, that had clung to me through all the intervening years, against the arbitrary fate that had "horned" me a girl instead of a boy.

Though cherished more secretly as womanhood drew on, the deeply ingrained conviction that the male had been singled out for special favors, while injustice was dealt to womankind at every turn, did not vanish at the marriage altar.

Not until I held in my arms a soft, tender, living little bundle that was actually my own—my very own—and felt the peculiar thrilling joy of little suckling lips drawing their sustenance from the new-made mother-breast; which tiny fingers, soft as feather-down, fondled possessively and played upon with most bewitching caresses; not until then did I find that old bugbear of being a girl slipping away from me—shed like an outgrown reptilian skin discarded and left behind forever, and a new-born realization of the wonder of motherhood taking its place.

Could any mere father experience this? Could a boy ever enter into this supreme compact of love that is different from anything else in all human experience? Impossible!

And when I bent my head, true to the instincts of childhood, to rub my nose over the sweet-smelling little pate—the odor of which is like to nothing else in all the world—and caught, with answering rapture, the little flickering smile that danced prophetically in infant eyes, and realized, miracle of miracles, that this baby was indeed my own, flesh of my flesh, blood of my blood, then, not for worlds of other joys would I have relinquished this one—this unspeakably precious crown-jewel purchased at so great a price—a price that already, strange to say, was almost forgotten in the compensating glory of motherhood.

I would not then have been a boy for a thousand worlds; for I had my "very own little real live meat-baby" at last.

Figure 50 Harriet Thurston and Aaron Buchheim Marriage, 1897

Figure 51 Harriet with Daughters (Augusta, Evelyn), 1907

EPILOGUE

After more than fifty-two years of single life, Joseph married Marie Harding, a sprightly young widow with two small daughters, and the village school mistress of Laguna, where they took up residence.

Figure 52 Joseph Thurston and Marie Harding Wedding, June 1921
with Virginia and Doris Frasier

Figure 53 Joseph Thurston and Marie Harding Wedding, Thurston Family Picture, 1921

Back Row, Left to Right: Helen Meredith, Richard Harding, Annie Thurston Korse, Ella Thurston, Minnie Reynolds Thurston, George Thurston Jr, Joseph Thurston, Marie Harding Frasier Thurston, Charles Ward, Sarah Thurston (mother), Artemisia Thurston Ward, Clara Thurston Garland, Harold Garland, Howard Jennings, Lafe Thurston, Florence Collins, Arthur Collins,

Front Row, Left to Right: Rosetta Thurston, June Harding, Violet Ward Case, Virginia Frasier, Doris Frasier, Clarabell Garland, Fred Garland, Ted Garland, Sadie Thurston Byers, Charlotte Thurston Jennings.

One day in June of Nineteen Twenty-Three, two years after that happy event, they went one evening to Hollywood to see "The Covered Wagon" then running in the theater of Sid Grauman, in the prologue of which, Indians played a prominent part. While carrying out their theater engagement, these Indians from Wyoming were camped in Cahuenga Pass above Hollywood.

As he sat watching this play, Joseph was forcibly impressed with the white wife of the Arapahoe Chief, Susie Broken Horn. Her build, size, and general appearance were so strikingly like the women of his mother's family—his own sisters—and her age appeared to correspond so perfectly with that required in the resemblance, that he was constrained to believe she might be the long lost Rosetta.

Mother, then eighty-two years of age, was in a delicate state of health, and in order to care for her, Charlotte with her husband was at the time living with Mother in her Santa Ana home. To Charlotte, Joseph communicated his surmisings, and together they went to Hollywood to obtain an interview with this white Indian woman.

Susie Broken Horn could speak no English. But without revealing their real purpose or suspicions, they succeeded in obtaining a personal interview with her through interpreters. They came away convinced from appearances alone that she was indeed their own long lost sister Rosetta.

Upon Charlotte's return, she found Mother in such a state of nervous excitement and worry over the whole affair, that complete collapse threatened to snap her slender life thread. To end her pitiful worrying, Charlotte, concealing her own convictions, quieted Mother by telling her that it was all a mistake, that the white woman could not possibly be Rosetta. So Mother settled down again from the upset and never knew of Charlotte's personal convictions.

Joseph wrote to Sid Grauman giving him the details of the ancient tragedy so far as he could remember from early accounts, he having been yet unborn at the time of his sister's disappearance, and asked him to investigate the case.

Sid Grauman became very much interested in doing all he could to help solve the mystery. With interpreters he visited Chief Broken Horn, plying him with questions. In answer to these, a very different story was elicited from the chief to account for the woman's presence among his tribe.

According to his version, she was one of two little white girls who had been captured by Indians in a raid on the covered wagon of whites in early days, the other being subsequently rescued by relatives. Years later, this sister, then grown, having located Susie, had tried to persuade her to leave the Indians and come to her home. But according to the story, the white Indian girl had refused to leave the tribe, so was among them of her own choice.

Sid Grauman was of course in no position to test the truth or falsity of this story, and could do nothing but accept it. The Chief himself, having been very young when the girl was taken, would in all probability not know personally whether the story was false or true. It could have been merely a clever invention to shield the actual abductors from accountability.

The whole matter was given out to the newspapers, who made a readable story out of it. But when this article came out in print, the tribe of Indians camped in Cahuenga Pass, having finished their engagement, picked up their tents and disappeared. And the incident was closed.

But we cannot help wondering if somewhere our very own sister might not be living under the name of Susie Broken Horn in the tent of her husband chief, knowing nothing of her early history and blood connection with the Children of Aliso.

Five years later, on April eleven, Nineteen Twenty-Eight, dear Mother went to her last long rest. She lies in the Evergreen Cemetery in the suburbs of Santa Ana, her sorrows and griefs and disappointments forever ended.[16]

REST

Scatter them gently, let them fall
Lightly, tenderly, over all,
Sifting, drifting, fluttering down-
Petals plucked from a rose-strewn mound;
Symbols only of peace—sweet peace,
From toil and turmoil, blest release.
Gone, the burden of pain and tears,
Gone the sorrow, the care, the fears.
Storms may bluster above her head,
Calm she sleeps in a quiet bed;
Dreamless, waits the Life-giver's call,
Whose trump awakes His children all.
Mother, loving and loved and gone,
Rest in hope of a bright beyond.

END NOTES

---

[1] The "Scott Case Collection on the History of Laguna Beach, California. MS-R181. Special Collections and Archives, The UC Irvine Libraries, Irvine, California" comprises research files, correspondence, photographs and ephemera. The collection also includes decades of research material that were gifted to Case as part of the Merle and Mabel Ramsey estate, historians and authors of several books on Laguna Beach history. https://oac.cdlib.org/findaid/ark:/13030/c8bc44q0/

[2] Photograph Reference. Golden Spike Ceremony at Promontory, Utah. National Archives and Records Administration, cataloged under the National Archives Identifier (NAID) 594940.

[3] George Thurston (born 1830 in New Haven, Ohio) was the son of Thomas and Rozetta Thurston. The Thurston family migrated with the Mormon community from Ohio to Illinois and to Utah (arriving October 1847). Thomas was a Bishop for the Morgan County, Utah region. Their pioneer life and biographies are documented in "Thomas Jefferson Thurston" (by Sharon Alice Miller McMullin in 2011) and "Rozetta Bull Thurston" (by Hulda Cordelia Thurston Smith in 1921 and updated by Sharon McMullin in 2011).

Sarah Lucina Snow (born 1841 in Pennsylvania) was the daughter of Erastus and Artimesia Snow. The Snow family migrated with the Mormon community from Vermont to Ohio to Illinois and Utah (arriving July 1847). Erastus was a member of the Quorum of the Twelve Apostles of the LDS Church. Erastus' life is thoroughly documented in Erastus Snow – The Life of a Missionary and Pioneer for the Early Mormon Church (by Andrew Karl Larson, published by the University of Utah Press in 1971).

[4] George Thurston's mission to England during 1854-1857, is summarized in Mormon Church records; and in his foreign correspondence letter published in Salt Lake City's Deseret News on March 1, 1855.

[5] "Artemisia" is the normalized spelling used throughout this manuscript since it matches census records, her death certificate and her children's birth records. Her grandmother, Artimesia Beman Snow, uses a different spelling.

[6] Figure reference. Example Side-wheeler steamship Senator. Article "The Old Side-Wheeled Senator" by Arthur Woodward, in The Journal of San Diego History, San Diego Historical Society Quarterly, July 1957, Volume 3, Number 3.

[7] Map Reference. Extract of United States Survey Maps 1873-1875, Townships 7&8 S, Range 8 W. US Department of the Interior, Bureau of Land Management (BLM), General Land Office Records. https://glorecords.blm.gov/default.aspx

[8] Map Reference. Homesteading Neighbors Near the Thurston Farm. The map underlay is the 1889 Map of Orange County compiled by S.H. Finley. Neighboring homestead locations are from land patent records at the United States Bureau of Land Management, General Land Office Records https://glorecords.blm.gov/search/default.aspx. Note: Lula Goff is the daughter of Hub and Lottie Goff. Leon Goff is the son of Frank and Emma Goff.

[9] Photograph from Case/Ramsey collection and the Historical Collection, First American Financial Corporation.

[10] George Thurston eventually submitted his fruit dryer invention for a patent in 1888, and was granted patent #426,478 on April 29, 1890. Reference United States Patent and Trademark Office (USPTO) patent search for "0426478" https://ppubs.uspto.gov/pubwebapp/static/pages/ppubsbasic.html.

UNITED STATES PATENT OFFICE.

GEORGE W. THURSTON, OF SAN FRANCISCO, CALIFORNIA.

FRUIT-DRIER.

SPECIFICATION forming part of Letters Patent No. 426,478, dated April 29, 1890.

Application filed August 17, 1888. Renewed February 19, 1890. Serial No. 341,004. (No model.)

To all whom it may concern:

Be it known that I, GEORGE W. THURSTON, a citizen of the United States, residing in the city and county of San Francisco, and State
5 of California, have invented a new and useful Fruit-Drier, of which the following is a specification, reference being had to the accompanying drawings and the letters referring thereto.

10 Figure 1 is a perspective view with portions broken out for the purpose of showing the construction of the interior; Fig. 2, a plan view; Fig. 3, an end elevation; Fig. 4, a sectional view showing the heating-pan cut
15 horizontally through the steam-passages just below the bottom or floor B; Fig. 5, a broken sectional view showing the construction and general arrangement of my improved drier. Fig. 6 is an enlarged view, partly in section,
20 of the condensed water-chamber.

My invention has especial relation to steam fruit-driers; and it consists in the combination of the following instrumentalities, by means of which the steam heat to which the
25 fruit is subjected can be regulated or tempered according to the varying conditions of the fruit during the process of drying, as will be fully understood from the following description.

30 This invention relates to an improvement in fruit-driers; and it consists in the combination and arrangement of devices, as will be hereinafter more fully described, and particularly pointed out in the claim appended.

35 I employ steam-pressure to regulate the heat of the steam employed under the drying-pan, thereby regulating the heat of the drying-floor B. I form the pans of the same material as that employed in the usual construc-
40 tion of that class of manufacture, such as sheet metal, &c. I form the partition S to serve as a support to the bottom of the pan as well as to divide the steam-space and form the passages C and C. The arrows show the
45 direction of the steam under the drying-floor B.

I form the steam-admitting space of any required size to allow a convenient space for attaching the steam-supply.

50 I form the condensed-water space E for the purpose of receiving the water as it is condensed and runs from the floor of the steam-passages C and C on its way to the condensed water chamber K. The condensed-water chamber K, I generally construct of sheet
55 metal of sufficient strength to sustain a pressure equal to that of the steam in the boiler, with which it is connected by the pipe P. I construct the float L, the connecting-rod M, the valve-lever N, the valve O, and connect-
60 ing-pipe P of such material and in the same manner as that class of machinery is generally constructed. I employ any suitable style of furnace and boiler. I place the steam-pressure valve H upon the top of the
65 boiler, as shown, and connect the same with the drying-pan by means of the opening U and pipe G. I connect the valve T with the gage-lever I and place the weight J at the distance out or in upon the beam or gage
70 lever I to insure the required amount of resistance or bearing upon the piston T, as will be more fully explained.

The following is the operation of my improved drier: The fruit to be dried is placed
75 upon the floor B of the drying-pan. The weight J is then adjusted upon the beam I to give the required bearing upon the piston T. The amount of pressure of steam to insure the required heat of steam I generally ascertain,
80 as well as the point where the weight is to be placed, by experiment, as they will vary according to the rapidity with which the steam is condensed, owing to the varying temperature of the pan in drying different kinds of
85 fruit; but the scale upon the beam is of advantage, for the reason that it may be relied upon in a general way and to limit the steam to ascertain the pressure of the steam in the boiler and limit the same. It will be seen
90 that the weight being set out upon the beam to a point where the steam must be heated to cause a given amount of pressure, as soon as the steam is heated above that point the pressure opens the passage through the open-
95 ing U, the pipe G, and continues to flow in as long as the heat is sufficient to raise the piston T above the opening U, thus filling the spaces C and C, and as fast as the steam radiates its heat to the pan and is condensed it
100 is replaced by fresh dry steam from the boiler, and the condensed steam in the form of water is allowed to flow through the pipe F into the condensed water and feed chamber

2 426,478

K. When the condensed water and feed chamber K is filled sufficiently, the float L is raised, operating the valve O by means of the connecting-rod M and lever N, thereby opening the passage through the valve O and at the same time admitting steam to the chamber K through the pipe Z.

It will be observed from the foregoing that I combine with an evaporating-pan having steam-circulating passages a regulated steam-supply and a reclaimer for the water of condensation, which water in a more or less heated state is returned as feed-water to the boiler automatically. By these means I am not only able to utilize the water and save fuel, but my main object is to maintain such a varying temperature of steam heat as the condition of the fruit requires.

It will be observed that I employ a water-box X, arranged on a pipe Y, leading to the condensed-water chamber K, and provide the pipe with a valve or cock G, whereby the said pipe may be opened when it is desirable to feed water to the chamber at the box X. It will also be understood from the foregoing description that when the float has been raised by the water in the chamber K, and the valve O being open to admit the water to the boiler, the valve at one end of the pipe Z will also be opened to admit steam into the chamber K.

What I claim as new, and desire to secure by Letters Patent, is—

The herein-described steam-heated fruit-drier, consisting essentially, of a pan having steam-passages C C below a floor B, a condensed-water space provided with an outlet-pipe F, a condensed-water-reclaiming chamber provided with a float-actuated valve O, applied to a return-pipe leading into a steam-boiler, a main steam-pipe leading from this boiler into a chamber F beneath the floor of the drier, and a branch pipe leading from the main pipe into the reclaiming-chamber, provided with a valve actuated by said float, all constructed and adapted to operate substantially as described.

GEORGE W. THURSTON.

Attest:
JOHN H. REDSTONE,
K. B. REDSTONE.

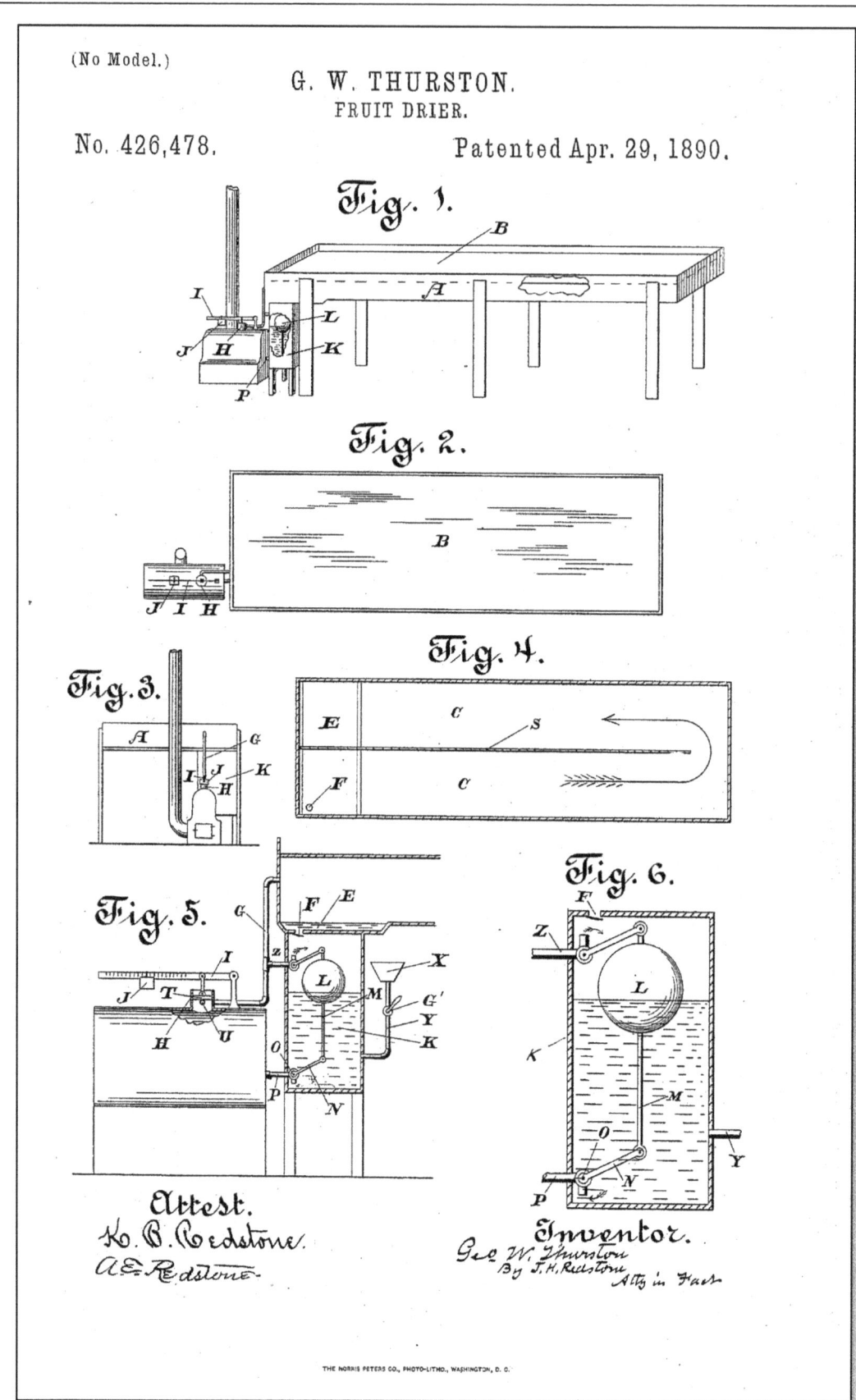

[11] Photograph from Case/Ramsey collection and the Historical Collection, First American Financial Corporation.

[12] Photograph from Case/Ramsey collection and the Historical Collection, First American Financial Corporation.

[13] George Thurston reluctantly agreed to leave the family in ~August 1887. His wife's brief biography (included as separate end note) summarizes their life hardships and his growing cruelty that forced the separation. He subsequently lived in Los Angeles, San Francisco and eventually Newton County, Texas (confirmed through census and voter registration records). It is believed that he perished as one of the thousands of victims in the great Galveston hurricane and flood of 1900. The following is a letter to his daughter Joan in December 1887, written from San Francisco.

This a letter written to Joan, Dec. 12th. 1887.By her father.

                              Franklin Hotel,
                                S. E. Corner of
                                  Sansome & Pacific Sts.
                                    Dec. 12th. 1887.

Dear Joan,
          Yours of the 4th. inst. came to hand yesterday.
          I was truly glad to learn that all my loved ones were
well for I have been so much afraid that some accident might
happen to some of you or that some of you might sicken & die
with no Father near to care for you or protect. O how I should
like to see you all & especially the dear little ones so helpless
& innocent. I hope they will not forget me? I seldom allow myself to think of those whom I have idolized lest existence itself become unendurable. When such thoughts come thronging into
my mind I hustle them out as soon as possible & force my thoughts
upon something else. No one can know how much I should like to
see you all, nor how I am interested in your wellfare, but I
trust I shall not always be reminded nor always remain una-
ppreciated.
          I have my faults- Who has not? But, no kinder or truer
or more sympathetic heart ever beat in human bosom than that
which throbs within my own, one capable of stronger attachment
to Family & Friends. There fore to be deprived of all at once
is truly hard to bear, but even this is far better than an in-
harmonious life with them.
          Some of my Children have taken pains to publish my
faults- but no one has ever heard me say a word of detraction
in regard to either of them or your Mother. I would scorn to
build my reputation upon the ruins of that of another & should
never expect to derive honour from the disgrace of my own
kindred ? And besides, I could never by any means justify myself
in putting a single straw in the way of their success & happiness in life.
          I donot mention this in bitterness- as having hard
feelings towards any one (for I have no child I don't dearly
love & for whom I would not gladly & freely make almost any
sacrifice) but to illustrate a principle.
          My whole cource in life has proven my integrity & my
love for my Family & I venture the assertion that not one man
in a million under the same circumstances would have done for
his Family what I have done for mine & have brought them up as
respectably as I have mine. I was a slave to them & was happy
in being so. I never dreampt of complaining. I considered
nothing a hardship. I was the means of brinking them into the
woeld & my duty- a pleasant duty, to provide for them & rear
them to become respectable & useful members of Society.
          I couldot therefore undo all the labour of my lifetime
by allowing myself to be forced into law by my own Family and
have my faults exposed and magnified in public & to justify
or paliate them, accuse or incriminate those who were dear to me
as life, injure their reputation and degrade them! No! I would
have died rather than that. It was on this account that I left
so unceremoniously & in order that you might in no way be
cramped and hampered- in order that you might sell the home
when a good opportunity might offer & make yourselves more
comfortable- which I realy desired. I made out that deed & and

and sent you- It cost $2.00 and how in the world it happened
that I did not sign it I cannot imagine. I was in haste and it
was the first deed I ever made out, that may be the reason. I was al
also despondent & at the time I thought I should never write
again to any of you nor to any soul on earth and the scrawl I
sent to you is the first & only one till now.

Ever since I made out that deed I have been afraid
that something might be wrong in regard to it- that perhaps
it failed to reach you, so I concluded to find out and I am
obliged by your sending it to me fix up. I guess it is all
right now but send me the patent & I will sign that over too
then you will surely have it all right.

I am still in good health, have a nice cozy little
room lighted by gas- well carpeted with a closet on one side
& a good bed in one corner. About 3 or 4 steps from this room
is a bath room where I take my daily bath.

I can sit here and read or write without any annoyance from any one & when I get tired take a walk for a rest.
Yet it is not home, all are kind & very obliging but where are
my loved ones- how are they & what are they doing.

I wish to write me all the news next time! Write of
all and every one in particular, Tell how all are getting along
& what they are doing.

Remember me kindly to all enquiring friends. Kiss all
the dear little children for me & teach them to lovr and respect
their Father. I wish I could send you all some of the brautiful
christmas presents I see here every where.

Above every thing I hope you will love one another
and stand by each other & never allow selfishness & greed to
suoolant affection- and sunder the ties of kindness.

Love, sustain and obey your Mother & do with cheer-
fulness all you can to lighten her burdens & make her happy
in her declining years. You can never repay your obligations
to her, but you can manifest your sence of gratitude for her
well fare by kindness and thoughtful solicitude.

Of course you have learned of the execution of those
brave and good men in Chicago called "Anarchists". Their execution was as foul a murder as was perpetrated by man! How I
do pity their poor families! And poor Nina Vanzand! What torture she poor girl has endured & alas is now undone! What is
the world coming to. I fear is a terrible & a bloody revolution
brewing. Either Humanity must fall or monopoly must go down.
Alas will it be in a sea of blood? I hope not.

With a long string of kisses for all, a Merry
Christmas & a Happy New Year I am

                    Your Father
                    C. W. Thurston Senior.

---

[14] Photograph from Case/Ramsey collection and the Historical Collection, First American Financial Corporation.

[15] Photograph from Case/Ramsey collection and the Historical Collection, First American Financial Corporation.

[16] Sarah Thurston authored the following brief biography in 1912.

```
             LIFE SKETCH OF MRS. SARAH LUCINA THURSTON
                    WRITTEN in 1912 at age 71

         I came with my parents from Pennsylvania to Utah when about
seven years old. Here, I lived an uneventful life until I was married
to George Washington Thurston in my 18th. year. (2months past 17)
         Our early married life was a series of moves. About the 5th.
one and first of importance, being in answer to the Church Presidents;
a call to go south and settle up the place , now St. George. We were
among the number called to go in the second year of the migration,
leaving Weber in the fall of 1862.
         On our arrival we found that the land allotted to us had been
disposed of to some one else, and a second offer of very inferior
land we refused. Our third piece, while satisfactory to us was after-
ward needed for public use; for which purpose we relinquished it,
after living on it for about two years.
         While in St. George, we experienced, in common with other fa-
milies, much sickness, on account of the water, which seemed to be
poisoning the children; and here , soon after the birth of our fourth
child,(1863), lost our second child, our little son Erastus, in his
fourth year, there being no competent physician in the country. Fear-
ing to lose our youngest child, who was also affected, we finally
moved back to Salt Lake City, from which place, my husband began
freighting to Montana.
         In this buisness, he accumulated sufficient means to purchase
an up-to-date Grist Mill and a mill site in Cache Valley, midway
between the two settlements of Mendon and Wellsville, three miles
apart; our location being off from the main road over a quarter of a
mile.
         Mr. Thurston himself, cut and snaked and hewed the main tim-
bers used in setting up this mill.
         Being hard pressed for means, he took in a business partner,
which proved to be a very unfortunate step, for various reasons. The
mill turned out to be an unprofitable investment for us.
         As soon as we settled in this place, Mr. Thurston, while
in Mendon on business, heard rumors that there had been an Indian
murderd covertly in that settlement.By inquiry, he satisfied himself
of the truth of the rumor, and was greatly troubled in mind, knowing
the treacherous nature of Indians, and their disposition to take
vengeance on the innocent indiscriminately with the guilty; and re-
gretted having located his family in such an isolated place. He was
persuaded by others that the affair would blow over; and having in-
vested all he had, saw no way out of the situation. He was however
scrupulously careful to be straight and honest in all dealings with
the Indians, of which there were many in the surrounding country;
and in giving no cause of offence to them. Not withstanding this,
his worst fears were more than realized,over two years later.
         The Indian Chief, Pocotello, with his band, came up to the
settlement for supplies, and camped for a while. They did not leave
without accomplishing thrie long cherished purpose of revenge on the
whites and we were the innocent victims; supposedly because our lonely
situation offered the least diffuculty, and our close prosimity to
the mill race would tend to divert suspicion from them.
         One cold raw morning in early spring, our little daughter
Rosetta, then in her third year, accompanied by her older sister,
went out of the house for a few minutes. The older sister came in
alone, saying that Rosetta was not quite ready to come in. I sent
her back immediately for the child, but she was no where to be found;
so quickly had she been spirited away by some unseen watcher. After
```

a fruitless search, fearing that she might have fallen into the mill race, we had the mill race emptied and the mill pond thoroughly dragged, without any result. The child had never given us any cause for anxiety in that direction, all the little ones having been taught to stay away from the places of danger. In this way, much valuable time was lost, giving her abductors opportunity to slip quietly away unseen while the rest of the tribe remained for a while.

The whole country was stirred up to search for the missing child, even the wily Indians joining in the search to allay suspicion, which by this time was directed to them; and later on confirmed in the general opinion. But no proof against individuals was procurable; and to have taken any rash steps against the tribe would have precipitated a race hatred and massacres.

Vague rumors from time to time kept us alternately in hope and dispair for years. Rewards were offered in vain; and not until all we had was spent in the useless searchh, and rumor after rumor ferreted out to no purpose did we give up hope of some day finding our child.

The year after the tragedy, we moved to Wver. where Mr. Thurston took charge of a saw mill for his father, in which he acquired an interest.

In 1871, we sold and came to California. After spending nearly a year in various places, we finally settled on an abandoned vlaim of Government land in Aliso Canyon., Los Angeles County; one half mile from the ocean, fifty five miles from the nearesr city, thirty five miles from the nearest settlement, and eight miles from the nearest neighbor; our sole possessions consisting of a small team of horses, a wagon, a tent, our trunks, a few dollars in money, and six children. There was however, a one room sheep- herders cabin on the place.

In the course of time, by the hard and persistent toil of all members of the family, through privation and hsrdships unnamable, we converted this place among the hills from a wilderness of sage and brush, sheep bones and rocks, to a beautiful and picturesque little home of gardens, orchards and vineyard. But the insurmountable drawback was lack of school facilities for the children; in default of which, we did what we could to educate them ourselves, with gratifying results, considering the circumstances.

It was the isolated situation of the Aliso farm, where the restraining influence of school environments were lacking, which made possible the development of the violent disposition, always overbearing, which was manifested by Mr. Thurston with increasing severity after we settled there, and which finally caused our separation on the grounds of cruelty to wife and children, 1887.

There were born to us in this place, seven children, making fifteen in all. The old homestead is still in the family, although some seventeen (1895 ,I with the minor children, moved to Santa Ana, twenty five miles from there;(a city built up since our settling in the country) where I have since resided, and where, at the age of seventy one, I now enjoy a comfortable home, and am within visiting distance, by car, of all my married children.

(Signed) Mrs. S. L. Thurston.

Dates to remember.
Father was last seen by a member of the family, in Feb. 1893.
Rosetta was born on Fathers birthday.
Annie was married on Lafe's birthday.
Luella was married Hulda's birthday.
The big flood at the ranch which changed the entire stream bed and roads was Feb. 14th. 1884.
Annie went to Arizona Aug. 9th. 1889, and stayed three years.The vineyard was dug up Dec. 1889. The new house was built in summer of 1891. We moved to Santa Ana in Aug. 1895.

INDEX